MODERN STUDIES IN PROPERTY LAW: VOLUME 10

This book contains a collection of papers presented at the Twelfth Biennial Modern Studies in Property Law Conference held at University College London in April 2018. The conference and its published proceedings are an established forum for property lawyers from around the world to showcase the latest research. This collection includes a keynote address by Dame Elizabeth Gloster, former Vice President of the Court of Appeal (Civil Division), on technology in property law. It also includes plenary addresses by Professor Henry Smith on the architecture of property law and the challenge of compiling the American Law Institute's Fourth Restatement of Property, and by Her Honour Judge Karen Walden-Smith on the role of the first instance judge in property cases. Sixteen further chapters address a wide range of issues, including the theory and taxonomy of land law, the re-evaluation of land obligations, the nature and operation of equitable property rights and shares, the role of property in commerce, comparative approaches to leases and trusts, and contemporary issues in land registration. Collectively, the chapters demonstrate the vibrancy, diversity and importance of property law and of current research in the subject.

Previous volumes in this series:

Modern Studies in Property Law: Volume 1
Edited by Elizabeth Cooke

Modern Studies in Property Law: Volume 2
Edited by Elizabeth Cooke

Modern Studies in Property Law: Volume 3
Edited by Elizabeth Cooke

Modern Studies in Property Law: Volume 4
Edited by Elizabeth Cooke

Modern Studies in Property Law: Volume 5
Edited by Martin Dixon

Modern Studies in Property Law: Volume 5
Edited by Susan Bright

Modern Studies in Property Law: Volume 6
Edited by Susan Bright

Modern Studies in Property Law: Volume 7
Edited by Nicholas Hopkins

Modern Studies in Property Law: Volume 8
Edited by Warren Barr

Modern Studies in Property Law: Volume 9
Edited by Heather Conway and Robin Hickey

Modern Studies in Property Law

Volume 10

Edited by
Ben McFarlane
and
Sinéad Agnew

•HART•
OXFORD • LONDON • NEW YORK • NEW DELHI • SYDNEY

HART PUBLISHING

Bloomsbury Publishing Plc

Kemp House, Chawley Park, Cumnor Hill, Oxford, OX2 9PH, UK

1385 Broadway, New York, NY 10018, USA

29 Earlsfort Terrace, Dublin 2, Ireland

First published in Great Britain 2019

First published in hardback, 2019

Paperback edition, 2023

A catalogue record for this book is available from the British Library.

A catalogue record for this book is available from the Library of Congress

ISBN: PB: 978-1-50997-423-8
ePDF: 978-1-50992-139-3
ePub: 978-1-50992-138-6

Typeset by Compuscript Ltd, Shannon

FOREWORD

This latest volume in the MSPL series comes as a splendid memorial to a truly excellent conference at UCL, both for those like me who were lucky enough to attend and for those who missed the wide-ranging, deep and perceptive insights into our shared property law, given by judges, academics and practitioners drawn from all over the common law world.

It doesn't seem to matter for how long one practises, studies or adjudicates on property law, the subject continues to present like an ever-expanding Swiss cheese, full of holes, gaps in the logic, awkward problems still to be resolved and, sometimes, controversies about the fundamentals which cause passionate disagreement among otherwise friendly colleagues. To this rich soup must now be added the ground-breaking change, both in daily practice and in the law, which will surely have to accompany the fast approaching invasion of digital communication and artificial intelligence. This will revolutionise the way in which we create, deal with and share real, personal and intellectual property, and how we then resolve the inevitable disputes which those activities generate.

The essays in this volume make a distinguished and wide-ranging contribution to the filling-in of those holes and gaps, and to a deeper understanding of some of the most elusive of the fundamentals. There is also some really perceptive guidance into the beneficial use which can be made of modern IT, in the context of land registration, with insights drawn from experience as far away in geography, culture and law as China. Precisely because each contribution is neither a text book, nor even a part of one, they each have their own refreshingly different approach and style, ranging from the almost ethereally academic to the intensely practical. They also draw together learning from the whole worldwide spectrum of the common law, where differences about the detail never quite seem to destroy the essential coherence of the whole. There is also a compelling study of the different ways in which the common law and civil law systems address shared social problems about property in a joined-up world.

This book is not going to be a standard text for busy students, practitioners or judges to grab off the shelf to solve some thorny problem under pressure of time. Rather it is going to be a treasured book for the legal bedside or fireside table, available to dip into for refreshment and the deepening of learning in moments of that precious disappearing commodity, legal leisure. Just take one essay at a time. Don't worry about the order in which they are presented, logical though it may be. Choose one that takes your fancy when the train is stuck in the wrong kind of leaves, the case is adjourned because they can't find the judge, or when the rest of the family is watching Strictly Come Dancing. And if one gets you really absorbed, there are footnotes galore to follow up on your laptop. I have already enjoyed many happy hours buried in these essays, and I am sure that you will too.

Lord Briggs of Westbourne

PREFACE

In deciding on the venue of the 2018 Modern Studies in Property Law (MSPL) Conference, the MSPL Board gave UCL the chance to be its first London host. We were delighted, but perhaps a little nervous, as Bentham House, home of the Faculty of Laws, was then in the midst of an extensive renovation. We had computer-modelled images of the conference venue: very impressive, but just impressions. And, as anyone who has studied property law will know, much can go wrong between plans and outcome. But thanks to the hard work of many in the Faculty and in UCL more broadly, and particularly due to the leadership of Professor Dame Hazel Genn, our then Dean, the three-year, £24m project was completed in March 2018. A short few weeks later, we then had the privilege of hosting the first conference to take advantage of the splendid new facilities. In those few weeks, as had been the case throughout the planning of the conference, we were wholly reliant on Lisa Penfold and the brilliant UCL Laws Events team, whose energy and commitment was exemplary. We were also very grateful for the continued support of the Faculty as a whole, particularly of our Dean, Professor Piet Eeckhout, who very kindly opened the conference.

The conference proceedings, we think, lived up to the setting, bringing academics, judges, practitioners, and post-graduate students together, from across the world, to exchange ideas and shed new light on some persistent questions about property. The standard of papers delivered in the Postgraduate Research Stream was very high, and the post-graduate speakers also presented posters during the main conference, giving their work a wider audience. We are grateful for the financial support provided to the post-graduate stream of the conference by the UCL Laws 'Back to Bentham Fund'. The 'Work in Progress' section showcased some fascinating research, and the practical importance of property law was highlighted in a plenary work in progress presentation by Lisa Whitehouse, discussing a pilot scheme where law students use their property law knowledge to assist occupiers threatened with the loss of their home. In addition to the full papers, which appear in this volume, Adam Hofri also presented his important empirical and analytical work on the use of offshore trusts, available in his paper in the 2017 volume of *Trust Law International.* Attendees at the conference were also informed by an update from Nicholas Hopkins on the Law Commission's plans for commonhold reform, and entertained by the after-dinner remarks of Lord Briggs of Westbourne, who has very kindly provided a foreword to this book. We are also very grateful to the chairs of the conference sessions, and to all those who attended and made the three days of property law discussion so stimulating. As Martin Dixon noted in an editorial in the *Conveyancer and Property Lawyer* ([2018] *Conv* 105), the new ideas presented at the conference inspired attendees to re-examine their existing views, and to guard against intellectual complacency. We hope this book, in setting out some of the challenges faced by modern property law, will do the same.

The volume, the tenth in the MSPL series, opens with the keynote address given by Dame Elizabeth Gloster. This engaging speech is reproduced here in essentially the same form as it was delivered. It challenged us to reflect on the way technology can assist in the development of property law, a theme that is taken up in relation to land registration in later chapters by Lu Xu and by Siôn Hudson and Brian Sloan. The plenary address by Professor Henry Smith was similarly inspiring, showing how undertaking a restatement project forces us to reflect on fundamental aspects of the structure of property law. Part I of the book is completed by the closing plenary address by Her Honour Judge Karen Walden-Smith, who reminded us of the modern challenges of applying property law in practice, particularly when those most affected by its rules may lack legal representation.

The challenge of managing complexity is one that emerges from Part I of the book, and the chapters in Part II certainly rise to it. Whereas Robin Hickey focuses on goods, and Donal Nolan on land, each of their chapters shows how a close attention to detailed rules of tort (and in, Robin's case, the criminal law too) can have important consequences for our understanding of key concepts such as ownership. Sue Farran's chapter similarly draws on wider aspects of the law, as well as aspects of contemporary urban land use, to reflect on how we should define and protect property. Commerce is the focus of both Larissa Katz and Magda Raczynska, but their chapters show how an understanding of the nature of such practically important tools as company shares and title-based financing depends on a consideration of how we define property rights. At a time when law faculties might be wondering whether to retain property law as a compulsory undergraduate module, the contributions in Part II demonstrate that a clear understanding of the nature of property is vital in many diverse contexts, from self-defence to retention of title.

Larissa Katz's chapter also contains a discussion of the prominence and primacy of land in thinking about property law, and Part III shows that regulating competing claims to the use of land has always been, and will continue to be, one of property law's most important challenges. Craig Rotherham considers 'ancient' forms of easement, looking at enforcement of rights to light and taking a historical perspective, whereas Susan Pascoe examines what may be (in English law at least) very new types of easement, employing a theoretical perspective to consider whether such easements should be recognised. Each of their chapters demonstrates the importance of changing social views to the development of property law, and the need to consider the roles both of statute and common law. A recent statutory intervention in New Zealand is the focus of Ben France-Hudson's chapter, and he very clearly points out the risk of legislating in a particular area without considering the wider scheme and principles of property law. The subsequent three chapters also consider the impact on property law of actual and proposed legislation and regulation. Emily Walsh examines changes to the position of landlord and tenant in the private residential sector: her analysis, combining empirical and theoretical work, has important lessons for the UK Government in its current review of the protection available to short-term tenants in England. Fabiana Bettini, looking at use of the Community Land Trust model as a means to provide affordable housing in England and France, shows how policy-motivated legislative reform can affect, and change, prior views as to fundamental aspects of property law: this echoes Sue Farran's premise that responding to modern social problems may require a more flexible approach to key concepts in property law. Sarah Nield also shows how theoretical work can have an important practical impact, by using an analysis of enduring property relationships to question whether the rules as to the regulation of mortgages are fully fit for purpose.

The law of land registration is considered in Part IV, and it is another area under review in England, where legislative changes are likely. By analysing the Chinese move to land registration, Lu Xu's chapter provides a new perspective on general problems, such as identity fraud, and suggests some specific solutions. Siôn Hudson and Brian Sloan identify a less well-known, but equally important, challenge to a land registration system: how to handle death. Like death, debates over the nature of equitable property rights are unavoidable, but in the first of the chapters of Part V, we argue that some progress can be made by considering precisely how a right under a trust binds a third party. John Mee's chapter, with its examination of the presumptions that may apply to payments, similarly helps to clarify a long-standing debate, this time over the operation of presumptions in resulting trusts. Mee's title quotes TS Eliot and James Fisher's chapter ensures that the book ends not with a whimper but a bang, as its study of the adoption of the trust in Japanese law provides more general lessons as to the nature of legal transplants and the perhaps surprising flexibility of property law.

What emerges very clearly from these varied contributions is the importance of property as a social, as well as a legal, institution and its continued relevance as an organising concept. For this reason, the need for modern research in property law cannot be doubted. We hope that this volume, like the conference that led to it, demonstrates the importance, quality, vitality and diversity of such research. We, and all the other contributors, are very grateful to the referees who made many helpful suggestions and ensured that every contribution to this volume has been rigorously peer-reviewed. Magda Raczynska thanks UCL for an award from the Global Engagement Fund, and Lu Xu thanks Fudan University and Professor Liu Shiguo for funding and supporting his early research for the chapter. We are very grateful to Hart Publishing for their ongoing commitment to the MSPL series and to Sinéad Moloney, Kate Whetter and Rosamund Jubber in particular for their work on this volume. We were lucky too to be able to call on Abe Chauhan as a research assistant and are grateful for his dedication in helping us to prepare the manuscript. We should end by thanking Robin Hickey and Heather Conway, editors of the previous volume, for sharing their expertise with us, and by hoping that this book whets the appetite for the 13th Biennial MSPL conference, which will be held at Northumbria University in 2020.

Sinéad Agnew and Ben McFarlane
September 2018

CONTENTS

PART III
LAND: RELATIONSHIPS AND REGULATION

PART IV
LAND REGISTRATION: PROBLEMS AND SOLUTIONS

PART V
TRUSTS: NATURE AND OPERATION

LIST OF CONTRIBUTORS

Sinéad Agnew is a Lecturer in Property Law at University College London. She is also a non-practising barrister and an Associate Member of Serle Court.

Fabiana Bettini is the Hulme Postdoctoral Fellow in Land Law at the University of Oxford and Brasenose College, Oxford.

Sue Farran is Professor of Laws at Northumbria University.

James C Fisher is a Project Associate Professor at the University of Tokyo.

Ben France-Hudson is a Lecturer at the University of Otago.

The Rt. Hon. Dame Elizabeth Gloster DBE, PC is the former Vice-President of the Civil Division of the Court of Appeal and now practises as an arbitrator from One Essex Court, Temple.

Robin Hickey is Professor of Law at Queen's University Belfast.

Siôn Hudson is a non-practising solicitor and was formerly a Partner in Wills, Trusts & Probate at Miller Sands Solicitors LLP.

Larissa Katz is an Associate Professor of Law and Canada Research Chair in Private Law Theory at the University of Toronto.

Ben McFarlane is Professor of Law at University College London.

John Mee is Professor of Law at University College Cork.

Sarah Nield is Professor of Property Law at the University of Southampton. She is also a non-practising solicitor (of England and Wales, and Hong Kong).

Donal Nolan is a Fellow of Worcester College, Oxford, and Professor of Private Law, University of Oxford.

Susan Pascoe is an Associate Professor of Law at Middlesex University. She is also a non-practising solicitor.

Magda Raczynska is a Lecturer in Law at University College London and Deputy Executive Director of the Secured Transactions Law Reform Project.

Craig Rotherham is Professor of Law at the University of Nottingham.

Henry E Smith is the Fessenden Professor of Law at Harvard Law School and the Reporter for the American Law Institute's Fourth Restatement of Property.

Brian Sloan is a College Lecturer in Law at Robinson College, Cambridge, and an Affiliated Lecturer, University of Cambridge.

Her Honour Judge Karen Walden-Smith, formerly a Specialist Chancery Judge of the Central London County Court, is the Designated Civil Judge for East Anglia and also sits as a Deputy Judge of the High Court.

Emily Walsh is a Senior Lecturer at the University of Portsmouth. She is also a non-practising solicitor.

Lu Xu is a Senior Lecturer at Lancaster University.

TABLE OF CASES

United Kingdom

Australia

Canada

China (People's Republic)

Germany

Hong Kong

Ireland

Japan

New Zealand

United States

European Court of Justice

TABLE OF PRIMARY LEGISLATION

United Kingdom

Australia

Canada

China (People's Republic)

Czech Republic

France

Germany

Ireland

Republic of Korea

Japan

New Zealand

United States

International Treaties and Conventions

TABLE OF SECONDARY LEGISLATION

United Kingdom

European Union

PART I

Modern Challenges in Property Law

1

Technology in Property: Putting You All on Notice

DAME ELIZABETH GLOSTER

I. Opening Remarks

It is a huge honour to have been asked to give the Keynote Lecture of the 2018 Modern Studies in Property Law Conference.[1] When I received the email from Professor Ben McFarlane asking me to do this, I must confess I found it a somewhat daunting prospect in light of the list of distinguished predecessors. I thought perhaps a look at the programme would calm my nerves but instead ended up struck by the breadth of expertise that would be represented in the room. At the time of my invitation, I was deeply engulfed in the fascinating world of synthetic credit default swaps. Although Ben emphasised that property law was 'broadly defined', I came to the conclusion that that subject might have only minority appeal for this audience. I opted instead for technology.

We judges are often portrayed in fiction and in the media as old-fashioned and otherworldly. I aim to persuade you today that – contrary to popular belief – I do own an iPhone, I am familiar with the concept of an 'App', but I have never been one for selfies, which is probably to the delight of the Lord Chief Justice.[2] In reality, most judges are committed users of technology and strive to embrace technological solutions that offer practical benefits in our everyday work. Counsel who appear before me are accustomed to requests from my clerk for electronic case files prior to a hearing. I am always grateful to the team of solicitors that puts these together and I can assure you they save me time both during the hearing and in the judgment-writing process. Although there will be some resistance, I expect the paper bundles that fill commercial and property courtrooms to follow the fate of tea trolleys and chauffeur-driven judicial limousines.

Judges regularly have to decide cases that consider the application of law to new technology. One such example is the open debate about email service of process, although perhaps fewer and fewer people remember email as being 'new' technology. There are two relevant cases from this year that I would like briefly to mention. The first is *Knight v Goulandris*[3]

[1] This chapter is the text of the keynote lecture given by Lady Justice Gloster (as she then was) at UCL on 11 April 2018. References to later developments in the footnotes below are included by way of editorial notes, in square brackets.

[2] Sir Ernest Ryder and Lord Burnett of Maldon, 'Guide to Judicial Conduct' (Courts and Tribunals Judiciary, 2018) 20, https://www.judiciary.gov.uk/wp-content/uploads/2016/07/judicial-conduct-v2018-final-2.pdf.

[3] *Knight v Goulandris* [2018] EWCA Civ 237, [2018] 1 WLR 3345.

in the Court of Appeal, and the second is *Barton v Wright Hassall LLP*[4] in the Supreme Court, which was handed down the day after *Knight*. *Knight* involved a party wall dispute, the facts of which were as follows: the appellant, Mr Knight, had built a basement extension to his house, involving a party wall extension. Damage was caused and Mr Knight and his neighbour, Mr Goulandris (the respondent), each appointed surveyors to determine its extent. They appointed a third surveyor under section 10(1)(b) of the Party Wall Act 1996. The surveyor made an award, which Mr Goulandris appealed in the Central London County Court. Mr Knight argued that the appeal was out of time. The appeal was issued on 17 September 2015 and, according to Mr Knight, the 14-day time limit under section 10(17) had expired on 15 or 16 September 2015. On 2 September 2015, the third surveyor had emailed the award to the surveyors of both parties. Mr Goulandris' surveyor had forwarded the email to him at 23:19 with the award attached as a PDF. He read it the next day. Also on 3 September 2015, Mr Goulandris's surveyor received a hardcopy in the post; however, Mr Goulandris did not receive the same. Section 15(1) of the Party Wall Act 1996 sets out the methods by which notices or documents 'may be served on a person'. It does not include email service. However, section 15(1A) adds that electronic communication can constitute service 'but only if the recipient has stated a willingness to receive the notice or document by means of electronic communication' and not withdrawn that statement.

Before I discuss the outcome of *Knight*, let me introduce the second case, *Barton*. In *Barton*, the defendants instructed solicitors who entered into desultory correspondence by email with the claimant, concluding that they would await service of the claim form and particulars. In June 2013, on the last day before expiry of the issue of the claim form, the claimant emailed the defendants' solicitors, attaching the claim form and particulars of claim in purported service of them, but without obtaining prior permission to do so as required by the Civil Procedure Rules (CPR), rule 6.3(1) and paragraph 4 of Practice Direction 6A supplementing Part 6. The defendants' solicitors served no acknowledgement of service but wrote to the claimant and to the court stating that they had not confirmed that they would accept service by email, that in the absence of such confirmation, email was not a permitted mode of service, that the claim form had expired unserved and that the action was statute-barred. The claimant made an application for an order under CPR, rule 6.15 to validate service retrospectively.

The district judge refused the application, finding that no good reason had been shown for the court to exercise its discretion to grant the order sought. The Court of Appeal affirmed the judge's decision on the basis that, despite the fact that the defendants' solicitors had been aware of the claim and had received the claim form before it had expired, the claimant had done nothing other than attempt service in breach of the rules through ignorance of what they were. The Supreme Court (Lady Hale and Lord Briggs dissenting), upheld that decision. This is in contrast to the decision in *Knight*, in which Patten LJ held that section 15(1A) need not be read restrictively and found that email service had been validly effected. His conclusion is different despite the clear similarities between the wording of CPR, rule 6.3(1) and section 15(1). Given the timing of *Knight*, the Supreme Court neither considered it, nor questioned whether the word 'may' was permissive in

[4] *Barton v Wright Hassall LLP* [2018] UKSC 12, [2018] 1 WLR 1119.

the context of CPR, rule 6.3(1) or whether the rule provides an exhaustive list of service methods. This has resulted in uncertainty in the law around whether email service is acceptable. That result is unavoidable given a 3–2 majority Supreme Court judgment, where the minority judgment is consistent with the reasoning of a unanimous Court of Appeal. It will be judges who will resolve this disparity when it inevitably arises again in a dispute.

Cases involving technology often highlight a tension between the force of precedent and a desire to ensure the law keeps abreast of recent developments in technology.[5] While English[6] law is ultimately adaptable and responsive to changes in technology, there is frequently a time lag during which it is judges that make the call.

This brings me to the essential theme of my talk, which is how I expect technology significantly to impact the way property disputes are litigated as well as the types of disputes which come before the courts. As Professor Richard Susskind has said, technology will disrupt and radically transform the way lawyers and courts act in all areas of practice.[7] What I intend to examine is the general relationship between new technological developments and English property law, focusing on relevant case law and commentary. I will argue that we should embrace the opportunity technology provides for property law, but approach this progress with caution. I will go on to analyse the tension which exists between technological progress and the development of an effective legal and regulatory framework.

I approach this in three parts:

- A brief overview of the use of technology in property litigation (section II).
- An assessment of the opportunities for technology in conveyancing (section III).
- An approach to resolving the tension between the technology and the law (section IV).

II. Technology in Property Litigation

A. The Courts

First, the courts: since 2014, there has been a major push – with which senior judges, politicians and officials have all been involved – to embrace technology across the court system. In July 2017, the Business and Property Courts were created as a single umbrella for separate civil jurisdictions across England and Wales.[8] In London, they are located in the Rolls Building on Fetter Lane, which is not too far from where we are right now. I know the Rolls Building well as I presided over the move into it of the Commercial Court, the Chancery Division and the Technology and Construction Court (TCC) in October 2011, as then Judge in charge of the Commercial Court. At the time, I saw the move

[5] See my comments in *Computer Associates UK Ltd v Software Incubator Ltd* [2018] EWCA Civ 518, [2018] 2 All ER (Comm) 398, [45], [55]–[56].

[6] Throughout, England refers to England & Wales.

[7] RE Susskind, *Tomorrow's Lawyers: an Introduction to Your Future* (Oxford, Oxford University Press, 2017) 15.

[8] Sir Geoffrey Vos, 'The Business and Property Courts Advisory Note' (13 October 2017) 1. The full note is to be found at: https://www.judiciary.gov.uk/wp-content/uploads/2017/09/bpc-advisory-note-13-oct2017.pdf.

as an exciting development in maintaining London's unrivalled position as a global centre for the resolution of high-value commercial, financial and property disputes. The new building provided a modern environment in which these disputes could be heard, incorporating the latest facilities, which reflected an understanding of the importance of technology to increasing efficiency in the litigation process.

Those specialist civil courts were recently rebranded as the Business and Property Courts. They remain committed to embracing technology to drive down costs and time frames in litigation. One such example was the introduction of mandatory e-filing in the Rolls Building in April of last year[9] and the provision of public access terminals and scanners in the reception area for those litigants with limited access to the necessary IT equipment.[10] I agree with the assessment that 'the new electronic case management and filing systems place the Rolls Building in the forefront of modern technology around the world.'[11] All of this will continue to make it cheaper, faster and hopefully easier to litigate large commercial and property cases.

B. Disclosure

Second, I move on to an issue on which I have spent much time: disclosure. This is a key procedural stage in most evidence-based claims, which can cost parties a significant amount of time and money. Those of us who have acted in document-heavy cases will understand the importance of disclosure to allowing claims to progress to trial and to facilitating settlements.

Following widespread concerns expressed by court users and the profession regarding the perceived excessive costs, scale and complexity of disclosure, I was pleased to chair the Disclosure Working Group, established in May 2016 by the previous Chancellor of the High Court, Sir Terence Etherton, now Master of the Rolls. In November 2017, we proposed a number of radical reforms to disclosure relevant to property lawyers. Our unanimous view was that there is a need for a wholesale cultural change, which is only achievable by the widespread promulgation of a completely new rule and guidelines. Professional attitudes must change and judges must shift to more proactive case management. In broad summary, we would remove the automatic entitlement to search-based disclosure and the court would only make an order of what is to be newly termed 'extended disclosure' in cases where there has been full engagement between the parties before the Case Management Conference (CMC). Such an order would be tailored to the issues in the claim. The overall approach is designed to be more flexible than the current Part 31 and to reflect developments in technology.[12]

[9] See: https://www.judiciary.gov.uk/you-and-the-judiciary/going-to-court/high-court/the-rolls-building/e-filing/.

[10] See V Jones, 'E-working to Become Compulsory in Rolls Building Courts as From April 2017' (*LexisNexis Dispute Resolution*, 16 December 2016) available at: http://blogs.lexisnexis.co.uk/dr/e-working-to-become-compulsory-in-rolls-building-courts-as-from-april-2017/.

[11] See: https://www.judiciary.gov.uk/you-and-the-judiciary/going-to-court/high-court/the-rolls-building/e-filing/.

[12] Dame Elizabeth Gloster, 'Disclosure Working Group Press Announcement' (Rolls Building Disclosure Working Group, 2018).

This is of particular relevance to property lawyers because the proposal is that the scheme will, subject to approval by the CPRC,[13] be piloted across the Business and Property Courts in all of the centres[14] for a two-year period.[15] I wholeheartedly agree with the Master of the Rolls' response to these reforms that:

> [i]t is imperative that our disclosure system is, and is seen to be highly efficient and flexible, reflecting developments in technology. Having effective and proportionate rules for disclosure is a key attraction of English law and English dispute resolution in international markets.[16]

That is why I consider it important to highlight recent cases such as *David Brown v BCA Trading Ltd, Robert Feltham, Tradeouts Ltd*.[17] This was a 2016 High Court decision in which BCA was permitted to use predictive coding in its disclosure process,[18] and the first case in which its use was contested.[19] The judge was correct first to consider whether predictive coding would be as effective at identifying the documents which would otherwise be identified through, for example, a keyword search. Having established that it would, he was right to find its significantly lower cost[20] rendered it the most reasonable and proportionate method of disclosure.[21] I would encourage parties and the courts at all levels to continue to be open to using technology to make disclosure less burdensome for all.

C. Access to Justice

Third, at a time like this, it is impossible to discuss the litigation process without commenting on access to justice. As has been widely reported, a greater number of litigants are appearing without lawyers. This is a point of concern at all levels of the court system. In the Civil Division of the Court of Appeal, of which I am the Vice President, the percentage of permission to appeal applications brought by litigants in person (LiPs) stood at 42 per cent in the 12 months ending 31 January 2018. The number of such applications has risen by 50 per cent in the last 10 years.[22]

This issue was further highlighted by the recent Supreme Court case of *Barton v Wright Hassall LLP*,[23] which I mentioned earlier. In that case, Mr Barton was a litigant in person,

[13] Civil Procedure Rules Committee.

[14] In the Rolls Building and in the centres of Bristol, Cardiff, Birmingham, Manchester, Leeds, Newcastle and Liverpool.

[15] Dame Elizabeth Gloster (n 12 above).

[16] Lady Justice Gloster, 'Proposals for a Disclosure Pilot for the Business and Property Courts in England and Wales Press Release' (Rolls Building Disclosure Working Group, 2017) 3.

[17] *David Brown v BCA Trading Ltd, Robert Feltham, Tradeouts Ltd* [2016] EWHC 1464 (Ch).

[18] ibid [9].

[19] See, 'BLP wins BCA battle in first predictive coding High Court trial', *The Lawyer* (London, 14 March 2018) available at: https://www.thelawyer.com/blp-marks-the-first-predictive-coding-win-at-high-court/.

[20] I also appreciate, as Mr Registrar Jones does at *David Brown* (n 17 above) [10], that cost is not the only relevant consideration.

[21] *David Brown* (n 17 above) [2].

[22] Sir Terence Etherton, 'Civil Justice After Jackson' (Conkerton Memorial Lecture, Liverpool Law Society, Liverpool, 15 March 2018) 10, available at: https://www.judiciary.gov.uk/wp-content/uploads/2018/03/speech-mor-civil-justice-after-jackson-conkerton-lecture-2018.pdf.

[23] n 4 above.

whose argument that he did not know about CPR rule 6.3, or presumably, Practice Direction 6A, because they were relatively inaccessible to a litigant in person such as him[24] was rejected by the Supreme Court. This rule required a claimant to secure the prior agreement of the defendant's solicitors prior to serving the claim form on them. It is Lord Sumption's comments that are most relevant for our present purposes:

> Turning to the reasons for Mr Barton's failure to serve in accordance with the rules, I start with Mr Barton's status as a litigant in person. In current circumstances any court will appreciate that litigating in person is not always a matter of choice. At a time when the availability of legal aid and conditional fee agreements have been restricted, some litigants may have little option but to represent themselves. Their lack of representation will often justify making allowances in making case management decisions and in conducting hearings. But it will not usually justify applying to litigants in person a lower standard of compliance with rules or orders of the court.[25]

Given this rise in LiPs, I would suggest – echoing the words of a number of my colleagues – that court systems must be simpler and less costly in order to increase their accessibility to this group. The traditional system is too costly, too slow, and too complex, especially for LiPs with small claims.[26] For those dealing with small property disputes, online dispute resolution as proposed by the Online Dispute Resolution Advisory Group (the ODR Group) in February 2015[27] and endorsed by Briggs LJ (Head of Civil Justice, as he then was) in his influential final report on his review of the structure of civil courts in July 2016[28] presents a real opportunity. It would increase access to justice and lead to substantial savings in costs: both for individual litigants and the court system. Internet-based dispute resolution has already been embraced by a number of other jurisdictions including Canada, Germany and the Netherlands. In the latter, there is a plan to widen the service from matrimonial disputes to landlord and tenant and neighbour disputes.[29]

I am not suggesting that online dispute resolution is the silver bullet. I accept the concern that careful thought needs to be given to the types of disputes that can appropriately be resolved in this way.[30] Further, it is important that litigants are able to continue to access legal advice in more complex cases. However, I am under no illusion as to how daunting using the civil courts can be for litigants, especially for the unrepresented. Property lawyers, particularly in the context of small disputes, should be open to how technology can play a vital role in restoring access to justice for some litigants. The use of tools such as online courts can release resources to assist those unable to use such a system. An added issue is whether low-value disputes should instead be resolved by online systems provided by the private sector.[31] Those in favour argue that the market may provide a cheaper and better

[24] [2018] UKSC 12, [11], Lord Sumption.

[25] ibid [18], Lord Sumption.

[26] Online Dispute Resolution Advisory Group, 'Online Dispute Resolution for Low Value Claims' (Civil Justice Council, 2015) 3, available at: https://www.judiciary.gov.uk/wp-content/uploads/2015/02/Online-Dispute-Resolution-Final-Web-Version1.pdf.

[27] Susskind (n 7 above) 115.

[28] Lord Justice Briggs, 'Civil Courts Structure Review: Final Report' (Courts and Tribunals Judiciary, 2016), available at https://www.judiciary.gov.uk/wp-content/uploads/2016/07/civil-courts-structure-review-final-report-jul-16-final-1.pdf.

[29] ibid 120.

[30] I agree with the conclusions of Lord Justice Briggs (as he then was) in his report (n 28 above) [6.95] and [6.101]–[6.102].

[31] Susskind (n 7 above) 115.

service than the public sector. However, I believe that one of the state's fundamental duties is to provide access to independent judges who resolve disputes in a manner that is binding and enforceable. I remain firmly of the view that this is a job for government.

One example of alternative dispute resolution technology in practice is one British student's free robot lawyer which can fight speeding tickets and rogue landlords. It is said to be able to pose an effective challenge to landlords over security deposits and house repairs.[32] This example shows that, as we consider access to justice in all areas of law, including property law, technology will be central to ensuring that more people can effectively protect their rights, and that is to be embraced.

III. Technology in Conveyancing

The next facet of the relationship that I want to consider is the conveyancing process, from which many property disputes arise. I want to address the opportunities for technology in this process and my expectations for how it will change the types of disputes coming before the courts.

A. Land Registration

I begin my analysis with three particular issues within the land registration process, for which I would suggest the solution may lie in disruptive technologies.

The first is the widely publicised 'registration gap'. As any property lawyer knows, the transfer of a registered interest in land does not take effect legally until the registration is completed.[33] The registration gap is a recurring problem with England's land registration system, which arises due to the delay[34] between completing a transaction, such as the sale of a home, and registration of that transaction at the Land Registry. The constant flow of cases before the courts highlights that it continues to be a problem for parties. One such example of a case is the 2016 High Court decision of *Baker v Craggs*,[35] in which Newey J (as he then was) held that land acquired by a purchaser was bound by an easement granted by the seller, without the purchaser's knowledge or consent, after the date of the relevant transfer but prior to the date that transfer was registered at the Land Registry. He held that the purchaser was in actual occupation of the relevant land but his rights had been overreached and subordinated to the right of way granted in favour of the second purchaser.[36]

[32] See C McGoogan, 'British Student's Free Robot Lawyer Can Fight Speeding Tickets and Rogue Landlords', *The Telegraph* (London, 13 July 2017) available at: https://www.telegraph.co.uk/technology/2017/07/13/british-students-free-robot-lawyer-can-fight-speeding-tickets/.

[33] Land Registration Act 2002, s 27(1).

[34] Often several weeks. [For recent discussion of the problems of the 'registration gap', see Law Commission, 'Updating the Land Registration Act 2002' (Law Com No 380, 2018) [5.175]–[5.194]. It is noted at [5.189] that: 'Consultees' comments have confirmed that the registration gap causes problems in practice.']

[35] *Baker v Craggs* [2016] EWHC 3250 (Ch), [2017] Ch 295.

[36] ibid [45]. [This finding was subsequently overturned on appeal: *Baker v Craggs* [2018] EWCA Civ 1126, [2018] 3 WLR 401, where it was held that the grant of an easement cannot overreach a purchaser's pre-existing equitable interest. The risk of an overreaching transaction occurring in the registration gap remains, however.]

This was a frustrating outcome for a purchaser, who completed his purchase initially free of such an encumbrance.

The second issue is avoidable mistakes. Here I turn to the well-known Court of Appeal case from 2013, *Parshall v Hackney*.[37] Mummery LJ called this a 'troublesome case' about 'title to a small piece of land.'[38] He went on: '[the land] is not big enough … to park a car on unless used in conjunction with adjoining land. Being in Chelsea … it is worth enough for the parties to survive three rounds of civil litigation'. The problem in this case was 'concurrent registration of title to the same piece of land in the names of different people' which '[e]ven someone who knows nothing about land registration would realise … is bad news.'[39] The issue is that both cannot be owners of a fee simple in the same piece of land.[40] The mistake was further exacerbated when, in the course of computerising the title plan to one of the homes, the Land Registry excluded the disputed land from the computerised title.[41] It was the Court that was left to the task of what Mummery LJ described as 'sorting out a muddle which has potentially serious, long-term consequences' by determining 'who has the better title to the disputed land and whether the land register should be rectified to reflect that.'[42] I suggest that such a mistake and thus the resulting dispute could have been avoided with the use of technology.

The third is an issue that unfortunately comes before the courts more and more often: fraud. There has been a considerable increase in registration fraud in the past 10 years.[43] In general, the incidence and value of fraud have increased – particularly identity fraud.[44] Some argue that the unlawful impersonation of a property owner is just one of the many facets of that wider trend. In the case of land registration, it is the Land Registry that must often deal with the consequences. Let me give an example of the types of property fraud cases that commonly come before the courts from a case I heard earlier this year: *P&P Property Limited v Owen White & Catlin LLP and Another*.[45] The claim related to the purchase of a property by the appellant property developer, for £1.03 million. The appellant claimed that the property was sold by a fraudster who impersonated the true owner. When the fraud was discovered, it became clear that the purchase monies, which were paid into an account in Dubai, could not be retrieved and the appellant had suffered a substantial loss. The appellant brought a claim against the fraudster's solicitors and estate agent for negligence, breach of warranty of authority and breach of trust.

One of the Land Registry's current technological solutions to fraud is to allow a party to track changes to the register or to apply for a restriction on the registered title.[46]

[37] *Parshall v Hackney* [2013] EWCA Civ 240, [2013] Ch 568.
[38] ibid [1].
[39] ibid [1] and [8], Mummery LJ.
[40] ibid [9], Mummery LJ.
[41] ibid [10], Mummery LJ.
[42] ibid [9], Mummery LJ.
[43] J Pownall and R Hill, 'The Land Registry's Perspective: The Practical Challenges of Land Registration' in A Goymour, S Watterson and M Dixon (eds), *New Perspectives on Land Registration: Contemporary Problems and Solutions* (Oxford, Hart Publishing, 2018) 12.
[44] [See too the discussion by Lu Xu, 'Updating Land Registration Law and Practice: Some Lessons from China' Chapter 15 in this volume.]
[45] *P&P Property Limited v Owen White & Catlin LLP and Crownvent Ltd* [2018] EWCA Civ 1082, [2018] Lloyd's Rep FC 445.
[46] See: https://www.gov.uk/protect-land-property-from-fraud.

Under the first method, the party can sign up to get property alerts if someone applies to change the register of his or her property, eg, by trying to use the property for a mortgage. Under the restriction method, a party can stop HM Land Registry registering a sale or mortgage of his or her property unless a conveyancer or solicitor certifies that the application was made by him or her. The continuing increase in registration fraud suggests this does not go far enough.[47]

B. E-Conveyancing

I am going to move my analysis onto what has been suggested as the long-term solution to all three of these identified issues: electronic conveyancing.

While it is possible to submit a number of Land Registry applications online through the Land Registry Portal, there is not yet an e-conveyancing system which facilitates the simultaneous completion and registration of a transaction, and thus eliminates the registration gap. That said, in February 2017, the Land Registry announced that it was 'to become the world's leading land registry for speed, simplicity and an open approach to data',[48] representing a commitment to using technology to improving its service offering. This was followed by a blog post entitled '[w]orld leading through digital transformation' in which John Abbott, the Director of Digital, Data and Technology at HM Land Registry wrote:

> For us at HM Land Registry, the most important aspect of adopting new technology is being sure it benefits users and makes the conveyancing process simpler, faster and cheaper, whilst enhancing the integrity and security of our register against threats from cyber-attacks and digital fraud.[49]

It is expected that digital technology will be disruptive to the traditionally paper-based conveyancing industry. I will watch with interest as the Land Registry tests what it has called a live 'Digital Street',[50] which will allow for the almost instantaneous execution of property transactions. I expect you all will too. It is the commitment to a fully digital register – something which has been mooted a number of times before[51] – in which I am most interested. According to HM Land Registry, such a register would 'contain as much information about a property as possible including links to other government agencies such as Companies House, Environment Agency, and Coal Authority, as well as possibly even to partners in the private sector';[52] this is a development to be welcomed. Last year, I heard a case called *Orientfield Holdings Ltd v Bird & Bird LLP*,[53] which highlighted the number of forms and

[47] [For a discussion of the problems that arise in relation to registration fraud in a succession context, see B Sloan and S Hudson, 'Death, Lies, and Land Registration' Chapter 16 in this volume.]

[48] HM Land Registry, 'Proposals to Amend the Land Registration Rules 2003: Government Response' (HM Land Registry, 2018) 6, available at: https://assets.publishing.service.gov.uk/government/uploads/system/uploads/attachment_data/file/674022/HMLR-Government-response-proposal-to-amend-land-registration-rules-2003-10.01.18.docx.

[49] J Abbott, 'World-leading Through Digital Transformation' (*HM Land Registry Blog*, 18 December 2017) available at: https://hmlandregistry.blog.gov.uk/2017/12/18/world-leading-through-digital-transformation/.

[50] ibid.

[51] Law Commission and HM Land Registry, *Land Registration for the Twenty-First Century: A Conveyancing Revolution* (London, The Stationery Office, 2001) 1.12.

[52] See Abbott (n 49 above).

[53] *Orientfield Holdings Ltd v Bird & Bird LLP* [2017] EWCA Civ 348, [2017] PNLR 31.

different agencies that can be involved in a single conveyance. In this case, we held that a firm of solicitors was not duty bound to obtain a Plansearch Plus report upon receipt of unsatisfactory responses from the seller in the property information form (PIF), when acting for a purchaser in a property transaction. However, having obtained the report, it had a duty to explain the results of the search to its client and had been negligent in unilaterally forming its own view that the report contained nothing adverse.[54] I would suggest that a fully digital register might allow for decreased reliance on a PIF because the title registration would have been linked to most of the information relating to that property, including that contained in a Plansearch Plus report. However, this provides no guarantee of protection from the negligence of the solicitor.

One of the potential methods being explored as a way of creating such a register is through the use of blockchain technology. I must first say that my blockchain expertise does not quite match my commercial law expertise. For this reason, I begin with a definition, which I helpfully adopt from the 2017 article of Rod Thomas and Charlie Huang, 'Blockchain, the Borg collective and digitalisation of land registries'. They explain that

> [t]he blockchain concept works as follows. Transactions are grouped into 'blocks'. Following verification, a new 'block' is added to the chain of previous transactions (prior verified blocks) and the distributed ledger updated instantaneously, permanently and irrevocably. The result can be seen by all users. The blockchain thus maintains a continuous growing record with every new block of verified transactions, incrementally building the chain as a unique matrix, thought to be practically impossible to corrupt and sabotage.[55]

For the purpose of this lecture, it is not necessary to delve deeper into the detail of the technology. However, I consider it slightly premature to request that my judicial pension be paid in bitcoin. The point I actually want to make is that we should all be on notice as to the potential for this innovative and hugely disruptive technology radically to transform property law and, in doing so, to deal with the issues I highlighted earlier in this part. Here are just some of the benefits of blockchain. First, the instantaneous updating of the ledger removes any registration gap. Second, it is transparent and immutable. This is because the distributed nature of the registry means it is impossible for it to be altered by any one entity without such a change being made clear to and accepted by the network as a whole.[56] This has the potential to prevent fraud and avoidable mistakes such as concurrent registration. Third, on the point of fraud, with blockchain technology, the expectation is that each property would be given a unique code which would be linked to a smart key held only by the owner. Without this key, it would be impossible for a party to represent themselves as that owner. This would be a much more effective way of preventing fraud.

This jurisdiction is not the first to consider blockchain as a means for recording property transactions. Internationally, the governments of Sweden,[57] the Republic of Georgia[58]

[54] ibid [26]–[34].

[55] R Thomas and C Huang, 'Blockchain, the Borg Collective and Digitalisation of Land Registries' [2017] *Conv* 14, 15.

[56] UK Government Chief Scientific Adviser, 'Distributed Ledger Technology: Beyond Blockchain' (Government Office for Science, 2015) 22, www.gov.uk/government/uploads/system/uploads/attachment_data/file/492972/gs-16-1-distributed-ledger-technology.pdf.

[57] See: https://chromaway.com/landregistry/.

[58] See: https://exonum.com/napr.

and Ghana[59] are already in various stages of exploring blockchain-based land registries. According to a 2017 report on the Swedish pilot, it resulted in 'a secure process for real estate transactions and mortgage deeds'. Each party to a transaction secured by blockchain had a digital file 'representing the agreement of ownership of the real estate, mortgage deeds and the transaction process'.[60] The pilot showed that transactions would be faster, more transparent, cheaper, and more secure.[61] Given this technology is still relatively new, I am not expecting a blockchain-based registry to be adopted within a matter of months. Nonetheless, I consider it important to discuss the potential opportunities it provides in a forum such as this in order to encourage property students, lawyers, judges and academics to engage with the issues relevant to its increasing prevalence to allow all to work together to improve the conveyancing process. While technologists may build the software, it is the lawyers and the legislators (assisted by lawyers) that will provide the legal and regulatory framework without which such technology will be unable to achieve its objectives. This includes providing solutions to the three issues identified at the beginning of this section.

I welcome the academic opposition to blockchain from individuals such as Rod Thomas and Charlie Huang who tentatively conclude that the use of blockchain systems for land registration is inherently problematic. In their article, they describe the difficulty that such a system has in overcoming what they call the 'multi-dimensional dilemmas that invariably arise from land ownership.' I find force in their argument that the 'concept of a decentralised registry is … problematic'.[62] Land is different from securities certificate entries, bank accounts and customers' Kindle e-book collections, all of which are entries in a list determining who owns what. Given its importance to individuals and the organisation of the state as a whole, I consider there is strength to Thomas and Huang's argument that 'some form of policing of the registry is required to avoid abuses or misuses of the system.'[63] One of the oft-cited benefits of blockchain technology is that it allows for trustless transactions in that a blockchain-based ledger does not require a centralised authority. Thomas and Huang write:

> Digital environments are unique in that their governance is regulated by two key sources of authority. The first one is the appropriate 'legal' code as may be enforced by the blockchain governance structure. The second is the technical code, being the software and protocols that the system actually operates through.

In terms of a public blockchain-based system, there is no single entity that can control the enforcement of any legal code. This is because of its decentralised, distributed nature. Consequently, its operation is enforced almost exclusively by its technical code. This could become problematic for a number of reasons.[64]

However, Thomas and Huang explain that there are two problems with this. First, while such a system is much less susceptible to fraud, the risk nevertheless remains. As a judge,

[59] See: http://bitlandglobal.com/.

[60] Lantmäteriet et al, 'The Land Registry in the Blockchain – Testbed' (March 2017) 4, available at https://chromaway.com/papers/Blockchain_Landregistry_Report_2017.pdf.

[61] ibid at 16.

[62] Thomas and Huang (n 55 above) 15.

[63] ibid.

[64] ibid 23.

I am concerned about how one ensures the enforcement of court orders under such a system where, for example, title has passed fraudulently and the court seeks to reverse the transaction. Second, a more mundane issue: if the idea is that each property would be given a unique code which would be linked to a smart key held only by the owner, how do we deal with the situation where an owner loses his code where there is no central registry to issue a replacement code?[65] These are just a couple of issues that show that while the technology may be exciting, more thought is required before it becomes viable.

C. Smart Contracts

As part of my discussion on e-conveyancing, I must take some time for smart contracts. Contract law owes much of its development to disputes arising from property transactions. The key principles affecting rectification, the construction of contracts, and implied terms hail from this practice area.[66] As with blockchain, I have chosen as my starting point the definition of a smart contract from a paper by a team of experts at UCL and Barclays:

> A smart contract is an automatable and enforceable agreement. Automatable by computer, although some parts may require human input and control. Enforceable either by legal enforcement of rights and obligations or via tamper proof execution of computer code.[67]

What are the benefits for property? The consensus appears to be that smart contracts could allow for all types of transactions, including those in property, to complete significantly faster when this technology is combined with a blockchain registry. For example, once the vendor receives funds into his account, title to the property could be automatically transferred to the purchaser. This would speed up the registration process. If we adopt a system where the ledger is immediately updated, there would no longer be a registration gap. Theoretically, this could lead to lower costs and greater efficiencies for the Land Registry. My view is that all those involved in property should be on notice as to the opportunity that smart contracts provide in the property arena. It is an area in which a range of voices must contribute to the development of the necessary legal and regulatory framework in order for the full benefits of smart contracts to be realised.

As with blockchain, one has to consider the disadvantages alongside the benefits. I will look at only two. The first is dealing with contractual interpretation. One can imagine the use of smart contracts in a simple asset ledger transaction, for example, the transfer of ownership of asset X from A to B. However, I question whether it is possible to produce code that would allow for the interpretation of complex legal concepts. If there is one thing my career at the Commercial Bar and on the Bench has shown me, it is that the meaning

[65] ibid.

[66] *Arnold v Britton* [2015] UKSC 36, [2015] AC 1619; *Marks & Spencer Plc v BNP Paribas Securities Services Trust Company (Jersey) Limited and another* [2015] UKSC 72, [2016] AC 742; *Chartbrook v Persimmon Homes Ltd* [2009] UKHL 38, [2009] 1 AC 1101.

[67] CD Clack, VA Bakshi and L Braine, 'Smart Contract Templates: Foundations, Design Landscape and Research Directions' (March 2017) available at: https://arxiv.org/abs/1608.00771v3. This definition is particularly useful for the purpose of our discussion because it is flexible as to the extent to which a smart contract may be fully implemented by computer code or instead combine aspects of traditional contracts and computer code.

of certain commonly used legal concepts is often not so common. It is here the courts play a key role in settling the wide range of interpretations on a case-by-case basis. Within the property context, let me take the example of overage clauses.[68] The most recent reported case on interpretation of an overage clause, and which helps to illustrate some of the difficulties that can arise, is the High Court case of *Gaia Ventures Ltd v Abbeygate Helical (Leisure Plaza) Ltd*,[69] decided this year. The issue in this case was whether a developer used 'reasonable endeavours' to achieve 'as soon as reasonably practicable' the satisfaction of certain conditions upon the fulfilment of which the developer itself became obliged to make an overage payment of £1.4 million. If it did not, the second issue was whether the overage payment or damages in lieu were payable. I am not yet persuaded that it is possible to execute and interpret such a contract without human involvement.

The second disadvantage to smart contracts relates to oral variations to contracts. There seems to be an incompatibility between the importance of freedom of contract, which allows for an oral variation, and the tamper-proof nature of the code from which smart contracts are made.

This takes me to the third issue – variations by the courts. There are questions as to how the tamper-proof nature of code would operate in the same environment as contract law concepts such as implied terms or contracts which are held to have been void from the outset. Unfortunately, I merely pose the question and hope somebody here may have the answer.

D. Electronic Signatures

I will end the third section of my lecture with a short point about electronic signatures. In April 2018, the first digital mortgage deed was entered into the Land Register following collaboration and testing with Coventry Building Society and Enact Conveyancing.[70] Through the use of the GOV.UK Verify service,[71] the borrower 'signed' the deed digitally. HM Land Registry is to be commended for its openness to embracing this technology. It reflects a commitment to transforming the conveyancing market through quicker and simpler digital services and improved use of technology. While this story does represent a move forward, we are still only talking about re-mortgages. The legal position of electronic signatures in the context of transfers of land remains unclear. Under section 2 of the Law of Property (Miscellaneous Provisions) Act 1989, a contract for the sale or other disposition of an interest in land in England must be in writing and signed by – or on behalf – of

[68] For other recent reported cases (the mere number of which in 2017 further demonstrates the scope for dispute in this area) on the interpretation of overage clauses see, for example: *Sparks v Biden* [2017] EWHC 1994 (Ch); *Sovereign Property Holdings Ltd v London and Ilford Ltd* [2017] EWHC 1773 (Ch) [An appeal has now been heard: [2018] EWCA Civ 1618]; *Minerva (Wandsworth) Ltd v Greenland Ram (London) Ltd* [2017] EWHC 1457 (Ch).

[69] *Gaia Ventures Ltd v Abbeygate Helical (Leisure Plaza) Ltd* [2018] EWHC 118 (Ch) [an appeal was heard but was unreported: *Gaia Ventures Ltd v Abbeygate Helical (Leisure Plaza) Ltd* (CA, 10 July 2018)].

[70] Enact Conveyancing, 'Digital Mortgage Signed by Borrower and Registered at HM Land Registry' (*Enact Conveyancing Blog*, 5 April 2018) available at: https://www.enact.co.uk/2018/04/digital-mortgage/.

[71] The Verify service provides a secure way to confirm one's identity online when accessing government services.

each party. It is not clear whether a land contract can be validly signed using an electronic signature.[72] It appears that there are also particular concerns around how an electronic signature should be witnessed.

Given this lack of clarity, I welcome the Chief Land Registrar's recent response to the proposals to amend the 2003 Land Registration Rules and the recognition that the rules around the types of transactions that can be carried out electronically must be clarified.[73] Much of modern business is conducted electronically and online. It is a step in the right direction that the Law Commission considers it appropriate to include a broader project on electronic signatures as part of its Thirteenth Programme of Law Reform.[74] This will have an impact much beyond the sphere of property. As I have already mentioned, the technology here provides an opportunity; however, the regulatory and legal response must ensure the result is a system that is both efficient and secure. If this means spending more time poring over the rules, then so be it.

IV. The Tension

I thus turn to the final aspect of the relationship: the tension between technological progress and the law. I mentioned this briefly at the beginning. I have already identified how technology is likely to transform the litigation process, through its increased use in the courts, changes to disclosure and ability to improve access to justice, particularly in smaller cases involving litigants in person. I have already expressed my view that within property law, it is the conveyancing process that is likely to see the greatest disruption from technology and this will impact the types of disputes coming before the courts. However, I have warned against viewing technology as the solution to all of the problems in the conveyancing process. While the technology in this area has met with the most excitement, I note that much of it remains in its infancy. The legal and regulatory framework must attempt to keep pace with its development in order to allow us to benefit from the advantages it offers while protecting us from the inevitable risks that flow from reliance on it. I want to end this lecture with some thoughts about how to approach the tension between the speed at which the technology develops and the lag of the law.

For a salient example, I will return to smart contracts. Let me compare them to traditional contracts. Both are agreements. In both, the parties have an intention to be legally bound by this agreement. However, smart contracts have two additional features.[75] The first is performance. A traditional contract is usually plain text (and sometimes merely an oral communication), which requires some act from the parties in order for it to be executed. However, a smart contract can be performed, at least partially, by computers, without the

[72] Guidance from the Law Society of England and Wales suggests that electronic signatures can be used for simple contracts, but a wet ink signature should be used for deeds and for any document which is filed at the Land Registry (https://www.lawsociety.org.uk/support-services/advice/practice-notes/execution-of-a-document-using-an-electronic-signature/). However, this is guidance only and not a statement of the law.

[73] HM Land Registry (n 48 above) 10.

[74] Law Commission, *Thirteenth Programme of Law Reform* (Law Com No 377, 2017) [2.11]–[2.13].

[75] I am grateful to Clifford Chance for their work on this topic, which has greatly informed my analysis.

direct intervention of the parties. The second additional feature is enforcement. Smart contracts can be enforced in two ways: either the traditional way (by the courts) or in a new way – through the tamper-proof execution of computer code.[76]

Now putting on my judicial hat, I am particularly interested in this issue of enforcement. It is clear that a court would only enforce a smart contract if it conforms to what a court recognises as a legal contract. As for tamper-proof execution, even this would only be legally effective if a court is willing to recognise the outcome of a technological execution process. If this outcome were to run contrary to a legal rule, it will be displaced by that rule. Let me provide a more concrete example. A wants to transfer a piece of land he owns to B. Both parties are early adopters of a blockchain solution, which I will call GlosChain. GlosChain includes an electronic ledger, on which ownership of real estate interests is represented by electronic coins. Using GlosChain, A executes a smart contract that transfers the coin representing his piece of land to B. On GlosChain, everything works correctly: the coin is transferred and B is represented on the ledger as the registered owner of that piece of land. There is, however, a problem. The law requires a transfer of that kind of estate in land to be effected by deed, signed and witnessed. The designers of GlosChain and the smart contract system did not consider this essential point.[77]

Now let us consider this issue comes before Lady Justice X. Despite the brilliant name of the blockchain solution, the outcome would have to be that without regulations specifically recognising such electronic transfers as valid, the court will not recognise B's title to the asset. If the blockchain is genuinely tamper-proof, then I am concerned that it would not be possible for a court to modify the result of the transfer on it. This takes me back to my earlier discussion on the potential importance of a central authority in this regard. Nonetheless, Lady Justice X's court would make its determination consistently with its interpretation of the relevant legal rules as they apply to the facts and not based on the outcome provided by the technology. The law will always sit above the technology – because even with smart contracts, it is the courts that must be the final arbiter of legal effect.

In accordance with my view of the importance of an open attitude to technology in property, I am pleased that the Law Commission announced last December a review of 'the current English legal and regulatory framework to ensure that it facilitates the use of smart contracts' as part of its Thirteenth Programme of Law Reform.[78] In doing so, it is recognising the increasing importance which smart contracts and this disruptive technology will play in all types of business, including property transactions. If conducted properly, the result should prevent disputes arising in the example I have just given.

In the meantime, the tension will remain, however, because the technology will inevitably develop faster than the law. Where a transaction is completed digitally, the Land Registry has made it clear that 'the requirements for a valid mortgage, transfer or lease of registered land will not change. All that will change is the way of preparing those documents. The documents, and the law behind them, will be fundamentally the same.'[79] Contrary to the

[76] Clifford Chance, 'Are Smart Contracts Contracts?' (*Clifford Chance Talking Tech*, 6 December 2017) 4, available at: https://talkingtech.cliffordchance.com/en/tech/are-smart-contracts-contracts.html.

[77] ibid.

[78] Law Commission (n 74 above) [2.39].

[79] HM Land Registry (n 48 above) 11.

Land Registry's view, however, I think there is a real need to make detailed rules by statutory instrument that give clear thought to the way the technological process is quite different from the status quo. Reliance on existing or previous rules will widen the gap between technology and the legal and regulatory framework and leave it to judges to make determinations on an issue-by-issue basis. I do not consider the uncertain position this leaves technologists in to be favourable. For technologists, the challenge is continuing to be innovative while ensuring the outcomes that flow from their technological solutions are legally effective. Lawyers and technologists will have to work together to resolve issues posed by an outcome that relies on both humans and code.

V. Conclusion

Drawing the threads together, I hope to have put you all on notice as to the way technology will transform the litigation and conveyancing processes in property law. There is good reason to think that England remains one of the most pro-technology jurisdictions in the world; further, that this is certain to continue, and possibly even increase, in the future. Yet, at the same time, it is impossible to ignore the tension between innovation and the much more conservative legal and regulatory framework. It will be for lawyers and technologists to work together to ensure that the advantages are realised and the risks are minimised. As disputes arise, it is judges who will be the final arbiters until the legislature is specific enough in its response to individual technologies. I do not expect to hear any of these disputes in my last couple of months on the Bench but I will be sure to recommend to some of my colleagues that they learn to code.

2

Restating the Architecture of Property

HENRY E SMITH

I. Introduction

The project for a 'Restatement of the Law Fourth, Property' sounds deceptively staid. However, each of the elements of its name – 'Restatement of the Law', 'Fourth', 'Property' – reflects a challenge. Property has been the laggard among areas of private law in receiving the Restatement treatment in the United States. Unlike contract and torts and even restitution, the First Restatement of Property was never finished and even lost the property torts to the Torts Restatement on account of excessive delay with the property project.[1] The Property Restatements started with an ambition to set the subject on a sounder, Hohfeldian footing, based on his scheme of jural relations – a vision that proved difficult to achieve for a variety of reasons.[2] And subsequent Restatements have only taken up selected topics, and never with the idea of filling in all the many areas – including adverse possession, most of personal property, real estate transfers, recording acts, groundwater, and mineral rights – left untouched by the First Restatement. As I will argue, the Restatement process, despite its ostensible conceptualism, treated property law as a heap of detachable rules, whose effects are additive. Once one accepts this (inaccurate) picture, piecemeal treatment can be (wrongly) regarded as only mildly problematic. The process and its results were in keeping with the conventional wisdom of the twentieth century in the United States: that nothing really holds the area of property together in terms of conceptual structure or subject-matter.[3] Property is a bundle of sticks, and it is sticks all the way down.

In 2014 The American Law Institute approved a new project for a Fourth Restatement of Property.[4] That is, we're now on the fourth round of restating the law of property. And yet, if it succeeds, it would be the first Restatement that would cover the entire subject. And 'Fourth' is not the only remarkable aspect of the project. We must still ask why Property and why a Restatement of the Law?

[1] *Restatement (First) of Torts* (Philadelphia, The American Law Institute, 1939) vii, intro.

[2] The Restatement relied heavily in its early sections on WN Hohfeld, 'Some Fundamental Legal Conceptions as Applied in Judicial Reasoning' (1913) 23 *Yale Law Journal* 16–59, (setting out eight 'fundamental jural relations' – right, duty, privilege, no-right, power, liability, immunity, disability – and their interrelations).

[3] TW Merrill and HE Smith, 'Why Restate the Bundle? The Disintegration of the Restatement of Property' (2014) 79 *Brooklyn Law Review* 681.

[4] I am the Reporter, and the Associate Reporters are Sara Bronin, John Goldberg, Daniel Kelly, Brian Lee, Tanya Marsh, Thomas W Merrill, and Christopher Newman.

One might think that the very reasons why there has been no comprehensive Restatement of Property would prevent there from being one now. I was once of that view,[5] and I can't prove that it's not true (at least not yet). Certainly the dominance of the bundle-of-rights picture of property in the United States complicates the possibility of any comprehensive Restatement effort.[6] As I will argue, the bundle picture simplifies property law in some ways that make some aspects easier to restate and others more difficult.[7] By treating property as a heap of rules and property interests as a collection of rights, privileges, duties, and so on, the bundle picture invites piecemeal treatment of the subject, making endurance the main factor in covering the entirety of property (whatever, on a nominalist view, that term is taken to cover). And yet, on the bundle view, the interconnection and interaction of the various components of property law are assumed away, making them all but impossible to capture in a Restatement. The coherence of the law and the doctrinal 'how', in addition to the substantive 'what' of property law, will inevitably get short shrift. Indeed on the bundle picture, comprehensiveness and coherence are not important goals at all.

Dissatisfaction with the limits of the bundle theory and its failure to deal well with complexity motivated me to start on the Restatement Project. More positively, the aim is to remedy these defects by capturing some of the architecture of property. The difference between a collection of rules and an architecture stems from the arrangement and interactions, the groupings, and the coherence (sometimes) of property law. In short, the need is for *system* in property law. To show why system is needed and to point to the kind of system that could be developed, I will employ the concepts and tools of complex systems theory (CST). In CST, a system is complex if it has many parts with many interactions, such that it is difficult to infer the properties of the whole from the properties of the parts.[8] Put differently, the effect of the system, here property law, is not the additive sum of the effects of the parts, such as rules or interests. Linear additivity is exactly what the bundle picture leads us to expect and exactly what a Restatement should transcend.

All this is very aspirational. There are many ways one might 'capture' the architecture of property – in articles, treatises, textbooks, and so on. Why a Restatement? Restatements are strange birds that are hatched from strange eggs. In this chapter I'd like to set out how the importance of architecture to the Restatement is almost exactly matched with the difficulty of implementing it in the Restatement process. Call it the 'Paradox of Architecture' in restating law in general and property in particular.

[5] Merrill and Smith (n 3) 708.

[6] On the status of the bundle picture as conventional wisdom in the United States, see eg BA Ackerman, *Private Property and the Constitution* (New Haven CT, Yale University Press, 1977) 26 (reporting that the bundle-of-rights conception of property is so pervasive that 'even the dimmest law student can be counted upon to parrot the ritual phrases on command'); EL Rubin, 'Due Process and the Administrative State' (1984) 72 *California Law Review* 1044, 1086 ('[P]roperty is simply a label for whatever "bundle of sticks" the individual has been granted.'); J Williams, 'The Rhetoric of Property' (1998) 83 *Iowa Law Review* 277, 297 ('Labeling something as property does not predetermine what rights an owner does or does not have in it.').

[7] For a variety of views on the bundle picture, see DB Klein and J Robinson, 'Property: A Bundle of Rights? Prologue to the Property Symposium' (2011) 8 *Econ Journal Watch* 193. For critiques of the bundle picture, see, eg J Penner, 'The "Bundle of Rights" Picture of Property' (1996) 43 *University of California, Los Angeles Law Review* 711; TW Merrill and HE Smith, 'What Happened to Property in Law and Economics?' (2001) 111 *Yale Law Journal* 357; HE Smith, 'Property as the Law of Things' (2012) 125 *Harvard Law Review* 1691.

[8] See, eg, M Mitchell, *Complexity: A Guided Tour* (New York, Oxford University Press, 2011); HA Simon, *The Sciences of the Artificial*, 2nd edn (Cambridge MA, MIT Press, 1981).

Section II sketches what I mean by the architecture of property and gives some examples from the law of possession and the property torts as we have been formulating provisions about them. In section III, I highlight how the Restatement process of drafting and its quasi-legislative aspirations make capturing the architecture of property more difficult. Section IV turns to the question of 'So what?' Why is it important to capture the architecture of property in a Restatement, especially in the United States? I will conclude on a necessarily optimistic note.

II. Architecture in Property Law

What is architecture in property law? The architecture of property, like that of other systems, is shaped by the problem of complexity. The notion of complexity in CST points to the need to organise people's interactions with scarce things. It even helps explain why we need to treat things as things. This view of complexity differs from that which motivated The American Law Institute in adopting its programme of restating the law. It also differs from the view implicit in strong versions of the bundle-of-rights picture of property, which in effect denies the importance of complexity in the sense of CST.

A. Architecture in the Complex System of Property Law

The words 'system' and 'systematic' are often tossed around in discussions of property law, both in a positive and negative sense. Before turning to how some of these favourable and unfavourable views of 'system' intersect with the Restatement process, this section will show how a specific sense of system will help sharpen the goals for a new Restatement.

Although the complexity of a system is hard to define, a common working definition in CST holds that a system is complex when it is difficult to infer the properties of the whole from the properties of its parts.[9] The reason is that the parts interact so strongly and interconnectedly that it is difficult to trace the combined effect of the parts and the net result. This leads to some properties of the system being emergent.[10] For example, it makes sense

[9] See sources cited in n 8 above. Lon Fuller recognised the problem of complexity under the heading of 'polycentricity', borrowed from Michael Polanyi: L Fuller, 'The Forms and Limits of Adjudication' (1978) 92 *Harvard Law Review* 353, 394–95 (introducing the concept of polycentric tasks) and M Polyani, *The Logic of Liberty: Reflections and Rejoinders* (London, Routledge and K Paul, 1951); see also E Kades, 'The Laws of Complexity and the Complexity of Laws: The Implications of Computational Complexity Theory for the Law' (1997) 49 *Rutgers Law Review* 403, 406–24.

[10] How seriously to take emergence and how much of a challenge it poses to reductionism is a large debate in philosophy and science, and one which we can largely sidestep here. The point for purposes of law and its restatement is that a fully reductionist (or constructivist) approach is prohibitively costly. Thus, even if in principle one could analyse legal relations into micro constituents and could track their contributions to macro effects, it would not be cost-effective to do so. Thus, where strong (and controversial) statements are about the 'ability' to reduce macro properties to micro foundations, we could more safely make statements about the 'efficacy' of reducing legal relations in a similar fashion and trying to build the world of law up from them: *cf* PW Anderson, 'More is Different: Broken Symmetry and the Nature of the Hierarchical Structure of Science' (1972) 177 *Science* 393, 393 ('The ability to reduce everything to simple fundamental laws does not imply the ability to start from those laws and reconstruct the universe … The constructionist hypothesis breaks down when confronted with the twin difficulties of scale and complexity … [A]t each level of complexity entirely new properties appear. Psychology is not

to deal with wetness and other properties of water as a whole without constant reference to the properties of oxygen and hydrogen atoms. Notions of emergence come in a variety of strengths, but for us a weak version is sufficient: the system effects are non-trivially related to the properties of the smallest constituents of the system, such that managing complexity requires us to speak in terms of system properties. We can engage in a holistic approach without giving up on reductionistic analysis where it is appropriate.[11]

The need to manage complexity also shapes how we organise systems like the law. Systems are organised into components (modules) in order to manage complexity. Each module contains elements that interact much more strongly internally than they do with elements outside the module. In a car, the brake system need not interact with the windshield wipers. If in a system every element could in principle interact freely with any other, the problems of multiple interaction and complexity effects would soon become intractable.

Such system effects are essential to explaining how property law works. This kind of complexity implicates views about property in the United States in the most fundamental way. Since the days of Legal Realism, conventional wisdom has held that property is a bundle of rights, or more metaphorically, a bundle of sticks.[12] By this is meant that 'property' is a meaningless label that does not denote any stable content. Property is not a right to a thing, because legal relations hold between persons, and not between persons and things. As to content, legal relations can be mixed and matched, such that, in more extreme versions of the bundle of rights, the bundle is in principle quite plastic. The notion of things disappears altogether, and denying that property is about things at all is, along with a denial of the systemic aspects of property law, one of the most important articles of faith in Legal Realism and its progeny.[13] The bundle-of-rights picture is seen as more hardheaded, realistic, less metaphysical and in keeping with a more complex age.[14]

There is a great deal of irony in this. Although the bundle of rights as an analytical device has its uses, the more extreme versions that present themselves as a substantive theory of property have exactly the opposite effect to that intended when it comes to complexity.

The mainstream conception of property in the United States is at its weakest when it comes to issues of complexity. On the bundle-of-rights picture of property, 'property' is only a label for some significant cluster of legal relations to which we choose to give that designation.[15] Instead of property being a right to a thing, with some special core

applied biology, nor is biology applied chemistry.'); and at 395 ('[W]e can now see that the whole becomes not merely more, but very different from the sum of its parts.'). See also HE Smith, 'Emergent Property' in J Penner and HE Smith (eds), *Philosophical Foundations of Property Law* (Oxford, Oxford University Press, 2013) 320.

[11] See Simon (n 8 above) 195. Thus, insisting on reductionism in principle does not provide an argument against the practical indispensibility of legal concepts that rest on weak emergence. But *cf* SN Glackin, 'Back to Bundles: Deflating Property Rights, Again' (2014) 20 *Legal Theory* 1.

[12] For a classic statement, see TC Grey, 'The Disintegration of Property' in JR Pennock and JW Chapman (eds), *NOMOS XXII: Property* (New York, New York University Press, 1980) 69.

[13] See Grey (ibid) 70. See also FS Cohen, 'Transcendental Nonsense and the Functional Approach' (1935) 35 *Columbia Law Review* 809, 815 (decrying 'the "thingification" of property,' which made possible a pretence that 'courts are not creating property, but are merely recognizing a pre-existent Something').

[14] See eg T Arnold, *The Folklore of Capitalism* (New Haven CT, Yale University Press, 1937) 114–116; see also eg JE Herget, *American Jurisprudence, 1870–1970: A History* (Houston TX, Rice University Press, 1990) 147–58; GE White, *Patterns of American Legal Thought* (Indianapolis IN, Bobbs-Merrill Co, 1978) 139.

[15] See eg WH Hamilton and I Till, 'Property' in ERA Seligman and A Johnson (eds), *Encyclopaedia of the Social Sciences*, vol 11 (New York, Macmillan, 1937) 528 (declaring that property is nothing more than 'a euphonious

status for the right to exclude or powers of licensing and transfer, we can instead mix and match various rights to use and exclude, powers to alienate, and so on. Such a theory also downplays the importance of the thing as well. The idea is that, because legal relations hold between persons, bilaterally, and not between persons and things, the thing must be unimportant. At most property is a set of legal relations with respect to a thing.

Downplaying things poses problems. On the bundle theory, the communication of legal relations through the thing is incidental to the way property works. In the real world, many property relations are communicated to a wide and impersonal audience through a thing.[16] In James Penner's famous car park, people generally know not to take or damage cars without needing to know anything about their owners or possessors: whether the car is on loan from the possessor's sister in law, whether it is subject to a security interest, etc.[17] And it is this need to communicate with a large and indefinite audience that forms a rationale for standardising *in rem* rights, for example as reflected in the closed number of forms, the *numerus clausus* principle.[18]

The bundle picture presents two major problems, one static and one dynamic. Both the static and dynamic problems are magnified in the Restatement process.

The static problem is one of delineation and definition. If property is a collection of use rights, how far do we distinguish uses? Is every use a separate stick? Is farming a use? Is growing tomatoes the relevant use? If legal relations are bilateral, how do we capture the *in rem* aspect of property? More fundamentally, it is infeasible to delineate property relations by starting at the atomic or subatomic level.[19] Interestingly, recognising this problem of delineation need not make us indifferent to how property is used or hostile to Hohfeld's analytical contributions. As Ben McFarlane and Simon Douglas argue, an appreciation of how property works points to the importance of rights to exclude as a wholesale and implicit way to protect privileges of use.[20] Thus, the Hohfeldian framework can be adapted to a more systemic view of property, something that may not be out of keeping with Hohfeld's unfinished programme.[21]

collocation of letters which serves as a general term for the miscellany of equities that persons hold in the commonwealth'); see also Grey, above n 12.

[16] See eg Smith (n 7 above).

[17] See JE Penner, *The Idea of Property in Law* (Oxford, Clarendon Press, 1997) 75–76 ('As I walk through a car park, my actual, practical duty is only capable of being understood as a duty which applies to cars there, not to a series of owners. … The content of my duty not to interfere is not structured in any way by the actual ownership relation of the cars' owners to their specific cars.').

[18] See TW Merrill and HE Smith, 'Optimal Standardization in the Law of Property: The *Numerus Clausus* Principle' (2000) 110 *Yale Law Journal* 1, 12–20 (explaining the standardisation of property as a response to benefits and costs of communicating rights to different audiences; see also B Rudden, 'Economic Theory v. Property Law: The *Numerus Clausus* Problem' in J Eekelaar and J Bell (eds), *Oxford Essays In Jurisprudence: Third Series* (Oxford, Oxford University Press, 1987) 239, 241 ('In all "non-feudal" systems with which I am familiar … there are less than a dozen sorts of property entitlements.'). The *numerus clausus* principle is discussed in a number of chapters in this volume: see eg, the contributions of Ben France-Hudson (Chapter 11) and Susan Pascoe (Chapter 10).

[19] See BA Lee and HE Smith, 'The Nature of Coasean Property' (2012) 59 *International Review of Law and Economics* 145; TW Merrill and HE Smith, 'Making Coasean Property More Coasean' (2011) 54 *Journal of Law & Economics* S77.

[20] S Douglas and B McFarlane, 'Defining Property Rights' in J Penner and HE Smith (eds), *Philosophical Foundations of Property Law* (Oxford, Oxford University Press, 2013) 219.

[21] See TM Sichelman, 'Very Tight "Bundles of Sticks": Hohfeld's Complex Jural Relations' in S Balganesh, T Sichelman and H Smith (eds), *The Legacy of Wesley Hohfeld: Edited Major Works, Select Personal Papers, and Original Commentaries* (Cambridge, Cambridge University Press, forthcoming), available at SSRN: https://ssrn.com/abstract=2947912.

The dynamic problem with the conventional bundle-of-rights picture of property is directly related to system effects. Changes to one attribute of a thing or one stick in the bundle will affect some other attributes and sticks, and some more than others.

Let's focus on the basic question of thinghood in property. The world could fit anywhere along a spectrum of complexity. Things are made up of attributes, and bundles of rights are made of more basic relations (whether they are actually delineated in those terms or not). If we regard a thing as a bundle of attributes or ownership as a bundle (in some sense) of legal relations, what is the relationship between and among the attributes of the thing or between and among the legal relations in the bundle?

There are three possibilities, which are really segments of a spectrum of complexity.[22] One possibility is that the constituents of a thing and the strands of ownership do not interact. Thus, a stick can be inserted into or removed from the bundle in a highly predictable way. We could subtract a right to exclude hikers or add a right to sunlight in the United States, or vice versa in England. Because the sticks are additive, the problem of whether to include the stick or not can be analysed in isolation from the rest of the bundle. In terms of improving the bundle, if we can be sure that the addition or subtraction of a stick makes an improvement on its own terms, we can be sure that we have improved the bundle overall. It is easy to see why this would appeal to legal interventionists, and it is no accident that the bundle of rights came to the fore in the New Deal era, and is in keeping with the high-modernist progressivism of the early twentieth century.[23]

At the opposite extreme, the law could be maximally complex: every pair of attributes in the thing, every pair of legal relations in the bundle, and every pair of rules could interact, leading to maximal complexity. The complexity is unstructured and irreducible. Changing one element, say, one stick in the bundle, could have untold ripple effects, and even small interventions would be highly unpredictable in their effects.

In the middle, between 'additive' complexity and fully interactive and intractable complexity is what is sometimes referred to as 'organized complexity.'[24] Attributes interact more with some attributes than others, and similarly for legal relations and rules. This structure can be exploited to manage complexity and make for a more usable system of law. Attributes that are complementary and interactive should be gathered into things, which is often the case in everyday ontology and is reflected in legal delineation. Thus, when it comes to property in land, attributes like soil and water go together but high reaches of the atmosphere do not. When it comes to the bundle of legal relations, similarly, sticks that interact should go together in a module and should interact more weakly with other sticks outside the module.[25] The internal cluster of privileges of a landowner are highly interactive but are left implicit and hidden behind the land boundary and protected by the relatively on/off character of trespass law. For important interactions outside the

[22] L Alston and B Mueller, 'Towards a More Evolutionary Theory of Property Rights' (2015) 100 *Iowa Law Review* 2255, 2262–72; HE Smith, 'Complexity and the Cathedral: Making Law and Economics More Calabresian' (2018) *European Journal of Law and Economics*, https://doi.org/10.1007/s10657-018-9591-x.

[23] *cf* Grey (n 12 above) 81 (discussing how the Legal Realists 'were on the whole supportive of the regulatory and welfare state, and in the writings that develop the bundle-of-rights conception, a purpose to remove the sanctity that had traditionally attached to the rights of property can often be discerned').

[24] W Weaver, 'Science and Complexity' (1948) 36 *American Scientist* 536.

[25] See eg CY Baldwin and KB Clark, *Design Rules: The Power of Modularity*, vol 1 (Cambridge MA, MIT Press, 2000) 58–59, 236–37, 257; Simon (n 8 above) 210.

land module and its associated modular package of rights, the interface to other such packages is constituted in the law of nuisance, easements, covenants, and the like. Importantly, tinkering with such packages and things can be done in a controlled way with due regard to the potential but manageable ripple effects. Packages of rights can be combined, split up and interact with each other to produce predictable (and, one hopes, desirable) macro effects.[26]

An analogy to architecture in its literal sense is instructive. In architecture the various elements, at the building level and above and below, are characterised by structured complexity. Various theories of architecture take for granted this structure, deny it, or try to harness it.[27] One feature of the high modernism of the mid-twentieth century was a partial understanding of complexity, comparable in many ways to what inspired the Restatements and Legal Realism. Urban planning of the era and urban renewal in particular were not sensitive to how order might emerge organically or spontaneously. The effects were treated as additive. Sometimes, as in zoning from the era, uses were separated ruthlessly, reflecting a lack of appreciation for how uses interact. Thus, as Jane Jacobs and now the New Urbanists emphasise, a vibrant street life fostered by ground-level retail businesses contributes to the informal social interactions important in a residential area.[28] How to modularise architecture has been a much contested topic, but it must be done in a way that does not kill off important sets of interactions on the one hand and allows for some degree of organic development.[29] The problem of modularisation in legal structures, especially 'bundles of legal relations', is similar: what to define in terms of things and relations and what to encode directly in the law versus allowing for extralegal development. Like architecture, property law falls in the middle ground of structured complexity, which profoundly shapes each field.

Elsewhere I have argued that a variety of problems addressed by property law fall squarely in this middle ground of structured complexity.[30] Far from being a peripheral aspect of property law, the importance of interactions between the elements of the legal landscape is at the centre of why property law has the architecture it does. Why is property a law of things?[31] Why isn't the bundle of rights fully protean, as many accounts would lead us to expect? Why has the drive since Legal Realism to make legal concepts in property and other areas shallow and fact-bound not been more successful?[32] And why have law reform efforts – including Restatements – often caused the law to become more and not less unmanageable in its complexity?

A part of an answer to all of the above is the failure to recognise that law is a complex system, the easy assumption that effects are linear, and the consequent disdain for

[26] AS Gold and HE Smith, 'Sizing up Private Law' (2016), available at SSRN: https://ssrn.com/abstract=2821354; Smith (n 7 above).

[27] See CM Herr, 'Generative Architectural Design and Complexity Theory' paper for the International Conference on Generative Art (2018), available at: https://www.researchgate.net/publication/30870757/download.

[28] J Jacobs, *The Death and Life of Great American Cities* (New York, Random House, 1961); P Katz (ed), *The New Urbanism: Toward an Architecture of Community* (New York, McGraw-Hill, 1994).

[29] Modularity theory is most famously applied to architecture in the work of Christopher Alexander. See C Alexander, S Ishikawa, M Silverstein, M Jacobson, I Fiksdahl-King and S Angel, *A Pattern Language: Towns, Buildings, Construction* (New York, Oxford University Press, 1977).

[30] See eg Smith (n 22 above).

[31] Smith (n 7 above).

[32] HE Smith, 'The Persistence of System in Property Law' (2015) 163 *University of Pennsylvania Law Review* 2055.

'metaphysical' doctrine. To begin with, the division of the world into legal things itself lends modularity to the system of property law.[33] If things are made up of attributes, which attributes are gathered together into a thing? Attributes that are highly complementary should go together and those that are not will tend not to. By defining legal relations like rights, duties, powers, and so on, over legal things, many of the internal aspects of things and their uses can be irrelevant to third-party actors. The laws of trespass to personal property and conversion do not depend on that information. Nor do those torts depend on the kind of engine the car has, whether it has leather seats, and on and on. In the case of personal property, the law can rely mostly on everyday ontology for what a thing is: chairs and pencils are things, etc. In some borderline cases, the law will specify that a collection, like a herd of animals, can also be a thing.

When it comes to real property, the thing subject to possession and ownership is more artificially constructed – boundaries need to be marked and possibly registries created and maintained. Once parcels are defined this way, much activity – farming, parking cars, reading books – can take place with no relevance to duty bearers under the law of trespass. The legal definition of real property also includes the *ad coelum* principle – one who owns the surface owns to the heavens above and the depths below – and here we find sensitivity to what is complementary to the use of the surface and what is not. Airspace at cruising altitudes is useful for airplanes (these days) and is not complementary or very interactive at all with activities at the surface. Thus, with the advent of airplane overflights it is not surprising that courts have defined the airspace used for navigation ('avigation') as a separate resource.[34]

Architecture is the solution to the complexity problem in property law as in many other complex systems. Property law provides devices to manage complexity that could not be replicated by private contracting.[35] What I mean by the architecture of property and what I think a Restatement should capture are a reflection of a fundamental aspect of property law in any legal system – its complexity. The solution is not to throw out the idea of reform altogether or to abolish Restatements. Instead, Restatements in general and a Restatement of Property in particular can put us on the road back to an appreciation of system in property law and a rebuilding of the architecture that would better implement it.

B. Solving the Problem of Architecture

Before turning to how to build architecture into a Restatement, it is worth considering what the system of property law requires. To see this, it is instructive to consider the very partial view of system and complexity that has characterised the Restatement process in the past.

[33] Smith (n 7 above); T Sichelman and HE Smith, 'Modeling Legal Modularity' (draft, 2017).

[34] See S Banner, *Who Owns the Sky? The Struggle to Control Airspace from the Wright Brothers On* (Cambridge MA, Harvard University Press, 2008).

[35] Lee and Smith (n 19 above); HE Smith, 'Economics of Property Law' in F Parisi (ed), *The Oxford Handbook of Law and Economics, Volume 2: Private and Commercial Law* (Oxford, Oxford University Press, 2017) 152; *cf* H Hansmann and R Kraakman, 'The Essential Role of Organizational Law' (2000) 110 *Yale Law Journal* 387, 406–07.

There is a traditional notion of architecture in the law, which is only partly what I have in mind. Some would see architecture and system as an aspiration of the civil law, perhaps tracing back to what was received from Roman law.[36] 'Architecture' and 'system' are associated with conscious design and abstract conceptualism. In contrast, the common law would be more spontaneously created and lack any designed architecture or system.

Here is not the place to wade into these debates. Instead, what I mean by 'architecture' and 'system' are as true of the common as of the civil law. A complex system can arise spontaneously or as a mixture of spontaneous and direct development. The point is that its organisation into components and the manner of the interaction determine both how the system works statically and how it shifts dynamically. Both are major aspects of CST.

The architecture of property law is reflected in doctrine. One might think – and a strain of conventional wisdom I am associating with the legacy of Legal Realism does hold – that any architectural features that property law exhibits are a matter purely of doctrinal carry-over and are decorative at best and distorting at worst. The architecture of property is something to overcome and not to celebrate.

This is mistaken and on a certain level clearly mistaken. Property has an architecture not because of blind adherence to tradition or false consciousness or the operation of hidden agendas. One can't rule out that some such may sometimes occur. However, as an explanation for all architectural aspects of property these nefarious sources and dismissible considerations fall far short of explaining why property has an architecture and why it should. For reasons familiar from CST that I will explore shortly, even in the absence of aesthetic and political considerations, a system that manages complexity is a necessity in property law. Especially in the United States, to say that property has an architecture one has to show why – on functional grounds – it has this architecture and why those reasons are good ones. A certain degree of functionalism is inescapable.

It is worth noting that uncertainty and complexity – paired together – were presented by the American Law Institute (ALI) as the reason for Restatements in the first place. The ALI commissioned a study in 1923, the Report of the Committee on the Establishment of a Permanent Organization for the Improvement of the Law, which formed the blueprint for the ALI and the Restatements. The authors of the report cited the number of decisions, the number of potentially applicable laws, and the number of facts that could be relevant to a case as the causes of the increased complexity of the law.[37] What the report does not mention is the potential for interaction among cases, statutes, regulations, and facts that can potentially be far more important than mere numerosity to the problem of complexity in the law. If the effects of additional legal materials and facts are additive, then a doubling of the legal materials and facts will lead to a doubling in their contribution to the cost of resolving a case. But with interaction effects the effect can be much greater than linear: each new case, each new rule, each new fact can potentially interact with all the existing ones. If a system has 100 elements, the addition of one element that can interact

[36] This is different from the totality of Roman law, which was quite casuistic and equitable. See, eg, F Schulz, *History of Roman Legal Science* (Oxford, Oxford University Press, 1946); A Watson, *The Spirit of Roman Law* (Athens GA, University of Georgia Press, 1995). The part of Roman law that travelled was more modular, and perhaps its modularity made it easier to adopt and adapt.

[37] The American Law Institute, *Report of the Committee on the Establishment of a Permanent Organization for the Improvement of the Law* (Philadelphia PA, The American Law Institute, 1923) 71–78.

with any of the existing elements increases the interactions by 100 (or by $n - 1$ for the addition of the nth element).

Because of these potential non-linear effects, the uncertainty in the law goes far beyond the kinds cited in the American Law Institute's 1923 Report. Interaction and nonlinear effects make inferences about the system as a whole – and how it bears on any situation – potentially more difficult to predict. This is a kind of uncertainty that dwarfs the problems of loose legal terminology and hard-to-find case law. It is also the kind of subtle effect that can be exploited by sophisticated actors. Consider an extreme example, tax law, where it is precisely the interaction of various provisions that provides the most fertile ground for tax evasion.[38] Only those who can afford expert help can make such a system work for them.

To illustrate how the incomplete view of complexity set forth in the 1923 ALI Report played itself out in the early parts of the Restatement (First) of Property, take the notion of an *in rem* right. In a conscious effort to follow Hohfeld, Harry A Bigelow, the Reporter, couched the early Sections of the Restatement in terms of rights, duties, privileges etc, closely tracking Hohfeld's scheme. Although not using Hohfeld's term 'multital,' the Restatement did implicitly adopt the Hohfeldian view that what we call '*in rem* rights' are really congeries of many similar rights availing bilaterally between owners and others.[39] If this weren't clear enough, Bigelow was challenged at an ALI meeting by one of the Council members, a Mr Beers, for failing to make mention of the idea that property 'is a right against all persons, against all the world.'[40] In Hohfeldian fashion, Bigelow replied that 'I do not believe that there is any such thing as a right against the world at large, against everybody.'[41] While there has been a lively discussion of what 'a right availing against others generally' exactly means, one advantage of thinking in terms of *in rem* rights is that it reflects the economising method of delineation that the law actually adopts: the law does not spell out *in rem* rights one by one as between each pair of members of society (much less with respect to each individual stick). Such a procedure would ignore the massive shortcut taken by delineating an *in rem* right wholesale: if someone has an *in rem* right, others generally have a duty unless they are specifically excepted.[42] Moreover, by acting as if, in principle, delineation occurred pair by pair and stick by stick, the door is opened to all sorts of complexity and intractability from the possible interaction of these fully articulated basic legal relations. In keeping with the ambition to capture rather than to tame

[38] DA Weisbach, 'Formalism in the Tax Law' (1999) 66 *University of Chicago Law Review* 860, 871 (arguing that responses to evasion rules increase complexity because of their potential interaction, making standards often more attractive in tax law).

[39] Hohfeld analysed '*in rem*' rights as a collection of bilateral rights. Where conventionally one would speak of an *in rem* right, Hohfeld said the right was 'multital,' meaning one of a cluster of many 'unital' or one-on-one right-duty pairs, availing against many others. Instead of *in personam* rights, Hohfeld saw 'paucital' rights, which were no different from *in rem* rights except in being paired with few similarly unital rights. WN Hohfeld, *Fundamental Legal Conceptions as Applied in Judicial Reasoning* (1917) 26 *Yale Law Journal* 710, 718–33. For discussion, see TW Merrill and HE Smith, 'The Property/Contract Interface' (2001) 101 *Columbia Law Review* 773, 780–89.

[40] HA Bigelow and RR Powell, 'Discussion of Property Tentative Draft No 1' (1929) 7 *The American Law Institute Proeedings* 199, 207, 211.

[41] ibid 215.

[42] A Kocourek, 'Rights in Rem' (1920) 68 *University of Pennsylvania Law Review* 322, 322; AS Gold and HE Smith, 'Scaling Up Legal Relations' in Balganesh, Sichelman and Smith (n 21 above), available at SSRN: https://ssrn.com/abstract=3091652.

complexity, Bigelow acknowledged that one person could hold a right against many people and the rights could be identical save in the identity of the duty bearer. Nevertheless, Bigelow cited the possibility of variation as the selling point for his Hohfeldian approach, on the grounds that the rights 'may vary according to the man.'[43] He went so far as to deny that 'accurately speaking,' there was '[any] such thing as a right against the world at large, or as the older authorities said, in rem.'[44] In the attempt to be accurate and perhaps to capture the complexity of modern life, the role of rules, the generality of the *in rem* right, and the converse generality of the duty to respect others' *in rem* rights that is facilitated by their impersonality are completely suppressed. This partial view of complexity has the perverse effect of leaving complexity completely untamed. Ironically, given its emphasis on context and complex social reality, the Restatements and the then-nascent American Legal Realism do a relatively poor job of dealing with the complexity of the law.[45]

The field of complex systems is suited to filling the gap left by traditional notions of legal complexity like that set out in the ALI's 1923 Report. The numerosity of legal rules, facts, and sources of law is important, but is only part of – and maybe the less important part of – the problem of complexity in the law. It is the interactions *between and among* rules, facts, and legal sources that make complexity so hard to deal with. The methods of dealing with this complexity include modular systems and concepts that organise this mass of interactions. The question then becomes how to implement these devices in a Restatement.

III. Restating: The Process

Restating architecture is a tall order because restating is itself not just a result but a process. That process includes meetings with advisory groups that go through sections one by one sequentially. Drafts are then evaluated and approved by the ALI Council and eventually the membership on a basis that is hardly more wholesale. The model is legislative and the goal is judiciousness. There is a lot to admire in this process, and it is designed to reflect a consensus. Consensus can be a mixed blessing: sometimes in the past it has been easy for those with intense preferences – reformers and industry lobbyists – to convince a sometimes academically-driven enterprise to adopt too easily cumbersome, multifactor balancing tests and vague standards.[46] And it is unlikely that a Restatement can provide detailed solutions in the absence of the on-the-ground knowledge that would be required, leading again

[43] Bigelow and Powell (n 40 above) 215.

[44] ibid. He went on to say that there is: 'nothing but a series of rights against various specified individuals and ordinarily while it is accurate to say you have got a right against everybody, against the world at large, yet when you come to the Restatement where it becomes essential to analyze your right more carefully, I do not want to find ourselves committed to the proposition that there is such a thing as a right against the world at large or against an indeterminably large number of people'.

[45] On complexity and realism, see HE Smith, 'On the Economy of Concepts in Property' 160 (2012) *University of Pennsylvania Law Review* 2097; Smith n 22 above.

[46] A Schwarz and RE Scott, 'The Political Economy of Private Legislatures' (1995) 143 *University of Pennsylvania Law Review* 595.

to over-reliance on vague standards.[47] To the extent that those with real-world knowledge are at the table, many areas can devolve into interest-group contests that are familiar from actual legislatures.

Let me highlight one less high-profile problem – or challenge – in the Restatement process for the area of Property. If the big problem with the received wisdom on property is the naïve bundle-of-rights picture, there is a lot in the Restatement process that reinforces it. Restating the law section by section makes it easy to think of the law in rule-by-rule terms. Everything is detachable and debatable in isolation. More specifically, the guidelines for Restatements have wound up focusing on 'selecting' the 'better rule', presumptively the 'majority rule' among American jurisdictions, or the 'minority rule' if a trend toward it can be discerned or good reasons for choosing it over the majority rule can be advanced.[48] At least insofar as the bundle of rights is concerned, the Restatement process and the vision of property implicit in the bundle picture go hand in hand.

There is some irony in this. The bundle-of-rights picture was espoused and entrenched in conventional wisdom by the Legal Realists of the 1920s and '30s, who were nothing if not sceptical of legal concepts. Indeed, some Realists poured scorn on the first generation of Restatements for being a conceptualist, and therefore inherently reactionary, enterprise (the Realists were prone to accusing anyone they disagreed with of conceptualism and formalism), but other Realists were not so negative especially after the Restatements themselves took a more Realist turn.[49] The Restatement enterprise could be accommodated to Realist ends, at least up to a point.

The common element between the Restatements and Realism is a disaggregated bundle-of-rights view. The First Restatement adopted a Hohfeldian framework (not carried through consistently), and the Hohfeldian framework was the inspiration for the bundle of rights.[50] It may well be that Hohfeld himself had planned to capture the unity of the law ('aggregate relations'), but when he died his system could be taken to be one of reductionism and disaggregation. Even as it stands, there are those who have employed Hohfeld's scheme in a more systematic and less reductionistic fashion,[51] but the Restatements were not among them. Partly, again, the Restatement process reinforced the reductionism of the bundle of rights. Restating rule by rule, interest by interest, as reflected in section-by-section drafting discussion and to some extent voting, meant that a disaggregated and linearly aggregated version of property was almost an inevitable product of the process. As a result, the Restatements, however conceptualistic they might at first have appeared to some Legal Realists, shared with Realism a lack of appreciation of the unity and system in the common law of property.

Another facet of the Restatement process contributes to the 'flattening' of the law: the search for direct solutions. Once the process focuses on problems in property law on a

[47] A Schwartz and RE Scott, 'The Common Law of Contract and the Default Rule Project' (2016) 102 *Virginia Law Review* 1523, 1527–32.

[48] The American Law Institute, *Capturing the Voice of the American Law Institute: A Handbook for ALI Reporters and Those Who Review Their Work*, revised edn (Philadelphia PA, The American Law Institute, 2015) 5–6.

[49] KD Adams, 'Blaming the Mirror: The Restatements and the Common Law' (2007) 40 *Indiana Law Review* 205.

[50] Merrill and Smith (n 3 above).

[51] Sichelman (n 21 above); McFarlane and Douglas (n 20 above).

section-by-section, rule-by-rule basis, the search for solutions is pushed into this mould. The kinds of solutions sought are direct ones that can be formulated in one or more sections. Thus, in the Restatement (Second) of Torts, different definitions of possession are offered and immediately used for purposes of defining real and personal property torts.[52] Because of the incompleteness of the Restatement, the commonalities of possession between real and personal property possession, and many of the implications of possession for other aspects of property law, were not addressed. Moreover, this treatment makes possession look less dependent on extralegal standards – what counts as control, what will be taken as objective manifestations of the intent to control – than it really is. Instead, each legal area is treated as a package of disconnected rules – separate from other areas of property law and lacking in much internal structure. The emphasis is more on finding solutions to problems than on providing a platform for private ordering. (This is even more of a problem in the related areas of contracts.)

Relatedly, when community standards and an articulated area of law are flattened, the tendency has been for Restatements to formulate the law as a series of balancing tests. Famously, the Restatement (Second) of Torts formulated the law of nuisance in this way.[53] Earlier law employed the locality rule and some adjustments to it based on considerations like ease of relocation.[54] The basic idea was a second-order adjustment of the mutual rights and duties of landowners in light of the conflict, in order to come up with a set of symmetric rights that maximised the freedom of a generic landowner.[55] This process was reflected in the common law maxim, *sic utere ut alienum non laedas* ('use what is yours so as not to harm another's'), which, not surprisingly, the Realists treated as an empty and conclusory slogan.[56] Taken as a first-order test it is. But seen in a more articulated – architectural – light, the maxim neatly expressed the process of conducting such a second-order adjustment. And the traditional mutual second-order adjustment and the 'modern' balancing test can differ substantively. Under the Restatement (Second) of Torts and in keeping with Realism, one can imagine a highly valuable land-use not counting as a

[52] *Restatement (Second) of Torts* (Philadelphia PA, The American Law Institute, 1965): § 157 ('Definition of Possession' of land); § 216 ('Definition of Possession of Chattel'). The First Restatement offers substantially similar definitions in two places (n 1 above) § 157 ('Definition of Possession' of land); *Restatement (First) of Torts* (Philadelphia PA, The American Law Institute, 1934) § 216 ('Definition of Possession of a Chattel').

[53] *Restatement (Second) of Torts* (Philadelphia PA, The American Law Institute, 1979) §§ 821D, 821F, 822.

[54] See *Campbell v Seaman*, 63 NY 568, 576–77 (1876). For discussion of the nature of nuisnace see D Nolan, 'The Essence of Nuisance' Chapter 5 in this volume.

[55] JCP Goldberg and HE Smith, 'Wrongful Fusion: Equity and Torts' in JCP Goldberg, P Turner and HE Smith (eds), *Equity and Law: Fusion and Fission* (Cambridge, Cambridge University Press, forthcoming).

[56] *Hale v Farmers Elec Membership Corp*, 99 P 2d 454, 456 (NM 1940) (holding that although *sic utere* is a good moral precept, it is useless as a grounds for decision because it does not determine any right or obligation, and citing cases and commentary to this effect); see also OW Holmes, 'Privilege, Malice, and Intent' (1894) 8 *Harvard Law Review* 1, 3 ('But whether, and how far, a privilege shall be allowed is a question of policy. Questions of policy are legislative questions, and judges are shy of reasoning from such grounds. Therefore, decisions for or against the privilege, which really can stand only upon such grounds, often are presented as hollow deductions from empty general propositions like *sic utere tuo ut alienum non laedas*, which teaches nothing but a benevolent yearning, or else are put as if they themselves embodied a postulate of the law and admitted of no further deduction, as when it is said that, although there is temporal damage, there is no wrong; whereas, the very thing to be found out is whether there is a wrong or not, and if not, why not.'). For a latter-day version, see *Lucas v South Carolina Coastal Council*, 505 US 1003, 1031 (1992) (criticising invocation of the *sic utere* maxim as conclusory).

nuisance even if it causes substantial physical damage, because the activity is more valuable, passes a cost–benefit test, or the like. On the traditional approach, which requires symmetry in the landowners' rights against each other, such a result is hard to reach, because it seems rather empty to say that one should put up with physical damage arising from the operation of a factory on one's neighbour's land because one has a symmetric right to open up a valued factory on one's own land too – unless the area is one in which factories are prevalent or generally expected.

Finally and more speculatively, the Restatement process may be tilted against system because abstractions are hard to track. The point of employing concepts in an architectural fashion is that the concept can link together and manage interactions in the system. The nature of the complexity problem is that interactions are hard to foresee. A modular system makes interactions and systems effects easier to track. However, modularity is not inevitable. One can adopt the pseudo-solution of denying the problem of complexity and flattening out the law, making it cumbersome and ill-equipped to serve its purposes. Eliminating interlocking concepts means that advisors, Council members, and those voting at an annual meeting can evaluate sections in isolation without worrying about unseen effects. Indeed, those functioning in these capacities might be suspicious that an abstraction might hide a hidden agenda – that an unseen interaction effect would produce a substantive outcome that the proponents are after but are hiding – and that the evaluator might not like. To me, this concern, which is a real one, is a reason to bring out the system latent in traditional law and to be explicit when deviating from it. Especially where the system is designed to be facilitative rather than to implement solutions, a crabbed and suspicious attitude to anything that looks at all abstract is misplaced.

IV. The Stakes in Restating

Let us turn finally to the question of stakes in restating property's architecture. Why does any of this matter? To ask this question in the UK might seem a little strange. In the UK, it is taken for granted that doctrine is important. Nonetheless, even in the UK, it is less clear how receptive lawyers and judges would be to drawing attention to the connective tissue of property law and how it all fits together. A common view of the common law is that the system involved in the common law is implicit, that the common law develops incrementally and semi-spontaneously. If so, then explicit attention to systemic aspects of the common law starts looking like incipient codification and a creeping civilian approach to law. Alternatively, one might think that in a common law system architecture is implicit and it is best to leave it that way, especially in formulating the law – as opposed to theorising about it. Indeed, in the late nineteenth century the organic development of the common law was cited as a reason to resist codification.[57]

Although I have much sympathy with the empirical or inductive view of the common law, I think there is not only value but great value in putting architecture front and centre in an American Restatement of Property. In an ideal world, the law might undergo its organic

[57] A Rodger, 'The Codification of Commercial Law in Victorian Britain' (1992) 109 *LQR* 570, 570–75.

growth and theoreticians would study it with a deep appreciation of its systemic aspects. That is decidedly not our world, especially in the United States.

Let me use some property torts as illustrations of how a Restatement can capture the architecture of property. I will focus on trespass to real property and trespass to personal property (although we are covering nuisance and conversion as well). Trespass to real property appears at first to be much simpler and less controversial than nuisance, and trespass to personal property has been a backwater until the recent rise of the Internet and the possibility of trespass to computer equipment and websites. Appearances are deceiving here.

Take trespass to real property first. The tort involves an interference with possession and it involves a boundary. Trespass turns out to harbour quite a number of difficult issues. First of all, like any kind of trespass it depends on the notion of possession. In the Restatement (Second) of Torts, each kind of trespass came with its own definition of possession.[58] And yet there is a sense in which real property and personal property both involve a legal thing that can be possessed.[59] In the case of personal property we can rely more easily on everyday ontology, whereas with land we need something like the *ad coelum* principle and demarcated boundaries to define the legal thing in question. Further, although there is great variation in the control to which land and various kinds of personal property are susceptible, it is possible and desirable to give a unified definition of possession; one that does not try to spell out what control and signs of intent to control are socially recognised as possession. Possession is different from the right to possess, which is a more purely legal construct.

More surprisingly, it turns out that defining trespass to land is not easy, because courts offer different definitions for different purposes – 'gist' and 'elements' definitions. At the macro level, courts sometimes offer a 'gist' definition, based on the interest protected and the purpose of the tort. For example, courts will define trespass in terms of a gist based on possession: 'The gist of an action of trespass to real property is in tort for the alleged injury to the right of possession.'[60] A little more specific is the idea of an invasion that interferes with possession: '[T]he gist of the action is the invasion of the plaintiff's possession.'[61] Such a definition is not fully operationalised: how do we know what constitutes an injury to the right of possession or even, for that matter, what is an invasion that interferes with possession?

Here is where elements definitions come in. Elements definitions often echo (even if faintly) the older forms of action. Courts offer such definitions in specifying the tort in detail; and courts zoom in on the element that is relevant in a given case. Courts don't really have an interest in spelling out what trespass is across the board. So a fairly general

[58] See n 52 above.

[59] JW Harris stresses the role of things in property and their close relationship to trespassory rules: JW Harris, *Property and Justice* (Oxford, Oxford University Press, 1996) 30–32, 119–61. For Harris, the 'essentials of a property institution are the twin notions of trespassory rules and the ownership spectrum.' These trespassory rules are defined in part in terms of things (at 5), or 'a resource' (at 25), and 'purport to impose obligations on all members of society, other than an individual or group who is taken to have some open-ended relationship to a thing, not to make use of that thing without the consent of that individual or group' (at 5).

[60] *McNeill v Rice Engineering & Operating, Inc*, 229 P 3d 489, 492 (NM 2010) (citation omitted).

[61] *Thurston v McMillan*, 108 Me 67, 78 A 1122, 1123 (1911).

elements-style definition would be: 'The elements of a cause of action sounding in trespass are an intentional entry onto the land of another without justification or permission, or a refusal to leave after permission has been granted but thereafter withdrawn.'[62] However, most courts offering elements definitions focus in on one kind of trespass at a time. Some trespasses are boundary crossings, some are overstaying one's welcome, and some involve failing to remove an object for which one is responsible. One could say that all of these involve being responsible for some object visible to the naked eye (including one's person) being on the wrong side of a land boundary without permission. Such a definition would elegantly cover the cases, but courts don't define trespass in such a general way. Cases come to courts as boundary crossings, overstayings, and failures to remove. Nevertheless, an elements definition is distinct from a gist definition, and occasionally a court will present them simultaneously: 'On the merits, a trespass claim represents an injury to the right of possession, and the elements of a trespass cause of action are an intentional entry onto the land of another without permission.'[63]

And then there is the further question of whether lack of permission is part of the main case or is a defence. This is a surprisingly muddled issue in the United States, and what authority there is on the question is split, with permission as a defence being the more usual approach.[64] Neither solution is entirely satisfactory.

Our tentative solution is to offer two kinds of definitions, a gist definition and an elements definition. The gist definition comes first:

> § 1. Trespass to Land
>
> A trespass to land is an intentional physical intrusion upon land possessed by another that interferes with the other's interest in exclusive possession.[65]

This definition defines trespass in terms of the interest protected. By invoking the notion of intrusion, it also implicitly includes a notion of lack of permission, without the need to elevate this into an element of the plaintiff's main case. Why is this important? In a sense, the only difference between lack of permission in the main case and permission as a defence would arise in a badly argued case where a defendant loses almost by default. And yet it bothers many – including many Advisors on the Restatement project – that we would all be presumptive trespassers most of the time unless we can provide a defence. So if one has permission or authorisation, an entry (or an overstaying or a failure to remove) is not really a trespass, even if (as we will see) one might reserve the permission issue for the defence phase. The gist definition captures this important everyday intuition about trespass. Moreover, even if the elements definition has to distinguish between kinds of trespass – boundary crossings, overstayings, and failures to remove – the gist definition brings them all under one notion, that of 'intrusion' – which captures the unity of the tort.

[62] *Volunteer Fire Association of Tappan, Inc v Cty of Rockland*, 956 NYS 2d 102 (App Div 2012) (citations omitted).

[63] *Ivory v International Business Machines Corp*, 116 AD 3d 121, 129, 983 NYS 2d 110, 116 (2014) (citations omitted).

[64] *Prosser and Keeton on the Law of Torts*, 5th edn (St Paul MN, West Publishing Co, 1984) § 18, at 112 and fn 2.

[65] *Restatement of the Law Fourth, Property* (Preliminary Draft No 3, Philadelphia, The American Law Institute, 2017) 23.

When it comes to the elements definition, we are more concerned with who has to prove what and when. It is tempting to think that because this is where the rubber hits the road, this is the only kind of definition that matters. As we will see, it is as important as one might think, but not exclusively so. Our tentative elements definition of trespass to land is:

§ 2. Trespass to Land: Prima Facie Case

An actor is subject to liability to another for trespass to land if the actor intentionally:

(a) enters or causes entry of a person or thing onto land in the other's possession, or
(b) remains on land in the other's possession, or fails to remove a thing that the actor is duty-bound to remove from land in the other's possession.[66]

Here we have grouped together overstayings and failures to remove – both involving trespasses that are based not on crossing a boundary. The definition here is much more precise and provides a roadmap for plaintiffs (and defendants). Instead of general intrusion as in the gist definition, the elements definition is framed in terms of familiar tort concepts of causation and intent as well as possession. The elements definition leaves the issue of permission to a defence. Here an actor 'is subject to liability' but may not be actually liable if the actor had permission for the activity in question (the boundary crossing, the remaining, or not removing a thing).

Why two kinds of definition? Here we get into at least a small architectural or systematic aspect of the law of property torts. There may be something systematically better about having two kinds of definition than one. The two kinds of definition serve different purposes: one gives a general sense of the tort, provides a direct line to its purpose, and serves as a bridge to everyday intuitions, especially moral intuitions about wrongful behaviour. The elements definition puts defendants on notice and sharpens the issues for litigation. Each can do what it does better because it doesn't try to do what the other does. A definition that provides elements and also captures the purpose of the tort might have to be very long and involved – quite complex. Perhaps more importantly, the two kinds of definition work in tandem – they interact productively. The elements definition should be read in light of the gist definition and vice versa. Thus if a question comes up at the borderline of the elements definition or a court wants to consider modifying the elements definition, reference can be made to the gist definition. Conversely, the elements definition gives a sense of what kinds of activity count as an intrusion; so not just statically but also dynamically, the two definitions may allow for a combination of flexibility and precision that is not possible with one integrated definition. At the very least it is an empirical question whether multiple definitions undermine each other and create excessive looseness or whether, as argued here, they allow for a combination of tightness, accuracy, and fidelity to purpose not possible in any other way. That courts historically have offered both kinds of definition is suggestive evidence in favour of such an approach. It also should count for something when doing a Restatement.

[66] ibid 26–27.

V. Conclusion

Restating property can be a test of different ideas about the nature of property law. Previous Restatements have suffered from the same deficiency as general discussions of property in the United States: a partial and misleading view of the complexity of property law. The greater complexity of modern life calls not for greater complication in the law's formulations or for more vagueness to avoid the issue altogether. What is needed is to manage complexity, and for that, the law already supplies some tools in its latent architecture. It is not too late to bring those tools out into the open.

3

'Judges are Human, Not Many People Know That': The Travails of the First Instance Judge

HER HONOUR JUDGE KAREN WALDEN-SMITH

I. Introduction

At the time of delivering this talk at UCL, I had spent the previous four and a half years as one of the two Specialist Senior Circuit Judges hearing Chancery cases in the County Court at Central London. In such a role, in addition to hearing cases involving partnership disputes, trusts, wills and all other Chancery disputes, I heard large numbers of property cases, including those transferred from the Chancery Division (now the Business and Property Court). However, property cases are not exclusively the preserve of the limited number of Specialist Circuit Judges around the country dealing exclusively with Business and Property cases. Many property cases are now dealt with in the Tribunals, and, as I have discovered in my new role as Designated Circuit Judge in an area outside London, many property cases are heard by Circuit Judges as part of their more varied diet of civil work.

While most of the lower value cases involving factual conflict, such as disrepair cases, boundary disputes, residential landlord and tenant disputes, and mortgage repossessions, will be heard in the First Tier Tribunals and on the District Bench, property work involving particular points of law and higher value disputes provides a substantial part of the diet of most Civil Circuit Judges. Significant points of law can arise in such property cases and Circuit Judges are often required to make decisions at first instance in areas where the law is still developing. Decisions need to be made on fine legal and factual distinctions. In some such cases, the Circuit Judge may be required either to carve a path through apparently conflicting decisions of higher courts in order to reach a soundly reasoned decision, or reach a determination where there is simply no clear guidance or authority. If the answer to a particular legal dispute is straightforward, then it is unlikely that parties who have the benefit of good legal advice will continue to litigate. It is those cases where the law is uncertain or where there is a factual conflict in need of resolution that make it to a full hearing. A first instance decision can thus provide the foundation for a new development in a particular area of the law, but it is likely to be limited in its importance unless it is adopted on appeal to a higher court so as to create binding authority. While very high value and lengthy cases will normally be retained by the High Court, the majority of property disputes are now dealt with in the County Court or the Tribunals. Leaving to one side the cases which are entirely determined on their facts, the decisions of the Circuit Bench and the Upper Tribunal could both provide a potentially rich vein of study.

The comment, 'Judges are human, not many people know that' was made by Horace Rumpole, John Mortimer's eponymous hero of Rumpole of the Bailey, a rather world-weary criminal law hack who spent his time treading the boards in the Central Criminal Court, and whose daily battles with the judiciary, whom he considered to be either incompetent or biased, or both, formed the central focus of his professional life. It was around these battles that John Mortimer fastened his stories. When I was invited to contribute a paper to the Modern Studies in Property Law conference 2018, I was asked to consider what matters to judges at first instance in deciding property and equity cases and whether academics were in danger of missing particular matters by focusing their attention upon appellate decisions.

While the Business and Property Courts, and other courts dealing with property and equity cases, may be far removed from the criminal courts, and certainly from the fictional world first created by John Mortimer in the 1970s, I did think I would use this as an opportunity for putting in a plea for an understanding that the life of a first instance judge is not always easy; there is a heavy and diverse workload and judges are, indeed, only human. As Alexander Pope said 'to err is human' and while doing our job conscientiously, so that we all try to get it right, we are more than capable of that very human failing of making mistakes. As first instance judges we do, of course, always have the benefit of the appellate court to correct our errors when we make them and the appellate courts always have the benefit of academics telling them how they get it wrong, should that ever be the case. There is an ongoing and important debate about the role of the judge as law-maker which would engage a whole separate chapter, if not a book. What seems clear to me is that the first instance judge has a very important role at the 'coal face' in interpreting the law as it operates in practice with real people in real situations.

Over the course of the conference, the delegates had the benefit of hearing numerous learned papers on a wide range of topics falling within the umbrella of modern developments in trusts and property law. My chapter does not deal with any particular area of property or trusts law and does not seek to match the level of knowledge and understanding brought by the academics from across the world in different jurisdictions. What my chapter addresses generally is the life of a first instance judge and how academic work in the detailed study of various aspects of property and equity law, aids and assists us in our understanding of the development of the law and in our application of that law. For the purpose of illustrating the work of the first instance judge, I will refer to some particular (albeit disparate) examples.

II. Recent Changes in the Work of the First Instance Judge

The work of the first instance judge, either in the High Court or in the County Court (District or Circuit) has changed in a considerable way over the last years as a result of two major changes: the 'push down' of work from higher to lower courts and the removal of public funding from a very large number of cases that are litigated.

The pushing down of work from the higher to the lower courts has been happening over many years and for a number of different reasons. In part, it is a consequence of increased workload and lack of judicial resource. It is also an unintended consequence of the reduction in the availability of public funding: more cases are now taken to the Court of Appeal when previously, with publicly funded lawyers involved, legal advice was given at a stage which would enable an individual to accept the outcome of a case or mediate a resolution. As a result of recent changes to the Civil Procedure Rules, the High Court now hears the majority of appeals from the Circuit Bench. For a number of years the Circuit Bench has been hearing cases that would previously, either due to value or complexity, have been heard in the High Court and, as a consequence of that change, cases that previously would have been heard by a Circuit Judge are heard by the District Bench.

As for public funding, while it is still possible to obtain funding in some instances where the protection of an individual's property is at stake, it is now much more limited. While there are still a number of litigants who act for themselves because that is the way they wish to conduct their litigation, there is a well-recognised modern litigant in person who is unrepresented, not through choice, but through an inability to fund representation privately where public funds are no longer available. Such litigants, who appear in court unrepresented, often feel out of their depth and in a disadvantaged position. It is the job of the judge to try to reassure such an individual that they are not at a disadvantage by being unrepresented, but plainly having access to representation by a trained advocate is an advantage, and any points of law really need a lawyer to deal with them.

As the years have passed, various charitable and academic institutions have stepped in to fill the void. These provide different forms of support, from practical and emotional support such as the PSU (Personal Support Unit), to pro-bono legal advice and representation from well-established institutions such as the CAB (Citizens Advice Bureau) and the Bar Pro Bono Unit, through to more newly created university legal support schemes, often run in direct collaboration with the local courts. While not a complete solution to the difficulties created by lack of public funding, this patchwork of support from a range of organisations and establishments is of enormous assistance not only to the individual faced with going to court alone, which can be an extremely frightening business, but also to the court. The duty of the judge to inform and reassure an unrepresented litigant is clear. What becomes much more difficult, particularly where both sides are unrepresented, is how far the judge should intervene to ensure that all relevant evidence is adduced and all legal arguments are presented. We operate in an adversarial system and judges are not investigators. However, it seems to me that while it is plainly essential that the judge does not descend into the arena of the dispute, the judge has an obligation to ask sufficient questions to get to the truth of the issues being presented. Without such intervention the judge is unable to reach a conclusion on the issues in a way which would ultimately be consistent with the judicial oath. It is in this area – the presentation of factual evidence and the development of legal argument – that the Third-Sector network of support has been of such importance. The ability of organisations such as the PSU to give emotional and practical support enables litigants to express themselves with more confidence, concentrating on those issues which are important to their case. Other organisations that are able to give legal support give the court invaluable direct assistance.[1] All judges are extremely grateful for all their work. They help us not to fall into error.

III. The Role of a First Instance Judge

A. Determination of the Facts

One of the most difficult tasks of the judge of first instance in a civil case is to determine what happened. Unless there is complete agreement with respect to the facts, a determination as to what happened has to be made by the judge before there can be any consideration of the applicable law. As Lord Justice Denning (as he then was) put it in *Jones v National Coal Board*,[2] fundamentally, the job of the English judge is 'to find out the truth, and to do justice according to law' and 'at the end to make up his mind where the truth lies.'[3] The core judicial responsibility is to think through the issues on which he or she must decide.

In determining what happened, the judge is (at least at the outset) in a disadvantaged position. Unlike the parties and their witnesses, who know what in fact happened, the judge, without second sight, has to piece together the evidence to come to a conclusion as to what happened. There may, of course, be some genuine misremembering or misinterpretation, but in essence the parties in dispute know whether, for example, there was an agreement and the terms of that agreement. The judge has to find that out for himself or herself and, in our jurisdiction, we rely on the adversarial system to come to a conclusion as to where the truth lies. More difficult still, and this is a scenario which not infrequently occurs in property disputes – particularly involving families or former business or personal partners – are those cases where there is a lack of truth on both sides. The judge has a duty to peel away the layers of the onion in order to reach a determination which it is hoped is entirely accurate. At the very least it has to be entirely logical on the evidence presented. The public at large expect (and are entitled to expect) the judge to get the factual findings right and for our part, even if we do not always succeed, judges do try very hard to get it right.

Leaving to one side the difficulties that can be caused when parties do not have the benefit of representation, the adversarial system that we rely upon within this jurisdiction greatly assists the judge in reaching a determination as to where the truth may lie. What the adversarial system does is to give the judge the benefit of having both sides explore every point which it is thought may benefit their own case or damage the case brought by their opponent. By the end of a properly managed but thoroughly contested case, a judge will have heard more than sufficient evidence to enable him or her to come to clear conclusions as to the facts. The importance of oral advocacy equally applies to the determination of contested points of law.

[1] To take just one example, at the Modern Studies in Property Law conference at UCL in April 2018, Dr Lisa Whitehouse presented a work in progress paper on a project, funded by the Ferens Education Trust, on the provision of a regular 'Clinic on Evictions and Repossessions' (staffed by, among others, Hull Law School students) designed to better prepare occupiers faced with the loss of their home for their court hearing.

[2] *Jones v National Coal Board* [1957] 1 QB 55.

[3] ibid 63.

As Sir Alan Ward put it in his last case sitting as a Lord Justice of Appeal:

> What I do want to emphasise is that this case demonstrates one aspect of our way of doing things which does represent the very best of British. That is our procedure for extended oral advocacy in our courts … Here we had [Counsel for the Appellant], a true expert in the field, marshalling his written and oral submissions in his usual measured and compellingly persuasive way. He has commanded my admiration over the many years I have been listening to him. [Counsel for the Respondents] is less well known to me. She had a rather torrid time when subject to a penetrating but ever-courteous Socratic inquisition from my Lord, Lloyd LJ, deploying a typical and invaluable judicial technique to tease out the issues and the arguments. She recovered and advanced her case with determination. The result was, as often happens, that the oral argument swayed the Court this way and that. That is the great triumph of oral advocacy and if it gives us more to ponder it eventually makes our task easier.[4]

To a litigant involved in a property dispute, findings of fact made by the judge are likely to be crucial. This is because most cases turn largely on the facts, and, once factual findings are made, they are very difficult to dislodge on appeal. As Lord Bingham remarked:

> To the judge, resolution of factual issues is (I think) frequently more difficult and more exacting than deciding pure points of law. In deciding the facts the judge knows that no authority, no historical enquiry and (save on expert issues) no process of reasoning will help him. He is dependent, for better or worse, on his own unaided judgment.[5]

There have, of course, been many attempts by academics and eminent judges to define how a judge reaches his or her determinations on the facts. The study of the decision-making process has become extremely important in the field of criminal law, particularly in relation to sentencing. By breaking down the way in which judges reach their decisions on sentences, it has been possible to assist judges in the decision-making process and, through the publication of Sentencing Guidelines, ensure greater consistency between sentencing decisions.

This exercise has not been undertaken with respect to civil decision-making (as far as I am aware), or at least not to the same extent or for the purpose of ensuring consistency. The factual matrix of civil cases, even within a particular field such as land ownership, is extremely diverse. Explanations as to how judges reach factual findings include matters such as how the judge will concentrate upon what is common ground between the parties; and how the judge will look to identify those matters which can be established by independent evidence, such as minutes of meetings or memoranda, which may have been written long before a dispute arose. In addition, the judge will look to evidence of that which plainly did happen, even if the parties do not agree that it happened. The most vexed issue for a judge determining disputed facts between parties is how to judge the credibility of one witness as against another when they are giving conflicting but seemingly plausible accounts. Such determinations are based on matters such as consistency with other evidence and consistency with what has been said at other times. Demeanour is not seen as a reliable indicator of where the truth may lie. A witness's sullenness or aggressiveness when challenged in the witness box may be as much to do with personality or cultural background as it is to do with whether that witness is telling the truth or not.

[4] *Malik v Fassenfelt & Others* [2013] EWCA Civ 798, [2013] 3 EGLR 99, [40].

[5] T Bingham, *The Business of Judging: Selected Essays and Speeches: 1985–1999* (Oxford, Oxford University Press, 2000) 3.

B. Application of the Law

The requirement to reach decisions on the facts is, of course, while crucial, not the only role of the first instance judge. The first instance judge also has to apply the law. A first instance judgment is very likely to follow the course of setting out in short form the parties and the issues between them, followed by the factual background, and only then the law and how it applies to the facts. With such a structure, the basis upon which the final conclusions are made should be easy to follow. Most importantly, the party who fails in their claim or defence needs to understand why they have failed. As Sir Stephen Sedley said:

> To simply adopt [a] party's submissions, however cogent they are, is to overlook what is arguably the principal function of a reasoned judgment, which is to explain to the unsuccessful party why they have lost. Such an omission is not generally redressed by a perfunctory acknowledgment of the latter's arguments. Even a party without merit is entitled to the measure of respect which a properly reasoned judgment conveys.[6]

A criticism that can be properly raised against at least some first instance judges, in the lower value and straightforward cases, is that they do not provide any reasoned judgment setting out the basis of their findings and final determination. In my view, that it is a failing. Quite plainly the detail and length of judgment will alter depending upon the length and complexity of a case. A case that takes two days' hearing of legal argument in the Court of Appeal or 10 days of evidence and law in the High Court or County Court will require a fully reasoned and detailed judgment, which may well be subjected to detailed scrutiny. A short possession hearing before a District Judge will not require any particular level of detail and, on a practical level, there is simply insufficient time for a detailed judgment to be given. However, the parties are entitled to understand why a decision has been made in a particular way. If someone is losing their home they need to know why. They are entitled to understand why this potentially life-altering event is taking place and, even if the judge considers it should be self-evident, no assumptions should be made about an individual litigant's understanding. If, by way of a simple example, someone loses their home because the arrears of rent have reached a certain level and the judge considers that there is no prospect of those arrears being paid off within a reasonable period, then the judge should explain why and say so. It does not take long to set out such reasons and it is important that the losing party understands why the decision is made. It is also another means by which a judge can provide a self-check against falling into error. The setting out of factual findings and legal reasons, however brief, is a way of ensuring the decision made is both logical and justifiable.

While I am not convinced that much can be gained by the academic writer giving a detailed deconstruction of how particular findings are reached, the academic article or journal can be of enormous value to the first instance judge when a particular point of law is still developing, or is in a state of change as a result of a legislative amendment or a Supreme

[6] *IG Markets Ltd v Crinion* [2013] EWCA Civ 587, [2013] CP Rep 41, [38].

Court decision that alters the course of the law. It is a given that the law does not stay still. The development of the law takes place not only through changes in legislation and by those occasional major and ground-breaking decisions of the Supreme Court, but also incrementally through judicial decisions – particularly those of the Court of Appeal, but also of the High Court and the lower courts.

IV. Should Academics Pay More Attention to First Instance Decisions?

In general, I would not expect academics to be interested in decisions made at first instance. The primary reason for that is that first instance judges are not generally bound by the decisions of other first instance judges. While a County Court judge may be bound by a first instance decision of a judge in the High Court, the occasions when that is going to occur are rare. It would require the same legal issue to have arisen in both jurisdictions and, given the way in which specialist property work is managed between the Business and Property Court of the High Court and the specialist judges of the Business and Property Court working within the County Court, that is unlikely to happen in a property law context. I am much more likely to hear a property case in the County Court than I would as a Deputy Judge of the High Court. Very often High Court judges will become involved in property cases either because of their extraordinary financial value or because there is an application for emergency interlocutory relief, such as obtaining an injunction to restrain entry onto property by trespassers, or when the High Court is the appellate court and hearing an appeal from a decision of the County Court on a property issue. In addition, sometimes a High Court judge or Deputy may sit as a judge of the Upper Tribunal – either the Lands Chamber or the Tax and Chancery Chamber.

Secondly, for the reasons I have already set out, the first instance decision has to start with a determination of the facts. It is highly likely that, even if two cases gave rise to the same legal issues within the same general factual area, the detailed factual findings would mean that the cases could properly and easily be distinguished from each other. In most cases, the law is likely to be relatively well-settled. The first instance judge is not there to alter the law and there is likely to be authority of a higher court to follow. Our job as judges of first instance is to ensure that we follow that authority accurately. If we fail to do so, or misunderstand the law as against the facts, then the higher courts will correct us.

While in general, as first instance judges, we are following the settled law and deciding the facts of any particular case, there are particular instances where the first instance judge has a greater role. First, there are examples of cases where it is the first instance judge who is shaping the ongoing development of the law, after the Supreme Court has determined a point of law. A good example of this may be seen in recent developments in housing law. Secondly, occasionally cases at first instance raise matters of general public interest on which authority is unsettled. These cases require first instance judges to make determinations which do not simply follow the decisions of higher courts. Both examples may prove to be exceptions to the general rule that academics are unlikely to be interested in cases decided at first instance.

A. First Instance Judges Developing the Law – Housing

An area of law which is constantly changing and developing and in which the County Court is particularly engaged, is housing law. The decisions of the County Court may provide a rich vein of material for the academic as these decisions are principally dictated by application of the law and, while the factual matrix is always of importance, the very nature of the legal challenge means that it is the *application* of the law that is of primary importance. By virtue of the provisions of the Housing Act 1996, the County Court is the forum for appeals against local authorities refusing housing obligations. Consequently, while the Administrative Court still deals with some challenges made by way of judicial review to the decisions of local housing authorities relating to homelessness, it is principally the County Court which deals with statutory appeals against the decisions of the housing authority. In the same way that a judge in the Administrative Court considering a challenge to a public law decision must not usurp the function of the decision-maker, the Circuit Judge must not fall into the error of substituting his or her own decision for that of the decision-making body, the housing authority. The role of the Circuit Judge is to review the housing decision and determine whether the authority has taken into account all relevant matters in reaching its conclusion.

Issues of vulnerability are currently engaging the Circuit Bench on a regular basis, despite the relatively recent clarification given by the Supreme Court in *Hotak v London Borough of Southwark.*[7] In *Hotak*, Lord Neuberger stated that in order to decide whether someone is vulnerable for the purpose of determining whether that person is in priority need of housing, a comparison must be made between the applicant and the ordinary person if rendered homeless, rather than between the applicant and the ordinary homeless person.[8] Further, a person is vulnerable if he or she is significantly more at risk of harm without accommodation than an ordinary person would be. In *Panayiotou v London Borough of Waltham Forest*[9] the Court of Appeal determined that *Hotak* created a qualitative test and that it did not set a quantitative threshold.

A relatively recent example of how the County Court has had to grapple with the issue of vulnerability is the decision of the Court of Appeal in *Rother District Council v Freeman-Roach.*[10] The applicant, Mr Freeman-Roach, had applied to Rother District Council for assistance under part 6 of the Housing Act 1996 ('the Act'). In his application for assistance he had disclosed that he had osteoarthritis in his hands, right knee and both ankles, and that he had suffered from two strokes in 2006 and 2013 which adversely affected his speech and mobility. He also suffered from depression and anxiety. The local housing authority determined that he was not in priority need, as he did not have a physical disability which would prevent him from accessing support services, and that neither the existence of osteoarthritis nor the strokes prevented him from undertaking normal daily tasks.

The decision that Mr. Freeman-Roach was not in priority need was challenged by way of a review pursuant to section 202 of the Act, but the decision was upheld on the basis

[7] *Hotak v London Borough of Southwark* [2015] UKSC 30, [2016] AC 811.

[8] ibid [52]–[55].

[9] *Panayiotou v London Borough of Waltham Forest; Smith v London Borough of Haringey* [2017] EWCA Civ 162, [2018] 2 WLR 1439.

[10] *Rother District Council v Freeman-Roach* [2018] EWCA Civ 368, [2018] HLR 22.

that none of his medical conditions prevented him from 'looking after himself and keeping himself free from harm on a day-to-day basis'. The *Hotak* test was set out within that review decision. An appeal was made pursuant to sections 204 and 204A of the Act and the Circuit Judge granted an interim injunction compelling the local authority to accommodate Mr Freeman-Roach and in due course allowed the appeals under sections 204 and 204A. The Circuit Judge determined that the authority had failed to carry out a comparative exercise, and as a consequence no comparison had been made of the personal circumstances of Mr Freeman-Roach and those of the hypothetical ordinary person who was made homeless. He rejected a submission that there had been a failure to expressly identify the characteristics of an ordinary person but did accept that there had been a failure to undertake a 'dual analysis' of Mr Freeman-Roach and the ordinary person.

Subsequently, the local authority succeeded in its appeal against the sections 204 and 204A decisions. The Court of Appeal held that it was for the appellant to establish that there was an error of law within the decision letter: it was not for the authority to establish that there was no error. It held further that the reviewing officer was not 'writing an examination paper in housing law',[11] and that a benevolent approach needed to be adopted by the court in considering the review decision so that it did not become too legalistic.

As can so often be the case, the reason for the appeal succeeding in *Rother DC v Freeman-Roach* masks the real issues of interest which remain live for the first instance judge. The Circuit Judge erred in this case because he had, in effect, reversed the burden of proof and made the respondent authority responsible for establishing that there was no legal error in the decision of whether he was in priority need. Of course the burden falls upon the appellant to establish an error of law, and *Holmes-Moorhouse v London Borough of Richmond upon Thames*[12] had already established the importance of the benevolent approach to decisions made by local authorities. What is really at stake in this type of case is what is meant by the ordinary person made homeless, when deciding whether a person is vulnerable for the purpose of establishing priority need. *Hotak* provided that the ordinary person was not someone who was already street homeless, and further provided that the ordinary person is not to be viewed with reference to the reviewing officer's own experience as that could lead to arbitrary and unpredictable outcomes. However, who is the ordinary person? Is it someone who has to be healthy and not suffering from any mental or physical frailties that are suffered by so many people? The Court of Appeal rejected the requirement to spell out the characteristics of the ordinary person. It would, in my view, be impossible to do so. Rose J said this:

> Mr Bolton [the reviewing officer] concluded that, although he accepted that Mr Freeman-Roach suffers from mental illness and physical disability, his several conditions were either controlled by medication or did not cause him any particular functional impairment. The comparison with the ordinary person who does not suffer from those disabilities is implicit when Mr Bolton describes the effect of each medical issue on Mr Freeman-Roach's ability to function.[13]

In other words, in each individual housing appeal where an issue of vulnerability arises, it will be for the Circuit Judge to determine whether the decision-making body has properly

[11] ibid [49], citing *South Somerset District Council v Secretary of State for the Environment* [1993] 1 PLR 80, 83 (Hoffmann LJ).

[12] *Holmes-Moorhouse v London Borough of Richmond upon Thames* [2009] UKHL 7, [2009] 1 WLR 413.

[13] *Rother DC v Freeman-Roach* (n 10 above) [32].

applied the test of determining whether the appellant is vulnerable as compared to the ordinary person made homeless. There is not one definition that will fit all cases and it is not so simple, as some might suggest, as to say that the ordinary person is someone who is both robust and healthy. In cases such as these, the first instance judge is undoubtedly developing the law.

There are also specific exceptions where a first instance decision is never appealed but nonetheless gives very clear guidance. An example might be *Re Beaney*,[14] in which Martin Nourse QC, sitting as a Deputy Judge of the Chancery Division, set out the common law test for capacity for lifetime gifts. This test has survived the test of time over four decades and it remains good law, even after the Mental Capacity Act 2015 came into force.

B. First Instance Judges Developing the Law – Public Interest Cases

In cases where there is no settled authority, or the facts of the case are of a particularly unusual nature, there may also be an opportunity for a first instance judge to push upon the boundaries so as to develop the law.

There are undoubtedly differences in approach between judges sitting at first instance. As Sir Stephen Sedley put it, some judges prefer to cling to the wreckage, holding close to the safety of the well-known, while others will strike out and swim out to deeper (and potentially more dangerous) waters in an effort to develop the law. It is those who are willing to abandon the security of the ship who will ensure that the law is vibrant and not sterile.[15]

The reality is not necessarily so black and white. The judge who strikes out and swims out to deeper waters may well be compelled to do so by reason of there being no settled authority which deals with the issues being raised. In such a case the first instance judge ultimately has no-one to rely upon other than him or herself, even though any decision will be made within the general framework that has already been established.

The case of *Malik v Fassenfelt*[16] was one such case. It raised the vexed question of whether Article 8 of the European Convention on Human Rights, the right to a private life, could ever apply where the property occupied was owned by a private landowner. It was one of a handful of first instance decisions which were precursors to the final decision of the Supreme Court in *McDonald v McDonald.*[17] The Supreme Court had previously avoided making a decision about whether Article 8 had any applicability in possession claims where the landlord was a private individual or body. The issue had arisen as a side question in *Manchester City Council v Pinnock*[18] in 2010, where a court of nine Supreme Court Justices had been especially convened to deal with the issue of Article 8. In that case, the Supreme Court expressly stated that it was not going to decide the issue as to whether

[14] *Re Beaney (Deceased)* [1978] 1 WLR 770 (Ch).
[15] S Sedley, *Ashes and Sparks: Essays on Law and Justice* (Cambridge, Cambridge University Press, 2011) 362–63.
[16] *Malik v Fassenfelt* (n 4 above).
[17] *McDonald v McDonald* [2016] UKSC 28, [2017] AC 273.
[18] *Manchester City Council v Pinnock* [2011] UKSC 45, [2011] 2 AC 104.

Article 8 applied to private landlords. Of the nine judges sitting, three determined that it most definitely did apply; three decided that it most definitely did not apply; and three were definitely not sure. With such a divergence of opinion between such eminent legal minds, it can be seen how difficult it is for the first instance judge to come to a determination.

Malik v Fassenfelt involved a piece of waste land ('the land'), which was in a little village to the west of London known as Sipson. It was likely to form part of the land that would need to be compulsorily purchased if a certain proposed plan for the development of a further runway at Heathrow came to fruition. The land had been speculatively purchased by two brothers who had unsuccessfully applied for planning permission to develop it. Thereafter the land had fallen into general misuse. At one time it was used as an area for the parking of taxis and hire cars, at another time it was let to someone who carried out car breaking and had been prosecuted for contaminating the land. The land had become an eyesore. It was contaminated by oil and petrol that had been allowed to seep into it; the local homeowners were despairing as to its future and the brothers who owned it appeared to have lost interest in it. A group of, plainly well intentioned, mainly young, people came onto the land. They styled themselves as 'Grow Heathrow' or 'Occupy Heathrow' and they were occupying the land as a protest against the further expansion of Heathrow Airport. They were undoubtedly keen to remain on the land in order to make it useful to the community and to oppose expansion. To that end, they cleaned up the land and turned it into a garden nursery[19] and into a bicycle repair centre. Many had started living on the site.

The community loved it, their local MP (John McDonald) supported the use of the land, and there was a happy and harmonious relationship between the squatters who were occupying the land without any authority whatsoever, and the local villagers. The landowner brothers finally decided to make use of the land and to that end brought possession proceedings against the squatters. At first instance, the judge ordered that the squatters give the brothers possession of their land. The decision at first instance (not overturned on appeal) was that Article 8 was capable of application in such a case, even though the landowners were private individuals and the occupiers of the land were trespassers, but that it would only apply in exceptional circumstances. It was also held that it was difficult to envisage a situation in which it would not be proportionate for a private landowner to obtain an order for possession, given the landowner's own rights to private property enshrined within Article 1 of the First Protocol to the ECHR.

A case such as *Malik v Fassenfelt* was particularly clear-cut as the occupiers had entered onto the land without any licence or consent and were in a totally precarious position. However, it raised a fundamental and important point of principle for which there was no guidance from higher courts. Until the clear determination of the Supreme Court in *McDonald v McDonald* that Article 8 is not directly enforceable as between private citizens so as to alter their proprietary or contractual rights and obligations,[20] any judge faced with the issue of a trespasser on privately owned land had to deal with that issue of whether Article 8 applied.

[19] This can perhaps be seen as an example of the phenomenon of 'guerilla gardening' discussed by Farran: S Farran, 'Redrawing The Law's Definition of Property in the Light of the Contemporary Use of Urban Surfaces' Chapter 6 in this volume.

[20] *McDonald v McDonald* (n 17 above) [40]–[41].

This is an example of an issue being determined at first instance that might be of interest to academics and other writers. Not only is there the academic interest created by the conflict between two European Convention rights, the right to a private life and the right to privately own property, but there is also the fact that a decision one way or the other could have considerable financial implications, given the size of the privately rented market. Indeed, there was much written in both academic journals and practitioner journals about the issue of the applicability of Article 8,[21] and such contributions were important in finding a route through the conflicting authorities but, of course, determinative guidance to first instance judges was not provided until the Supreme Court's decision in 2016.

There are other areas, particularly involving evolving areas of law, where the judge at first instance is forced into casting away from the coastline into deeper waters. While the judge at first instance may have to do all the hard work in both dealing with the facts and clarifying the law, it is a truism that all Court of Appeal and Supreme Court decisions have to start somewhere.

City of London Corporation v Samede[22] (commonly known as the *St Paul's Churchyard case*) is another example of such a case. Just as in *Malik v Fassenfelt*, the defendants were unlawful occupants of land, raising defences pursuant to Articles in the European Convention on Human Rights. They did not rely on Article 8 (right to a private life) but on Article 10 (freedom of expression) and Article 11 (freedom of assembly).

It may be recalled that from October 2011 until the court proceedings were finalised in 2012, a large number of tents (which had risen to between 130 and 200 tents by the time of the hearing in December 2011) had been erected on both the highway owned by the City and the churchyard surrounding St Paul's Cathedral owned by the Church. The tents were being used both for accommodation but also for a library, a self-styled 'Tent City University', a welfare centre and for the provision of food and drink. The occupiers of the camp had called themselves the Occupy Movement and they were concerned with a large number of issues including the perceived crisis of capitalism, the banking industry, climate change, social and economic injustice, the culpability of Western governments in various conflicts, and many other issues besides. The protesters asserted that the camp was part of a worldwide movement.

Lindblom J (as he then was) heard the case over five days and provided a detailed and well-reasoned decision. He quickly concluded that the only arguments properly available to the defendants were those that had been raised under Articles 10 and 11 of the Convention. The defendants were convinced that their protest was profoundly important and that its success was reliant upon the manner in which it had been conducted by protesting on land around St Paul's Cathedral. The City of London Corporation argued that: the protest camp on the land was plainly at odds with the purpose of the statutory schemes created by the Town and County Planning Act 1990 and the Highways Act 1980, alongside other legislation; it interfered with the Article 9 rights of others who wished

[21] See eg S Nield, 'Clash of the Titans: Article 8, Occupiers and their Home' in S Bright (ed), *Modern Studies in Property Law*, vol 6 (Oxford, Hart Publishing, 2011). For discussion of the position after the decision of the Court of Appeal in *McDonald v McDonald*, and before the Supreme Court's decision in that case, see eg S Nield, 'Article 8 and Horizontal Effect' [2015] *Conv* 77 and E Lees, 'Horizontal Effect and Article 8' (2015) 131 *LQR* 34.

[22] *City of London Corporation v Samede* [2012] EWHC 34 (QB), (2012) 109(5) *Law Society Gazette* 21.

to worship at the Cathedral; the effects and presence of the camp had created significant disturbance to the Cathedral staff; and the camp was causing a strain on the local drainage system, a nuisance both because of the noise and the smell, a loss of open space, and interference with use of the highway. Lindblom J carried out a balancing exercise between these competing arguments, and concluded that the City had undoubtedly 'convincingly established a pressing social need not to permit the defendant's protest camp to remain in St Paul's Churchyard'.[23]

Stanley Burnton LJ listed a 'rolled up hearing' for a full Court of Appeal to hear both the permission to appeal application and, if permission were granted, the appeal itself. This course was taken partly on the basis that Stanley Burnton LJ thought it important that the Court of Appeal should consider whether the City had been right to concede that Articles 10 and 11 applied. That issue was swiftly dealt with by the Court of Appeal,[24] who determined that Articles 10 and 11 were engaged. Lord Neuberger MR held that the question that required determination was 'the limits to the right of lawful assembly and protest on the highway'.[25] He held that the factors that need to be taken into account in determining that question include: the extent to which the continuation of the protest breaches domestic law; the importance of the precise location to the protesters; the duration of the protest; the degree to which the protesters occupy the land; and the extent of the actual interference the protest causes to the rights of others, including the property rights of the owners of the land and the rights of any members of the public. Permission to appeal was refused and the decision of Lindblom J was upheld.

The Court of Appeal recognised the thorough and careful judgment given at first instance by Lindblom J, and expressed the hope that the guidance given in the Court of Appeal in the *St Paul's Churchyard case* itself, and in the other recent case of *Hall*,[26] together with the first instance decisions in both cases, would assist judges in any future cases.[27] It seems to me implicit in the judgment dismissing the application for permission to appeal, that the Court of Appeal were acknowledging that the 'heavy lifting' had been undertaken at first instance, and that the judge had been required to come to conclusions with little guidance from higher courts as to the correct course to take. This is one of those rare cases where, before the decision of the Court of Appeal, writers would have been interested in reporting the outcome – both because of the interesting legal issues that arose but also because of the general public interest.

V. Conclusion

And so, to try to draw some threads together. The role of the judge at first instance is, in essence, to make determinations on the facts and then apply the law accurately. Regardless

[23] ibid [166].

[24] *City of London Corporation v Samede* [2012] EWCA Civ 160, [2012] 2 All ER 1039.

[25] ibid [38].

[26] *Mayor of London (on behalf of the Greater London Authority) v Hall and others* [2010] EWCA Civ 817, [2011] 1 WLR 504.

[27] *City of London Corporation v Samede* (n 24 above) [61].

of the complexity of the decisions that are being made, there is generally nothing remarkable about that which should excite the interest of the academic writer. That may be different if the case involves novel points of law which have not yet been determined by a higher court, and I have given two examples of where that has happened in *Malik v Fassenfelt* and the *St Paul's Churchyard case*. There are also those cases, such as the housing appeals, where the first instance judge has to develop the law so as to deal with the particular facts of each case, leading on from the statement of legal certainty made by the Supreme Court.

As Lord Bingham put it:

> In the hierarchy of legal skills, pride of place is given, and quite rightly, to the great exponents of legal principle, those (whether academic or judicial) who weave disparate threads of authority into coherent doctrine or plant the flag of legal principle in hitherto untrodden factual territory. In comparison with these mandarin arts, the judicial determination of factual issues occupies a somewhat lowly place, an activity of its nature ephemeral, uncreative and particular.[28]

In my view, academics not only help shape the law by creating coherent structures from decided cases, but they can also assist judges in finding a pathway through the complexities, so that our decisions at first instance accurately reflect the law as it currently stands. Academics studying and writing about principles of property and equity law ought properly to concentrate upon those decisions of the Court of Appeal and Supreme Court that shape and develop the law. While what we say may be of occasional interest, what you say can be of great assistance to us.

[28] Bingham (n 5 above) 3.

PART II

Property: Definition and Protection

4

Defending Property: Self-help Remedies, the Use of Force, and the Concept of a Property Right

ROBIN HICKEY

I. Introduction

If, without my consent, you have something that belongs to me, do I have the right to take it back? And can I use force to do so? The common law has no definitive answer to these deceptively simple questions, and the uncertainty surrounding the putative 'right to recaption' has long been the subject of lament by distinguished lawyers. It remains, however, a matter of some importance, and one likely to bear considerable significance where it is at stake in proceedings, especially in criminal matters, where potentially it affords a defence to a charge of theft or criminal damage.[1] It also serves as a central manifestation of the fundamental conception of ownership at work in the common law. While it seems almost unbearably trite to say that, if O is the owner of something, she is entitled to have it, this proposition underpins and enables many very ordinary dealings with things in our daily lives. Indeed, it could be said to be the very essence of a liberal conception of ownership,[2] since, at a general level, 'having' a thing creates the conditions for that exercise of decision-making authority in respect of it which has been identified as the hallmark of ownership.[3] An account of ownership which takes seriously the foundational place of a 'right' to possess needs to be able to explain the extent of any ability to defend or retake property, and to account for the complex interplay of values at stake in framing its limits. While we might assume that a 'right' to recaption follows automatically from, or indeed is included within, O's general right to exclude others from her thing, we will see that in analytical terms this is

[1] See for example the set of decisions concerned with the removal of wheel-clamping devices for parking violations on private land, where the general issue concerns whether the remover of the clamp can set up as a defence to a charge of criminal damage that he removed the clamp to protect his property in the car: *R v Mitchell* [2003] EWCA Crim 2188, [2004] RTR 14; *Stear v Scott* [1992] RTR 226 (Note) (DC).

[2] Honoré calls the right to possess 'the foundation upon which the whole superstructure of ownership rests': AM Honoré, 'Ownership' in AG Guest (ed), *Oxford Essays in Jurisprudence* (Oxford, Oxford University Press, 1961) 113.

[3] See for example L Katz, 'Exclusion and Exclusivity in Property Law' (2008) 58 *University of Toronto Law Journal* 275, describing the essence of ownership by analogy to sovereignty and the 'agenda-setting authority' of the owner.

not straightforwardly the case, and to understand rigorously the owner's ability to recapture or defend we need to pay attention to the broader relationship between property, tort and criminal law.

A first glance at the authorities suggests that the common law uncontroversially recognises a self-help remedy to take back wrongfully-taken goods.[4] The possibility is generally framed in terms of the 'right' of the owner or prior possessor ('the right of recaption'), and this right is considered to be of ancient provenance. Thus, in an influential review of the law within the Report that informed the drafting of the Torts (Interference with Goods) Act 1977, the Law Reform Committee was of the opinion that: 'There is little doubt that, under the existing law, an owner is entitled to retake his chattel peaceably from any person who is unlawfully in possession of it …'.[5]

However, the Report goes on to express some frustration at the opacity of the law on recaption, and struggles to state its parameters exactly.[6] It also notes a tension between the state of the law and the lay-person's likely perception of her rights in this regard.[7] The analytical result has been a tendency to account for the law on recaption through discursive analysis of a series of apparently discrete propositions which bear no necessarily linear relation to each other, and have no overarching conceptual framework.[8] Correspondingly, more recent authorities have taken the view that the availability and extent of the right to recaption are far from clear, and its principles have not been very thoroughly developed.[9] In part, this might be referable to what we might term an ordinary judicial wariness of self-help as an alternative to litigation, in light of readily appreciable concerns for the risks to society which might arise as citizens are encouraged to pursue justice by their own hand.[10] But it is equally clear that the conceptual basis of the law on defence and recaption has not been authoritatively articulated, and this is a concern insofar as it reflects the intellectual poverty of a basic and foundational component of our property thought.

[4] *Blades v Higgs* (1861) 10 CB NS 713, 142 ER 634. It would be more accurate, if less pithy, to say: 'to take back goods which have been the subject of wrongful interference', since it is clear that scope of the relevant wrongs to which this self-remedy responds is broader than acts of taking.

[5] Law Reform Committee, *Eighteenth Report: Conversion and Detinue* (Cmnd 4774, 1971) [116].

[6] ibid [121].

[7] ibid [122]: 'This is a field of law which touches very closely the ordinary man's conception of his fundamental rights and in our view it is of the essence of a good law on the subject that it should allow self-help where the majority of the community think it reasonable'.

[8] For example: O can peacefully recapt something wrongfully taken; O can use reasonable force to recapt something wrongfully taken where the taking disturbs her possession; O's servants can peacefully recapt something, or use force to recapt something taken; O is entitled to enter onto the land of the trespasser to retake goods wrongfully taken. For an analytical account of the law written in this style, with close attention to the authorities, see: CA Branston, 'The Forcible Recaption of Chattels' (1912) 28 *LQR* 261.

[9] 'The law has not been clarified since the Law Reform Committee Report and one certainly cannot deduce from such scant authority as there is on recaption of chattels the general rule that a person is entitled to use reasonable force to recover a chattel of which he has been wrongfully deprived': Tuckey LJ in *R v Mitchell* [2003] EWCA Crim 2188, [2004] RTR 14, [16].

[10] See eg *Southwark London Borough Council v Williams* [1971] Ch 734, 745–46. Also note Tuckey LJ's observation in *Mitchell* that there are other routes to recovery: 'We can understand that the appellant felt annoyed by what happened because we accept that he believed that he had been lawfully parked and Metro had no right to clamp his car. But self-help was not his only reasonable remedy. He could in fact have paid the £60 (he had the cash on him), and then sought to recover it *via* Metro's appeal process or through the civil courts': *R v Mitchell* (n 9 above) [19].

Accordingly, this chapter concerns itself mainly with the overarching conceptual framework of the law of defence and recaption, rather than the details of particular doctrinal propositions.[11] Leaving aside the possible judicial preference to eschew the development of self-help remedies for public safety concerns, the argument here is that there are at least two broader jurisprudential reasons which explain why it has proved so difficult to state the law on recaption clearly. The first is an analytical issue: accounts of the law tend to assume rather lightly that a *right* to recaption actually exists, when there are reasons of first principle to doubt that it does. In particular, since in English law there is no perfect duty on anyone to restore personal property taken or withheld from an owner,[12] there can be no straightforward entitlement to take something back as a matter of right.[13] Secondly, having assumed the existence of such a right, available commentary and analysis focuses on its extent, chiefly through consideration of a number of (admittedly important) matters of policy concern (eg, can O enter the land of another to retake? is O justified in applying force in retaking?). While such matters are clearly important in determining the sphere of O's ability to act, they have no necessary connection to the presence or absence of any *right* to retake that O may have – they refer instead to the scope of duties *to which O is subject*, and which shape and constrain her authority in relation to the thing in ways extrinsic to her core property right. Each of these reasons gestures towards a deeper and counter-intuitive possibility: there is no specific right to recaption at common law. Sometimes it might seem as if there is, as where goods are retaken by a claimant as a self-help alternative to damages for the defendant's conversion, or where a defendant escapes a criminal charge by relying on an argument that the goods were hers; but when these kinds of phenomena are analysed rigorously, it turns out that each is better explained by reference to applicable rules of tortious or criminal liability, and does not necessarily depend on the existence of a formal right to recaption. This, in turn, has important and far-reaching implications for the nature and structure of property rights at common law, particularly to the extent that uncritical rehearsal of the existence of a general right to recaption has obscured the prominent role of the law of obligations in delineating property rights, resolving property loss, and implicating a broader range of human values than those prima facie at stake in a property dispute.

Each of these claims is developed in the successive parts of this chapter, and taken together they articulate both an original conceptual framework for the ability to defend and recapture property, and an account of the broader significance of this framework for the nature and justification of ownership. Section II examines the doctrinal structures that enable the protection of title to goods in English law, which for present purposes comprise

[11] For discussion on the doctrinal propositions, including commercial applications and suggestions for reform, see eg: L Aitken, 'The Abandonment and Recaption of Chattels' (1994) 68 *Australian Law Journal* 263; C Hawes, 'Recaption of Chattels: the Use of Force Against the Person' (2006) 12 *Canterbury Law Review* 253.

[12] At least as early as Bracton it was observed that actions to recover movables in English law 'will only be *in personam*, because he from whom the thing is sought is not bound to return the thing absolutely but disjunctively, to restore it or its value. By simply paying its value he is discharged, whether the thing itself is in existence or not': GE Woodbine (ed), *Henri De Bracton on the Laws and Customs of England*, vol 2, SE Thorne (tr) (Cambridge MA, Harvard University Press, 1968) 292.

[13] At least in the sense of an owner having a freestanding claim-right to take something back. This point is explored below.

liability rules implemented by the tort of conversion.[14] It argues that, in the context of interference with goods, while a given interferer, X, will come under a duty to compensate O for the loss caused by the interference, this is best understood as a remedial duty flowing from the wrong of X's conversion. Recaption represents one means of satisfying this duty, but this is analytically distinguishable from the proposition that O has a *right* to recapt, and on this view the latter proposition serves to obscure rather than clarify the functions of the law of obligations in property contexts. Section III argues that, in a related way, difficult questions pertaining to the social limits of defence and recaption have been addressed and implemented through adjustments of tortious and criminal duties, rather than by adjustments to O's ownership per se. Indeed, properly construed, even the most difficult political question about the limits of property defence – can O use disproportionate force to defend her home? – is analytically agnostic as to the nature and extent of O's property. At the level of doctrine and value, the law on the application of force to defend or recapture property is best understood as an example of the law shaping and constraining O's exercise of authority in relation to her thing in ways extrinsic to the right to exclude that forms the content of her ownership. Section IV draws the implications of these arguments together to offer a general observation on the nature of ownership in the common law: the substance of O's relation to her thing is constructed and implemented through the law of obligations. While the chapter resists the reductionist turn that would disaggregate the essence of property into obligations, it does suggest that the obligations-based structure of property protection has significant implications for the nature and justification of property rights at common law. Specifically, this structure reveals the potential of property institutions to encompass and reflect a broader range of human values than those ordinarily thought to underpin conceptions of property as a right to exclude. The potential for the social limits of this core right to be delineated and refined through competing, countervailing adjustments to extrinsic norms of tort law and of criminal law locates the doctrinal institutions which resolve property disputes in a more plural, more reflexive frame; but not one which derails ownership or its analytical form in such a way as to threaten the autonomy-serving and transactional value championed by exclusion accounts. In this way, attentiveness to the obligation-based doctrinal and analytical structures of ownership offers a solution to the persistent theoretical and practical problem of framing property institutions to reflect plural, incommensurable values in ways consistent with the demands of the rule of law.

II. There is No *Right* to Recaption

Whilst it might seem deeply counter-intuitive to suggest that an owner of something might not have a right to take it back, here I argue that this is the most accurate rendering of O's position. The argument develops, first, through some observations of first principle about the protection of title to goods, and then by noting some corroborating features of the current law.

[14] On the general distinction between property rules and liability rules, see G Calabresi and AD Melamed, 'Property Rules, Liability Rules, and Inalienability: One View of the Cathedral' (1972) 85 *Harvard Law Review* 1089.

In English law, protection of ownership interests in goods is achieved through the law of torts, and chiefly the tort of conversion.[15] The evolution of tortious norms in this respect is deeply contingent, and the history of the procedural development of conversion is fascinating and frustrating in equal measures;[16] but English law has arrived at a position that appears to effect and protect a very pure notion of property as a right to exclude. If, abstractly construed, O's ownership of something consists in everyone else coming under a duty not to interfere with O's control of that thing,[17] in English law this finds doctrinal expression in the general duty not to convert O's thing. What counts as a conversion – that is, what counts as a breach of the duty not to interfere with O's control – has not entirely succumbed to satisfactory definition; but the gist is that conversion is 'an act of deliberate dealing with a chattel in a manner inconsistent with another's right whereby that other is deprived of the use and possession of it'.[18] It is clear that this catches even transient, non-exhaustive uses.[19] Accordingly, in English law, the content of O's ownership of something can be understood to comprise the general duty on everyone else not to interfere with O's control of the thing; and correlatively, O has the *right* to exclude everyone else from control of the thing.

Where a given interferer, X, converts O's thing, he comes under a specific duty[20] to remedy O's loss.[21] Importantly, this does not inevitably entail that O recovers the thing *in specie*. Damages is the ordinary remedy for conversion (as it was in the Roman *vindicatio*; often, though perhaps a little uncritically, taken as the paradigm property claim).[22] Specific recovery is possible but exceptional. Section 3 of the Torts (Interference with Goods) Act 1977 preserves established jurisdictions at common law and in equity to order a defendant to deliver-up converted goods, but such an order is expressly at the discretion of the

[15] See generally S Green and J Randall, *The Tort of Conversion* (Oxford, Hart Publishing, 2009); *Clerk and Lindsell on Torts*, 22nd edn (London, Sweet & Maxwell, 2017) ch 17; P Birks 'Personal Property: Proprietary Rights and Remedies' (2000) 11 *King's College Law Journal* 1.

[16] For an excellent overview, see S Douglas, *Liability for Wrongful Interference with Chattels* (Oxford, Hart Publishing, 2011); and JB Ames, 'The History of Trover' (1897–98) 11 *Harvard Law Review* 277, continued 374.

[17] B McFarlane, *The Structure of Property Law* (Oxford, Hart Publishing, 2008) 140; J Penner, *The Idea of Property in Law* (Oxford, Oxford University Press, 1997); TW Merrill and HE Smith, 'The Morality of Property' (2007) 48 *William & Mary Law Review* 1849, 1850; TW Merrill, 'Property and the Right to Exclude II' (2014) 3 *Brigham-Kanner Property Rights Conference Journal* 1, 3.

[18] *Kuwait Airways Corpn v Iraqi Airways Co (Nos 4 and 5)* [2002] UKHL 19, [2002] 2 AC 883, [38], Lord Nicholls approving the general statement of the law taken from the 17th edn of *Clerk and Lindsell*. Now see *Clerk & Lindsell* (n 15 above), [17-06].

[19] *Aitken Agencies Ltd v Richardson* [1967] NZLR 65; *Petre v Heneage* (1701) 12 Mod 519, 88 ER 1491; *Vandrink and Archer's Case* (1591) 1 Leon 221, 74 ER 203; *Walgrave v Ogden* (1591) 1 Leon 224, 74 ER 205.

[20] For present purposes the important point is that, as a consequence of facts relating to X's conduct, X becomes obligated to respond to O. There is an important debate about whether X immediately comes under a legal duty to O, or whether X incurs a liability which is perfected by a later court order: see eg S Smith, 'Duties, Liabilities, and Damages' (2012) 125 *Harvard Law Review* 1727, arguing that only a liability arises. Either way, O's recovery follows from the remedial responsibilities of X.

[21] Remedies for conversion are uncontroversially compensatory in nature and aim, and damages is the ordinary award: 'The action in conversion is a purely personal action and results in a judgment for pecuniary damages only. The judgment is for a single sum of which the measure is generally the value of the chattel at the date of the conversion together with any consequential damage flowing from the conversion and not too remote to be recoverable in law', Lord Diplock in *General and Finance Facilities Ltd v Cooks Cars (Romford) Ltd* [1963] 1 WLR 644 (CA), 650. See generally *Clerk & Lindsell* (n 15 above), [17-93].

[22] In substance and form, the *vindicatio* is much closer to conversion than is commonly assumed: see R Hickey, 'Wrongs and the Protection of Personal Property' [2011] *Conv* 48, 55.

court, and it is clear that the jurisdiction will not be exercised where damages would be an adequate remedy.[23] This means in practice that litigation will rarely enable O to get her thing back, unless she can establish that the asset bears deep personal significance, or that for other reasons it would be impossible to replace it in the current state of the market.[24] Accordingly, the content of O's remedial right is best understood as comprising a duty on X to compensate for O's loss, which in most cases will be achieved by paying her the value of the thing at the date of its conversion. The compensatory aims of this remedial right are corroborated and further reflected in a number of ancillary rules, such as the courts' ability to require O to accept the tender of equivalent goods in satisfaction of her loss.[25]

It bears emphasis that, where it arises, the operative cause of O's remedial right is X's *wrong* (specifically, X's conversion of O's goods to X's own use).[26] In the absence of a conversion, O can assert no specific right against X in relation to the thing in question. This is outstandingly (and perhaps absurdly) demonstrated in a set of cases where O fails to recover her goods notwithstanding that X agrees that an asset in dispute belongs to O.[27] In *Clayton v Le Roy*,[28] for example, the claimant's watch was stolen, and the claimant told the jeweller from whom he had earlier bought the watch of the theft. Following the theft, a serendipitous chain of transactions, which included a good faith purchase, culminated in the purchase of the watch by a Mr Bennett, who sent the watch to the same jeweller for repair. The jeweller recognised the watch, and wrote to the claimant to advise that Mr Bennett was willing to return the watch if the claimant would pay the purchase price. Incensed at the suggestion, the claimant ill-advisedly purchased and served on the jeweller a writ of detinue (for present purposes, a forerunner of conversion);[29] *ill-advisedly* because he did so prior to making a formal demand that the defendant jeweller re-deliver the watch to him. Since the defendant had not refused a formal request prior to the purchase of the writ, the court held that the defendant had committed no wrong at the date of the writ, and the claimant had no remedial entitlement.[30] Cases in this line serve to demonstrate that owning something is not, without more, sufficient to generate a specific right against X to its value or recovery, the latter depending entirely on X's commission of a recognised wrong.

This wrongs-based structure of the law has crucial implications for the analytical nature of property rights, and in turn for the idea of a freestanding right to recaption. Other things being equal, and absent any conduct amounting to a wrong, O's ownership consists solely in the general duty of others not to interfere with her control of the thing.[31] This general duty

[23] *Clerk & Lindsell* (n 15 above) [17-89]; Green and Randall (n 15 above) 207–08.

[24] *Howard E Perry Ltd v British Railways Board* [1980] 1 WLR 1375.

[25] *Solloway v McLaughlin* [1938] AC 247.

[26] For the more general view that this linkage between wrong and corresponding right of action has critical implications for our understanding of tort law, see J Goldberg and B Zipursky, 'Civil Recourse Defended: A Reply to Posner, Calabresi, Rustad, Chamallas, and Robinette' (2013) 88 *Indiana Law Journal* 569.

[27] For the view that the results in these cases are 'absurdly unfair', see N Palmer, 'The Abolition of Detinue' [1981] *Conv (NS)* 62, 68.

[28] *Clayton v Le Roy* [1911] 2 KB 1031.

[29] See generally S Douglas, 'The Abolition of Detinue' [2008] *Conv* 30.

[30] *Clayton v Le Roy* (n 28 above) 1050, 1052.

[31] McFarlane (n 17 above) 22–23, 140; Penner (n 17 above). For an overview of the theoretical position which emphasises the right to exclude as the basis of ownership, see Katz (n 3 above), 279–85, and the discussions cited there.

protects and preserves a sphere of freedom for O to deal with the thing as she sees fit – to use and enjoy it, to paint it pink, to give it away, and so on.[32] But this is understood as a negative liberty,[33] which, though it safeguards and enables O's ability to make decisions about how to use the thing,[34] nevertheless entails no further enumerated claim-rights, including no claim-right to retake.[35] When O in fact retakes something in circumstances where no one has committed any wrong, as for example where she loses something in a public place and later retraces her steps to take it back, the jural position is more accurately rendered by saying that O has a liberty to retake the thing,[36] that liberty consisting in the absence of a duty on O *not to retake* the thing: ie, O is not in breach of duty to X (or Y, or Z, or anyone else) if O does retake the thing, and correlatively, X (or Y, or Z, or anyone else) has no-right of redress if O does retake the thing. This proposition is evident, though only impliedly articulated, in the cornerstone principle of relativity of title at common law. Any possessor of goods acquires a property right good against the whole world except those who can prove an earlier, and therefore better, title.[37] From the opposite end, only those with an earlier, better title can exclude a possessor of goods from the thing in question. Unless she comes under such a duty of non-interference, O is free to take the thing in question; and it is this freedom – the absence of a duty *not to interfere* – that accounts for O's ability to take things that belong to her in circumstances where she has not been wronged.

Other things being equal, the model applied where O simply loses a thing in a public place and goes to get it back would also fall to be applied where the thing is in X's possession. On this model, O has a liberty against X to recapture. It follows that if O is to be considered to have something more than this – if she is considered to have a technical claim-right to recapture goods, as appears to be the orthodox view – this claim-right plausibly could arise only in response to some further breach of duty by X occasioned on the facts. This means that, if it exists, the right to recaption it is at best a remedial claim-right corresponding to X's duty to compensate O for the loss occasioned by X's interference with O's control. Here, however, the general remedial structure of conversion discussed above,

[32] JW Harris, *Property and Justice* (Oxford, Clarendon Press, 1996) 29–32.

[33] I Berlin, 'Two Concepts of Liberty' in I Berlin, *Four Essays on Liberty* (Oxford, Oxford University Press, 1969).

[34] The duty of non-interference is a 'protective perimeter': see HLA Hart, 'Legal Rights' in HLA Hart, *Essays on Bentham: Studies in Jurisprudence and Political Theory* (Oxford, Clarendon Press, 1982) 162, 171–73; Penner (n 17 above) 40; and J Penner, 'Ownership, Co-ownership, and the Justification of Property Rights' in T Endicott, J Getzler and E Peel (eds), *Properties of Law: Essays in Honour of Jim Harris* (Oxford, Oxford University Press, 2006) 167–68.

[35] Thus equally, for example, O has no claim-right to use her thing: see eg S Douglas and B McFarlane, 'Defining Property Rights' in J Penner and HE Smith (eds), *Philosophical Foundations of Property Law* (Oxford, Oxford University Press, 2013) 219. Indeed, strictly speaking, no Hohfeldian claim-right is a claim-right of the holder to do a particular thing, since a claim-right can only be about the conduct of somebody else: J Finnis, 'Some Professorial Fallacies About Rights' (1972) 4 *Adelaide Law Review* 377, 379. So a claim-right to recapture, like a claim-right to use, does not make analytical sense. The most that could be said is that X may be under a duty to O to allow O to retake the thing.

[36] A liberty is properly distinguished from those rights (called 'claim-rights') which correlate to legal duties. Indeed, a liberty consists exactly in the absence of any such duty. Where O has a liberty to do something, in so doing O breaches no duty to X. Correlatively, X has no-right that O shall not do so, and is not entitled to redress if O does: WN Hohfeld, 'Some Fundamental Legal Conceptions as Applied in Judicial Reasoning' (1913–14) 23 *Yale Law Journal* 16, 32–33.

[37] WJ Swadling, 'Property' in A Burrows (ed), *English Private Law*, 3rd edn (Oxford, Oxford Universty Press, 2013) [4.422].

which leans against specific recovery and favours damages as a standard award, argues against conceiving a remedy of recaption as a matter of right. To the extent that it is permitted, successful recaption surely satisfies O's claim against X, but that is exactly the point: like the court's function to compel O to accept an equivalent,[38] recaption provides one means of satisfying X's obligation to remedy the loss caused by his conversion. Beyond this, it is not clear that the idea of a right to recaption has any analytical value, and indeed to conceive of O's entitlement to retake in terms of a claim-right serves to obscure rather than clarify the nature of property at common law.

This is not to say, of course, that the law does not sometimes facilitate O's self-help recovery of things taken from her. Clearly it does so in a number of important ways: for example, the potential for a refusal to re-deliver on demand to amount to a conversion provides an encouragement to X to avoid liability by returning a thing he knows is not his;[39] and the potential for O to evade a possible competing liability for improvements made to the thing by X,[40] to say nothing of evading the general costs and probative challenges of litigation, seems to incentivise self-help over recourse to the courts.[41] The point here is just that none of these things entails that O has a *right* to retake something that belongs to her. Strictly speaking she does not. Generally she is at liberty to retake her thing, and in appropriate circumstances she will acquire a remedial right that X compensates her for her loss, which might be satisfied by retaking; but in analytical terms this is not the same as holding that she has a right to recaption.

III. Policy-Ends Effected by Obligations, Not Property

As noted above, cases and commentary on recaption tend not to be concerned with the existence of a right to recaption per se, and rather assume its availability and ancient provenance. The purpose of this section is not to object further to this analytical mistake, but rather to highlight a related consequence. The kinds of issues which have troubled courts and commentators about the practice of self-help have concerned what we might term the social limits of O's behaviour, reflected for example in particular questions about whether and to what extent O can access X's land to take back her thing, or use force to secure its recovery. These kinds of limits are self-evidently of interest and import to a stable and peaceful society, and there is no question that they represent an appropriate matter for adjudication. Here I wish to observe, though, that the accomplishment of these ends bears no necessary connection to the presence or absence of any right to retake that O may have. It depends instead on the scope of duties *to which O herself is subject*, and which shape and constrain her exercise of authority in relation to the thing in ways extrinsic to her core property right.

[38] *Solloway v McLaughlin* (n 25 above); Green and Randall (n 15 above) 209–10.
[39] *Howard E Perry Ltd v British Railways Board* (n 24 above); *Issack v Clark* (1614) 2 Bulst 306, 80 ER 1143.
[40] *Greenwood v Bennett* [1973] QB 195.
[41] Green and Randall (n 15 above) 209–10.

The report of the Law Reform Committee which informed the Torts (Interference with Goods) Act 1977 engaged in specific discussion of defence and recaption; and, whilst its recommendations relating to defence and recaption were not enacted in the 1977 Act, it continues to represent a useful and authoritative account of the law.[42] Instructively, having briefly rehearsed the availability of a general right of peaceable recaption,[43] the report took the view that the law was far from clear on the extent of the right, principally as to whether force might be used to retake property, and whether it was possible without permission to enter onto the land of another to retake property.[44] Having considered but rejected the value of an absolute prohibition on retaking in either of these scenarios, the report proposed to resolve the current ambiguity with the proposition that neither should be permitted unless the person retaking had acted reasonably.[45] This would require judgements on the facts of particular scenarios, and while it leaves open the question of whether such context-sensitive patterns of reasoning are consistent with the lay-person's wish to know very clearly in a stipulated context how she should behave, nevertheless the proposed approach is consonant with the historical development of the law in this area. Consider the following quotation from Blackstone:

> If, for instance, my horse is taken away, and I find him in a common, a fair, or a public inn, I may lawfully seize him to my own use: but I cannot justify breaking open a private stable, or entering on the grounds of a third person, to take him, except he be feloniously stolen; but must have recourse to an action at law.[46]

The aim of this quotation is to delineate when O's entry onto land for the purposes of retaking will be *lawful*. Other things being equal, like everyone else in the world, O is under a duty not to enter land belonging to X unless and until she is permitted to do so (eg, unless and until X exercises his power to alter the prevailing jural relation by releasing O from her duty not to enter on the land). The proposition at stake is that this is otherwise where X has taken O's goods onto X's land. If this is true, and the authorities seem to suggest that it is, analytically there are two possibilities, each of which comes to the same thing in practice. Either: (i) X's general right to exclude others from the land is not available against O for so long as X retains on his land goods he has taken wrongfully from O, such that correlatively we can regard O as being under no duty not to enter X's land in these circumstances (ie O has a liberty to enter X's land for the purpose of recaption); or (ii) while O is still under a prima facie duty not to enter X's land where X has wrongfully taken O's goods, on the facts this duty is waived by operation of law, such that O has an immunity to enter the land for the purposes of retaking.[47] Either way, the net result is that O can enter to retake the goods, and this result is effected analytically by an adjustment of the prima facie duty to

[42] Law Reform Committee (n 5 above).

[43] ibid [116].

[44] ibid [117]–[119].

[45] ibid [125].

[46] E Christian (ed), *Commentaries on the Laws of England by Sir William Blackstone*, vol 3, 15th edn (London, Cadell & Davies, 1809) 4.

[47] In Hohfeldian terms an immunity is the opposite of a liability, and correlates to a disability ('no-power'). So if O has an immunity against X, X has no power to sue O, and so O is not under a liability to be sued by X: (n 36 above) 55.

which O is subject (the duty not to enter X's land). Instructively, then, the question whether O can enter X's land to retake something is analytically agnostic as to O's property rights: irrespective of whether O is accurately regarded as having a formal right to retake her goods, the matter of her entry to X's land can be addressed and resolved by considering the scope of the duties O owes towards X.

A similar pattern emerges in respect of O's ability to use force to defend goods. Again the cases and commentaries seem to proceed on a default assumption that in at least some circumstances it is permissible for O to retake goods and to use force in so doing; and again this assumption is perhaps adopted too uncritically.[48] However, for present purposes the broader point is that cases of this kind are not strictly about the scope of O's rights. All of the pertinent questions of law which have occupied judges in reported decisions are questions concerned with the scope of possible justifications for criminal or civil liability in light of the context provided by a defendant's assertion that she was defending property. This is true of the well-known decision in *Blades v Higgs*,[49] where the formal matter at stake was whether the defendants could justify an assault by pleading that they were taking steps to protect the goods of their master. The same matter was at stake more recently in *R v Burns*, where the defendant's use of force to eject a passenger from his car was held to be unlawful because on the facts there were other more reasonable methods by which the defendant could have regained exclusive possession of his car.[50] It is also true of *Green v Goddard*,[51] argued before Holt CJ, which *Clerk & Lindsell* cites to justify the possibility of applying force to defend or resist violent trespass.[52] The short report of *Green* records:

> [I]t is lawful to oppose force to force; and if one breaks down the gate, or comes into my close *vi et armis*, I need not request him to be gone, but may lay hands on him immediately, for it is but returning violence with violence: So if one comes forcibly and takes away my goods, I may oppose him without any more ado, for there is no time to make a request.[53]

This reasoning makes particularly clear that the operative concern is about the appropriate limits of the application of force, with the property interest of the defendant (O) supplying the context rather than the analytical content of the reasoning. Without more, recognition that O might defend herself and her goods in this context has no analytical bearing on the content of her property. This is not to say that it does not shape her behaviour in respect of the asset – clearly whether O is able to apply force to resist taking has a significant bearing on her ability to exercise decisional autonomy with respect to the thing, and we will return to this point shortly. But for present purposes, the important point is again that the outcomes of these cases depend on adjustment of the duties to which O is subject, through the recognition of appropriate defences, rather than on any augmentation of her property rights.

[48] For example, *Clerk & Lindsell* (n 15) [30-06], makes the general point in reliance on the case of *Dean v Hogg and Lewis* (1824) 10 Bing 345, 131 ER 937, where the conclusion was that a hirer did not have exclusive possession of a boat, and therefore was *not* in a position to justify force employed to eject an intruder, so the first difficulty here is the attempt to justify a proposition on its negative. The reported judgment of Tindal CJ similarly assumes that, other things being equal, a possessor would be justified in using force, but no authority is cited: ibid.

[49] See n 4 above.

[50] *R v Burns* [2010] EWCA Crim 1023, 1 WLR 2694, [14].

[51] *Green v Goddard* (1704) 2 Salk 641, 91 ER 540.

[52] *Clerk & Lindsell* (n 15 above) [30-14].

[53] *Green v Goddard* (n 51 above).

These outcomes find an important and instructive parallel in the more recent law on defence of a household. As is readily apparent, this is a matter of enormous political and popular concern. In April 2018, the month of the 12th Modern Studies in Property Law conference, there was a widely reported incident in Hither Green, London (nine miles from the location of that MSPL conference) in which an alleged burglar was fatally-stabbed, and a homeowner arrested on suspicion of murder before being released without charge.[54] The case provoked strong reaction and interest, including significant controversy arising from a sense that victims of crimes were being treated as perpetrators. Major news outlets carried analysis on what counts as reasonable force 'when someone is defending their home'.[55]

So far as the law is concerned, it has for some time been clear that an appropriate measure of force can be justified in defending land or a home: as Millett LJ put it in *Revill v Newberry*, 'violence may be returned with necessary violence'.[56] The difficult question is what counts as reasonable force. The common law position now finds statutory expression in section 76 of the Criminal Justice and Immigration Act 2008, as amended by the Legal Aid Sentencing and Punishment of Offenders Act 2012 and the Crime and Courts Act 2013. Reflecting the premise that a defendant under pressure may not be able to weigh with nicety the various factors in play,[57] these provisions entitle the matter to be judged on the circumstances as the defendant honestly (even if mistakenly or unreasonably) believed them to be; and in the general case of self-defence or defence of property they provide that force will not be considered reasonable 'if it was disproportionate in those circumstances'.[58] As part of its more general policy to 'fight back against crime' and 'put the criminal justice system on the side of responsible citizens',[59] in 2010 the Conservative Party professed a commitment to 'give householders greater legal protection if they have to defend themselves against intruders in their homes'.[60] Through section 43 of the Crime and Courts Act 2013, the Coalition Government implemented this policy by amending section 76 of the 2008 Act to augment the standard of force at stake in judging the reasonableness of action in householder cases,[61] such that 'the degree of force used by D is not to be regarded as having been reasonable … if it was *grossly disproportionate* in the circumstances'.[62] It follows from this that it *can* be reasonable for O *to use disproportionate force* to defend her household.[63]

[54] BBC News, 'Hither Green "burglary death" Suspect to Face No Action', *BBC News* (London, 6 April 2018) available at: https://www.bbc.co.uk/news/uk-england-london-43676359.

[55] See eg BBC News, 'What Are Your Rights in Tackling Burglars?', *BBC News* (London, 6 April 2018) available at: https://www.bbc.com/news/uk-43652308; T Powell, 'Hither Green Burglar Stabbing: Ministry of Justice Says Homeowners Can Defend Themselves "if life at risk"', *London Evening Standard* (London, 5 April 2018) available at: https://www.standard.co.uk/news/uk/hither-green-burglar-stabbing-ministry-of-justice-says-homeowners-can-defend-themselves-if-life-at-a3807141.html.

[56] *Revill v Newberry* [1996] QB 567, 580. Note this echoes very closely the language in *Green v Goddard* (n 51 above).

[57] Criminal Justice and Immigration Act 2008, s 76(7).

[58] Criminal Justice and Immigration Act 2008, s 76(6).

[59] Conservative Party, *Invitation to join the government of Britain: the Conservative Party Manifesto 2010* (London, Conservative Party, 2010) 55.

[60] ibid 56.

[61] Criminal Justice and Immigration Act 2008, Explanatory Notes, [430].

[62] Criminal Justice and Immigration Act 2008, s 76(5A).

[63] *R (on the application of Collins) v Secretary of State for Justice* [2016] EWHC 33 (Admin), [2016] QB 862. Note that this does not necessarily mean that it *will* be reasonable for O to use disproportionate force. As *Collins* makes

While this change is a potentially significant departure from the ordinary (ie non-householder) position that force is not to be regarded as reasonable if it was *disproportionate*,[64] for our purposes it is important to note that it is a measure directed at enhanced protection for the person of the householder, rather than her property. This is true in two senses.

First, consistently with my earlier comments on the use of force for retaking, in the example of the householder provision we see O's exercise of decisional autonomy constrained not by any adjustment in her ownership per se, but rather through the adjustment of duties to which she is subject. To the extent that section 76(5A) increases the scope and extent of defences available to O in respect of action she takes in her home, it correspondingly reduces the scope and extent of potential liabilities for a range of criminal offences, including fatal offences. Again, adjustments are delivered though the medium of obligations, not property: it's not that, as owner, O has the expressly enumerated right to defend her home; it's that in the context of taking steps to defend her home she may be permitted to apply a higher standard of force without transgressing the ordinary duties to which she is subject.

Moreover, secondly, although in the explanatory notes and the Bill readings, section 76(5A) was expressly orientated towards protection of 'homes', that O is a property-holder is of little analytical significance. The availability of the defence does not turn on the presence or absence of a property right in respect of the premises defended, it requires only that O is 'not a trespasser at the time the force is used' and that she believed the intruder to be a trespasser: O could be a tenant, a guest, a plumber engaged to carry out repairs, or anyone else lawfully on the premises.[65] Of course, a highly likely scenario for such criteria to be satisfied is the context of O defending a home which she owns, but since O can be protected even if she has *no* property right in respect of the land, the question of the use of force is very clearly separated from the content of any property right she may have. Consistently with this, the householder provisions are squarely suffused with concern for the persons and relationships at stake rather than O's decisional autonomy in respect of the building itself. Consider the following justifications offered for the introduction of the augmented defence:

> Few situations can be more frightening than when someone's own home is violated. Faced with that scenario, a person will do what it takes to protect themselves and their loved ones.[66]
>
> The home is the one place where a person should have the right to feel safe. Being confronted by an intruder in those circumstances would be particularly terrifying. The feeling of anguish or panic would be heightened if someone knew that family members or close friends staying with them in the house were in imminent danger.[67]

While we might reasonably expect a government that purports to be committed to the reduction of crime to have more ambitious expectations of where we might be entitled to feel

clear, this remains a matter to be determined on the facts of the case: s 76(5A) operates to permit consideration of whether the use of disproportionate force was reasonable in the circumstances, in contrast to the use of *grossly* disproportionate force, which may not be considered reasonable. This reasoning in *Collins* has subsequently been affirmed by the Court of Appeal: *R v Ray* [2017] EWCA Crim 1391, [2018] 2 WLR 1148.

[64] Criminal Justice and Immigration Act 2008, s 76(6).

[65] Criminal Justice and Immigration Act 2008, s 76(8A).

[66] HC Deb, 14 January 2013, vol 556, col 641.

[67] Crime and Courts Bill Deb, 5 February 2013, col 277.

safe (the *one* place?), these quotations make very plain that the enactment of section 76(5A) aims at the protection of the person of the householder and her family, rather than protection of the buildings and land.[68] Moreover, it implicates a distinct range of values. Exclusion-based accounts of property are premised on the idea that ownership preserves O's autonomy to deal with the thing as she sees fit, incentivising investment and facilitating efficient transactions.[69] In contrast, the householder provision directs its concern to O's interpersonal attachments and commitments, to responsibilities of care and protection for others, and indeed to O's dignity. The context of home provides a reason for augmenting the applicable norms of self-defence because it heightens the depth and strength of the commitments at stake – the particular terror of a violation of one's home, the particular anguish that comes from a family member being placed in danger. These harms, and their effects on O's decision-making, can easily be distinguished from the more facilitative ends served by ownership in the ordinary case. As Joshua Getzler has argued in the context of burglary offences, the gist of burglary is that the burglar's invasion of physical space makes for a serious crime, and that the harm caused by burglary is distinct from the harm occasioned by related offences like theft. Burglary constitutes 'an *injuria* or attack on personality, security and dignitary interests', and this justifies configuring its constituent elements differently.[70] So it is with the householder provisions, which are premised on the self-defence of the householder and the defence of her family, and accordingly protect a set of concerns and values different from those which underlie any ownership right she might have in respect of the premises.

IV. Property, Obligations, and Values

The arguments in the foregoing sections are significant. First, they supply an overarching conceptual framework to the law on recaption and defence which can shape the persistently difficult doctrinal debates on its availability and extent. Secondly, they cast wider light on the nature, and in turn the justification, of property rights at common law. In headline terms, the analysis reveals that the substance of O's dealings with property is shaped by the law of obligations. This is clear at every step of the argument, from the way in which conversion supplies the contours of the core content of ownership; to the relevance of remedies rules in framing the entitlement to recaption; and via the impact of rules of tort and crime on the limits of O's ability to take forceful steps to recover and defend her property. Indeed, to the extent that such an avowedly central incident of ownership as the entitlement to possess one's own thing depends for its implementation not on a specifically enumerated right, but instead on the construction and confluence of tortious and criminal duties in a given case, it could plausibly be argued that the whole content of property collapses into the law of obligations. Such a reductive and iconoclastic position is tempting, but is probably

[68] Importantly, this is corroborated by the drafting of section 76, through which it is clear that the householder provision specifically relates to the self-defence of persons rather than defence of property: *Archbold: Criminal Pleading, Evidence and Practice*, 66th edn (London, Sweet & Maxwell, 2017) [19-48a].

[69] Merrill (n 17 above) 9–13; Katz (n 3 above) 279–80; and see generally HE Smith, 'Mind the Gap: The Indirect Relation Between Means and Ends in American Property Law' (2009) 94 *Cornell Law Review* 959, 971–72.

[70] J Getzler, 'Use of Force in Protecting Property' (2006) 7 *Theoretical Inquiries in Law* 131, 150.

worth avoiding. In particular, it risks concealing the differing functions of the various obligations at work, and as with the legal-realist view which sought to disaggregate property to a bundle of sticks,[71] it especially obscures the generality of the duty not to interfere with O's control.[72] The doctrinal existence of that general duty is important. As we have said, the duty not to convert is a duty not to interfere wrongfully with a thing which O is entitled to possess; and correlatively, O enjoys a right to keep everyone else in the world from interfering with the thing. This protects a large measure of freedom for O to determine how the thing is to be used, and signals this freedom to the world in a manner apt to minimise information costs, exactly the values prefigured in exclusion-based accounts of property. So, far from undermining ideas of property in common law, a conversion-led, obligations-based system of property protection seems to implement a very pure conception of property as a right to exclude. And the other provisions and obligations at stake in a given case in many ways will operate to reinforce it. For example, adjustments to duties owed by O which allow O to repel interferers and dis-incentivise intrusion are at least plausibly consistent with a conception of ownership that has at its core O's right to exclude others.

However, it is also clear that the content of O's right to exclude does not exhaust the considerations at stake in determining the limits of O's autonomy or action in relation to retaking or defending her things. In the first place, the rules on defence and recaption are not solely *about property rights*. It would be impossible to give an accurate account without being sensitive, for example, to the influence of heavily discretionary remedial rules in determining whether O is entitled to recover a specific thing in litigation, or the circumstances in which it is necessary for O to demand that X desists before applying force to defend her thing. This means, more generally, that the carte blanche, prima facie freedom to retake afforded to O by the right to exclude is necessarily constrained by countervailing rules of obligations. These rules may not always be easy to state exactly, and they may have different bases; that is, there may be differences in aim and underpinning values between the propositions we encounter in laws about defence and recaption, and those we encounter in laws about the content of ownership represented by a core right to exclude. Recall, by way of comparison, Getzler's observations on burglary, as constituting 'an *injuria* or attack on personality, security and dignitary interests'.[73] The offence of burglary has been constructed to address something more than the harm addressed by theft and trespass, something more than the autonomy- and utility-based considerations that underpin and justify O's core right to exclude others from O's land. So it is with the law on recaption and defence, which plausibly responds to interpersonal values, commitments and attachments, and to dignity concerns, and to the personhood values respected at least some of the time in permitting O to be reunited with specific things. This is deeply significant for the practice of property. When property law is accurately understood to be implemented through patterns of interlocking and offsetting obligations (liability for burglary operating beyond the ordinary basis of theft; the prima facie extent of O's right to exclude constrained by defence rules that turn on a reasonableness standard, which seeks to make some reference

[71] F Cohen, 'Dialogue on Private Property' (1954) 9 *Rutgers Law Review* 357.

[72] TW Merrill and HE Smith, 'Making Coasean Property More Coasean' (2011) 54 *Journal of Law and Economics* S77, S82.

[73] Getzler (n 70 above).

to attachment and dignity concerns), property disputes can be seen to implicate a much broader range of values than is entailed by exclusionary conceptions of ownership.

Property, as any legal institution, requires to be justified in terms of the values it promotes,[74] but the extent to which property implicates a plural range of values has been a persistent matter of controversy in property theory. Indeed, it can fairly be said that disagreements about the conceptual essence of property in large measure reflect disagreements about the sufficiency of the underpinning values themselves. Exclusion accounts of property are premised on the interest we have in the use of things,[75] and justify property institutions by relying on: the autonomy-maximising potential for the owner; the extent to which exclusion rights provide reasons to invest in or maximise the use-potential of the thing; and the extent to which exclusion rights facilitate efficient transfers of and dealings with things, especially in the sense in which they minimise information costs. Progressive property theory pushes back on the individualistic turn in exclusion accounts, emphasising the other-regarding features of property institutions and the extent to which they implicate deeper moral and political ideas of just social relationships and just distributions.[76] On this view, property is premised on a broad and incommensurable range of human values, which includes individual values but moves beyond them to further encompass social interests like stewardship, civic responsibility, and aggregate wealth. If this is right, it challenges the dominance of exclusion-based theories in justification debates,[77] but also highlights the disadvantages of exclusion rights as a basis for dispute resolution. The modern realist perspective of Hanoch Dagan might be thought of as a middle way, agreeing on the value pluralism of property but focusing attention on how the institutions of property law should respond, emphasising the need for the forms of property to be re-evaluated and reshaped continually.[78] On this view, some of the time an exclusion right will be the appropriate institutional response, but in other contexts the law should design and implement a different doctrinal structure that better reflects the values at stake.[79]

Whichever theoretical position is adopted, the assumption seems to be that each property institution (ownership, lease, etc) corresponds to and (more or less effectively) implements a particular balance of values in the available range. The task of adjusting these institutions is understood to be a serious and constitutionally important matter: even Dagan's view, which stresses the 'ongoing (probably endless) process of reshaping property',[80] equally recognises the need for the number of property forms to be limited (a *numerus clausus*) and for caution in reconstitution of property rights.[81] The law on defence and recaption suggests that, as far as ownership is concerned, the common law is able to accomplish and implement such shifting balances of values not only by adjusting the basic form of ownership (a duty not to interfere with O's control), but through the continuous reflexive interplay of further obligations. Some of the time this happens through the introduction of legislative

[74] H Dagan, *Property: Values and Institutions* (Oxford, Oxford University Press, 2010) 29.

[75] Penner (n 34 above); Smith (n 20 above) 1693.

[76] GS Alexander and others, 'A Statement of Progressive Property' (2009) 94 *Cornell Law Review* 743.

[77] But compare Smith (n 20 above) and Merrill (n 17 above), which in different ways caution against treating exclusion accounts as *only* committed to these values.

[78] Dagan (n 74 above) 35.

[79] See for example Dagan's arguments about institutions of marital property, especially ibid ch 9.

[80] Dagan (n 74 above) 4.

[81] ibid.

amendments which specifically address the values under consideration and expressly tailor the limits of O's action in light of those values, as in the householder provisions added to section 76 of the 2008 Act, or indeed the general clarifying work of the Law Reform Committee which did much to illuminate the common law of recaption notwithstanding the omission of its recommendations from the text of the 1977 Act. At other times, these adjustments will happen though the interpretive work of the courts, as in seminal cases like *Blades v Higgs*,[82] which determine the permissible bounds of activity in forceful retaking cases. In either situation, refinements to existing obligations allow for the incremental extension and revision of the outer limits of ownership, while retaining the stability of its basic form. This provides a doctrinal mechanism to manage the complex interplay of values engaged in the circumstances of defence or retaking, and at a general level attests to the law's effectiveness in promoting the plural values underpinning property. It does not of course mean that the range of property institutions is overly or infinitely revisable. On the contrary, the countervailing propositions of obligations at stake are themselves relatively settled, such that in cases of this kind we are really dealing with marginal adjustments to the countervailing effects of the content of other duties. However, to see any of this, we need first to appreciate that, in the common law, the substance of an owner's position and the ordinary limits on her behaviour in respect of a thing are delineated by obligations beyond her right to exclude. This right, and the correlative duty it entails, may represent the core of law's intervention to protect O's decisional autonomy; but there is a broader range of obligations and values at stake in framing the full content of her position.

V. Conclusion

It seems deeply counter-intuitive to suggest that there is no right to recaption at common law, but this is the best rendering of the position as a matter of principle, and the analytical moves necessary to make this argument have deep significance for property law. They serve to illustrate the pre-eminent function of the law of obligations in protecting property interests and in framing the limits of an owner's autonomy in dealing with her things. An appreciation of this function supplies not only an overarching conceptual framework for the law on defence and recaption, but also a pertinent example of the common law implementing a process of responsiveness to the demands of the plural range of values that underlie and justify property institutions. This implementation occurs in a manner that is compatible with those theories that emphasise exclusion as the essential core of property, but the law on defence and recaption makes equally clear that the substance of an owner's freedom to deal with a thing is shaped by considerations and doctrines extrinsic to her core right to exclude. Accordingly, notwithstanding the counter-intuitive headline which denies a specific right to recaption, a sharper understanding of the law on defence and recaption provides a fuller picture of property. The dominance of the law of obligations in framing the substance of the right to possess is perhaps surprising, but it manages at once to retain an essential concept of property as a right to exclude while at the same time tempering its

[82] See n 4 above and generally section III above.

limits through the operation of countervailing obligations. This in turn suggests that the aims and values which inhere in a right to exclude conception of property do not exhaust the range of values at stake in resolving property disputes, an observation which serves to underscore and increase the range of incommensurable values implicated in a property problem. In this way, a deeper understanding of the doctrinal and conceptual structures implementing self-help remedies reveals much more about the nature of ownership in the common law, and its broader commitment to the values and interests that justify private property rights.

5

The Essence of Private Nuisance

DONAL NOLAN

I. Introduction

When we refer to the 'essence' of something, we might mean a number of different things. One established usage of the word essence is 'a perfume or scent', for example. What, we might then ask, is the 'essence' of private nuisance in this sense? The stench of sewage?[1] The unmistakeable odour of a pig farm?[2] The pong of a waste disposal facility?[3] Or perhaps the 'pungent and nauseating' smell of oil from an oil depot?[4]

Happily, here I want to focus on a different meaning of the word 'essence': what my dictionary refers to as 'the indispensable quality or element identifying a thing or determining its character',[5] or in other words the feature or set of features that defines a thing. And my claim is that the essence of private nuisance in this sense is interference with (or impairment of) the usability of the claimant's land. Although I would accept that a full definition of the tort of private nuisance requires the addition of certain qualifications (for example, that the interference must be non-trespassory), I maintain that this idea of interference with the usability of land is the central defining feature of the cause of action, in the sense that (subject to those qualifications) anything that interferes with the usability of land can in principle amount to a private nuisance, and anything that does not, cannot.

Since my claim is best understood as a clarification of the orthodox view that the central defining feature of a private nuisance is an interference with the use and enjoyment of land, you might be asking yourself why I feel it necessary to make it. There are three reasons for doing so. The first is that the clarification turns out to be an important one. The second is that, although this central defining feature of private nuisance is well-established, it has been the subject of very little sustained analysis, and one of the aims of this chapter is to begin the task of plugging that gap.[6] And the final reason is that the orthodox conception of private nuisance has come under attack recently, and there is a danger that without a robust defence of it the coherence and utility of the tort will be compromised. In this chapter I seek to provide such a defence.

[1] *Dobson v Thames Water Utilities Ltd* [2011] EWHC 3523 (TCC), 140 Con LR 135.

[2] *Bone v Seale* [1975] 1 All ER 787 (CA); *Wheeler v JJ Saunders Ltd* [1996] Ch 19 (CA).

[3] *Barr v Biffa Waste Services Ltd* [2012] EWCA Civ 312, [2013] QB 455.

[4] *Halsey v Esso Petroleum Co Ltd* [1961] 1 WLR 683 (QB).

[5] *The Concise Oxford Dictionary*, 12th edn (Oxford, Oxford University Press, 2011).

[6] It has been said, for example, that 'there is a relatively limited body of case law addressing the scope of what may possibly constitute the "interference" that is actionable in private nuisance' (*Shogunn Investments Pty Ltd v Public Transport Authority of Western Australia* [2016] WASC 42, [62] (Kenneth Martin J)).

The chapter is divided hereafter into three main sections. In section II, I show just how orthodox it is to define private nuisance by reference to interference with the use and enjoyment of land, seek to clarify this defining idea as concerned with the abstract usability of the land, and consider the implications of this analysis for the scope of the private nuisance action. In section III, I summarise and then critique a recent challenge to the orthodox conception of the tort, which I call the 'physical invasion' view. And in section IV, I briefly consider some of the implications for property theory of the orthodox conception of private nuisance, properly understood. It is important to emphasise that the scope of the chapter is limited to the question of identifying what is capable of amounting to a private nuisance, or (put differently) what is the key defining characteristic of all instances of private nuisance. I am not concerned with other questions, such as whether in a particular case an interference that is capable of being a private nuisance does actually amount to a nuisance on the facts (or for that matter with the question of what determines whether an interference capable of amounting to a nuisance is in fact one).[7]

II. The Orthodox Conception of Private Nuisance

There are countless examples in the case law and the academic literature of definitions of private nuisance in terms of interference with the use and enjoyment of land. To give you a flavour of these, just consider the following examples, which come from a range of different jurisdictions:

> Private nuisance may be described as unlawful interference with a person's use or enjoyment of land, or some right over, or in connection with it.[8]
>
> A private nuisance is an unreasonable interference with the use and enjoyment of land.[9]
>
> A private nuisance is a nontrespassory invasion of another's interest in the private use and enjoyment of land.[10]
>
> [T]he main role [of nuisance in Scots law] is as a doctrine of property law or neighbourhood protecting interests in the use and enjoyment of land ...[11]

Furthermore, this focus on the protection of interests in the use and enjoyment of land is not confined to the common law (and Scots law) of nuisance, but is also key to

[7] It seems that I am not alone in my view that the orthodox definition of private nuisance needs defending, and in preparing my defence I have had the advantage of reading C Essert, 'Nuisance and the Normative Boundaries of Ownership' (2016) 52 *Tulsa Law Review* 85, where the author trenchantly critiques the physical invasion view of the tort. I have few quibbles with Essert's analysis, and there are some significant overlaps between my criticisms and his. It is, however, important to emphasise that our agendas are different, in that Essert's concern in his article is to put forward what he calls a 'normatively attractive vision of nuisance law' as a whole, while my concern is the narrower one of identifying the appropriate definition or conception of the cause of action.

[8] *Winfield & Jolowicz on Tort*, 19th edn (London, Sweet & Maxwell, 2014) [15-008].

[9] K Barker et al, *The Law of Torts in Australia*, 5th edn (Melbourne, Oxford University Press Australia, 2012) 185. For an identical definition, see also AM Linden and B Feldthusen, *Canadian Tort Law*, 10th edn (Markham, Ont., LexisNexis Canada, 2015) 608.

[10] Restatement (Second) of Torts (Philadelphia, The American Law Institute, 1977) § 821D.

[11] *The Laws of Scotland: Stair Memorial Encyclopedia*, vol 14 (Edinburgh, Law Society of Scotland, 1988) [para 2017].

understanding principles of neighbour law in civilian systems. According to §906(1) of the German Civil Code (*Bürgerliches Gesetzbuch*, BGB), for instance:

> The owner of a piece of land is not entitled to prohibit the intrusion of gases, vapours, smells, smoke, soot, heat, noises, shocks and similar interferences emanating from another piece of land to the extent that the interference does not or only immaterially prejudices the use of his piece of land.

Although the orthodox conception of private nuisance is well-established, it has been the subject of very little analysis, and in the remainder of this section of the chapter, I propose to clarify and to explore that conception, and to consider its implications for the scope of the cause of action.

The first thing to notice is that the word 'land' in the orthodox definition of private nuisance refers to the legal conception of land, which encompasses not only the physical land itself, but also the buildings and other things attached to it (trees, shrubs, crops etc), as well as acquired rights that run with the land.[12] Thus it is that private nuisance encompasses interferences with acquired rights or servitudes (easements and *profits à prendre*),[13] and that buildings and other fixtures fall under its protective cloak.

A second, crucially important, point to notice about the orthodox definition is that strictly speaking there is a flaw in it. This is because private nuisance is a 'tort against land'[14] – meaning (among other things) that the gist of the wrong is the diminished utility of the land itself, as opposed to the inconvenience and discomfort suffered by the occupiers. Hence, for example, '[a] sulphurous chimney in a residential area is not a nuisance because it makes house-holders cough and splutter but because it prevents them taking their ease in their gardens'.[15] And it follows from this that the wrong in nuisance is not interference with the use and enjoyment of the land per se, as the orthodox definition suggests, but rather interference with the capacity of the land in question to be used and enjoyed (its fitness 'for the ordinary purposes of life'[16]) – a more general notion of the 'usefulness'[17] or 'usability'[18] of the land that 'abstracts from the particularity of specific uses'.[19] This explains

[12] See in particular the definition of 'land' in the Law of Property Act 1925, s 205(1)(ix). On the legal conception of land, see K Gray and SF Gray, *Elements of Land Law*, 5th edn (Oxford, Oxford University Press, 2009) ch 1.2.

[13] See D Nolan, 'Nuisance' in K Oliphant (ed), *The Law of Tort*, 3rd edn (London, LexisNexis Butterworths, 2015) [22.25]ff. For the avoidance of doubt, it should be made clear that in the case of an easement, nuisance requires a substantial interference with the usability of the easement (right of way, etc), and not with the usability of the dominant tenement (though of course the former may entail the latter).

[14] See D Nolan, '"A Tort Against Land": Private Nuisance as a Property Tort' in D Nolan and A Robertson (eds), *Rights and Private Law* (Oxford, Hart Publishing, 2012). The definitive judicial statement of this understanding of the tort and its implications is to be found in Lord Hoffmann's judgment in *Hunter v Canary Wharf Ltd* [1997] AC 655 (HL).

[15] FH Newark, 'The Boundaries of Nuisance' (1949) 65 *LQR* 480, 489.

[16] See *Appleby v Erie Tobacco* (1910) 22 OLR 533 (Ontario DC) 538 (Middleton J).

[17] See NM McBride and R Bagshaw, *Tort Law*, 6th edn (Harlow, Pearson Education, 2019) 395.

[18] Restatement (Second) of Torts (n 10 above) § 821D, comment b. The extent to which the concept of 'ordinary use' is built into this abstract notion of usability is a difficult question that I do not have the space to explore here. Clearly the ordinariness of the affected use is a consideration in nuisance cases, by virtue of the 'abnormal sensitivity' principle (as to which, see Nolan (n 13 above) [22.44]–[22.45]), but whether this goes to the defining notion of interference with the usability of the land or instead to the subsequent issue of 'substantial interference' is less obvious.

[19] EJ Weinrib, 'Ownership, Use, and Exclusivity: The Kantian Approach' (2018) 31 *Ratio Juris* 123, 130 (discussing Kant's theory of property).

why the test of substantial or unreasonable interference is an objective one, that takes no account of any abnormal sensitivity either of the claimant or of the use to which she puts her property,[20] and also why the damages in an amenity nuisance case are assessed objectively, in the sense that they compensate for the diminished utility of the land attributable to the wrongful interference, rather than the actual impact of the nuisance on the occupiers of the land.[21]

This turns out to be a critically important clarification. For a start, the clarification renders the orthodox conception of private nuisance compatible with rejection of a 'right to use' property – as opposed to a 'right to usability' of property – a right which property theorists have correctly identified as problematic.[22] It also explains, for instance, why it is that Roderick Bagshaw falls into error when he defines private nuisance in terms of 'some forms of interference with a claimant's use and enjoyment of his or her land', and then gives as an example of a form of such interference that falls outside the scope of the tort, 'injuring or imprisoning the claimant'.[23] In fact, private nuisance is not concerned with whether the claimant can use or enjoy her land at all, but only with whether (and to what extent) her land is capable of being used and enjoyed. Furthermore, this clarification shows that on the orthodox conception of private nuisance one cannot plausibly explain the cause of action by reference to the resolution of competing uses of land,[24] since the law's concern is revealed as being with the usability of the claimant's land, not the specific uses to which the claimant puts it (and certainly not with the uses to which the defendant puts his land, not least because private nuisance liability can attach to conduct that does not amount to a use of the defendant's land at all[25]).

What more can we say about this definitional idea of interference with the capacity of the land in question to be used and enjoyed? The concept is certainly a broad one, which includes, for example, causing an alteration of the physical condition of land that reduces its utility[26] – hence the fact that physical damage to land falls within the scope of private nuisance.[27] On the other hand, the concept nevertheless excludes from the scope of private nuisance certain conduct which could be said to 'harm' the claimant's land, but without affecting its usability. Hence, for example, conduct that reduces the market value

[20] See *Network Rail Infrastructure Ltd v Williams* [2018] EWCA Civ 1514, [43] (Sir Terence Etherton MR).

[21] See *Hunter* (n 14 above) 696 (Lord Lloyd), 706 (Lord Hoffmann).

[22] See, eg, JE Penner, *The Idea of Property in Law* (Oxford, Clarendon Press, 1997) 72–73 (though in concluding from this implausibility that 'the concept of exclusion, not use, dominates the legal analysis', Penner throws the 'usability' baby out with the 'use' bathwater).

[23] R Bagshaw, 'The Edges of Tort Law's Rights' in Nolan and Robertson (n 14 above) 417–18.

[24] cf, R Coase, 'The Problem of Social Cost' (1960) 3 *Journal of Law & Economics* 1; G Calabresi and AD Melamed, 'Property Rules, Liability Rules, and Inalienability: One View of the Cathedral' (1972) 85 *Harvard Law Review* 1089. For an illuminating discussion highlighting this aspect of these economic approaches to nuisance, see HE Smith, 'Exclusion and Property Rules in the Law of Nuisance' (2004) 90 *Virginia Law Review* 965, 967–69.

[25] See Nolan (n 14 above) 475–76.

[26] See the Restatement (Second) of Torts (n 10 above) § 821D, comment b.

[27] Commentators sometimes question whether physical damage claims should be classified as nuisances (see, eg, C Gearty, 'The Place of Private Nuisance in a Modern Law of Torts' (1989) 48 *CLJ* 214), but while there is admittedly a case for separating such claims off from amenity nuisance claims and dealing with them in negligence – though also a case against doing this – the law's assumption that to physically damage land is substantially to interfere with its capacity for use and enjoyment seems a reasonable one. For a prominent example of judicial reasoning based on this assumption, see *Hunter* (n 14 above) 705–06 (Lord Hoffmann), and for a defence of this assumption, see M Lee, 'What is Private Nuisance?' (2003) 119 *LQR* 298, 308–10.

of real property without impairing its utility is not wrongful,[28] so that a company which triggers a collapse in house prices in an area by closing down the main source of local employment does not thereby create a nuisance.[29]

Nor does the concept of interference with the usability of land extend to conduct that has a deleterious effect on a commercial enterprise operating on the claimant's land without diminishing the utility of the property more generally.[30] The classic illustration of this principle is *Victoria Park Racing and Recreation Grounds v Taylor*,[31] where the first defendant built a platform on his land which overlooked the plaintiff's racecourse and the second defendant stood on the platform and gave a live radio commentary on the races and announced the results, with the result that fewer people attended the races. According to the majority of the High Court of Australia, these actions of the defendants infringed no legal right of the plaintiff's, and in particular the mere fact that they had reduced the market value of the plaintiff's property and diverted custom away from its business did not make them a nuisance. According to Latham CJ, the defendants had 'not interfered in any way with the use and enjoyment of the plaintiff's land', since the racecourse remained 'as suitable as ever it was for use as a racecourse'.[32] Similarly, Dixon J said that 'the substance of the plaintiff's complaint' went to interference, not with 'its enjoyment of the land, but with the profitable conduct of its business'.[33]

The rejection of the private nuisance claim in *Victoria Park Racing* seems clearly to have been correct, and its key reasoning is reflected in more recent Australian case law rejecting nuisance claims for conduct that had affected the profitability of a business on the plaintiff's land, but was not considered to have interfered with the use and enjoyment of the land itself.[34] There are, however, also more borderline cases in the law reports. Three relatively recent decisions from across the common law world are instructive. The first is *Smith v Inco*,[35] where deposits from the defendant's factory led to an increase in the nickel content of the soil in the plaintiffs' neighbouring properties, which reduced their market value because of an (apparently false) community perception that these deposits might pose a health risk to occupiers. In this case, the Ontario Court of Appeal held that since the deposits had not objectively diminished the land's utility they were incapable of grounding a nuisance claim. On one level, this decision – which is consistent with the Court of Appeal's conclusion in *Birmingham Development v Tyler*[36] that a nuisance claim cannot lie in respect

[28] For clear statements of this principle, see *Soltau v De Held* (1851) 2 Sim (NS) 133, 158, 61 ER 291, 301 (Sir RT Kindersley VC); *Harrison v Good* (1871) LR 11 Eq 338 (Ch) 353 (Sir James Bacon VC); and *Network Rail Infrastructure* (n 20 above) [46]–[48] (Sir Terence Etherton MR).

[29] For discussion, see R Kidner, 'Nuisance and Rights of Property' [1998] *Conv* 267, 276–79.

[30] See *Ricket v The Metropolitan Railway Company* (1865) 5 B&S 156 (Exch) 162–63, 122 ER 790, 795 (Erle CJ) (aff'd *Ricket v The Metropolitan Railway Company* (1867) LR 2 HL 175 (HL)).

[31] *Victoria Park Racing and Recreation Grounds v Taylor* (1937) 58 CLR 479 (HCA).

[32] ibid, 493. Note the way in which the usability of the land is here tied to its use 'as a racecourse'. The extent to which the usability idea that underlies nuisance is tied to the use of the affected land in a general sense (as, for example, a home, factory, shop, farm, racecourse, etc) is a difficult one that lies beyond the scope of this chapter.

[33] ibid, 508.

[34] See *Deepcliffe Pty Ltd v Council of the City of Gold Coast* [2001] QCA 342, 118 LGERA 117 (parking restrictions on street near restaurant); *Shogunn Investments* (n 6 above) (removal of turning lane in median strip near entrance to commercial car park).

[35] *Smith v Inco* [2011] ONCA 628, 107 OR (3d) 321.

[36] *Birmingham Development v Tyler* [2008] EWCA Civ 859, [2008] BLR 445.

of a false belief that the defendant's property may collapse onto the claimant's land – seems right.[37] We should be concerned in private nuisance with actual (not perceived) interferences with the capacity of the land to be used and enjoyed, just as a claimant in a battery case must establish that there was actually a touching, and not merely that she reasonably perceived that there was. On the other hand, the capacity of land to be used and enjoyed cannot be completely separated from the subjective perceptions of those occupying it; a noise or smell is more likely to be a nuisance if generally perceived as unpleasant, for example.[38]

The second difficult decision is *D Pride & Partners (a firm) v Institute for Animal Health*,[39] where Tugendhat J rejected an argument that the defendants could be liable in private nuisance for causing an outbreak of foot-and-mouth disease that led to the introduction of government restrictions on the movement of the claimants' livestock. Intuitively, this seems right. After all, although the defendant's actions did (albeit indirectly) affect the ability of this particular land to be used for a particular purpose, namely raising cattle, they did not affect the usability of the land in a more general sense, and while blocking or substantially interfering with the access to the claimant's land can amount to a private nuisance, that seems a far cry from acting in such a way as to bring about a situation in which the claimant is prevented by the act of a third party from moving a particular class of chattels on or off her land.[40]

The third case, *Marsh v Baxter*,[41] raises similar questions. In this instance, occasional escapes of genetically-modified canola from the defendant's property caused most of the plaintiffs' farmland to be stripped of its organic certification by an association with which it had a contractual relationship, even though none of the plaintiffs' crops or livestock could acquire any genetic traits from the canola. A nuisance argument was rejected by both the Supreme Court and the Court of Appeal of Western Australia, and again, this seems intuitively to be correct. At its highest, you could say that the canola escapes interfered – also via a third party's intervention – with the use of the plaintiffs' land to 'farm organically', but given that in fact there was no risk of any transfer of genetic material, this would seem to blur the important distinction drawn in the earlier cases between interfering with *the land* and 'interfering with' (or making less profitable) *a business* conducted on it. Having said that, it is noteworthy that both courts dismissed the claim on the grounds, not that there had been no interference with the use and enjoyment of the plaintiffs' land, but that any such interference had not been substantial, bearing in mind the abnormal sensitivity of the plaintiffs' use in the locality.

[37] See also *Adkins v Thomas Solvent Co* 487 NW 2d 715 (Mich 1992); and *Adams v Star Enterprise* 51 F 3d 417 (4th Cir 1995).

[38] Commentators have been more sympathetic to claims based on unfounded fears than have the courts: see, eg, JPS McLaren, 'Nuisance in Canada' in AM Linden (ed), *Studies in Canadian Tort Law* (Toronto, Butterworths, 1968) 342–43; J Lowry and R Edmunds, 'Stigma Damages, Amenity and the Margins of Economic Loss: Quantifying Perceptions and Fears' in J Lowry and R Edmunds (eds), *Environmental Protection and the Common Law* (Oxford, Hart Publishing, 2000); Bagshaw (n 23 above) 420–21.

[39] *D Pride & Partners (a firm) v Institute for Animal Health* [2009] EWHC 685 (QB).

[40] cf, *Exxon Corporation v Yarema* 516 A 2d 990 (Md App, 1986) where recovery was allowed in private nuisance after groundwater contamination caused by the defendants led to the imposition of severe controls on properties in the locality not otherwise affected by the contamination, including prohibitions on the use of groundwater, on the building of homes on the land, and on the sale of the land.

[41] *Marsh v Baxter* [2014] WASC 187, 46 WAR 377 (aff'd *Marsh v Baxter* [2015] WASCA 169, 49 WAR 1).

Also tricky are the so-called 'affront' cases, of which the best known in England are *Laws v Florinplace*,[42] where it was held that there was a triable issue as to whether the mere presence of a sex shop in the locality of the claimants' properties could potentially amount to a nuisance, and the similar earlier decision in *Thompson-Schwab v Costaki*,[43] where the Court of Appeal issued an interlocutory injunction to close down a brothel that had opened in the claimant's street. In retrospect these decisions certainly come close to countenancing liability for diminution in value per se.[44] In *Laws*, for example, Vinelott J quoted (as if relevant) the evidence of a home owner 'that the continuance of the defendants' business would severely injure the value of his property',[45] as well as the evidence of two estate agents who had expressed divergent opinions on the effect of the sex shop on local property prices.[46] Then again, a respectable argument can be made to the effect that – at least in extreme cases – the mere presence of a particular activity in the vicinity of a property could be so upsetting to an ordinary occupier as to amount to an interference with the capacity of the property to be used and enjoyed for normal purposes, and there are certainly some American cases to this effect.[47]

As these borderline cases suggest, it seems fair to say that the full implications of the orthodox conception of private nuisance have not yet been identified.[48] Could, for example, shutting off the supply of essential utilities such as water, gas and electricity to a property come within the orthodox conception of private nuisance, on the grounds that the absence of such amenities is capable of significantly diminishing the utility of the property?[49] In a first instance case, *Anglian Water Services Ltd v Crawshaw Robbins & Co Ltd*,[50] it was held that interrupting the supply of gas to a property could not be a nuisance, but the reasons given were unpersuasive. The first – that the right to the supply of gas was not a property right but a contractual right vis-à-vis the supplier – looks conclusory (after all, the right could be both contractual and proprietary). And the second – that the interference could be regarded as being with the use of gas appliances on the claimant's land, rather than with the use and enjoyment of the land itself – rests on a false dichotomy, since the fact that gas appliances cannot be used on my property may itself diminish the property's utility.[51] The decision is also hard to square with that of the Court of Appeal in *Guppys (Bridport) Ltd v Brookling*, where a landlord was held liable in nuisance for trying to force a tenant out of the demised property by, inter alia, cutting off the supply of water and electricity.[52]

[42] *Laws v Florinplace* [1981] 1 All ER 659 (Ch).

[43] *Thompson-Schwab v Costaki* [1956] 1 WLR 335 (CA).

[44] For telling criticism of the decisions, see Kidner (n 29 above) 277–78.

[45] *Laws* (n 42 above) 662. See similarly the mention of a plaintiff's concern about the effect of the defendants' activity on property values in *Thompson-Schwab* (n 43 above) 339.

[46] *Laws* (n 42 above) 663–64.

[47] See, eg, *Foley v Harris* 286 SE 2d 186 (Va 1982) (junkyard). See further, RR Coletta, 'The Case for Aesthetic Nuisance: Rethinking Traditional Judicial Attitudes' (1987) 48 *Ohio State Law Journal* 141.

[48] For an insightful exploration of these issues, see Bagshaw (n 23 above) 417–21.

[49] For an analogous case, see *Barratt Homes Ltd v DWR Cymru Cyfyngedig (Welsh Water) (No 2)* [2013] EWCA Civ 233, [2013] 1 WLR 3486, where Lloyd Jones LJ said (at [53]) that the claimant's ability to connect its properties to water and sewerage services was 'an essential adjunct' of its use of land, interference with which was arguably capable of amounting to a nuisance.

[50] *Anglian Water Services Ltd v Crawshaw Robbins & Co Ltd* [2001] BLR 173 (QB).

[51] cf, *Network Rail Infrastructure Ltd v CJ Morris* [2004] EWCA Civ 172, [2004] Env LR 41, where the nuisance claim failed, but it was not argued that the interference was incapable of being a nuisance because it interfered only with the use of certain devices on the claimant's property.

[52] *Guppys (Bridport) Ltd v Brookling* (1984) 14 HLR 1 (CA).

One final point about the orthodox conception of private nuisance as an interference with the capacity of land to be used and enjoyed is a reminder that this is only the start of the nuisance enquiry. Even if the defendant's conduct falls within the scope of the nuisance cause of action in this sense, there are a host of other issues to consider, such as whether on the facts the interference was substantial, whether it was foreseeable, whether the claimant has standing to sue, whether any defences apply and so on. For the most part, the distinction between the definitional issue being explored in this chapter and the other issues that may arise in a nuisance claim is reasonably clear, but there is at least one exception, where the blurring of the distinction has sometimes obscured analysis of the essential nature of the cause of action.

Although nuisance litigation is usually focused on whether, on the facts of the case, a particular interference with the use and enjoyment of land is a substantial one, another (often overlooked) question is whether the type of interference with the use and enjoyment of land in question is potentially actionable in private nuisance at all. This is because, as I have argued elsewhere,[53] the umbrella right instantiated by the tort of private nuisance – which we can loosely call 'the right to the usability of land' – is underlain by a complex substructure of more specific natural rights and acquired rights, and furthermore the tort does not protect against certain kinds of interference with the usability of land at all. Hence, close inspection of private nuisance law reveals a threefold classification of natural rights (which attach automatically to the land), acquired rights (which the law recognises, but which must be acquired by grant or prescription) and 'no rights' (which the law does not recognise at all), that operates as a preliminary filter in nuisance cases independent of, and anterior to, the question of whether, on the facts, the interference with the usability of the land is substantial.[54] For present purposes, the important thing to note about this substructure is that it is concerned with the classification of types of interference with the usability of land, and hence it is analytically posterior to the definitional question that is the subject-matter of this chapter. It follows that on the view of the tort taken here, it is a mistake to try to explain the 'no rights' cases at a definitional level, as falling outside the basic conception of the tort; rather, these cases should be understood as falling within that conception, but as nevertheless not actionable on the grounds that this particular type of interference is not considered to merit a legal response.

This observation can be illustrated by reference to perhaps the most prominent examples of these 'no rights' in English law, namely the rules that an occupier has no right that others not obstruct the view from her land,[55] and no right to receive percolating water from a neighbour's property.[56] Now it seems fairly obvious that blocking a beautiful sea view from her house or causing her well to dry up are actions that interfere with the capacity of a neighbour's property to be used and enjoyed. Hence in theory such conduct could be held to amount to a private nuisance, even if English courts happen to have taken the view that such forms of interference are permissible.[57] What follows from this is that we cannot learn

[53] Nolan (n 14 above) 465–68.

[54] For the details, see Nolan (n 13 above) [22.18]–[22.38].

[55] See *Aldred's Case* (1610) 9 Co Rep 57b, 58b, 77 ER 816, 821 (Wray CJ).

[56] *Chasemore v Richards* (1859) 7 HL Cas 349, 11 ER 140; *Bradford Corp v Pickles* [1895] AC 587 (HL).

[57] I emphasise 'English law' here because it is characteristic of the substructure of private nuisance that the classification of particular interference types is context-sensitive, so that different common law systems may classify the same kind of interference in different ways.

anything about the essential nature of the private nuisance tort from the fact that such forms of interference are not actionable. Nevertheless, it seems clear that the failure to grasp this distinction between the basic scope or definition of the cause of action and its 'substructure' is one of the key drivers of the recent challenge to the orthodox conception of the tort.[58] That challenge is what I will call the 'physical invasion' view of private nuisance, and it is to that challenge that I now turn.

III. The Physical Invasion View

A. Summary of the Physical Invasion View

In broad terms the physical invasion view of private nuisance seeks to reformulate the cause of action as a sort of 'mini-trespass' tort, in which the focus is no longer on interference with the use and enjoyment of the claimant's land as such, but instead on the defendant being responsible for a physical invasion of the claimant's land that falls short of a trespass of the traditional kind.[59] In this section I seek to give an outline of this view, and to identify its most prominent proponents. The motivations that appear to lie behind this view are varied, and the proponents include scholars of libertarian, Kantian and utilitarian persuasions. This reflects the broader point that (in the words of Larissa Katz), exclusion-based accounts of property 'emerge from a range of very different normative and methodological approaches'.[60] The question of what motivates this unlikely alliance of adherents to adopt forms of the physical invasion view is an interesting and important one, but unfortunately I do not have the space to explore that question here.[61] Instead, I seek simply to summarise the various forms of the physical invasion view that have been put forward, in order both to demonstrate the extent of its influence and to set the scene for my defence of the orthodox conception of private nuisance.

The first clear statement of the physical invasion view appears to be in a 1979 article by Richard Epstein.[62] Epstein there defined nuisances as 'invasions of the plaintiff's property that fall short of trespasses but which still interfere in the use and enjoyment of land'.[63]

[58] See, eg, RA Epstein, 'Nuisance Law: Corrective Justice and Its Utilitarian Constraints' (1979) 8 *Journal of Legal Studies* 49, 60ff; RW Wright, 'Private Nuisance Law: A Window on Substantive Justice' in Nolan and Robertson (n 14 above) 512–13; S Douglas, 'The Content of a Freehold: A "Right to Use" Land?' in N Hopkins (ed), *Modern Studies in Property Law*, vol 7 (Oxford, Hart Publishing, 2013) 374–75; S Douglas and B McFarlane, 'Defining Property Rights' in J Penner and HE Smith (eds), *Philosophical Foundations of Property Law* (Oxford, Oxford University Press, 2014) 231–32.

[59] There are weak echoes of the physical invasion view in dicta in a few English cases, of which the most prominent is the statement by Lord Goff that for an action to lie in private nuisance 'in respect of interference with the plaintiff's enjoyment of his land, it will generally arise from something emanating from the defendant's land' (*Hunter* (n 14 above) 685). In some subsequent cases Lord Goff's remark has in effect been taken as at least raising a presumption against a nuisance analysis where there is no such emanation: see, eg, *Anglian Water Services* (n 50 above) 197 (Burnton J).

[60] L Katz, 'Exclusion and Exclusivity in Property Law' (2008) 58 *University of Toronto Law Journal* 275, 279.

[61] For the beginnings of an explanation, see ibid, 279–85; and H Dagan, *Property: Values and Institutions* (Oxford, Oxford University Press, 2011) ch 2.

[62] Epstein (n 58 above).

[63] ibid, 53.

Note that this version of the physical invasion view was not a full-scale assault on the orthodox conception of private nuisance, for two reasons: first, because (as his definition makes clear) Epstein still tied the physical invasion to the use and enjoyment of the claimant's land; and, second, because Epstein accepted that utilitarian considerations justified (in his words) 'making certain forms of noninvasive conduct actionable within the nuisance context',[64] giving as an example the removal of lateral support from the claimant's land.

Six years later, Thomas Merrill argued in the same journal that the law of nuisance was concerned with 'the right to exclude intrusions by others', and that the difference between trespass and nuisance was that while the former governed 'relatively gross invasions by tangible objects', nuisance applied to 'more indirect and intangible interferences'.[65] Merrill's thesis, which was based on what he called 'a simple economic model',[66] proved influential in property law circles, and other property scholars have since used economic analysis to explain private nuisance as a doctrine rooted (to a greater or lesser degree) in a property owner's core right to exclude. A good example is a sophisticated economic analysis of nuisance by Henry Smith,[67] who posited that '[i]nformation costs go a long way toward explaining why and how nuisance law rests on a foundation of exclusionary property rights',[68] while accepting that this was not the whole picture, and that more open-textured 'governance' rules also played a part in the determination of nuisance cases. Smith's take on nuisance is summed up in a more recent paper in which he claims that '[m]uch of nuisance is "mini-trespass", and otherwise it constitutes a fine-tuning of the exclusionary regime through governance'.[69]

The association of nuisance with a physical intrusion onto the claimant's land is not, however, limited to the work of property lawyers, for endorsement of the physical invasion view can also be found in the writings of tort lawyers of a Kantian persuasion, such as Richard Wright.[70] It is important to note, though, that not all Kantian private law scholars share this view of private nuisance, and that two of the most prominent such scholars, Ernest Weinrib and Arthur Ripstein, seem perfectly comfortable with the orthodox conception of the tort.[71] Indeed, in a recent article Weinrib characterises Kant's theory of property in terms of 'usability', an analysis that chimes with the central message of this chapter.[72]

That brings me to the most sustained and radical assault on the orthodox conception of private nuisance, which can be found in recent work by Simon Douglas and Ben McFarlane. Douglas and McFarlane's endorsement of the physical invasion view of private nuisance

[64] ibid, 94.

[65] TW Merrill, 'Trespass, Nuisance, and the Costs of Determining Property Rights' (1985) 14 *Journal of Legal Studies* 13, 13–14.

[66] ibid, 14.

[67] Smith (n 24 above).

[68] ibid, 970.

[69] HE Smith, 'The Persistence of System in Property Law' (2015) 163 *University of Pennsylvania Law Review* 2055, 2079.

[70] See Wright (n 58 above) 512. See also the more nuanced argument in support of the claim that 'a person's right to land … is exclusionary' in JW Neyers and J Diacur, 'What (is) a Nuisance?' (2011) 90 *Canadian Bar Review* 213, 219–20.

[71] See EJ Weinrib, *The Idea of Private Law*, revised edn (Oxford, Oxford University Press, 2012) 191; and A Ripstein, *Private Wrongs* (Cambridge MA, Harvard University Press, 2016) 137.

[72] Weinrib (n 19 above) 131 maintains that for Kant, ownership is 'the legal concept that pertains to the usability of things', and that '[u]sability lies at the heart of the Kantian account of ownership'.

law does not appear to rest on either an economic or a Kantian foundation, but instead arises in the course of a broader argument to the effect that private law does not (or at least should not) recognise a right to use and enjoy one's property, an argument summed up in the following statement:

> It thus seems that A, a freeholder of land, is owed no legal duty by B, C, D etc … not to impair A's ability to use his land. Rather, A is merely owed a duty by B, C, D etc … not to physically interfere with his land.[73]

Note that, although this broader argument appears to be completely at odds with the orthodox definition of private nuisance, the tension between the two is certainly reduced (and possibly even eliminated) by the clarification of that definition made earlier in this chapter, since in fact what private nuisance protects on the orthodox view is not the *use* but the *usability* of land. On the other hand, in an earlier sole-authored paper Douglas argued that it followed from the fact that there was or should be no claim-right in a freeholder to use her land that 'the gist of liability in nuisance is not the impairment of the utility of the freeholder's land, but the physical interference with it',[74] and this narrower claim is quite obviously inconsistent with the orthodox conception of the tort, even as clarified.

Three further observations should be made about the arguments of Douglas and McFarlane at this point. The first is that, whereas previous adherents of the physical invasion view (such as Epstein, Wright and Smith[75]) had maintained the connection with the claimant's use and enjoyment of land, Douglas and McFarlane break that link completely. The second point is that Douglas and McFarlane specifically connect their physical interference analysis with the idea of a boundary crossing, and endorse Merrill's distinction between trespass and nuisance as marking the difference between invasions by tangible and 'less tangible' things.[76] And the third point is that Douglas in particular acknowledges the difficulties that the traditional conception of private nuisance poses for his broader argument, and concedes that there are (in his words) a 'small number' of nuisance cases that are impossible to rationalise in terms of a physical interference with the claimant's land.[77]

B. Critique of the Physical Invasion View

In this subsection, I subject the physical invasion view of private nuisance to critical analysis and defend the orthodox conception of the tort. It is important to note that while some of my observations apply to all the various different forms of the physical invasion view that have been put forward, others are limited to one or more particular iterations of it.

The first and most obvious difficulty with the physical invasion view of nuisance is that it does not even come close to fitting the actual law. As Christopher Essert points out, '[t]he case books are rife with cases' in which liability does not rest on any kind of emanation

[73] Douglas and McFarlane (n 58 above) 232.
[74] Douglas (n 58 above) 373.
[75] See Smith (n 24 above) 992, 997.
[76] Douglas and McFarlane (n 58 above) 225–56. See also Douglas (n 58 above) 369.
[77] Douglas (n 58 above) 373.

onto the claimant's land.[78] We might start with four types of case that Nicholas McBride and Roderick Bagshaw have aptly categorised as concerned with 'earth, water, air and light':[79]

> *Earth*: the rule that a removal of lateral support that causes your neighbour's land to collapse is actionable in nuisance.[80]
>
> *Water*: the rule that a person who diverts a natural stream or substantially alters its flow to the detriment of a downstream riparian owner is liable in private nuisance.[81]
>
> *Air*: the rule that a person who obstructs the flow of air through a defined channel or aperture onto the claimant's land is liable in private nuisance if a right to the flow of air has been acquired by grant or prescription;[82] and
>
> *Light*: the rule (in English and Commonwealth law, but not in American law[83]) that a person who substantially interferes with the light reaching the windows of a building on the claimant's property is liable in private nuisance if a right to light has been acquired by grant or prescription,[84] a rule explicitly understood in the case law as concerned with the effect of the diminution of the light on the 'comfort and convenience or *usefulness*' of the building in question (emphasis added).[85]

Two other examples of well-established types of nuisance that do not involve any physical invasion of the claimant's land are substantial interference with a private right of way, and impeding the access to the claimant's property from the highway.[86]

In addition to these well-established forms of private nuisance, there are several other examples of cases or types of case where nuisance liability has been imposed despite the absence of any kind of 'boundary crossing':

- The 'affront' cases, such as *Laws v Florinplace*, discussed earlier.[87]
- The suggestion in *Birmingham Development Co Ltd v Tyler*[88] that if the state of the defendant's property is such as to pose an actual danger of its collapsing onto the claimant's neighbouring land then this could amount to a nuisance.
- The unanimous view of the Court of Appeal in *Barratt Homes Ltd v Welsh Water (No 2)*,[89] that although in the light of the particular statutory context no action lay in nuisance for damage resulting from a refusal by a sewerage undertaker to allow a developer to

[78] Essert (n 7 above) 96. See also Nolan (n 13 above) [22.12], and for judicial rejection of the suggestion that nuisance is so limited see, eg, *Victoria Park Racing* (n 31 above) 506-507 (Dixon J); *Thompson-Schwab* (n 43 above) 656 (Romer LJ); and *Barratt Homes* (n 49 above) [60] (Lloyd Jones LJ), [81] (Arden LJ).

[79] NM McBride and R Bagshaw, *Tort Law*, 5th edn (Harlow, Pearson Education, 2015) 453–45.

[80] *Hunt v Peake* (1860) John 705, 70 ER 603; *Backhouse v Bonomi* (1861) 9 HL Cas 503, 11 ER 825.

[81] *Mason v Hill* (1833) 5 B & Ad 1, 110 ER 692; *Orr-Ewing v Colquhoun* (1877) 2 App Cas 839 (HL); *Fear v Vickers* (1911) 27 TLR 558 (CA). This rule forms part of a more complex set of principles that govern riparian rights: for further details, see J Getzler, *A History of Water Rights at Common Law* (Oxford, Oxford University Press, 2004).

[82] *Bass v Gregory* (1890) 25 QBD 481 (QB).

[83] See, eg, *Fontainebleau Hotel Corp v Forty-Five Twenty-Five Inc* 114 So 2d 357 (Fla Ct App 1959).

[84] *Bowry and Pope's Case* (1589) 1 Leon 168, 74 ER 155; III Bl Comm 216–17.

[85] See *Kine v Jolly* [1905] 1 Ch 480 (CA), 493 (Vaughan Williams LJ). The seminal case on the nature of the right is *Colls v Home and Colonial Stores Ltd* [1904] AC 179 (HL).

[86] On the right of access, see Nolan (n 13 above) [22.85]. This right is a private right appurtenant to the property, distinct from the public's right to pass along the highway: see, eg, *Toronto Transit Commission v Swansea (Village)* [1935] SCR 455 (SCC) 457 (Davis J).

[87] See text to nn 42ff, above.

[88] n 36 above.

[89] n 49 above.

exercise its statutory right to connect newly built properties to a public sewer, the undertaker's conduct was capable of amounting to a nuisance.

- The decision in the Canadian case of *Nor-Video Services v Ontario Hydro*[90] that interference with television reception amounted to a private nuisance (a possibility also left open by the House of Lords in *Hunter v Canary Wharf*[91] unless the interference was caused by a building on the defendant's land).

Nor can the types of case I have described be dismissed as peripheral to some alleged paradigm of physical invasion, as Lord Goff suggested in the *Hunter* case.[92] On the contrary, if one looks, for example, at the chapter on nuisance in *Baker and Milsom's Sources of English Legal History*[93] (which covers English private law up to 1750), one finds that *all* of the cases in the first part of the chapter[94] concern rights of way, rights of common and diversion of watercourses, a clear indication that for much of its history the law of nuisance was dominated by cases that do not correspond with the physical invasion view of the tort. This ties into a broader weakness of the physical invasion view, namely that it fails to account for the operation of private nuisance in acquired rights cases (ie, those involving interference with easements and profits). Although these acquired rights cases are frequently underemphasised in the modern literature on the tort of nuisance, they are in no way tangential, but are instead central to a proper understanding of both the historical and the contemporary operation of the cause of action.

In addition to the many examples of nuisance that do not involve a physical intrusion onto the claimant's land, there are a number of other problems with the physical invasion view (or versions of it). One, rather fundamental, such difficulty is that while the physical invasion view tells us that only things that cross the boundary can be nuisances, it then gives us little guidance as to which intangible boundary crossings are nuisances, and which are not (and why). (The problem with the physical invasion view, in other words, is not just that not all nuisances are boundary crossings, but that not all boundary crossings are nuisances – or trespasses.) In particular, if we follow Douglas and McFarlane in rejecting the idea that a nuisance is an interference with the use and enjoyment of the claimant's land, then we must obviously also reject the idea that nuisance liability turns on whether that interference is substantial or unreasonable. However, Douglas and McFarlane do not tell us what should replace that central stage of the nuisance enquiry, and yet *something* has to replace it, unless we are to believe that *every* sound wave, odour, ray of light, etc crossing the boundary of a person's property is wrongful, a proposition which is self-evidently nonsensical.[95] In his more moderate version of the physical invasion view, Epstein explains the focus on *substantial* interference (as encapsulated in the 'rule of give and take, live and let live',[96] the locality rule and so on) as a 'utilitarian constraint' on a pure form of

[90] *Nor-Video Services v Ontario Hydro* (1978) 84 DLR (3d) 221 (Ontario SC).

[91] *Hunter* (n 14 above).

[92] ibid, 685. See also the reference by Douglas (text to n 77 above) to 'a small number of claims successfully litigated in nuisance' where there was no physical emanation onto the claimant's land; and Douglas and McFarlane (n 58 above) 230 ('a small number of cases').

[93] J Baker, *Baker and Milsom's Sources of English Legal History: Private Law to 1750*, 2nd edn (Oxford, Oxford University Press, 2010).

[94] ibid, 640–52.

[95] See also Essert (n 7 above) 97–98 (discussing light rays in particular).

[96] *Bamford v Turnley* (1862) 3 B&S 66, 84, 122 ER 27, 33 (Bramwell B).

corrective justice, focused on the boundary crossing *simpliciter*.[97] But, while this enables him formally to square his theory with the law, the suggestion that the conceptual apparatus that determines the vast majority of nuisance actions – and which lies 'at the heart of nuisance law'[98] – is a peripheral 'constraint' on the true nature of the cause of action rings hollow, and only goes to demonstrate 'the central failure of his account'.[99]

This first difficulty shades into a second one, which is that some versions of the physical invasion view fail plausibly to account for central doctrines of the law of private nuisance, most obviously the requirement that the interference with another's use and enjoyment must be substantial, or unreasonable.[100] Here the logic of the orthodox conception of the tort is clear: you begin by asking whether there is an interference with the capacity of land to be used and enjoyed at all, and then (if there is) you move on to consider how significant that interference is. By contrast, if you try to break the link with the land's utility, then the substantial interference question either makes no sense at all (substantial interference *with what*, on the Douglas/McFarlane approach?), or is pushed, rather implausibly, to the conceptual periphery (Epstein). Nor is this the only instance of a central aspect of private nuisance law which is clearly derivative of the conception of the tort as an interference with the usability of land. Another good example is the holding of the House of Lords in *Hunter v Canary Wharf* that the basic damages in a nuisance case are to be assessed by reference to the diminution in the value of the land attributable to the nuisance, and that in amenity nuisance cases (as opposed to physical damage cases) what this meant was the diminution in the *use or utility value* of the property.[101]

Sticking with the law itself, a further weakness of the physical invasion view is that the account its proponents give of the distinction between trespass and nuisance is unpersuasive. The alleged dichotomy between 'tangible' and 'intangible' things is clunky in the extreme;[102] makes little sense from a functional perspective (why should invasions of tangible and intangible things be subject to different legal regimes?); and is a poor match for the law, since there are many examples of nuisances that do involve boundary crossings where the thing that crosses the boundary is eminently 'tangible' and not remotely 'ethereal',[103] such as stray golf balls[104] and cricket balls,[105] a collapsing fence or wall,[106] and encroaching tree branches and roots.[107] Although not free from difficulty, the traditional way of

[97] See Epstein (n 58 above) 82ff.

[98] Essert (n 7 above) 104.

[99] ibid, 104, fn 97. It is also worth noting that there is in fact nothing 'utilitarian' about these rules, but that is an argument for another day.

[100] For discussion of this requirement, see Nolan (n 13 above) [22.39]ff.

[101] *Hunter* (n 14 above) 696 (Lord Lloyd), 706 (Lord Hoffmann).

[102] See Essert (n 7 above) 112, emphasising the arbitrary nature of the distinction. Unsurprisingly, the suggestion made to a US court that the two causes of action be distinguished in this way was roundly rejected: see *Martin v Reynolds Metals Co* 342 P 2d 790, 221 Or 86 (1960).

[103] See Smith, 'Nuisance' (n 24 above) 998 ('nuisance is about invasions of a more ethereal sort').

[104] *Lester-Travers v City of Frankston* [1970] VR 2 (Victoria SC); *Segal v Derrick Golf & Winter Club* (1977) 76 DLR (3d) 746 (Alberta SC).

[105] *Miller v Jackson* [1977] QB 966 (CA).

[106] *St Anne's Well Brewery Co v Roberts* (1928) 140 LT 1 (CA) 6 (Scrutton LJ); *Mann v Saulnier* (1959) 19 DLR (2d) 130 (New Brunswick SC).

[107] For judicial confirmation that encroachment of tree branches or roots is a nuisance not a trespass, see, eg, *Lemmon v Webb* [1894] 3 Ch 1 (CA) 24 (Kay LJ); *Davey v Harrow Corpn* [1958] 1 QB 60 (CA) 70 (Lord Goddard CJ).

drawing the distinction, which asks whether the interference is direct (trespass) or indirect (nuisance)[108] tracks the historical division between trespass and case, is easier to justify,[109] and is a much better fit with the cases.

Yet another difficulty with the physical invasion view is that the positive arguments that have been put forward for it are weak, and usually rely on what I hope to have shown is a misunderstanding of the orthodox conception of private nuisance (coupled, as argued earlier, with a failure to appreciate the role played by what I have called the 'substructure' of the tort[110]). Douglas, for example, says that what he terms a 'duty of non-impairment of use' owed to a freeholder of land could prove 'very onerous', since it could potentially entail 'a duty to refrain from doing any act that could prevent [the freeholder] from making a specific use of his land', and gives as an example buying up building materials that the freeholder needs in order to erect a building on his land.[111] As we have seen, however, what the tort of private nuisance protects is a relatively abstract notion of the usability of the claimant's land, rather than the ability of the claimant to actually use her land, whether generally or in specific ways. Once this is understood, the duty that Douglas thinks very onerous turns out to be entirely reasonable, and the building materials example is revealed as a red herring. Similarly, Douglas's other argument against a duty of non-impairment of use, that a freeholder will not usually be overly prejudiced by the loss of a specific liberty to use her land,[112] again misses the point that what private nuisance in fact protects is a more general interest in the usability of land, substantial interference with which is likely to be highly prejudicial to both freeholders and tenants alike.

Finally, the physical invasion view, and in particular the rejection of a right to the usability of land, is counter-intuitive, and fairly obviously misses the point. After all, how plausible is an account of real property law according to which it is not an interference with your property rights to block all the access to your land, or to suck out all the air from your flat using a pump, or to make your house uninhabitable by cutting off all the utilities that service it?[113] And do we really believe that, as Douglas and McFarlane argue, an 'affront' case like *Thompson-Schwab*[114] is possibly explicable on the basis that the presence of the brothel or those frequenting it causes light rays to cross the boundary of the claimant's land[115] (which, we might note, is also true of the presence of every other person, building or thing visible from the claimant's property, including a cloud flitting past on the horizon or a star shining in the night sky)?

[108] *Southport Corpn v Esso Petroleum Co* [1953] 2 All ER 1204 (QB) 1208 (Devlin J).

[109] For such a justification, see Nolan (n 14 above) 481–82. See also the not dissimilar justification put forward by Essert (n 7 above) 112–24. Both justifications for the direct/indirect distinction centre on the fact that in nuisance it is necessary to show that the interference is substantial/unreasonable, but that no such limitation applies in trespass.

[110] See text following n 53 above.

[111] Douglas (n 58 above) 376.

[112] ibid, 376–77.

[113] Note that Douglas accepts that denying a person all access to his or her chattel can amount to a wrongful interference with it, actionable in conversion: S Douglas, *Liability for Wrongful Interferences with Chattels* (Oxford, Hart Publishing, 2011) 99.

[114] See n 43 above.

[115] Douglas and McFarlane (n 58 above) 232.

IV. Implications for Property Theory

Since it seems clear that at least some manifestations of the physical invasion view of private nuisance are rooted in attempts to square the tort with particular theories of property, it is now time to turn the tables, and to ask what implications the orthodox conception of the cause of action, properly understood, might have for property theory. After all, as Essert points out, '[u]nderstanding property requires understanding nuisance'.[116]

The most obvious such implication is that private nuisance demonstrates that it cannot be right to conceive of property rights solely in terms of a right to exclude others. While many private nuisance cases do in fact involve boundary crossings, many do not, and (more importantly) the essence of private nuisance does not lie in the idea of a physical invasion of the claimant's land, but rather in the impairment of the land's usability. A theory of property that cannot explain the essence of a cause of action so central to the lived reality of land law is not a persuasive one. Furthermore, the fact that the role nuisance plays in the protection of incorporeal hereditaments is such a problem for the physical invasion view of the tort serves as a useful reminder that theories of property need to be capable of explaining property rights of this kind, which clearly rest not on a right to exclude but on (something like) a right not to be excluded.

Beyond the relatively simple claim that property rights cannot be conceived solely in terms of a right to exclude others, the implications of the orthodox conception of private nuisance for property theory become less clear-cut. After all, the claim that a plausible theory of property must be capable of accommodating a usability right is not necessarily inconsistent, for example, with the suggestion that the right to exclude is 'fundamental to the concept of property',[117] or indeed that exclusion or the right to exclude is the 'essence'[118] or 'core'[119] of property. On the other hand, the practical significance of private nuisance in common law systems of real property casts doubt even on these weaker claims, for, as Hanoch Dagan points out, doctrines such as nuisance 'are not marginal or peripheral to the life of property, but deal instead with some of our most commonplace human interactions'.[120]

Then again, my analysis of the essence of private nuisance is entirely consistent with some of the central arguments that have been made by commentators who have endorsed exclusion-based accounts of property, which suggests that, properly understood, private nuisance might not be as much of a problem for these theorists as it is for their theories. Take, for example, Douglas and McFarlane's 'core argument' that 'the distinctiveness of property rights is best understood, not by looking at the positive uses available to A, but rather at the negative duties owed to A by the rest of the world'.[121] Here the clarification of

[116] Essert (n 7 above) 119–20. See also at 86, where he says that 'a complete theory of property would help explain what counts and what does not count as a nuisance', and that conversely 'a complete theory of nuisance would help explain the rights definitive of ownership of real property'.

[117] TW Merill, 'Property and the Right to Exclude' (1998) 77 *Nebraska Law Review* 730, 731.

[118] M Cohen, 'Property and Sovereignty' (1927) 13 *Cornell Law Quarterly* 8, 12–13. See also Penner (n 22 above) 71 (describing exclusion as the 'formal essence' of the right to property).

[119] TW Merrill and HE Smith, *Property: Principles and Practice* (New York, Foundation Press, 2007) 22. For discussion of this idea, see Dagan (n 61 above) 38ff.

[120] Dagan (n 61 above) 41.

[121] Douglas and McFarlane (n 58 above) 220.

the orthodox conception of private nuisance is significant, since it shows that what nuisance protects is not A's 'right to use' her land in particular ways, but a perfectly plausible 'right to usability' that corresponds to a duty not substantially to impair the usability of other people's land. Similarly, while the orthodox conception of private nuisance, properly understood, is incompatible with James Penner's argument that the interest we have in the use of property grounds only a formal right of exclusion,[122] it is perfectly consistent with what appears to be his more foundational claim that 'there is simply no basis in the legal institution of property rights to individuate or identify particular use-rights as legally recognised elements of the bundle [of rights]'.[123] And, again, by avoiding the high information costs associated with the delineation of specific use rights, an abstract usability right would appear to be consistent with Smith's 'information-cost rationale for broad rights'.[124]

Tying these threads together, we can see that recognition of the underlying nature of private nuisance as a cause of action demonstrates that property rights need not (as many property theorists seem to assume[125]) be conceived of in strictly binary terms as either rights of exclusion or specific use rights: nuisance shows that there is a plausible third possibility, a right of usability that can profitably operate in tandem with an exclusion rule, as exemplified by its sister tort of trespass.

Finally, although my focus in this chapter is on the law of private nuisance, and so on property rights in land, we should also note the possibility that an exclusion/usability model may also underlie the protection of interests in chattels. As in the case of land, the implausibility of a 'right to use' personal property in particular ways[126] is not inconsistent with a more abstract right to the usability of chattels, and indeed there is some evidence of such a right in the law governing wrongful interference with personal property.[127] At the same time, it would be a mistake to ignore the important differences between land and chattels, and their implications for any usability analysis. In particular, the immovability or 'stuckness' of land means that it is more likely to be rendered unusable by the activities of others, whereas chattels are by definition movable and hence problems caused by their being rendered unusable in one location can generally be avoided by relocating them.[128]

[122] J Penner, 'Hohfeldian Use-Rights in Property' in JW Harris (ed), *Property Problems From Genes to Pension Funds* (London, Kluwer Law International, 1997) 168.

[123] ibid, 172. Furthermore, it is also compatible with Penner's claim that 'the right to property does not enable use' (ibid, 171), since we have seen that a proper understanding of the orthodox conception of nuisance shows it to be concerned with the usability of the land, not the ability of the claimant to use it.

[124] Smith (n 24 above) 971. Similarly, a usability right would appear to satisfy Smith's test of a 'gatekeeper right that protects the owners' interests in a wide and indefinite class of uses without the need to delineate … those uses at all' (973).

[125] See, eg, Merrill and Smith (n 119 above) 21. This assumption may reflect the influence of early law-and-economics scholarship, which characterised nuisance disputes as conflicts between particular land uses: see in particular the works by Coase and by Calabresi and Melamed, cited in n 24, above.

[126] As to which, see Douglas (n 58 above) 376–77.

[127] See Douglas, *Liability for Wrongful Interferences with Chattels* (n 113 above) 66–68, 99, 117–18, 157. See also the discussion of a 'right to use' chattels in S Green, 'Rights and Wrongs: An Introduction to the Wrongful Interference Actions' in Nolan and Robertson (n 14 above).

[128] Though not always. If, for example, the defendant prevents the claimant from taking her car out of her garage he renders it immovable and hence unusable for its core purpose of transportation. See further, Bagshaw (n 23 above) 417. See also *England v Cowley* (1873) LR 8 Ex 126 (Exch) 128 (Pollock B). In the famous German 'Fleet case', it was held that trapping a ship in a canal for nine months amounted to a violation of ownership rights in the ship: BGH 21 Dec 1970, BGHZ 55, 153.

V. Conclusion

In this chapter, I have sought to defend and clarify the orthodox conception of private nuisance as a tort that responds to interference with the use and enjoyment of land. In doing so, I have argued for the rejection of an attenuated vision of real property which rests not only on a misguided 'isomorphism between the boundaries of the property right and the physical boundaries of the land',[129] but also (by ignoring incorporeal hereditaments) on a misconception of 'land' in its legal sense as a three-dimensional physical space, as opposed to a normative idea.[130] I hope thereby to have shown not only that private nuisance is a complex and sophisticated cause of action, but also that by looking through the lens of nuisance we can more clearly see the complexity and sophistication of the institution of property itself.[131]

[129] See RG Bone, 'Normative Theory and Legal Doctrine in American Nuisance Law: 1850 to 1920' (1986) *Southern California Law Review* 1101, 1157.
[130] See Essert (n 7 above) fn 107. On the legal conception of land, see n 12 above.
[131] See Dagan (n 61 above) 37 (referring to property as 'a complex and heterogenous legal construct').

6

Redrawing the Law's Definition of Property in the Light of Contemporary Use of Urban Surfaces

SUE FARRAN

I. Introduction

There has been recent debate about whether a new 'Banksy' work entitled 'Draw the Raised Bridge!' on a disused bridge in Hull should be cleaned off or celebrated as a significant contribution to Hull's 2017 city of culture status.[1] A local Conservative councillor was reported as stating that the piece 'should be cleaned off. It should be photographed and the photograph kept because Banksy is not without talent', while a BBC Arts Editor stated,

> I don't think you can remove it … I think the whole point of Banksy's work is they are what is called site-specific … they work because of the places they've been put and if you remove the location the work loses its power.[2]

The debate reflects opposing views about graffiti and the relationship of power and place. Who (particularly if, as in this case, ownership of the locus is unclear) has the right to make the decision to remove or leave this Banksy, and why? How is power over location or places – particularly those which physically and sometimes legally traverse the private/public divide – exercised and regulated (and the two may not be synonymous)? And what does this tell us about the law that governs property?

Kevin Brown has comprehensively covered much of the law relating to public space, particularly the use of criminal sanctions to control human activity.[3] In this chapter I seek to unravel the legal underpinnings, primarily but not solely of private law, which inform both the Hull councillor's point of view and the observation of the Arts Editor. In order to do this I first look at the idea of taxonomies and how different taxonomical approaches to concepts may provide scope for defining property more broadly. Drawing on Kevin Gray's work, I then consider how a more flexible, contextually aware definition of property

[1] Banksy is a recognised but unidentified graffiti 'artist', whose 'pieces' are deemed to be highly collectible and of considerable economic value. See eg L Collins, 'Banksy Was Here', *The New Yorker* (New York, May 14 2007).

[2] BBC News, 'Hull Banksy Mural "should be cleaned off"', *BBC News* (London, 27 January 2018): http://www.bbc.co.uk/news/uk-england-humber-42844953.

[3] K Brown, 'The Hyper-regulation of Public Space: the Use and Abuse of Public Spaces Protection Orders in England and Wales' (2017) 37 *Legal Studies* 543.

might accommodate changing, practical realities. To do this, the focus is on the surfaces of the built environment (the ground, walls, bridges, roofs, etc) and activities that challenge or reframe the concepts underpinning Gray's definition, particularly the right to exclude. This can be illustrated by the Banksy controversy but also by other activities taking place in cities, towns and villages, particularly about property falling within the public domain. The chapter concludes by suggesting that the way in which we define property can inform our approach to the taxonomy of property law.

II. The Taxonomy of Law

Sheehan and Arvind[4] suggest that, in its broadest sense, there are three dimensions to the taxonomy of law: 'the selection of sets of ideas, categories and concepts used to describe and order the subject of study'; 'the basis on which we constitute and give content to these concepts and categories'; and 'the relationship between the various categories, concepts and ideas we use to describe the area of study'. The taxonomy of law is used to determine whether or not a set of facts is subject to a set of rules that give rise to legal consequences: 'Taxonomy in law *is* about how we treat the subject of our taxonomy.'[5] Sheehan and Arvind argue that 'the shape of a taxonomy depends on its purpose'.[6] In this chapter I suggest that we might reverse this proposition by starting with the realities of how people relate to urban space, using this to inform a definition of property which can accommodate the reality, and using the concept (or subject) to determine the taxonomy.

Not everyone regards the taxonomy of law in the same way.[7] In private law, for example, there is considerable debate chiefly among those who support Peter Birks's line of reasoning and those who do not.[8] This chapter does not intend to engage with that debate but instead to try to extract some bare bones that might be applied in the field of property law. Sheehan and Arvind point to two main schools of thought: 'interpretivists' and 'contextualists'. While the former prefer to rely on legal principles of general application justified by context-neutral norms (and so are aligned jurisprudentially with legal positivists), the latter allow more room for policy and consideration of the actual context in which the law is applied (and so are aligned jurisprudentially with legal realism). Contextualists may be more ready to accept change because their realist view of the law is more 'socially and empirically grounded',[9] and their understanding of concepts 'more *evidently* linked to social facts and circumstances'.[10] The interpretivist school of thought instead adopts a more rigid,

[4] D Sheehan and RR Arvind, 'Private Law Theory and Taxonomy: Reframing the Debate' (2015) 35 *Legal Studies* 480.

[5] ibid 484.

[6] ibid 483.

[7] See for example E Sherwin, 'Legal Taxonomy' (2009) 15 *Legal Theory* 25. Sherwin adopts a threefold approach: formal, function, reason-based taxonomy.

[8] For this see for example P Watts, 'Taxonomy in Private Law – Furor in Text and Subtext' (2014) *New Zealand Law Review* 107; K Low, 'The Use and Abuse of Taxonomy' (2009) 29 *Legal Studies* 355; and Sheehan and Arvind (n 4 above).

[9] Sheehan and Arvind (n 4 above) 496.

[10] ibid 497.

socially detached, static view of concepts and the categorisation of these into legal subjects (contract, tort etc), preferring certainty and clear rules.

Significantly for this chapter, Sheehan and Arvind argue that taxonomies can work in different ways. They can be descriptive: used primarily as an organisational tool at a particular moment in time or for a particular purpose – such as might be deployed for example in outlining the content of a law module; prescriptive, in which case they tend to be rather static – such as the taxonomy of the law of contracts; or developmental, dynamically recognising and accommodating change in both the process and appearance of the law – as found for example in the evolution of equitable solutions to novel problems. The prescriptive approach, while it might create certainty and consistency in the application of the law may be of limited use in hard or novel cases. If, then, one adopts a 'contextualist' and 'developmental' approach to the taxonomy of law it might be possible to propose a new taxonomy, taking into account social change, challenges to existing normative underpinnings, and the identification of new values in society that need to be reflected in the law. This aligns with 'the realist taxonomic enterprise', which Dagan describes as 'both backward and forward looking, constantly challenging the continued validity and desirability of the normative underpinnings of existing legal categories'.[11]

Sheehan and Arvind suggest that 'Taxonomies that seek to be useful … must not only prescribe an ideal answer, but also chart a path by which the legal system gets from its current position to the proposed position.'[12]

To do this it is necessary to understand, or to determine the concepts used in the taxonomy of any legal category. This task can be divided into considering how concepts are constructed – what is their content, and how are they used to determine what falls within and what falls without the concept? Sheehan and Arvind suggest that concepts are individuated one from the other and use the example of estoppel.[13] Within this concept are sub-concepts; representation in respect of property interests (at least for proprietary estoppel), reliance on that representation in some way, and detriment which would not have been incurred were it not for the representation and reliance. There is an interrelationship between these sub-concepts that must all be met to satisfy our understanding of proprietary estoppel. To determine whether something falls within the concept, a set of facts is tested against the sub-concepts. Sheehan and Arvind refer to this approach of looking at concepts as 'intension' and 'extension'. The intension of a concept is 'the set of conditions that a thing must satisfy to fall under the concept',[14] while the extension is 'the set of things that …"fall under" the concept'.[15] Some concepts might look similar by extension but their intension is different. Sheehan and Arvind use Frege's example of the planet Venus,[16] the intension of which may differ because it is referred to as both the Evening Star and the Morning Star, but the extension of which is the same.

[11] H Dagan, 'Legal Realism and the Taxonomy of Private Law' in C Rickett and R Grantham (eds), *Structure and Justification in Private Law* (Oxford, Hart Publishing, 2008) 147, 161.

[12] Sheehan and Arvind (n 4 above) 488.

[13] ibid 489.

[14] ibid.

[15] ibid.

[16] ibid.

These, however, are shifting sands, especially if one adopts a contextualist approach, which Sheehan and Arvind suggest is one not so much interested in there being 'some inherent quality about a concept',[17] as the application of the concept in particular circumstances.

An example might be found in the case of estoppel. The influence of a contextual approach which looks at the application of a concept in particular circumstances has seen a shift away from the 'five probanda' (or sub-concepts of proprietary estoppel) of *Willmott v Barber*,[18] to a looser set of sub-concepts or criteria: representation, reliance and detriment.[19] Indeed, it might be argued that the concept of estoppel now overlaps with the concept of constructive trust.[20] So, the intension of estoppel has changed. At the same time, however, those very sub-concepts that make up the concept of estoppel are subject to variation, so while we may teach students that these three elements are required, in fact the case-law suggests there are many variations of, for example, representation, so it is difficult to be absolute about what constitutes a representation[21] and whether the concept is the same in domestic or commercial contexts, or situations of imperfect gift, unilateral mistake or common expectation cases.[22] There is, then, scope for manipulating (depending on one's viewpoint or theoretical approach) the constituent elements of a concept and their importance. For example, in *Taylors Fashions*, Oliver J observed (regardless of the category of estoppel being referred to) that what was required was:

> a very much broader approach which is directed rather at ascertaining whether, in particular individual circumstances, it would be unconscionable for a party to be permitted to deny that which knowingly, or unknowingly, he has allowed or encouraged another to assume to his detriment than to enquiring whether the circumstances can be fitted within the confines of some preconceived formula serving as a universal yardstick for every form of unconscionable behaviour.[23]

Sheehan and Arvind ask 'What are the consequences of highlighting certain factors while omitting others?'[24] The answer either must be that certain sets of facts or circumstances fall outside the concept or are brought within it, and this intended or unintended result is determined by the normative underpinnings of the concept and its sub-concepts. So, if judges find on the facts and through a broad application of the sub-concepts that there

[17] ibid.

[18] *Willmott v Barber* (1880) 15 Ch D 96.

[19] *Taylors Fashions Ltd v Liverpool Victoria Trustees Co Ltd* [1979] EWHC (Ch) 1. Following with approval Buckley LJ in *Shaw v Applegate* [1977] 1 WLR 970, 978: 'I do not … think it is clear that it is essential to find all the five tests set out by Fry J (in *Willmott v Barber*) literally applicable and satisfied in any particular case. The real test, I think, must be whether upon the facts of the particular case, the situation has become such that it would be dishonest or unconscionable for the plaintiff, or the person having the right to be enforced, to continue to seek to enforce it'.

[20] Sheehan and Arvind (n 4 above) 499 suggest there is also an overlap with the concept of contract but it is unclear here if they are referring to promissory or proprietary estoppel. On the taxonomy of proprietary estoppel see Lord Neuberger of Abbotsbury, 'The Stuffing of Minerva's Owl – Taxonomy and Taxidermy in Equity' [2009] *CLJ* 537.

[21] See, for example, comments by Lord Walker in *Yeoman's Row Management Ltd and Another v Cobbe* [2008] UKHL 55, [2008] 1 WLR 1752. Contrary to the usual meaning of representation, it would seem that standing by or simply allowing would be sufficient for representation.

[22] This is a classification proposed by K Gray and SF Gray, *Elements of Land Law*, 4th edn (Oxford, Oxford University Press, 2005) [10.189], cited by Lord Walker in *Cobbe* (n 21 above) at [48].

[23] *Taylors Fashions Ltd v Liverpool Victoria Trustees Co Ltd* (n 19 above) 151–52.

[24] Sheehan and Arvind (n 4 above) 491.

is an estoppel, then this might undermine or eventually change the intension of estoppel. Changing the content or meaning of concepts by themselves will not necessarily create a new taxonomy, but from a contextual/realist perspective, it is important that a taxonomy of property law should be sufficiently dynamic to accommodate the judicial development of concepts, particularly if this judicial response is in reaction to changing norms reflecting changes in society. The taxonomy we adopt may have consequences for how flexible we can be in developing and applying individual concepts within that taxonomy.

The question for taxonomy appears to be how this evolution of norms or the 'moral element'[25] of concepts can be used to marry conceptual and contextual approaches to create new taxonomies, or, how do we taxonomise shifting concepts? One approach suggested by Sheehan and Arvind is to adopt a Hegelian teleological approach, ie what is the purpose of the law? This can be both 'backwards-looking and forwards-looking',[26] but it does require engagement with, and revaluation of concepts and categories as well as a recognition of the ways in which concepts and categorisation 'constrain and shape the manner in which the law responds',[27] which may sit uneasily with contextualists' view of the 'inherently indeterminate nature of concepts'.[28] The danger of a teleological approach is that it may be very undemocratic, reflecting the interests of a dominant elite or a particular political agenda. Alternatively, in looking forward it could strive to be more democratic, less party-politics orientated, and more inclusive. A teleological shift in housing law, for example, might involve the expansion or reduction of social housing.

III. The Taxonomy of Property Law

Eveline Ramaekers points out that before we can decide what property law is, we have to be sure that there is such a category as 'property law' that can be marked out from other areas of law.[29] She highlights the many different ways of looking at property. The fact that we might refer to the teaching of 'Land Law', or of 'Commercial Property Law' underscores the challenge and the way in which lawyers subsequently think about property based on the pragmatic considerations of legal education. As will be seen in the examples below (and as became very evident at the 2018 Modern Studies in Property Law conference), there are not always clear boundaries between, say, property law and tort law,[30] or contract law[31] or even criminal law.[32] Ramaekers focuses in particular on the fuzzy boundaries between the law of property and the law of obligations and the different ways in which these are delineated in different authorities and in different legal systems. If one accepts these overlapping

[25] ibid 493.
[26] ibid 500.
[27] ibid.
[28] ibid.
[29] E Ramaekers, 'What is Property Law' (2017) 37 *OJLS* 588.
[30] See eg D Nolan, 'The Essence of Private Nuisance' Chapter 5 in this volume.
[31] See eg F Bettini, 'Long Leases and Affordable Housing: A Comparative Analysis of French and English Law' Chapter 13 in this volume.
[32] See eg R Hickey, 'Defending Property: Self-help Remedies, the Use of Force, and the Concept of a Property Right' Chapter 4 in this volume.

boundaries then the categorisation of property law needs to be based on concepts which are themselves not subject-bound. So, for example, if one bases property law on the law of things, or the 'thinginess' of the subject-matter, then one is immediately faced with the challenges of new forms of property. Similarly, one might argue the same for the term 'resource' used by Gray, insofar as while this suggests a 'thing' to which a value is attached, what is valued will change as society changes. For the purposes of this chapter, I propose to adopt Gray's view[33] that property is about control over access and the power to exclude:

> 'Property' is the power-relation constituted by the state's endorsement of private claims to regulate the access of strangers to the benefits of particular resources. If, in respect of a given claimant and a given resource, the exercise of such regulatory control is physically impracticable or legally abortive or morally or socially undesirable, we say that such a claimant can assert no 'property' in that resource.[34]

This categorisation, based on a number of separate but inter-related concepts (control, access, power, exclusion, etc), avoids too much consideration of the nature of the 'thing' or 'resource' and focuses instead on relationships. It also, I think, lies at the essence of the diverging views of the Hull councillor and the BBC Arts Editor and, when the concepts are examined in the context of the examples below, admits the possibility of a new taxonomy.

Gray's definition is attractive (for my purposes) because he argues that dominium is not limitless but may be 'curtailed by limitations of a broadly "moral" character'.[35] Property, he argues, is limited to the control exercised over access.[36] He also points out that property is not a thing; that some resources are not propertised – and therefore belong to no one or to everyone. Even if they are propertised, dominium is subject to limitations, incursions and restrictions, and property is dynamic and potentially a morally limited concept because 'physical, legal and moral conditions of excludability may vary according to time and circumstance'.[37] Together this suggests that there is some room for change, but the starting point is that something is property if it has the attribute of excludability: 'A resource is "excludable" only if it is feasible for a legal person to exercise regulatory control over the access of strangers to the various benefits inherent in the resource.'[38] He suggests that there are three grounds on which non-excludability may rest: physical, legal, and moral. Gray acknowledges that what is an excludable or non-excludable resource – and therefore property – is fluid. What might not be property today could be property tomorrow.

Most importantly, Gray suggests that 'the test of moral excludability is much more closely concerned with those social conventions or mores which promote integrative social existence than with any normative judgment about individual human conduct.'[39] He is referring to what we might regard as the global commons or resources for the common good, but his test does not have to be limited to these, because as he states:

> In setting the moral limits of 'property', the courts effectively recognise that there is some serial ranking of legally protected values and interests: claims of 'property' may sometimes be overridden

[33] K Gray, 'Property in Thin Air' (1991) 50 *CLJ* 252.
[34] ibid 294.
[35] ibid 287.
[36] ibid 294.
[37] ibid 295–96.
[38] ibid 268.
[39] ibid 280.

> by the need to attain or further more highly rated social goals … The predominating emphasis expressed in the notion of moral non-excludability is the need to afford especial protection to those values which promote human communication and social intercourse.[40]

The important point, for this chapter, is that 'property rights are merely prima facie rights which may be abridged or overridden by other moral concerns'.[41] Gray goes on to point out that these moral limits can include land. He cites the example of the Australian case of *Gerhardy v Brown*.[42] In this case the requirement for non-Pitjantjatjaras (the Pitjantjatjara are an Aboriginal peoples) to have permission to enter lands designated under the Pitjantjatjara Land Rights Act 1981 was challenged as being contrary to the Racial Discrimination Act 1975 and the normal incidents of ownership. The High Court of Australia held that in the context of this particular land, the exclusion by operation of statute was lawful. Commenting on the case, Gray concludes

> Although accepting that the right to exclude strangers is ordinarily an incident of ownership of land the Court was able to contemplate circumstances in which this right of exclusion might be abridged by more highly valued social objectives. In thus delineating the limits of 'property', the High Court significantly emphasised the need to promote those moral or political standards which enrich life and constructive social interaction within a community of equals.[43]

In this case, the statutory restrictions were a special measure to address historical racial inequalities.[44]

The consideration of moral grounds for non-excludability calls into play the intersection of public and private. Although he is primarily referring to private property Gray points out that no property is truly private,[45] 'and in underpinning the law of 'property' the state indirectly adjudicates an exceedingly broad range of the power-relations permitted within society'.[46] If our taxonomy of property focusses only on private law, there is a danger that the influence and impact of the state or the public parts of property law will be overlooked. This is significant not only in practical terms but also for informing the norms underpinning concepts. This is played out in the debate as to the Hull Banksy work. Both spokespersons are private individuals representing public bodies – the council and the BBC. Both are expressing what might be private or official (public) views and both are drawing on certain understandings of valued social objectives.

Adopting a developmental/contextualist approach which, as suggested by Sheehan and Arvind, is 'more 'socially and empirically grounded',[47] and 'more *evidently* linked to social facts and circumstances',[48] and drawing on the concept and sub-concepts in Gray's definition, it may be possible to define property in a way that is sufficiently flexible to take into account changing realities and values, without abandoning established tenets entirely. The following table suggests how Gray and Sheehan and Arvind might be brought together.

[40] ibid 281.
[41] ibid 283.
[42] *Gerhardy v Brown* (1985) 159 CLR 70. This was essentially a case concerned with the scope of the Racial Discrimination Act 1975, especially positive discrimination in favour of Aboriginal peoples.
[43] Gray (n 33 above) 289.
[44] *Gerhardy v Brown* (n 42 above). See on this the *dictum* of Justice Brennan, [33]–[34].
[45] Gray (n 33 above) 304.
[46] ibid.
[47] Sheehan and Arvind (n 4 above) 496.
[48] ibid 497.

Gray	**Sheehan and Arvind**
Excludability	Primary concept
Power	Sub-concept the extension of which is endorsement by the state
Access	Sub-concept the extension of which is regulation of benefits
Control	Sub-concept the extension of which is a physically possible, legally effective and morally defensible power to exclude

If we apply the concepts to a set of facts, then where the state endorses the exercise of the power to exclude through its legal frameworks and agents; regulates access to the benefits by determining who may and may not have access; and – through affording remedies or imposing sanctions – upholds the control of the subject-matter, then there is property. This might be illustrated by considering how courts determine if there is a lease rather than a lesser right. An interpretivist, preferring certainty, might hold that unless there is a term certain and exclusive possession there is no lease, whereas the contextualist might argue that the rigour of exclusive possession needs to be subject to a further set of sub-concepts because of the unscrupulous behaviour of some landlords. An example of this can be found in the case of *Antoniades v Villiers*.[49] This then raises the question of what norms underpin the inclusion/exclusion determined by the extension of these concepts. It is here that we can see the relevance of Gray's three grounds on which non-excludability based on control may rest.

To illustrate this I focus on the contextual and factual interaction of people with surface areas – largely but not solely – in urban environments. In doing so I intend to draw attention to Gray's three grounds for non-excludability (physical, legal and moral), and thereby challenge 'the continued validity and desirability of the normative underpinnings of existing legal categories'.[50] In this way it might be possible to arrive at a slightly different set of sub-concepts which then inform a new 'realist taxonomic enterprise'[51] that is compatible with Dagan's aim of 'constantly challenging the continued validity and desirability of the normative underpinnings of existing legal categories'.[52]

IV. Guerilla Gardeners, Graffiti Artists, and Park-Runners

There is a broad spectrum of human interaction with the surfaces of the physical environment from lawful to beyond the law, or 'outlawed' activity, which takes place on horizontal and vertical surfaces that may be regarded as private or public property, or private or public space, or may fall somewhere in between (the abandoned bridge in Hull is a case in point). For purposes of illustration, the social interaction of three groups of people with the

[49] *Antoniades v Villiers* [1990] 1 AC 417. See S Bright, 'Beyond Sham and into Pretence' (1991) 11 *OJLS* 136.
[50] Dagan (n 11 above) 147, 161.
[51] Sheehan and Arvind (n 4 above) 485.
[52] Dagan (n 11 above).

physical space of urban areas will be considered: guerrilla gardeners, graffiti artists, and park-runners. Each of these groups engages with the surfaces of the environment in different ways and their engagement reflects something other than property interests as currently defined, but does raise issues of power, access, and control. This is not to suggest the law is irrelevant; rather that the law both shapes and influences social action and operates as a trigger for resistance and rebellion. The past (backward-looking) therefore informs the present, and prompts us to think about change (forward-looking). These activities have been selected because they challenge excludability, either physically, legally and/or morally, and therefore our understanding of what property is.

In urban areas while the physical boundaries of place may be more apparent due to the hard-edged environment, the boundaries of spaces are more porous and may be more volatile.[53] Spaces may be 'claimed' by city parks authorities, private householders, individuals or collectives, relying on legal concepts informed by accepted and often-unchallenged normative or moral underpinnings. Skateboarders, graffiti artists, gangs, rough sleepers, guerrilla gardeners, and people on the move may make claims to place, either temporarily or more permanently. If Gray's emphasis on excludability as a defining characteristic of property is applied, then the question is who controls these places, who has access, who benefits and therefore which set of facts or objects falls within the definition of the concept? For example, the graffiti artist who throws up a 'piece' claims the wall, railway siding, fence, as his or her 'spot' or place – 'this is mine, I was here'. The person sleeping in a doorway defends his or her place, marking it with a selection of paraphernalia to indicate its boundaries; the seed-bomber planting in the small gaps around council trees in the pavement, makes a fleeting claim to the garden created; residents cultivating vegetables on the mini-roundabout in a residential street may make a longer-term commitment. The relationship of people in these examples to the places they use are empirical facts and socially grounded: people do these things and they do them for a social reason. The claims they make in respect of the surfaces/property they use may not be claims of ownership as generally understood, because the space may be 'owned' by others, even if within the public domain (here used in a non-legal sense). However, these acts of engagement demonstrate the relationship – perhaps merely transient – of the individual or collective with the physical environment in which they are located and with society, and various values in society. A descriptive or prescriptive taxonomy of property law cannot accommodate these engagements. A developmental taxonomy might do so in so far as 'developmental taxonomies see the law as being in a process of change'.[54] If, following a realist or contextualist approach, the law is to respond to change, then the concepts that inform it also have to change. The following practical realities are used to demonstrate how Gray's concept of property might be developed by incorporating some sub-concepts into the idea of exclusion as a defining characteristic of property.

[53] Space and place are distinguished in human geography and architecture. Space is open, abstract and subjective, while place refers to how people claim or use a location or part of space. Layard has drawn attention to the abstract nature of property law and the physical materiality of place and the way in which law has encroached on space to enclose it within the law and exclude multiple claims. A Layard, 'Shopping in the Public Realm: The Law of Place' (2010) 37 *Journal of Law and Society* 412. See also Willmore's use of these terms in C Willmore, 'Planning Law Reform and Reconceptualising the Regulation of Land Use' in H Conway and R Hickey (eds), *Modern Studies in Property Law*, vol 9 (London, Hart Publishing, 2017) ch 14.

[54] Sheehan and Arvind (n 4 above) 485.

A. Guerrilla Gardeners

The guerrilla gardening movement in its present form first started in New York in the 1970s as part of the counter-culture movement of the time.[55] Today it might be seen as part of a much wider socio-cultural movement of individual and community engagement with gardening in diverse ways, which reflects growing concern with the environment, with sustainable development, with the accountability of public authorities, and with the retention or safeguarding of public space.[56] Guerrilla gardening might also be carried out as a form of protest.[57] For example, a recent manifestation of guerrilla gardening is the construction of miniature gardens in potholes in roads to draw attention to poor road maintenance.[58] Alternatively, it may also be viewed positively as a social and cultural phenomenon which brings people together either as individual members of the movement or as groups initiating community projects. There is therefore a certain moral ambivalence surrounding guerrilla gardening: Is it a constructive or destructive use of property? Is it beautification or vandalism? Is it anti-social, because it is often secretive or done without permission? Or is it in fact socially constructive, bringing people with common concerns together? Are there in fact moral grounds for non-excludability? If so, what are these and how extensive should they be?

In principle, there is legal excludability, not least because of the legal control of spaces. In practice, however, the available legal tools appear weak. Firstly, on the face of it, guerrilla gardening engages less with property law and more with the law of tort and potential breaches of the criminal law (although prosecution of guerrilla gardeners in the UK seems very rare).[59] While gardening on some locations may raise health and safety issues,[60] the positive actions of guerrilla gardeners might counteract the negative actions of the local authority or private landowner who might otherwise be charged with health and safety offences – for example, because of the rubbish fly-tipped on land, or the use to which it is put for drug-dealing and prostitution. The moral grounds for an owner's right to exclude are thus undermined. Similarly, while the tort of trespass is available to landlords or owners of guerrilla gardened spaces, the quantum of damages is likely to be negligible, especially if the guerrilla gardeners have cleared the space of rubbish and enhanced it aesthetically by planting. Suing in the tort of nuisance is also unlikely to be successful, especially where the gardeners may have removed a number of pre-existing potential nuisances.

[55] M Fraser, 'How Guerrilla Gardening Took Root', *BBC News (Scotland)* (London, 15 March 2010) available at: http://news.bbc.co.uk/1/hi/scotland/8548005.stm.

[56] S Farran, 'Earth Under the Nails: The Extraordinary Return to the Land' in N Hopkins (ed), *Modern Studies in Property Law*, vol 7 (Oxford, Hart Publishing, 2013) 173–91; O Zanetti, *Guerrilla Gardening: Geographers and Gardeners, Actors and Networks: Reconsidering Urban Public Space* (MA/MSc dissertation, Queen Mary, University of London, 2007) available at: http://www.guerrillgardening.org/books/ZanettiGG.pdf.

[57] G McKay, *Radical Gardening: Politics, Idealism and Rebellion in the Garden* (London, Francis Lincoln Limited, 2011).

[58] BBC Trending, 'Thai Women Take Dip in the Road in Pothole Protest', *BBC News* (London, 29 September 2016) available at: https://www.bbc.com/news/blogs-trending-37485461.

[59] A search of reported cases on the legal data base Westlaw revealed very few cases in which prosecutions were brought. See also B Daniel, '"Guerrilla Gardeners" in Morpeth Risk Prosecution to Carry Out Clean Up', *Chronicle Live* (Newcastle, 29 September 2014) available at: https://www.chroniclelive.co.uk/news/north-east-news/guerilla-gardeners-morpeth-risk-prosecution-7847167.

[60] For example the embankments or roundabouts.

Moreover, these activities may take place on 'orphaned' or abandoned land the ownership of which is unclear, so from a property law perspective there is no one to bring an action. There is also land that has been purchased for development, often by speculative absentee investors or local councils, which is left undeveloped. So it may be many years before the guerrilla gardening activity is challenged. The issue of legal excludability is also undermined by the 'adoption' of guerrilla projects by local councils or communities keen to gain the moral high ground on green or environmentally sensitive policies,[61] or an owner's willingness to tolerate the projects as a form of 'harmless' protest.[62]

B. Graffiti Artists

Mixed attitudes towards graffiti are evident in the example at the start of this chapter. In some cases and in some places graffiti may be regarded as cultural heritage – indeed attendees at the 2018 Socio-Legal Studies Association conference in Bristol were offered a cultural tour of the works of Banksy. Others share the view of the Hull city councillor and have suggested that graffiti is no more than vandalism, anti-social behaviour, and an attack on private property;[63] still others have ambivalent views.[64] Negative stereotyping may be due to the failure to distinguish between different forms of graffiti, or because the line between what might be regarded as mere 'tagging'[65] and what is regarded as 'art' in the world of graffiti is contentious.[66] Not all share the view that graffiti is 'street art', not least because of the location of the expression. Banksy himself is quoted as asking, 'Is graffiti art or vandalism? That word (art) has a lot of negative connotations and it alienates people, so no, I don't like to use the word "art" at all.'[67] Indeed the very term 'art' may be contrary to the political and social messaging behind graffiti.

Clearly, the act of graffiti breaches the physical excludability of the sites where it appears. As with guerrilla gardening, from the perspective of legal excludability graffiti straddles public and private law. It is categorised as criminal damage,[68] and potentially attracts a

[61] R Hudson, 'Guerrilla Gardens: What Happens When Communities Take Over Council Land' *The Guardian* (London, 3 June 2014) available at https://www.theguardian.com/local-government-network/2014/jun/03/guerrilla-gardens-communities-council-land-social.

[62] O Kolokouris, 'Urban Gardening in Greece – A New Form of Protest' (2015) 11 *Green European Journal* 43.

[63] Crime Concern, 'Vandalism, Graffiti and Environmental Nuisance on Public Transport – Literature Review' (London, Department of Transport, Local Government and the Regions, 2004); A Akbar and P Vallely, 'Graffiti: Street Art – or Crime?', *The Independent* (London, 16 July 2008) available at: http://www.independent.co.uk/arts-entertainment/features/graffiti-street-art-ndash-or-crime-868736.html.

[64] Akbar and Vallely (ibid); D Rogers, 'Speaking With: Cameron McAuliffe on Graffiti, Art and Crime', *The Conversation* (Melbourne, 24 March 2015) available at: http://theconversation.com/speaking-with-cameron-mcauliffe-on-graffiti-art-and-crime-39183.

[65] The artistic presentation of 'signatures'.

[66] N Sanchez, 'Graffiti: Art Through Vandalism: A Look at the Urban Art Movement Through the Scope of Aesthetics and Illegality' (Communication Over the Internet, University of Florida, undated) available at: http://iml.jou.ufl.edu/projects/fall07/Sanchez/art.html; N Patel, 'Graffiti in Austin: Crime or Art?' (*Graffiti vs Art*, April 2010) available at: https://whatisart320.wordpress.com/.

[67] C McAuliffe and K Iveson, 'Art and Crime (and Other Things Besides …): Conceptualising Graffiti in the City' (2011) 5 *Geography Compass* 128, 130.

[68] Graffiti falls under section 1 of the Criminal Damage Act 1971, which states 'A person who without lawful excuse destroys or damages any property belonging to another intending to destroy or damage any such property

punishment of imprisonment for adult offenders if the damage (usually assessed by the cost of removal of the graffiti) exceeds £5,000.[69] Minor graffiti offences are punishable by a penalty notice of £50 issued under the Anti-Social Behaviour Act 2003,[70] or a caution.[71] In other words while some graffiti is criminalised as being merely anti-social, other graffiti is criminalised as damage to property.

However, criminalising graffiti is not without its problems. Firstly, there is the issue of whether a specific piece of graffiti – or all graffiti (and the law makes no distinction) – is 'damage'. This term is not defined in the legislation but has been explained as being when the value or usefulness of a thing is impaired,[72] permanently or temporarily.[73] The limits of this definition are evident in the decisions of the courts, where it has been held that whether or not there is damage is a matter for the jury to decide so that graffiti *may* be damage, but equally it *may* not.[74] As Edwards points out,

> the spatial contexts in which graffiti is situated need to be considered if its social, aesthetic and legal significance is to be appreciated. They (the court decisions) also show the contested economic, social and political value of some publicly situated property.[75]

Secondly, if the property is neither destroyed nor damaged, and there is no intent to do so, can this be labelled criminal damage?[76] Much may depend on the phrase 'without lawful excuse'. Does the creation of a work or art amount to a lawful excuse – which might undermine legal excludability, or is this merely a moral argument – which if upheld could undermine moral excludability? What is art is a very subjective point of course and may have no place in informing legal concepts: the Hull Banksy is a case in point. For many (including Banksy) the term 'art' may have negative connotations and be rejected by the artist even though others may refer to the work as 'art'. Could, however, the aesthetic enhancement of an ugly hoarding or boarded up warehouse afford a 'lawful excuse' for an otherwise potentially criminal act, thereby providing a defence to the charge?[77] Under the

or being reckless as to whether any such property would be destroyed or damaged shall be guilty of an offence'. Damage that is evidently less than £5,000 in value is tried as a summary offence (subject to a fixed fine) in the Magistrates' Court (Magistrates' Courts Act 1980). Where the damage is less than £5,000 the maximum sentence is three months' imprisonment or a fine of £2,500 for adult offenders.

[69] For those aged 12–17 years, the maximum custodial penalty is a detention and training order of up to 24 months.

[70] In England and Wales, s 48 of the Anti-Social Behaviour Act 2003 gives local authorities the power to serve graffiti removal notices on certain bodies responsible for the surface where graffiti has appeared. These bodies include the owners of street furniture (bus shelters, street signs, phone boxes, etc). In England and Wales, the Clean Neighbourhoods and Environment Act 2005 enlarges the powers of local authorities and the police.

[71] Guidelines issued by the UK Government suggest a caution for the minor offence of writing graffiti on a bus shelter: https://www.gov.uk/caution-warning-penalty.

[72] *R v Fiak* [2005] EWCA Crim 2381, [2005] Po LR 211.

[73] *Morphitis v Salmon* [1990] Crim LR 48.

[74] See cases cited by I Edwards, 'Banksy's Graffiti: A Not-so-Simple Case of Criminal Damage' (2009) 73(4) *Journal of Criminal Law* 345–61.

[75] ibid 351.

[76] Criminal Damage Act 1971 s 1: 'A person who without lawful excuse destroys or damages any property belonging to another intending to destroy or damage any such property or being reckless as to whether such property would be destroyed or damaged shall be guilty of an offence'.

[77] Edwards (n 74 above).

relevant criminal law, a 'lawful excuse' rests on the belief of consent.[78] Such is the nature of graffiti that this is unlikely – except where work is commissioned or surfaces are intentionally provided for graffiti. If, however, the artist is an eminent graffiti artist then he/she might presume consent – the graffiti will after all enhance the value of the building. If the surface is a public building, even if in 'private' ownership, could the consent of the public be relevant? It might be argued that the possibility of subsequent public approbation of damage to publicly owned buildings allows a defendant to meet the test for the lawful excuse defence in section 5(2)(a) of the Criminal Damage Act 1971 by showing that

> he believed that the person or persons whom he believed to be entitled to consent to the destruction of or damage to the property in question had so consented or would have so consented to it if he or they had known of the destruction or damage and its circumstances.

In Hull one visitor to the new Banksy described seeing the piece as 'a dream come true', and when vandals tried to deface it, a window cleaner was hailed in the local press as saving it after cleaning whitewash off it.[79] Subsequent plans by the publicly elected council for regeneration of the area through graffiti also suggest ex post facto approbation.

While in principle the law may provide for excludability, Gray's warning that there is no such thing as wholly private property should be borne in mind. Indeed, in England public authorities may order graffiti to be cleaned off private property even if the owner of that property wishes to retain the graffiti.[80] Further, despite the reach of the criminal law, some boroughs and councils set aside graffiti areas known as 'free walls' or adopt a no-prosecution policy in respect of certain areas, which become 'graffiti tolerance zones',[81] or identify graffiti as local or national heritage.[82] This suggests that whatever the criminal law might say, private property owners are adopting rather different standpoints.

Leaving aside the public law, there are also dilemmas in the private law of intellectual property.[83] The creator of a work of graffiti has intellectual property rights to that work, provided graffiti is regarded as a 'work',[84] although because of the potential criminal consequences or desire for anonymity, the 'artist' may not wish to be identified.[85] Even if these rights are limited to moral rights[86] because of the 'unlawfulness' of the activity,[87] these are

[78] Section 5(2)(a) of the Criminal Damage Act 1971, set out in the text below, provides this defence.

[79] BBC News, 'Hull Window Cleaner Saves Defaced Banksy Mural', *BBC News* (London, 29 January 2018) available at: http://www.bbc.co.uk/news/uk-england-humber-42857424.

[80] Under the Town and Country Planning Act 1990 a local authority can serve notice on the property owner if, in the authority's opinion, the graffiti it is detrimental to the amenity of an area (s 215).

[81] In 2011 in Bristol, for example the city hosted the UK's largest ever permanent street art project 'See No Evil'.

[82] After one of Banksy's works was scrubbed off a wall in Bristol in 2014, the Mayor of Bristol said 'He (referring to Banksy) is part of what gives Bristol its artistic, creative and subversive spirit which makes us such a sparky place': P Flanagan, 'Banksy's Boost for Bristol Youth Club', *The Telegraph* (London, 15 April 2014) available at: http://telegraph.co.uk/culture/culturenews/10768697/Banksys-boost-for-Bristol-youth-club.html.

[83] See C Lerman, 'Protecting Artistic Vandalism: Graffiti and Copyright Law' (2013) 2 *New York University Journal of Intellectual Property and Entertainment Law* 295.

[84] Copyright, Designs, and Patents Act 1988, s 4(1), amended in parts by the Intellectual Property Act 2014.

[85] Anonymous work may still be subject to copyright for a statutory period of time – see, s 12(2), Copyright, Designs and Patents Act 1988 in the UK.

[86] Section 78, Copyright, Designs and Patents Act 1988.

[87] J Davies, 'Art Crimes? Theoretical Perspectives on Copyright Protection for Illegally Created Graffiti Art' (2012) 65 *Maine Law Review* 28–55.

still control and benefit rights recognised in law, and the law itself makes no reference to whether the act of creativity has to be lawful. Moreover, with art extending to encompass installations, public art, and performance art, it has been suggested, at least in the Banksy case, that the removal of the mural and its sale by auction could be a breach of the rights pertaining to the original artwork (removal of the medium of expression ie the wall).[88] The implication of a continuing intellectual property right was manifest in 2014 when Banksy gave his permission for one of his works 'Mobile Lovers' – originally attached to the building but subsequently removed for safe-keeping – to be sold by a youth centre in Bristol to raise funds.[89] Alternatively, any act aimed at the physical property that damages the graffiti could be viewed as a breach of the copyright to the integrity of the work.[90] Potentially therefore there could be a clash of property interests between, for example, the owner of a wall and the graffiti artist whose work adorns that wall.[91]

As with guerrilla gardening, the property rights of others may be infringed because of the potentially law-breaking nature of both activities, but the moral grounds for excludability may be undermined where these activities are adopted and/or 'legitimised' by the public or private sector: in the case of graffiti through commissioning, public approbation or the dedication of specific public and private surfaces for graffiti artists.[92] Normative controversy surrounds both. These activities also show that the intensions of concepts such as 'art', 'damage', 'trespass', 'greening the environment' could all apply to these extensions, thereby presenting challenges for a taxonomy, given that very different concepts could apply to the same extension. So for example, those interested in the artistic dimension of graffiti might ask 'is it art?', whereas those interested in the political dimension would perhaps focus on the use of art and/or graffiti as protest;[93] while lawyers might see only an infringement of property rights. An interpretivist definition of property law would place guerrilla gardening or graffiti outside the law because of non-compliance with certain concepts, while a more liberal, socially attuned, contextualist approach might bring the activity within the law because of the creative and communal qualities it fosters. Alternatively we might see these

[88] P McGrath, 'Banksy Under the Hammer: Graffiti and the Law' (*Incorporated Council of Law Reporting Blog*, 6 March 2013) available at: http://www.iclr.co.uk/banksy-under-the-hammer-graffiti-and-the-law/.

[89] Flanagan (n 82 above); I Johnston, 'Banksy Breaks Cover to Join Debate over "Mobile Lovers" Artwork', *The Independent* (London, 8 May 2014) available at: http://www.independent.co.uk/arts-entertainment/art/news/banksy-breaks-cover-to-join-debate-over-disputed-mobile-lovers-artwork-9335129.html. Banksy gave permission to the Broad Plain and Riverside Youth Project to take ownership of the piece 'Mobile Lovers'. The mayor of the city is reported to have said 'I hope it will be respected and protected as we would want for *any other legitimate work of street art*' (emphasis added).

[90] Integrity refers to the artist's right to object to any derogatory treatment. See E Bonadio, 'Banksy Strikes Again: Basquiat, Graffiti, and the Issue of Copyright Law', *The Conversation* (Melbourne, 22 September 2017).

[91] Under a Lockean approach to property both the graffiti artist and the guerrilla gardener might seek to assert the property rights of their labours.

[92] See for example, the annual Dundee Graffiti Jam; but note too G Ogston, 'West End of Dundee Hit by "Paris" Graffiti Tag', *The Courier* (Dundee, 3 January 2015) available at: https://www.thecourier.co.uk/news/local/dundee/125125/west-end-of-dundee-hit-by-paris-graffiti-tag/.

[93] M Dragićević-Šešić, 'The Street as Political Space: Walking as Protest, Graffiti and the Student Carnivalization of Belgrade' (2001) 17 *New Theatre Quarterly* 74; E Pindado, 'Graffiti Artists Turn Mexico City's Walls into a Collective Cry of Protest', *Splinter News* (13 March 2015) available at: http://fusion.net/story/102767/graffiti-artists-turn-mexico-citys-walls-into-a-collective'cry-of-protests/; S Jacobs, 'The Graffiti in Greece Shows Just How Angry its Citizens Really Are', *Business Insider UK* (London, 24 June 2015) available at: http://uk.businessinsider.com/greeces-graffiti-artists-send-powerful-messages-of-protest-2015-6.

surfaces of the urban landscape as neutral or 'negative space' – a term used by graffiti artists interviewed by Halsey and Young in their studies in Australia,[94] where claims of 'property' are overridden.[95]

C. Park-Runners

As Gray suggests, 'The predominating emphasis expressed in the notion of moral non-excludability is the need to afford especial protection to those values which promote human communication and social intercourse'.[96] This possibility is illustrated by the debate, which erupted in April 2016, surrounding 'park-runs'. These running events held in public spaces are proving popular, but have provoked controversy regarding fee-charging by councils (on grounds such as costs of maintenance) and policies regarding group-users, and complaints from other park-users. The controversy started with Stoke Gifford Parish Council, which said it would exercise its powers under the Local Government Act 1976 to charge a fee. This local council decision escalated though social media, the press and television, culminating in a petition to Parliament.[97] It was argued that firstly, parks were community assets and secondly, there was a tradition of free use by the public. While it would have been possible to physically exclude the runners, the non-excludability on moral grounds can be seen in the arguments put forward against fees. For example, the benefits of the activity were that park-runs were open to all; they promoted health, wellbeing and community spirit and encouraged runners to 'get back to nature'. Park-running was also supported as an antidote to the commercialisation of running in organised events: they were aimed at getting the local community involved in exercising and participating by removing barriers to equality of opportunity such as fees, equipment/dress requirements. Given that today park-running attracts sponsors and supporters and the umbrella organisation 'Parkrun' has a large complement of staff, the non-commercial angle may be rather suspect.[98] Nevertheless, a number of interesting normative claims relating to the contested space emerge. Supporters excluded from running at their local park described themselves as 'exiles', while officials pointed to the environmental degradation of the ground subjected to park-runners and problems of obstruction for other users, and the infringement of the 'well-being' of non-runners.

While tensions between different park or green space users are not unusual – see for example the frequent notices prohibiting ball games, skate-boarding and so on – it has been suggested that the controversy over park-runs is a symptom of a broader contemporary concern: the 'battle of the parks'.[99] Increasingly people have more leisure and are being encouraged through various government and non-government programmes to 'get out'

[94] M Halsey and A Young, '"Our Desires are Ungovernable": Writing Graffiti in an Urban Space' (2006) 10 *Theoretical Criminology* 275, 286.

[95] Gray (n 33 above) 281.

[96] ibid.

[97] The petition was rejected on the grounds that the Health Secretary did not have the power to intervene in the Parish Council's decision.

[98] See the Parkrun website: http://www.parkrun.org.uk/aboutus/.

[99] J Glover, 'The Parkrun Furore and the Battle for Parks' (Local Government Information Unit, 13 May 2016) available at: http://www.lgiu.org.uk/2016/05/13/the-parkrun-furore-and-the-battle-for-parks/.

more and engage in healthy lifestyle choices. At the same time upper tier local authorities have responsibility for public health, while in the UK local authorities at all levels and the public sector in general are finding budgets drastically cut and are having to make decisions regarding non-essential services. The maintenance of parks and gardens may be one area where savings can be made or income increased – for example by charging professional dog walkers permit fees,[100] or by levying charges on specific groups of park-users. In urban areas, the problems of equitable sharing of facilities may be particularly acute because of the pressure on and shortage of green spaces and the competing demands for building land. This is the contextual reality. At the same time, there is the rhetoric of engaging more with local communities – for example under the Localism Act 2011, Part 5. Under this legislation, local communities can apply to get green spaces listed as an asset of community value, and thereby prevent the sale or change of use of such spaces for six months.[101] However, getting a green space listed is only a temporary measure and unless the community can raise the funds to buy the green space that is at risk, it is likely to be lost. The focus is therefore on ownership of green space rather than the maintenance of it, but this does present the possibility of public/private/hybrid ownership and/or control of parks and other spaces, and the opportunity for rethinking the relationships between local and central state and non-state agencies, organisations and communities and the physical environment.[102]

V. Conclusion: Is it Time for a New Approach to Defining Property?

The possibility of a new taxonomy is inspired by Siems's comment that:

> Since taxonomies can never be a perfect representation of the complexities of the real world, they can be seen as, more or less refined, conjectures – and it is then also the tasks of subsequent researchers to critically scrutinise these conjectures and try to develop better ones.[103]

Using Gray's definition of property and the sub-concepts that comprise the intension of 'excludability', which determines whether a 'thing' is property or not, I have tested these sub-concepts against the facts of various social activities taking place in contexts in which property rights may be claimed, but where there may be at the very least moral grounds for non-excludability. I suggest that the examples I have chosen prompt us to think about when, and in what contexts, the 'right of exclusion might be abridged by more highly valued social objectives'? Might there be, as the High Court of Australia recognised, a case for

[100] In London, the Royal Parks charge £300 a year for a permit.

[101] Localism Act 2011, Part 5 chapter 3.

[102] E Wallis, *Places to Be: Green spaces for active citizenship* (London, Fabian Society, 2015). In 2017 the UK Government held a consultation on preventing councils from charging fees for park-runs: Department for Communities and Local Government, *Running Free: Consulation on Preserving the Free Use of Public Parks* (London, Department for Communities and Local Government, 2017).

[103] MM Siems, 'A Network-Based Taxonomy of the World's Legal Systems' (Durham, Durham Law School Working Papers, 2014) 5.

emphasising the need to promote those 'moral or political standards which enrich life and constructive social interaction within a community of equals'?[104]

To do this we might have to move away from a purely legal taxonomy to a more interdisciplinary perspective. The value of adopting a different approach is expressed by Moore who argues: 'Many lawyers and law professors view law as an instrument for controlling society and directing social change, but most anthropologists are concerned with law as a reflection of a particular social order.'[105] Moving away from an interpretivist/positivist approach towards a more developmental/contextual approach, it might be possible to consider a 'consensus' theory of law that conceives of legal norms in broad (and largely sociological) terms, in other words the 'living law' is what people do,[106] and the repeated iteration of the lived experience may give rise to a legal framing.[107] This ties in with Sheehan and Arvind's implied question: 'What do we want a taxonomy of the law to do?' Alternatives have been suggested by writers such as Barker,[108] Hughes,[109] and Bannister and Kearns,[110] and, although primarily focused on criminal law controls, such analyses could be used to inform a new taxonomy of the law, not least, because, as the examples in this chapter show, the ways in which people interact socially with property may not be the extension of an existing legal concept but their persistence and reiteration may mean that the concept or concepts have to be rethought. The moral grounds for doing so might be prompted by a greater commitment to environment, citizenship, community, humanity or indeed democracy. Current property taxonomy means that some lived experiences remain precarious in law or indeed unlawful – the 'occupation' of doorways, railway arches or park benches by the homeless may be one example, and degrees of tolerance are inconsistent and very much a 'post-code lottery'.[111] At the same time, it is important to recognise that the lived experience is constantly changing so that the standards to which the High Court of Australia referred are neither static nor absolute; they constantly encounter resistance and undergo negotiation. If our taxonomy leads to a rigid definition of property then it will not be able to accommodate possible changes in the law when the law adapts to changing circumstances – the consultation by the UK Government on the prohibition of fees for park-runners is but one example.[112]

A dynamic taxonomy (rather than a prescriptive one) does not have to mean an abrupt severance with the historical development of the current law – indeed the activities described above take place within, but in resistance to, the current taxonomy – but it may

[104] Gray (n 33 above) 289.

[105] SF Moore, *Law as Process: An Anthropological Approach* (London, Routledge and Kegan Paul, 1978) 244.

[106] E Erlich, *Fundamental Principles of the Sociology of Law* (Cambridge MA, Harvard University Press, 1936).

[107] Y Tuan, *Space and Place: The Perspective of Experience* (Minneapolis, University of Minnesota Press, 1977).

[108] A Barker, 'Mediated Conviviality and the Urban Social Order: Reframing the Regulation of Public Space' (2016) 57 *British Journal of Criminology* 848.

[109] G Hughes, 'Communitarianism and Law and Order' (1996) 16(49) *Critical Social Policy* 17.

[110] J Bannister and A Kearns, 'The Function and Foundations of Urban Tolerance: Encountering and Engaging with Difference in the City' (2013) 50 *Urban Studies* 2700.

[111] Evidence of intolerance and 'criminalisation' was recently demonstrated in Oxford where the belongings of homeless people left to 'mark' their 'place' were confiscated and warning notices issued, but media backlash prompted a change of approach. See further on this criminalisation aspect, K Brown, 'The Hyper-Regulation of Public Space: the Use and Abuse of Public Spaces Protection Orders in England and Wales' (2017) 37 *Legal Studies* 543.

[112] Department for Communities and Local Government (n 112 above).

mean moving the law in a more morally justifiable direction. In the twenty-first century, this may require taking into consideration equality of opportunity, human rights, health and well-being, and more generally inclusion rather than exclusion.[113] Already there are indications that the law's definition of property has to shift to encompass things like security of the home; accessible and affordable housing; healthy and sustainable environments; greener cities; and inter-generational equity of resources.

If the definition of property law remains static, it will become irrelevant. So how might it be developed? As a start, and without deviating too far from Gray, a new set of sub-concepts might be introduced. So that if we refer back to the definition: '"Property" is the power-relation constituted by the state's endorsement of private claims to regulate the access of strangers to the benefits of particular resources', we could introduce 'reasonableness' into regulation, bringing with it sub-concepts of proportionality and necessity (both concepts which are encountered frequently, if fluidly, in law). Further, some consideration might be given to the intrusion of 'power-relation' reflecting an acknowledged imbalance between the power of the state, the private property owner, and the third-party stranger. An extension example can be found in the construction of physical barriers to prevent rough sleepers using doorways, benches and bus shelters which has given rise to public protest and adverse media coverage, to the extent that in some cases the state has been forced to back down.[114] Here, it is suggested, the power-relationship has shifted. As with park-runs, social media communication creates a powerful fourth estate. Even where an owner, be it a local authority or a private landlord, has the legal right to exclude, moral indignation may mean abandoning or not enforcing that right. This is particularly so if the state can no longer endorse the exercise of that right or is ambivalent about doing so. The fourth estate might argue that the guerrilla gardener, the graffiti artist, the park-runner and the rough sleeper are all part of the *demos* reflected in our understandings of democracy. Consequently, the 'state' might need to rethink the moral grounds of endorsement and thus exclusion, and this in turn might ultimately lead to limits on the legal right to exclude. So, a new sub-set of concepts informing the existing definition of property could allow a definition of property that more nearly reflects the meaning of property in the lived experience of many urban dwellers and perhaps better reflects the values of social justice which are beginning to emerge in the second decade of the twenty-first century. If it is to be relevant, a taxonomy of property law needs to reflect this reality.

[113] See too S Pascoe, 'Re-evaluating Recreational Easements – New Norms for the Twenty-First Century?' Chapter 10 in this volume, where the relevance of health and well-being to the law's definition of permitted easements is discussed.

[114] See Brown (n 111 above).

7

Corporate Shares as Shares

LARISSA KATZ

I. Introduction

In this chapter, I ask whether shares in corporations ought to command more attention within theories of property. Contemporary liberal property theorists typically take land (and sometimes goods) as the basic case of property. Shares tend to be left out of these accounts or treated as imitations or mutations of the basic case. Economists, for their part, have transformed the idea of ownership: 'owner' refers to the ultimate beneficiary of the *value* of assets. Shares are treated as a central case of property by those who take this approach. Shareholders are taken to own the corporation insofar as they are the ultimate beneficiaries of its value.

In this chapter, I concede shares do not fit within the traditional property framework.[1] This does not mean, however, that the traditional idea of property is obsolete and that a new property framework is in order.[2] The reason why shares fit awkwardly within the property framework is that shares are not, at their core, rights in the nature of property, even though property-related institutions of bankruptcy, expropriation, taxation, etc, have adapted to treat them as such. The legal concept of a 'share' is better accounted for as a right in a procedure for dividing a shifting mass of value. I introduce a distinction between a share and a part: a part, in contrast to a share, is defined in relation to a mass of unchanging size.[3]

[1] For a non-proprietary account of shares, see A Pretto-Sakmann, *The Boundaries of Personal Property* (Oxford, Hart Publishing, 2005) (explaining shares in terms of *in personam* obligations.) The alternative account I offer, which emphasises the procedural aspects of a share and the similarities to equitable interests, is consistent with Pretto-Sakmann's conceptual claim.

[2] TC Grey, 'The Disintegration of Property' in JR Pennock and JW Chapman (eds), *NOMOS XXII: Property* (New York, New York University Press, 1980). D Markovits and A Schwarz, 'Who Owns What? Re-Thinking Remedies in Private Law' (North American Private Law Theory Workshop, New Haven CT, October 2018) (cited with the authors' permission). For a more balanced take on the centrality of property in the conventional sense, see B Rudden, 'Things as Things and Things as Wealth' (1994) 14 *OJLS* 81.

[3] For a conflation of the two ideas see *Popat v Shonchhatra* [1997] 1 WLR 1367 (CA), 1372. Nourse LJ states that a partner's interest in partnership assets cannot be understood as a 'share' for as long as the partnership continues because no partner has a right 'to require the whole or even a share of any particular asset to be vested in him.' Nourse LJ goes on to say that the only stage at which a partner can be said to have a *share* in anything is at the point of division of the ultimate residue, which 'will be a share of cash.' With great respect, I think the idea of a share to which Nourse LJ refers is the idea of a part (as in a part of a whole). It is of course quite right that there can be no part-entitlement in a pool of assets of fluctuating value until the point when the mass is fixed in some form and ready to be divided into parts; that is to say, to be allocated as property.

Share-entitlements are inherently rights in a procedure, whereas part-entitlements are rights in the nature of property.[4] Share-entitlements and part-entitlements sometimes stand in an important relationship to one another. A procedure for dividing a mass of shifting value (with respect to which a right is held as a share) *ends* when the mass is fixed in size, at which point the entitlements with respect to the mass are held as part-entitlements.[5]

The account I offer here of corporate shares is of the corporate share *as a share* in this more general sense. Corporate shares, I argue, derive many of their features from this concept of a share although of course there are accretions to the idea of a share that reflect the particular context of shares in a corporation, given the corporate form (eg, voting rights). Corporate shares are rights in a procedure, ongoing during the operation of the corporation and complete only at the time of the dissolution of the corporation and the final distribution of corporate assets – the point at which share-entitlements turn into part-entitlements.[6] The normative idea of a fair procedure for dividing a mass of value explains many of the familiar features of shareholding: its regulative principles of proportionality, non-oppression and non-forfeiture, and finally the limits of contract in this context.

The idea of shares as rights in a procedure presupposes the very idea of property that *does* command centre stage in property theory today, viz, rights in the nature of property, of which property in land or goods are the central cases. The relationship of shares to traditional property is analogous in some ways to the relationship of equity derivatives to shares. Almost 100 years ago, Berle and Means described the immense shift of wealth from traditional property to corporate shares.[7] More recently, wealth has shifted again, from shares to derivative rights (roughly speaking, contractual rights to the future sale of shares at a fixed price) and the like.[8] More and more, the ultimate beneficiaries of the value of corporations hold that value in the form of derivative rights.[9] And yet equity derivatives[10] presuppose the idea of a share. Shares are no more the central case of property than derivatives are the central case of shareholding. Both are rights defined in relation to the acquisition of rights in another form: derivatives are in relation to shares, and shares in relation to classical property rights.

[4] I argue elsewhere that a litmus test for distinguishing rights in a procedure from rights in the nature of property is whether the right in question admits of self-help: while self-help is available with respect to property, a private actor can never help herself to a procedure. I set out and defend this thesis in other work on equity. See L Katz, 'Equity: Pathways to Legal Rights' in D Klimchuk, P Miller, I Samet and HE Smith, *Philosophical Foundations of Equity* (Oxford, Oxford University Press, forthcoming.)

[5] Note that bankruptcy is a way of avoiding the completion of the initial procedure. Through bankruptcy, shareholders are re-routed to another procedure in which they accept new rights in place of their original rights.

[6] It follows that all corporations must be *in principle* dissoluble, an idea we find, for example, in 8 Delaware Code § 276 (2015).

[7] AA Berle and GC Means, *The Modern Corporation and Private Property*, 1st edn (Piscataway NJ, Transaction Publishers, 1932).

[8] Other examples include options (the right to buy stock for a certain exercise price during an exercise period) and other equity incentives like phantom stock (that yields a cash payout keyed to the value of shares).

[9] See HTC Hu and B Black, 'Equity and Debt Decoupling and Empty Voting II: Importance and Extensions' (2008) 156 *University of Pennsylvania Law Review* 625, focusing on derivatives and the uncoupling of economic interests, which lie with the derivative interest-holder, and voting rights, which remain with the shareholder. In recent years, this decoupling of voting and economic interest has been used to acquire major stakes in companies without triggering disclosure rules that would otherwise apply if a person held more than a certain stake (eg 5% in Switzerland).

[10] When using the term derivatives for the purposes of this chapter, the discussion is limited to instruments whose ultimate value is tied to underlying shares of capital stock, ie, equity derivatives.

The conclusion I defend is that a person 'owns' shares only in a weak sense of *having* rights to the shares. Owning shares in the first sense of 'having rights' is not the kind of owning that a theory of property ought to take as central.[11] And what is more, 'having rights' in this context presupposes someone else's – the Corporation's – 'having *property* rights' in the traditional sense. The concept of a share in a corporation is formally tied to the allocation of the value of its assets remaining on dissolution. Two features of the corporation emerge as central to this account: corporations are always in principle purposive and so in principle dissoluble (when the purpose is exhausted); secondly, the primary source of a corporation's power is property, or some right with respect to property, as it is conventionally understood in property theory.

II. Land as the Paradigmatic Case of Property

Why is land taken to be the paradigmatic case of property in property theory?[12] One reason is that the moral salience of property and its conceptual contours are plainest in the context of land. In contemporary liberal property, property is understood to solve a problem arising from an unavoidable feature of human existence: people are necessarily located somewhere in space.[13] When people find themselves in proximity to others, there is a need for some system for coordinating their activities so that peaceable co-existence is possible. The idea of property solves the problem of co-existence in space. Property gives the standing to set the agenda with respect to land, with the result that no one is subject to the arbitrary (ie, unauthorised) decisions of anyone else within that space.

While property in land and property in goods are often taken to be on equal footing in property theory, there are normative reasons to start with land.[14] To see why that is so, consider the relation between material goods and land. Material goods are themselves necessarily located somewhere in space and exercising ownership rights over material goods (accessing, possessing, using and even abandoning goods[15]) is itself a *land-based activity*.

[11] See eg, JW Harris, *Property and Justice* (Oxford, Oxford University Press, 1996) 9 ('"My", "yours", "his" may signify relationships that have nothing to do with owning.')

[12] See eg, J Waldron, *The Right to Private Property* (Oxford, Oxford University Press, 1988); A Ripstein, *Force and Freedom* (Cambridge MA, Harvard University Press, 2009); Harris (n 11); R Epstein, *Takings: Private Property and the Power of Eminent Domain* (Cambridge MA, Harvard University Press, 1985); RC Ellickson, 'Property in Land' (1993) 102 *Yale Law Journal* 1315; AM Honoré, 'Ownership' in AG Guest (ed), *Oxford Essays in Jurisprudence* (Oxford, Oxord University Press, 1961) (the 11 incidents of ownership are not offered as land-specific but Honoré clearly has land in mind: he uses land throughout to illustrate how the incidents of ownership work and why they are important). There is a long tradition of thinking about land as the basic case of property outside of legal theory: see eg U Vogel, 'When the Earth Belonged to All: the Land Question in Eighteenth-century Justifications of Private Property' (1988) 36 *Political Studies* 102.

[13] Kant wrote: 'Had the surface of the earth been an infinite plane, men could have been so dispersed upon it that they might not have come into necessary communion with each other.' I Kant, *Metaphysics of Morals*, M Gregor (tr) (Cambridge, Cambridge University Press, 1996) § 13. Modern property theorists like Bob Ellickson have put the point this way: 'Because human beings are fated to live mostly on the surface of the earth, the pattern of entitlements to use land is a central issue in social organization.' R Ellickson, 'Property in Land' (1993) 102 *Yale Law Journal* 1315, 1317.

[14] Note that many contemporary property theorists take material goods to serve just as well as land as a core example of the conceptual structure of property. See B McFarlane, 'Property and the New Doctrinalism: Comment' (2015) 163 *University of Pennsylvania Law Review* 293.

[15] See EM Peñalver, 'The Illusory Right to Abandon' (2010) 109 *Michigan Law Review* 191, 202–08 on the centrality of land in this context.

Property in material goods may be held independently of property in the land on which they are located. Alternately, property in material goods may be derivative of ownership of land. If it is the latter, property in land must be established first: we know who owns the apple only once we know who owns the land on which the apple tree is located. If it is the former, we still cannot overlook the way in which ownership of material goods (eg, cars, baseballs, etc) is dependent on the prior configuration of rights over the space in which the thing is located and used. Fully-fledged ownership of goods requires that the owner of the goods be free from arbitrary interference within the space she requires for exercising her property rights. To be clear, it is not necessary for the owner of goods *herself* to own the land required to access and use the goods. A system of property can accommodate the possibility that someone other than the owner of goods is in charge of the space where the goods are. It does so through rules about access and control that temper the landowner's right to exclude. These accommodations range from allowing the creation of subordinate property rights in land (eg, leaseholds, easements, profits); recognising individualised privileges to use publicly-owned land (eg, privileges to use roads for the purposes of parking or driving one's car); or implying privileges to enter another's land, eg, to retrieve goods left there (eg, a tenant entering the land to pick up her personal property after the end of a lease). Accommodations that enable land-based use of property in goods must be consistent with the continued and separate ownership of land by another. At some point the possibility of accommodation runs out. The law of fixtures reflects this kind of line-drawing exercise. Where a chattel is permanently attached to someone else's land, so that use of the good would either depend on the landowner's say-so or undermine the landowner's authority, the common law shifts ownership of the chattel to the owner of the realty.[16] The key thought here is that ownership of material goods entails land-based activity and so depends on our already having solved coordination problems involving our activities in time and space. Property in goods depends, in other words, on property in land.

Contemporary property theory and common-law thinking also offer conceptual reasons for treating land or goods as the paradigm of property. Land ownership invokes most clearly the conceptual core of property, understood in liberal property theory and common law today as a right to exclude or perhaps exclusive and bounded decisional authority.[17] Because of land's durability and usability, land brings to bear the full range of ownership powers: the authority to set the agenda, to grant subordinate rights, to appoint a successor, etc, as well as

[16] A system of property will avoid a situation where ownership of the object *requires* long-term cooperation with a separate owner of space. It is difficult to imagine a situation in which it would make good normative sense for a system of property to allow that an object be separately owned but that treats it as permanently out of reach of the owner.

[17] On the conceptual core of property see Waldron (n 12 above); Harris (n 11 above); J Penner, *The Idea of Property in Law* (Oxford, Oxford University Press, 1997); McFarlane (n 14 above); B McFarlane, *The Structure of Property Law* (Oxford, Hart Publishing, 2008); L Katz, 'Exclusion and Exclusivity in Property Law' (2008) 58 *University of Toronto Law Journal* 275; L Katz, 'Philosophy of Property – Three Ways' in J Tasioulas (ed), *Cambridge Companion to Law and Philosophy* (Cambrige, Cambridge University Press, forthcoming); HE Smith, 'Property as the Law of Things' (2012) 125 *Harvard Law Review* 169; HE Smith and TW Merrill, 'What Happened to Property in Law and Economics?' (2001) 111 *Yale Law Journal* 357; HE Smith and TW Merrill, 'The Property/Contract Interface' (2001) 101 *Columbia Law Review* 773. All but Penner and McFarlane take land to be the basic case. See also CM Newman, 'Using Things, Defining Property' in J Penner and M Otsuka (eds), *Property Theory* (Cambrige, Cambridge University Press, forthcoming).

rights that accede to the office of ownership[18] (eg, rights to the yield of the thing, to chattels that are affixed, to airspace above[19]) and duties (to neighbours, the state and subordinate rights-holders) that an owner might have.[20] It makes less sense to work out what it means to be an agenda-setter or gatekeeper in the context of goods that are designed for a single use by a single user, such as a stick of chewing gum. For this reason, much of the contemporary conceptual work on property starts with the idea of land and is then extended to other things that operate like increasingly weak versions of property in land.[21]

III. Shares as Property: Imitation, Mutation or Transformation

There are three main approaches to thinking about shares as property. The most straightforward way to account for shares as property in the traditional sense is to reify shares, introducing the idea of an intangible 'thing', such as an income stream, that a shareholder can be said to own, an approach once defended by James Penner.[22] Seen this way, as rights with respect to an intangible thing, shares are understood as property rights on equal footing with land or goods.

How else might shares fit within the traditional idea of property? A second approach involves thinking of shares not as an imitation but as a mutation of the central case.[23] Shares are property in this broader sense because they 'define [the shareholder's] position so far as access to and control of material resources is concerned.'[24] Shares, on this view, arise out of the fragmentation and recombination of traditional property rights, achieved where an original owner transfers her property rights to the corporation in order then to split and combine them in new ways. Waldron drew an explicit analogy between a share in a corporation and a mortgagee's interest or the interest of a beneficiary of a trust, all three of which he suggests are created by the power of an owner to fragment property. He writes

> individual owners have the power acting with others to constitute corporate persons and to transfer *their* holdings to it. Once that has been done *those* holdings will be used, controlled and managed on a basis that is different from the paradigm of private ownership, where an individual's determination is taken as socially decisive (emphasis added).[25]

Seen this way, shares are not distinct forms of right, but merely mutations of property. Latent in this understanding of shares as fragments of property is that shareholders collectively own the corporation's assets.[26]

[18] See L Katz, 'Property's Sovereignty' (2017) 18 *Theoretical Inquiries in Law* 299, 308–09.

[19] Whether airspace is just land on a vertical dimension, protected by trespass, or is better understand as a use-right like an easement, protected by nuisance, is the subject of controversy. See eg, *Didow v Alberta Power Ltd* 1988 ABCA 257, [1988] 5 WWR 606.

[20] See Honoré's 11 incidents of ownership (n 12 above). See D Attas, 'Fragmenting Property' (2006) 25 *Law & Philosophy* 119, 147 suggesting that these can be reduced to four.

[21] ibid.

[22] Penner (n 17 above) 214–15.

[23] Waldron (n 12 above) 57–59 (rejecting the view that shares involve ownership of intangible things) and 37.

[24] ibid 37.

[25] ibid 58.

[26] ibid.

Finally, there is a third approach that takes shares to be ownership rights, and the object of ownership, the corporation itself.[27] This view is associated with economists who have characterised shareholders as the true owners of corporations because of their economic interest in the company and its affairs. This approach relies on transforming the idea of ownership so that it is centrally concerned with entitlements to value. The economists' view of ownership as entitlements to value emerges from Berle and Means' famous insight that wealth in corporate form has split the 'property atom', by severing control-rights from 'beneficial ownership of this property – or in less technical language from the legal right to enjoy the fruits.'[28] For Berle and Means, the traditional idea of property served as a model for how to structure incentives in corporate property to avoid what economists now recognise as agency problems, where incentives between managers and owners are misaligned.[29] For economists today, ownership is conceptually independent from control and yet functionally dependent on it.

This third approach has its counterparts within legal theory. Thomas Grey drew attention to the proliferation of rights to value: in the modern era of corporations, he argued, property just means rights to value; the traditional idea of property is obsolete.[30] Bernard Rudden's distinction between things as value, and things as things, also allows for the place of value in property.[31]

Recently, Daniel Markovits and Alan Schwarz have argued that shares are entitlements to value (EV) in contrast to entitlements to things (ET).[32] In their view,

> the modern corporation … is a legal device for embedding property in contract and thus for constructing a shareholder's ownership entitlement in the corporation's property as an EV rather than an ET with managers – charged to exercise their business judgement to manage the corporation's assets – as the decider who fixes the V [value].

What is transformative about Markovits and Schwarz's account is the idea that 'property' is grounded in contract, a matter of private ordering, and not as conventional accounts of property understood, in the power of the state to define and enforce rights with respect to things.[33]

[27] This was the dominant view of the nature of shares and shareholding in corporate law and economics. As we will see, the idea of ownership invoked there has nothing to do with shareholding per se and everything to do with identifying the ultimate beneficiary of value, who may not hold shares but rather some right against those shares, like a derivative right.

[28] AA Berle and GC Means, *The Modern Corporation and Private Property*, revised 1st edn (Piscataway NJ, Transaction Publishers, 1967).

[29] OE Williamson, 'The Economics of Organization: The Transaction Cost Approach' (1981) 87 *American Journal of Sociology* 548.

[30] Grey (n 2 above).

[31] See Rudden (n 2 above). As Joshua Getzler has shown, Roman law has the conceptual apparatus necessary to foreground different aspects of property in different institutional contexts. Common law thinking about property has tended to settle on one or other of these contexts as central. See J Getzler, 'Plural Ownership, Funds and the Aggregation of Wills' (2009) 10 *Theoretical Inquiries in Law* at 250.

[32] Markovits and Schwarz (n 2 above) ('[P]roperty is predominantly protected by liability rules'). Markovits and Schwarz seems to conflate the dominance of liability rule protection with the proportion of assets protected by *in personam* obligations. See also Grey (n 2 above). The traditional view in law and philosophy of property is that property does not exist in the air but relates to particular subject matter or things: see eg, Lord Mustill in *Re Goldcorp Exchange Ltd* [1995] 1 AC 74, 91. See also, B Fried, 'Wilt Chamberlain Revisited: Nozick's "Justice in Transfer" and the Problem of Market-Based Distribution' (1995) 24 *Philosophy and Public Affairs* 226 for the distinction between things and value.

[33] See Markovits and Schwarz (n 2 above) ('On this account, the shareholder's entitlement is not fixed by the state but rather by the shareholders themselves, through the contracts that establish the corporation.')

Markovits and Schwarz, like others before them,[34] argue that property is mainly concerned with entitlements to value (protected by what Calabresi and Melamed identified as 'liability rules'[35]) as opposed to entitlements to things (protected by property rules), and conclude from this that EVs have now displaced ETs as the central case of property. Thus, they say '[i]n the United States today, nearly 85 percent of all non-residential private fixed assets are held on terms that leave them under non-owner management.' The ubiquity of EVs does not signal that rights to value are now to be taken as the central case of property. For one thing, the ubiquity of EVs is hardly a modern phenomenon. John Baker describes a case from 1502 acknowledging that by the end of the fifteenth century, most land in England was held on use (the precursor of the modern trust).[36] A *cestui que use* (what we would call today the beneficiary) did not herself have the entitlement to the thing (the ET) but merely a right in respect of her feoffee's ET that funnelled the benefits of ownership to her (after subtracting any costs associated with providing those ownership services). This is the kind of right that, like shares, Markovits and Schwarz would characterise as EV: the ultimate beneficiary of the value of the land was, for the most part, not the manager/ET-holder. And yet few would deny that 'classic' property in land was fundamental and basic to the architecture of property law then as indeed I think it is now. Then, as now, the entire scheme depends on securing the ETs (the rights of the manager/corporation/trustee) with respect to which others' EVs are then defined.

IV. From Property to Procedure

There are difficulties with all three approaches to fitting shares within the idea of property. A shortcoming of the first approach, treating shares as rights to an intangible thing, is the artificiality of 'conjuring'[37] an intangible thing for the purpose of treating shares as property. A more serious shortcoming is that in this context the 'intangible thing' does not itself refer to a sphere of decision-making over which the shareholder has jurisdiction, in anything like the way that land or material goods do. Shareholders are not in charge of any sphere of

[34] See n 32 above.

[35] G Calabresi and AD Melamed, 'Property Rules, Liability Rules and Inalienability: One View of the Cathedral' (1972) 85 *Harvard Law Review* 1089. Calabresi and Melamed suggested that private rights might be classified according to the kind of remedy they attract: liability rules respond to violations of rights with monetary awards; property rules respond with injunctions. The different types of rules, and the circumstances in which one kind of rule is to be favoured over the other, have been the subject of extensive discussion within law and economics. The liability rule/property rule distinction roughly tracks the distinction between things as value and things as things.

[36] JH Baker, *An Introduction to Legal History*, 4th revised edn (London, Butterworths, 2005) 251. As a cautionary note, there is a longstanding debate among trust scholars as to whether the beneficiary's interest in a trust is *in rem* (proprietary) or *in personam*. (Indeed this mirrors the debate about the proprietary nature of shares.) A Canonical description of the two positions is FW Maitland, *Equity: A Course of Lectures* (Cambridge, Cambridge University Press, 1936) 115. My own view, which I do not have space to defend here, is that the beneficiary's interest as a right in respect of property rights, is fundamentally an *in personam* right, even allowing that it can attach serially to one constructive trustee after another. See also S Agnew and B McFarlane, 'The Paradox of the Equitable Proprietary Claim' Chapter 17 in this volume for a discussion of how a beneficiary's right under a trust has proprietary effect in equity.

[37] Waldron (n 12 above) 57.

human interactions demarcated by the intangible thing itself. Of course, shareholders have transactional powers enabling them to act on the rights they have, such as the powers to assign, bequeath, or to sue to enforce the right itself, just as owners of land do. But owners of land hold those transactional powers over a right that in substance is very different: the underlying right that the owner of land can sell, fragment, etc, is a kind of authority to set the agenda for a thing that commands deference from the world at large. To equate shares with traditional property because both convey similar transactional powers is to miss a deeper and more profound difference between the underlying rights of shareholder and owner. In a corporation, it is the board of directors not the shareholders who have decision-making power.[38] Shareholders elect the members of the board of directors and have the power to change the composition of the board, but shareholders do not have the power to direct the board to take an action. The board has the power to, and in fact must as a matter of law, exercise its business judgement independently, subject to its fiduciary duties to determine the best interests of all shareholders and, in certain jurisdictions and instances, other stakeholders.

I also reject the second approach that shares are simply the combining, splitting and recombining of property rights. What is mistaken about this view is the creation story: the thought that shares emerge out of the powers of owners to fragment property, and then to split and recombine the fragments in different ways. It is also difficult to reconcile a conclusion from this premise, that shareholders are the real owners of the corporate assets,[39] with corporate law's insistence on a distinction between shareholding and ownership of the underlying assets.[40] Indeed, one danger of the property-in/property-out model implicit in the Waldron approach is that it undermines a signature feature of the corporate form, one that helped to distinguish it from a tenancy in common and a partnership. In a corporation, capital is genuinely locked in. There is no basis for a shareholder of a corporation to call for the return of 'his' contribution because he has no property interest in the assets of the corporation.[41] Shareholders also have no ability to force a board to declare a dividend

[38] But see J Armour, 'Companies and Other Associations' in A Burrows (ed), *English Private Law*, 3rd edn (Oxford, Oxford University Press, 2013) 3.50ff (describing situations where the decisional capacity of the board of directors is seriously impaired such that shareholders can step in, and situations where courts will 'pierce the corporate veil' in order to hold shareholders liable.)

[39] Waldron implies that shareholders as owners of the underlying asset are only missing an incident or two in much the same way that owners in other contexts might (eg, landlords).

[40] See E Freund, *The Legal Nature of Corporations* (Chicago, University of Chicago Press, 1897) 34: 'A shareholder of a railway company has no distinct right of property in the rolling stock … he cannot use the cars at his pleasure, he can give no orders to the employees and if he performs an act of ownership, he is a trespasser.' *cf* Bernard Rudden's account of shares in New River Corporation, understood as a fractional interest in *underlying corporeal assets of the company* (Rudden (n 2 above) 94). See also Pretto-Sakmann (n 1 above).

[41] See MM Blair, 'Locking in Capital: What Corporate Law Achieved for Business Organizers in the Nineteenth Century' (2003) 51 *University of California, Los Angeles Law Review* 387. Modern partnership law departs from the traditional common law property-in/property-out structure of a tenancy in common with respect to capital contributions. Section 24(1) of the Partnership Act of 1890 clearly establishes a default rule of equal sharing with respect to partnership assets (capital and revenue profits) but more controversially seems also to provide for the equal distribution of capital contributions, subject to implied or express agreement to the contrary. See Nourse LJ's discussion *in obiter* (neither party challenged pro-rata distribution of capital in the case) in *Popat v Shonchhatra* (n 3 above) 1372 (saying that s 24(1) clearly alters the common law rule as to partners' pro-rata entitlements to capital but suggesting that the slightest of implied intentions to share according to pro-rata contributions would displace this provision.)

and so no right *to* dividends but only a right to their share if a dividend is declared. The corporate structure is designed to sever the connection between the capital contributions of the shareholders and the assets of the corporation. Shareholders who contribute value to the corporation are acquiring something new through the payment of value rather than maintaining rights to value in some new form.

The third approach (ownership as rights to value) leads to conceptual and functional instability. Conceptually it is unstable because, in attaching 'real ownership' to value, ownership becomes a fugitive quality, not bound to any particular legal structure. Ownership moves from one form of right to another, from conventional property to shares to pure contract, as rights to value become lodged in the contractual arrangements *behind* shares. The ultimate entitlements to value today are largely constructed out of contractual devices, like derivatives, options and, even further removed from traditional property, swaps and phantom shares.[42] The last kind of financial instruments are indeed *just* contractual rights to the payment of money, tied to the value of shares without involving any rights to the shares themselves or even to their acquisition.

Among the dangers in locating 'ownership' in a foundation of contract is the risk of overlooking differences in the ways rights to value perform on bankruptcy and insolvency, and on the dissolution of the company, depending on whether they are embedded in conventional property, corporate shares or pure contract (eg, phantom shares).[43] Contractual rights cannot separate or fuse entitlements in the way that property rights can be fragmented or merged into one undivided whole. Roughly speaking, the effect of property rights is that the creditor of one owner is not able to satisfy their claims out of the assets of another. Where the assets have a common owner in the traditional property law sense, *all* the assets are available to meet the claims of creditors of the owner, even where through contract there are separate 'owners' in the sense of separate holders of entitlements to value.[44] Conversely, where separate legal entities own assets, the assets of one are not usually available to meet the creditors of the other, even if there is a contractual overlay that brings both legal entities under common management.

Nor can contract have free rein in delineating the boundaries of shareholders' interests in a way that holds on the bankruptcy or dissolution of the corporation, suggesting again that we should not conceive of shares just as rights to value grounded in contract. Imagine that shareholders of a corporation have a contractual arrangement that allocates profits from one class of assets that the corporation owns (car factories) to type 1 shareholders and

[42] See *Re Lehman Brothers International (Europe)* [2010] EWHC 2914 (Ch), [27]. The dispute turned in large part on the question of whether contract generates property or merely replicates some of its costs and benefits in a way that, when put to the test, does not amount to property.

[43] Note in common law and theoretical work on property, the effects of bankruptcy on rights is often the litmus test of property. See Penner (n 17 above) 132 on the proprietary character and treatment of choses in action in bankruptcy. See also: S von Pufendorf, *On the Law of Nature and Nations*, CH Oldfather and WA Oldfather (trs) (Oxford, Clarendon Press, 1934)) 763 (book V chapter VIII section 2) on the dissolution of partnerships. See *Re Lehman Brothers International (Europe)* (n 42 above) Lord Briggs [276]ff, distinguishing personal obligations that 'synthetically' created benefits equivalent to property (during the solvency of obligor) from proprietary interests.

[44] See H Hansmann and R Kraakman, 'The Essential Role of Organizational Law' (2000) 110 *Yale Law Journal* 387 (emphasising the organizing role of legal personality); J-P Robé, 'The Legal Structure of the Firm,' (2011) 1 *Accounting, Economics, and Law* 5 (explaining the role of corporations to partition assets within firms); see also EM Iacobucci and GG Triantis, 'Economic and Legal Boundaries of Firms' (2007) 93 *Virginia Law Review* 515, 525, 527.

allocates the profits of another type of corporate assets (mines) to type 2 shareholders. Say that shareholders have agreed among themselves that on dissolution this division of assets will hold, so that creditors of the car business will be paid out of the first class of assets and the creditors of the mining business will be paid out of the second. Imagine further that the contract stipulates that shareholders have residual claims on dissolution only to 'their' assets – car factories or mines. These contractual rights might create entitlements to value that are tied to specific assets but the kind of partitioning that contract achieves does not hold on bankruptcy or dissolution: the creditors of the corporation have claims that hold as against all the corporation's assets, notwithstanding the attempt to partition entitlements to value. Similarly, the interest shareholders have in the assets of the corporation at dissolution cannot be restricted to a particular class of assets, but relates rather to all the assets of the corporation remaining after prior claims have been satisfied. The rank-ordering of shareholders and the preference of some to others does not belie this point: the rank ordering is a contract-driven prioritising of interests in relation to what necessarily remains an undifferentiated pool of assets. All this is to say that contractually-created rights to value do not perform in the same way as property rights, even though shares can be subjected to a contractual overlay adjusting the value of what shareholders in the end receive.

There is an instability in the concept of ownership as a right to value. As it turns out, even those who think of ownership as rights to value, with shares as a primary example, ultimately recognise that rights to value depend to some extent on accompanying control rights.[45] A right to value simply does not function optimally in the total absence of control rights: the pure separation of control and value invites agency problems that reduce value. The conventional wisdom is to couple the right to value with *sufficient* control to guard against agency problems.[46] This suggests that traditional property, with its coupling of control and value, continues to serve as a model for how to structure property rights. It would be an odd thing to define ownership in a way that leaves out a constitutive part.

Even if the functional instability of the idea of ownership on the third approach is solved by aligning control and economic interests, there remain further difficulties with thinking of shareholding as tantamount to ownership of the corporation. Too *much* control is clearly as problematic as too little control. By too much control I do not mean here control *in excess* of economic interest (as where shareholders acquire 'empty votes' by buying up shares the value of which has gone to the holders of derivative rights).[47] A problem of too much control can arise where control and 'ownership' are actually perfectly aligned, as in the case of the shareholder who owns 100 per cent of the shares of a corporation and has

[45] R Romano, 'After the Revolution in Corporate Law' (2005) 55 *Journal of Legal Education* 342, 347 with reference to MC Jensen and WH Heckling, 'Theory of the Firm: Managerial Behavior, Agency Costs, and Ownership Structure' (1976) 3 *Journal of Financial Economics* 305.

[46] SJ Grossmann and OD Hart, 'The Costs and Benefits of Ownership: A Theory of Vertical and Lateral Integration' (1986) 94 *Journal of Political Economy* 691; OD Hart and J Moore, 'Property Rights and the Nature of the Firm' (1990) 98 *Journal of Political Economy* 1119.

[47] Decoupling of voting and economic interest and then the acquisition of these empty votes by shareholders in excess of their economic interest is a problem that economists recognise is consistent with their view that economic interest and control should be aligned, see, for example: JM Barry, JW Hatfield and SD Kominers, 'On Derivatives Markets and Social Welfare: A Theory of Empty Voting and Hidden Ownership' (2013) 99 *Virgina Law Review* 1103.

100 per cent of the control. A sole (or majority[48]) 'owner' of the corporation can put in place a board of directors that allows the 'owner' to use the corporation and its assets in self-serving ways, eg by directing corporate assets to the use of the shareholder. The puzzle that the 100 per cent shareholder presents is that it is precisely where there is union of control and value that there is also the greatest risk of the perversion of the corporate form.

My point is certainly not that we see an abuse of corporate form in all cases of a 100 per cent shareholder; but it is precisely in these cases that there is the greatest *potential* for abuse of the corporate form: the tendency toward perversion increases with the consolidation of control. Courts are far more likely to find such perversion in the context of a 'one person' corporation than in public corporations where 'ownership' as entitlement to value is diffuse. This concern with perversion is manifest in the phenomenon of piercing the corporate veil, where a court disregards the corporate entity and attaches liability to the individual shareholder.

The third approach does not have the resources to explain why the concentration of ownership of a corporation in the hands of a few or even a single shareholder tends to destabilise the corporate form (even if problems do not materialise in every case).[49] While this one-person corporation structure raises the greatest potential for abuse of the corporate form, it is the logical conclusion of the third approach: surely an owner of the corporation, understood as having a right to value, ought to be able to enhance the value of the corporation *to her* as best she is able, subject to the equal claims of other shareholders. Thus, the economists' approach seems to embrace an account of ownership which fails to explain why sole ownership, in the sense of an entitlement to value, can be problematic.

V. Shares as Shares: A Right in a Procedure

A share on my account is just a share: a right to share in the division of a mass of value along with ancillary rights that are in service of this primary right. The conceptual anchor for the idea of a share is a relationship to an ultimate pool of value accumulated as the corporation operates and that stands ultimately to be divided on dissolution. The idea of a share then gives conceptual priority to the right of the shareholder to a share of the assets of the corporation remaining at the time of dissolution (that is, those remaining after other creditors have been satisfied). This right has understandably been downplayed in accounts of the nature of the share, as it is a priority right that usually ends up placing shareholders precisely last, and also because corporations, although always in principle dissoluble, are in practice often meant to continue indefinitely. My account shows why, nonetheless, this ultimate right to share in the division of corporate assets is conceptually important to the very idea of a share even while the corporation is ongoing. This is so even if empirically speaking the

[48] The takeover of the corporation by a majority stakeholder presents similar problems but I avoid this example here because it also raises worries of oppression, forfeiture and the potential violation of proportionality requirements as among shareholders.

[49] The threat of uniting ownership and control, through takeover, has been used as a tool for disciplining underperforming managers. See eg, R Romano, 'A Guide to Takeovers: Theory, Evidence and Regulation' (1992) 9 *Yale Journal on Regulation* 119, 122–33.

value of a share to most actual shareholders is constituted by secondary markets, or by the exercise of important but conceptually secondary rights like the right to share in declared dividends. This right to share fairly in the division of a mass of value gives rise to what are in effect procedural safeguards regulating how that mass is dealt with in what we can now see as the interim: the period between the start of corporate operations and the end point at which the quantum is fixed and available for division. The fact that sometimes a shareholder may receive nothing, because as it turns out there is nothing left, or that the shareholder may be re-routed through a bankruptcy procedure and required to take up another position in relation to the available assets, does not change the fundamental nature of the share.[50] We still work out the idea of a share in relation to the right of a shareholder to a fair procedure for dividing a mass of value (for instance, we assess the justice of the shareholder's position in bankruptcy proceedings against the position they would have had in the event that the corporation was dissolved and assets distributed outright.)

A share in a corporation is, in short, fundamentally *a share*, an idea concerned with appropriate principles for dividing a mass of shifting magnitude. In this, a share in a corporation bears some similarity to other notions of shares and shareholding in private law, eg, the shares that equity recognises in a partition and sale where, in addition to the original contributions (which can be returned on an arithmetical basis), there are also losses and profits to allocate. The pro-rata shares that co-owners of an intermixture claim where the mixture has greater or lesser value than the original contributions is also a geometric principle for division that adds something to the basic idea in property law of the continuation of pre-existing property rights. A share, as a right in a procedure, properly attracts principles we might usually associate with public law:[51] principles of proportionality, non-oppression and non-forfeiture. I will turn to these principles, which I take to be important regulative principles appropriate to the very idea of a share, below. These principles offer a partial normative explanation of the bundle of rights conventionally associated with shares: rights to dividends, capital and voting, and the freedom to tailor the configuration of that bundle through contract.[52] My account suggests, however, that voting rights do not fall directly out of the basic idea of a share in a corporation but require further explanation. The idea that the right to vote comes apart from the idea of shareholding is consistent with the reality in corporate law that there can be voting and non-voting stock, a division that is not inherently problematic. Shares may convey additional rights relating to the governance of corporations, eg voting shares. But not all shares convey voting rights. Rights to vote have to do with membership in a corporation, not shareholding. Membership and shareholding

[50] A shareholder generally cannot be made worse off, in the bankruptcy proceeding, than she would be in the case of the dissolution of the corporation.

[51] And Equity, too. But then in my view Equity has a public law feel to it because Equity too emerges from the executive branch, and the prerogative, and so implicates a certain role of the state in relation to citizens, rather than the purely private relationality found in private law frameworks. See L Katz (n 4 above).

[52] See eg, Pretto-Sakmann (n 1 above); Harris (n 11 above) 51 ('Shares in companies consist in rights to money (dividends when declared and a share in the company's residuary assets on dissolution), and rights to vote in company resolutions.'). Some reduce this to two ideas. See Markovits and Schwarz (n 2 above) ('The purchaser of a share of stock in a company buys two things: the right that the company administer its property to maximize profits and the right to vote on important decisions, such as who should be directors and whether the company should be sold.').

are separate ideas (and so we can have non-stock corporations with members), and shares may or may not come with membership rights like voting rights. Voting rights relate to an idea of membership in an association, corporate or otherwise. Voting rights follow from the status of a shareholder as a fully-fledged *member* of a corporation.

A. Principles of Proportionality, Non-Domination and Non-Forfeiture

The regulative principles appropriate to the idea of a share in a corporation are principles of proportionality, non-domination and non-forfeiture. These are manifest as a right (exigible against the human managers of the corporation) to be treated with horizontal proportionality (fairness vis-à-vis fellow shareholders); a right that managers deal with corporate assets so as to maximise profits; and a right to a share of the corporate assets remaining on dissolution, or to its equivalent[53] in bankruptcy proceedings.[54] The right to proportionality is manifest as a right to any dividends declared. It is a matter of horizontal proportionality that if corporations declare a dividend, shareholders have a right to their share, subject to any contractual modification of that right. But of course a right to purely horizontal proportionality cannot trigger a right *to* income. The power to declare a dividend remains exclusively a decision of the corporation.

A principle against forfeiture also explains why assets cannot actually be removed from the pool available on dissolution to satisfy shareholders' pro-rata claims. *How* the mass is ultimately divided may be established contractually, but the mass of assets – *what* is to be divided in that way – is beyond the reach of contract. The share is a right that floats over the entire mass until the division is complete, leaving only the manner of division to be established through contract.[55] To limit a shareholder's right to a procedure for dividing only a part of the mass is a forfeiture of a kind: she forfeits a right to share in the division of the whole mass of value, whatever its size. This is so even if in practical terms she does not end up with less in her pocket: what is lost or forfeit is the position in relation to a mass, the accumulation, retention and division of which are all subject to her procedural rights.

A shareholder's right against forfeiture is generally manifested as a right that the corporation, through its human managers, *maximise* profits. The right against forfeiture echoes but it is importantly different from Milton Friedman's claim that the social responsibility of a corporation is to maximise profits.[56] On my account, the responsibility of the corporation to the shareholders is indeed to maximise profits. But a corporation can only discharge that

[53] The equivalence between bankruptcy and dissolution is an equivalence as between two procedures. The idea of a share as a right in a procedure fits better this understanding of equivalence than the idea of a share as a property right that is lost and replaced with some other kind of right altogether, in the bankruptcy context.

[54] See eg: s 211(7)(d) Canadian Business Corporations Act (RSC, 1985, c C-44) (distribution of remaining property among shareholders according to their respective rights after dissolution) and ss 141, 140.1 Canadian Bankruptcy and Insolvency Act (RSC, 1985, c B-3) (rateable pay of (postponed) equity claims).

[55] *cf* Grossmann and Hart (n 46 above); Hart and Moore (n 46 above).

[56] M Friedman, 'A Friedman Doctrine – The Social Responsibilty of Business Is to Increase Its Profits' *The New York Times* (New York, 13 September 1970).

responsibility consistently with its own agency.[57] A corporation, in exercising its powers of ownership, its powers to contract, and its by-law-making powers, must do *its* utmost to maximise profits, but its utmost is just that: a bounded capacity. The gist of my argument is this: owners occupy an office of ownership that does not in itself require decisions about things to be made in the public interest. And yet the nature of the agent or officeholder shapes the kinds of decisions open to that agent within that otherwise unlimited office.[58] Any of the private powers that the corporation holds can only be exercised in a manner that is consistent with its nature as a corporation. The key feature of a corporation – one that follows the corporation into the office of ownership and constrains the reasons for which it can act in the exercise of any power it has – is the corporation's inherent, formal purposiveness.

B. Purposiveness of Corporations

A reason to resist conflating shareholding with ownership of a corporation (and so ownership with entitlements to value) is that corporations are formally structured as purposive entities. The structure of managerial decisions about the corporation is distinct from the structure of ownership decisions. Ownership decisions are inherently self-serving: owners are not formally constrained by some external purpose of the thing in making decisions about it. By contrast, managerial decisions about the corporation are structured, at least formally speaking, by the *purposiveness* of corporations. The purposiveness of corporations is a positive feature, not something to be avoided. Corporations gain their powers largely from their ownership of assets but they have capacity to own *because* they are legal persons who owe their existence to an act of government.[59] As legal persons created always by an act of government (legislative or executive), they are inherently purposive: government could not use its public authority to confer legal personhood for no purpose at all (because all exercises of public authority are for a public purpose). There is some purpose or end for which corporations are always designed, even if that purpose (as is mostly the case today) is very broadly construed. Corporations are *structurally* purposive agents even in contexts where there is very little content poured into this structure. And so the manner in which a corporation exercises any of its powers is constrained by the purposive nature of its agency. Indeed, we might say precisely the same thing about trustees: a trustee has an office that is inherently purposive (to benefit another in the exercise of ownership).

[57] A similar phenomenon of officeholder shaping office applies where state actors hold private property. The nature of the official/agent affects the way the office is held. See also: Waldron (n 12 above) 40–41; Harris (n 11 above) 104–06.

[58] See for example: *Sun Indalex Finance, LLC v United Steelworkers* [2013] 1 SCR 271, 2013 SCC 6; *Rollins v Rollins*, 755 SE 2d 727 (Ga 2014) in particular on the implications of the business judgement rule; REN, 'The Trust Corporation: Dual Fiduciary Duties and the Conflicts of Institutions' (1961) 109 *University of Pennsylvania Law Review* 713 (note); PB Miller, 'Multiple Loyalties and the Conflicted Fiduciary' (2014) 40 *Queen's Law Journal* 301; similar conflicts can arise in the case of for-profit providers of healthcare, housing, education, etc but will be attenuated when similar services are provided by non-profit corporations as provided for, eg in the Ontario Not-for-Profit Corporations Act 2010 (SO 2010, c 15).

[59] For the American history of creating corporations, by government act or by prescription (period of time after which lost grant presumed, see TC Spelling, *A Treatise on the Law of Private Corporations* (New York, LK Strouse & Co Law Publishers, 1892) 22–23.

That purposiveness colours everything the office of trustee touches, including for example the exercise of powers which the trustee has as owner of particular assets.

The purposiveness of the private corporation has receded from view and manifests itself now as a merely formal structuring principle. Few private corporations have clearly articulated purposes that actually do any work in shaping corporate decision-making. But as a conceptual matter, a corporation remains a legal person with delegated powers to act for purposes, no matter how broadly construed. Even in a world in which corporate law has thinned the notion of purposiveness dramatically, there remain institutional indicia of this bedrock idea.[60] The formal idea was given legal expression in the idea of visitorial jurisdiction. A visitor, holding a common law office, has an administrative rather than a judicial role: to supervise corporate conduct to ensure consistency with the corporation's nature and purposes.[61]

The formal purposiveness of corporations explains in part what is problematic about the total unity of economic interest and control, as in the case of the shareholder who has 100 per cent of the shares in the corporation and uses that position to strip the corporation of its value, for self-serving reasons. The point is that corporations are meant to be structured as powers for purposes and so are not meant to be available for the purely self-serving ends of a shareholder. The fact that the purposes of most private corporations are underdeveloped conceals this formal structural constraint on corporations and their capacity to serve the interests of shareholders, whatever those might be. The problem with treating corporations as totally non-purposive does not emerge as clearly where there are multiple shareholders, whose economic interests are often best served by enhancing the value of the corporation itself rather than stripping it of value in order to achieve some ulterior gain. Concerns about horizontal proportionality and non-oppression among shareholders will tend to operate as the primary check on value-stripping for the benefit of one shareholder among many, even if the purposiveness of the corporation is overlooked.

Finally, it is important to acknowledge the reasons why there is strong resistance to requiring a more substantive purposiveness of private corporations (and, it is worth adding, why there has been the move to erode the purposiveness of corporations in Anglo-American law). It is plain that there is a demand for a sphere for private ordering beyond the goal-oriented or managerial purview of the state. Indeed, it seems that Maitland understood the dominance of the trust and unincorporated associations, and the relatively late adoption of the corporation, to reflect precisely this worry about the link between corporations and the state.[62] The worry about state overreach may have something to do with the origins of

[60] See eg, Companies Act 2006, ss 31, 39, 42.

[61] See eg R Pound, 'Visitorial Jurisdiciton over Corporations in Equity' (1936) 49 *Harvard Law Review* 369; Judge Glock, 'The Forgotten Visitorial Power: The Origins of Administrative Subpoenas and Modern Regulation' (2017–18) 37 *Review of Banking & Financial Law* 205, 213: 'The position of "visitor" is almost unknown today, but it once carried great weight. Under English law, from at least the fifteenth century, a visitor was the representative of the founder of a religious or charitable corporation.' See too, *King v Lee* (1690) 1 Shower KB 251, 89 ER 554, 555: 'Every private corporation has a visitor.'; S Kyd, *A Treatise on the Law of Corporations* (London, J Butterworth, 1793) 286; 1 Bl Comm 480; FW Wegenast, *The Law of Canadian Companies* (Toronto, Carswell, 1931) 775–76. I am grateful to Lionel Smith for drawing my attention to the role of visitors and to these sources. For the distinction between visitorial and judicial oversight see: *Cuomo v Clearing House Association, LLC*, 557 US 519 (2009).

[62] See F Maitland, 'Trust and Corporation' (1904) in M Ryan and D Runciman (eds), *Maitland: State, Trust and Corporation* (Cambridge, Cambridge University Press, 2003), discussed by J Getzler, 'Frederic William Maitland – Trust and Corporation' (2016) 35 *University of Queensland Law Journal* 171.

the corporate form in the Royal prerogative, an exercise of state power to rule, based on *salus populi*.[63] Fear of corporations began as fear of an overreaching royal prerogative; the same fears that dogged equity. The worry is a larger worry about the state in a managerial mode, foisting its purposes on citizens rather than establishing a non-purposive framework for legal relations, available then for private purposes.[64] Eventually, Parliament reined in the prerogative in relation to the corporation (just as it did in relation to equity): the legislature took over the creation of corporations (and the regulation of commerce too).[65] A worry about the managerial state operating within the private sphere is heightened where the state sets down the ends of private action. This worry, however, is not warranted where the purposiveness of corporations is understood formally: a corporation is purposive in the formal sense where the purposes themselves are set privately.

VI. Conclusion

The view of the nature of shares as rights in a procedure for dividing a mass of value helps to resolve a number of unresolved questions about the nature of shares. It also defends against claims that so-called 'corporate property' ought to dominate theories of property.

On rights-based accounts of shares, a shareholder's right is a right to an intangible thing, 'an income stream in an economic enterprise.'[66] Seen this way, the right to income is taken to be a normal and indeed central incident of shareholding. My account offers a different way of explaining shares that does not foreground rights to income nor does it require the invention of an intangible thing. By accounting for shares as rights in a procedure for dividing a mass of value, I explain why dividends are in a sense foreign to the idea of a share, while at the same time explaining why *if* cash is paid out in the form of dividends, management has a duty to make these payments consistently with the shareholders' rights in the procedure (rights to fairness, non-domination and proportionality). A right to dividends, far from being a constitutive element of a share as a share, is understood better as a consequence of a more basic claim of fair treatment or horizontal proportionality.[67]

My account builds on some of the central insights of Waldron's approach, for instance that shares are in some respects *like* the equitable rights of mortgagors and of beneficiaries of a trust. The analogy refers not to splitting and recombining property rights, but rather to setting out and regulating rights in a procedure. Equitable rights take the form of rights in

[63] DEC Yale (ed), *Sir Matthew Hale's The Prerogatives of the King* (London, Selden Society, 1976).

[64] See eg, M Oakeshott, *Rationalism in Politics and Other Essays*, reprint edn (Indianapolis IN, Liberty Fund, 1991); T Poole, *Reasons of State: Law, Prerogative and Empire* (Cambridge, Cambridge University Press, 2015).

[65] Corporations by legislation are not as obviously concerned with governance and purposes as those created by prerogative. And yet there remains a close relationship between these. This is the same kind of analogy I think that Pomeroy employed when he suggested that that unregistered property rights in recording acts were like equitable rights (*Pomeroy's Equity Jurisprudence and Equitable Remedies*, vol I, 3rd edn (San Francisco, Bancroft-Whitney, 1905) 82–83 (§ 76). Creatures of statute can behave like equity.)

[66] Penner (n 17 above) 214.

[67] This account fits well with the economist's view that payment of cash to shareholders in the form of dividends tends to be inefficient. See notably, F Black, 'The Dividend Puzzle' (1976) 2 *Journal of Portfolio Management* 5; R La Porta, F Lopez-de-Silanes A Shleifer and RW Vishny, 'Agency Problems and Dividend Policies around the World' (2000) 55 *Journal of Finance* 1, with further references.

respect of other people's rights, and concern the pathways to legal rights that equity regulates. It is no coincidence that shares share some of the features of equitable rights. Both corporations and equity emerged out of the exercise of the royal prerogative.[68] The purposive and managerial quality of governmental power beyond the creation of corporations and the doing of equity has left its mark on both. In understanding shares as rights in a procedure, I aim to show how that is so. Whereas the Waldron approach conceives of corporate shares in terms of arithmetical principles of division and so presupposes fragments of property (eg, a slice of a fixed pie), I suggest that we think of shares as geometric principles of division: principles for dividing a magnitude subject to increase and decrease. A principle of arithmetical division presupposes a whole comprised of fixed parts: it is just a matter of dishing out each predetermined 'slice', to continue the pie metaphor. In contrast, a principle of geometric division (only) anticipates an allocation of part-entitlements.

My account suggests why ownership theories of shareholding are also conceptually problematic, whether or not the shares are dispersed among many or concentrated in the hands of a few. Shares are *relational* by design, and the relation they concern is the relationship of proportionality among fellow participants within a procedure. This concern about horizontal proportionality generates constraints on management decisions. Where there are no such allocative questions or concerns about horizontal proportionality among shareholders, as in the case of the 100 per cent shareholder, the idea of a share ceases to be a relational idea about a fair procedure for dividing something. Shareholding in those contexts operates like ownership but without the authority and responsibility built into the office of ownership. Economists are right to worry about the inefficiencies in these cases, and courts are right then to pierce the corporate veil. The explanation for why it is a perversion of the corporate form can be understood in terms of the nature of shares themselves.

[68] See further for the royal prerogative: S Whittaker, 'Public and Private Law-making: Subordinate Legislation, Contracts and the Status of "Student Rules"' (2001) 21 *OJLS* 108, fn 30 with reference to 1 Bl Comm 472; F Pollock and FW Maitland, *The History of English Law before the Time of Edward I*, reprinted 2nd edn (Indianapolis IN, Liberty Fund, 1968) 669.

8

The Proprietary Nature of Title-based Financing Interests

MAGDA RACZYNSKA

I. Introduction

The recent work on secured transactions, conducted separately by two expert groups, the Secured Transactions Law Reform Project[1] and the City of London Law Society,[2] makes it clear there is a case for reform in this area. While a consensus exists in relation to a number of aspects of the future regime, one unresolved debate concerns the legal relationships arising through retention-of-title clauses in contracts of sale, hire-purchase and lease agreements and their variants such as lease-back or buy-back agreements. Their common feature is that an owner of an asset (A) delivers possession of the asset to another – the buyer, the lessee or the hirer (B) – whilst retaining ownership of the asset. Such relationships are often used functionally as security interests because they enable B to raise finance (typically, to acquire goods on credit) from A while protecting A from the credit risk through the retention of ownership.

The interests created in A through contracts of sale with retention-of-title clauses, hire-purchase and finance lease agreements will be referred to in this chapter as 'title-based financing interests'.[3] The functional similarity between such interests and security interests has led to a debate as to whether title-based financing interests ought to be governed by rules similar to those that apply to security interests.[4] English law has traditionally resisted functionalism in favour of a more conceptual approach. One of the arguments against regulating title-based financing interests in a way similar to security interests is that the former are created through retention of a right A already has, not a grant of a new property right by B in favour of A. But this does not say much about the nature of A's interest following

[1] For the work of the Project, see: https://securedtransactionslawreformproject.org.

[2] See *Discussion Draft of the Secured Transactions Code* (22/07/2015) available on the pages of the Financial Law Committee of the City of London Law Society, at: http://www.citysolicitors.org.uk.

[3] Such terminology is also adopted elsewhere (see eg H Beale, M Bridge, L Gullifer and E Lomnicka, *The Law of Security and Title-based Financing*, 3rd edn (Oxford, Oxford University Press, 2018)) but does not yet seem to be universal.

[4] A number of jurisdictions have based their regulation of secured transactions on a functional definition of security: see eg Article 9 of the Uniform Commercial Code in the USA, New Zealand Personal Property Securities Act 1999; Saskatchewan Personal Property Security Act 1993; the Ontario Personal Property Security Act 1990; and in Australia, Personal Property Securities Act 2009 (Cth).

such retention. In discussion on the future of the law, it would be helpful to gain a better understanding of the right that A obtains. This chapter contributes to this understanding. In so doing, it also hopes to cast new light on the list of property rights in English law. While the list may generally be closed (*numerus clausus*), this chapter seeks to make a case, based on the current law, for the recognition of a new type of property right.

The purpose of this chapter is to examine the proprietary nature of title-based financing interests and their place in property law. It explores whether title-based financing interests confer as much protection on the owner as absolute ownership, ie, whether it is correct to say that A simply retains title to an asset, so no new property right is involved. If a new form of property right is created, which is distinct from ownership, but has not been granted by B to A, it is necessary to consider whether the law regulates it appropriately, taking into account the interests of third parties on whom the right impacts. The chapter does not seek to debate the accuracy of the functional approach to title-based interests.[5] Instead, it seeks to open a wider discussion of whether, from the perspective of property law, title-based financing interests are better understood in a different way than through the prism of ownership, and whether they should be regulated accordingly.

The chapter is structured as follows. First, title-based financing interests are discussed as forms of proprietary disposition, which are different from security interests. The argument made here is that, whilst the courts make it clear that title-based financing interests do not constitute grants of a property right by *the debtor* (B) to the creditor (A), there is nothing to preclude us from regarding A's retention of title as involving the creation of a new right by *A herself*. Second, it is considered whether A's new right constitutes ownership or a new type of property right, which would have implications for the *numerus clausus* principle. On the one hand, from A's perspective, based on A's intention relating to the proprietary disposition of the asset, the right that A holds is not new: it is simply ownership. However, as a matter of practice, title-based financing interests give rise to the same types of problems for third parties (eg, information costs) as property rights lesser in scope than absolute ownership, such as security rights. Furthermore, even under English law, which does not re-characterise title-based interests as security rights, there are important differences between ownership and title-based financing interests, in particular, with respect to damages available for interference with the asset subject to such an interest and to the applicability of exceptions to the *nemo dat* principle. These factors tend to support the argument that the right that A holds is not ownership but a new type of property right. Third, the chapter looks at the impact of regarding A's right as a new type of property right. Section III identifies different responses that could be adopted in law to take this new perspective on title-based interests into account. One response could be to say that, since title-based interests are to some extent already different from simple ownership, the law could go further and treat them like security interests by adopting a Uniform Commercial Code/Personal Property Security Act approach. Another is to say that whilst allowing A the freedom to retain an interest, English law deals with some of the *numerus clausus* concerns through other means, such as by limiting the effect on a third party of A's title-based interest. It considers whether the current approach of English law

[5] For a critique of functionalism, see M Bridge, RA Macdonald, RL Simmonds and C Walsh, 'Formalism, Functionalism and Understanding the Law of Secured Transactions' (1999) 44 *McGill Law Journal* 567.

appropriately balances A's interests with those of third parties, and whether it responds to some of the policy questions around title-based interests.

II. Title-based Financing Interests as a Form of Proprietary Disposition

Before we look at the nature of the retained ownership, it is important to consider whether a retention-of-title clause contained in a contract is a result of the exercise of freedom to contract, understood as the freedom to shape rights and obligations arising between the parties, or the freedom of the owner to dispose of its property, governed by property law. If it is the former, it is not generally the case that the law will restrict or regulate that freedom; if the latter, social control seems justifiable to a greater extent, because the imposition of duties and liabilities on third parties needs to be considered, and so the law is more likely to interfere with that freedom. As this section shows, courts will generally give effect to parties' intentions to retain ownership. While the courts have consistently drawn a sharp distinction between title-based financing interests and security interests, there is nothing to suggest that the former could not be a further form of a property right, different from both security interests and ownership.

A. Freedom of Contract or Freedom to Dispose (Retain)?

Consider first a party seeking to purchase goods. That party may obtain credit directly from the supplier in the form of deferment of time for payment of the price for the supplied goods. To reduce the credit risk, the seller may withhold the passage of property in the goods until a stipulated condition is fulfilled, typically payment of the price.[6] The legislative basis for retention of title in the context of sale of goods is section 19(1) of the Sale of Goods Act 1979, which provides that where there is a contract for the sale of specific goods or where goods are subsequently appropriated to the contract, the seller may, by the terms of the contract or the appropriation, reserve the right of disposal of the goods until certain conditions are fulfilled.[7] While retention of title is thought to be based on freedom of contract (understood narrowly as freedom to undertake personal obligations) because it often arises on the basis of terms of contract, section 19(1) suggests recognition of a property-based freedom to dispose, which may or may not be exercised at the same time as freedom to contract. That retention of title is based on a freedom to dispose of property (including freedom to retain property) is further supported by evidence from cases that identify the property-based limits of this freedom. While a contract governing the transaction between A and B can specify the nature of the interest in the asset, and courts will generally give effect to the intentions expressed in the contract, an attempt

[6] Note that the term 'conditional sale' has a specific meaning in the Sale of Goods Act 1979 as an installment sale.
[7] See also Sale of Goods Act 1979, s 17.

to extend a retention-of-title clause to the proceeds and/or products of the goods supplied will not generally be successful.[8] A 'buyer'/debtor who manufactures a product out of goods supplied becomes the owner of that product (a new thing) through a property doctrine of original (ie, non-derivative) acquisition of ownership, so the proprietary effect of a clause purporting to retain title is to grant a new proprietary interest in the product in favour of the financier, even if the financier sought to 'retain' its ownership in the product.[9] The consequences of this are that the new right will be seen as a proprietary right granted by the 'buyer'/debtor in favour of the 'seller'/creditor by way of security; that is, a charge. If the 'buyer'/debtor is a company, the charge will be invalid against the liquidator, administrator or creditors unless registered.[10]

The exercise of the freedom to dispose (retain) also occurs in hire-purchase and lease agreements. Such agreements in practice usually involve three parties: title to an asset is acquired from the seller by a financier, who then retains it in the contract with the debtor. The debtor under a hire-purchase agreement has an option to purchase the asset at the expiry of a certain period or the completion of a set of payments, whereas the agreement with the financier under a lease contract is so structured that the financier retains property in the goods while the debtor has neither a right nor a power to acquire property in the asset upon payment of the instalments – even if, by the end of the payment period, the economic value of the asset is negligible so that the financier has no interest in obtaining the asset back.

It should be added that unlike hire-purchase agreements, leases are not necessarily a financing arrangement. Leases of goods have been recognised in English law from at least as early as 1703, when Lord Holt CJ in *Coggs v Barnard*,[11] describing various forms of bailment, included delivery of possession of goods to the bailee (B) 'to be used by him for hire'.[12] In modern times, delivery of A's goods for B's use in return for rent is very common, as it enables B to gain use of goods for however short or long a term desired without having to pay the purchase price for them. Typical examples are a holiday rental of a car or the hiring of a construction crane. However, leases have also come to be used precisely so that B can finance acquisition of an asset whilst obtaining use of it. This involves a purchase of the asset by A from a manufacturer or a supplier, and then the grant of a lease of the asset by A to B. Such leases, known as finance leases, by contrast to operating leases,[13] are concluded

[8] Note that following *PST Energy 7 Shipping LLC v OW Bunker Malta Ltd* [2016] UKSC 23, [2016] AC 1034, contracts expressed to be contracts for sale with retention-of-title clauses where selling-on or consumption of goods is envisaged prior to property passing will likely not be classed as contracts for sale of goods.

[9] *Clough Mill Ltd v Martin* [1985] 1 WLR 111 (CA), 120 (Robert Goff LJ) although see 124 (where Oliver LJ was more doubtful); *Borden (UK) Ltd v Scottish Timber Products* [1981] Ch 25 (CA). A clause purporting to retain title to proceeds is very likely to amount to a grant of a charge: *Re Peachdart* [1984] Ch 131; *E Pfeiffer Weinkellerei-Weineinkauf GmbH v Arbuthnot Factors* [1988] 1 WLR 150. See generally M Raczynska, *The Law of Tracing in Commercial Transactions* (Oxford, Oxford University Press, 2018) ch 5.

[10] Companies Act 2006, s 859H.

[11] *Coggs v Barnard* (1703) 2 Ld Raym 909, 92 ER 107; see also M Bridge, L Gullifer, K Low and G McMeel, *The Law of Personal Property*, 2nd edn (London, Sweet & Maxwell, 2017) [13-001].

[12] *Coggs v Barnard* (ibid) 912–13.

[13] The terminology refers to the (now) historical accounting distinction between finance and operating leases whereby, in relation to operating leases, risks and rewards of the ownership of goods were the lessor's while, in the case of finance leases, they were the lessee's: see International Accounting Standards (IAS) 17 Leases; Institute of Chartered Accountants, Statement of Standard Accounting Practice (SSAP) No 21, cited in: *Gallagher v Jones*

typically for a period envisaged to cover the working life of the asset at a rental which is calculated to cover the market price of the asset (its capital value) with a return on capital.[14] The development of finance leasing of goods has been fuelled in practice by tax advantages in relation to commercial customers.[15]

A simpler way of *expressing* the owner's freedom to retain title is to say that it is based on freedom of contract, but one understood broadly as including *freedom to retain* title to property as well as creation of personal obligations between the parties. The freedom to retain title is particularly wide if one considers that parties may agree that the title will not pass until all debts owed on any account are paid.[16]

B. Title-based Financing Interests Distinguished from Security Interests

The courts have consistently maintained that there exists a deep conceptual divide between security interests and title-based financing interests, as this section illustrates. For current purposes, it is particularly important to observe that in drawing this distinction the courts have said nothing that would contradict the view, advanced in this chapter, that the retained interest is a new type of property right, different from absolute ownership (and different also from security interests). To show the basis on which the courts have differentiated title-based financing interests from security interests, it is convenient to start by outlining the ways in which the two types of interests can be seen as similar.

Title-based financing interests and security interests are similar in at least two aspects. First, they perform a similar function as each enables the creditor/financier to resort to an asset[17] in order to discharge the ('secured') obligation prior to other creditors of the debtor, whilst also facilitating the debtor's use of the asset.[18] Secondly, title-based interests can be seen as non-possessory interests, which are similar to a legal mortgage in the sense that the financier holds title but not possession.

(Inspector of Taxes); Threlfall v Jones (Inspector of Taxes) [1994] Ch 107, 117 (Sir Thomas Bingham MR); and in the CA in *On Demand Information plc v Michael Gerson (Finance) Ltd plc* [2000] 4 All ER 734 (CA), 737 (Robert Walker LJ), reversed without impact on the point just made: *On Demand Information plc v Michael Gerson (Finance) Ltd plc* [2002] UKHL 13, [2003] 1 AC 368. The new accounting standards, IFRS (as of January 2019) treat all leases as the same for accounting purposes, requiring all lessees of leases of at least one year to recognise assets and liabilities unless the asset is of low value: International Financial Reporting Standards (IFRS) 16 Leases: https://www.ifrs.org/issued-standards/list-of-standards/ifrs-16-leases/.

[14] R Goode and E McKendrick (eds), *Goode on Commercial Law*, 5th edn (London, LexisNexis Butterworths, 2016) [22.05].

[15] Bridge et al (n 11 above) [13-004], citing HMRC, CA23810-PMA: Long funding lease: lessees; *Barclays Mercantile Business Finance Ltd v Mawson* [2004] UKHL 51, [2005] 1 AC 684.

[16] *Armour v Thyssen Edelstahlwerke AG* [1991] 2 AC 339 (HL). For an academic argument (now of historic interest) that a contract of sale purporting to retain title until all liabilities due under any other contracts are discharged creates a security interest, see W Goodhart, 'Clough Mill Ltd v Martin – A Comeback for Romalpa?' (1986) 49 *MLR* 96.

[17] The term 'resort to an asset' is not commonly used in relation to title-based financing interests but it should be understood in this context to mean the power that the owner has to re-possess its asset, including in insolvency of the possessor.

[18] Note, too, that courts have an inherent equitable jurisdiction to give relief against forfeiture (*On Demand Information plc v Michael Gerson (Finance) plc* (n 13 above (HL)) which is said to be indicative of a security character of the interest: *Shiloh Spinners Ltd v Harding* [1973] AC 691 (HL); Beale et al (n 3 above) [7.04].

However, it is clear that the courts do not regard these similarities as normatively significant, as will be shown immediately below. As to the similarity of function, the courts have consistently refused to treat a transaction as secured borrowing simply because the right which the creditor retains is intended to function, and in fact functions, economically as security.[19] Instead, in determining the nature of the transaction, the courts aim to find the 'substance of the transaction'[20] by reference to the nature of the obligations between the parties, as objectively manifested in the agreement,[21] rather than the purpose of the transaction itself.[22] For example, parties to a contract expressed as a sale of debts may agree that the seller of the debts is under a duty to pay the buyer any shortfall in payment arising when the buyer realises the value of the assets by collecting the debts.[23] In such cases, the courts determine the character of the transaction as a sale, based on the wording of the agreement, including the labels that the parties use, unless the agreement contains obligations which are inconsistent with a sale.[24]

As to the second common feature, the courts have implicitly denied its relevance and instead have focused on the difference in the way the two interests are created. In the case of a security interest, the person who has or will obtain title to the asset *grants* (confers) a new proprietary interest *in favour of the creditor* (the charge,[25] the equitable mortgage[26] and the pledge[27]) or conveys title to the creditor for the purposes of security (the mortgage[28]). By contrast, title-based financing interests are created *by retention* of title *by the creditor*:[29] the property right is not conferred upon the creditor but stems from

[19] *Welsh Development Agency v Export Finance Co* [1992] BCC 270 (CA), 300 (Staughton LJ).

[20] See *Re George Inglefield* [1933] Ch 1 (CA), 26–28 (Romer LJ); *Lloyds & Scottish Finance Ltd v Cyril Lord Carpets Sales Ltd* (1979) [1992] BCLC 609 (HL); *Re Curtain Dream plc* [1990] BCLC 925 (Ch); *Welsh Development Agency v Export Finance Co Ltd* (ibid); *Orion Finance Ltd v Crown Financial Management Ltd* [1996] 2 BCLC 78 (CA). See also L Gullifer, 'Quasi-security interests: functionalism and the incidents of security' in I Davies (ed), *Issues in International Commercial Law* (Aldershot, Ashgate Publishing, 2005); A Berg, 'Recharacterisation after Enron' [2003] *Journal of Business Law* 205.

[21] If a document does not manifest the real intentions of the parties, it is regarded as a sham and as such it has no effect between the parties or against third parties, although an innocent third party may be able to argue that a party to a sham document is estopped from relying on the sham transaction: *Snook v London and West Riding Investments Ltd* [1967] 2 QB 786 (CA), and see *Midland Bank plc v Wyatt* [1995] 1 FLR 696 (Ch), 699 (Young QC sitting as a deputy High Court judge).

[22] See *Helby v Matthews* [1895] AC 471 (HL) 475 (Lord Herschell LC): 'the substance of the transaction evidenced by the agreement must be looked at, and not its mere words … But the substance must, of course, be ascertained by a consideration of the rights and obligations of the parties, to be derived from a consideration of the whole of the agreement.'

[23] See *Lloyds & Scottish Finance Ltd v Cyril Lord Carpets Sales Ltd* (n 20 above) (there was a sale of debts even though the buyer had a recourse against the seller for a shortfall); *Welsh Development Agency v Export Finance Co* (n 19 above) 279–80 (Dillon LJ).

[24] See *Orion Finance Ltd v Crown Financial Management Ltd (No 1)* (n 20 above). This assumes the document is not a sham: see n 21 above.

[25] *Carreras Rothmans Ltd v Freeman Mathews Treasure Ltd* [1985] Ch 207 (Ch), 227 (Peter Gibson J); *Re Bank of Credit and Commerce International SA (in liquidation) (No 8)* [1998] AC 214 (HL), 226 (Lord Hoffmann) and *Bond Worth* [1980] Ch 228 (Ch), 250 (Slade J) (drawing a distinction between a grant of a charge and conveyance in mortgage).

[26] Beale et al (n 3 above) [6.08]–[6.11].

[27] See eg *Coggs v Bernard* (n 11 above) 112 (Holt CJ); *Donald v Suckling* (1866) LR 1 QB 585, 595 (Shee J), 606 (Mellor J), 614 (Blackburn J) referring to 'special property' conferred on the possessor.

[28] Beale et al (n 3 above) [6.05].

[29] *McEntire v Crossley Bros* [1895] AC 457 (HL), 470 (Lord Shand); *Clough Mill Ltd v Martin* (n 9 above), 123 (Oliver LJ) and 125 (Sir John Donaldson MR); *Armour v Thyssen Edelstahlwerke AG* (n 16 above) 353 (Lord Jauncey). See also *Goode and Gullifer on Legal Problems of Credit and Security*, 6th edn (London, Sweet & Mawell, 2017) [1-31].

a proprietary entitlement to the asset which the creditor already held. Even in the case of a sale and lease-back or buy-back, where the debtor first transfers title to the asset to the creditor, the proprietary interest which the creditor holds in the asset is created not by a grant by the debtor but by withholding the passage of title.

The contrast between a grant and a retention of a proprietary interest is at the heart of the distinction between security interests and title-based financing interests. This means that the courts recognise the proprietary effect of a transaction depending on whether they find that a proprietary interest was retained or granted. The way a proprietary interest arises does not necessarily define its nature. In the absence of judicial guidance, it is possible to argue that even though the title-based financing interests are different from security interests, this does not mean that they are necessarily the same as simple ownership.

III. Title-based Financing Interests: Simple Ownership or a New Type of Property Right?

It is important to know whether the proprietary nature of title-based financing interests amounts simply to ownership, or a new type of property right, in order to know whether any of the concerns that underpin the *numerus clausus* principle apply to them. There are two main arguments which support the view that title-based financing interests amount to simple ownership. One is that they are created as retained ownership, and the law gives effect to that intention by treating them like ownership. Another is that the courts have consistently distinguished them from security interests, emphasising the conceptual divide under English law between security interests and absolute interests,[30] the latter being ownership or possession in relation to personal property.[31] The merits of the first argument are discussed below. The second argument was dealt with in the section above,[32] where it was seen that the recognition of the distinction between security interests and title-based financing interests does not preclude us from saying that retained ownership is in fact a new type of property right.

A. Simple Ownership – The Intention to Retain Ownership

When A enters into an agreement with B for sale of an asset on retention-of-title terms, hire-purchase or lease, the proprietary effect that the parties aim to achieve is that A is to remain the owner subject to certain terms, eg performance of an obligation by B, while B obtains possession of the asset. For A to be able to contract on retention-of-title terms, A must already own the asset, even if for a short period and even if the asset was

[30] Beale et al (n 3 above) [4.01]; S Worthington, *Personal Property Law: Text, Cases and Materials* (Oxford, Hart Publishing, 2000) 57–58.

[31] *Goode on Commercial Law* (n 14 above) ch 2, particularly [2.20]–[2.27]. See also W Blackstone, *Commentaries on the Laws of England, vol II*, reprint edn (Chicago IL, University of Chicago Press, 1979) referring to things in possession as divided into 'an absolute and a qualified property', the latter being pledge and bailment (at 395–96).

[32] See section II.B above.

acquired from a third party specifically so that A could enter into a title-based transaction with B.[33] Moreover, A can only retain the interest that she has. For example, an absolute owner of goods cannot retain only equitable ownership because it is not the case that an absolute ownership is a composite interest comprising legal and equitable ownership.[34] For this reason, a purported retention of equitable ownership will amount to creation of a charge.[35]

Since A's intention is to retain what A already has, it can be said that by giving effect to a retention-of-title clause the law simply gives effect to that intention by recognising A's proprietary right after the transaction as the same right (ie ownership) prior to the dealing with B. The courts have made it clear that it does not matter what purpose or motive A might have in retaining the ownership. For example, the fact that A chooses to retain ownership for the purpose of securing B's obligation to pay will not of itself preclude the effectiveness of the clause.[36]

B. Title-based Financing Interests Differentiated from Ownership

The legal position of a person who reserves title appears equivalent to that of a person who holds absolute title and who has not entered into any transaction, as far as its strength against third parties is concerned.[37] After all, one could simply say that such a person retains *ownership*. The simplicity of this point betrays its importance. It is sometimes raised in the reform debate as the reason why there is no perceived need to regulate title-based interests (by, eg, requiring registration and/or re-characterising such interests as security interests); ownership is thought to be beyond regulatory concerns.

What follows is an argument that the protection afforded by a title-based interest to its holder vis-à-vis third parties is weaker than that offered by absolute title (ownership). This is so: (i) as a matter of policy, because the public aspects of private legal relations relating to things are different in the case of title-based interests as compared to absolute interests; and (ii) as a matter of principle under the current law, because there are instances where title-based interest holders receive less protection of their interest compared to owners.

[33] This is so generally with (finance) leases and hire-purchase agreements, which involve the financier purchasing an asset from the supplier.

[34] *Westdeutsche Landesbank Girozentrale v Islington London Borough Council* [1996] AC 669 (HL).

[35] *Re Bond Worth* (n 25 above).

[36] See, eg, *Welsh Development Agency v Export Finance Co* (n 19 above) 273 (Dillon LJ) (indicating that factoring of debts or invoice discounting, which are forms of outright assignment, are legitimate ways to raise finance, and it is not necessary to use a charge). An analogous point can be made about title-based financing transactions. See also *McEntire v Crossley Bros* (n 29 above), 465–66 (Lord Herschell LC) and JH Dalhuisen, 'Security and Ownership Based Funding Techniques (2)' [1998] *European Business Law Review* 118, 123. *Cf* the position in Germany in the 19th century where retention of title clauses seemed to have become common because buyers were not able to easily borrow money from lending institutions: see R Pennington, 'Retention of Title to the Sale of Goods under European Law' (1978) 27 *ICLQ* 277. In modern times in England, a person who seeks finance is free to choose sale credit (from, eg, a supplier) over loan credit (from, eg, a bank) and will make the decision based on the usual factors such as cost of credit transaction, ease of transaction. It is not clear to what extent personal or institutional biases play a role, for example whether a debtor takes sale credit as a matter of habit.

[37] Each form of title-based transaction gives rise to rights and powers, duties and liabilities between the parties. For example, a contract of sale of an asset with a retention-of-title clause gives rise to a (self-executing) duty on the seller to transfer property in the asset upon the fulfilment of the contractual condition.

(i) Policy

An absolute owner does not need to be concerned with publicising her interest to third parties, at least in the case of assets that do not have registers in which ownership would be registrable.[38] The owner need not even be particularly careful with the asset. For example, if an owner carelessly loses a gold watch, she is no less protected and third parties do not become more worthy of protection if they take the asset.[39] However, the law's response is different in the case of title-based financing interests because the owner has entrusted the possession of its object to a third party, and at the very least must be taken to have accepted the risk that the third party might deal with the asset, and that when they do, an innocent party may require protection. The entrustment of possession is not a unique feature of title-based financing interests but for current purposes it need not be; it simply shows that the *public aspects* of private legal relations relating to things are different in the case of title-based interests compared to absolute interests.

(ii) As a Matter of Principle under Current Law

The strength of a property right can be measured by considering the extent to which it empowers the right-holder to exclude various third parties from the asset. This is based on a view that the distinctiveness of property rights lies not in A's liberty to use an asset but in the duty, owed to A, that it imposes on the rest of the world.[40] For the purposes of this chapter, it is convenient to separate different categories of third parties: (i) strangers who interfere with the possession of the physical asset; (ii) disponees to whom the possessor[41] purports to sell the asset, give a security interest in the asset, or with whom she enters into a title-based arrangement; and (iii) insolvency officers (an administrator, a liquidator or a trustee in bankruptcy) of the possessor.

a. Enforceability against wrongdoers through the tort of conversion

As a general rule, when a third party interferes with a physical asset, the possessor or a person with an immediate right to possess can sue the wrongdoer for conversion to recover damages,[42] calculated by reference to the full value of the asset[43] at the time of the conversion.

[38] The obvious example is the land register.

[39] See *Farquharson Brothers & Co v King & Co* [1902] AC 325 (HL), 332 (Earl of Halsbury LC).

[40] J Penner, *The Idea of Property in Law* (Oxford, Clarendon Press, 1997) 71; TW Merrill, 'Property and the Right to Exclude' (1998) 77 *Nebraska Law Review* 730; HE Smith, 'Exclusion versus Governance: Two Strategies for Delineating Property Rights' (2002) 31 *The Journal of Legal Studies* S453; HE Smith, 'Property as The Law of Things' (2012) 125 *Harvard Law Review* 1691; S Douglas and B McFarlane, 'Defining Property Rights' in J Penner and HE Smith (eds), *Philosophical Foundations of Property Law* (Oxford, Oxford University Press, 2013) 219. The terminology in the text closely mirrors the last-mentioned work.

[41] The term 'possessor' is used here to mean the person who entered into the title-based financing arrangement, and it is assumed for simplicity that they remain in possession of the asset.

[42] Other remedies for conversion are delivery up of the asset and injunction: Torts (Interference with Goods) Act 1977, s 3.

[43] *Solloway v McLaughlin* [1938] AC 247 (PC); *BBMB Finance (Hong Kong) Ltd v ED Holdings Ltd* [1990] 1 WLR 409 (PC), 412–13 (Lord Templeman); *Malkins Nominees Ltd v Société Financière Mirelis SA* [2004] EWHC 2641 (Ch), [34] (Laddie J); *McGregor on Damages*, 20th edn (London, Sweet & Maxwell, 2017) [36.011].

It is debated whether damages for the tort of conversion (as well as other torts and breach of contract) are meant to provide a substitute for, and so to vindicate, the right that was infringed,[44] or to compensate for the actual loss suffered, which involves taking into account the rules on causation, remoteness and mitigation. The latter is the mainstream view.[45] In the context of the tort of conversion, authorities suggest that damages are awarded for the loss suffered,[46] and the consideration of causation, remoteness and mitigation is relevant.[47]

When goods are bailed, damages are not generally limited by reference to the value of the claimant's interest in the converted asset.[48] For example, a pawnbroker may recover from a third-party wrongdoer damages that amount to the full value of the converted goods, although this is subject to a duty to account to the pawnor for the surplus.[49] This would suggest that a title-based interest holder should be able to recover the full value of the asset when, eg, the possessor is permanently deprived of the asset by the third-party wrongdoer. But this is not so. Cases involving hire-purchase agreements suggest that the financier is only able to recover damages that amount to the financial value of its interest.

In *Wickham Holdings v Brooke House Motors Ltd*[50] the financier (the 'owner') sought damages for the entire value of a car, which had been let on hire-purchase and had subsequently been converted by a third party. The financier claimed damages without taking into account payments already received from the debtor. The Court of Appeal held that the financier could not recover more than the damages for its actual loss and required a deduction to be made for payments already made.[51] The rule was explained in the following terms by Fox LJ in *Chubb Cash v John Crilley*:

> The court regarded it unjust that, if the hire-purchase owner had only a limited interest in the goods (i.e., the outstanding instalments), he should recover their full value. The damage, therefore, was limited to the actual amount of the loss, that is to say the amount still outstanding under the hire-purchase agreement.[52]

[44] R Stevens, *Torts and Rights* (Oxford, Oxford University Press, 2007); R Stevens, 'Damages and the Right to Performance: A Golden Victory or Not?' in JW Neyers, R Bronaugh and SGA Pitel (eds), *Exploring Contract Law* (Oxford, Hart Publishing, 2009) 171.

[45] See eg *McGregor on Damages* (n 43 above); and R Hickey, 'Defending Property: Self-Help Remedies, The Use of Force and the Concept of a Property Right' Chapter 4 in this volume. For arguments against the substitutive damages thesis, see A Burrows, 'Damages and Rights' in D Nolan and A Robertson (eds), *Rights in Private Law* (Oxford, Hart Publishing, 2012) 275.

[46] *VFS Financial Services (UK) Ltd v Euro Auctions (UK) Ltd* [2007] EWHC 1492 (QB), [94] and [102] (Richard Seymour QC).

[47] *Kuwait Airways Corporation v Iraqi Airways Co (Nos 4 and 5)* [2002] UKHL 19, [2002] 2 AC 883. For the relevance of mitigation, see *Uzinterimpex JSC v Standard Bank Ltd* [2008] EWCA Civ 819, [2008] 2 Lloyds Rep 453, 469–70 (Moore-Bick LJ); regarding remoteness, see *Kuwait Airways Corporation v Iraqi Airways Co (Nos 4 and 5).* See also generally S Green and J Randall, *The Tort of Conversion* (Oxford, Hart Publishing, 2009) 191–201.

[48] *The Winkfield* [1902] P 42 (CA); Green and Randall (n 47 above) 172.

[49] *Swire v Leach* (1865) 18 CB (NS) 479, 492, 141 ER 531, 536 (Erle CJ). Between the bailor and bailee the party who recovers must account to the other: *The Winkfield* (ibid) 60–61 (Collins MR) (duty to account by the recovering bailee), *O'Sullivan v Williams* [1992] 3 All ER 385 (CA) (duty to account by the bailor).

[50] *Wickham Holdings Ltd v Brooke House Motors Ltd* [1967] 1 WLR 295 (CA). See also *Belvoir Finance Co Ltd v Stapleton* [1971] 1 QB 210 (CA) (note that the hire-purchase contracts in this case were illegal, but since the contracts were fully executed the claimant financier obtained property in the lorry and could therefore sue in conversion). *Wickham* was followed in *VFS Financial Services (UK) Ltd v Euro Auctions (UK) Ltd* (n 46 above), especially [102], [104] (Richard Seymour QC).

[51] *Wickham Holdings* (n 50 above) 299–300: Lord Denning MR said that the plaintiff finance company was 'only entitled to what it had lost by the wrongful act of the defendants'.

[52] *Chubb Cash Ltd v John Crilley & Son* [1983] 1 WLR 599 (CA), 601.

In hire-purchase cases the actual loss recoverable by the financier is measured by reference to the amount that the financier has yet to be paid under the agreement. This is so even though the hire-purchase agreement does not confer on the financier any duty to pass property in the asset at the end of the hiring period to the hirer. Analogous reasoning can apply to the interest of the seller who retained ownership and a lessor in the context of asset finance.

One explanation of the difference between the pledge cases and hire-purchase cases is that a pledgee has a duty to account to the pledgor for any surplus (over the amount of the discharged secured obligation) inherent in the nature of the pledge, while in hire-purchase agreements there is nothing to oblige the title-based interest holder to account to the hirer for the rentals paid.[53]

A second explanation, suggested here, starts from the premise that title-based interests differ from security interests.[54] While security interests are dependent on the extent to which a secured obligation remains unperformed,[55] title-based interests are not. Thus, a limitation of the title-based interest became necessary to prevent the title-based holder from benefiting unduly from its legally advantageous position and to preclude opportunistic behaviour. The limited interest referred to in *Chubb* must mean a limited financial interest, determined by reference to the capital value of the retained asset in accordance with the terms of the agreement. This second explanation is meant to complement, rather than contradict, the explanation referring to the duty to account.

On either view, it would seem reasonably clear that the measure of damages for conversion is more generous in the case of absolute interests than it is in the case of title-based financing interests.

b. Enforceability against disponees – *nemo dat* and its exceptions

A title-based financing interest held by A in goods possessed by B binds a third party disponee (C) because, unless A consents, B cannot pass to, or create in favour of, C a greater interest than B has (*nemo dat*). There are some statutory exceptions to this derivative title rule. However, as the discussion that follows shows,[56] their scope of application is rather narrow, and displays an idiosyncratic nature, commensurate with their development as responses to specific concerns to protect certain innocent buyers. They all require that B should be in possession of the goods with A's consent.[57] While some exceptions initially developed to protect innocent buyers when goods were entrusted by an absolute owner to a professional seller for onward resale,[58] nowadays the circumstances in which an owner

[53] *McGregor on Damages* (n 43 above) [38-065], noting that this point was made in an analogous case of a buyer, who has not paid the price for the goods, seeking to recover damages from the seller for reselling the goods to third party: in *Chinery v Viall* (1860) 5 H & N 288, 157 ER 1192 the buyer was held able to recover the full value of the goods less the agreed price.

[54] See section II.B above.

[55] In Civilian and mixed jurisdictions, the dependence on the secured obligation is known as accessoriness (or accessority) of security rights.

[56] What follows is an abbreviated discussion of exceptions to *nemo dat* found in Raczynska (n 9 above) [2.102]–[2.111].

[57] A Tettenborn, 'Transfer of Chattels by Non-owners: Still and Open Question' (2018) 77 *CLJ* 151 calls for a recognition of a background rule of entrustment in the context of exceptions to *nemo dat*.

[58] Factors Act 1889, ss 8 and 9.

entrusts goods to another are probably more likely to occur instead under a title-based arrangement.

A seller supplying goods under a contract of sale with a retention-of-title clause may lose its title if C successfully raises a defence based on section 25 of the Sale of Goods Act 1979 (section 9 of the Factors Act 1889). For the defence to be available, a number of factors must be met. C must show that B was a 'buyer', ie a person who agreed to buy goods, and that she was in possession of the goods, with A's consent, at the time of disposition to C. B must have been in possession of the goods under the contract of sale with the retention-of-title clause, not under another agreement.[59] Where these requirements are fulfilled, the disposition to C has 'the same effect as if the person making delivery or transfer were a mercantile agent in possession of the goods or documents of title with the consent of the owner'. These words are not easy to understand but were eventually interpreted by the Court of Appeal in *Newtons of Wembley Ltd v Williams*[60] as impliedly importing the requirements of section 2 of the Factors Act 1889. Thus, C can only raise the defence if the disposition was made in a manner in which it would have been made had the buyer been disposing in the ordinary course of business of a mercantile agent.[61] This limitation of section 25 to buyers in the ordinary course of business was intended to protect A's ownership,[62] but its denial of protection to buyers not buying in the ordinary course of business is unfortunate and unjustified on any rational policy grounds.[63]

Where goods are supplied under a hire-purchase agreement, B's position somewhat resembles that of a buyer under a contract of sale with a retention-of-title clause. However, section 25 of the Sale of Goods Act 1979 does not apply, since B does not undertake an obligation to buy but merely has an option to purchase. Thus, she is not a person who 'bought or agreed to buy' for the purposes of the section.[64] This caused significant problems in practice as innocent buyers were exposed to the risk of acquiring goods subject to ownership of another, without knowing and without having an opportunity to inspect the seller's title. Eventually, a new statutory defence under Part III of the Hire Purchase Act 1964, was introduced. It is limited to purchasers who are innocent private purchasers of a motor vehicle. B must be in possession of the vehicle under the hire-purchase agreement at the time the vehicle is disposed of to C, so the hire-purchase agreement must be concluded before the vehicle is disposed of to C.[65] It is not entirely clear what constitutes 'disposition' in section 27 of the 1964 Act but it seems to have been interpreted restrictively, as synonymous with 'sale'. For example, a transaction whereby B passed property

[59] The practical difficulty of meeting the requirements of s 25 of the 1979 Act is illustrated by, eg, *Fadallah v Pollak* [2013] EWHC 3159 (QB), [55] (the defence failed, as the buyer acquired possession prior to the agreement to buy).

[60] *Newtons of Wembley Ltd v Williams* [1965] 1 QB 560.

[61] Contrast the approach in Australia, *Langmead v Thyer Rubber Co Ltd* [1947] SASR 29, 39 (Reed J) and New Zealand, *Jeffcot v Andrew Motors Ltd* [1960] NZLR 721.

[62] *Newtons of Wembley Ltd v Williams* (n 60 above) 564 (Sellers LJ).

[63] R Goode, 'Sale by Seller with Voidable Title' (1965) 115 *Law Journal Newspaper* 4. See also *Forsyth International (UK) Ltd v Silver Shipping Co Ltd (The Saetta)* [1994] 1 WLR 1334 (QB), 1351 (favouring the contrary view to that in *Newtons of Wembley* but being bound by it).

[64] *Helby v Matthews* [1895] 2 QB 537; *Belsize Motor Supply Co v Cox* [1914] 1 KB 244; *Modern Light Cars Ltd v Seals* [1934] 1 KB 32, 43 (Roche J); *United Dominions Trust (Commercial) Ltd v Parkway Motors Ltd* [1955] 1 WLR 719 (QB).

[65] *Kulkarni v Manor Credit (Davenham) Ltd* [2010] EWCA Civ 69, [2012] 2 Lloyd's Rep 431.

in a vehicle to C in return for C's forbearance from suing B for part of a debt B owed to C does not amount to a disposition on the basis that it would also not be a sale,[66] and the court indicated there were no reasons to expand this protection.[67]

In some circumstances, C might look to rely on the 'seller in possession' defence under section 24 of the Sale of Goods Act 1979 (section 8 of the Factors Act 1889). The defence might arise where B first sells the goods to A, who lets them back to B on a hire-purchase agreement. Unlike section 27 of the Hire Purchase Act 1964, it is not restricted to sales by B to C, and C need not be a 'private purchaser'. The likely challenge for C with section 24 is to show that B is a seller who 'continues in possession'. Contrary to previous thinking,[68] it is not necessary that the seller must continue in possession as a seller,[69] which suggests that, upon taking the possession of the goods under a hire-purchase agreement and becoming a bailee, B constitutes a 'seller in possession' for the purposes of section 24.

A disposition of the leased goods by a lessee cannot, generally, deprive the lessor of its title to the goods. The 'seller in possession' defence under section 24 of the Sale of Goods Act 1979 might, however, be raised where the lessor-to-be (A) first buys the goods from the lessee-to-be (B) and then A leases them back to B. Such lease-back transactions are not uncommon if B seeks to use the asset to raise finance. If B then sells the goods to a third party (C), the third party might raise a 'seller in possession' defence, as discussed above in the context of hire-purchase agreements, so long as there is no break in B's possession between the sale from B to A and the second sale from B to C.[70]

Apart from the complexity of the picture, the obvious conclusion is that the current law gives the holder of a title-based financing interest less protection against third parties compared to an absolute owner. An owner who retained title in a title-based financing transaction will, however, be protected as strongly as an absolute owner in cases where the innocent third party is a secured creditor. This is a sensible rule insofar as it gives the title-based interest holder a strong position when the debtor has not paid much towards the capital value of the asset. However, once much of the capital value of the asset has been paid for by the debtor, the question arises whether the debtor should be able to deal with the asset unencumbered (eg, by granting security interests in order to obtain further finance against the asset), at least to the extent that the asset has been paid for. There is ultimately a policy choice as to whether financing should be encouraged in this way, but if it should, it is worth considering how the law might need to adjust.

[66] For authorities that exchange of property in return for a forbearance of debt (where no money is paid at all) is not a sale, see eg *Simpson v Connolly* [1953] 1 WLR 911 (QB), 915 (Finnemore J) (in relation to land but stating that the same principles are relevant as in the case of sale of chattels); *Robshaw Bros Ltd v Mayer* [1957] Ch 125 (Ch), 129 (Upjohn J).

[67] *VFS Financial Services Ltd v JF Plant Tyres Ltd* (n 46 above) [18]–[19] (Judge Mackie QC); *Royscott Trust v Burno Daken Ltd* (QB, 9 July 1993) (Astill J) cited in relevant part in *VFS Financial* at [10]. See also *Kulkarni v Manor Credit (Davenham) Ltd* (n 65 above) [15]–[16].

[68] *Staffs Motor Guarantee Ltd v British Wagon Co Ltd* [1934] 2 KB 305; *Eastern Distributors Ltd v Goldring* [1957] 2 QB 600.

[69] *Pacific Motor Auctions Pty Ltd v Motor Credits (Hire Finance) Ltd* [1965] AC 867 (PC), followed by the Court of Appeal in England: *Worcester Works Finance Ltd v Cooden Engineering Co Ltd* [1972] 1 QB 210 (CA), 217 (Lord Denning MR).

[70] *Pacific Motor Auctions Pty Ltd v Motor Credits (Hire Finance) Ltd* (n 69 above). See also *Mitchell v Jones* (1905) 24 NZLR 932.

c. Enforceability against insolvency officers

As against the insolvency officers of the possessor, title-based interests are enforceable in the same way as absolute ownership: anyone holding such interests may take the asset outside insolvency of the possessor.[71] To that extent, as a matter of current law they are as robust as absolute interests.

However, there are cases where the owner cannot simply take what is his. In *Re Piggin*[72] Carey Evans J held that a clause in a hire-purchase agreement which gave the owner a right to terminate the agreement if the hirer or other counterparty were to go into insolvency was not enforceable. The owner had to accept what was owing to it under the agreement, and accept that the trustee in bankruptcy was able to exercise the option to purchase, which meant that the owner lost its ownership under terms other than those agreed. There were two reasons given for this decision. One was that the trustee in bankruptcy should take on the rights and powers of the hirer for the benefit of the hirer's creditors, since the hirer acquired them for valuable consideration. The second reason was based on the equitable jurisdiction against forfeiture, which prevented the hirer from forfeiting the benefit of the hire-purchase agreement. Whilst the reasons for the decision have been doubted,[73] the decision has not been overruled and the outcome has its proponents.[74] This suggests that it is at the very least arguable that in some circumstances an owner of an asset under a hire-purchase agreement may lose its ownership whilst an absolute owner would not.

The above discussion has shown that, under the current law, whilst title-based interests are protected in broadly the same way as absolute ownership, there are nonetheless circumstances where title-based interests will not be protected as strongly against third parties as absolute ownership. This is consistent with a policy recognising that the public aspects of private legal relations relating to things are different in the case of title-based interests compared to absolute interests.

IV. The Ways Forward?

In many jurisdictions across the world title-based financing interests and security interests are treated in the same way in the sense that they are governed by a uniform set of rules relating to priority conflicts, title transfers, opposability against execution creditors, and the effect of the interest in insolvency. They are treated in the same way because they perform the same

[71] For an order of claims in liquidation, bankruptcy or administration, see *Re Nortel Companies; Bloom v Pensions Regulator* [2013] UKSC 52, [2014] AC 209, [39]–[40] (Lord Neuberger); *Re Lehman Brothers International (Europe) (In Administration)* [2015] EWCA Civ 485, [2015] BCC 431. The transactions, which give rise to the claims made are subject to the claw-back rules in insolvency law: see Insolvency Act 1986, ss 238, 339 (transactions at an undervalue) and ss 239, 340 (preferences), both sets of provisions read in conjunction with ss 240, 341 of the 1986 Act, and ss 423–425 of the 1986 Act (defrauding creditors).

[72] *Re Piggin* (1962) 112 LJ 424.

[73] F Oditah and A Zacaroli, 'Chattel Leases and Insolvency' [1997] *Company Financial and Insolvency Law Review* 29, favouring the decision in *Roe on the demise of Hunter v Galliers* (1787) 2 Term Rep 133, 100 ER 72 in which a clause conferring on the lessor of land a right of re-entry was held valid. The decision in *Galliers* focused on why the clause was not contrary to principle or policy and did not purport to lay down a broader rule that such clauses should always be valid in the lessee's insolvency.

[74] This is based on the view that the hirer's option is a valuable asset, making the hirer's interest more than contractual: F Oditah, 'Assets and the Treatment of Claims in Insolvency' (1992) 108 *LQR* 459, 483–85.

function; the location of title is not decisive.[75] Thus, a supplier of goods purporting to retain title does not retain title to an asset; instead, the law recognises the parties' intention to be that the supplier (the creditor) is to hold an interest in property for the purposes of security while the buyer or hirer of the goods (the debtor) obtains possession of the asset.[76] That the supplier's interest is a security interest is made explicit in the Uniform Commercial Code (UCC)[77] and is referred to as re-characterisation of the transaction.[78]

The functional approach was first adopted in Article 9 UCC, and then in various Personal Property Security Acts (PPSA's).[79] In England and Wales, a wholesale reform along those lines was proposed by the Law Commission in 2004[80] but the final recommendations, which, owing to certain objections and time constraints, were more limited,[81] were not enacted in the Companies Act 2006. The need for and shape of further reform of the English law of secured transactions continue to be debated.[82]

There are two key arguments in favour of treating title-based financing interests in the same way as security interests.[83] The first is that the forms of transactions are similar and should be treated alike. The premise is that a multiplicity of proprietary interests, where each interest is governed by its own different rules, makes the law unduly complex. Simplification of the rules based on function is a means to achieve this. Against this, it could be said that characterisation of transactions based on their economic function goes against the traditional and current approach of English law, as set out above.[84] Conceptually, the functional approach is underpinned by a legal realist idea, propounded by the Chief Reporter for the UCC, Karl Llewellyn, that abstract concepts (such as title) cannot serve as a basis for resolving commercial disputes[85] because, as another legal realist put it, they are in fact masking policy preferences 'in the cloak of legal logic' and ought to be made explicit.[86] On the continent, including in the UK, legal realism has much less traction.

[75] Title has even more diminished role in the context of sale of goods under Article 2 UCC, see generally WL Tabac, 'The Unbearable Lightness of Title Under the Uniform Commercial Code' (1991) 50 *Maryland Law Review* 408; H Kripke, 'The Principles Underlying the Drafting of the Uniform Commercial Code' [1962] *University of Illinois Law Forum* 321, 328.

[76] See UCC § 9-109(a)(1): 'any transaction, regardless of its form, that creates a security interest in personal property or fixtures by contract'. See also, eg, Saskatchewan Personal Property Security Act 1993, s 3(1)(a); New Zealand Personal Property Securities Act 1999, s 17(1)(a) and the Australian Personal Property Security Act 2009, s 12(1).

[77] See UCC § 1-201(35): 'The retention or reservation of title by a seller of goods notwithstanding shipment or delivery to the buyer … is limited in effect to a reservation of a "security interest"'.

[78] M Bridge, 'Secured Credit Legislation: Functionalism or Transactional Co-Existence' in SV Bazinas and O Akseli (eds), *International and Comparative Secured Transactions Law Essays in Honour of Roderick A Macdonald* (Oxford, Hart Publishing, 2017) 1, 18.

[79] Personal Property Security Acts in all Canadian Provinces except Québec, which did not follow Article 9 UCC when promulgating its new Civil Code; New Zealand Personal Property Securities Act 1999; Australian Personal Property Securities Act 2009 (Cth); also in other jurisdictions, eg Malawi.

[80] Law Commission, *Company Security Interests: A Consultative Report* (Law Com CP 176, 2004); Law Commission, *Registration of Security Interests: Company Charges and Property other than Land* (Law Com CP 164, 2002).

[81] Law Commission, *Company Security Interests: Final Report* (Law Com No 296, 2005).

[82] See the work of the Secured Transactions Law Reform Project (n 1 above) and the City of London Law Society Financial Law Committee (n 2 above). See also L Gullifer and O Akseli, *Secured Transactions Law Reform. Principles, Policies and Practice* (Oxford, Hart Publishing, 2016) particularly ch 12 therein (L Gullifer and M Raczynska, 'The English Law of Personal Property Security: Under-reformed?').

[83] See Gullifer (n 20 above); Attorney-General's Department, *Review of Personal Property Security Act 2009: Final Report* (2015) [4.1]–[4.3] (review of the PPSA in Australia).

[84] See section II.B above.

[85] See KN Llewellyn, 'Through Title to Contract and a Bit Beyond' (1938) 15 *New York University Law Quarterly Review* 159.

[86] F Cohen, 'Transcendental Nonsense and the Functional Approach' (1935) 35 *Columbia Law Review* 809.

Concepts are important in achieving justice in like cases because of their invariance in response to context.[87] They also help us keep track of the significance of legal changes in legal doctrines.[88] Additionally, as Gullifer noted, it is no more logically necessary to distinguish between title-based financing interests and absolute ownership than it is to distinguish between security interests and title-based financing interests.[89] The choice must be based on policy.[90]

As argued earlier, the question is whether title-based financing interests should protect a public goal. If title-based financing is to be encouraged as, eg, an alternative to loan finance, whilst protecting an efficient use of resources, it would be necessary to recognise that the debtor (buyer, hirer, lessee) acquires, to the extent that the price or rent for the asset has been paid, a sufficient interest in the asset which they can use to, eg, raise further capital, or which can be used to the satisfaction of execution creditors. It is unlikely that financiers would perceive this as a negative development if, as a result, the demand for such form of finance were to increase (and this is likely). A drastically different way to try to increase the proliferation of title-based finance interests would be to strengthen their proprietary protection, eg, by giving full damages in the case of conversion. This option, however, might be perceived as less attractive by those seeking title-based finance, as their own interest would be less protected in case of an interference by a third party with the asset.

The second argument in favour of treating title-based finance interests and security interests similarly is that both forms of transaction share a common need for publicity. This argument used to be driven primarily by the desire to do away with the impression of false wealth posed by all non-possessory interests.[91] Now, it is better seen as driven by the desire to lower the costs of due diligence, since a third party seeking to deal with the debtor would only need to check an (online) register in the first instance. The argument supports registration of both forms of transactions, but it does not necessarily support the view that both security interests and title-based financing interests should be treated in the same way for all other purposes.[92] In addition, it is necessary to consider whether lack of registration should necessarily invalidate the interest on the possessor's insolvency.[93] Hire-purchase agreements and finance leases are already registrable in privately-operated

[87] For a discussion of the importance in property law of standards with a relatively high degree of invariance to context, see HE Smith, 'Emergent Property' in Penner and Smith (n 40 above) 320.

[88] J Waldron, 'Transcendental Nonsense and the System in the Law' (2000) 100 *Columbia Law Review* 16.

[89] Gullifer (n 20 above).

[90] See section III.B(i) above.

[91] D Baird and T Jackson, 'Possession and Ownership: An Examination of the Scope of Article 9' (1983) 35 *Stanford Law Review* 175; R Goode, 'The Modernisation of Personal Property Security Law' (1984) 100 *MLR* 234. The premise of false wealth was critiqued because both security interests and title-based interests are so common that possession no longer indicates ownership and creditors are not misled: C Mooney, 'The Mystery and Myth of 'Ostensible Ownership' and Article 9 Filing: a Critique of Proposals to Extend Filing Requirements to Leases' (1988) 39 *Alabama Law Review* 683, 739–40.

[92] It should be added that contracts of sale with retention-of-title clauses in the context of inventory, that is where goods supplied are eg on-sold, consumed or used in the process of manufacture give rise to separate considerations than asset finance, in particular they do not appear to give rise to the same concern about publicity as asset finance. See further the work of the Secured Transactions Law Reform Project, *Case for Reform* (April 2017) (n 1 above).

[93] As is the position in New Zealand, although there the lack of invalidation on insolvency applies across all interests, including security interests. It is said to be underpinned by the policy against 'false wealth' or 'secret liens', premised on the idea that prospective creditors make lending decisions on the basis of the appearance of wealth and on the fact that once the debtor is insolvent, no prospective creditor is prejudiced by the false wealth, so there is no need to penalise an unregistered interest. This position fails to take into account execution creditors. See D Dugdale, 'The Proposed PPSA' [1998] *New Zealand Law Journal* 383.

registers (such as Experian, HPI Check), which could support public registration. However, such a reform would need to introduce some added value, eg, by enabling third parties to rely on a register for the purposes of proving detrimental reliance, which is currently not possible.[94]

V. Conclusion

One of the recurring tensions in property law is between contract freedom and private volition on one hand and social control on the other.[95] To address this conflict, the law has adopted a simple principle, namely that it is generally not the case that a contract between A and B can impose a new duty or liability on a third party. This principle is said to underpin the rationality of the *numerus clausus* principle.[96] The principle stipulates that there exists a fixed list of property rights and unless the content of a right already matches one on the list, it cannot be regarded as having a proprietary status. The principle is said to exist in English law,[97] although it is not without sceptics.[98] Alongside various efficiency justifications,[99] there are also those that have focused on explaining the internal content of the standard forms of property right.[100]

Of particular interest is a view, propounded by Davidson, that having a fixed list of property rights plays a regulatory role, as property law is used as a means of defining, controlling and regulating the public aspects of private legal relations with respect to things.[101] There are two interesting aspects of this view that lead to valuable conclusions when dealing with title-based financing interests. One is that although standardisation is a stable, persistent feature of property law,[102] the list of forms and their substance have always been dynamic, representing inevitable trade-offs between the choices that a holder of a property interest might make with respect to that property, and the effects those

[94] *Moorgate Mercantile Co Ltd v Twitchings* [1976] QB 225.

[95] See eg R Epstein, 'Notice and Freedom of Contract in the Law of Servitudes' (1981–82) 55 *Southern California Law Review* 1353.

[96] B McFarlane, 'The *Numerus Clausus* Principle and Covenants Relating to Land' in S Bright (ed), *Modern Studies in Property Law*, vol 6 (Oxford, Hart Publishing, 2011) 311, 315.

[97] W Swadling, 'Property' in A Burrows (ed), *English Private Law*, 2nd edn (Oxford, Oxford University Press, 2007) [4.09] and [4.129]. For an illustration of this aspect of *numerus clausus* in relation to land, see *Keppel v Bailey* (1834) 2 My & K 517, 536, 39 ER 1042, 1049 (Lord Brougham LC). See generally B Akkermans, *The Principle of Numerus Clausus in European Property Law* (PhD thesis, Maastricht University 2008) 473; NM Davidson, 'Standardization and Pluralism in Property Law' (2008) 61 *Vanderbilt Law Review* 1597, 1605.

[98] B Rudden, 'Economic Theory v Property Law: The Numerus Clausus Problem' in J Eekelaar and J Bell (eds), *Oxford Essays in Jurisprudence: Third Series* (Oxford, Clarendon Press, 1987) 239.

[99] TW Merrill and HE Smith, 'Optimal Standardisation in the Law of Property: the Numerus Clausus Principle' (2000) 110 *Yale Law Journal* 1; H Hansmann and R Kraakman, 'Property, Contract, and Verification: the Numerus Clausus Problem and the Divisibility of Rights' (2002) 31 *Journal of Legal Studies* S373; Davidson (n 97 above) 1597; McFarlane (n 96 above) 311, 315.

[100] See, eg, H Dagan, 'The Craft of Property' (2003) 91 *California Law Review* 1517, 1558 and 1562 (arguing, broadly, that the patterns of social relationships map onto the property categories); D Lewinsohn-Zamir, 'The Objectivity of Well-Being and the Objectives of Property Law' (2003) 78 *New York University Law Review* 1669.

[101] Davidson (n 97 above) 1601. This is based on Bentham's approach to property as 'entirely the work of law': J Bentham, *The Theory of Legislation*, 2nd edn, R Hildreth (tr) (London, Trübner, 1871) 111.

[102] See HE Smith, 'The Persistence of System in Property Law' (2015) 163 *University of Pennsylvania Law Review* 2055.

choices have on others.[103] This means that one should keep an open mind to change. Just because title-based financing interests emerged from the exercise of the owner's freedom to withhold passing of property under a contract, this does not mean that the title which the owner holds is the same as absolute ownership. Nor does it mean that it ought necessarily be conflated with another category of property right. But it is an encouragement to consider the trade-off of choices which the holder makes with the effects of those choices on others. This leads to the second point, which is that one should consider the social aspect of title-based financing interests and consider the public goals which a particular type of property right should protect.[104] If the idea is that title-based financing interests should be just an incidental exercise of the owner's freedom, nothing needs to be done. However, if these interests are thought to correspond to an existing or new public goal or social priority (eg, financing the acquisition of assets other than through banks), there may well be a need for considering a new category or subsumption of title-based finance interest under an existing category of property right other than ownership.

This chapter sought to show that framing the balance between preserving parties' bargains and the effects those have on third parties through consecration of ownership as the basis of title-based financing arrangement is unsatisfactory. From the perspective of property law, title-based financing interests should be recognised as a new form of property right, created by the financier (or the seller) when retaining ownership. Whether this justifies a statutory reform of registration and streamlining of the rules applicable to various interests is a separate matter, which requires the resolution of practical concerns.

[103] See for example the discussion in S Pascoe, 'Re-evaluating Recreational Easements – New Norms for the Twenty-First Century?' Chapter 10 in this volume.

[104] Davidson (n 97 above) 1648, 1649.

PART III

Land: Relationships and Regulation

9

Remedies for Breaches of Rights to Light: Averting a Tragedy of the Anticommons

CRAIG ROTHERHAM

I. Introduction

An occupier who enjoys light through a window in England, Wales or Northern Ireland for 20 years acquires an easement, the breach of which will amount to a nuisance.[1] While other common law jurisdictions inherited the English law on 'ancient lights', such easements have largely been eliminated by legislatures in Commonwealth jurisdictions[2] and rejected State by State by courts in the USA.[3] This chapter explores the concerns generated by such rights and asks whether, in view of these, they should be enforced. It considers, in particular, whether right holders should always, or almost always, be entitled to an injunction or whether they might, instead, often be limited to monetary relief. An examination of reported right to light cases demonstrates the effect that the judicial approach to injunctions has on levels of litigation. A historical perspective emphasises that the courts have, at times, been sensitive to the special difficulties to which rights of light give rise and have been prepared to treat these entitlements as *sui generis*. An approach that, in contrast, insists that those enjoying an easement of light are entitled to an injunction as a matter of course is likely to encourage protracted disputes that will pose a significant obstacle to urban development.[4]

[1] While claimants generally rely on s 3 of the Prescription Act 1832, oddly, that legislation did not abrogate the common law principles of prescription, and claimants occasionally rely on the doctrine of 'lost modern grant' in circumstances in which the Act would not confer protection. Any easement arising under the Act is inchoate until a suit is brought to enforce the right (s 4).

[2] The fate of easements of light in Australia and New Zealand is detailed in Law Commission, *Rights to Light* (Law Com CP No 210, 2013). See also F Burns, 'The Future of Prescriptive Easements' (2007) 31 *Melbourne University Law Review* 3. These rights still exist in the sparsely populated Canadian Provinces of New Foundland and Prince Edward Island, while in Nova Scotia such easements may arise on land not found in cities, or in unincorporated towns. Easements of light have been eliminated in all the other Provinces: see M Bowden, 'Protecting Solar Access in Canada' (1985) 9 *Dalhousie Law Journal* 261, 263–64. Another exception is the Republic of Ireland, which inherited both the common law on rights of light and the Prescription Act 1832 but now regulates prescriptive rights pursuant to the Land and Conveyancing Law Reform Act 2009. Curiously, however, rights of light have given rise to little litigation in that jurisdiction.

[3] There appears to be no extant authority recognising an easement of light in any American State. See *Fontainebleau Hotel Corp v Forty-Five Twenty-Five Inc* 114 So 2d 357, 359 (Fla App, 3d Dist 1959).

[4] In practice the effect of rights of light has been limited by local authorities' use of powers to enable developers to overcome private rights (see below text accompanying nn 134–135).

II. Concerns about Easements of Light

A. The Anomalous Nature of Negative Prescriptive Easements

It appears that rights of light were initially understood to be natural rights appurtenant to the claimant's tenement.[5] Subsequently, however, these entitlements came to be conceptualised as a type of servitude arising by prescription through long use.

Prescription generally results in the acquisition of a positive easement, giving the owner of the dominant tenement a right to make some limited use of the servient tenement. Rights of light, in contrast, amount to negative easements, limiting the owners of the servient tenement in their use of their property. Positive prescriptive easements are generally explained on the basis that it is not in the interest of public order to permit land owners to enforce their rights following a long-standing failure to respond to open and continuous breaches. In this vein, Fry J observed:

> [I]t is plain good sense to hold that a man who can stop the asserted right, or a continued user, and does not do so for a long time, may be told that he has lost his right by his delay and his negligence, and every presumption should therefore be made to quiet a possession thus acquired and enjoyed by the tacit consent of the sufferer.[6]

English accounts from the thirteenth century onwards have emphasised the importance of an owner's acquiescence to conduct that is adverse to his rights.[7] There was, as a result, a tendency to deny the suggestion that prescriptive rights might be acquired where the activity of the party claiming an easement was perfectly legal during the period in question.[8] On occasion, the courts have suggested that the owner of the servient tenement burdened by a right of light could be said to have acquiesced by having failed to take steps to obstruct the light in question.[9] The common view, however, is that rights of light are anomalous because, as Willes J in *Webb v Bird* remarked:

> In general a man cannot establish a right by lapse of time and acquiescence against his neighbour, unless he shews that the party against whom the right is acquired might have brought an action or done some act to put a stop to the claim without an unreasonable waste of labour and expense.[10]

For this reason, negative prescriptive easements have generally been treated with suspicion, and the courts have suggested that this class of rights is unlikely to be extended.[11]

Of course, just because this class of easements cannot be explained by reference to notions of acquiescence does not mean that it is indefensible. In *Dalton v Henry Angus & Co*,

[5] Janet Loengard provides perhaps the fullest account of the historical development of this area of law in J Loengard, 'Common Law and Custom: Windows, Light and Privacy in Late Medieval England' in S Jenks, J Rose and C Whittick (eds), *Laws, Lawyers and Texts: Studies in Medieval Legal History in Honour of Paul Brand* (Leiden, Brill, 2012) 279.

[6] *Dalton v Henry Angus & Co* (1881) 6 App Cas 740 (HL), 774 (advising HL).

[7] See generally J Getzler, 'Roman and English Prescription for Incorporeal Property' in J Getzler (ed), *Rationalizing Property, Equity and Trusts* (Oxford, Oxford University Press, 2003) 281.

[8] *Sturges v Bridgman* (1879) LR 11 Ch D 852, 863 (Thesiger LJ).

[9] *Cross v Lewis* (1824) 2 B & C 686, 689, 107 ER 538 (Bayley J).

[10] *Webb v Bird* (1861) 10 CB (NS) 268, 285, 142 ER 455.

[11] *Hunter v Canary Wharf* [1997] AC 655 (HL), 726 (Lord Hope).

Blackburn J effectively dismissed as doctrinaire the view of his fellow judges that a prescriptive easement in the form of a right to support for a building should be rejected because it could not be explained in these terms.[12] On the other hand, the burden of justifying such easements is inevitably a heavy one. If the use of land that gives rise to the easement does not involve an interference with the rights of the owner of the servient tenement, not only is it implausible to argue that there is acquiescence, but it is difficult to see that the practice can be supported on the grounds of 'quieting title'. Instead, the creation of an interest out of a use that was not adverse to anyone's rights is likely to sow fresh discord. Some other justification is needed to explain negative easements that arise by prescription.

B. Justifying Prescriptive Easements: Four Considerations

(i) The Extent of the Benefit and Burdens Resulting from an Easement

An obvious starting point for evaluating the appropriateness of particular classes of prescriptive easements is that there is no reason why we should develop proprietary rights arising by operation of law if the benefits they conferred did not generally exceed the burdens they imposed. The general rule that, for a prescriptive easement to arise, the use in question should amount to a breach of the owner of the servient tenement's rights, serves a useful function in providing a strong indication that the use does not impose a significant burden. It is reasonable to assume that, if it were burdensome, the owner of the servient tenement would have acted to enforce his rights.[13] Equally, the fact that the occupier of the dominant tenement used the servient tenement in a certain way continuously for an extended period is likely to indicate that the benefit derived from that use was substantial.

In the absence of toleration of continuous and apparent adverse use, there can be no assumption that the long enjoyment of light indicates that the benefit such an easement confers normally exceeds the burden it imposes. It does not follow from this that negative easements should never be recognised; rather, their utility has to be established by some fact other than long enjoyment. It might be accepted that a class of negative easements is socially beneficial. However, if this were so, there is no reason to provide that they arise by prescription, as the long enjoyment of the benefit in question adds nothing to the argument for protecting it. Thus, in the case of a right of lateral support for a building – another form of negative prescriptive easement – the benefit in question appears to be compelling and the burden relatively modest.[14] Indeed, as Lord Penzance suggested in *Dalton v Henry Angus & Co*, the real objection to the legal treatment of easements of support is that there is no good reason why they should arise by prescription following long enjoyment rather than being recognised as rights that come into being immediately.[15]

[12] *Dalton v Henry Angus & Co* (n 6 above) 817.

[13] As Lord Blackburn observed 'presumably such rights if not exercised are not of great value': *Dalton v Henry Angus & Co* (n 6 above).

[14] A factor stressed by a number of their Lordships in *Dalton* (ibid) 804 (Lord Penzance) and 827 (Lord Blackburn).

[15] ibid 804.

Easements of light place a burden on the servient tenement which generally outweighs the benefit conferred on the dominant tenement. Thus, typically the 'book value' of the light lost by the owner of the dominant tenement is a fraction of the value gained by the owner of the servient tenement as a result of developing his property in breach of the easement.[16]

It is probable that the notion that easements of light were socially beneficial was plausible when these rights were first recognised. Demographic pressures were less acute and a sensible accommodation was afforded whereby the common law respected a custom of the City of London that permitted owners within that area to build without restriction on 'ancient foundations'.[17] There was little in the way of building regulations, let alone the comprehensive planning system that was established in the middle of last century.[18] Natural light was particularly highly prized because alternative sources of illumination were relatively expensive and unpleasant.[19] In the Wisconsin Supreme Court in *Prah v Maretti*, Abrahamson J explained the extinction of rights to light in American law thus: 'Since artificial light could be used for illumination, loss of sunlight was at most a personal annoyance, which was given little, if any weight by society.'[20]

(ii) The Identifiability of these Interests

The courts have emphasised that we should be wary of recognising interests if their existence would not be readily apparent to interested parties.[21] There are several reasons for concern. For one thing, we need to consider the position of owners of servient tenements. On the one hand, prescriptive rights of light generally arise without owners being aware of the danger and having the opportunity to take steps to stop the process (by, for example, developing their property while they still have the right to do so). On the other hand, once these rights have come into being, further unfairness may result for owners of servient tenements who may invest resources in developing their property only to find their plans thwarted when the existence of an easement of light is brought to their attention.

In addition, the identifiability of an easement is an issue for potential purchasers of an affected property for at least two reasons. First, there is a risk of unfairness resulting from purchasers' acquiring land in the belief that there are no limits on their right to develop it, only to discover that their options are limited by a prescriptive easement.[22] Secondly, there is a general concern that the presence of rights that are difficult to identify encourages parties

[16] This explains the growing interest in release fee awards which effectively provide a way for the owner of the dominant tenement to capture some of this difference in value. See, below nn 120–121 and accompanying text.

[17] The Prescription 1832 Act, s 3 effectively abrogated the 'ancient foundations' custom for most purposes: *The Salters Company v Jay* (1842) 3 QB 109.

[18] The Town and Country Planning Act 1947.

[19] In cases decided before the twentieth century, much is often made of the inconvenience of having to light more candles (eg *Wells v Ody* (1836) 7 Car & P 410, 410, 173 ER 182) or to 'burn gas' (eg *Cooper v Hubbuck* (1862) 12 CB (NS) 456, 461, 142 ER 1220).

[20] *Prah v Maretti* 321 NW 2d 182, 189 (Wis 2d, 1982).

[21] *National Provincial Bank Ltd v Ainsworth* [1965] AC 1175 (HL), 1247–48 (Lord Wilberforce); *Hunter v Canary Wharf* (n 11 above) 726 (Lord Hope).

[22] As legal easements likely to have been used in the year prior to the transfer of the servient tenement, rights to light will in practice be protected as overriding interests and thus bind successors in title even in the absence of the entry of a notice on the register (Land Registration Act 2002, Sch 3, para 3).

to investigate the matter, and difficulties in satisfactorily determining the existence of a right mean that such investigations are liable to be relatively expensive. In this vein, Merrill and Smith argue that the *numerus clausus* principle reflects a policy that property rights should be standardised in order to limit costs that would come from the need to investigate title. Unusual rights *in rem* are liable to impose externalities on subsequent potential purchasers of the land in question.[23]

Where the traditional preconditions for prescriptive easements are fulfilled, such policy concerns are unlikely to be acute. The principle that a use should be open, continuous and adverse for a prescriptive easement to come into existence should ensure that it occurs to affected owners and any interested third parties that there is an issue to be addressed. In contrast, the fact that a neighbour's windows enjoy a good level of natural light is not likely to give either the owner or a potential purchaser of land a moment's pause.

Difficulties of identification have been exacerbated by a judicial insistence that these rights persist in circumstances in which it would have been difficult even for an observer well versed in the law to identify the possibility of the existence of an easement of light. The courts will protect rights of light even where there is no longer a window of longstanding that might serve to signal the existence of the interest. Thus, the owner of the dominant tenement might rebuild a structure that he has chosen to demolish or that was destroyed in a fire and still enjoy protection for 'ancient lights' provided that the number, size and location of the new windows broadly correspond to those in the original building.[24] A purchaser of the servient tenement would only be likely to see that his neighbour's premises were recently constructed and, in the unlikely event that he was alert to the issue, he could be forgiven for assuming that he was within his rights in building without fear of any easement of light.[25]

Equally, the courts were traditionally very loath to infer from the fact windows were blocked up for many years that an easement had been abandoned.[26] Even more strikingly, the courts held that an easement remained even if the original building was demolished, there was no structure on the site of the dominant tenement and there was no guarantee that anything would be rebuilt.[27] Other signs that an objective observer might have interpreted as militating against prescription were treated as irrelevant. Thus, prescription might operate even if, for much of the relevant 20-year period, the dwelling on the dominant tenement was unused and uninhabitable.[28] It is, however, likely that, following recent reforms designed to limit overriding interests, no easement of light would now be enforceable against a purchaser of property in such cases in the absence of a notice being entered

[23] TW Merrill and HE Smith, 'Optimal Standardization in the Law of Property: The Numerus Clausus Principle' (2000) 110 *Yale Law Journal* 1. See too the discussion of the *numerus clausus* principle in this volume: S Pascoe, 'Re-evaluating Recreational Easements: New Norms for the Twenty-First Century?' (Chapter 10) and B France-Hudson, 'The Recognition of Covenants in Gross in New Zealand: A Dangerous Advancement?' (Chapter 11).

[24] *Cooper v Hubbuck* (1862) 30 Beav 158, 54 ER 849; *Tapling v Jones* (1865) 20 CB (NS) 166, 144 ER 1067.

[25] See *Newson v Pender* (1884) 27 Ch D 43 (CA). *Moore v Rawson* (1824) 3 B & C 332, 107 ER 756 is a rare case in which the court held that owner of the dominant tenement's actions amounted to an abandonment of his easement. Abbott CJ observed that the plaintiff's actions 'may have induced another person to become the purchaser of the adjoining ground for building purposes' (ibid 336).

[26] *Stokoe v Singers* (1857) 8 EL & BL 31, 120 ER 12.

[27] *Ecclesiastical Commissioners for England v Kino* (1880) 14 Ch D 213 (CA).

[28] *Courtauld v Legh* (1869) LR 4 Exch 126 (Ex).

on the register of the servient tenement. Rights of light will now bind a purchaser only if they have been 'exercised' in the year leading up to the relevant disposition of land.[29]

(iii) Uncertainty as to the Scope of Rights

A second source of uncertainty concerns the scope of protection provided by an easement of light. The difficulty in this case is not in determining whether an easement has arisen but in judging at what point obstruction of light by the owner of the servient tenement would become actionable.

From its inception, an actionable interference with an easement of light was treated as a nuisance.[30] After considerable judicial indecision on the matter, the House of Lords in *Colls v Home and Colonial Stores*[31] early last century settled on an entitlement of 'sufficient light according to the ordinary notions of mankind'.[32] The judiciary long explored the possibility of favouring a more or less quantifiable threshold for determining when an obstruction of light becomes a nuisance. In the late nineteenth century, there was an attempt to derive guidance from a standard prevalent in building regulations of the time. It was suggested that there would not be an actionable nuisance if sunlight reached the sill of the window in question at an angle of not more than 45 degrees from the horizontal. The suggestion met with a mixed response from the judiciary.[33]

Eventually, a considerable degree of predictability was ensured by experts generally adopting a methodology finalised by Percy Waldram in the 1920s. According to this approach, at least 50 per cent of a room should enjoy illumination of one lumen at the height of a standard table, essentially the amount of light received at a distance of one foot from a candle in a darkened room.[34] However, in *Ough v King*,[35] Lord Denning MR emphasised that Waldram's method was a rule of thumb rather than a definitive test and that judges were entitled to reach their own view on the matter.

One concern with uncertainty in identifying the existence and/or scope of rights of light is that individuals may be deterred from developing land because of the possibility of a breach, even if it is likely that an easement of light either does not exist or would not be breached by the contemplated development. In this way, such uncertainty effectively adds to the burden imposed on the servient tenement by such easements.

[29] Land Registration Act 2002, Schedule 3, para 3.

[30] For discussion of the implications of this for different models of nuisance law see D Nolan, 'The Essence of Nuisance', Chapter 5 in this volume.

[31] *Colls v Home and Colonial Stores Ltd* [1904] AC 179 (HL).

[32] ibid 204 (Lord Davey), 208 (Lindley LJ). The phrase was first formulated by James LJ in *Kelk v Pearson* (1871) LR 6 Ch App 809, 811 (Ch App).

[33] *City of London Brewery Co v Tennant* (1873) LR Ch App 212, 220 (Ch App) (Lord Selborne viewed the 'rule' as prima facie evidence that there was no actionable interference); *Hackett v Baiss* (1875) LR 20 Eq 494 (Ch) (standard favoured by Jessel MR); *Ecclesiastical Commissioners for England v Kino* (1880) 14 Ch D 213 (CA) (James, Brett, and Cotton LJJ rejecting the relevance of the standard); *Parker v First Avenue Hotel* (1883) 24 Ch D 282 (Ch) (North J issued a prohibitory injunction that the defendant should respect the standard); *Colls v Home and Colonial Stores* (n 31 above) (standard endorsed by Lord Lindley).

[34] The essential tenets of Waldram's method were accepted by Eve J in *Charles Semon & Co v Bradford Corporation* [1922] Ch 602 (Ch).

[35] [1967] 1 WLR 1547 (CA).

(iv) The Risk of Holdouts – A 'Tragedy of the Anticommons'?

Private property is often justified by reference to the 'tragedy of the commons', which focuses on the potential of proprietary rights to ensure that users bear the costs as well as enjoying the benefits of exploiting resources that could be unsustainably over-exploited if held in common.[36] More recently, however, scholars have noted that difficulties can arise too from a proliferation of property rights. If there are too many people with property rights that confer a power of veto over the use of a particular resource, the problems in securing the consent of all those with an interest are liable to result in that resource being under-utilised, a fate that Michael Heller characterises as the 'tragedy of the anticommons'.[37] This spectre looms large for easements of light, which tend to place much greater constraints on the potential development of the servient tenement than, for example, a right of way.

The objection to the fact that the burden imposed by easements of light typically outweighs the benefit might be regarded as essentially a question of distributional fairness if owners of servient tenements could easily negotiate a relaxation of such rights. As Ronald Coase postulated, if legal rules allocate rights to someone who is not the most valued user of a resource, in the absence of transaction costs, that misallocation will be corrected in the market.[38] As Coase himself recognised, however, transaction costs are often a problem. For example, a development scheme will often obstruct the light enjoyed by several dwellings, thereby giving rise to risks of strategic behaviour that are present when a buyer has to secure the consent of numerous sellers. As Calabresi and Melamed noted, each seller has an incentive to exaggerate the value he attaches to his right and to 'hold out' in order to maximise his own share of the gains from trade. If all sellers act in this way, the likelihood is that they will collectively demand too much and the negotiations will break down.[39]

Other commentators have observed that, in the absence of a market price for the right at issue, there can be substantial obstacles to bargaining even when there are only two parties who need to reach an agreement. One difficulty when bargaining in 'thin markets' is that one party's valuation of the entitlement at issue is 'private information' that the other party cannot objectively verify.[40] In addition, such bargains might break down simply because there is no obvious basis for dividing up the potential gains from trade that would result from a concluded agreement.[41] Finally, the dangers of parties not reaching agreement are heightened by any uncertainties as to the existence and/or scope of entitlements that may result in the parties having different views as to their rights.

In the face of substantial obstacles to bargaining, owners of servient tenements are likely to struggle to secure a release from owners of dominant tenements, even if such an arrangement providing for a relaxation of an easement of light would be mutually advantageous.

[36] G Hardin, 'The Tragedy of the Commons' (1968) 162 *Science* 1243.

[37] MA Heller, 'The Tragedy of the Anticommons: Property in the Transition from Marx to Markets' (1998) 111 *Harvard Law Review* 621.

[38] RH Coase, 'The Problem of Social Cost' (1960) 3 *Journal of Law & Economics* 1.

[39] G Calabresi and AD Melamed, 'Property Rules, Liability Rules and Inalienability: One View of the Cathedral' (1972) 85 *Harvard Law Review* 1089.

[40] I Ayres and E Talley, 'Solomonic Bargaining: Dividing a Legal Entitlement to Facilitate Coasean Trade' (1985) 104 *Yale Law Journal* 1027.

[41] R Cooter, 'The Cost of Coase' (1982) 11 *Journal of Legal Studies* 1.

III. Remedies for Breaches of a Right to Light

A. The Significance of Remedies for Interfering with an Easement of Light

The likelihood that holdouts will complicate efforts to buy out easements of light is largely dependent upon the extent to which the owner of the dominant tenement can veto any attempt to develop the servient tenement in breach of the easement. Such bargaining power is determined in large part by the willingness of the courts to enjoin the actions of the defendant. If, instead of being entitled to an injunction, claimants were limited to recovering damages for loss of amenity, the leverage conferred by easements of light would be greatly reduced.

B. The Rise of the Right to Light

(i) Remedies in Right to Light Actions before the Chancery Amendment Act 1858

Before the latter part of the nineteenth century, rights of light litigation was largely conducted in the courts of common law. While litigants might seek an interim injunction as a prelude to the matter being determined at law, the courts of equity would not entertain awarding a permanent injunction in response to an alleged breach of a common law right if the merits of the matter had not been tried in a court of law.[42]

Even though the courts of common law did not at this point have the remedy of an injunction in their armoury, plaintiffs were not expected to be satisfied with the remedy of damages. Plaintiffs could recover only for loss resulting from past breaches and not for anticipated damage on the assumption that a breach would continue.[43] The standard order upon a finding that a structure erected by the defendant interfered with the plaintiff's easement of light was a verdict for the plaintiff with an award of nominal damages.[44] As, Lord Tindal CJ remarked in his directions to the jury in *Parker v Smith*, the effect of such a verdict would be 'that of a notice to the defendants, that they must pull down the building of which the plaintiff complains.'[45]

Odd as it might seem now, one possibility was that the plaintiff might take the matter into his own hands and abate the nuisance by pulling down the offending structure.[46] Another option for resolving a continuing breach in these circumstances was to go to the Court of Chancery to seek an injunction. However, an alternative was to bring a further action in the court of common law that had already found in favour of the plaintiff. As Jervis CJ suggested in *Battishill v Reed*, 'if the defendant persists in continuing the

[42] *Fishmongers v East India Co* (1752) Dick 163, 21 ER 232.
[43] *Battishill v Reed* (1856) 18 CB 696, 139 ER 1544.
[44] ibid, 714 (Jervis CJ).
[45] *Parker v Smith* (1832) 5 Car & P 438, 440, 172 ER 1043.
[46] *Perry v Fitzhowe* (1846) 8 QB 757, 775, 115 ER 1057 (Lord Denham CJ).

nuisance, then they may give such damages as may compel him to abate it.'[47] He also quoted Blackstone's *Commentaries* for the proposition that, 'very exemplary damages will probably be given if, after one verdict against him, the defendant has the hardiness to continue the nuisance.'[48]

The effectiveness of this approach can be seen in the one reported right to light case where the plaintiff sued the defendant a second time for the same nuisance. In *Shadwell v Hutchinson*,[49] the court delivered a verdict for the plaintiff and awarded nominal damages. Two years later, the plaintiff brought a further action in response to the defendant's failure to abate the nuisance. The court awarded damages of £100.[50] A ruling was subsequently granted reducing the damages after the defendant acted to abate the nuisance.[51]

(ii) The Jurisdiction to Grant Damages in Lieu of an Injunction

The mid-to-late Victorian period saw a boom in rights to light litigation. In giving his judgment in *Dent v Auction Mart Co* in 1866, Sir William Page Wood VC observed that, 'the cases have become more frequent of late, in consequence of the increased desire to erect, in the metropolis and elsewhere, buildings of considerable magnitude, which must, of course, more or less affect houses in their immediate neighbourhood.'[52] One indication of this rise in litigation is provided by reported cases on such disputes. Of course, only a fraction of disputes are litigated, only a subset of contested cases will reach the higher courts and only some of these will be reported. Nonetheless, the number of cases reported is likely to reflect relative levels of litigation in the higher courts. Reflecting Wood VC's perception, there was an explosion in reported cases in the 1860s. Levels of reported litigation remained relatively elevated for the following four decades as shown in Table 1.[53]

Certainly, as Wood VC suggested, some of this rise in litigation can be attributed to demographic pressures: the period of 1860–1900 saw the population of inner London (which provided the backdrop to most reported right to light cases) increase from 3 million to 5 million. Yet, the population of that area had already tripled from 1800 to 1860, without a significant rise in reported cases.[54] It is likely that changes in the legal environment in the mid-nineteenth century encouraged those whose rights were being infringed to resort to litigation. One of the most obvious changes in the juridical landscape came in the form of the Prescription Act 1832, which is sometimes regarded as having encouraged plaintiffs to assert prescriptive rights.[55] However, with the exception of its elimination of the 'ancient

[47] *Battishill v Reed* (n 43 above) 714.
[48] ibid, 712.
[49] *Shadwell v Hutchinson* (1829) 3 Car & P 615, 619, 172 ER 569.
[50] *Shadwell v Hutchinson* (1830) 4 Car & P 333, 334, 172 ER 728.
[51] *Shadwell v Hutchinson* (1831) 2 B & AD 97, 99, 109 ER 1079.
[52] *Dent v Auction Mart Co* (1866) LR 2 Eq 238, 245 (Ch).
[53] The data in this and the following tables is drawn from cases involving rights of light, whether arising by prescription or by implied or express grant, on the basis that the issues of enforcement are largely the same regardless how the easement arises. The data includes different stages of the litigation of the same dispute where these are reported.
[54] Great Britain Historical Geographical Information Systems Project, A Vision of Britain through Time (2017). Data on Inner London population available at: http://www.visionofbritain.org.uk/unit/10076845/cube/TOT_POP.
[55] See M Lobban, in W Cornish et al, *The Oxford History of the Laws of England, vol 12: 1829–1914 Private Law* (Oxford, Oxford University Press, 2010) 1071.

Table 1 Reported Right to Light Cases

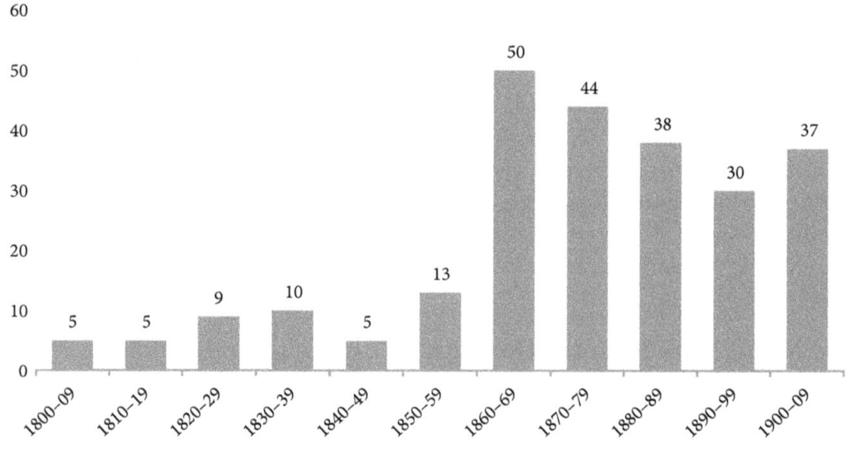

foundations' custom that had hitherto prevailed in the City of London, the reforms of the Act were largely relatively minor matters of procedure and there was no significant increase in reported lights cases in the 30 years that followed its enactment.

The 1850s saw a series of institutional reforms that presaged the integration of the common law and equity realised by the Judicature Act 1873. One such reform was the passing of the Common Law Procedure Act 1854, section 79 of which granted the courts of law powers to award injunctions for repetitive or ongoing breaches. Had this power been exploited in right to light cases, such litigation might have remained largely the province of common law courts. The power was, however, little used in this context before being superseded by the more fundamental reforms of the 1870s.[56] Instead, the reported cases suggest that the rise in rights of light litigation coincided with these disputes being heard in the Chancery Courts, as Table 2 demonstrates.

A number of institutional reforms enabled parties to litigate disputes over common law rights in the courts of equity. The Court of Chancery Procedure Act 1852 gave the courts of equity the jurisdiction to decide points of law, allowing courts of equity to go beyond providing interlocutory relief and to hear rights of light disputes on their merits. The powers given by the Act were initially little used,[57] and, a decade later, Parliament passed the Chancery Regulation Act 1862, better known as Rolt's Act, to force the Chancery Courts to assume a greater role.[58] While by the time the latter Act came into force the rise of lights litigation was already underway, it may have contributed to a spike in cases in the Courts of Chancery in the mid-1860s.

[56] The jurisdiction was used after considerable discussion in a right to light case in *Jessel v Chaplin* (1856) 2 *Jurist (NS)* 931. It also appears to have been used in another dispute of this type in *Crofts v Haldane* (1867) LR 2 QB 194 (QB), where the plaintiff's pleading appears to be phrased in the wording of s 79, and an injunction was apparently awarded.

[57] Although the Act was used in *Potts v Levy* (1854) 2 Drewry 272, 61 ER 723.

[58] The role of Rolt's Act and Lord Cairns' Act is discussed by counsel for the plaintiff in *Durell v Pritchard* (1865) LR 1 Ch 244, 247 (Ch App).

Table 2 The Migration of Lights Litigation to the Courts of Chancery

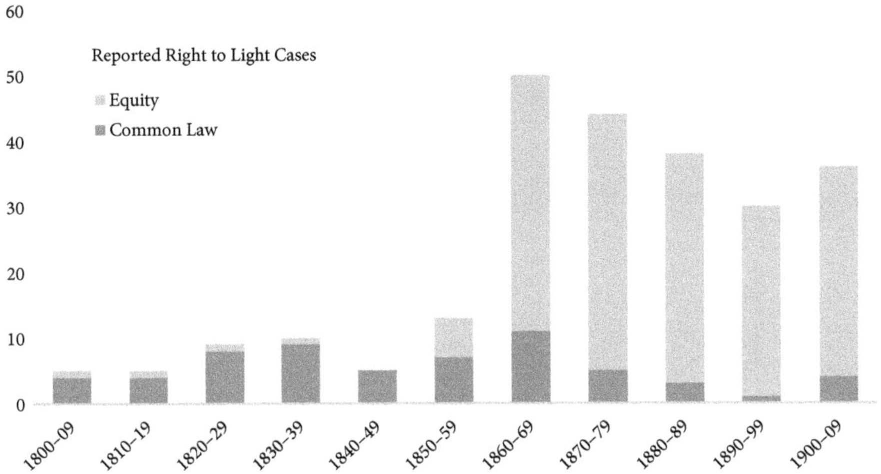

It would be tempting to attribute the increase in reported cases to the Chancery Amendment Act 1858. Lord Cairns' Act, as it was more commonly known, was designed to allow the Courts of Chancery to award claimants damages in lieu of equitable remedies so that they did not have to initiate a separate suit at law in order to recover monetary relief. Although it was not foreseen by the drafters of the legislation, the courts of equity asserted a power unavailable at common law to award damages for the future loss that would result from a Court's denial of a permanent injunction.[59] The increase in rights of light litigation and its shift to the Courts of Chancery were contemporaneous with that Act coming into force. However, a close examination of cases of this type heard in equity in the late 1850s and early 1860s suggests that litigants were slow to rely on the new powers and judges tended to ignore them or interpret them restrictively.

Instead, a more proximate cause of the growth of right to light litigation in the Courts of Chancery would appear to be the courts' adoption of a strict approach to awarding injunctions to protect private rights, most authoritatively signalled by the House of Lords in *Imperial Gas Co v Broadbent*.[60] The plaintiff, a market gardener, brought an action in the Court of Common Pleas claiming that the defendant's gas manufacturing operation was causing an actionable nuisance. The parties agreed to refer the case to a referee, who found in favour of the plaintiff and made an award of damages for past harm. When the defendant thereafter sought to expand the operation in dispute, the plaintiff brought the matter to the Court of Chancery, where Sir William Page Wood VC granted an injunction. On appeal, Lord Cranworth resisted the suggestion that the court might have regard to considerations of public convenience in deciding whether an injunction

[59] *Isenberg v East India House Estate Company* (1863) 3 De GJ & Sm 263, 46 ER 637.
[60] *Imperial Gas Co v Broadbent* (1859) 7 HLC 600, 11 ER 239.

should be available.[61] The House of Lords rejected the defendant's subsequent appeal, with Lord Campbell concluding that, where a plaintiff 'has established his right at law he is entitled as of course to an injunction to prevent the recurrence of that violation.'[62]

Table 3 Reported Right to Light Cases 1850–1869

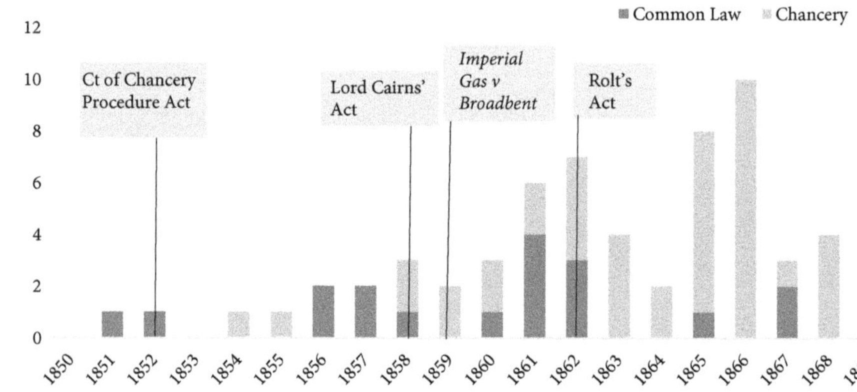

In the 1860s, it became increasingly commonplace for plaintiffs in right to light cases to initiate an action in the Courts of Chancery seeking injunctive relief. For a time, it appeared that the possibility of awarding damages in lieu of an injunction provided by Lord Cairns' Act might lead to the courts' being more reluctant to enjoin such nuisances. Thus, Lord Westbury, whose period as Lord Chancellor began shortly after the passage of that Act, showed himself to be particularly cautious about the use of injunctions. In *Isenberg v East India House Estate Company*,[63] despite the fact that he was faced with a defendant who had accelerated the construction of a development after the plaintiff complained that the completed building would interfere with his light, Westbury LC refused to grant an injunction. His Lordship remarked that, 'The exercise of that power is one that must be attended with the greatest possible caution.'[64] In his view, the Court should not, 'deliver over the Defendants to the Plaintiff bound hand and foot, in order to be made subject to any extortionate demand that he may by possibility make'.[65]

Sir John Romilly MR adopted a more cautious attitude towards the use of the jurisdiction conferred by Lord Cairns' Act in right to light cases. Thus, in *Dunball v Walters*,[66] he remarked:

> An Act of Parliament alone can give any person the right of taking the property of another without his consent on payment of an adequate pecuniary compensation, and the right to light and air is as much property as the land which enjoys this easement on the land of another.[67]

[61] *Broadbent v Imperial Gas Co* (1857) 7 De G M & G 436, 462, 44 ER 170.
[62] *Imperial Gas Co v Broadbent* (n 60 above) 609.
[63] n 59 above.
[64] ibid 272.
[65] ibid 273.
[66] *Dunball v Walters* (1865) 35 Beav 565 (Ch), 55 ER 1106.
[67] ibid 567.

Further decisions of the Courts of Chancery in this period suggested that Lord Westbury's approach to injunctions in right to light cases might prevail. In *Curriers' Company v Corbett*,[68] Sir RT Kindersley VC refused to grant a mandatory injunction for the reason that, 'The Defendant's new buildings are of considerable magnitude and importance, while the two houses of the Plaintiffs are comparatively of small value and importance …'[69] Similarly, later that year, in the Court of Appeal in Chancery in *Durell v Pritchard*,[70] Sir George Turner LJ remarked that, 'this Court will not interfere by way of mandatory injunction, except in cases in which extreme, or at all events very serious, damage will ensue from its interference being withheld.'[71] Subsequently, Romilly MR himself awarded damages in lieu of an injunction in *Calcraft v Thompson*,[72] modifying his approach to the jurisdiction in response to Sir George Turner LJ's judgment in *Durell*.

A change of attitude was soon apparent. After Lord Westbury's resignation, later Lord Chancellors took a less active judicial role and the law was shaped primarily by successive Masters of the Rolls and Vice Chancellors.

While Wood VC expressed some dissatisfaction with the constraints imposed by easements of light, he nonetheless viewed this as a matter for the legislature.[73] He concluded that the courts should respond to breaches of these rights in the manner proposed in *Broadbent*, whereby injunctions should be available as of right, and that this approach should not be affected by the recognition of the jurisdiction to grant damages in lieu of an injunction. Thus, in refusing to award damages in the place of a mandatory injunction in *Dent v Auction Mart Co*,[74] Wood VC remarked,

> it cannot be contended that those who are minded to erect a building that will inflict an injury upon their neighbour have a right to purchase him out without any Act of Parliament for that purpose having been obtained.[75]

While Wood VC awarded damages in lieu of an injunction on more than one occasion in this context, he stressed that mandatory injunctions could be denied only in exceptional circumstances. Thus, in two cases in which he exercised the jurisdiction in the defendant's favour, he concluded that the fact that the plaintiffs had expressed a willingness to consent to the proposed development for the right price provided a good indication that the harm in question could fairly be compensated by money.[76]

The Judicature Act 1873 came into effect shortly after Romilly's successor as Master of the Rolls, Sir George Jessel, began his tenure. The Act permitted courts of law to award equitable remedies. Nonetheless, most rights to light litigation continued to be initiated

[68] *Curriers' Company v Corbett* (1865) 2 Dr & Sm 355, 62 ER 656.

[69] ibid 361.

[70] n 58 above.

[71] ibid, 250.

[72] *Calcraft v Thompson* (1866) 35 Beav 559 (Ch), 55 ER 1013; affirmed by Chelmsford LC: *Calcraft v Thompson* (1867) 15 WR 387.

[73] *Stoke v City Office Co* (1865) 12 LT (NS) 602 (Ch), 603.

[74] n 52 above.

[75] ibid 246. For similar remarks by the same judge, see *Senior v Pawson* (1866–67) LR 3 Eq 330 (Ch), 333. Such comments should not be taken to suggest that the defendant missed the opportunity to obtain a Private Act of Parliament to enable him to proceed without fear of an injunction. There is no trace of a practice of the legislature authorising private developments in this way.

[76] *Senior v Pawson* (ibid); *Viscount Gort v Clark* (1868) 18 LT Rep NS 343 (Ch).

in the Courts of Chancery, perhaps because claimants preferred the greater certainty that was afforded by avoiding the jury that remained a feature of common law trials.

In *Aynsley v Glover*,[77] in considering an application for an interlocutory injunction, Jessel MR showed himself to be well aware of the potential that awarding damages instead of an injunction had for reducing the 'holdout' problem. His Lordship suggested that the discretion had been conferred in order to prevent plaintiffs using their position to 'obtain a very large sum of money from defendants'.[78] Nonetheless, he concluded that it would be appropriate to award damages only where the plaintiff's injury was 'very slight' and the hardship that would be visited upon the defendant as a result of imposing the injunction considerable. Jessel MR suggested that an upper limit of £40 would be appropriate. Such a sum would be the equivalent of around £4,500 in 2018.

The judiciary had initially proved willing to deny injunctions even in cases where the building at issue was in the early stages of construction when the matter was heard or where the defendant had completed construction after the plaintiff had commenced the action.[79] Subsequently, however, the courts tended to limit relief to damages only in cases where the building in question was complete;[80] and even then, it was not certain that the court would exercise its discretion in the defendant's favour.[81] As a result, the denial of mandatory injunctions became increasingly uncommon. The only reported case in which damages were granted in lieu of a mandatory injunction in a right to light dispute in the last two decades of the nineteenth century was *Martin v Price*, where Kekewich J's use of the discretion was overturned on appeal.[82]

Table 4 Applications for Mandatory Injunctions in Reported Right to Light Cases

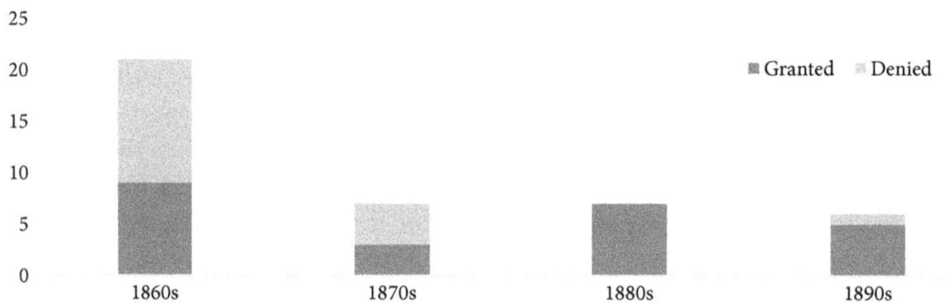

The judicial attitude to the award of damages in lieu of an injunction was most definitively expressed in the Court of Appeal's decision in *Shelfer v City of London Electric Lighting Co*,[83] where the Court unanimously upheld the plaintiffs' appeal against Kekewich J's refusal

[77] *Aynsley v Glover* (1874) LR 18 Eq 544 (Ch).

[78] ibid 555. Jessel MR remarked, 'I do not like to use the word extort', thereby conveying the impression that he had something of the kind in mind.

[79] See eg *Jackson v The Duke of Newcastle* (1864) 3 De GJ & S 275, 46 ER 642 (construction in progress at the time the matter was heard); *Isenberg v East India House Estate Company* (n 59 above) (building completed after action initiated).

[80] This was a feature of most of the handful of cases in the 1870s where an injunction was denied. See *City of London Brewery Co v Tennant* (n 33 above); *Lady Stanley of Alderley v Earl of Shrewsbury* (1875) LR 19 Eq 616 (Ch); and *National Provincial Plate Glass v Prudential Assurance* (1877) 6 Ch D 757 (Ch).

[81] See eg *Lazarus v Artistic Photographic Co* [1897] 2 Ch 214 (Ch).

[82] *Martin v Price* [1894] 1 Ch 276 (CA).

[83] *Shelfer v City of London Electric Lighting Co* [1895] 1 Ch 287 (CA).

of an injunction for a nuisance caused by the defendant's electricity-generating operation. AL Smith LJ formulated his 'good working rule', which was to represent the orthodoxy on this issue for much of the next 120 years. In his view, damages should be awarded as a substitute for an injunction only:

> (1) If the injury to the plaintiff's legal rights is small, (2) And is one which is capable of being estimated in money, (3) And is one which can be adequately compensated by a small money payment, (4) And the case is one in which it would be oppressive to the defendant to grant an injunction ...[84]

Once again, the court was uncomfortable with the implication that it might undermine property rights by limiting plaintiffs to damages in lieu of an injunction. This concern was expressed most succinctly by Lindley LJ when he remarked, 'Expropriation, even for a money consideration, is only justifiable when Parliament has sanctioned it.'[85] It is apparent, however, that *Shelfer* was far from revolutionary. That decision was foreshadowed by the approach of Wood VC in the 1860s and Jessel MR in the 1870s.[86]

C. The Balance Restored in *Colls*

As noted, the latter half of the nineteenth century saw a sharp and sustained rise in rights of light litigation. In addition to the judicial tendency to award injunctions as a matter of course in response to breaches of rights to light, plaintiffs were encouraged by decisions that strengthened the scope of protection conferred by an easement of light. The courts rejected the notion that the level of lighting that one might legitimately expect depended in part on the location in which the dispute arose.[87] In addition, various authorities, culminating in the Court of Appeal decision in *Warren v Brown*,[88] concluded that the owners of dominant tenements were permitted to retain an exceptional level of natural light if that was necessary for the profession practised on the premises in question.[89] Moreover, *dicta* in some cases[90] appeared to suggest that owners of dominant tenements were essentially entitled to the same level of light enjoyed at the moment the easement arose.

The high degree of protection provided to rights of light compromised urban development. The facts of *Colls v Home and Colonial Stores*[91] usefully illustrate the constraints that the prevailing state of the law imposed. The plaintiff, whose three-storey premises benefited from electric lighting, complained of the defendant adding a third storey to its premises on the opposite side of a street with a width of 40 feet in the City of London. It seems scarcely credible that such a modest expansion in the centre of the metropolis could have resulted in the highest court in the land hearing an appeal by the defendant

[84] ibid 322–23.
[85] ibid 315–16.
[86] Indeed, subsequently in *Slack v Leeds Industrial Co-operative Society* [1924] 2 Ch 475 (CA), 487, Pollock MR remarked that, 'The rules that are laid down in *Shelfer* ... are also to be found in *Aynsley v Glover*, if not in the same terms, at any rate in words to much the same effect ...'.
[87] *Yates v Jack* (1866) LR 1 Ch App 295 (Ch App).
[88] *Warren v Brown* [1900] 2 QB 722 (CA).
[89] See eg *Lazarus v Artistic Photograph Co* (n 81 above).
[90] Eg: *Calcraft v Thompson* (1867) 15 WR 387; *Scott v Pape* (1886) 31 Ch D 554 (CA).
[91] n 31 above.

against an order that it pull down the storey it had added. However, the state of the authorities was such that, with considerable reluctance, the Court of Appeal had reached the view that it was obliged to order a mandatory injunction.[92] In upholding the defendant's appeal, the House of Lords sought to restate numerous aspects of right to light law.

A key feature of *Colls* was the choice of a single objective standard for the degree of light to which plaintiffs were entitled, without regard to the fact that the plaintiff might have enjoyed an exceptional amount of light, or to any need for an extraordinary level of illumination that the plaintiff might claim. This was most succinctly captured by Lord Lindley's conclusion that claimants were entitled to 'sufficient light according to the ordinary notions of mankind for the comfortable use and enjoyment of [the premises]'.[93]

Their Lordships concluded that the obstruction in question did not amount to a nuisance. While this was sufficient to dispose of the case, both Lords Macnaghten and Lindley addressed the issue as to whether it would have been appropriate to award an injunction had they found the defendant liable. Lord Macnaghten doubted that 'the amount of damages which may be supposed to be recoverable at law offers a satisfactory test' for determining whether the courts should limit the plaintiff to monetary relief. Instead, his Lordship suggested that the issue should turn primarily on the quality of the defendant's behaviour. He concluded,

> if there really is a question as to whether the obstruction is legal or not, and if the defendant has acted fairly and not in an unneighbourly spirit, I am disposed to think that the Court ought to incline to damages rather than to an injunction.[94]

For his part, Lord Lindley struck a much less strident tone than he had in *Shelfer*. In an analysis that featured none of the absolutist property rights rhetoric that marked the judgments of that earlier decision, his Lordship was content to conclude that this would have been an appropriate case in which to grant damages in lieu of an injunction. He concluded by counselling moderation in right to light disputes, observing that:

> There are elements of uncertainty which render it impossible to lay down any definite rule applicable to all cases. First, there is the uncertainty as to what amount of obstruction constitutes an actionable nuisance; and, secondly, there is the uncertainty as to whether the proper remedy is an injunction or damages. But, notwithstanding these elements of uncertainty, the good sense of judges and juries may be relied upon for adequately protecting rights to light on the one hand and freedom from unnecessary burdens on the other. There must be consideration for both sides in all these controversies.[95]

The apparent relaxation in the approach toward exercising the discretion conferred by Lord Cairns' Act signalled in *Colls* had an immediate effect on the Court of Appeal in *Kine v Jolly*.[96] The defendant had built a house which interfered with the plaintiff's right to light, substantially diminishing the value of the plaintiff's property. While denying the

[92] *Home and Colonial Stores v Colls* [1902] 1 Ch 302.
[93] *Colls* (n 31 above) 208.
[94] ibid 193.
[95] ibid 208.
[96] *Kine v Jolly* [1905] 1 Ch 480 (CA); affirmed *Jolly v Kine* [1907] AC 1 (HL).

appeal on the question of liability, the Court of Appeal reversed Kekewich J's decision at first instance on the choice of remedy and so denied the plaintiff a mandatory injunction. Cozens-Hardy LJ observed that:

> I think it is impossible to doubt that the tendency of the speeches in the House of Lords in *Colls* … is to go a little further than was done in *Shelfer* …, and to indicate that as a general rule the Court ought to be less free in granting mandatory injunctions than it was in years gone by.[97]

Given rights to light are qualified in that an actionable nuisance arises only when the interference is so significant that it renders the premises 'substantially less comfortable and convenient',[98] it is unclear that any such breach could be said to have satisfied the first of AL Smith LJ's tests in *Shelfer*, whereby it must be demonstrated that 'the injury to the plaintiff's legal rights is small'.[99] Moreover, given that a majority of the Court of Appeal accepted Kekewich J's finding that the value of the premises had been 'substantially diminished', it is difficult to understand how the breach could have satisfied AL Smith LJ's third test that the injury 'is one which can be adequately compensated by a small money payment'.[100]

Within a few years of *Colls*, there was a marked decrease in rights of light litigation. In the next 20 years, the courts seldom ordered a mandatory injunction in response to a breach of a right to light,[101] and in at least four instances damages were ordered as an alternative to that remedy.[102] Almost two decades after *Colls*, Younger LJ summarised the consequences of that decision:

> It has become a commonplace amongst us that the restatement of the law and proper practice in such cases made by the House of Lords in *Colls' Case* reduced the hitherto abundant flow of actions for injunctions in light and air cases to a mere trickle. Injunctions became no longer a matter of course; the real damage did not translate itself into a sum sufficiently substantial to be attractive. Cases of trivial interference no longer troubled the Courts.[103]

Twenty years after *Colls*, in *Leeds Industrial Cooperative v Slack*,[104] the House of Lords concluded by a narrow majority that the courts had the jurisdiction to grant damages for prospective harm in substitution for a *quia timet* injunction. The plaintiff had halted the defendant's building development by obtaining an interim injunction and thereby prevented the threatened breach of his easement of light occurring. The case was sent back to the Court of Appeal, which did indeed exercise its discretion to grant damages.[105] The willingness of

[97] *Kine v Jolly* (ibid) 504.
[98] *Colls v Home and Colonial Store* (n 31 above) 187 (Lord Macnaghten).
[99] *Shelfer* (n 83 above) 322.
[100] ibid.
[101] The one exception is *Higgins v Betts* [1905] 2 Ch 210 (Ch).
[102] *Kine v Jolly* (n 96 above); *Ankerson v Connelly* [1907] 1 Ch 678 (CA); *Bailey v Holborn & Frascati* [1914] 1 Ch 598 (Ch); *Wills v May* [1923] 1 Ch 317 (Ch).
[103] *Slack v Leeds Industrial Co-operative Society Ltd* (n 86 above), 461. His Lordship was dissenting on the question of the jurisdiction to grant damages in lieu of a *quia timet* injunction, expressing a view that was subsequently adopted by the majority of the House of Lords on appeal.
[104] *Leeds Industrial Cooperative Society Ltd v Slack* [1924] AC 851.
[105] *Slack v Leeds Industrial Co-operative Society Ltd* (n 86 above).

the House of Lords to sanction the use of the jurisdiction not only to permit continuing nuisances but to authorise future transgressions of the plaintiff's rights was starkly at odds with the restrictive attitude apparent in the line of cases culminating in *Shelfer*.[106]

The retreat from the late Victorian approach to the award of remedies in right to light cases continued in *Fishenden v Higgs & Hill*,[107] when the Court of Appeal once again overturned a refusal of the first instance court to award damages in lieu of an injunction. Lord Hanworth MR was critical of AL Smith LJ's rule[108] and suggested that 'we ought to incline against an injunction if possible'.[109] Romer LJ concluded that, while he was sure that an injunction would be refused if *all* of the criteria in *Shelfer* were fulfilled, AL Smith LJ could not be taken to have asserted that an injunction would invariably be denied if *any* of them were not satisfied.[110] Consistently with Lord Macnaghten's analysis in *Colls*, Lord Hanworth MR and Romer LJ justified overturning the decision of the court below in large part because the defendants had acted in good faith.[111]

Echoing Lord Lindley's coda in *Colls*, members of the Court of Appeal in Fishenden suggested that rights of light cases should be treated differently from other nuisances. Both Maugham LJ and Lord Hanworth MR sought to restrict *Shelfer* to its facts by emphasising that it was a case in which the nuisance physically damaged the plaintiff's property.[112] Maugham LJ concluded that AL Smith LJ's approach did not offer 'a universal or even a sound rule in all cases of injury to light'.[113]

The choice of the majority of their Lordships in *Colls* to favour an absolute, objective standard for nuisance by interference with an easement for light rather than one that was dependent upon the level of light previously enjoyed by the defendant no doubt did a great deal to stem the flow of litigation. Not only did this approach impose a higher threshold for claimants; it offered the possibility that the standard might be reduced to a measurable benchmark that would bring greater certainty to light disputes. This opportunity was, to a degree, realised with the development and widespread use of Percy Waldram's method.[114]

There appear to be no reported right to light cases in the *Law Reports*, the *Weekly Law Reports* or the *All England Reports* between 1937 and 1967.[115] While no doubt attributable in part to the distractions of the Second World War, the consequences of the temporary extension of the period of prescription provided for in the Rights to Light Act 1959 and the establishment of a comprehensive planning regime, this pause in litigation is nonetheless remarkable.

[106] Damages were ordered in lieu of a *quia timet* injunction in a right to light case by Pearson J *Holland v Worley* (1884) LR 26 Ch D 578 (Ch). However, it was quickly treated as bad law by Bacon VC in *Greenwood v Hornsey* (1886) 33 Ch D 471 (Ch).

[107] *Fishenden v Higgs & Hill* (1935) 153 LT 128 (CA).

[108] ibid 139.

[109] ibid.

[110] ibid 141.

[111] ibid 139 (Lord Hanworth MR) and 141 (Romer LJ).

[112] ibid 138 (Lord Hanworth MR) and 144 (Maugham LJ).

[113] ibid 144.

[114] See above n 34.

[115] The only reported case in this period I have found is *Blake & Lyons Ltd v Lewis Berger and Sons* [1951] TLR 605 (Ch).

Table 5 Reported Right to Light Cases Since 1850

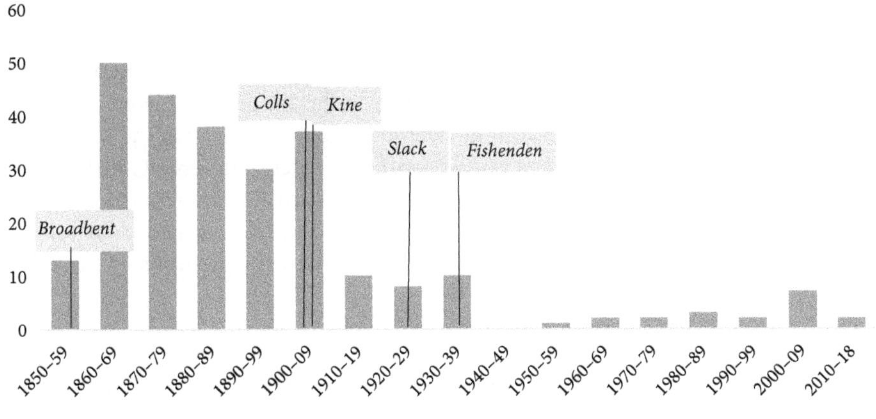

D. A Brief Return to *Shelfer*

The danger of such a lengthy hiatus is that the hazards of treating easements of light in the same way as any other proprietary interest may fade from the collective memory of the legal community. In 2006, in *Regan v Paul Properties DPF (No 1)*,[116] the Court of Appeal ordered a mandatory injunction in a case in which a defendant had proceeded with a development after having been advised by an expert that any interference with the claimant's right to light that was likely to result would be minor. In overruling the decision of the judge at first instance to award damages as a substitute for a mandatory injunction, Mummery LJ suggested that Lord Macnaghten's remarks in *Colls* had been treated as carrying an authority that he had never intended them to have.[117] While the diminution in value to the claimant from the development was not more than £5,500 and the cost of complying with the injunction for the defendant would have been £200,000, the Court concluded that the *Shelfer* test was not satisfied. A similar result was seen four years later in the High Court decision of *HKRUKII (CHC) Ltd v Heaney*.[118]

The availability of injunctive relief was also affected by the emergence of awards of release fees in lieu of an injunction following *Wrotham Park Estate Co Ltd v Parkside Homes Ltd*.[119] The practice has developed of granting claimants awards of around a third of any profit attributable to the breach of the right in question. Awards made on this basis are said to reflect what the claimant might reasonably have charged the defendant in return for relaxing the rights in question.[120] It was suggested both in *Regan* and *Heaney* that such awards should be taken into account for the purposes of AL Smith's test in determining whether 'the injury to the plaintiff's legal rights is small' and/or 'is one which can

[116] *Regan v Paul Properties DPF (No 1)* [2006] EWCA Civ 1391, [2007] Ch 135.
[117] ibid [39].
[118] *HKRUKII (CHC) Ltd v Heaney* [2010] EWHC 2245 (Ch), [2010] 3 EGLR 15.
[119] *Wrotham Park Estate Co Ltd v Parkside Homes Ltd* [1974] 1 WLR 798 (Ch).
[120] For an example of this in the context of a right to light dispute, see *Tamares (Vincent Square) Ltd v Fairpoint Properties (Vincent Square) Ltd (No 2)* [2007] EWHC 212 (Ch), [2007] 1 WLR 2167.

be adequately compensated by a small money payment'.[121] This approach would have the rather perverse result of meaning that claimants who are in the privileged position of being entitled (if no injunction were granted) to awards far exceeding the diminution in value suffered as a consequence of a breach of a right to light would as a result always be entitled to an injunction. It might be argued that such awards should not be treated as relevant to the *Shelfer* test because they are based on the defendant's gain rather than the claimant's loss. Such an objection would, however, be at odds with the recent Supreme Court decision in *Morris-Garner v One Step (Support) Ltd*,[122] where their Lordships concluded that a release fee awarded in lieu of an injunction is properly regarded as compensation for loss on the basis that, 'the refusal of an injunction effectively deprive[s] the plaintiffs of the benefit of their right, and therefore of its value'.[123]

E. Reimagining Remedies for Nuisance: *Lawrence v Fen Tigers Ltd*

The status of *Shelfer* was reconsidered by the Supreme Court in *Lawrence v Fen Tigers*,[124] a dispute involving two claimants who had moved to an isolated bungalow near a stadium used for motor sports. While upholding the claimants' appeal on the question of liability, the Court sent the matter back to the court of first instance to consider whether damages should be awarded instead of an injunction.

There was agreement amongst their Lordships that the exercise of the jurisdiction to grant damages in lieu of an injunction should no longer be constrained by a strict application of AL Smith LJ's rule from *Shelfer*. Importantly for the purpose of this analysis, Lords Neuberger and Sumption treated *Regan* as wrongly decided.[125] Lord Neuberger, giving the lengthiest judgment, suggested that, prima facie, a claimant should be entitled to an injunction on proof of a nuisance and that the burden lay on the defendant to persuade the court that damages should be granted instead.[126] However, the effect of his Lordship's approach was to greatly reduce the obstacles to discharging that burden. Echoing Romer LJ's analysis in *Fishenden*,[127] Lord Neuberger stated that if the tests listed by AL Smith LJ are all met, a court should deny an injunction and grant damages; if they are not all fulfilled, however, the court might still exercise its discretion in the defendant's favour.[128] Their Lordships agreed that the judiciary might do well to take more account of the public interest in choosing between remedies than courts had previously done. They agreed that the court might have regard to the fact that planning permission had been granted for a particular development, although they varied on how much weight should be attached to the matter.[129]

[121] *Regan v Paul Properties DPF No 1 Ltd* (n 116 above) [72] (Mummery LJ); *HKRUK II v Heaney* (n 118 above) [80]–[81] HHJ Langan QC.

[122] *Morris-Garner v One Step (Support) Ltd* [2018] UKSC 20, [2018] 2 WLR 1353.

[123] ibid [54] Lord Reed (with Lady Hale, Lord Wilson and Lord Carnwarth concurring).

[124] *Lawrence v Fen Tigers Ltd* [2014] UKSC 13, [2014] AC 822.

[125] ibid [119]–[120] (Lord Neuberger), [159] (Lord Sumption).

[126] ibid [121].

[127] See above text to nn 107–113.

[128] *Lawrence v Fen Tigers Ltd* (n 124 above) [123].

[129] ibid [167] (Lord Mance), [246] (Lord Carnwath).

The decision in *Lawrence* may have particular significance for right to light disputes. Lord Neuberger remarked, 'I do not see such cases as involving special rules when it comes to this issue.'[130] Perhaps he thought it important to make this claim because, in proposing a departure from *Shelfer*, he relied on the 'more open-minded approach' that he argued was apparent in *Colls*, *Kine* and *Fishenden*,[131] all cases involving rights of light. Lord Mance, in contrast, observed that he was not sure that the same considerations arose in right to light cases compared with a nuisance of the kind found in *Lawrence*.[132] Given that Lord Mance was the most cautious of the judges in favouring a departure from *Shelfer*, he may have intended to indicate that the fact that the courts are often prepared to deny injunctions in right to light cases does not mean that they should be ready to do so for other types of nuisance.

One reading of *Lawrence* is that cases of 'coming to the nuisance' and right to light disputes can be viewed as two special categories where the courts might readily decline to grant an injunction.[133] In contrast, in other cases of nuisance, the case for awarding damages in lieu of an injunction might be more difficult to justify.

F. Takings for Quasi-Public Purposes

One reason that large building schemes can still be completed is the sleight of hand formerly enabled by section 237 of the Town and Country Planning Act 1990 and now provided for by section 203 of the Housing and Planning Act 2016. The latter provision indicates that, where a local authority has appropriated land for planning purposes, 'easements and other rights' may be overridden. This applies whether the development is carried out by the local authority or by someone deriving title from it, thus allowing public bodies to acquire title to land temporarily and pass it on to a developer who may then build without the danger of being enjoined.[134] The owner will have to pay compensation pursuant to the usual principles applying to land that is compulsorily purchased. However, these principles stipulate that compensation is paid according to the market value of the right and not on the basis of a release fee that the owner of a dominant tenement benefiting from a right to light might have hoped to extract from the developer.[135]

IV. Conclusion

Rights of light are anomalous. There is much to be said for the view that England and Wales would do well to follow the lead of so many other common law jurisdictions and eliminate these easements. As long as they do exist, however, there are good reasons to

[130] ibid [122].
[131] ibid [117].
[132] ibid [167].
[133] Treating coming to the nuisance cases as special in this way would equally explain the Court of Appeal's decision to refuse an injunction in *Miller v Jackson* [1977] QB 966 (CA).
[134] *Midtown Ltd v City of London Real Property Col Ltd* [2005] EWHC 33 (Ch), [2005] 14 EG 130.
[135] ibid [34].

treat them differently from other rights. What is more, there is a judicial tradition recognising this: briefly established in the 1860s in the decisions of Lord Westbury and Sir George Turner LJ, and later sustained for decades in a line of appellate authority from *Colls* to *Fishenden*. Rights of light pose special problems because they are burdensome, difficult to identify and vague in scope, and because the obstacles to bargaining around these entitlements are potentially acute. The Supreme Court's decision in *Lawrence* appears to acknowledge this understanding and will hopefully serve to encourage the courts to be more willing to grant damages instead of injunctions in this context.

10

Re-evaluating Recreational Easements – New Norms for the Twenty-First Century?

SUSAN PASCOE

I. Introduction

This chapter evaluates the underpinnings for the validity of recreational and sporting easements in English law. Recognition of such easements represents a wider functional and progressive approach to easements, incorporating new norms of twenty-first-century active lifestyles into what constitutes an easement. The chapter will seek first to analyse recreational easements by reference to Dyal-Chand's sharing model of servitudes and to Alexander's arguments on the promotion of human flourishing. Secondly, by reference to van der Walt's analysis of the rationale and function of anti-fragmentation strategies, it will be evaluated whether rights to use sporting and recreational facilities should be recognised as easements, and to what extent the proliferation of land burdens represents a shift away from the certainty and predictability of a *numerus clausus* of land rights. Thirdly, the complex dynamics of human and property relationships require a re-evaluation of the potential for greater conflict between dominant and servient landowners in maintaining the facilities for use of the easements, and necessitate a reappraisal of what constitutes possession and control of the servient land. Lastly, an assessment is made of the ex ante restrictions on easements versus their ex post regulation and the need for provisions for modification and discharge of easements. It is argued that sporting and recreational easements should be recognised as valid within the parameters analysed below.

This evaluation is prompted by the decision in *Regency Villas Title Ltd v Diamond Resorts (Europe) Ltd* (hereinafter referred to as *Regency Villas*),[1] which raises some of these issues and acts as a useful starting point for this analysis. An appeal was heard in the Supreme Court on 4 and 5 July 2018. The Supreme Court's decision was published too late for detailed examination in this chapter, but recognises the importance of recreation in modern life and has confirmed that there is room for development in English law, making the analysis of broader conceptual issues in this chapter, which of course apply across different jurisdictions, highly relevant. Prior to the decision, stability rather than innovation had been at the heart of the structural parameters which underlay the instrumentalist approach to

[1] *Regency Villas Title Ltd v Diamond Resorts (Europe) Ltd* [2018] UKSC 57 on appeal from [2017] EWCA Civ 238, [2017] 3 WLR 644.

recreational rights as easements. *Regency Villas* represents an extension to the scope of the decision in *Re Ellenborough Park*,[2] where rights to enjoy a park by landowners of surrounding properties were acknowledged to be valid easements. The reference to easements to play tennis and bowls in *Re Ellenborough Park*[3] was *obiter* and the case did not extend the rights generally to sporting and recreational easements.

In the Supreme Court in *Regency Villas*, Lord Briggs (with whom Lady Hale, Lord Kerr, and Lord Sumption agreed, with Lord Carnwath dissenting) demonstrated twenty-first-century vigour in acknowledging that 'recreational and sporting activity … is so clearly a beneficial part of modern life that the common law should support structures which promote and encourage it, rather than treat it as devoid of practical utility or benefit',[4] and in recognising the necessary quality of utility and benefit to the dominant tenement for there to be easements over the Italianate gardens, two outdoor hard-surfaced tennis courts, three indoor squash courts, a putting green, a croquet lawn, the new indoor swimming pool and the 18-hole golf course. The Supreme Court disapproved of the approach of the Court of Appeal in looking at the facilities grant as if it were a grant of separate rights to each facility:

> the Facilities Grant is in my view in substance the grant of a single comprehensive right to use a complex of facilities, and comprehends not only those constructed and in use at the time of the 1981 Transfer, but all those additional or replacement facilities thereafter constructed and put into operation within the Park as part of the leisure complex during the expected useful life of the Regency Villas timeshare development …[5]

Lord Briggs was clear 'that the common law should, as far as possible, accommodate itself to new types of property ownership and new ways of enjoying the use of land'.[6] He was dismissive of past attitudes to 'mere recreation or amusement' as in the *dictum* of Baron Martin in *Mounsey v Ismay*,[7] stating instead that

> the advantages to be gained from recreational and sporting activities are now so universally regarded as being of real utility and benefit to human beings that the perjorative expression 'mere right of recreation and amusement, possessing no quality of utility or benefit' has become a contradiction in terms.[8]

Nevertheless, the decision in *Regency Villas* needs to be seen in the context of timeshare owners, where the servient estate was large and run as a commercial business open to the public as well as to timeshare owners – potentially over 150 timeshare owners who were able to act collectively through the Regency Villa Owners' Club.

In relation to indoor easements, the Supreme Court rejected the distinction which the Court of Appeal drew between outdoor and indoor recreational easements.[9] The incorporation of value judgements about land use and recreation was particularly evident in the rejection by the Court of Appeal of recreational indoor games, activities and facilities on

[2] See *Re Ellenborough Park* [1956] Ch 131.
[3] ibid 168 (Evershed MR).
[4] *Regency Villas* (n 1 above) [81] (Lord Briggs).
[5] ibid [26].
[6] ibid [76].
[7] *Mounsey v Ismay* (1865) 3 H & C 486, 498, 159 ER 621.
[8] *Regency Villas* (n 1 above) [59] (Lord Briggs).
[9] ibid [90] (Lord Briggs), rejecting the approach of the Court of Appeal at [80] (Vos LJ).

the servient land from the scope of easements. These value judgements about the utility and benefit to the dominant tenement were incorporated into the analysis in determining that the modern approach to taking physical exercise is not applicable to recreational indoor games, and this distinction was rightly rejected by the Supreme Court. It is unfortunate that disparate activities such as playing snooker, which is a sport, and watching television, a leisure activity, were grouped together without differentiation by the Court of Appeal, for the ostensible reason that they were all to be carried on in the same area (the ground floor of the Mansion House) and on the basis of the reasoning that the right was really no more than a personal right to use chattels and services provided by the defendants. Watching television was rightly rejected for this reason as an easement, but the Court of Appeal was too hasty in rejecting a right to play snooker, because similar objections could be raised in relation to playing tennis or squash, and this was acknowledged by the Supreme Court. As Lord Briggs noted, the fact that the exercise of a claimed recreational easement involves the use of the servient owner's chattels is not in itself a decisive objection: 'it is no objection to the recognition of a right as an easement that it may be exercised over, or with the use of, chattels or fixtures on the land, rather than merely over the land itself.'[10] Differentiation between playing snooker indoors and playing tennis outdoors might also lead to a result which is inconsistent with general norms against discrimination on the grounds of disability, such as seen, for example, in the Equality Act 2010. Because use of many of the facilities relevant to both indoor and outdoor recreation is not possible without the use of chattels, the approach of the Supreme Court is correct.

The Supreme Court also acknowledged that 'while it may be that a restaurant, viewed on its own, is not a recreational or sporting facility, it is perfectly capable of being viewed as part of a sporting or recreational complex.'[11] The Supreme Court did not specifically make a decision in relation to the Court of Appeal's rejection of a claimed easement to use the reception area and its back office, but Lord Briggs acknowledged that it was unlikely that communal parts of the ground floor and basement could have been intended to be excluded from the scope of the easements.[12] The grouping together by location in the basement of the Mansion House of the gym, sunbed and sauna area, and the rejection by the Court of Appeal of claimed easements to use those facilities, was thus rightly overruled by the Supreme Court, which adopted instead a far more balanced and nuanced approach to the use of chattels, allowing the recognition of such easements.

II. Recreational Easements, the Sharing Model of Servitudes and Human Flourishing

A. Sharing Model of Servitudes

Easements always involve some degree of the sharing of land. However, the sharing model of servitudes advocated by Dyal-Chand[13] appears to play no discernible role in the recognition

[10] ibid [91] (Lord Briggs).
[11] ibid [89].
[12] ibid.
[13] R Dyal-Chand, 'Sharing the Cathedral' (2013) 46 *Connecticut Law Review* 647.

of recreational easements in English law, because, as she acknowledges, exclusion – the conceptual opposite of sharing – is the thematic foundation of property law. Exclusion may be considered the defining characteristic of property ownership as a presumptive means of enhancing property's role as a stable basis for market transactions. Sharing appears as the exception to the rule of exclusion. Her view is that it is somewhat ironic that courts recognise sharing by creating exceptions to rights rather than by more actively fashioning remedies to enforce sharing. In doing so, they regularly fail to respond to the core problem of exclusion that they are drawn to redressing.[14]

Using a vantage point provided by Oliver Wendell Holmes in the realm of contract law, Dyal-Chand develops a model for enhancing property outcomes and, in particular, for promoting sharing as a preferred outcome in core doctrinal areas, such as those involving claims of nuisance, adverse possession, implied easements and trespass.[15] She develops the 'interest-outcome approach' to better resolve core property disputes based on a model that provides both a modern and specific template for enriching outcomes in property law, since property sharing can be a very modern means of addressing distributional concerns such as those featured in *Regency Villas*. When a property law system is focused on outcomes in any given dispute, it is more likely to recognise opportunities to share. Shared uses are not just a matter of most effectively internalising the externalities of property ownership and use; they also can increase the 'size of the pie', providing more individuals with access to property for the purpose of productive use.[16] This approach also recognises the importance of use and possession over (and, at times, in lieu of) formal title, because use and possession are often legitimate interests that can serve as the basis for finding more equitable outcomes. Implied easements are a pertinent example of courts creating shared interests in land by granting limited rights of access and use to non-owners.

It is true that focusing on legitimate interests, or justified expectations, will muddy crystalline rules that prioritise formal title and exclusion,[17] and a focus on outcomes and reliance interests also could add 'mud'.[18] Indeed, Dyal-Chand acknowledges that there are certain challenges to the model, the most significant of these probably being that the model would create uncertainty and unpredictability of property rights and that this would cause market instability.[19] Nevertheless, the most important feature of sharing under the interest-outcome approach is that it results in outcomes that represent compromises of some sort between the parties' varying interests and require the tangible sharing of land as exhibited in *Regency Villas*. The use of tennis courts, swimming pools and golf courses may be an extension of the meaning of 'utility and benefit',[20] but recognition of the benefits of physical activity in upholding the validity of recreational easements demonstrates elements of the sharing model, enabling incorporation of analysis of broader interests relevant in a dispute. For Dyal-Chand, sharing is a remedial option, but the sharing model is already implicit in some well-recognised easements and the decision in *Regency Villas* demonstrates its osmotic incorporation into the corpus of the definition of easements.

[14] ibid 652.
[15] ibid 654.
[16] ibid 668.
[17] CM Rose, 'Crystals and Mud in Property Law' (1988) 40 *Stanford Law Review* 577.
[18] Dyal-Chand (n 13 above) 679.
[19] ibid 681.
[20] J Bray, 'More than just a walk in the park: a new view on recreational easements' [2017] *Conv* 418, 439.

B. Sharing Servitudes and Human Flourishing

It is illuminating to compare Dyal-Chand's analysis with Alexander's examination of governance property.[21] Alexander rarely undertakes specific analysis of sharing, but his discussion of governance property,[22] defined as multiple-ownership property that requires governance norms to regulate the internal relations between the multiple owners,[23] overlaps significantly with what Dyal-Chand describes as sharing remedies. In van der Walt's view, it could be said that all sharing remedies, in Dyal-Chand's terminology, create such governance property.[24] Governance property aims at achieving certain values, including autonomy, aggregate welfare and the Aristotelian idea of human flourishing. Human flourishing is a pluralistic moral value comprising multiple values, including individual autonomy and freedom, social welfare, community and sharing, and personhood and self-realisation.[25]

Easements are a governance property arrangement because of the proprietary interests of the dominant and servient owners who have conflicting interests, which require mechanisms to co-ordinate and maximise the values of their respective interests.[26] Recreational easements encourage and enable the flourishing of the owners of the dominant tenement, but inevitably inhibit the servient owners by restricting the use of their own land, even if the original servient owners entered into the consensual arrangements freely. The rivalrous nature of property is particularly highlighted by recreational easements and balancing the interests of the owners of the dominant and servient tenements, for example in relation to the allocation of responsibility between them to maintain the facilities, may accordingly be too complex an issue for governance property.

Information theorists would argue for the optimal level of standardisation or the optimal level of systemic complexity for recreational easements.[27] By way of contrast, progressive theorists are attentive to a wide array of factors and concerned that property should not employ simplifying rules that are insufficiently attentive to the values at stake. Adopting a progressive theorist's approach to recreational easements, it is necessary for property to reflect democracy, promote freedom and advance human flourishing with the focus on ends rather than function. Progressive theorists affirmatively value ongoing considerations of whether property rules are serving the proper values and creating appropriate relationships.[28] These regulate how property works as a social ordering device. The result in *Regency Villas* is consistent with a progressive property approach to easements to avoid a result which is unjust to the timeshare owners.

[21] See GS Alexander, 'Governance Property' (2012) 160 *University of Pennsylvania Law Review* 1853.

[22] For a critique of Alexander's definition of governance property, see S Blandy, S Bright and S Nield, 'The Dynamics of Enduring Property Relationships in Land' (2018) 81 *MLR* 85, 94–95.

[23] Alexander (n 21 above) 1856.

[24] AJ van der Walt, 'Sharing Servitudes' (2015) 4 *European Property Law Journal* 162, fn 1.

[25] Alexander (n 21 above) 1875. See further R Walsh, 'Property, Human Flourishing and St Thomas Aquinas: Assessing a Contemporary Revival' (2018) 31 *Canadian Journal of Law and Jurisprudence* 197.

[26] Alexander (n 21 above) 1862–63. Legal mechanisms could, for example, facilitate increased use of landlords' and tenants' associations.

[27] See TW Merrill and HE Smith, 'Optimal Standardization in the Law of Property: The *Numerus Clausus* Principle' (2000) 110 *Yale Law Journal* 1. See also JB Baron, 'The Contested Commitments of Property' (2010) 61 *Hastings Law Journal* 917, 920, 940, 950.

[28] Baron ibid 965.

By way of contrast to English law and the approach in *Re Ellenborough Park*,[29] American courts and legislatures have been very responsive to the demands for increasing the availability of servitudes since the time of the Industrial Revolution. By creating exceptions, adopting new categories and changing the content of doctrines received from English law, the courts freed American law from the most severe constraints imposed by classical servitudes doctrine in the nineteenth and early twentieth centuries.[30] The Restatement (Third) of Property Servitudes (2000) adopted the principle that landowners may freely create servitudes unless they are illegal or unconstitutional or violate public policy, and instead shifted the focus to rules of interpretation and doctrines governing modification and termination of servitudes.[31]

The desire for servitudes far outstripped those that could be supplied within traditional limits, and American courts and legislatures responded with pragmatic changes and exceptions that left only vestigial traces of traditional principles.[32] They were able to do so, because American law provided easy access to land title records and provided nearly complete protection against servitudes to purchasers without notice. If the Law Commission reforms are introduced to overhaul implied easements, so that easements are implied only where they are necessary for the reasonable use of the land,[33] recreational easements would have to arise by express grant and be registered, so a similar approach to recreational easements could arguably be adopted in English law. This would not, however, deal with concerns over a proliferation of easements sterilising the use of the servient land. Since the American approach allows for more flexible discharge or variation of servitudes, English law would need to extend its means of ex post control of easements, as discussed in section V.B below.

C. Indoor Recreational Activities

The law of easements has not drawn a general distinction between outdoor and indoor easements, and easements which make use of indoor parts of the servient land have been recognised as valid.[34] If a legal system were simply to exclude recreational indoor games, activities and facilities on the servient land from the scope of easements,[35] this would constitute a rejection of a sharing-oriented outcome approach and of a progressive property approach, instead incorporating an exclusionary, ownership-focused model to indoor activities. An interest-outcome approach would instead take full account of both parties'

[29] *Re Ellenborough Park* (n 2 above).

[30] S French, 'The American Restatement of Servitude Law: Reforming Doctrine by Shifting from *Ex Ante* to *Ex Post* Controls on the Risks Posed by Servitudes' in S van Erp and B Akkermans (eds), *Towards a unified system of land burdens* (Antwerp, Intersentia, 2006) 109.

[31] ibid 112.

[32] ibid 111. French gives examples of enforceable servitudes for condominium regimes, scenic highways, conservation of agricultural land and wildlife habitat and historic preservation: ibid 109.

[33] Law Commission, *Making Land Work: Easements, Covenants and Profits à Prendre* (Law Com No 327, 2011) [3.45] and clause 20 of Law of Property Bill.

[34] See, for example, *Wright v Macadam* [1949] 2 KB 744, *Miller v Emcer Products Ltd* [1956] Ch 304, *Heywood v Mallalieu* (1883) 25 Ch D 357.

[35] The approach preferred by the Court of Appeal in *Regency Villas* (n 1 above) [85] (Vos LJ), but rejected by the Supreme Court [90] (Lord Briggs).

actual use (or non-use) of the property, in its physical, social and economic context and with due regard for its effect on the community and society at large, and would possibly enable some kind of physical or temporal sharing of the property.[36] Exclusion from the category of easements in relation to indoor activities should not be decided on the basis of what van der Walt terms an on/off switch. An on/off switch only allows the binary option between two opposite outcomes, whereas outdoor easements demonstrate a glider-switch approach,[37] which enables a range of options in between the two extremes.

Use of a gym as an easement requires individual analysis due to the benefits of physical activity and exercise. With the ever-increasing popularity of gyms, which encapsulate a modern approach to exercise, an easement over a gym would be a natural progression of a modern approach to easements. British Columbia is a common law jurisdiction and easements over a pool, gym and sauna were ruled valid in *Strata Plan NW 1942 v Strata Plan NW 2050*.[38] More recently, in *Strata Plan NWS 3457 v Strata Plan LMS 1425*,[39] a recreational facilities easement was accepted as valid with the recreational facilities including a community building with a sauna, whirlpool, kitchen, exercise room, amenity room, changing room and meeting room. The easement had been registered at the Land Title Office when the lands were developed in the early 1990s and the dispute was over responsibility to pay for the upkeep of the easement.

The potential for human flourishing and the 'community' or 'social' interest in land would be acknowledged in taking a broad approach to indoor activities and would not result in the prioritisation of the individualism of private ownership. According to the social obligation norm,[40] property is subject to social obligations and community-driven obligations, and private ownership entails obligations to act or refrain from acting for the purpose of promoting the collective good of the community.[41] Models of sharing and human flourishing are nullified if all indoor recreational facilities are rejected as easements and it is therefore commendable that the Supreme Court in *Regency Villas* did not take that path. Questions over the interpretation and application of the test of utility and benefit, amidst an unarticulated apprehension of opening the floodgates to indoor easements, highlight some of the incongruencies and conflicts with interpersonal relationships which could arise, and which will be examined in section IV.

III. Anti-Fragmentation Strategies and Certainty and Predictability of *Numerus Clausus*

The purpose of anti-fragmentation strategies or controls is to prevent an undesirable proliferation of real rights in land.[42] The strategic, systemic application of anti-fragmentation

[36] Van der Walt (n 24 above) 166.

[37] ibid 176–77 and see also Dyal-Chand (n 13 above) 664–66 who also uses the switch terminology.

[38] *Strata Plan NW 1942 v Strata Plan NW 2050* (2008) 69 RPR (4th) 67 (BCSC).

[39] *Strata Plan NWS 3457 v Strata Plan LMS 1425* 2017 BCSC 1346, [2017] BCWLD 5382.

[40] GS Alexander, 'The Social-Obligation Norm in American Property Law' (2009) 94 *Cornell Law Review* 745, 757.

[41] An example in English law can be seen in Empty Dwelling Management Orders established under the Housing Act 2004. See S Pascoe, 'The Social Obligation Norm and the Erosion of Land Ownership?' [2012] *Conv* 484, 487–91.

[42] AJ van der Walt, 'The Continued Relevance of Servitudes' (2013) 3 *Property Law Review* 3.

controls might have resulted in a refusal to recognise *any* of the easements in *Regency Villas*. Van der Walt examines the normative framework within which the control strategies are applied and developed and analyses two justifications for anti-fragmentation controls, which are the anti-feudalism narrative and the efficient land-use narrative.[43] The latter narrative explains anti-fragmentation strategies with reference to their promotion of efficient land use or economic efficiency, which focuses on utility.

A. Relevance of the Anti-feudalism Narrative and *Numerus Clausus* to Recreational Easements?

As van der Walt has argued, the anti-fragmentation restrictions that characterise modern property law are, for civil lawyers, specifically anti-feudal guarantors of liberty and autonomy, bulwarks against a slide back into feudalism and oppression.[44] The anti-feudalism narrative describes the abolition of feudalism as a move away from a proliferation of fragmented land rights towards unified and absolute ownership. The problematic remnants of feudalism in English law re-emerge from time to time,[45] but are not an explicit rationale for constructing boundaries for the validity of easements and are at best an implicit force only. In relation to *profits à prendre*, the Law Commission has recognised how they were originally created to facilitate a system of feudal landholding.[46] Medieval law did not have much experience of easements apart from rights of way and rights to water, and profits were much more common and important.[47]

Post-feudal civil law property doctrine, which, according to the anti-feudalism narrative, was aimed at ensuring that ownership remains a unitary, unfragmented right, finds its clearest expression in the *numerus clausus*, or closed catalogue, of nominate real rights in land.[48] Based on the assumed value of a unitary and absolute right of ownership, the idea of a *numerus clausus* of property rights was to promote legal certainty, predictability and transparency as central values of the post-revolutionary scheme of rights. Anti-fragmentation controls such as *numerus clausus* ensured that the limited use-rights that the private owner is allowed to create do not contribute to a renewed erosion or fragmentation of ownership.[49]

In relation to French and Belgian law, Sagaert argues that the restrictive function of the *numerus clausus* is especially relevant because, in the civil law, servitudes are 'the modern translation of feudal burdens'.[50] Van Erp argues that the strict civil law *numerus clausus*

[43] ibid 4–5.

[44] ibid 7.

[45] See, for example, I Williams, 'The Certainty of Term Requirement in Leases: Nothing Lasts Forever' [2015] *CLJ* 592, 606–09 in relation to abolition of the *escheat* of freehold land and the feudal underpinnings of the certainty requirement for leases.

[46] Law Commission, *Easements, Covenants and Profits à Prendre* (Law Com CP No 186, 2008) [6.1].

[47] See AWB Simpson, *A History of Land Law*, 2nd edn (Oxford, Oxford University Press, 1986) 107–08.

[48] Van der Walt (n 42 above) 9.

[49] ibid 11.

[50] V Sagaert, 'Party Autonomy in French and Belgian Law: The Interconnection between Substantive Property Law and Private International Law' in R Westrik and J van der Weide (eds), *Party Autonomy in International Law* (Munich, European Law Publishers, 2011) 119, 127 discussed in van der Walt (n 42 above) 9.

doctrine should develop towards a *numerus quasi-clausus*, because some flexibility is needed to regulate new forms of rights in property.[51] He argues that what civil law could learn here from common law is flexibility, which enables property law to be more responsive to economic developments. What the common law could learn from civil law is that closing legal categories creates more legal security and reduces information costs. The question remains what the starting point should be: common law pragmatism or civil law theory? In van Erp's view, neither should be the starting point, but rather historical-comparative analysis, taking into account socio-economic factors, should lead the way towards the most workable approach.

Information theorists focus on *numerus clausus* in order to avoid the tremendous information costs that would be imposed if parties were free to create any kind of property rights they might desire,[52] whereas progressive theorists do not take direct issue with the *numerus clausus* principle, but the values which they wish to further cannot necessarily be vindicated in the 'standardized, stripped down form' which information theorists value.[53] Chang and Smith argue that in between the strict *numerus clausus* principle and the restriction-free *numerus apertus* principle, a compromise is to allow property customs, such as complex divisions of property rights or idiosyncratic customs, to create new, *de jure* property forms, where they impose tolerable information costs and prevent *numerus clausus* from becoming a straitjacket on property.[54] Such an approach arguably enables recreational easements to adapt to the twenty-first century.

De Waal argues for an approach that is similar to that adopted in English law, which is an approach that is flexible enough to allow a landowner to do something that was patently not possible in Roman law and that is directly in conflict with the anti-fragmentation impulse of a strict *numerus clausus*: a landowner who has built and established a hotel business on her land could, in terms of the flexible approach, contract with a neighbouring landowner for the right of her hotel guests to stroll and picnic along the shore of a dam on the neighbouring land, and also to register that right as a praedial servitude[55] in favour of the dominant property.[56] Rural servitudes could not be acquired in Roman law purely for the right to stroll on another's land, whereas a different approach was taken to urban servitudes.

In English law, as McFarlane has stated, the significance of *numerus clausus* is how the courts police the most important boundary in land law between personal rights, on one side of the line, and estates and interests in land, on the other, a boundary on which the whole

[51] S van Erp, '*Numerus Quasi-Clausus* of Property Rights as a Constitutive Element of a Future European Property Law?' (2003) 7.2 *Electronic Journal of Comparative Law*, available at: https://www.ejcl.org/72/art72-2.PDF 11-2. See also B Akkermans, *The Principle of Numerus Clausus in European Property Law* (Antwerp, Intersentia, 2008) 118.

[52] Merrill and Smith (n 27 above) 1.

[53] Baron (n 27 above) 920, 922.

[54] Y Chang and HE Smith, 'The *Numerus Clausus* Principle, Property Customs, and the Emergence of New Property Forms' (2015) 100 *Iowa Law Review* 2275, 2279, 2292–93.

[55] The term praedial servitude derives from Roman law and is used in civil law systems to describe a right which is granted over servient land for the benefit of dominant land. For the distinction between praedial and personal servitudes, see AJ van der Walt, *The Law of Servitudes* (Claremont, Juta, 2016) chs 5 and 6.

[56] MJ de Waal, '*Die vereistes vir die vestiging van grondserwitude in die Suid-Afrikaanse reg*' (1990) 1 *Stellenbosch Law Review* 1 discussed in van der Walt (n 42 above) 19–20. See also the South African decision in *Hotel De Aar v Jonordon Investment (Edms) Bpk* 1972 (2) SA 400.

map of property law depends.[57] In common law, the goal of legal certainty and stability is promoted through the requirements for a valid easement under *Re Ellenborough Park*.[58] Although ownership is routinely fragmented, *Regency Villas* highlights an enduring tension at the heart of easement law between, on one hand, freedom to create property rights, which is an embodiment of individual autonomy and economic liberty, and on the other hand, preservation of the unity and absoluteness of ownership, which is an embodiment of legal certainty and security of title. This tension still shapes the doctrinal debate about precisely where the line should be drawn in deciding on the permitted scope of easements.

B. Relevance of the Efficient Land-use Narrative to Recreational Easements?

The efficient land-use narrative is more suited to the analysis of recreational easements and focuses more directly on the utilitarian goal of ensuring or promoting efficient land use. As van der Walt recognises, the efficient land-use argument is sometimes used to argue for the abolition of restrictions, and sometimes for a qualified and flexible adaptation of some of the restrictive devices.[59] The efficient land-use argument usually holds that restrictive strategies serve a legitimate function in modern law, but when circumstances change, overly strict adherence to the restrictive measures and inflexibility have a negative effect on the efficient use of land. On the basis of changed circumstances, they therefore usually argue, in one form or another, for a flexible approach that would retain the beneficial features of the anti-fragmentation strategies while allowing for some deviation where necessary.[60] Recognition of the validity of outdoor recreational easements represents elements of this approach, suggesting that new categories of easements can be created even though they may appear to conflict with traditional restrictions.

A consequence of the recognition of outdoor recreational easements is that a proliferation of land burdens can create an anticommons, which potentially results in underuse of a valuable resource, so that restrictive strategies like *numerus clausus* are justified in so far as they counter the anticommons effect of the proliferation of land burdens. A tragedy of the anticommons occurs when too many parties have the right to exclude and nobody has an effective use privilege with the result that the property is underused.[61] This is potentially foreseeable with recreational easements, where the neighbouring owners may be seeking to avoid concurrent use of the land. Economic efficiency therefore justifies both retaining the traditional anti-fragmentation strategies and introducing new ex post strategies that would

[57] B McFarlane, '*Keppell v Bailey* (1834); *Hill v Tupper* (1863) The Numerus Clausus and the Common Law' in N Gravells (ed), *Landmark Cases in Land Law* (Oxford, Hart Publishing, 2013) 1, 3. See also K Gray, 'Property in Thin Air' (1991) 50 *CLJ* 252, 302.

[58] *Re Ellenborough Park* (n 2 above).

[59] Van der Walt (n 42 above) 12–14.

[60] ibid discussing Sagaert (n 50 above) 123–24. See also B Rudden, 'Economic Theory v Property Law: The Numerus Clausus Problem' in J Eekelaar and J Bell (eds), *Oxford essays in jurisprudence – Third series* (Oxford, Oxford University Press, 1987) 237, 245.

[61] MA Heller, 'The Boundaries of Private Property' (1999) 108 *Yale Law Journal* 1163; MA Heller, 'The Tragedy of the Anticommons: Property in the Transition from Marx to Markets' (1998) 111 *Harvard Law Review* 621 cited in van der Walt (n 42 above) 21.

reinforce their efficiency in facilitating consolidation of fragmented land-use rights, such as the American mechanisms for discharging or varying easements.[62]

The most significant feature of the efficient land-use narrative is that the normative framework within which it functions is unwaveringly utilitarian. Efficient land use, that is economic efficiency, optimisation of the conditions for free and wealth-maximising use of private property, is the only normative guideline. The real issue with recreational easements in *Regency Villas* might not be fragmentation of ownership, but commercialisation of land rights in the context of timeshare owners who wish to make full use of recreational easements granted to them. However, if an opportunity arose for the servient land to be used for other purposes, more efficient overall land use could be prevented by the holders of the recreational easements.

IV. Dynamics of Human and Property Relationships and Conflict Between Dominant and Servient Landowners

There is the potential for conflict and friction between dominant and servient landowners, because easements limit the owner of the servient tenement in use and enjoyment of land for the sake of enhancing the use of the dominant tenement. This conflict can be exacerbated when conditions under which an easement is exercised change significantly over time as well as when there are changes in ownership. Principles of 'give as well as take'[63] are necessary to allow a co-existence of rights between landowners, reflected in formal or informal ground rules. Consequently, decisions as to validity of easements must not lay foundations for potential contention. Conflict could arise from the parties having to determine what would be reasonable charges that the servient owner could make for use of services or for the use of chattels, although use of the easement itself would be without payment of any charge or fee for the exercise of those rights.[64] Another source of contention might be establishing what would be reasonable provisions made by the servient owner for regulation of the easements in the ordinary course, such as timings for use, obtaining access to the servient land, provision for use of chattels, tidying, cleaning, etc. A further potential source of tension may derive from the servient owner replacing facilities with those of the same or similar kind. Such factors may add to the problematic relationship between the parties depending on the circumstances.

A. Conflict in Recreational Easements Between Landowners

The issue arises whether potential conflict over the use of land should be a relevant factor in determining the validity of easements and its importance in ex post regulation. The analysis

[62] Van der Walt (n 42 above) 21.

[63] *R (on the application of Lewis) v Redcar and Cleveland BC* [2010] UKSC 11, [2010] 2 AC 70, [48] (Lord Walker) discussed in A Baker, 'Recreational Privileges as Easements: Law and Policy' [2012] *Conv* 37, 42–43. See also Purle J in *Regency Villas Title Ltd v Diamond Resorts (Europe) Ltd* [2015] EWHC 3564, [48].

[64] *Regency Villas* (n 1 above) Court of Appeal [86] and Supreme Court [32], [67]–[73].

of Blandy, Bright and Nield of enduring property relationships in land has particular resonance in the context of recreational easements due to the need to avoid conflicts in sharing land in order to use the recreational easements. The dynamics approach acknowledges the broad range of legal, regulatory, social and commercial norms that touch on property relationships and recognises that those norms are not rigid, but evolve responsively to the spatial, temporal and lived dimensions of property in land.[65] Such an approach recognises that property relationships are lived relationships that are sustained by their evolution over time to accommodate changing patterns and understandings of spatial use, new rights-holders, relationship needs, economic realities, opportunities and technical innovations,[66] and so can be particularly pertinent to sporting and recreational easements.

Under the dynamics approach, it is necessary to develop a more collective and co-operative way of living to make the easement 'work'.[67] The schema draws attention to variety and fluidity, and in particular draws out the relational, that is the contextual and 'between persons' relations, recognising that these property relationships are in part socially constructed. The authors apply to property relationships the key idea from relational contract theory that parties to contracts are 'embedded in complex relations',[68] which is particularly germane to recreational easements. The continuing nature of the relationship is an important feature, affecting the way in which the governing norms are articulated at the outset, and accommodating the possibility that these may need to evolve and be adjusted over time to reflect the dynamics of the relationship between right-holders.[69] Woven within the idea of 'enduring' property relations, therefore, is recognition that as the relationship is sustained through time, there may be a degree of 'give and take' to accommodate changes in the use of land, in the identity of the rights-holders, in external regulatory and economic forces, as well as in the parties' preferences for rigidity or flux. Where there is a dispute over shared space, it may be necessary to resolve not only the disputed property relationship, but also the personal relationship between the parties. If the personal relationship cannot be maintained, the property relationship may also falter.[70] The need to police the easements may, however, militate against recognition of such easements.[71]

Particularly important in the context of recreational easements is the parties' unwritten understandings as to the use of the land which may be factored into the interpretation of the factual matrix. This is demonstrated well by the case of *Bradley v Heslin*,[72] where the temporal nature of enduring property relationships meant that the formal legal easements no longer reflected how the land was laid out or the practices about usage that had developed over the 30 harmonious years before the relationship broke down between successors

[65] Blandy et al (n 22 above) 85–86.

[66] ibid.

[67] ibid 86.

[68] ibid 87, citing IR Macneil, 'Relational Contract Theory: Unanswered Questions' (2000) 94 *Northwestern University Law Review* 877, 881.

[69] ibid 87–88.

[70] ibid 89.

[71] This is similar to the rule in contract that specific performance will not be granted if the relationship between the parties requires constant supervision. See, for example, *Cooperative Insurance Society Ltd v Argyll Stores (Holdings) Ltd* [1998] AC 1.

[72] *Bradley v Heslin* [2014] EWHC 3267, discussed in Blandy et al (n 22 above) 97–98, 102, 108–110. I am very grateful for an unpublished case note on *Bradley v Heslin* [2014] EWHC 3267 shared with me by Professor Alison Clarke.

in title. The decision of Norris J, recognising an easement by estoppel to open and close gates, demonstrates how formal property rights changed over time and how the 'real deal' differed from the 'paper deal'.[73] The parties had evolved self-generated norms throughout the harmonious 30 years and such norms resulted in solutions moulded from 'mud' being transformed into 'crystallised' rights,[74] acquiring proprietary effect. In the majority of lived relationships, the parties simply cannot afford the expense of litigation, so it is the muddy rights that endure in uncrystallised form. The consequence in relation to sporting and recreational easements is that courts should be amenable to recognising their validity, because the parties will develop their own norms to deal with practical difficulties that may arise over use of such facilities.

B. Impact of Occupation or Possession on the Relationship?

Van der Walt also acknowledges the more complex and contested image of human relationships,[75] and how a progressive approach to easements may lead to conflicts between landowners due to a shift in power between dominant and servient owners, with greater power for owners of dominant land.[76] An easement will not be valid in English law if it requires the dominant owner to exercise a right to joint occupation or deprives the servient owner of proprietorship or legal possession.[77] If the owner of the dominant land had to take actual occupation or possession of part of the servient land in order to give continued effect to the easement, that might point against the existence of such an easement in the first place. This test appears to be closest to the test of possession and control from *Moncrieff v Jamieson*[78] where Lord Scott rejected the 'ouster' principle that asks whether the servient owner is left with any reasonable use of his land and would instead 'substitute for it a test which asks whether the servient owner retains possession and, subject to the reasonable exercise of the right in question, control of the servient land'.[79] Some of the claimed easements in *Regency Villas* may have been so extensive as to leave the servient tenement without viable use.

Such conflicts will be heightened even further if the servient owners were to go out of business and cease to maintain the facilities, and the owners of the dominant tenement would be at liberty to enter the servient tenement to maintain and repair the facilities at their own expense. There would need to be examination of the nature of the works that the dominant owner would undertake, since on one view that could prevent the right claimed being an easement if those activities became so extensive that they amounted to possession or occupation by the dominant owner.[80] This would be a question of fact and degree in

[73] Blandy et al (n 22 above) 98.
[74] ibid 108 discussing Rose (n 17 above).
[75] Van der Walt (n 42 above) 6.
[76] Van der Walt (n 55 above) ch 3.
[77] *Regency Villas* (n 1 above) Court of Appeal [60] (Vos LJ) deriving from *Re Ellenborough Park* (n 2 above) 164 (Evershed MR) and see Supreme Court [61] (Lord Briggs).
[78] *Moncrieff v Jamieson* [2007] UKHL 42, [2007] 1 WLR 2620.
[79] ibid [59]. See also the discussion in Law Commission (n 33 above) [3.188]–[3.211].
[80] *Regency Villas* (n 1 above) Court of Appeal [49]; but see the different view of Lord Briggs in the Supreme Court [64]–[65].

each case and would require an individual assessment of each right claimed and the level of maintenance that each relevant facility would require.[81]

The potential impact on the human relationship between the parties of invasive interventions on the servient land must not be overlooked. If the dominant owners can provide their own water supply when they need to fill the swimming pool – if necessary from a tanker – and potentially provide even a filtration plant for the pool, and this would not be regarded as sharing possession of the land on which the pool is constructed,[82] that would nevertheless be intrusive, and there would need to be an analysis of the logistics of organisation on the servient owner's land. Equally intrusive would be if the dominant owners provide their own electricity to light squash courts with a generator or by other means if the owner of the servient tenement cannot be required to provide that electricity through a coin-operated meter system.[83] Further, the dominant owners could mow the grass[84] and take other necessary steps to make the golf course or croquet lawn playable, although if a golf course requires daily mowing to be properly playable, it was acknowledged by the Court of Appeal that might require taking 'actual occupation or possession', but the majority in the Supreme Court did not take such a view.[85]

Due to the problematic effect on the relationship between the parties, rather than securing the right by way of an easement, if the law is reformed to enable positive covenants to bind successors in title, an alternative way this could be dealt with would be for a positive covenant on the servient owner to maintain the pool and the dominant owner to pay a fair share of the cost of this.[86] Servient owners may rightly not wish to be constrained in the use of their own land in such a way, although that would not apply in the *Regency Villas* kind of situation, where the timeshare developer retains land specifically in order to provide the agreed rights and thereby obtains a much higher price for the timeshares. In other scenarios, this would, however, circumvent the limitation in the law of easements that no positive obligation could be imposed on the servient owner. This could impose undesirable clogs on title, except in the context of communal facilities where the sharing of running costs would minimise the burden on individuals.[87]

C. Property Relationships in the Domestic Context – A Proportionality Test?

There needs to be differentiation between, on the one hand, the situation where the servient estate is run as a commercial business providing sporting and recreational facilities and,

[81] See also N Pratt, 'A Proprietary Right to Recreate: *Regency Villas Title Ltd v Diamond Resorts (Europe) Ltd* [2017] EWCA Civ 238' [2017] *Conv* 312.

[82] *Regency Villas* (n 1 above) Court of Appeal [72] and compare the broad brush approach taken by the Supreme Court [64]–[65] and [67]–[73].

[83] ibid, Court of Appeal [68].

[84] See in relation to mowing the grass airfield, *Dowty Boulton Paul Ltd v Wolverhampton Corporation (No 2)* [1976] 1 Ch 13, 24 (Russell LJ).

[85] *Regency Villas* (n 1 above) Court of Appeal [60] and see too Lord Carnwath in the Supreme Court [101]–[105], disagreeing with the approach of the majority at [64]–[65].

[86] Law Commission (n 33) [5.69], [6.30]–[6.31]. See also Baker (n 63 above) 52.

[87] Baker ibid.

on the other hand, the situation where the servient and dominant owners are domestic neighbours.[88] Although there is not a distinct demarcation currently, as the law evolves, what may be an easement in a commercial context may not necessarily be an easement in the domestic context, although in both cases it will need to be established whether there is the required element of utility and benefit to the dominant land. Baker has suggested that rights between neighbours which would interfere with reasonable notions of domestic privacy should not be recognised as easements, and where recreational rights interfere with domestic privacy, even expressly conferred privileges should be regarded as merely personal arrangements.[89] Indoor easements have, however, been recognised, such as an easement to use a toilet,[90] and an easement to use a kitchen belonging to the owner of a neighbouring tenement for particular purposes was implicitly recognised as valid in *Heywood v Mallalieu*,[91] although failed for other reasons. As Baker states, rights to share kitchen facilities are more important to commodious living than the use of a tennis court, so greater leeway can be expected with the former.[92] In relation to the upmarket residential context, he argues that recreational facilities could perhaps be supported only where the facility was out of the way of the alleged servient house and covered only a small proportion of its grounds. Such an argument could be used to justify an easement allowing the use of indoor squash courts and tennis courts, and perhaps indoor and outdoor table-tennis tables.

Van der Walt and van Staden suggest a proportionality test to be incorporated in balancing two prominent common law principles, namely, that the servitude holder has all the rights necessary for the effective exercise of his servitude, and that the servitude must be exercised *civiliter modo*, so as to impose the least possible burden on the servient land.[93] The *civiliter* principle protects the interests of the servient proprietor by requiring that the servitude be exercised reasonably, in a manner that will cause the least damage or inconvenience to the servient property. In the balancing or proportionality analysis, the question is whether avoiding the harm that not awarding the servitude will cause for one party justifies the harm or loss that awarding it will cause for the other.[94] The focus would be on actual use, use interests and the potential for sharing, and a contextual assessment of all competing or conflicting rights and interests is required. In the context of easements in English law, it would, however, be very cumbersome to introduce a proportionality test into the ex ante recognition of easements.

A proportionality analysis can be contrasted with the strong undercurrents of exclusion in the domestic context. This was demonstrated by the *obiter dictum* concerning use of a swimming pool in *Moncrieff v Jamieson*[95] where Lord Scott doubted whether the grant

[88] Purle J in *Regency Villas* (n 63 above) [64] differentiated the domestic context, but the Court of Appeal did not do so specifically. The Supreme Court did acknowledge some differentiation.

[89] Baker (n 63 above) 48, 53.

[90] *Miller v Emcer Products Ltd* (n 34 above).

[91] *Heywood v Mallalieu* (n 34 above).

[92] Baker (n 63 above) 48.

[93] AJ van der Walt and S van Staden, '"Progressive" Judicial Interpretation of Servitudes and Ancillary Servitude Entitlements – *Jersey Lane Properties (Pty) Ltd t/a Fairlawn Boutique Hotel & Spa v Hodgson*' (2016) 79 *Journal of Contemporary Roman-Dutch Law* 671, 675–76.

[94] Van der Walt (n 24 above) 197.

[95] *Moncrieff v Jamieson* (n 78 above) [47] referred to in *Regency Villas* (n 1 above) Court of Appeal [71] and Supreme Court [66]. Compare *Grant v McDonald* [1992] 5 WWR 577 where the right to build and use an outdoor swimming pool was regarded as capable of being an easement by the British Columbia Court of Appeal after consideration of *Re Ellenborough Park* (n 2 above).

of a right to use a neighbour's swimming pool could ever qualify as an easement, because the swimming pool owner would be under no obligation to keep the pool full of water and the grantee would be in no position to fill it if the grantor chose not to do so. Lord Scott's concern in *Moncrieff* was the considerable and disproportionate imposition on the servient tenement that filling and using a swimming pool would require.[96] English law may now be different from Scottish law on this point, since the right to use an outdoor pool in English law is capable of being an easement, and it would entitle, though not require, the dominant owner to fill the pool if the servient owner did not do so.[97] Nevertheless, a right to swim or play golf may lie on the edge of what can be accepted as a servitude in Scottish law.[98]

Although in van der Walt's and van Staden's analysis, proportionality includes constitutional goals, and there are no such defined constitutional goals in English law, a proportionality test could serve a useful function in the context of recreational easements, especially in the domestic context. It may be that the proportionality test would then be merely a different means of undertaking utilitarian calculus. In practice, in nearly every case where a servient owner grants a dominant owner the rights to use sporting facilities, it is because the servient owner is in the business of providing sports facilities or is a charitable or public body whose purposes include the provision of sporting facilities. However, in the domestic context, access to indoor facilities may be far more problematic than access to outdoor facilities, and the impact of enduring property relationships in land and the significance of human relationships within them must not be overlooked in decisions relating to the validity of easements.

V. Ex ante Restrictions versus Ex post Regulation of Easements

Ex ante controls prevent or restrict the creation of easements from the outset, while ex post controls provide for the amendment or termination of already existing easements.[99] In English law, the common law mostly provides for ex ante controls as laid down in *Re Ellenborough Park*,[100] while ex post controls would need to be created in or derived from statutory provisions,[101] which would require legislation by way of a reformulated section 84 of the Law of Property Act 1925 to modify or terminate easements in English law. There is some limited ex post control at common law, because an easement will end if an irreversible change of circumstances means that the easement no longer benefits the dominant tenement.[102]

[96] *Moncrieff v Jamieson* ibid [47] as analysed in *Regency Villas* (n 1 above) Court of Appeal [26]. Vos LJ in *Regency Villas* Court of Appeal [71]–[74] and Lord Briggs in the Supreme Court [66]–[67], [71], [75], [92] disagreed with the *obiter* in *Moncrieff*; in contrast, Lord Carnwath, dissenting in the Supreme Court, saw Lord Scott's concern as being 'unanswerable' in relation to the claimed easement to use the golf-course: [105].

[97] *Regency Villas* (n 1 above) Court of Appeal [72].

[98] See KGC Reid and GL Gretton, *Conveyancing 2016* (Edinburgh, Avizandum Publishing, 2017) 140. See also more generally on servitudes in Scottish law, GL Gretton and AJM Steven, *Property, Trusts and Succession*, 3rd edn (London, Bloomsbury, 2017) ch 13. I am very grateful to Dr Andrew Steven for very helpful discussions and information on servitudes in Scotland.

[99] Van der Walt (n 42 above) 4.

[100] *Re Ellenborough Park* (n 2 above).

[101] Van der Walt (n 42 above) 4.

[102] See *McAdams Homes Ltd v Robinson* [2004] EWCA Civ 214, [2005] 1 P & CR 30, [12].

A. Ex Ante Restrictive Controls

Ex ante restrictive controls, in prioritising security and stability of land rights, are justified insofar as they limit the rights which can burden properties perpetually by controlling the freedom of landowners to create new land burdens that will bind successive owners, which might result in inefficient fragmentation. Questions of intergenerational fairness focus analysis on allowing current owners to impose burdens on future generations which may be irremovable.[103] Stricter ex ante regulation of easements also minimises the dangers of idiosyncratic burdens on land. However, ex ante restrictions can be viewed as an infringement of the private autonomy of the parties to an easement and from a contractarian perspective, stability may arguably result from absolute private autonomy.[104]

Crystal rules are exemplified by the traditional rules of easement law which regulate easements ex ante, determining beforehand the content of an easement and denying consideration of anything falling outside those boundaries.[105] French has taken the extreme view in proposing that no restrictive ex ante rules should regulate the creation of servitudes, and all that should be required for the creation of a servitude is that there is a valid contract which is aimed at the creation of a servitude that complies with the formal requirements for transactions involving land.[106] Other authors have taken more nuanced approaches, such as Sagaert who asserts that the value of ex ante measures of regulation are found in the extent to which they ensure that burdens placed on land are objectively useful.[107] However, he agrees that a better way to realise the goal of continued usefulness of burdens on land would be to enable the abolition of these rights when they become obsolete. Nevertheless, English law has confirmed the importance of ex ante restrictions in determining the validity of sporting or recreational easements and the need to determine the nature of the works and level of maintenance which the servient owners would be required to undertake for maintenance or repair.[108]

B. Ex Post Regulation of Easements

Van der Walt has argued that the traditional ex ante strategies of preventing fragmentation are becoming increasingly more unsuitable and ex post strategies of correction are more suitable to the dynamic economy of the twenty-first century.[109] In his view, both common law and civil law jurisdictions are gradually shifting away from 'an *ex ante*

[103] See S van Staden, 'Ancillary Rights in Servitude Law' (LLD thesis, Stellenbosch University 2015) 159, citing S Sterk, 'Freedom from Freedom of Contract: The Enduring Value of Servitude Restrictions' (1985) 70 *Iowa Law Review* 615, 616.

[104] Van Staden ibid 157 citing RA Epstein, 'Notice and Freedom of Contract in the Law of Servitudes' (1982) 55 *Southern California Law Review* 1353, 1358; BWF Depoorter and P Parisi, 'Fragmentation of Property Rights: A Functional Interpretation of the Law of Servitudes' (2003) 3 *Global Jurist Frontiers* 1, 6; Sterk ibid 616.

[105] Van Staden ibid 172 discussing Rose (n 17 above).

[106] French (n 30 above) 112, discussed by Van Staden ibid 173; S French, 'Servitudes, reform and the new Restatement of Property: Creation Doctrines and Structural Simplification' (1988) 73 *Cornell Law Review* 928, 948.

[107] V Sagaert, 'The Fragmented System of Land Burdens in French and Belgian Law' in van Erp and Akkermans (n 30 above) 31, 51 discussed by van Staden ibid 173.

[108] *Regency Villas* (n 1 above) Court of Appeal [60] and compare the Supreme Court [67]–[73].

[109] Van der Walt (n 42 above) 21–22.

(common-law rule) preventing the creation of "atypical property arrangements" to *ex post* (statutory and judicial intervention) remedying the negative effects of such arrangements'.[110] The American Restatement (Third) of Property Servitudes provides a good example of a move to ex post controls.[111] Flexibility is mostly linked to new, corrective ex post controls that can rectify the problems caused by inflexible application of the preventative ex ante controls, without abandoning them altogether. The most commonly used argument in support of flexibility is that the law should allow termination or amendment of ageing, obsolete and unworkable land burdens and should allow variation of existing land burdens for the sake of better planning. Permanent, inflexible land burdens create restraints on alienability and produce inefficiency in land markets.[112] The counterarguments are that registration can overcome most problems caused by land burdens and that allowing ex post variation or termination could cause uncertainty.[113]

The ex post regulation envisaged in *Regency Villas* was for the servient owners to make reasonable provisions for regulation of the easements in the ordinary course.[114] However, as already noted, if the grant does not provide agreed regulatory structures regarding, for example, timings and resolution of disputes, then any shared enjoyment must be exercised reasonably, which again is likely to be contested. Another manner of ex post regulation would be to impose time-limits on the existence of all easements. Lovett and Rose[115] support durational limitations on the protection of servitudes, and Lovett proposes a period of 30 years as appropriate for the initial protection stage.

One of the factors that tends to make the law reluctant to add extra rights to the *numerus clausus* is the difficulty of removing a right once it has been attached to land as a burden, so the easing of that will have a knock-on effect on any judicial inclinations towards *numerus clausus*. Even though in practice, problematic easements may be removed by negotiation and payment of compensation, ex post corrective measures to amend or terminate easements to address flexibility problems should be introduced, as the Law Commission has recognised with its proposal that section 84 of the Law of Property Act 1925 be amended and extended so as to apply to easements and profits.[116] Its recommendation is that an easement should only be modified if the Lands Chamber of the Upper Tribunal is satisfied that the modified interest will not be materially less convenient to the benefited owner and will be no more burdensome to the land affected,[117] which will inevitably restrict the

[110] ibid 22.

[111] See French (n 30 above).

[112] Van der Walt (n 42 above) 18, 29–30.

[113] ibid 18 citing JA Lovett, 'Creating and Controlling Private Land Use Restrictions in Scotland and Louisiana: A Comparative Mixed Jurisdiction Analysis' (2008) 19 *Stellenbosch Law Review* 231, 244–245. See also B France-Hudson, 'The Recognition of Covenants in Gross in New Zealand: A Dangerous Advancement?' Chapter 11 in this volume, where the author expresses doubts on the effectiveness of ex post controls in analysing covenants in gross in New Zealand.

[114] *Regency Villas* (n 1 above) Court of Appeal [86].

[115] Van Staden (n 103) 176–77, citing CM Rose 'Servitudes, Security and Assent: Some Comments on Professors French and Reichman' (1982) 55 *Southern California Law Review* 1403, 1414.

[116] Law Commission (n 33 above) [7.35], [7.49], [7.55], [8.52], [8.54], [8.56] and see Law of Property Bill, clauses 30–32 and Sch 2. Note that in *Regency Villas* (n 1 above) Lord Briggs at [79] referred to the Law Commission's proposals.

[117] ibid [7.60], [8.57].

jurisdiction for modification. Nevertheless, such reforms are long overdue and will incorporate significant ex post regulation into English law, which will have consequential impact on ex ante restrictions and, accordingly, encourage flexibility. Conversely, if the ex ante controls are relaxed as *Regency Villas* suggests, this makes the case for expanding the ex post controls even more compelling.

VI. Concluding Remarks

A new normative framework has emerged in the academic literature within which the validity of recreational and sporting easements should depend on a range of contextual factors, recognising that the categories of easements are in need of modernisation in order to be fitting for the twenty-first century. Policy considerations in recognising easements which encourage physical activity are a welcome development. The Supreme Court has removed a potential dichotomy between indoor and outdoor activities, so the negative externalities of indoor easements no longer represent a central paradox, and this development in the law has significant implications for the normative content of easements, conceivably removing a legal lacuna in cases with complex factual scenarios.

This chapter has analysed different conceptual approaches through which recreational and sporting easements can be evaluated. Such evaluation will now be crucial in English law: following the Supreme Court's innovation in *Regency Villas*, the courts will now need to determine the precise scope of recreational and sporting easements. Incorporating notions of sharing and human flourishing would encourage a progressive approach to easements, whilst balancing anti-fragmentation controls such as *numerus clausus* with the efficient land-use narrative may be a catalyst for flexibility within the law. Questions of how to manage the long-term relationship between dominant and servient owners will require co-operative arrangements and mechanisms for the usage of recreational easements. Although the decision in *Regency Villas* needs to be seen in the specific context of timeshare owners, a holistic approach to recreational easements means that there cannot necessarily be neat lines between commercial and non-commercial contexts. The floodgates are unlikely to be opened in the domestic context where a narrow view of recreational easements is likely to prevail.

The conceptual analysis undertaken in this chapter will provide a valuable framework for scrutinising the future development of recreational and sporting easements, not only in England, but also in other jurisdictions. Certainly, a nuanced application of the test of utility and benefit is needed to incorporate fairness and address distributional concerns and anxiety over intrusion on the servient land in recognition of the complex dynamics of human and property relationships. One lesson from the chapter, however, is that the common law rules form only one part of a more complex picture. For example, statutory intervention would be required for a significant shift in the regulation of easements from an ex ante approach, focusing on stability of land rights, to flexible, ex post regulation of easements. Such a shift would add value to land arrangements and enable the law to develop in a progressive but incremental way.

11

The Recognition of Covenants in Gross in New Zealand: A Dangerous Advancement?

BEN FRANCE-HUDSON

I. Introduction

Although New Zealand is a relatively small country it has a tradition of being adventurous when it comes to the law of property. Since 1987 it has allowed parties to agree to positive covenants, which will bind successors in title. It was one of the first countries in the world to experiment with individual transferable quotas for fishing.[1] It legislated to make it clear that no one owns 'the common marine and coastal area' (in other words, the foreshore and seabed).[2] Recently, it has legislated to vest legal personhood in the Whanganui River and Te Urewera mountain range.[3] These developments, although sometimes controversial, have generally been positive and have furthered the distinct New Zealand law of property while utilising existing forms of proprietary interest.

The most recent innovation is an amendment to the Property Law Act 2007, which allows for the creation of covenants in gross.[4] From 2019[5] it will be possible to create a covenant that will burden the land of a covenantor, but not benefit land held by a covenantee, and that will be able to run with the land so as to bind successors in title. While the creation of covenants in gross is not, in and of itself, objectionable (particularly in a country that has comfortably recognised positive freehold covenants), aspects of this reform are troubling. In particular, as finally enacted, there is arguably no requirement that a covenant in gross be intrinsically linked to the burdened land. There is no explicit 'touch and concern' test; rather the covenant must simply require the covenantor to do, or not do, something in relation to the land. This wording may allow for the content of covenants in gross to include a wide range of obligations only distantly related to the land itself. Moreover, it also appears arguable that the legislation will allow the original covenanting parties to agree that it will bind people with only a limited connection to the burdened land, such as licensees or short- to mid-term lessees.[6] It follows that, on one plausible

[1] See Fisheries Act 1983; Fisheries Act 1996. Please note that, unless otherwise indicated, all statutory provisions come from New Zealand legislation.

[2] Marine and Coastal Area (Takutai Moana) Act 2011, s 11 (2).

[3] See Te Urewera Act 2014, s 11; Te Awa Tupua (Whanganui River Claims Settlement) Act 2017, s 14.

[4] Amendments to the Property Law Act 2007 contained within the Land Transfer Act 2017, ss 242–246.

[5] Land Transfer Act 2017, s 2.

[6] See section III.B, text around n 91 below.

interpretation, private parties may now agree to a wide range of quite personal obligations that are only remotely related to the ownership, use, occupation, or value of the land, and that may be binding in perpetuity.

Although this potentially wide scope appears to have been unintentional, it may allow for the creation of proprietary rights that go well beyond anything that has previously been contemplated in New Zealand or elsewhere. This inevitably engages a discussion of the *numerus clausus* principle and raises questions about its continuing application to property law, particularly where property rights are created by statute.

This chapter begins by outlining the nature of covenants in gross and the reasons why New Zealand has chosen to adopt them as a tool for managing obligations in relation to land. It undertakes a close analysis of the new statutory provisions, observing that they may result in problematic outcomes, particularly when viewed in light of the practical and jurisprudential concerns which the *numerus clausus*, at least in part, aims to avoid. Finally, it suggests that the *numerus clausus* still has a role in influencing the shape of property law.

This chapter serves not only as an introduction to the creation of a novel interest in land, but also as a cautionary tale. Although covenants in gross are not problematic per se, far greater attention ought to have been paid to the principles that underpin the presence of the *numerus clausus* at common law. In expanding the categories of recognised proprietary rights, legislatures should be cautious and cognisant of the risks the *numerus clausus* principle aims to avoid. This time, New Zealand may have gone too far, too fast.

II. Covenants in Gross

In essence, a freehold covenant in gross is an obligation contained in a deed that burdens servient land but that benefits a person (or body corporate) rather than dominant land.[7] While there is no difficulty enforcing such a covenant as between the original parties to the deed it was not possible for such a covenant to run with the servient tenement so as to bind successors in title at common law or equity in New Zealand.[8]

A covenant in gross can be contrasted with both a restrictive covenant (which involves an obligation not to perform a certain activity on land) and a positive covenant (which involves an obligation to perform a certain activity on land). Legislation in New Zealand allows the creation of both of these types of covenant as interests in land providing, in either case, that the covenant burdens land and benefits other land.[9] 'Benefit', in this context, means that the covenant must 'touch and concern' the dominant land.[10] If it takes effect on

[7] *ANZCO Foods Waitara Ltd v AFFCO New Zealand Ltd* [2005] NZCA 166, [2006] 3 NZLR 351 [46]; New Zealand Law Commission, *A New Land Transfer Act* (NZ Law Com Report 116, 2010) [7.4].

[8] Prior to 2005, there had been debate about this issue. See *Staples v Co (Ltd) v Corby* (1899) 17 NZLR 734 (CA); *ANZCO Foods Waitara Ltd* (n 7 above), which affirmed the position that covenants in gross cannot bind successors in title; EM Brookfield, 'Restrictive Covenants in Gross' [1970] *New Zealand Law Journal* 67.

[9] Property Law Act 2007, ss 301–303.

[10] D Brown, 'Easements, Profits and Covenants' in E Toomey (ed), *New Zealand Land Law*, 3rd edn (Wellington, Thomson Reuters New Zealand, 2017) 1106. The 'touch and concern' test operates as shorthand for the fact that

or after 1 January 1953 (for restrictive covenants) or 1 January 1987 (for positive covenants), it can be notified on the Torrens certificate of title. It will operate to bind successors in title providing they are either owners or 'occupiers'.[11]

The rationale for requiring a dominant tenement is found deep in the doctrinal arguments contained in the English cases that followed, and refined, the initial outcome in *Tulk v Moxhay*.[12] As arguably finally established in *London County Council v Allen*[13] the doctrine in *Tulk v Moxhay* 'does not extend to the case in which the covenantee has no land capable of enjoying, as against the land of the covenantor, the benefit of the restrictive covenant'.[14]

Precisely how such *dicta* can be justified on a principled basis has exercised scholars for generations and is one of the reasons why discussions of the *numerus clausus* principle often focus on freehold covenants.[15] The *numerus clausus* 'metaprinciple'[16] connotes the strictness of the common law's attitude towards property rights, especially in relation to land. It is present in some form in almost all legal systems[17] and tends to recognise fewer than a dozen classes of property rights in land, which can be loosely grouped into three categories: rights to present or future possession; securities; and the non-possessory, non-security rights that are often termed servitudes.[18] Overall, the principle indicates that property owners are not able to fashion the characteristics of the rights that accompany their ownership,[19] and 'any new rights must fit within firmly established pigeonholes, of

the covenant 'must either affect the land as regards mode of occupation, or it must be such as per se, and not merely from collateral circumstances, affects the value of the land' (*Rogers v Hosegood* [1900] 2 Ch 388 (CA), 395 (Farwell J), affirming the definition of Bayley J in *The Mayor, etc of Congleton v Pattison* (1808) 10 East 130, 138, 103 ER 725, 728). See also, JC Fisher, 'Rethinking the Rules for the Proprietary Effect of Freehold Covenants' in H Conway and R Hickey (eds), *Modern Studies in Property Law*, vol 9 (Oxford, Hart Publishing, 2017).

[11] Property Law Act 2007, s 303(2). See text to n 90 below for the meaning of the word 'occupier'.

[12] *Tulk v Moxhay* (1848) 2 Ph 774, 41 ER 1143. New Zealand's land law owes its foundations to English law although there has also been reform of some of the more undesirable aspects of that law. See GW Hinde, 'Land Law in the Legal System' in GW Hinde, DW McMorland, NR Campbell, JL Foster, TN Gibbons, S Scott and P Twist (eds), *Principles of Real Property Law*, 2nd edn (Wellington, LexisNexis New Zealand, 2014) [1.004]. It should also be noted in this context that New Zealand has a comprehensive code governing residential tenancies (contained in the Residential Tenancies Act 1986), which has allowed the law in relation to covenants (both leasehold and freehold) to develop in ways it may not have done if residential tenancies were still subject to it.

[13] *London County Council v Allen* [1914] 3 KB 642 (CA).

[14] ibid 660 (Buckley LJ).

[15] Eg, in discussing both the fundamental justification of the *numerus clausus* and its importance in the context of reform of the English law of freehold covenants, McFarlane suggests that the *numerus clausus* is the product of the 'general and simple idea' that it is not generally accepted that duties can be imposed on third party strangers (X) simply as a result of an agreement between others (A and B). Of course, this is the essence of what occurs when individuals enter into an agreement giving rise to a freehold covenant. See B McFarlane, 'The Numerus Clausus Principle and Covenants Relating to Land' in S Bright (ed), *Modern Studies in Property Law*, vol 6 (Oxford, Hart Publishing, 2011) 326, 330.

[16] B Edgeworth, 'The *Numerus Clausus* Principle in Contemporary Australian Property Law' (2006) 32 *Monash University Law Review* 387, 390. By metaprinciple, Edgeworth indicates that it is a higher order norm that helps to influence more specific rules of property law.

[17] M Weir, 'Pushing the Envelope of Proprietary Interests: The Nadir of the *Numerus Clausus* Principle?' (2015) 39 *Melbourne University Law Review* 651, 653.

[18] B Rudden, 'Economic Theory v. Property Law: The *Numerus Clausus* Problem' in J Eekelaar and J Bell (eds), *Oxford Essays in Jurisprudence: Third Series* (Oxford, Clarendon Press, 1987) 241–42.

[19] McFarlane (n 15 above) 312.

which the law permits only a small and finite number'.[20] As Brougham LC noted in *Keppell v Bailey*,[21]

> it must not … be supposed that incidents of a novel kind can be devised and attached to property at the fancy or caprice of any owner … great detriment would arise and much confusion of rights if parties were allowed to invent new modes of holding and enjoying real property;[22]

in another's words, '"fancies" are for contract, not property'.[23]

There is no universally accepted justification for the *numerus clausus* principle, and in recent years it has come under sustained criticism. In particular, it is very difficult to reconcile with economic analysis of law and the efficiencies that are said to flow from market ordering.[24] The rise of modern registration systems, such as New Zealand's Torrens title regime, have also led to ongoing questions as to its utility as a guiding principle in property law.[25] Moreover, the principle has never been viewed as acting to limit the ability of legislatures to create new types of property right via statute.[26]

Nonetheless, a number of commentators suggest that it maintains a useful metric by which to guide the development of the law.[27] There is nothing necessarily objectionable about increasing the categories of rights recognised as proprietary. In fact, cases that closed the door on development (such as *Keppell v Bailey*[28] and *Hill v Tupper*[29]) may well have inhibited some desirable growth in common law and equity.[30] However, overall, the goal should be that property law develops on a 'principled basis'.[31] The *numerus clausus* can be seen as one element of that principled development. As the common law desire to avoid a proliferation of different sorts of property rights is generally accepted as well founded,[32] the boundaries spelt out by the *numerus clausus* are a very useful way to avoid the negative consequences that flow from the creation of new types of property interest by statute.[33]

Notwithstanding the doctrinal nuances and theoretical arguments, changing urban growth and social and political developments over the twentieth and twenty-first centuries have led to pressure for change in a number of jurisdictions.[34] New Zealand in 1987 responded by enacting legislation that overturns the general common law principle that it is not possible to create positive burdens that run with the land. This move appears driven, in part, by a desire to avoid some of the problems other jurisdictions experience with imposing positive obligations on landowners, such as an obligation to

[20] Edgeworth (n 16 above) 387.

[21] *Keppell v Bailey* (1834) 2 My & K 517, 39 ER 1042.

[22] ibid 536–37, 1042.

[23] Rudden (n 18 above) 243.

[24] ibid 261. But see TW Merrill and HE Smith, 'Optimal Standardization in the Law of Property: The Numerus Clausus Principle' (2000) 110 *Yale Law Journal* 1.

[25] McFarlane (n 15 above) 314. See also RA Epstein, 'Notice and Freedom of Contract in the Law of Servitudes' (1982) 55 *Southern California Law Review* 1353; Rudden (n 18 above).

[26] P O'Connor, 'Contractual Specification of New Property Rights in Resources: The Problem of Measurement Costs' (2012) 39 *Monash University Law Review* 38, 41.

[27] See, eg, Edgeworth (n 16 above); O'Connor (n 26 above); Weir (n 17 above); Merrill and Smith (n 24 above).

[28] *Keppell* (n 21 above).

[29] *Hill v Tupper* (1863) 2 H & C 121, 159 ER 51.

[30] S Bright, 'Of Estates and Interests' in S Bright and J Dewar (eds), *Land Law: Themes and Perspectives* (Oxford, Oxford University Press, 1998) 546, as cited in Edgeworth (n 16 above) 399 and 418–19.

[31] ibid 546 as cited in Edgeworth (n 16 above) 419.

[32] Weir (n 17 above) 657.

[33] ibid 669.

[34] Law Commission for England and Wales, *Easements, Covenants and Profits à Prendre: A Consultation Paper* (Law Com No 186, 2008); Edgeworth (n 16 above); O'Connor (n 26 above); Weir (n 17 above).

maintain or repair a party wall, right of way, or drain.[35] This reform has not proven to be problematic and is now seen as a very normal part of the background of conveyancing practice.

Unsurprisingly, this pressure has also been felt in relation to the inability to create covenants in gross. Many individuals and bodies corporate have wished to be able to ensure that a burden will run with a piece of servient land notwithstanding the absence of dominant land to which it relates. In particular, local authorities desired the ability to impose ongoing burdens on land, for example to ensure a condition against further subdivision is enforceable against later owners of the land. They were eventually given this power by legislation.[36] A number of other species of covenant have also been created by way of legislation, some of which operate as covenants in gross, such as open space covenants under the Queen Elizabeth the Second National Trust Act 1977.[37]

However, these statutory innovations do not extend to other groups who may wish to take advantage of covenants in gross, such as developers who wish to ensure that future owners in a subdivision are required to enter into a contract with a specified utility provider (such as an electric supply company); businesses that wish to create restraint of trade obligations forbidding, for example, competitor retail or fast food outlets from leasing space within a development;[38] or bodies corporate (or management companies) running apartment buildings[39] wanting to ensure that owners join a residents' association. While any one of these purposes, on its own, might be unobjectionable, there is a real risk that if taken too far the use of covenants in gross could allow a form of private government to emerge, created by developers to regulate the behaviour of all those in a particular area or development.

A. Encumbrance Instruments

As a result of this demand, and in line with the worldwide ability of conveyancing lawyers to invent ways to circumvent irksome rules, a method of securing what is, in essence, a de facto covenant in gross was devised by New Zealand practitioners utilising 'encumbrance instruments'.[40] These instruments were initially designed to secure either a rentcharge[41] or annuity,[42] both of which have their origins in English property law and both of which are now uncommon.[43]

[35] *McMorland on Easements, Covenants and Licences*, 3rd edn (Wellington, LexisNexis New Zealand, 2015) [17.040].

[36] See Resource Management Act 1991, s 221.

[37] See also Resource Management Act 1991, ss 108, 221 and 240; Crown Pastoral Land Act 1998, s 97; Heritage New Zealand Pouhere Taonga Act 2014; T Gibbons, 'Land Covenants: Challenges and Opportunities' (2015) 5 *Property Law Review* 113, 115–16.

[38] New Zealand Law Society Property Law Section, 'Review of the Land Transfer Act 1952 – Instruments of Encumbrance' (submission to the New Zealand Law Commission, 11 May 2009) sch B, attached to I Haynes et al, 'Torrens in the Digital Age – A New Land Transfer Act' (Property Law Conference, Te Papa, June 2014); New Zealand Law Commission (n 7 above) [7.8].

[39] See Unit Titles Act 2010.

[40] Land Transfer Act 1952, s 101 (4).

[41] Law Commission (n 7 above) [7.6]: 'A rentcharge is a sum of money paid periodically to someone who is not entitled to any future estate in the land'.

[42] ibid: 'An annuity is a sum payable yearly as a personal obligation of the grantor or out of property not consisting exclusively of land.'

[43] ibid.

Encumbrance instruments are provided for by a range of provisions that must be read together.[44] A memorandum of encumbrance is deemed to be a form of mortgage, although the amount secured by the rentcharge is typically nominal.[45] The overall purpose is to ensure that the covenants contained in the memorandum of encumbrance bind third-party successors in title.[46] This is achieved because where a person accepts a transfer of land subject to mortgage, they become personally liable to the mortgagee for the payment of all amounts and the performance of all obligations secured by the mortgage and for the observance and performance of all other covenants expressed or implied in the mortgage.[47] As a result, any covenant included within the instrument will bind the owner of the encumbered land, and any successor in title, while the encumbrancee will retain the benefit.[48]

Importantly, case law suggests that, due to the wording of section 97(2) of the Property Law Act 2007 (the effect of which is that a mortgagee must only discharge a mortgage where there has been 'payment to the mortgagee of all amounts and *the performance of all other obligations*'[49] (emphasis added)), a mortgagee or encumbrancee is not required to provide a discharge of the mortgage until all the obligations that are secured have been performed.[50] Thus, the use of this mechanism does not amount to clog on the equity of redemption and can run with the land, potentially in perpetuity. Where a covenantor or successor in title fails to perform, all the usual remedies of a mortgagee apply.[51]

The attractiveness of this mechanism is probably self-evident. Encumbrance instruments have been used:

- In a subdivision to require owners of the lots to join a residents' association and pay annual fees;
- In a subdivision to require owners to enter into standard contracts with a utility provider and to pay charges for use of utilities;
- To require owners to enter into a franchise or supply agreement;
- To set out restraint of trade provisions;
- In place of car parking/signage easements or to secure compliance under a car parking/signage licence;
- To secure compliance with a right of first refusal to offer a property back to a third party; and,
- In place of covenants in gross to record on the title all manner of contractual obligations.[52]

[44] See Land Transfer Act 1952, ss 2 and 101; Property Law Act 2007, ss 4 and 203.

[45] Gibbons (n 37 above) 116.

[46] *Menere v Jackson Mews Management Ltd* [2009] NZCA 563, [2010] 2 NZLR 347, [45] (Hammond and Chambers JJ), [60] (Baragwanath J).

[47] Property Law Act 2007, s 203(1)(a)(i)–(ii).

[48] Brookfield (n 8 above) 70.

[49] Property Law Act 2007, s 97(2).

[50] *Menere* (n 46 above) [47].

[51] E Toomey, 'Mortgages' in E Toomey (ed), New Zealand Land Law, 3rd edn (Wellington, Thomson Reuters New Zealand, 2017) 836.

[52] New Zealand Law Society Property Law Section (n 38 above) [7] and sch B.

B. A Move to Covenants in Gross

In 2010, the New Zealand Law Commission issued a report recommending that Parliament pass a new Land Transfer Act to facilitate the creation of a modern land transfer system.[53]

Having become aware of certain problems associated with the practice of using the encumbrance mechanism, the Law Commission dedicated a chapter of its report to analysing these concerns. Moreover, a degree of dissonance had crept into New Zealand's law of covenants, given the statutory recognition or creation of covenants in gross in particular circumstances.[54]

Overall, the Law Commission reached the conclusion that use of the encumbrance mechanism should cease. The Law Commission viewed them as artificial on the basis that encumbrances are aligned to mortgages, while covenants relate to how land is used, and noted that, if the covenant is not in gross, the Property Law Act already contained provisions allowing for its recognition and effect.[55] Moreover, the encumbrance mechanism was seen as giving the protections of registration to a type of covenant that had never been recognised by the common law or equity as an interest in land. They could not be easily challenged or removed from a title, and it also appeared unlikely that they could be redeemed, leading to negative results overall.[56] Importantly, the Law Commission stressed that 'some such covenants [were] apparently used to record on title to land "all manner of contractual obligations"'.[57] In the Law Commission's view, it was not appropriate for many personal contractual obligations to run with the land. Nor, from the point of view of public policy, should all such covenants be supported, 'for example, those that are essentially in restraint of trade rather than strictly related to land use'.[58]

This led to the Law Commission recommending that the encumbrance mechanism should no longer be allowed to be used to create de facto covenants in gross.[59] Nonetheless, recognising that the practice of using encumbrances to bind third parties was now so longstanding and widespread that it should not now be held invalid,[60] the Law Commission accepted that there was an unmet demand for such interests to be recognised and recorded on the title.[61] Interestingly, the Law Commission's discussion contains no reference to any of the theoretical arguments for and against covenants in gross. As a result, and following fairly consequentialist reasoning, it considered there was a strong case for the express

[53] New Zealand Law Commission (n 7 above) Foreword.

[54] See n 37 above.

[55] Via the recognition of restrictive and positive covenants attached to servient and dominant land: New Zealand Law Commission (n 7 above) [7.28].

[56] ibid [7.29]. In *Menere* (n 46 above), the person bound by the covenant would carry on being bound to use a particular service provider, even if it was not performing its obligations.

[57] New Zealand Law Commission (n 7 above) [7.31], citing New Zealand Law Society Property Law Section (n 38 above) sch B.

[58] ibid [7.32].

[59] ibid [7.33].

[60] New Zealand Law Society Property Law Section (n 38 above) [6].

[61] New Zealand Law Commission (n 7 above) [7.35]. Although not referred to by the Law Commission, this echoes the observation made by Rudden (n 18 above) that, given that people can get around the restrictions imposed by the *numerus clausus* principle by utilising complicated mechanisms (such as rentcharges), it can be more efficient to let people achieve such ends directly.

recognition of covenants in gross. It recommended that the new Land Transfer Act 2017 amend the Property Law Act 2007 to provide for covenants in gross 'to ensure their validity and make their creation transparent'.[62] It suggested that they be treated in the same way as restrictive and positive covenants, be recognised as interests in land, run with the burdened land, and be assignable to a new covenantee.[63]

Crucially, in its discussion the Law Commission outlined a number of provisos and limitations. In particular, it considered that there needed to be some limits on the use of covenants in gross to prevent interests that are personal in nature being treated as interests in land that would run with it indefinitely.[64] It considered and rejected a number of ways this could be achieved, settling on a 'touch and concern'[65] the land test, whereby the covenant must have a close link with the burdened land rather than being merely personal.[66] Although it noted the criticisms of this type of test,[67] and the fact that the test was a somewhat difficult fit where there was no dominant tenement, it remained of the view that the covenant needed some connection with the use of the land burdened by the covenant. However, the Law Commission recognised that on its own, this test would be insufficient to address all of the possible problems with covenants in gross. Consequently, it also suggested that the court have a wide power to modify or remove such covenants.[68]

These suggestions were collated by the Law Commission into a draft Bill which formed the basis for the legislative process that led to the Land Transfer Act 2017 and its amendments to the Property Law Act 2007. For the purposes of this chapter, only two provisions need to be highlighted (with emphasis added):

> **307A Covenants in gross**
>
> In sections 307B to 307H, covenant in gross in relation to land, means a covenant that—
>
> (a) is contained in an instrument; and
> (b) requires the covenantor to act or to refrain from acting in a particular way *in relation to the occupation or use of the land or part of the land*; and
> (c) benefits another person; and
> (d) is not attached to other land.
>
> **307B Legal effect of covenant in gross**
>
> (1) A covenant in gross, *unless a contrary intention appears*, is binding in equity on—
>
> (a) every person who becomes the owner of the burdened land,—
>
> …
>
> (b) every person who is for the time being the occupier of the burdened land.[69]

[62] ibid [7.35].
[63] ibid [7.37].
[64] ibid [7.39].
[65] See text to n 75 below.
[66] New Zealand Law Commission (n 7 above) [7.48]–[7.52].
[67] ibid [7.48]. See, eg, *London Diocesan Fund v Avonridge Property Co Ltd* [2005] UKHL 70, [2005] 1 WLR 3956, [26], where Birkenhead LJ noted that the distinction between those covenants in leases that touch and concern the land and those that do not 'has long been criticised as illogical and not easily drawn in practice'.
[68] New Zealand Law Commission (n 7 above) [7.53]–[7.57].
[69] ibid (Land Transfer Bill) 310.

In my view, if these provisions had been enacted in this form, there would have been no problem. Certainly, in a jurisdiction that already recognises positive covenants, has created a range of statutory covenants in gross, and organically adapted the use of encumbrance instruments to the purpose of a covenant in gross, the statutory recognition of covenants in gross appears to be a logical next step.

Regrettably, the final text of the legislation is quite different from that suggested by the Law Commission. In particular, there is no explicit reference to the requirement that the covenant be in relation to the occupation or use of the land. Moreover, the legislation appears to allow the original covenanting parties to agree that it will bind a range of people at the election of the parties, rather than the parties being limited to binding only owners or 'occupiers'. In my view, both of these factors are problematic and may take covenants in gross in New Zealand significantly outside anything ever contemplated under the guiding principles of the *numerus clausus*.

III. The Land Transfer Act 2017 Amends the Property Law Act 2007

As enacted, the following provisions are to become law by early January 2019.[70] The problems can be stated relatively simply, although the ramifications are harder to quantify.

A. Covenants in Gross Need Only Be 'in Relation to' the Servient Land

Section 307A defines covenants in gross (with emphasis added):

> **307A Covenants in gross**
>
> In sections 307B to 307F and 318A to 318E, **covenant in gross** means a covenant that—
>
> (a) is expressed in an instrument coming into operation on or after the commencement of this section; and
>
> (b) requires the covenantor to do something, or to refrain from doing something, *in relation to the covenantor's land*; and
>
> (c) benefits another person, but is not attached to other land.[71]

This provision only provides that the covenant in gross require the covenantor to do, or refrain from doing, something 'in relation to' the covenantor's land. While it could be argued that this language is aimed at ensuring covenants in gross do 'relate' to the land in the same manner as the touch and concern test (in line with case law that suggests they can be used

[70] Land Transfer Act 2017, s 2.

[71] Property Law Act 2007, s 307A to be inserted by Land Transfer Act 2017, s 242.

as synonyms),[72] the commentary on the provisions so far questions whether the touch and concern test has actually been retained.[73]

The Law Commission had suggested that the phrase read: 'requires the covenantor to act or to refrain from acting in a particular way in relation to the *occupation or use of the land* or part of the land'.[74] It stressed that although the traditional touch and concern test was not immediately applicable in this context (as covenants in gross do not have a dominant tenement which the covenant must 'touch and concern'), it was nonetheless important that a covenant in gross 'has some connection with the use of the land burdened by the covenant'.[75] Arguably, this wording was stricter than the somewhat amorphous test implied by the language of touch and concern.[76] A possible reason for the change can be found in the New Zealand Law Society's submission on the Law Commission's Draft Bill. The Society was concerned that a requirement to join a residents' or precinct society and pay dues would not be caught by the phrase 'in relation to the occupation or use of the land or part of the land', although it did accept that such an interpretation was at least arguable.[77]

Presumably in order to remedy this potential objection, the final wording removes any reference to 'occupation or use'. This is problematic as it is potentially wider than necessary and could go well beyond the restrictions or limits contained within the traditional test. While the final wording would enable a covenant requiring membership of a residents' society to be enforced, as relating to the land, it may also cover membership of residents' walking groups, golf clubs, gyms, and other organisations or amenities only distantly related to the land. It may also cover situations such as a requirement not to hang washing outdoors or not to park a trade vehicle on the driveway, both of which may be unlikely to have met the Law Commission's wording.

This means that the content of the property right that can be created via a covenant in gross is potentially much wider than first envisaged. If the courts interpret the 'in relation to' test in a wide manner, it would create an inconsistency with the test for positive covenants, which are also potentially unlimited in content[78] but are limited by the fact that they must benefit (ie touch and concern) the dominant land.[79]

The requirement at both common law and equity that a covenant benefit (or touch and concern) dominant land can be seen as one of the ways in which parties are limited in their ability to create novel proprietary rights.[80] The *numerus clausus* principle can be seen as controlling the boundary between that which is proprietary and that which is

[72] See, eg, *Federated Homes Ltd v Mill Lodge Properties* [1980] 1 WLR 594 (CA) 604.

[73] Brown (n 10 above) 1111; E Toomey, *Land Transfer Act Handbook 2017* (Wellington, Thomson Reuters New Zealand, 2017) 20.

[74] New Zealand Law Commission (n 7 above) (Land Transfer Bill) 310.

[75] ibid [7.49].

[76] For a review of the criticisms of this test, see Fisher (n 10 above).

[77] New Zealand Law Society, 'Land Transfer Act Review – Government Response' (submission to Land Information New Zealand, 11 October 2010) [2.3.3](c).

[78] McFarlane (n 15 above) 328.

[79] Property Law Act 2007, s 303 (1)(a); *McMorland on Easements, Covenants and Licences* (n 35 above) [17.028]–[17.029].

[80] O'Connor (n 26 above) 45.

purely personal.[81] By imposing a requirement that the covenant must 'affect the nature, quality, mode or user or value of the land of the dominant owner',[82] the law operates in an attempt to ensure that only obligations that intimately affect the land are vested with proprietary status. The rule operates both to recognise the lack of consent by successors in title to the initial bargain and also to restrict the sorts of contractual fancies that can attach to land.[83] Although difficult to apply in practice,[84] and admittedly somewhat lax,[85] it does act as a yardstick by which to measure whether an interest is purely personal or not. While the traditional touch and concern test is undoubtedly problematic and probably does not function as a failsafe way of limiting the type of obligations capable to be recognised as proprietary,[86] it does seem generally accepted that there ought to be 'a connection of some meaningful kind between the land itself and an obligation aspiring to proprietary effect'.[87] As suggested by Fisher, in improving the rules relating to land obligations, the rules 'should be more intrinsically "land centred" and less open to idiosyncratic human agreements than the touch and concern criterion'.[88]

Unfortunately, although the Law Commission's suggested wording may well have been a step in the right direction towards a clearly stated requirement that covenants be intrinsically related to the land affected, the final wording may not achieve this purpose.

B. The Covenanting Parties May Be Able to Bind Others to the Covenant in Gross

Landowners, however, are not the only group that may become bound to a covenant in gross, and it is in this sphere that another problem with New Zealand's new legislation becomes evident. Section 307C of the amendments to the Property Law Act addresses the legal effect of covenants in gross (as opposed to the question of whether the parties to the deed actually intended to create a proprietary right, which is governed by s 307B). It states (with emphasis added):

> **307C Legal effect of covenant in gross**
>
> (1) A covenant in gross is binding in equity on—
>
> (a) every person who becomes the owner of the burdened land,—
>
> …
>
> (b) every person who is for the time being the occupier of the burdened land.
>
> (2) A covenant in gross ceases to be binding on a person referred to in subsection (1) when that person ceases to be the owner or occupier of the burdened land, but without prejudice to that

[81] B McFarlane, '*Keppell v Bailey* (1834); *Hill v Tupper* (1863): The *Numerus Clausus* and the Common Law' in N Gravells (ed), *Landmark Cases in Land Law* (Oxford, Hart Publishing, 2013) 1.

[82] See *P & A Swift Investments v Combined English Stores Group* [1989] AC 632 (HL), 642.

[83] O'Connor (n 26 above) 45.

[84] See text to n 67 above.

[85] Fisher (n 10 above) 27.

[86] ibid 27–30.

[87] ibid 29.

[88] ibid 37.

person's liability for breach of the covenant arising before that person ceased to be the owner or occupier of the land.

(3) *Subsections (1) and (2) are subject to any contrary intention that appears in the instrument in which the covenant is expressed.*

(4) The benefit of a covenant in gross is capable of being assigned.

(5) This section overrides any other rule of law or equity ….[89]

It is important to note that 'occupier' is limited in the legislation to those who are in occupation under a lease or licence for a term of greater than 10 years.[90]

The drafting of section 307C is problematic.[91] On a narrow reading, it may simply mean that the presumption is that a covenant in gross will bind owners and occupiers but that under section 307C(3) the parties may agree that it will not bind either the owner (or a person who becomes the owner) or an occupier. If this reading is correct (and this was probably the intention), section 307C is unproblematic and in line with the provisions relating to positive and negative covenants that attach to dominant and servient land.

However, an alternative reading of the section is that while the presumption is that the covenant in gross will bind owners and occupiers, this is subject to 'any contrary intention' appearing in the instrument recording the covenant. This reading suggests that the parties to the covenant in gross can agree that it will bind those, such as licensees and lessees with leases for terms of less than 10 years, who do not fall within the statutory definition of an owner or an occupier.

This is probably unintentional,[92] but if accepted as a valid interpretation, it would be extraordinary for a number of reasons. Firstly, it would be very odd if the parties could agree that a covenant in gross can bind non-owner/occupiers when it is not possible to bind such a person to a positive covenant.[93] Secondly, if the intention was to allow parties to bind non-owners and non-occupiers, then it seems odd that this was not made explicit. Thirdly, and perhaps most importantly, the apparent width of the new section 307C(3) suggests that parties can bind anyone in the world to any agreement made between the parties providing only that it requires them 'to do something, or to refrain from doing something, in relation to the covenantor's land'.[94] Thus, not only can A and B agree to bind a successor in title, C, but they could also bind any other stranger, X, who has acquired

[89] Property Law Act 2007, s 307C to be inserted by Land Transfer Act 2017, s 242.

[90] 'Occupier' is primarily defined as a person 'who is in occupation of the land under a lease, or a licence to occupy the land in consideration of rent or a payment in the nature of rent, for a term of not less than 10 years certain or a renewal for a term of any length', or a person 'who remains in occupation of the land, with the consent of the lessor, after the term … has expired'. See Property Law Act 2007, s 4.

[91] It can be contrasted to the draft s 307B suggested by the Law Commission, which states that '[a] covenant in gross, *unless a contrary intention appears*, is binding in equity on' an owner or occupier (see text to n 69 above). The location for the words 'unless a contrary intention appears' in the first and second subclauses of the draft section arguably makes the intention clearer that if the parties chose, they could *limit* the binding nature of the covenant in gross so that it was personal to them and did not bind future owners or occupiers. This is in line with the wording used in relation to positive and restrictive covenants and the approach to those sections (see Property Law Act 2007, ss 301, 302 and 303(2)).

[92] New Zealand Law Commission (n 7 above) 310.

[93] See Property Law Act 2007, s 306(a), which notes that nothing in s 303 (dealing with the legal effect of covenants running with land) limits or affects, among other things 'the duty owed by a person holding an interest in land (other than the occupier of the land) to observe the terms of any *restrictive covenant* burdening the land' (emphasis added).

[94] Property Law Act 2007, s 307A(b).

no rights from A and indeed may be a non-owner or non-occupier. Overall, it would appear that New Zealand has now legislated so that it is not only possible for B to acquire a right that is capable of binding A's successor in title, C; but also for B to have a right which will bind X (a stranger) but not A; for B's right to bind X but never C; or for B's right to bind A, C and X! Some of these permutations go well beyond anything ever contemplated by the common law or equity.[95] For example, a covenant in gross requiring the owner of a property in a subdivision to be a member of a residents' gym could be drafted to also bind a visitor, member of the owner's family, or other distantly related party. In another context, not only could a publican (for the time being and whether an owner, long-term lessee, or short-term lessee) be required to purchase a particular type of beer, but her patrons might be restricted from drinking anything else.

I can find no record explaining why the Law Commission's draft section, which connected the contrary intention much more closely to the owner/occupier provisions, was not adopted in full. My suspicion is that the placement of the words reflects a modern drive towards clear and simple statutory drafting and a general dislike of having more than one thought in a clause. However, in this case, the potential result has been to alter the meaning and effect of the clause from that suggested by the Law Commission and from that used for restrictive and positive covenants. I suspect that this was not the intention and does not reflect an explicit policy choice. If the interpretation I have noted is adopted by the courts, there are likely to be significant consequences not only for individuals and legal entities bound by obligations that they did not bargain for and cannot avoid but also for New Zealand's law of property more generally.

IV. The Potential Problems Created by Covenants in Gross as Enacted

As enacted, there is the potential for covenants in gross in New Zealand to create proprietary interests in land the content of which can be so wide so as to contain very personal obligations not closely connected with the land burdened. In addition, the class of persons potentially bound may be very wide. This seems to run contrary to the three mischiefs, identified by Edgeworth, that the *numerus clausus* aims to avoid:[96] it is unlikely to maximise the uses to which land can be put; it will not make things as simple as possible for third parties looking to purchase land; and it will not protect the integrity of the 'science of the law'[97] (by which is meant the rationality and coherence of the law).

A. Maximisation of Land Use

The goal of enacting a statutory covenant in gross in New Zealand was to recognise the legitimate demand for a tool to manage and enforce obligations that were not directly

[95] For a detailed discussion, see McFarlane (n 81 above).
[96] Edgeworth (n 16 above) 394–95.
[97] See *Keppell* (n 21 above) 535–36, 1049.

covered by existing property instruments. However, the enactment of the provisions may arguably have gone too far, which may have the effect of restricting the ways in which land can be used and developed.

If the test of 'in relation to the covenantor's land' in section 307A(b) is read at its widest, it may, for example, encompass agreements that require an owner to sell their land on particular terms or to a particular class of purchaser. This may occur particularly in situations of imbalance of power between those seeking to impose the conditions and those who will be bound by them, such as in retirement villages.[98] While such a term could be rendered void by the courts on the grounds that it is contrary to public policy,[99] the potential remains that such an owner would be restricted in the way they use their property. Similar concerns arise in situations that may be more closely aligned with restraint of trade clauses. There is a risk that the legislation overreaches and tips over into creating a situation whereby land use is unduly restricted. Over time, this may have a chilling effect and is likely to decrease the uses to which the land can be put.

One of the goals of the legal developments during the nineteenth century, as reflected by the *numerus clausus*, was to provide for the efficient commodification of land.[100] Covenants in gross on the New Zealand model appear to allow for rights that may shackle land with all manner of duties and could well severely limit the uses to which land may be put. While there are provisions for covenants and covenants in gross to be extinguished or amended,[101] these require an application to a court and the associated costs, uncertainty, and delay. The freedom of a present owner to deal with their property as they choose should be circumscribed to an extent so that such costs will not be borne by future owners.[102]

B. Simplicity of Conveying Land

One of the difficulties with the provisions as enacted is the wide range of potential subject-matter that may be covered by a covenant in gross and the parties that may be bound by it. This has the potential to seriously complicate the conveyancing process. While notice of the covenant and a record of its content will be easily ascertained from the register of title, precisely how the agreement will work and its effect on various parties will be a matter for the interpretation of the purchaser's advisors. This will add uncertainty and cost to the process of buying property. While it could be argued that purchasers will simply be free to make the choice about whether to purchase a property or not, particularly pertinent in New Zealand with its robust registration system,[103] this may accord too much sophistication to people who may have very little understanding of the intricacies of land law,[104] and who, at least in New Zealand, almost always enter into the standard form contract to purchase the land before seeking legal advice.

[98] New Zealand Law Commission (n 7 above) [7.32].

[99] See Property Law Act 2007, s 318D(1)(f) to be inserted by Land Transfer Act 2017, s 246.

[100] Edgeworth (n 16 above) 394.

[101] Property Law Act 2007, ss 317 and 318D, which are substantially similar.

[102] Edgeworth (n 16 above) 406 and McFarlane (n 15 above).

[103] See for example Epstein (n 25 above) who argues more generally that a robust registration system is a substitute for the *numerus clausus*.

[104] P O'Connor, 'Careful What You Wish For: Positive Freehold Covenants' (2011) 75 *Conv* 191, 204.

The potentially open-ended nature of covenants in gross is likely to significantly increase transaction costs and runs contrary to the balancing act the *numerus clausus* undertakes in seeking the optimal number of standardised property rights within the system of conveying land.[105] The Torrens register, with all its simplicity, allows for a much wider range of property rights to be created than recognised at common law or equity and the register means that extra transaction costs may be minimal.[106] In principle, in New Zealand, there is no problem from this point of view in recognising covenants in gross. However, given the potential problems in interpretation of the sections as enacted, it is inevitable that there will be disputes about the operation and effect of the legislation and the validity and effect of particular covenants in gross. This, of course, involves both cost and risk. We should not underestimate the costs that novel and unusual property rights will create for others.[107]

In addition, while the Torrens register will no doubt bring such obligations to the attention of a purchaser, to the extent covenants in gross may be able to bind non-owners or non-occupiers, such individuals may not have any need to consult the register. Consequently, the notice that the register confers will be ineffective, and yet such a person may still be bound by the covenant in gross. Consequently, the Torrens system provides little protection to more distantly related parties and cannot be seen as operating in substitution for the protections provided by the *numerus clausus*.

C. Rationality and Coherence of the Law

The statutory recognition of covenants in gross may well have contributed to the coherence of the law in one sense in New Zealand. Removing the ad hoc encumbrance system and replacing it with a statutory covenant in gross certainly provided a sense of order to an area of the law that had become unwieldly. Given the use and adaptation of the encumbrance mechanism to bind servient owners to obligations not attached to dominant land, there was clearly a need to rationalise the manner in which this was achieved. However, enacting the legislation in its current form, which potentially allows private parties to create a very wide range of sui generis contractual rights, and allowing these to become vested with a proprietary mantel, runs the risk of seriously undermining any coherence in the covenant system; the different treatment of positive convenants and convents in gross is notable in this regard. It is likely to make it very difficult for judges, lawyers, and commentators to accurately assess whether a particular agreement does, or ought to, fall within the category of a covenant in gross. It will also make it more difficult to assess what should or should not amount to a proprietary interest more generally. For example, if such a wide range of agreements may amount to property as a covenant in gross, this may impact on other questions, such as whether a licensee should have standing to sue in trespass.[108] Judges, who do not necessarily have a strong grounding in property law, may fail to appreciate the subtle differences between the boundaries of what is (or ought to be)

[105] Edgeworth (n 16 above) 394; Merrill and Smith (n 24 above).
[106] Edgeworth (ibid) 406.
[107] O'Connor (n 26 above) 63.
[108] See, eg, *Manchester Airport v Dutton* [2000] QB 133 (CA), discussed by McFarlane (n 81 above) 24.

purely personal and that which is proprietary, and this may undermine the common law scheme of property generally.

It could be argued that protecting the 'science' or rationality and coherence of the law becomes somewhat otiose when property is created by legislation; Parliament can do as it chooses and may be as incoherent as it wishes. Moreover, as Edgeworth notes, this justification for the *numerus clausus* was never particularly strong.[109] Modern developments such as unit or strata title schemes provide an example of very complex novel regimes of property that have not rendered the law incoherent or incapable of reasoned analysis. Indeed, such developments are welcome and, providing that a right can be carefully and precisely articulated, there need not be problems with classification. In particular, the ability to record these property rights on a Torrens register allows for customisation of rights that goes far beyond anything ever contemplated by the common law or equity. This, it is suggested, avoids the imposition of undue transaction costs on third parties as they can easily discover the content of a particular right from the register.[110] Nonetheless, the property rights that are able to be recorded on the register ought still be certain, predictable, and coherent for a number of reasons, including as noted above, the uncertainty and costs that are likely to creep in. Regardless of the source of law, it should still operate as an internally coherent system.[111]

It follows that, even though there is a strong argument that new types of property can be beneficial in allowing modern society to evolve, the goal ought to be the optimal number of accepted proprietary interests.[112] If New Zealand's covenants in gross are taken at their widest, they do not reflect such an optimisation. As Edgeworth presciently notes:

> [T]here will always be a need for an optimal number of interests for which property law is the legitimate gatekeeper. … At the very least, novel interests should be close in form to those presently on the list. Any change in the *numerus clausus* should be incremental. In gaining admission to the list, it would also make sense to impose a requirement of some kind of public benefit test before being recognised. Examples of contractual rights that would have difficulty passing this test would include covenants that do not 'touch and concern' the land, such as covenants to provide personal services that contracting parties might wish to annex to land.[113]

As enacted, it seems that New Zealand's legislation has failed to heed these warnings. There seems to be no reason why I could not covenant with the owner of a hairdressing salon that he or she provides me with hairdressing services or with a kindergarten to provide childcare. The obligation would require the covenantor to do something, and the obligation would be 'in relation to' the covenantor's land to the extent that it would bind the owner (or the occupier or anyone else) for the time being of that land to that obligation. In pushing out the boundaries of property law, there are good reasons to be careful, and New Zealand has not been.

[109] Edgeworth (n 16 above) 407.
[110] ibid 407.
[111] See, eg, HLA Hart, *The Concept of Law* (Oxford, Oxford University Press, 1961).
[112] Edgeworth (n 16 above).
[113] ibid 406.

V. The *Numerus Clausus* is Dead; Long Live *Numerus Clausus*

As noted by Pollock CB in *Hill v Tupper*:

> A new species of incorporeal hereditament cannot be created at the will and pleasure of the owner of property; but he must be content to accept the estate and a right to dispose of it subject to the law as settled by decisions or controlled by act of Parliament.[114]

There can be no doubt that the generally accepted forum for property-making has moved to Parliament. It is therefore tempting to think that the *numerus clausus* as a guiding metaprinciple is, or should be, dead. As Epstein suggests, it can be argued that the law should operate so that individuals are free to create any property interest they choose and that there is only a problem in relation to covenants if a successor in title is bound by undiscoverable burdens.[115] If such a right is unattractive to others, that will be reflected in the price people are willing to pay,[116] and as a result, the operation of the market will serve to dictate the types of rights property holders are prepared to create. Certainly, such a view could explain the New Zealand approach to covenants in gross. A number of commentators have suggested, however, that simply because legislators have the ability to create property rights via statute, this does not necessarily mean they should do so without reference to the potential reasons why the class of property rights has historically been closed.[117] The New Zealand experience helps to demonstrate the truth of this position. The way in which covenants in gross have been allowed for indicates that, although there are no impediments to the legislative creation of property rights,[118] the *numerus clausus* still provides 'useful lessons'[119] for legislators and for the lawyers and judges that will have the task of defining the ambit of covenants in gross in New Zealand.

The risks of ignoring the *numerus clausus* principle are manifold. Dangers stem from the risk of excessive fragmentation and a resulting stagnation driven by numerous conflicting property interests, leading to gridlock.[120] Issues of cost arise, including those associated with determining disputes in relation to new forms of property that may not align with existing common law concepts, especially the effects on subsequent owners. In addition, problems can arise where the scope and content of a new property interest is not clearly defined and where the parties who enter into the agreement leading to the interest are not clear about which aspects of it are intended to bind subsequent owners.[121] The avoidance

[114] Hill (n 29 above) 127–28.
[115] Epstein (n 25 above).
[116] ibid 1360.
[117] See, eg, O'Connor (n 26 above); Weir (n 17 above).
[118] New Zealand has a very strong tradition of Parliamentary sovereignty and there are few, if any, limits on what the legislature can do via statute. See *Rothmans of Pall Mall (NZ) Ltd v Attorney-General* [1991] 2 NZLR 323 (HC), 330.
[119] O'Connor (n 26 above) 43.
[120] Weir (n 17 above) 669, citing MA Heller, 'The Tragedy of the Anticommons: Property in Transition from Marx to Markets' (1998) 111 *Harvard Law Review* 621, 624 and 674–75.
[121] O'Connor (n 26 above) 64, cited by Weir (n 17 above) 668.

of each of these hazards could be said to be at the heart of the function of property law, and helps to explain why it is so different from contract. Simply creating a property right by statute does not remove these concerns or the potency of the *numerus clausus* as a guiding principle.

There is a strong argument that in creating new property rights by statute legislatures should pay close attention to the *numerus clausus*, and that a new right should only be created where: there is a clear public interest at issue; the drafting is sensitive to economic and stagnation issues and designed to ensure as little conflict as possible between the new interest and existing common law concepts; the provisions are sensitive to the possibility of changes in public policy; and the property rights created are able to be modified in light of changing circumstances.[122]

The legislation providing for covenants in gross in New Zealand does allow for a court to modify or extinguish them for a range of reasons, including a change in the character of the neighbourhood or if the covenant is 'contrary to public policy or to any enactment or rule of law'.[123] While this runs into the difficulties associated with 'ex post facto restraints on the content of covenants'[124] and the fact that it is up to the third party eventually bound by the covenant to take the active steps, risk, and cost of challenging it, it does provide a mechanism for judicial oversight and for changing circumstances to be catered for.

I accept that it could be that New Zealand has unconsciously opted for a regime of covenants in gross that is in accordance with Epstein's laissez-faire model. Indeed, in light of New Zealand's approach to deregulation and free markets over the last decades, this is not outside the realm of possibility.[125] However, this seems unlikely in light of the Law Commission's original recommendations. While the creation of covenants in gross is not necessarily a problem in itself, dangers flow from ignoring the basic lessons of the *numerus clausus* when creating property, including making the law of property both cluttered to the point of gridlock and unduly complex.[126] In my view, the legislature should have carefully circumscribed the content and scope of the right, rather than (consciously or unconsciously) creating a wide range of interpretative possibilities. Had a quite restrictive approach to covenants in gross been adopted, and found to be unduly limiting, this could have been subsequently remedied. An incremental approach would have provided a useful response to a legitimate problem but also would have taken account of the lessons of the *numerus clausus*. Nonetheless, it may not be too late, as judges can use the *numerus clausus* when interpreting the legislation. As a result, it would be possible for judges to view section 307C as allowing the parties to limit the scope of who is bound, so that it is not expanded beyond owners and occupiers. Certainly, New Zealand's Supreme Court is aware

[122] Weir (n 17 above) 669.
[123] Property Law Act 2007, s 318D(1)(f) as to be inserted by Land Transfer Act 2017, s 246.
[124] McFarlane (n 15 above) 329. For discussion of the difference between ex ante and ex post control of property rights in land, see too S Pascoe, 'Re-evaluating Recreational Easements – New Norms for the Twenty-First Century?' Chapter 10 in this volume.
[125] B Easton, *The Commercialisation of New Zealand* (Auckland, Auckland University Press, 1997).
[126] Weir (n 17 above) 679.

of the principle, discussing it in a recently decided case.[127] However, its ultimate conclusion in that case, that it could

> see no sensible reason why a party bound by a covenant cannot be prevented by injunction from acting inconsistently with the promise it contains even if the practical effect of that is that the party must allow another onto its land[128]

does not inspire a great deal of confidence in the Court's application of the principle.

VI. Conclusion

A range of pressures are being brought to bear on property law. The challenges posed by climate change, environmental issues, technological change and globalisation are all pushing property law to develop in interesting and exciting ways.[129] There is no doubt that property law has the capacity to grow and develop in line with these pressures.[130] It is appropriate that the forum for creating property interests has shifted to the legislature, which is much better placed than the courts to effect evolution in property law in line with changing social mores.[131] Undoubtedly, in line with the perceived needs of a changing society, we will see legislatures expanding the boundaries of the recognised common law property interests.[132] Clearly, the statutory provisions allowing for positive covenants to bind successors in title and, most recently, the creation of covenants in gross, are archetypal examples of the legislature pushing the boundaries of the common law and, by extension, the *numerus clausus* principle. This is a good thing, and while covenants in gross are not necessarily a bad thing, the New Zealand approach serves as a cautionary tale. Insufficient attention has been paid to the precise wording of the legislation, and there was no discussion of what effect it might have on the broader scheme of property law. The discussion focused on the problems raised by the encumbrance mechanism, and covenants in gross appear to have been a consequentialist reaction to these concerns. It does not appear that anyone stopped to think about how covenants in gross might impact on property law more generally or what lessons property law, and in particular the *numerus clausus*, might be able to provide.

The New Zealand experience illustrates that the *numerus clausus* may continue to have valuable lessons for property law, notwithstanding the ability of legislatures to do what they want. This also tells us something about property law more generally and in particular about the principle of the *numerus clausus*. There remains a place for it in discussions about how property law should develop into the future and we ignore it at our peril.

[127] *Escrow Holdings Forty-One Ltd v District Court at Auckland* on appeal from *Body Corporate 341188 v District Court at Auckland* [2016] NZSC 167, [2017] 1 NZLR 374.

[128] ibid [59].

[129] Weir (n 17 above) 652, 663, and 673–78.

[130] See B France-Hudson, 'Surprisingly Social: Private Property and Environmental Management' (2017) 29 *Journal of Environmental Law* 101.

[131] Edgeworth (n 16 above) 418.

[132] Weir (n 17 above) 656 and 662.

12

Security of Tenure in the Private Rented Sector in England: Balancing the Competing Property Rights of Landlords and Tenants

EMILY WALSH

I. Introduction

There has been a significant increase in the percentage of people living in privately rented accommodation in England in the last decade.[1] Tenants living in the private rented sector (PRS) have very limited security of tenure; they typically sign a six- or twelve-month assured shorthold tenancy agreement[2] after which they often become statutory periodic tenants. This means that the tenancy can be brought to an end without the tenant either being at fault or being given a reason, on two months' notice at any time after the initial term.[3] Charities such as Shelter have been calling for some time for tenants in the PRS to have increased security of tenure,[4] and the government has issued a consultation to examine how the barriers to longer tenancies might be overcome.[5] Not only has the size of the PRS increased in recent years but there has also been significant growth in the number of families making long-term homes in the sector.[6] This chapter examines whether no-fault evictions in England should continue in the light of these changes in the sector, while taking account of the competing proprietary interests of landlords and tenants.

[1] The tenure share of the PRS has grown from 11% in 2003–04 to 20% in 2016–17 according to the Ministry of Housing, Communities and Local Government, *English Housing Survey 2016–2017: Headline Report* (London, Ministry of Housing, Communities and Local Government, 2018).

[2] 81% of tenancies in the PRS are for this initial term according to the Department for Communities and Local Government, *English Housing Survey Private Rented Sector 2015–2016* (London, Ministry of Housing, Communities and Local Government, 2017) 20.

[3] Housing Act 1988, s 21.

[4] L Reynolds, *Safe and secure? The Private Rented Sector and Security of Tenure* (London, Shelter, 2005).

[5] Ministry of Housing, Communities and Local Government, *Overcoming the Barriers to Longer Tenancies in the Private Rented Sector* (London, Ministry of Housing, Communities and Local Government, 2018). This consultation commenced after presentation of this paper at the *Modern Studies in Property Law* conference at UCL in April 2018 and the results of the consultation were not known at the time of the final submission of this chapter.

[6] 38% of households in the PRS had children in 2016–17 up from 34% in 2006–07, according to the Ministry of Housing, Communities and Local Government (n 1 above).

Section II of the chapter provides a brief historical background to housing law and policy in so far as it relates to the PRS. It also provides a context to the current size and composition of the sector in terms of the characteristics of both landlords and tenants. Section III of the chapter considers the removal of the no-fault ground for eviction from the perspective of landlords. The narratives of landlords are provided by responses to a Scottish Government consultation which took place in 2014. These were selected on the basis that at the time Scotland, like England, had a no-fault ground for eviction of tenants in the PRS and the Scottish Government asked consultees whether the no-fault ground for eviction should be removed. The answer from Scottish landlords and letting agents was a resounding 'no'. Section III of the chapter analyses the reasons respondents gave for their negative response to this question and considers the impact of these concerns on the question of reform in England. Having considered the landlord's perspective, Section IV looks at security of tenure from a tenant's point of view. Section IV takes a different approach from that taken in section III by examining the considerable interdisciplinary scholarship on the importance of home and how this can be applied specifically to tenants in the PRS. In so doing, theories of property and personhood and recent debates on ontological security are considered. Section V examines the proposals for reform in England raised in the recent consultation by the government and considers how these proposals may be received by landlords and the extent to which, if they were to be adopted, they would be sufficient for tenants to be able to make a home in the PRS.

II. The Background: The Private Rented Sector in the UK

The private rented sector represented about 90 per cent of housing in 1900.[7] Most of the century to follow saw a steady decline in the sector so that by the end of the century it comprised the smallest tenure type.[8] The decline in the PRS is sometimes attributed to the rise in regulation.[9] However, some experts argue that the sector was already severely stressed.[10] The onset of the First World War led to Britain, like many other nations, adopting rent control.[11] In order to prevent rent control leading to eviction, the legislation also provided for security of tenure.[12] Unlike other nations involved in the war, Britain retained rent control after the war ended. Indeed controls, although amended to remove certain

[7] M Partington, A Marsh, R Lee and FH Stephen, *Ensuring Compliance: The Case of the Private Rented Sector* (Centre for Market and Public Organisation, Working Paper No 06/148, 23 March 2006).

[8] D Rhodes, 'The Fall and Rise of the Private Rented Sector in England' (2015) 41(2) *Built Environment* 258.

[9] P Kemp, 'Rebuilding the Private Rented Sector' in M Malpass and R Means (eds), *Implementing Housing Policy* (London, Open University Press, 1992); A Crook, 'Private Rented Housing and the Impact of Deregulation' in J Birchill (ed), *Housing Policy in the 1990s* (London, Routledge, 1992).

[10] S Lowe, 'The New Private Rented Sector – Regulation in a Deregulated Market' in S Lowe and D Hughes (eds), *The Private Rented Housing Market Regulation or Reregulation* (London, Ashgate, 2007); R Forrest and A Murie, *Selling the Welfare State the Privatisation of Public Housing* (London, Routledge, 1988).

[11] J Melling, *Housing, Social Policy and the State* (London, Croom Helm, 1980).

[12] Increase of Rent and Mortgage (War Restrictions) Act 1915.

categories of property,[13] remained in place until 1957.[14] The Rent Act 1957 aimed at increasing supply and investment through decontrol but largely failed in its goal.[15] The Rent Acts which followed in the 1960s and 1970s provided for 'fair rents' set by rent officers and increased security of tenure by extending succession rights. Whilst the Rent Act 1977 remains in force, it is of diminishing importance, since lettings created after 15 January 1989 are regulated by the Housing Act 1988.[16]

The Housing Act 1988 was introduced by a Conservative Government concerned that the decline in the private rented sector was the result of rent control. The legislation took all new private lettings out of rent control, instead providing for a new type of letting known as the 'assured tenancy', which allowed landlords to charge whatever rent the market would allow. In terms of security, the assured tenant enjoyed statutory security and a limited form of succession on death. Inception of the Housing Act 1996 diminished this security by providing that from 28 February 1996 any new tenancy would be an 'assured shorthold' tenancy (AST) unless the parties agreed that it would be an assured tenancy. The effect of this in terms of tenant security was that the landlord could regain possession by serving a notice under section 21 of the Housing Act 1988 without demonstrating any fault on the part of the tenant.[17] Where possession is sought under section 21 an accelerated procedure can be used whereby the court will make its decision on the papers and an order for possession within 14 days can be made. During the fixed term the landlord can seek possession in accordance with section 8 of the 1988 Act on one or more of the grounds contained in Schedule 2. These grounds are divided into two types, mandatory grounds for possession, where the court must order possession, and discretionary grounds, where the court may order possession if it considers it reasonable to do so. Mandatory grounds include: a landlord needing to return to the property to live, the mortgagee's entitlement to exercise the power of sale, demolition and reconstruction of the property by the landlord, and serious rent arrears. Discretionary grounds include persistent rent areas, breach of obligation, deterioration of the property, nuisance or annoyance, or conviction for illegal or immoral use.

Since the early 1990s the fortunes of the PRS have reversed.[18] The deregulation of the sector may well have played a part in the resurgence in popularity of private tenancies, but other factors, such as the increasingly limited access to social housing,[19] the availability of new 'buy-to-let' mortgages, a tax regime which has, until recently, been favourable to

[13] The Rent and Mortgage Interest Restrictions Act 1923 removed controls from new lettings and, as investment in building public housing eased shortage; the Rent and Mortgage Interest Restrictions (Amendment) Act 1933 removed rent controls from all but the lowest value properties.

[14] The onset of the Second World War led to reintroduction of general controls.

[15] JB Cullingworth *Essays on Housing Policy* (Hemel Hempstead, Allen & Unwin, 1980) 64; P Kemp 'Ideology, Public Policy and Private Rental Housing Since the War' in P Williams (ed), *Directions in Housing Policy Towards Sustainable Housing Policies for the UK* (London, Paul Chapman Publishing Ltd, 1997).

[16] As amended by Housing Act 1996.

[17] This section has recently been amended by the Deregulation Act 2015. In summary, the landlord must give two months' notice in writing to the tenant and where the tenancy is fixed term, this may not be during the first four months.

[18] Rhodes (n 8 above).

[19] K Scanlon and B Kochan, *Towards a Sustainable Private Rented Sector the Lessons from Other Countries* (London, LSE, 2011) 8.

buy-to-let landlords,[20] the growth in student numbers and increased mobility of young people, may also have facilitated growth in the sector.[21]

The popularity of the sector with young professionals and students is clear, and for these groups the ease of access and exit make it a desirable tenure; 46 per cent of occupiers in the PRS in 2016–17 were aged 25–34 (up from 27 per cent in 2006–07).[22] The extent to which this group envisages a successful transition to owner-occupation is less certain; in 2016–17 only 60 per cent of private renters envisaged buying.[23] The average age for first-time buyers has also increased by three years in the last decade, from 30 in 2006–07 to 33 in 2016–17.[24] Recent trends point towards increasing permanency for some in the sector, including families and previously homeless households.[25] Furthermore, the increasing proportion of households in the PRS with children (38 per cent in 2016–17, up from 34 per cent in 2006–07)[26] has led charities to call for more security of tenure in the sector to support family life.[27] The problem is particularly clear in London where the percentage of residents living in private rented accommodation is much higher than elsewhere in the country. In the country as a whole the tenure share of the PRS has grown from 11 per cent in 2003–04 to 20 per cent in 2016–17.[28] In London in the last 10 years the sector has grown from 16 per cent to 30 per cent. London has also seen growth in the number of children occupying private rented accommodation, a rise from one in five children in the capital living in private rented accommodation in 2004 to one in three in 2014.[29]

One of the challenges in regulating the PRS has been the fact that it is largely a cottage industry. In a report published in 2016 the housing charity Shelter found that 56 per cent of landlords own a single property and 88 per cent are private individuals rather than companies.[30] The Law Commission has referred to such landlords as 'hobby landlords'.[31] Some of these landlords were forced into the sector when the property slump prevented them from selling their homes; others have inherited a property or ended up with an extra property when they have moved in with a partner. Faulkner describes these types of landlords as 'accidental landlords', a term she defines as 'a homeowner who is letting their property due to circumstance rather than having actively pursued buying a property to let it out'.[32] She estimates that 23–42 per cent of landlords are 'accidental' and that this group

[20] Recently Stamp Duty Land Tax has been increased to 3% for private landlords and mortgage interest relief is being reduced incrementally between 2017–18 and 2019–20.

[21] Partington et al (n 7 above); T Crook and PA Kemp, 'England' in T Crook and PA Kemp (eds), *Private Rental Housing: Comparative Perspectives* (Cheltenham, Edward Elgar Publishing Ltd, 2014); PA Kemp, 'Private Renting after the Global Financial Crisis' (2015) 30(4) *Housing Studies* 601; and J Rugg and D Rhodes, *The Private Rented Sector: its Contribution and Potential* (York, York Centre for Housing Policy, University of York, 2008).

[22] Ministry of Housing, Communities and Local Government (n 1 above).

[23] ibid 13.

[24] ibid.

[25] Rugg and Rhodes (n 21 above).

[26] Ministry of Housing, Communities and Local Government (n 1 above).

[27] R De Santos, *A Better Deal Towards More Stable Private Renting* (London, Shelter, 2012).

[28] Ministry of Housing, Communities and Local Government (n 1 above).

[29] London Assembly, *At Home with Renting Improving Security for London's Private Renters* (London, Greater London Authority, 2016).

[30] L Reynolds, *Research Report Survey on Private Landlords* (London, Shelter, 2016).

[31] Law Commission, *Renting Homes the Final Report: Volume 1* (Law Com No 297, 2000) 18.

[32] K Faulkner, *The Impact of Accidental Landlords on the Private Rented Sector* (August 2016) 14.

accounts for 10–20 per cent of lettings. Arguably accidental or 'hobby' landlords create issues with regard to professionalism, as they may lack the specialist knowledge required to comply with their obligations.[33] It is perhaps unsurprising that amateur landlords struggle to comply with the regulations as, according to the London Assembly Housing Committee, there are around 50 Acts of Parliament and 70 sets of regulations that apply to the PRS.[34]

It is difficult to identify landlords and tenants because registration and licensing is not compulsory in all parts of the UK,[35] making communication challenging.[36] Indeed in England there is no register of landlords and licensing is only required for Houses of Multiple Occupation (HMOs)[37] in areas where individual local authorities deem it to be necessary. There have been calls for compulsory licensing[38] but these have to date been ignored by governments.

There has been consistent cross-party consensus regarding the value of the PRS and the need for it to be professionalised. This consensus is evidenced by policies produced by both of the main political parties. In 2010, before losing the general election, the Labour Government launched a consultation on measures to increase investment in the PRS.[39] In 2012 the Department for Communities and Local Government (DCLG) commissioned a report on the barriers to institutional investment in private rented homes: the 'Montague Report'.[40] Following publication of the Montague Report the Coalition Government introduced a number of incentives and initiatives to encourage institutional investment in the sector.[41] The Housing White Paper in 2017[42] made a number of proposals including: changing the National Planning Policy Framework (NPPF) to explicitly refer to build-to-rent as a model that planning authorities should consider; allowing developers to more easily offer affordable private rent instead of other types of affordable housing; encouraging the use of 'family-friendly' tenancies; and establishing a joint committee of government, industry and the public sector to address wider barriers to build-to-rent. Calls for improvements in the sector have not led to change in England as quickly or radically as they have in other parts of the UK.

[33] J O'Connor 'Issues in the Management of Private Rented Accommodation' in L Sirr (ed), *Renting in Ireland: the Social, Voluntary and Private Sectors* (Dublin, Institute of Public Administration, 2014).

[34] London Assembly (n 29 above).

[35] In Scotland there has been compulsory registration since 2006. In Wales registration became compulsory in November 2016. Landlords must then either obtain a licence or use licensed managing agents. Those seeking a licence must pass checks to ensure they are fit to let property, undergo training and comply with a code of practice. Northern Ireland has a national registration scheme but licences are only required for Houses of Multiple Occupation (HMOs).

[36] T Moore and R Dunning, *Regulation of the Private Rented Sector in England Using Lessons from Ireland* (York, Joseph Rowntree Foundation, 2017) 7.

[37] HMOs are properties occupied by two or more people who are not living together as a couple or as part of the same family (Housing Act 2004, s 254). They have been perceived as more likely to fall below acceptable housing standards.

[38] Rugg and Rhodes (n 21 above) xxiii.

[39] HM Treasury, *Investment in the UK Private Rented Sector* (London, HM Treasury, 2010) 28.

[40] A Montague, *Review of the Barriers to Institutional Investment in Private Rented Homes* (London, Department for Communities and Local Government, 2012).

[41] Incentives and initiatives included the 'build to rent fund', the 'housing stimulus package' and the 'private rented sector taskforce'.

[42] Department for Communities and Local Government, *Fixing our Broken Housing Market* (London, Department for Communities and Local Government, 2017).

The reason for the different regulatory regimes in different parts of the UK is that housing policy has been devolved in the UK since the late 1990s. Wales and Scotland have increased regulation to provide tenants with stronger rights. The only change with regard to security of tenure in England has been an attempt to put a stop to 'retaliatory eviction', the practice of landlords serving a section 21 notice where a tenant has complained about the condition of the property or a want of repair. The Deregulation Act 2015 prevents a landlord from serving a section 21 notice where the tenant has made a complaint in writing regarding the condition of the property and this complaint has not been adequately addressed. This is clearly a positive step for tenants, but it addresses only one small issue with regard to security of tenure. In addition to the changes aimed at ending retaliatory eviction, landlords are now required to safeguard tenants' deposits in accordance with a government-approved deposit protection scheme[43] and to provide tenants with prescribed information and a copy of the government's *Renting Homes* leaflet. Failure to comply with these requirements can result in a fine of not less than the amount of the deposit and not more than three times the deposit.[44]

In Wales when the Renting Homes (Wales) Act 2016 comes into force, existing tenancy arrangements will be replaced with two types of contract: secure contracts, modelled on secure tenancies; and standard contracts, modelled on assured shorthold tenancies.[45] It seems likely that private landlords will adopt the standard contracts which have a minimum term of six months. Since the Private Housing (Tenancies) (Scotland) Act 2016 came into force on 1 December 2017 the short assured tenancy has been replaced with a 'private residential tenancy'.[46] Under the old short assured tenancy regime the landlord could give the tenant two months' notice, to end no earlier than the end of the fixed term.[47] This mirrored the section 21 provisions in England and meant that the tenant had very limited security of tenure. Under the new 'private residential tenancy' regime, unlike the previous short assured tenancy, there is no 'no-fault' ground for possession. However, the landlord can regain possession for occupation for herself or for a family member[48] or in order to sell the property.[49] Since 1 December 2017 the First-tier Tribunal in Scotland has the jurisdiction to deal with disputes in the PRS. The aim of moving these disputes from the Sherriff Court to the First-tier Tribunal is to allow disputes to be dealt with more quickly in a specialist setting.[50] The rationale behind these changes and the consultation undertaken by the Scottish Government are considered further in section III of this chapter.

III. The Landlords' Perspective: Evidence from Scotland

This section of the chapter examines the narrative of landlords and letting agents in Scotland with the aim of creating a picture of the potential tension between the needs

[43] Housing Act 2004, s 213 as amended by Localism Act 2011, s 184 and Deregulations Act 2015, ss 30–40.
[44] Housing Act 2004, s 214(3) and (4) as amended by Localism Act 2011, s 184.
[45] Renting Homes (Wales) Act 2016, s 1.
[46] Private Housing (Tenancies)(Scotland) Act 2016, s 1.
[47] Housing (Scotland) Act 1988, s 33.
[48] ibid, Sch 3 para 4 and 5.
[49] ibid, Sch 3 para 1.
[50] L Robertson, *Consultation on a New Tenancy for the Private Sector* (Edinburgh, Scottish Government, 2014).

of tenants with regard to security of tenure, and the concerns of landlords and letting agents in providing this security.

In October 2014 the Scottish Government published a consultation regarding changes to the private rented sector.[51] The overall aim was, 'to improve security of tenure for tenants, while giving suitable safeguards for landlords, lenders and investors'.[52] The consultation ran from 6 October 2014 to 28 December 2014 and received 2,543 responses. The majority of the responses – 1,982 of them – were campaign responses where standard answers were produced multiple times. There were campaigns on both sides of the debate, with a total of 74 campaign responses from landlords and letting agents over two separate campaigns and 1,908 responses from the Living Rent campaign which represented tenants' interests.[53]

The following section of this chapter is a thematic analysis of the negative responses given to the first consultation question: 'Do you agree that the no-fault ground for a landlord to repossess their property should be excluded from the new tenancy system?'[54] This was clearly a key question in the consultation, as 99 per cent of respondents provided an answer to it; a larger percentage than to any other question.[55] Applied thematic analysis (ATA) was used to code the data for analysis.[56] These codes were collated into potential themes which were then refined.[57] As this was a relatively small data set, manual coding was employed.[58] The main themes revealed in the analysis of the data are considered below.

Approximately one third of respondents who answered 'no' to the first question mentioned the deterrent effect of excluding the no-fault ground for a landlord to repossess their property. The concern of these individuals and groups was that without the no-fault ground for possession landlords would leave the sector and that future investment in the sector would be curtailed. Some landlords specifically referred to the impact the proposed change would have on them personally, claiming that they would leave the sector altogether, or sell their rental properties in Scotland and buy instead in England. Many of the landlords who referred to the deterrent effect of the proposed changes stated that the perceived resultant drop in investment in the PRS was contrary to the government's policy and some even stated that it would result in an increase in homelessness. Closely aligned to the idea of deterrence to landlords was the concern expressed by some that mortgage lenders would be unwilling to lend. For example, one respondent stated, 'lenders will be less likely to provide finance and potential reductions in the value of a rented property with a tenant in occupation [mean that lenders] are likely to increase charges and reduce the amount of borrowing available'.[59]

[51] ibid.
[52] ibid.
[53] Living Rent are a Scottish tenants' union.
[54] Responses are available at: http://www.gov.scot/Publications/2015/01/8970/downloads.
[55] ibid 6.
[56] See G Guest, KM MacQueen and EE Namey, *Applied Thematic Analysis* (Los Angeles, Sage, 2012) for further details on undertaking applied thematic analysis.
[57] See V Braun and V Clarke, 'Using Thematic Analysis in Psychology' (2006) 3 *Qualitative Research in Psychology* 77, 79 for the process adopted.
[58] As opposed to using a qualitative data analysis software package such as NVivo.
[59] Consultation response (see nn 50 and 54 above) PRS 314.

The adverse impact of the proposed change was expressed not only as a deterrent effect on individuals and organisations entering the sector, but also as potential adverse changes in landlords' behaviour towards tenants. The argument here was that if landlords could not easily remove tenants they would become more risk averse and would therefore let only to tenants whom they felt they would not need to evict. This argument is illustrated by one landlord who stated, 'I would be much more particular about who I rented to if that happens, and might stop renting out'.[60]

Another popular theme was the need for the landlord to maintain flexibility and control of his or her property. This theme arose in more than 10 per cent of responses analysed. In these instances respondents often did not specify why they needed to retain flexibility. Where the response was more specific it was clear that the landlord wanted to be able to sell the property if required. For example, 'the majority of landlords, whether they are individuals or institutional investors, need the flexibility of being able to repossess their property if required for financial circumstances'.[61] Less frequently, the need for flexibility and/or control appears to relate to sector-specific issues such as lettings to students or HMOs; or because of tenant behaviour. Occasionally respondents stated that flexibility was advantageous not only to landlords but also to tenants. This perhaps slightly missed the point, as under the Scottish Government's proposals tenants were to be permitted to retain flexibility whilst at the same time this flexibility was to be reduced for landlords.[62] The theme of flexibility and control was sometimes linked to the theme of incentive/deterrent described above. For example, 'making it more difficult for landlords to repossess will discourage both individuals and larger landlords who need flexibility in dealing with their assets'.[63] The theme of flexibility was also occasionally linked to the theme of landlords' rights which is discussed further below.

Initial coding revealed a number of themes which could be grouped together under the overall theme of 'unfairness'. Here the respondents were concerned that their rights were not being acknowledged or respected. This was sometimes expressed on the basis that the property belonged to them and that they should therefore be allowed to do with it as they pleased, 'it detracts from the concept that the houses are owned by the landlords'.[64] Interestingly, on one occasion the landlord not only emphasised the ownership of the property but referred to the property as home. A further concern was that removal of the no-fault ground was 'an erosion of the landlord rights',[65] and that the balance of the rights between landlords and tenants had tipped too far in favour of the rights of tenants: 'in our view, granting security of tenure to tenants will swing the balance heavily towards tenants and away from landlords, lenders and investors in a way likely to cause disruption'.[66] Although not often articulated expressly, this notion of landlords' rights might be considered to be an expression of the proprietary nature of those rights. This notion was made explicit by one respondent who stated: 'such an interference with personal property rights is too great an

[60] ibid PRS 252.
[61] ibid 042.
[62] Robertson (n 50 above) 27.
[63] Consultation response (see nn 50 and 54 above) PRS 214.
[64] ibid 003.
[65] ibid 154.
[66] ibid 416.

infringement of the right to property in Scots law and does not respect the traditional Scots law doctrine of the right of the owner to the fruits of the property'.[67]

The final sub-theme which emerged from the broader theme of unfairness related to the contractual nature of tenancies and the role of the government in regulating these contractual relationships. In a response which was repeated a number of times, respondents stated that 'this would represent a fundamental shift in contract law and security of tenure'.[68] Aligned to this notion of the individual right to private property is an aversion to intervention by the state, which was also occasionally expressed in the data. The current regulation was referred to as 'overbearing'.[69] One respondent explained the concerns particularly clearly: 'the PRS is currently heavily regulated and the Scottish Government must be careful this does not tip the balance so that current or potential investors feel it is not worth their efforts or money to invest'.[70]

The inadequacy of the fault-based grounds for obtaining possession was the second most popular theme. Many landlords felt that the fault-based grounds did not cover all situations where a tenant was at fault, or that it was sometimes difficult to prove tenant fault. Landlords reported that this was particularly the case with regard to anti-social behaviour. The word 'behaviour' arose 84 times in 29 responses.[71] The concern may be summarised as follows: 'one of the most difficult breaches to prove is that of anti-social behaviour. Often it boils down to one person's word against another's'.[72] Landlords also complained that even with regard to eviction for rent arrears the fault-based system was flawed, as tenants sometimes 'play the system'[73] by paying off some arrears at the last minute. Furthermore, where the tenant was in arrears the mechanics of the fault-based procedure meant that the amount of arrears accrued by the time of eviction was much higher than where the no-fault based approach was used. Landlords expressed concern that the fault-based system was time-consuming, costly and complex.

Most landlords did not refer to the proposal that disputes would be heard in the First-tier Tribunal. Those who did refer to the new tribunal service were not convinced that it would cope with demand: 'it is also a "leap of faith" at this stage to expect landlords to trust that the new Tribunal Service will not be overwhelmed by expected high numbers of referrals if the no-fault ground for possession is removed'.[74] The idea that there will be a large increase in fault-based evictions contradicts what the same respondent claimed about the low level of no-fault evictions. Indeed a number of respondents claimed that no-fault evictions were rare, many expressing the view that 'few landlords ask perfectly good tenants to leave for no reason'.[75] A further criticism of the use of the First-tier Tribunal was that it would be no 'cheaper, quicker or more effective'.[76] A number of landlords stated that the no-fault ground

[67] ibid 270.
[68] ibid 310, 311, 334, 339, 430 and 690.
[69] ibid 511.
[70] ibid 332.
[71] Five of the responses were identical in the wording of their concern with regard to behaviour.
[72] Consultation responses (see nn 50 and 54 above) PRS 059, 161, 511, 394 and 395.
[73] ibid 161.
[74] ibid 310.
[75] ibid 526.
[76] ibid 458.

for possession was actually better for the tenant, as it resulted in less acrimony,[77] prevented strain on the landlord and tenant relationship,[78] and meant that there was no 'black mark' against the tenant that might prevent future letting.[79]

This section of the chapter has provided an insight into the views of landlords with regard to the properties they rent out and the tenants who occupy them. Most landlords felt that security of tenure in the private rented sector should not be increased and that the sector needed to remain flexible in the interests of both landlords and tenants.

IV. The Tenants' Perspective: Property and Security of Tenure

This section considers the tenants' perspective on possible reforms to the PRS and asks what weight should be given, in the face of potential resistance from landlords, to tenants' desire for secure occupation of a home. In doing so, this section draws on the considerable body of scholarship relating to the importance and meaning of home, and on the personhood theory of property.

The personhood theory of property is usually attributed to Hegel's examination of the concept in the *Philosophy of Right*.[80] His justification of property is based on concern for an individual's free will, rather than promotion of the collective good. Freedom for Hegel was inextricably linked with personality. As Alexander and Peñalver put it, 'Property is the necessary medium through which the process of individual and social development occurs'.[81] They explain that in their view, the modern significance of Hegel's theory is that it both justifies and limits private ownership of property on the basis of self-development and it establishes the essential relationship between private property, personal identity and community.

The most influential modern theorist to draw inspiration from Hegel's theory is Margaret Radin. Radin, like Hegel, is interested in the relationship between property and self-development. She states that 'to achieve proper self-development – to be a person – an individual needs some control over resources in the external environment'.[82] In considering the connection between property and personhood Radin explains that most people possess objects that they feel strongly connected with, to the extent that these objects are felt to be almost part of themselves. It is possible to assess the strength of the relationship between owner and object by considering the kind of pain that would result from its loss. An object, she says, 'is closely related to one's personhood if its loss causes pain that cannot be relieved by the object's replacement'.[83] She contrasts the effect of a wedding ring being stolen from a

[77] ibid 314.
[78] ibid 119.
[79] ibid 006.
[80] GWF Hegel, *Philosophy of Right*, TM Knox (tr) (Oxford, Clarendon Press, 1952).
[81] GS Alexander and EM Peñalver, *An Introduction to Property Theory* (Cambridge, Cambridge University Press, 2012) 61.
[82] M Radin, *Reinterpreting Property* (Chicago, University of Chicago Press, 1993) 35.
[83] ibid 37.

jeweller and a wedding ring being stolen from its wearer. In the former situation insurance proceeds can reimburse the owner; in the latter, money will not adequately compensate for the loss.

Radin categorises property under two separate headings: 'personal' and 'fungible'; personal property being objects which are bound up with the person, and fungible property being property the loss of which can be relieved with money. Radin acknowledges that even to the extent that there may be a consensus as to what property could constitute 'personal' or 'fungible' property, the distinction must be a continuum and not a dichotomy. A 'home' which is owned and occupied would clearly be a category of 'personal' property. Home ownership is, and has been since the 1970s at least, the preferred tenure in the UK and indeed most developed Anglophone countries.[84]

It is clear then that an owner-occupied home is, in Radin's terms, personal property. What is less clear is whether, from the tenant's point of view, a rented home occupied under an assured shorthold tenancy is such personal property. It could be argued that a tenant does not have the same connection to their 'home' as an owner-occupier, or a party occupying under a long lease. A home owner can make and profit from home improvements, from decorating and gardening to structural home improvements designed to add value as well as amenity. Assured shorthold tenants in the PRS, on the other hand, have fewer opportunities to put their own personality into their home. They may be permitted to decorate, often on the precondition that the property is returned to the landlord in the condition in which it was let, but their ability to engage in home improvements is likely to be very limited. The short-term nature of the letting is also likely to prohibit the tenant from making improvements, or indeed really feeling 'at home'.

Historically this might be seen as a justification for not affording extra weight to the rights of private residential tenants; they were merely renting for a short time before purchasing a more permanent home. Poorer long-term renters were able to access security of tenure through council housing. However, government policy since the 1970s has been to marginalise the public rented sector, making it a mere 'welfare net' for those who cannot afford home-ownership.[85] Radin argues that where tenants are transient rather than occupying an established home, then their claim no longer appears obviously weightier than the landlord's.[86] In the past young renters planning to buy their own home and saving for a deposit may have viewed their rented home as fungible rather than personal, on the basis that they were looking forward to putting their personality into their first owned property.[87]

As we have seen, however, the PRS now serves a different function with many tenants needing to stay longer and families forming a more significant proportion of occupants of this tenure type. A family with children who have no realistic prospect of ever buying a

[84] J Kemeny, 'A Political Sociology of Home Ownership in Australia' (1977) 13(47) *Journal of Sociology* 47; R Ronald, *The Ideology of Home Ownership* (London, Palgrave Macmillan 2008); and P Saunders, *A Nation of Homeowners* (London, Unwin Hyman, 1990).

[85] L Whitehouse (1998) 'The Home Owner: Citizen or Consumer' in S Bright and J Dewer (eds), *Land Law Themes and Perspectives* (Oxford, Oxford University Press, 1998).

[86] Radin (n 82 above) at 80.

[87] Indeed this dream of home links to the 'paradise' signifier of home identified in Somerville's research and considered further below.

home or finding a more secure form of tenure might only have their private rented house to call home.[88] In this situation, if the home they occupy cannot be called personal property, this surely must only be because the tenure type is insecure, and this in turn raises questions as to the impact on the sense of self of those living in the PRS. Radin also acknowledges that if not all interests of tenants have the same relationship to personhood, then not all interests of landlords are fully fungible.[89] Looking at the position of the PRS in England and Wales, it is clear that landlords often rent out property in which they once lived themselves, or have inherited from parents (the 'accidental' landlords referred to above). Clearly landlords renting out these homes may have an attachment to the property in a way in which a landlord who bought the property for investment purposes would not. Indeed, in the responses to the Scottish Government consultation analysed in section III above, there were a number of times in which the close attachment of the landlord came through in the consultation data. One of the best examples of this is the following comment from a letting agent:

> the vast majority of properties we let are our landlord's homes, their parent's homes … to remove the right of the person who not only owns it but also whose home it may have been to require it to be handed back at their discretion … is ridiculous.[90]

There are numerous landlord–tenant combinations but one might imagine a situation in which a family are renting a property which was the former home of a landlord and this being problematic, as both landlord and tenant have personal ties to the property. In such a situation Radin's theory of property and personhood provides no clear solution as to whose claim should be afforded the strongest protection.

Defining home is challenging, and the problem arises not only in the tenancy context, but also where there is occupation under a licence or as a trespasser. Some writers have provided a historical or linguistic analysis[91] to demonstrate how the concept of home has evolved in the English language and other languages over time. Home is an area of interdisciplinary research, with contributions from sociology, anthropology, human geography, history, architecture and philosophy.[92] A comprehensive definition has proved elusive. Benajmin provides the following attempt:

> The home is that spatially localised, temporally defined, significant and autonomous physical frame and conceptual system for the ordering, transformation and interpretation of the physical and abstract aspects of domestic daily life at several simultaneous spatio-temporal scales, normally activated by the connection to a person or community such as a nuclear family.[93]

More manageable than a definition are the attributes of home provided for in the literature. Tognoli listed five such attributes: centrality; continuity; privacy; self-expression and

[88] Rugg and Rhodes (n 21 above) and De Santos (n 27 above).
[89] Radin (n 82 above) at 84.
[90] Consultation response (see nn 50 and 54 above) PRS 137.
[91] J Moore, 'Placing Home in Context' (2000) 20 *Journal of Environmental Psychology* 207, 208.
[92] S Mallett, 'Understanding Home: a Critical Review of the Literature' (2004) 52(1) *The Sociological Review* 62, 64.
[93] D Benjamin, *The Home: Words, Interpretations, Meanings and Environments. Ethnoscapes: Current Challenges in the Environmental Social Sciences* (Aldershot, Avebury Publishing, 1995) 158 (as cited in Moore (n 91 above) 208).

personal identity; and social relationships.[94] Després reviewed the literature from 1974 to 1989 and elicited 10 general characteristics.[95] Blunt and Dowling compared Després' list to those of Somerville and Mallett and found considerable similarity.[96] For the purposes of this chapter, Somerville's seven 'key signifiers' will be considered further. These are: shelter; hearth; heart; privacy; roots; abode; and paradise.[97] Home as shelter connotes the physical structure of a dwelling or a roof over one's head. Home as hearth connotes comfort and welcome. Somerville states that home as heart is similar to the connotation of hearth, but the latter is more related to emotional security and happiness, and the former is more related to physiological security. Home as privacy involves control and the power to exclude others. Home as roots relates to personal identity and could be conflated with the concept of 'ontological security' as expounded by Giddens:

> The confidence that most human beings have in the continuity of their self identify and the constancy of their social and material environments. Basic to a feeling of ontological security is a sense of the reliability of persons and things.[98]

Home as abode is perhaps the sparsest and most basic of the signifiers. It relates to where one currently resides whether it be 'a palace or a park bench'.[99] Somerville's final signifier is home as paradise. This attribute is an ideal rather than a reality: the notion of what home could or ought to be.

Research on perceptions of home for homeless people and feminist research on the concept of home for women in abusive relationships has added further nuances to the notion of home. Some research argues that you may not need a roof over your head to have a sense of home,[100] yet other research argues against this idea, finding that homeless people frequently refer to the need for a house in order to be at home.[101] Yet more research has examined the extent to which homeless men and women retain a dream of home while living on the streets.[102] To this extent Somerville's signifier of 'paradise' may be retained by some homeless people. Those suffering domestic abuse may own a house yet lack a sense of home. The notion of 'homeless at home' is a theme that also runs through

[94] J Tognoli, 'Residential Environments' in D Stokols and I Altman (eds), *Handbook of Environmental Psychology* (New York, Wiley, 1987).

[95] C Després, 'The Meaning of Home: Literature Review, Directions for Future Research' (1991) 8(2) *Journal of Architectural and Planning Research* 96.

[96] A Blunt and R Dowling, *Home* (Abingdon, Routledge, 2006) 10, referring to Mallett (n 92 above) and Somerville (n 97 below).

[97] P Somerville, 'Homelessness and the Meaning of Home: Rooflessness or Rootlessness' (1992) 16 *International Journal of Urban and Regional Research* 529, 532.

[98] A Giddens, *The Consequences of Modernity* (Cambridge, Polity Press, 1991).

[99] Somerville (n 97 above) 533.

[100] Gurney found that rough sleepers may have a sense of home from the 'cultural mileu of life on the street': C Gurney *The Meaning of Home in the Decade of Owner-Occupation: Towards an Experiential Perspective* (Working Paper 88, School of Advanced Urban Studies, University of Bristol, 1990) (cited in Somerville (n 97 above)).

[101] A study of people sleeping rough in public places in Brisbane found that all participants spoke of home as a physical structure and none described the public places in which they slept as their home. More specifically, home was a home of one's own allowing the assumption of control: C Parsell, 'Home is Where the House is: the Meaning of Home for People Sleeping Rough' (2012) 27(2) *Housing Studies* 159.

[102] J Wardhaugh, 'The Unaccommodated Woman: Home, Homelessness and Identity' (1999) 47(1) *The Sociological Review* 91.

some of the research.[103] Blunt and Dowling state that 'home is undeniably connected to a built form such as a house, but home is not always a house'.[104]

Discussion of the literature has established that 'home' is a complex and, to a certain extent, a contested concept. Many researchers have used a list of phenomena or indicators to establish the extent to which individuals experience a sense of home. One of these aspects, 'ontological security' has proved to be particularly difficult to measure.[105] How then does tenure type relate to this notion of ontological security? Owner-occupiers may obtain more ontological security from home but this is not necessarily as a result of the tenure itself; rather it is to do with having 'wealth, living in a nice area, living in a larger and better quality dwelling and being settled in relationships and work'.[106] Other research has found that housing tenure is more than a mere proxy for socio-economic status and that there is a gradient in housing tenure and psychological distress; with short-term renters reporting the highest levels of distress and mortgage-free owner-occupiers, the lowest levels.[107] The extent to which home is perceived as a 'safe haven' and how secure occupants feel in their home has been found to be dependent upon tenure type. However, the binary measure of housing tenure (home owners versus renters) is a limitation of this research. Those who choose to live in the PRS because they want the benefit of the flexibility it affords are unlikely to experience negative impacts on their well-being as compared to those who are tenants as the result of economic necessity and would prefer more security.

Research has shown that those in the lowest income group of renters are more likely to worry about housing with 30 per cent of this group expressing concern compared to 12–21 per cent of richer groups.[108] A higher percentage of private renters (35 per cent) have been found to be worried about housing than Local Authority or Housing Association renters (27 per cent and 25 per cent respectively), and a relatively low percentage (11 per cent) of owner occupiers were found to be worried about housing.[109] Interestingly one of the key concerns expressed by the lowest income group with regard to housing is the lack of control; 88 per cent felt that they could do little or nothing to improve their situation.[110] The need to differentiate between different groups within tenures is important, as is the need to acknowledge that the relationship between tenure and home, and

[103] ibid; K Bennett, 'Homeless at Home in East Durham' (2011) 43(4) *Antipode* 960.

[104] Blunt and Dowling (n 96 above) 10.

[105] Kearns and others unpacked the concept in their research by selecting three phenomena on which to focus: home as a haven, a site of autonomy, and providing social status. They state that Somerville illustrates how domestic privacy is required for self-identity but that ontological security can only be maintained whilst the self is viewed positively in relation to others and this requires the additional concept of status. A Kearns, R Hiscock, A Ellaway and S Macintyre, '"Beyond Four Walls". The psycho-social benefits of home: evidence from West Coast Scotland' (2000) 15(3) *Housing Studies* 387.

[106] R Hiscock, A Kearns, A Ellaway and S Macintyre, 'Ontological Security and Psycho-Social Benefits from the Home: Qualitative Evidence on Issues of Tenure' (2001) 18 *Housing Theory and Society* 50, 62. However, the interviewees in Hiscock and others' study were all owners or renters in the social rented sector in Scotland. Some did have experience of renting in the private rented sector, either personally or via the testimony of family and friends, and this form of tenure was represented as insecure.

[107] J Cairney and M Boyle, 'Home Ownership Mortgages and Psychological Distress' (2004) 19(2) *Housing Studies* 161.

[108] E Taylor and M Toomse-Smith, *Social and Political Attitudes of People on Low Incomes 2017 Report* (London, NatCen Social Research, 2017) 11.

[109] ibid 12.

[110] ibid 13.

indeed the importance of the concept of home, may vary across an individual's housing career.[111] Older people it seems have a stronger sense of identification with home and therefore housing insecurity may be particularly problematic for this group.[112] Self-esteem can be negatively affected by re-possession of owner-occupied property but may also be affected by an inability to buy a property or adapt it to reflect an individual's personality.[113] This supports Radin's thesis on the relationship between personal property and personhood.[114] Gurney carried out an analysis of certain landmark policy documents[115] and concluded that the frequency with which the word 'home' is used is greatest with regard to home ownership and smallest with regard to private renting.[116]

This section of the chapter provides a theoretical counter-balance to the concerns of landlords analysed in section III of this chapter. Whilst landlords wish to maintain flexibility by retaining the right to evict tenants without demonstration of fault, theoretical and empirical research has demonstrated that home is important to personhood and that insecure tenancies are less likely to provide a sense of home. Assured shorthold tenants in the PRS who can be served notice without explanation under section 21 are therefore more likely to be subject to psychological distress than other types of tenants or owner occupiers. With the increase in families occupying in the PRS the argument for reform has grown in force. The final section of this chapter looks at the government's proposals for increasing the length of tenancies in the PRS in England and the extent to which these will successfully balance the rights of landlords and tenants.

V. Balancing the Competing Rights of Landlords and Tenants

Not all tenants in the PRS want or need increased security of tenure, but some do and this chapter has demonstrated that insecure tenancies are likely to have a detrimental effect on tenants who have no choice but to make their home in a privately rented property. There is currently nothing to prevent tenants asking for and landlords offering longer tenancies; however, tenancies in this context are rarely for a fixed term of more than a year. This section of the chapter considers how the law could be changed to give tenants longer tenancies where these are desired, while addressing the concerns of landlords that were identified in section II.

The consultation into longer tenancies issued by the government in July 2018 proposes tenancies with a duration of a minimum of three years but with an opportunity for either

[111] D Clapham, 'Happiness Wellbeing and Housing Policy' (2010) 38(2) *Policy and Politics* 253, 259; and P Sissons and D Houston, 'Changes in Transitions from Private Renting to Homeownership in the Context of Rapidly Rising House Prices' (19.02.2018) *Housing Studies* (online).

[112] W Stone, T Burke, K Hulse and L Ralston, *Long-term Renting and its Outcomes in a Changing Australian Private Rented Sector* (Final Report No 209, Melbourne, Australian Housing and Urban Research Institute, 2013).

[113] ibid.

[114] Radin (n 82 above).

[115] Most importantly Gurney analysed the 1995 Housing White Paper: Department of the Environment and Welsh Office, *Our Future Homes: Opportunity, Choice, Responsibility* (Cmd 2901, 1995).

[116] C Gurney, 'Pride and Prejudice: Discourses of Normalisation in Public and Private Accounts of Home Ownership' (1999) 14(2) *Housing Studies* 163.

party to end the tenancy after six months. After this six-month period has expired, the tenancy would continue, with only the tenant having the option of earlier determination (on two months' written notice). Landlords would be able to recover possession only on the existing grounds set out in Schedule 2 of the Housing Act 1988 by serving a notice under section 8 of the Act, or by serving notice where they intend to sell the property.[117] This section of the chapter looks at this proposal in the light of the concerns of landlords summarised in section III, and the needs of tenants demonstrated in section IV.

In the thematic analysis of landlords' concerns presented in section III of this chapter, a number of themes emerged. The most commonly occurring theme was that increasing security of tenure in the PRS would be a deterrent to new landlords joining the sector and would cause some existing landlords to leave the sector. One of the key concerns was that landlords needed the flexibility to remove problematic tenants and also to sell with vacant possession when required. The changes in Scotland have reduced flexibility, as landlords in the sector can no longer serve notice on their tenants without either the tenant being at fault or the landlord needing the property back to live in or to sell.[118] Flexibility is also slightly reduced by the longer notice periods required where the tenant has lived at the property for longer than six months and the landlord wishes to regain possession to live in the property or to sell.[119] The changes proposed by the government for England may be met with fewer objections by landlords than the changes in Scotland because a higher level of flexibility will be preserved. The English proposals allow the landlord to serve notice on the tenant at the end of the first six months of the tenancy, creating a kind of probationary period. As is the case in Scotland, the English proposals also allow the landlord to regain possession if she needs the property for her own occupation, for a family member, or to sell with vacant possession.[120] However, there is no proposal to increase the notice period from the two-month period already in use.[121] The other key difference between the changes to the PRS in Scotland and those proposed in England is that in Scotland tenancies are now entirely open-ended whereas the proposals in England are for a minimum three year tenancy. Scottish landlords and letting agents felt that the proposed changes were unfair and that the changes would shift the balance too far in favour of the tenants. The proposed changes in England are less radical so it is likely that that English landlords will not object so strongly on the grounds of fairness.

The other main objection voiced by the Scottish landlords was that the fault-based grounds for eviction were inadequate and that the process was too slow. It would seem that landlords wanted to keep a no-fault ground for possession to use when tenants were at fault. Landlords suggested that they did not evict tenants who were not at fault unless they needed to regain the property for their own use. Issues regarding tenant behaviour and rent arrears were a particular concern. It is likely that landlords in England might express similar objections. The government has acknowledged that there are concerns regarding the time it takes for a landlord to gain possession.[122] It is quite clear that the process is

[117] Ministry of Housing Communities and Local Government (n 1 above).
[118] Private Housing (Tenancies)(Scotland) Act 2016, Sch 3 paras 1, 4 and 5.
[119] In this case the tenant must have at least 84 days' notice.
[120] Ministry of Housing Communities and Local Government (n 1 above) 19.
[121] ibid.
[122] Ministry of Housing Communities and Local Government (n 5 above) 14.

not quick, but it may be that the perception is worse than the reality. Research carried out for the Residential Landlords Association (RLA), which represents landlords in the PRS, stated that it takes an average of 41 weeks for a landlord to repossess.[123] The data cited in the RLA report came from the Ministry of Justice but the way that it is used in the RLA report is rather misleading, as the Ministry of Justice breaks down this data further, showing that in the PRS the average time it takes to repossess is 22 weeks.[124] The same RLA research found that 70 per cent of landlords stated that they would be encouraged to offer longer tenancies if the section 8 process was reformed so as to allow possession to be gained more quickly.[125]

The next question to consider is the extent to which the government's proposals would improve the ability of tenants in the PRS to create a home. In Scotland now the starting point for tenants in the sector is that they are able to remain in their rented home for as long as they like. There are limited opportunities for the landlord to remove a tenant who is not at fault (eg where the landlord requires possession so she can occupy herself, or to sell the property) but even in such a case, where the tenant has occupied the property for more than six months, she will get a longer period of notice. The position for tenants in England would be much less secure, even if the proposed changes were to become law. The tenant would have to wait until after the first six months to enjoy the remaining two-and-a-half years of security that the tenancy would afford. Clearly the suggested three years is a considerable improvement for tenants on the six- or twelve-month term most tenants are currently offered; however three years is a relatively short period of time compared to the average time an owner occupier remains in a property, and is less than the five years suggested by Shelter.[126] Three-year tenancies would bring England into line with some other European countries such as France and Ireland, but would offer less security than Spain, where contracts last five years, and Scotland and Germany, where the contract lasts indefinitely.

VI. Conclusion

Tenants in the PRS in England have had to wait a long time for the government to seriously consider making longer tenancies available and this move will surely be welcomed by families living in the sector. It is likely that the proposals will be met with resistance from landlords who currently benefit from considerable flexibility, and fear being trapped in a relationship with problematic tenants. The content of such objections can perhaps be anticipated as a result of the review, undertaken in section III of this chapter, of responses to the Scottish Government's 2014 consultation. It is important to balance such objections with a careful consideration, as in section IV of this chapter, of the potential importance of long-term occupation to at least some tenants in the PRS. A recognition of the tenant's

[123] Ministry of Housing, Communities and Local Government (n 1 above) 14.
[124] Ministry of Justice, 'Mortgage and Landlord Possession Statistics in England and Wales, October to December 2017 (Provisional)' (2018).
[125] ibid.
[126] De Santos (n 27 above).

perspective suggests that the solution lies not in maintaining the ability for landlords in England to regain possession with two months' notice at any time after the expiry of an initial six- or twelve-month period,[127] but rather in improving the speed with which tenants can be evicted if they are at fault.[128] A discussion of how that might be done is beyond the scope of this chapter, but a faster and better resourced court system would certainly facilitate this. Consideration should be given to use of a tribunal system, as has been adopted in Scotland, and perhaps introduction of a paper-based eviction process for serious rent arrears (tempered by an appropriate appeals process) to reduce losses suffered by landlords where there are long delays.

[127] As currently occurs under s 21 of the Housing Act 1988.
[128] As currently occurs under s 8 of the Housing Act 1988.

13

Long Leases and Affordable Housing: A Comparative Analysis of French and English Law

FABIANA BETTINI

I. Introduction

In the last few decades long-term housing affordability has become a crucial concern in the political agenda of many European cities. Rising housing prices and soaring private rents have increasingly prevented middle-income households from getting access to decent and affordable housing, especially in major cities; at the same time, the supply of public housing has proved inadequate in the face of low-income households' growing demand.[1] In response to the housing crisis, new policy measures have been adopted at the institutional level to promote social housing. Moreover, resident- or community-led collaborative housing initiatives, such as co-housing, housing cooperatives, and Community Land Trusts, have re-emerged as valid alternatives to open-market and public housing; these initiatives often provide affordable housing while promoting community values such as environmental sustainability, mutual solidarity, cooperation, and sharing.[2]

In all this, the Community Land Trust (CLT) model has started to appeal both to groups of residents and institutional actors throughout Europe for its ability to foster housing affordability and revitalise community neighbourhoods. The CLT model was originally used in the United States in the late 1960s by African-American farmers to gain access to agricultural land,[3] and has spread rapidly since the 1990s as a means to provide affordable housing to low- and medium-income households unable to access open-market ownership.[4]

[1] Housing Europe, *The State of the Housing in the EU 2017* (2017) 15.

[2] Eg DU Vestbro (ed), *Living together – Co-housing Ideas and Realities Around the World: Proceedings from the International Collaborative Housing Conference in Stockholm, 5–9 May 2010* (Stockholm, Division of Urban and Regional Studies, Royal Institute of Technology in Collaboration with Kollektivus NU, 2010).

[3] JE Davis, 'Origins and Evolution of the Community Land Trust in the United States' in JE Davis (ed), *The Community Land Trust Reader* (Cambridge MA, The Lincoln Institute of Land Policy, 2010) 3–47. See also International Independence Institute, *The Community Land Trust: A Guide to a New Model for Land Tenure in America*, reprint edn (Cambridge MA, Center for Community Economic Development, 2007).

[4] According to Abramovitz, the reasons for the increased emphasis on affordability in the US are to be linked to 'the massive number of low- and moderate-income rental units built under various subsidy programs in the late 1960s and early 1970s that have been in danger of being lost as affordable housing through mortgage prepayment. … In addition, the rapid housing price inflation experienced in many parts of the country during

In the United States, the CLT is legally defined by the Housing and Community Development Act 1992 as a non-profit community housing development organisation established for the purpose of

> (A) acquir[ing] parcels of land, held in perpetuity, primarily for conveyance under long-term ground leases;
> (B) transfer[ring] ownership of any structural improvements located on such leased parcels to the lessees; and
> (C) retain[ing] a preemptive option to purchase any such structural improvement at a price determined by formula that is designed to ensure that the improvement remains affordable to low- and moderate-income families in perpetuity.[5]

In practice, CLTs rely on various forms of subsidies to acquire a parcel of land and hold it in perpetuity for the benefit of a local community, present and future. CLTs build or renovate homes on the land and sell them to low-income or moderate-income households. Normally, CLTs vest in the homeowner a leasehold interest in the land through long-term ground leases (usually 99-years long).[6] However, as the definition suggests, the interest is accompanied by or includes deeded ownership of the house (and other improvements), which can be transferred independently from the land. Although this legal arrangement would be the most desirable, in some US jurisdictions CLTs have been advised 'to use a lease that does not recognize separate, deeded ownership of the improvements, but does provide for the purchase of a long-term leasehold interest in the entire property (both land and improvements)'.[7] Besides this, CLT leases feature specific clauses that ensure long-term housing affordability. First, the ground leases normally contain restrictions, such as buyer-eligibility and resale price restrictions, according to which residents can re-sell homes only to income-qualified persons approved by the CLT and for a price calculated pursuant to a predetermined formula. Secondly, the CLT may retain an option to purchase homes located on the land in case residents wish to sell them or in case of mortgage default, with the purpose of reallocating them to income-eligible candidates.[8] The separation of interests in the property, coupled with several types of restrictions on disposition of the dwellings, is what enables CLTs to keep homes available and affordable for present and future generations of homebuyers.

the 1980s further strained the ability of the private housing market to sustain an adequate supply of affordable units': DM Abramowitz, 'Focus: Long-term Affordability. Community Land Trusts and Ground Leases' (1992) 3 *ABA Journal of Affordable Housing & Community Development Law* 5.

[5] The definition also clarifies that a CLT's corporate membership 'is open to any adult resident of a particular geographic area specified in the bylaws of the organization' and that the board of directors 'includes a majority of members who are elected by the corporate membership' and is composed of 'equal numbers of (i) lessees, (ii) corporate members who are not lessees, and (iii) any other category of persons described in the bylaws of the organization': see Housing and Community Development Act 1992, s 213 (a)(3). This section amends s 233 of the Cranston-Gonzalez National Affordable Housing Act (42 USC 12773).

[6] A Model Lease is provided by the Community Land Trust Network: see K White (ed), *The CLT Technical Manual* (London, National Community Land Trust Network, 2011) ch 11-A. However, it is possible (and frequent) that CLTs rent homes to income-qualified residents at affordable rents.

[7] White (n 6 above) ch 10, p 5. The manual also clarifies that 'the Model Lease not only prohibits removal of the improvements but provides that title to the improvements shall revert to the CLT upon the termination of the lease' (ibid) 2.

[8] White (n 6 above) chs 8 and 11.

These features of the American CLT model have made it attractive for many European countries as a means to tackle the shortage of affordable housing.[9] In English law, the CLT is defined within the Housing and Regeneration Act 2008 as a corporate body which acquires and manages land and other assets for the express purpose of furthering the social, economic and environmental interests of a local community.[10] In the framework of English CLTs, long-term housing affordability is often realised by selling homes to income-eligible purchasers either in freehold or in leasehold, and by attaching restrictive covenants to the sale.[11] According to the National CLT Network, more than 40 CLTs have developed over 800 affordable homes across the country up to March 2018, hundreds of others are being planned or built, and it is estimated that a further 3000 homes will be developed by 2020.[12]

Likewise, a great interest in the CLT model has grown in France among citizens and institutional actors. In 2013 the association Community Land Trust France 'Pour un foncier solidaire' was created and it started to campaign for the adoption of the CLT model.[13] In 2014, the Loi ALUR introduced a French version of the CLT, allowing public and private legal persons to be recognised with the status of *organisme de foncier solidaire* (OFS).[14] Despite this legislative recognition, the development of the CLT model in France has run up against the inadequacy of existing legal devices – notably existing forms of long leases – to ensure long-term housing affordability.[15] This has led French reformers to introduce in 2016 a new type of lease, the *bail réel solidaire* (BRS), to be used exclusively by the OFS with the goal of achieving affordable housing for low-income households.[16]

Against the background of the recent development of the CLT model, this chapter adopts a theoretical perspective to compare the institution of the lease in England and in France as a valuable device used in the context of Community Land Trust for achieving housing affordability goals. In section II, the chapter presents the development of the CLT model in England and explains how the long lease is used in this context. It proceeds with an analysis of the nature of the English lease, suggesting that its hybrid nature – part contract, part property – has played a significant role in the development of the model in

[9] For example, the Interreg North-West Europe 'Sustainable Housing for Inclusive and Cohesive Cities' (SHICC) project began in Lille, France, on 22 May 2018 with a Conference focused on 'Community Land Trusts – A Model for Permanently Affordable Housing in European Cities?'. More information on the project can be found at: http://www.nweurope.eu/projects/project-search/shicc-sustainable-housing-for-inclusive-and-cohesive-cities/.

[10] See Housing and Regeneration Act 2008, s 79.

[11] English CLTs may pursue housing affordability through other legal models as well, for example shared ownership and shared equity (see unpublished data from the National CLT Network, on file with the author). These models are not discussed in this chapter.

[12] Data on the growth of the CLT movement across the UK are provided by the National CLT Network and available at: http://www.communitylandtrusts.org.uk/article/2018/3/6/newly-updated-map-of-clts-in-england-and-wales.

[13] See the association's press release, available at: http://www.communitylandtrust.fr/clt-en-france--c1/creation-de-l-association-clt-france--66.

[14] The rules on OFS are now contained in the *Code de l'urbanisme* art L. 329-1 and two implementing decrees (décret n° 2016-1215 du 12 septembre 2016 and décret n° 2017-1037 du 10 mai 2017) have recently been adopted. See below for further discussion on this point.

[15] The first French OFS has been created by the metropolitan council of Lille at the end of 2017, but no CLT schemes have been completed so far.

[16] Ordonnance n° 2016-985 du 20 juillet 2016, art 1er-2°. The new provisions for the BRS have later been included in the *Code de la construction et de l'habitation* (CCH), articles L. 255-1 to L. 255-19. Detailed regulations for the BRS implementation were adopted in May 2017 (Décret n° 2017-1038 du 10 mai 2017).

England. Section III then focuses on the development of CLTs in France, exploring the gradual transformation of the long lease and the hybrid nature of the BRS. The chapter argues that, while the French and English conceptions of ownership greatly differ, both legal systems conceive of the lease as a hybrid creature, part contract and part property, and it is precisely this hybrid nature that has enabled the CLT model to be implemented in both countries.

II. The Development of the CLT Model in England and the Hybrid Nature of the English Lease

The CLT movement emerged in England in the early 2000s when academics and professionals started to explore its potential to meet the need for affordable housing.[17] From 2006 to 2008 a National CLT Demonstration Programme was run with the purpose of studying 14 existing CLTs and fostering the development of the model.[18] The programme led to subsequent empowerment programmes between 2008 and 2010 and to the creation of intermediary bodies (umbrella CLTs) on a county-wide basis.[19] A few years later the institutional framework was strengthened with the establishment of a National CLT Network, with the purpose of advocating and lobbying on behalf of CLTs at a national level.[20]

As a concept, a CLT has been legally defined by the Housing and Regeneration Act 2008 as a corporate body:

> established for the express purpose of furthering the social, economic and environmental interests of a local community by acquiring and managing land and other assets in order—
>
> (a) to provide a benefit to the local community, and
> (b) to ensure that the assets are not sold or developed except in a manner which the trust's members think benefits the local community.[21]

[17] See eg KT Dayson et al, *Investing in People and Land: Sowing the Seeds for Rural Regeneration* (Manchester, University of Salford, 2001) 55; The Countryside Agency, *Capturing Value for Rural Communities: Community Land Trusts and Sustainable Rural Communities* (Wetherby, Countryside Agency Publications, 2005).

[18] The programme was run by Community Finance Solutions (CFS) of the University of Salford with the support of the Department for Communities and Local Government and other UK charities. For more information see R Patterson and KT Dayson, *Proof of Concept – Community Land Trusts* (Manchester, Community Finance Solutions and University of Salford, 2011). See also Department for Communities and Local Government, *Community Land Trusts: A Consultation* (London, Department for Communities and Local Government, 2008) 11.

[19] For a detailed discussion of the genesis of the movement in England, see T Moore and K McKee, 'Empowering Local Communities? An International Review of Community Land Trusts' (2012) 27(2) *Housing Studies* 282; T Moore, 'Replication Through Partnership: the Evolution of Partnerships Between Community Land Trusts and Housing Associations in England' [2018] 1 *International Journal of Housing Policy* 82.

[20] The CLT Network became an independent charity in June 2014. For a concise history of the emergence of the CLT Network in England, see information available on the Network's website: http://www.communitylandtrusts.org.uk/what-is-a-clt/history-of-clts. A more detailed analysis of the creation and role of the Network is provided by T Moore and D Mullins, 'Scaling-up or going-viral: comparing self-help housing and community land trust facilitation' (Third Sector Research Centre, Working Paper No 94, 2003) 21.

[21] Housing and Regeneration Act 2008, s 79(4).

The English definition further requires that a CLT:

> is established under arrangements which are expressly designed to ensure that—
> (a) any profits from its activities will be used to benefit the local community (otherwise than by being paid directly to members),
> (b) individuals who live or work in the specified area have the opportunity to become members of the trust (whether or not others can also become members), and
> (c) the members of the trust control it.[22]

While this definition has prompted the development of CLTs across England, it does not clarify which legal arrangements are the most suitable for setting up a CLT. To begin with, the definition does not indicate a specific type of corporate body, with the consequence that any prospective CLT will have to choose a legal format that meets the requirements laid down in the definition quoted above. As the National CLT Network indicates, the most suitable legal formats to set up a CLT in England are a Community Benefit Society, a Community Interest Company Limited by Guarantee, and a Company Limited by Guarantee which is also a registered charity.[23] In any case, all these legal structures are membership-based corporate bodies, which allow individuals who live or work in a defined geographical area to become members and take part in the management and control of the asset, as the definition specifies. Moreover, unlike the US definition, the English one does not refer explicitly to housing affordability and does not identify the lease as the legal mechanism through which this goal should be achieved.

Despite this, English CLTs generally set housing affordability as their primary goal and the lease is considered a useful legal device to achieve that goal. CLTs normally receive land at little or no cost from the public or acquire a site at open-market value through 'subsidies' from government, charities or benefactors, or through community shares.[24] While holding land in freehold, CLTs undertake to renovate or build homes on the land and to make them available to income-qualified households for rent, purchase, or a mix of both at affordable prices.[25] When CLT homes are up for sale, property interests are usually sold on a 'long leasehold' basis. Long leases are today often preferred over freehold for the sale of residential properties, especially (but not only) in the case of units in block of flats.[26]

[22] Housing and Regeneration Act 2008, s 79(5).

[23] These legal formats are identified by and their suitability discussed in a document provided by the CLT Network. See National CLT Network, 'Introduction to the Legal Formats', available at http://www.communitylandtrusts.org.uk/_filecache/3d8/4e6/196-introduction-to-legal-formats--for-website.pdf.

[24] These sources are mentioned in the National CLT Network website, available at: http://www.communitylandtrusts.org.uk/what-is-a-clt/about-clts.

[25] Sometimes a CLT holds land as a leaseholder under a head-lease, with a private or public entity, usually a local Council, remaining the freeholder of the site. At other times, CLTs may grant a lease to a housing association and work in partnership to build and manage homes. Homes are then either rented out or sold through shared ownership (unpublished data from the National CLT Network, on file with the author).

[26] See, however, the UK Government's consultation paper published to seek views on the most pressing areas for reform, namely the possibility to limit or ban the sale of new-build leasehold houses: Department for Communities and Local Government, *Tackling Unfair Practices in the Leasehold Market* (London, Department for Communities and Local Government, 2017). The consultation received a massive response with over 6,000 replies: see Department for Communities and Local Government, *Tackling Unfair Practices in the Leasehold Market. Summary of Consultation Responses and Government Response* (London, Department for Communities and Local Government, 2017).

Through a long lease the CLT grants to an income-eligible purchaser (leaseholder) the exclusive possession of a dwelling, in exchange for the payment of a premium, a small ground rent, and a portion of the service charge. The duration of the lease is fixed and depends on the specific project, but it is normally very long (eg 250 years). CLT leases may also contain specific clauses that, by prohibiting or restricting the use and enjoyment of the premises, are tailored to the preservation of housing affordability. First, occupancy and use restrictions may establish that homes shall be used as private dwellings for occupation by a defined number of persons, and that any lodging agreement or licence to occupy/sublet should require the prior written consent of the CLT. Secondly, buyer-eligibility and resale price restrictions may affect the alienation of CLT homes. While the assignment of the lease is normally permitted, the CLT may retain a right to nominate a purchaser or a time-limited option to purchase the homes in order to reallocate them to income-eligible candidates. Thirdly, restrictive covenants concerning the price of resale are normally imposed; these restrictions require that the price is calculated according to a formula specified in the lease, instead of being set at a market level, thus enabling the CLT to keep homes affordable for the next generation of homebuyers.[27]

To summarise, English CLTs may rely on long leases to pursue the primary goal of providing and keeping homes available at affordable prices for the benefit of a local community. Indeed, long leases allow CLTs to vest in the leaseholders a substantial interest in the property: the sum paid as a premium by the leaseholder, although set below market value, reflects the capital value of the lease, while the ground rent paid is very small. Indeed, CLTs seem less concerned with the value of the reversion than with maintaining a strong degree of control over how properties are used and transferred. In this respect, long leases normally include restrictive covenants to limit the use and alienation of CLT properties; as a result, subsidies obtained in the form of financial grants from public and private entities are not recaptured by the market and long-term housing affordability is secured.

The reason why the lease is seen as a valuable means in the context of CLTs to secure housing affordability relates to its ambivalent, hybrid nature. Indeed, while being rooted in the law of contract, the lease has progressively acquired a proprietary nature, with the consequence that modern leases are governed by both proprietary and contractual rules.

In the early common law, 'the right to occupy another's land for a defined period of time was originally considered … merely to create rights *in personam*'.[28] The lease was founded on a simple contractual relationship between landlord and tenant and the lessee's remedies were restricted to a personal action in damages against the lessor on his covenant to give enjoyment of the land.[29] As Birks observes, 'the term of years was no different from a contract of hire [of land]'.[30] Over time, however, the lease underwent a transformation into

[27] See the model lease used for the St Clements site in Tower Hamlets, the flagship project of London Community Land Trust. According to the lease, homes are normally purchased on a 250-year lease basis, with restrictive covenants linking the resale price to increases in median income in the specific borough, and with the CLT retaining a purchase option for six months before homes can be sold to a buyer chosen by the leaseholder. See East London CLT, *Model Lease for Units in Block of Flats, St Clements Hospital, Tower Hamlets*, 2016 (on file with the author).

[28] *Street v Mountford* [1985] AC 809, 814E (Lord Templeman).

[29] AWB Simpson, *A History of the Land Law*, 2nd edn (Oxford, Clarendon Press, 1986), 71; F Pollock and FW Maitland, *The History of English Law*, vol 2, 2nd edn (Cambridge, Cambridge University Press, 1898) 106ff.

[30] P Birks, 'Five Keys to Land Law' in S Bright and J Dewar (eds), *Land Law: Themes and Perspectives* (Oxford, Oxford University Press, 1998) 457, 474–75.

a proprietary interest due to the accumulation of a series of remedies that enabled the lessee to recover possession of the land against third parties.[31] In particular, the development of the action of ejectment during the Middle Ages converted the personal relationship of landlord and tenant into a new type of relationship based on the recognition of some form of estate ownership vested in the tenant.[32] It is 'by virtue of this metamorphosis [that] the leasehold began to cross the critical conventional borderline between contract and property'.[33]

The leasehold is today primarily regarded as an estate in land that is considered to have proprietary character.[34] Historically, the notion of 'estate' represents the conceptual apparatus to analyse property relations in land. Although land is primarily conceived of as a physical reality, and de facto possession is the measure of the degree of control and use that a claimant can assert on a piece of land,[35] what is owned is not the land but an estate in land, which represents 'a time-related segment – a slice of time – of the rights and powers exercisable over the land'.[36] As a result of this, English law can contemplate disaggregation of property – possibly of different intensity and duration – through the grant of different estates in land. The landlord–tenant relationship offers an example of the ease with which English land law deals with the simultaneous allocation of different quantums of property in relation to the same piece of land. The tenant (or leaseholder) enjoys physical possession and occupation of the property against payment of a rent, while the landlord (or freeholder) owns the reversion expectant on the lease and receives the rent and profits. For this reason it is argued that the 'principal purpose of the lease (and a vital feature) is to achieve a division of interests, or a split in the ownership, in the property as a whole'.[37] The lease also allows further fragmentation of ownership, since property rights can be sold or transferred while the lease is in existence: the leaseholder may sell to an assignee that becomes the new leaseholder, and the freeholder may sell the reversion to a person that becomes the new freeholder; and both assignee and reversioner may in turn sell or transfer their interest further.[38]

[31] J Morgan, 'Leases: Property, Contract, or More?' in M Dixon (ed), *Modern Studies in Property Law*, vol 5 (Oxford, Hart Publishing, 2009) 419, 421.

[32] TFT Plucknett, *A Concise History of the Common Law*, 5th edn (London, Butterworth, 1956) 373; *Megarry and Wade, The Law of Real Property*, 8th edn (London, Sweet and Maxwell, 2012) 96.

[33] KJ Gray and SF Gray, *Elements of Land Law*, 5th edn (Oxford, Oxford University Press, 2009) 307, observe that 'the leasehold estate provides the pre-eminent historic demonstration of the transformation of contractual right into proprietary title'.

[34] Law of Property Act 1925, s 1 (1)(b). See, however, *Bruton v London & Quadrant Housing Trust* [2000] 1 AC 406, 415 where Lord Hoffmann affirmed that the term 'lease' or 'tenancy' 'is not concerned with the question of whether the agreement creates an estate or other proprietary interest which may be binding upon third parties'. For comments on the case see M Dixon, 'The Non-Proprietary Lease: the Rise of the Feudal Phoenix' (2000) 59 *CLJ* 25; S Bright, 'Leases, Exclusive Possession and Estates' (2000) 116 *LQR* 7. For a broader discussion, see A Goymour, '*Bruton v London & Quadrant Housing Trust* [2000]: Relativity of Title, and the Regulation of the "Proprietary Underworld"' in S Douglas, R Hickey and E Waring (eds), *Landmark Cases in Property Law* (Oxford, Hart Publishing, 2015) 151ff.

[35] KJ Gray and SF Gray, 'The Idea of Property in Land' in Bright and Dewar (n 30 above) 15, 19.

[36] Gray and Gray (n 33 above) 58. As Bright observes, 'the doctrine of estates focuses on the quantum of time for which land is held but not explicitly on the nature of ownership': S Bright, 'Of Estates and Interests: A Tale of Ownership and Property Rights' in Bright and Dewar (n 30 above) 529, 530.

[37] D Clarke, 'Long Residential Leases: Future Directions' in S Bright (ed), *Landlord and Tenant Law: Past, Present and Future* (Oxford, Hart Publishing, 2006) 171, 172.

[38] M Dixon, *Modern Land Law*, 10th edn (Abingdon, Routledge, 2016) 217–18.

Although the proprietary nature of the lease is now accepted, its contractual nature persists in modern law. While in its most basic form the lease is 'a contract for possession only', which 'involves no more than the grant of land for a time to the tenant', modern leases are 'contracts for possession "plus"', which have come to contain many other promises beyond the grant of land to the tenant.[39] As Luxton observes, through the lease it is possible to 'impose on the parties a whole range of covenants which can result in the common law incidents of estate being overwhelmed'.[40] This does not mean, however, that the lease has lost its proprietary character and become contractual in nature; on the contrary, the lease shows a hybrid nature – 'part contract, part property'[41] – and, as such, both ordinary contract law rules and property-based rules apply.[42] In particular, despite the fact that covenants are contractual promises, the law recognises their 'enforceability' based on the proprietary nature of the lease. This results in both negative and positive covenants being enforceable not only against the current landlord and tenant but also against subsequent assignees, even though they are not in a contractual relationship.[43] Thus, through a combination of proprietary and contractual elements, the lease achieves far more than a division of property between the parties and it constitutes 'an effective way of maintaining control over land through the medium of covenants'.[44]

In the light of its hybrid nature, the lease has proved to be particularly useful in the context of CLTs. First, the lease allows the CLT to achieve a division of interests in property between the CLT/freeholder and residents/leaseholders. Secondly, by relying on the lease, CLTs are able to attach and enforce restrictive covenants that guarantee the control over the use and alienation of CLT properties. Thus, it is precisely its hybrid nature that makes the lease a suitable legal device for the promotion of housing affordability in the context of CLTs.

III. The Development of the CLT Model in France

The need for long-term affordable housing has grown in France. Over the last 15 years, an increasing number of households encountered serious difficulties in getting access to housing due to the economic, financial, and real estate crisis. In particular, middle-income households – until then protected by their level of education and social integration – have seen their chances of getting access to decent and affordable housing, especially in major

[39] S Bright, '*Street v Mountford* Revisited' in Bright (n 37 above) 31.

[40] P Luxton, 'Termination of Leases: From Property to Contract?' in J Birds, J Bradgate and C Villiers (eds), *Termination of Contracts* (London, Wiley Chancery Law Publishing, 1995) 179.

[41] *Linden Gardens Trust v Lenesta Sludge Disposals Ltd* [1994] 1 AC 85, 108 (Lord Browne-Wilkinson).

[42] While contract law doctrines primarily come into consideration for the termination of the lease (eg frustration, rescission for fraud, termination for breach), property-based rules mostly concern the 'possession-rent' relationship (forfeiture, distress, certainty of term, and covenant enforceability). The contractual and proprietary aspects of the lease are thoroughly examined by S Bridge, 'Leases – Contract, Property and Status' in L Tee (ed), *Land Law: Issues, Debates, Policy* (Portland OR, Willan Publishing, 2002) 98, 113ff.

[43] *Megarry and Wade, The Law of Real Property* (n 32 above) 937.

[44] Clarke (n 37 above) 176.

cities and towns, seriously undermined.[45] This scenario has served as the breeding ground for the re-emergence and spread of residents-led housing initiatives, which culminated in the legal recognition of *habitat participatif* (a French version of co-housing).[46] At the same time, the observation of the growing practice of CLTs across the US and Europe led to the creation in 2012 of the French association 'Community Land Trust France "Pour un Foncier Solidaire"' and to the recognition in 2014 by way of legislation of the *organisme* (or *office*) *de foncier solidaire* (OFS), with the explicit purpose of introducing in France a model for the supply of affordable housing for low-income households.[47]

OFS, the French version of the CLT, is defined by the law as a non-profit organism whose activity is totally or partially devoted to the acquisition and management of improved or unimproved building land and whose main goal is to provide affordable housing to be rented or sold to income-qualified people.[48] First of all, it should be noted that, like the English CLT, an OFS is not in itself a legal format but a status conferred on a legal person, regulated under either public or private laws; thus, there is freedom to choose the most suitable legal form to set up an OFS, provided that it complies with the requirements established by the law.[49] Secondly, differently from English law, the French definition explicitly recognises housing affordability as the OFS's main goal and mentions the lease as the mechanism through which such goal should be achieved.[50] However, compared to English law where CLTs could easily develop by relying on long leases and restrictive covenants, the practical development of the CLT model in France has run up against the absence of a type of long lease that could realise the main effects of the CLT. Because of all this, the French legislator adopted in 2016 a new form of long lease, the *bail réel solidaire* (BRS), to be used by the OFS. Although modelled on existing types of long lease, the BRS constitutes a remarkable innovation, as it combines an *in rem* nature (hence the label 'real') with buyer-eligibility and resale price restrictions, thus keeping housing units affordable for first and subsequent generations of purchasers.

[45] S Bresson and L Tummers, 'L'habitat participatif en Europe. Vers des politiques alternatives de développement urbain?' in *Métropoles*, 15, 2014.

[46] Loi n° 2014-366 du 24 mars 2014 pour l'accès au logement et un urbanisme rénové (ALUR), art 47, available at: https://www.legifrance.gouv.fr/eli/loi/2014/3/24/ETLX1313501L/jo/article_47.

[47] Loi n° 2014-366 du 24 mars 2014 (ALUR), art 164, which incorporated the OFS into the *Code de l'urbanisme*, art L. 329-1. The OFS belongs to a broader range of instruments of 'housing aid policies', as they have been defined in the *Code de la construction et de l'habitation* (CCH) at articles L. 301-1 to L. 301-6. A recently adopted enabling decree (*Décret* n° 2016-1215, 12 septembre 2016) has provided a more detailed regulatory framework for the creation and organisation of the OFS, which now features in the regulatory portion of the *Code de l'urbanisme*, articles R329-1 to 329-17. For a comment on the introduction of the OFS in France, see V Le Rouzic, 'L'organisme de foncier solidaire, un nouvel acteur?', *Actes pratiques et ingénierie immobilière*, n° 3, 2 Septembre 2017, 39–41.

[48] CCH, art L. 329-1. As to the structure and organisation of the OFS, art R. 329-3 specifies that the management of the OFS shall be modelled on some basic principles: (i) all benefits of the OFS must be allocated to the continuation and development of its activity; (ii) financial reserves cannot be distributed among OFS members but must be entirely dedicated either to the management of the *baux réels solidaires* or to the development of the OFS activity; and (iii) revenues of the OFS activity must be entirely dedicated to the OFS's main purpose as well.

[49] According to articles R. 329-6 to R.329-10, the recognition of an OFS status by the Prefect requires the OFS to have specific purpose, bylaws, and a governing body, and to set out the mechanisms used to control the *baux réel solidaire* and the residents' revenues. The Prefect can at any time suspend or revoke the OFS status if the legal entity no longer complies with the conditions required or in case of violation of its obligations.

[50] See CCH, art R. 329-1, alinéa 1.

A. From Contract to Property: The Evolution of the French Long Lease

While a general feature of the English lease is its ambivalent nature – part contract, part property – the same does not hold true in relation to the French lease, which is generally seen as a contract. However, in certain specific contexts such as urban development and housing, ad hoc legislative interventions have conferred on the lease a more pronounced proprietary character. In this sense, the adoption of the BRS in the context of the French OFS does not mark a break with the past; rather, it represents the culminating point of a process of transformation of the nature of the lease. Explaining this evolution sets the scene for the subsequent discussion of the BRS and of the implications of its hybrid nature for the development of the CLT model.

The French lease is a contract by which the lessor transfers to the lessee a personal right of use and enjoyment of the leased property against payment of a rent. According to article 1709 of the French Civil Code, the lease is the contract where 'one of the parties is under the obligation to allow the other to use the thing for a specified period of time and against payment of an agreed price, with the other party undertaking the obligation to pay'. Supported by most of the early commentators of the Civil Code and upheld by early court decisions,[51] this view is anchored in the traditional French conception of ownership. The French legal system has been underpinned by a unitary notion of ownership as absolute *dominium* since the French Revolution of 1789. Indeed, article 544 of the Civil Code embodies a conception of ownership as the widest and most absolute control that a person can exercise on a thing, to the exclusion of the rest of the world.[52] According to this conception, the owner has the right to use (*usus*), to enjoy (*fructus*), and to dispose of (*abusus*) the thing. The two main theoretical consequences that followed from this conception of absolute ownership were the *summa divisio* between real and personal rights and the *numerus clausus* principle. The possibility to carve out of ownership less extensive rights *in rem* (*démembrements de la propriété*)[53] and to vest them in different persons was admitted, but severely restricted to those rights mentioned by the law (usufruct, use, use of a dwelling, and easement).[54] No rights *in rem* other than those could be created

[51] For an overview of the doctrinal debate on the nature of the lease in France, see TJR Stadnik, 'The Doctrinal Origins of the Juridical Nature of Lease in the Civil Law' (1980) 54 *Tulane Law Review* 1094, esp 1103–12. This view could be still considered the traditional view today: P Malaurie, L Aynes and P-Y Gautier, *Droit des contrats spéciaux*, 9th edn (Paris, Librairie générale de droit et de jurisprudence, 2017) 367. Early case law also confirmed the view: see eg Req. 6 mars 1861, synd. Vollot, DP 1861, I. 417, which argued that 'the lease does not allow the dismemberment of ownership, which stays undivided in the hands of the lessor, for whom the lease is only a means of rendering land productive and of reaping its benefits; as to the difference from emphyteusis and usufruct, the lessee does not have a proper and personal possession; rather, he possesses for the proprietor of whom the lessee is the representative under this relationship, and to whom alone the lessee's possession is a benefit'.

[52] See French Civil Code, art 544: 'Ownership is the right to enjoy and dispose of things in the most absolute manner, provided they are not used in a way prohibited by statutes or regulations'.

[53] As Pfister observes, the term '*démembrements*' was used for the first time by R-J Pothier, *Traité du droit de domaine de propriété* (Paris, Debure, 1764): see L Pfister, 'Propriété démembrée ou démembrements de propriété' in M Cornu, J Rochfeld and F Orsi (eds), *Dictionnaire des biens communs* (Paris, Presses Universitaires de France, 2017) 964.

[54] See French Civil Code, art 543: 'a person can have on a thing a right of ownership, a simple right of enjoyment, or a mere easement'.

by way of contractual agreement and, as they deprive the owner of the ability to use and enjoy his property, those rights had to be limited in time so that the original owner could reconstitute ownership at its fullest after the expiry of the relevant period. Again for the purpose of protecting the absolute character of ownership, the French Civil Code did not conceive explicitly of the possibility to split ownership of land between two persons. Having simultaneous ownership on the same thing was considered a remnant of the feudal *double domaine*, where ownership of land was commonly split between the landlord, who owned the ground, and the vassals, who owned the surface layer of the ground (what was cultivated and built on it or what was under it) (*propriété divisée*).[55] In opposition to the past, the principle '*superficies solo cedit*' was established as the rule and divisions of interests in the property treated as an exception.[56] It is for these reasons that English scholars view the civil law conception of ownership as an indivisible unity and believe that the fragmentation of ownership is unacceptable to the eye of a Continental jurist.[57]

The unitary and absolutist conception of ownership has impacted on the way of understanding the lease, which has been systematised as a contract that vests in the lessee only a right *in personam* to use and enjoy the land. Since the second half of the nineteenth century, however, French courts have started to challenge the view that the parties could never transfer rights *in rem* carved out of ownership.[58] At the same time, courts began to recognise a right of superficies on constructions or plantations standing upon land, thus enabling a split in the ownership of the property between the ground and the surface layer.[59] This innovative judicial approach was confirmed in 1902 by the legislative introduction of the *bail emphytéotique* (emphyteutic lease),[60] a contract which vests in the leaseholder – for a duration of between 18 and 99 years – a right *in rem* to use and enjoy the land (emphyteusis) against payment of a ground rent, which is transferable both *inter vivos* and *mortis causa* and capable of being mortgaged and seized.[61] Moreover, the lessor also vests in the

[55] P Legal, 'Les vertus de la propriété partagée. Des fondements de l'Ancien droit aux attentes contemporaines' in L Andreu (ed), *Liberté contractuelle et droits réels* (Paris, Institut Universitaire Varenne, 2015) 11; L Pfister, 'Propriété divisée' in M Cornu et al (n 53 above) 969–72.

[56] See the French Civil Code, art 456–577. According to the principle expressed by the Latin maxim '*superficies solo cedit*', ownership of a piece of land extends to all buildings and other constructions erected on or linked with the land. The only exception to the principle is in article 553 of the French Civil Code, which admits that 'all constructions, plantings and works on or inside a piece of land are presumed made by the owner, at his expenses and belonging to him, *unless the contrary is proved*' (emphasis added). The principle '*superficies solo cedit*' is also a feature of English land law, through the rule of accession: see eg Gray and Gray (n 33 above) 28.

[57] See Gray and Gray (n 33 above) 6; P Matthews, 'The Compatibility of the Trust with the Civil Law Notion of Property' in L Smith (ed), *The Worlds of the Trust* (Cambridge, Cambridge University Press, 2013) 320.

[58] For example, see Cass. Civ., 24 August 1857, DP 1857, 1, 326; Cass. Civ. 24 January 1864, 1, 83.

[59] See CA Besançon, 12 déc. 1864 and Cass. Req., 21 nov. 1877 : DP 1878, 1, 301, cited in A-M Patault, *Introduction historique au droit des biens*, 1st edn (Paris, Presses Universitaires de France, 1989) 253. The difference between a *right in rem* and a right of superficies lies in the type of fragmentation they enable. With a right *in rem*, the owner transfers some of the rights associated with ownership (*usus* and *fructus*) to a third party and retains the right to dispose of the thing (*abusus*); with a right of superficies, the owner vests in the lessee all the rights associated with ownership (*usus*, *fructus*, and *abusus*) in relation to a specific portion of the thing owned (eg, the ownership of buildings erected on a piece of land). See generally S Laporte-Leconte, 'Le droit de superficie', *JurisClasseur Construction-Urbanisme*, 2016, fasc. 251–30.

[60] The emphyteutic lease is contained in the *Code rural* (Rural Code), articles L. 451-1 to L. 451-13.

[61] J-P Moreau, 'Bail Emphytéotique. – Commentaires', *JurisClasseur Construction-Urbanisme*, 2013, fasc. 109, 1ff; J-L Tixier, 'Bail emphytéotique', *Repertoire de droit civil*, 2017, §§ 1–84; C Saint-Alary-Houin, 'Bail emphytéotique (droit privé)', *Dalloz Action Droit de la Construction*, 2013, Dossier 140, §§ 140.50–140.410.

lessee a right of superficies on plantations or buildings, the contract resulting in a separation of ownership of land and improvements between the lessor and the lessee for the duration of the contract.[62] The emphyteutic lease represents the first attempt of the French legislator to push the nature of the lease in a proprietary direction. Although initially envisaged only in relation to agricultural land, the lease proved to be sufficiently flexible a device to serve commercial and residential purposes as well.[63]

In more recent times, the legislator has further intervened to develop tools specifically targeted at urban improvements and housing provision and, for this reason, introduced two new forms of long lease, modelled on the hybrid structure of the emphyteutic lease. The *bail à construction* (building lease)[64] is a contract by which the lessee undertakes as its main obligation to build on the leased land and to keep the buildings in good condition for the duration of the lease. Like the emphyteutic lease, the building lease must have a duration of between 18 and 99 years and must vest in the lessee an *in rem* right of enjoyment of the land, which can be transferred and mortgaged. However, land improvement being the primary obligation of the lessee, the building lease invariably vests in the lessee a right of superficies over the buildings. The result is that, within a building lease, ownership of land and buildings is split between lessor and lessee for the duration of the contract.[65] A second hybrid form of lease – the *bail à rehabilitation* (renovation lease) – was introduced in 1990 in response to the pressure of social housing providers (*organismes HLM*).[66] The main feature of the renovation lease is the possibility for a landowner to lease an already existing building to a qualified lessee,[67] who undertakes renovation works on the building and rents out apartments to residential tenants for the duration of the lease. The contract vests in the lessee an *in rem* right of enjoyment of the buildings, which allows the lessee to manage them during the lease, to enter into residential lease agreements with income-qualified residents, and to collect the rent.[68]

[62] Laporte-Leconte (n 59 above) 11–12. However, land and improvements revert to the owner-lessor at the end of the lease, who does not have any obligation to pay a compensation sum to the lessee: see Rural Code, art 451-10.

[63] The flexible nature of the emphyteutic lease led to the introduction in 1988 (Loi 5 janvier) of a specific form of emphyteutic lease to be used by local and regional authorities in relation to public land, called *bail emphyteotic administratif*.

[64] The *bail à construction* was adopted by the Loi n° 64-1247 on 16 December 1964 and Decret n° 64-1323 on 24 December 1964, and it was later included in the *Code de la construction et de l'habitation* (CCH), articles L. 251-1 to L. 251-9 and R. 251-1 to R. 251-3.

[65] B Stemmer and H Périnet-Marquet, 'Bail à construction', *JurisClasseur Construction-Urbanisme*, 2010, fasc. 110, 1; C Saint-Alary-Houin, 'Bail à construction (droit privé)', *Dalloz Action Droit de la Construction*, 2013, Dossier 120, §§ 120.60–120.330.

[66] Art 1, Loi 90-499 du 31 mars 1990, then included in the CCH, articles L. 252-1 to L. 252-4. See generally J Hugot and C Le Marchand, 'Bail à réhabilitation', *JurisClasseur Construction-Urbanisme*, 2017, fasc. 120-10; Saint-Alary-Houin, 'Bail à rehabilitation', *Dalloz Action Droit de la Construction*, 2013, Dossier 130, §§130.40–130.270.

[67] Invariably, a social housing provider, a local authority, or a mixed-economy company whose main purpose is to provide housing.

[68] However, unlike the forms of lease previously examined, this contract does not vest in the lessee a right of superficies; nor could the parties stipulate to do so, since the main obligation of the lessee is to renovate existing buildings while the lessor remains owner of both land and buildings for the duration of the lease. Thus, in a sense, this form of lease presents a less pronounced proprietary character than either the emphyteutic or the building lease. This is also confirmed by the existence of a set of statutory provisions limiting the freedom of the lessee to dispose of its right *in rem*. In particular, the lessee can mortgage and transfer its right only to other eligible legal entities (social housing promoters) and upon approval by the lessor, and can only use the building for the specific purpose of renting it.

Thus, in all these forms of long lease, the legislator has attempted to transform gradually the nature of the lease by adding proprietary elements. While the standard lease remains a pure contract, these long leases stand as exceptions, strictly regulated by the law, and justified by the pursuit of specific purposes, most notably the promotion of urban development and housing. Indeed, these arrangements provide both parties with substantial advantages. On the one side, the lessee is given strong protection through *in rem* rights or a right of superficies to renovate existing buildings or build new ones, while obtaining mortgage funding and recovering the cost of the investment via renting out the housing units. On the other side, since ownership of land and buildings normally reverts to the lessor at the end of the lease, the lessor itself benefits from improvements and buildings that it did not pay for. Despite their usefulness in the context of housing, these types of long lease have fallen short of ensuring the affordability of the housing stock. Indeed, the French courts have shown hostility towards anti-speculative and buyer-eligibility clauses by either declaring them void[69] or demoting the lessee's right *in rem* to a right *in personam*.[70] Clearly bearing the legacy of the French traditional conception of ownership as an absolute right, the courts justified these rulings on the ground that these sorts of clauses would represent undue restrictions on the lessee's enjoyment of his rights.

B. The French OFS and the Hybrid Nature of the *Bail Réel Solidaire*

Given the resistance shown by French courts, existing types of long lease proved to be inadequate to achieve long-term housing affordability. To overcome this, the French legislator in 2016 decided to adopt a new type of long lease, the *bail réel solidaire* (BRS), to be used by the OFS.[71] Although the BRS relies on the structure of pre-existing long leases (notably, the emphyteutic and the building lease), the legislator has envisaged a device with a truly hybrid nature, in which contractual rules and property-based rules do not conflict with one another but rather work together to accomplish the main goal of ensuring housing affordability.

The BRS is a contract by which the lessor vests in the lessee rights *in rem* over the land and a right of superficies over the buildings for a term of between 18 and 99 years.[72] The basic structure clearly resembles that of the emphyteutic and building leases. Indeed, the BRS enables the splitting of ownership of land and improvements between the lessor/OFS and the lessee/purchaser for the duration of the contract. While the lessor must invariably

[69] In relation to the building lease, see Cass. 3e civ., 24 sept. 2014, n° 13-22.357, P+B, D. 2014. 1939. See M Poumarède, 'Nullité d'une clause d'agrément stipulée dans un bail à construction', *Revue de droit immobilier*, 2014, n° 12, 640.

[70] In relation to the emphyteutic lease, see Cass. 3e civ., 10 April 1991, n° 89-20276, *Bulletin Civil*, III, n° 114, and Cass. 3e civ., 29 avr. 2009, n° 08-10944. For a discussion on this point see S Brange et al, 'Genèse du bail réel immobilier et du bail réel solidaire', *Actes pratiques et ingénierie immobilière*, n° 3, 2 Septembre 2017, 9–10.

[71] The relevant texts are: the Loi n° 2015-990 du 6 août 2015 'pour la croissance, l'activité et l'égalité des chances économiques' (so-called Loi Macron), art 94, which first envisaged the possibility to adopt a new long-term real lease; the *ordonnance* n° 2016-985 du 20 juillet 2016, articles 1–2, which adopted the BRS and included it in the *Code de la Construction et de l'habitation* (CCH), articles L. 255-1 to L. 255-19; the Loi n° 2017-86 'égalité et citoyenneté' du 27 janvier 2017, which ratified the previous ordonnance; the decree n° 2017-1038 of 10 May 2017, which fixed the economic conditions of the BRS (income ceilings, sale and rent thresholds).

[72] CCH, article L. 255-1.

be an OFS, the lessee may be either an income-eligible person or a real estate developer. In the first case, the OFS concludes a BRS directly with a resident who thus obtains ownership of an individual dwelling for the duration of the lease. In the second case, the OFS vests in the developer a right of superficies to build homes on the land for purchase or rent. If the housing units are sold, each purchaser must enter into an individual BRS with the OFS, and the rights of the developer on the housing unit will be withdrawn from the original BRS. In either case, thus, through a contract the lessor/OFS confers upon the lessee/resident the temporary ownership of the housing units.

Given that the BRS's specific objective is to pursue housing affordability, the legislator has added a series of mandatory terms specifically designed to achieve this goal, which represent the main innovation of the BRS. First, the law provides for buyer-eligibility restrictions: whether the lease is stipulated by the OFS with an individual directly or through the intermediation of a developer, the lessee must have an income which meets the requirement established by the law. Secondly, the law ensures that housing remains affordable in the long term by regulating the rights of all parties and the transmissibility of these rights. While the lessee can transfer ownership and rights further by way of sale, the prospective purchaser must comply with the income-eligibility criteria specified by the law; moreover, he must be approved by the OFS, which also retains a right of pre-emption whenever a right is transferred.[73] Thirdly, the law provides that, where the OFS has agreed on the person of the purchaser, the duration of the contract is 'recharged' for a period equivalent to that of the original contract;[74] in this way, the transferee is able to enjoy ownership for another full term, instead of being entitled only to the remainder of the lease and suffering the devaluation of his asset. Finally, the prices of the housing units must be calculated on the basis of a legislatively set formula that limits real estate speculation and that applies to both first-time lessees and the subsequent transferees.[75]

The division of interest in property obtained through the lease, coupled with the 'rechargeable' character of its duration, have the ultimate effect of realising potentially perpetual fragmentations of ownership. Indeed, the OFS retains ownership of the land while accepting that ownership of the housing units could be potentially separated in perpetuity. On the other side, buyer-eligibility and resale price restrictions, coupled with the exercise of the OFS's right of pre-emption, ensure that homes will remain affordable for future generations of income-eligible purchasers. Although this mechanism is limited to the specific context of the OFS, it is precisely the flexible nature of the lease – part property and part contract – which has made it a privileged legal device in the hands of the legislator to develop the Community Land Trust model in France.

[73] According to articles L. 255-10 to L. 255-13, the concept of 'transfer' includes both the sale and gift of the lessee's rights. The law also regulates the case of death of the lessee by providing that, while his rights are automatically inherited, successors must comply with the income-based criteria; if they do not fall within the legally prescribed ceilings, successors must sell their rights, or the OFS can decide to bring the contract to an end.

[74] See article L. 255-12, which provides that 'the lease is extended by operation of law to allow the lessee to benefit from an *in rem* right of the same duration of that of the initial contract'.

[75] The price of the transfer of ownership and real rights are established for each year in relation to different geographical zones: see CCH, article R. 255-1.

IV. Conclusion

In the midst of a profound housing crisis that has hit Europe in the last few decades, the Community Land Trust model has come to be seen both in England and France as an innovative solution to providing affordable housing to low- and moderate-income households. While it remains to be seen whether or not CLTs will actually help to tackle the housing crisis in either system, the adoption of the CLT model has offered the opportunity to explore the hybrid nature of the lease and to illuminate a convergence between the French and English ways of understanding property. As the chapter has highlighted, both the English CLT and the French OFS may rely on long leases and covenants to obtain the doubly beneficial effects of vesting leaseholders with a property interest in their homes while retaining control over the use and resale of the properties. These two main effects are the result of the hybrid nature that the lease possesses both in English and French law. Transcending the narrow boundaries of the landlord–tenant relationship, the lease reveals itself as a flexible and adaptable legal device that is crucial for the implementation of broader public and social goals in the housing context. In turn, the similarity of effects that the lease generates in the contexts of CLT and OFS is also remarkable in the light of the different property traditions embedded in the two legal systems. While reliance on the lease is not surprising in the English context, its adoption in the form of BRS in French law is striking. Indeed, the fragmentation of ownership has always been a fundamental feature of English land law, with the consequence that a mechanism of the 'lease plus covenants' type constitutes a natural application of this way of understanding property relations in land. By contrast, the historical insistence of French law on the idea of ownership as *dominium* has made it difficult to realise fragmentation of ownership, a corollary of this being that the lease is not generally seen as a device to separate property ownership among different persons. In the light of this, the introduction of the BRS has put pressure on French traditional property categories. Indeed, French scholars have presented the BRS as 'a small revolution of property law' that has accomplished 'a modernisation of the Napoleonic conception of ownership'.[76] In its journey from contract to property, the long 'real' lease has called into question the sanctity of the traditional conception of ownership. The multiplication of long real leases and, more importantly, the ascendancy of the BRS demonstrate that the concept of absolute and perpetual ownership as modelled on *dominium* is no longer the 'flagship model for the use and enjoyment of the thing'.[77] By contrast, the different utilities associated with a given resource can be better exploited through mechanisms of separation of land and buildings. In this sense, the evolution of the lease – and ultimately the development of the CLT model – suggests that English and French property law, despite their structural differences, share points of contact and can converge towards similar solutions when pressing social needs so demand.

[76] V Le Rouzic, 'Le bail réel solidaire: une petite révolution du droit de propriété à mettre en perspective', *Gazette du Palais*, 2017, n° 30, 69; J Picard, 'Le bail réel solidaire: la reconnaissance de l'emphytéose rechargeable' *Les Petites Affiches*, 2016, n° 233, 6ff.

[77] B Mallet-Bricout, 'Baux réels et solidarité', *Revue trimestrielle de droit civil*, 12/2016, n° 4, 943.

14

How is the Fit? The Regulation of Mortgages as Enduring Property Relationships

SARAH NIELD

I. Introduction

The English law of mortgages has long been described as a work of fiction.[1] The legal charge by way of mortgage only meets the demands of modern lending through a layering of consensual, legislative, regulatory and other sources to produce a working credit relationship. In seeking to understand the mortgage as an enduring property relationship, the purpose of this chapter is to consider the fit between the key strands of this complex web.[2] It will argue that the dynamics of the enduring mortgage relationship are compromised by the lack of a logical fit between consensual and regulatory norms, which consequently highlights key regulatory challenges.

The chapter will do so by outlining the diverse network of sources from which the mortgage relationship is constructed. It will then consider two case studies – one from the residential context and the other from commercial lending – to examine the fit between particularly significant layers of this network. The residential case study looks to the interface between the mortgage conduct of business rules (MCOB), to which regulated mortgage providers should adhere, and their inherent right to possession. The commercial case study examines the remedial deficit resulting from the intersection of common law and regulatory redress for the mis-selling of interest rate hedging products (IRHPs) to small and medium-sized enterprises (SMEs). These examples have been chosen as they are drawn from the contrasted contexts of residential and commercial borrowing, and different points in time during the credit relationship. IRHPs look to the sales process whilst the residential mortgage case study examines mortgage enforcement. Both case studies demonstrate that the fit between the parties' legal relationship and their regulatory treatment is not seamless but in fact raises fundamental questions both in respect of the parties' rights and obligations (and their attendant remedies) and the behavioural norms with which the parties are expected to comply. The chapter concludes by identifying some of the questions that this unsatisfactory interface presents for the regulation of mortgages as enduring property relationships.

[1] G Watt, 'The Lie of the Land: Mortgage Law as Legal Fiction' in E Cooke (ed), *Modern Studies in Property Law*, vol 4 (Oxford, Hart Publishing, 2007).

[2] This chapter builds on work on S Blandy, S Bright and S Nield, 'The Dynamics of Enduring Property Relations' (2018) 81 *MLR* 85.

II. Diverse Network of Sources

The mortgage, as a property right, has an internal and external face. Externally, the mortgage confers priority on the mortgagee over third parties, including both secured and unsecured creditors. But it is the internal life of the mortgage between the parties with which this chapter is primarily concerned.[3] Alexander has used the term governance property to describe 'what happens inside the [property] box'[4] and suggests that to overlook this perspective gives 'a distorted and misleading view of property'.[5]

A. The Theoretical Frame

Complex consensual relations are initially outlined by the stated terms of the contract from which they emanate. Macneil described a spectrum of contractual behaviour from discrete to relational contracts.[6] Contracts at the discrete end of this spectrum tend to show high levels of what Macneil described as 'presentiation', evidenced by detailed written agreements in which the parties (or at least one of them) set out terms which attempt to crystallise the parties' future relations at the point of formation.[7] For instance, lenders require borrowers to enter into highly presentiated loan and security documentation to try and determine their future relationship. Yet enduring consensual relationships are frequently maintained by mutual trust and reciprocity, as evidenced by understandings generated beyond the stated terms. These informal understandings are the hallmarks of contracts towards the relational end of the spectrum. Macaulay and Bernstein therefore argued that it is necessary to consider the 'real deal' beyond the 'paper deal' to look at how the parties actually conduct their relationship.[8]

Underpinning relational contract theory is the core idea that contracts, including loan contracts, are 'embedded in complex relations'.[9] Macneil viewed contracts as an exchange between individualism and communalism, taking place within a social structure through which contracts are seen as linked horizontally and vertically with other exchange relations.[10] Accordingly, it is helpful to look both at the norms that emanate from the

[3] The phrase 'the internal life of property' is attributed to H Dagan, 'Remedies, Rights and Properties' (2011) 4 *Journal of Tort Law* 1, 19.

[4] GS Alexander, 'Governance Property' (2012) 160 *Pennsylvania Law Record* 1853, 1855. Others use the term but with a slightly different meaning: see HE Smith, 'Exclusion versus Governance: Two Strategies for Delineating Property Rights' (2002) 31 *Journal of Legal Studies* 453 and TW Merrill and HE Smith, 'The Property/Contract Interface' (2001) 101 *Columbia Law Review* 773.

[5] Alexander (ibid).

[6] D Campbell (ed), *The Relational Theory of Contract: Selected Works of Ian Macneil* (London, Sweet & Maxwell, 2001) 42–58.

[7] ibid.

[8] S Macaulay, 'The Real Deal and the Paper Deal: Empirical Pictures of Relationships, Complexity and the Urge for Transparent Simple Rules' (2003) 66 *MLR* 44 and L Bernstein, 'Merchant Law in the Merchant Court: Rethinking the Code's Search for Immanent Business Norms' (1996) 144 *University of Pennsylvania Law Review* 1765.

[9] IR Macneil, 'Relational Contract Theory: Unanswered Questions' (2000) 94 *Northwestern University Law Review* 877, 881.

[10] Campbell (n 6 above) 51–52. See also JM Feinman, 'Introduction' in D Campbell, L Mulcahy and S Wheeler (eds), *Changing Concepts of Contract: Essays in Honour of Ian Macneil* (Basingstoke, Palgrave Macmillan, 2013).

parties' internal relationship and at those that are external as part of the parties' interaction with society as whole. He reflected this interaction in the 10 contract norms he identified as essential to contractual behaviour.[11] Austen-Baker has since rationalised these norms into four more general norms, namely: satisfying performance expectations, preservation of the relationship, substantial fairness, and harmonisation with the social matrix.[12] The first three norms are self-explanatory, but harmonisation with the social matrix seeks to capture the call for contracts to observe social values both as regards generic contractual rules and in how those rules are utilised in individual contractual relations.[13]

Progressive property theory, too, looks beyond property as a wealth maximisation vehicle promoted by self-interest, and instead promotes a relational view of property as embedded within community.[14] Accordingly, property rights should embrace not just individual advancement but also a social obligation norm to promote human flourishing.[15] The concept of community is fluid and expansive and not confined to the state. Alexander and Peñalver explain that such communities 'are mediating vehicles through which we come to acquire the resources we need to flourish and to become fully socialised into the exercise of our capabilities'.[16] Communities, whilst encompassing physical neighbourhoods, thus look also to the socio-economic environments in which property relations, including those constructed by secured lending, operate.

Sarah Blandy, Sue Bright and I have argued that when considering the governance of enduring property relations we need to be similarly sensitive to the 'real deal' within the communities of which they form part.[17] Thus, for instance, if we are to understand the dynamics of the enduring mortgage relationship we need to consider the network of sources that shape the 'real deal' in the socio-economic landscape against which that relationship is conducted. A loan is rarely an end in itself – it is the purpose of the borrowing which provides this landscape.

Black has described 'two key ways' in which 'the state provides institutional structures for their [the financial markets] constitution and operation'.[18] First, are the 'facilitative structures' provided by the rules of contract and property to structure financial transactions, and secondly, 'regulative structures' which require 'markets, organisations, and behaviours

[11] Campbell (ibid) 153–55. Namely (i) role integrity, (ii) reciprocity, (iii) implementation of planning, (iv) effectuation of consent, (v) flexibility, (vi) contractual solidarity, (vii) the 'linking norms' (restitution, reliance and expectation interests), (viii) the 'power norm' (creation and restraint of power), (ix) proprietary of means, and (x) harmonisation with the social matrix.

[12] R Austen-Baker, 'Comprehensive Contract Theory: A Four Norm Model of Contract Relations' (2009) 25 *Journal of Contract Law* 216.

[13] ibid, 226.

[14] GS Alexander, EM Peñalver, JW Singer and LS Underkuffler, 'A Statement of Progressive Property' (2009) 94 *Cornell Law Review* 743; K Gray and S Gray, 'Rhetoric of Reality' in J Getzler (ed), *Rationalising Property, Equity and Trusts: Essays in Honour of Edward Burns* (London, LexisNexis, 2003) 24, also promote a relational view of property.

[15] GS Alexander, 'The Social Obligation Norm in American Property Law' (2009) 94 *Cornell Law Review* 745 and EM Peñalver, 'Land Virtues' (2009) 94 *Cornell Law Review* 821.

[16] GS Alexander and EM Peñalver, 'Properties of Community' (2009) 10 *Theoretical Inquiries in Law* 127, 139.

[17] See n 2 above.

[18] J Black, 'Seeing, Knowing, Regulating Financial Markets: Moving the Cognitive Framework from the Economic to the Social' (2013) 13 *Journal of Corporate Law Studies* 401, 414. K Lynch-Shally, 'Borrowers and Lenders in the Residential Mortgage Context: Legacy of the Financial Crisis on Regulatory Frameworks in Ireland and Spain' (PhD Thesis, National University of Ireland Galway, 2016) 3.5.3, uses a different nomenclature of 'the constitutive private sphere' and 'the facilitative public sphere'.

to be organised in particular ways'.[19] It is important to note that Black argues that these structures do not stand alone but need to be understood against a social conception, not just an economic conception, of financial markets. It is the interaction between these facilitative and regulatory structures with which this chapter is concerned and it is thus convenient to consider the network of sources that constitute the mortgage relationship by utilising this distinction.

B. The Facilitative Sphere

The parties' facilitative relationship is founded upon their consensual relationship within the parameters permitted by the rules of property and obligations. Performance is monitored by the parties and in the case of dispute – whether as to the content of, or compliance with, those rules and obligations – determined and enforced through the judicial system at the suit of the injured party.

(i) The Interaction of Property and Obligation

In English law, property and obligation have a complex inter-relationship. Contracts are used to create and transfer property rights and some property rights, so created, remain at a crossroads between property and obligation. This is the case with the mortgage relationship, the creation of which results in an enduring contractual relationship, constituted by the loan contract, and an enduring property relationship with attendant rights and power of enforcement conferred upon the mortgagee over the mortgaged property as security for the mortgagor's performance of the loan contract. Although in the case of mortgages, the contractual and property rights remain distinct throughout the parties' relationship, the parties' property relationship cannot be understood in isolation from their contractual relationship. It is thus important to be sensitive to the dynamics that arise from this interface.

The loan contract is a personal obligation on the part of the borrower to repay their indebtedness to the lender and remains the source of the borrower's obligation to repay even if the mortgage has been exercised by sale of the property. The loan contract also contains an agreement to create a legal charge, the 'mortgage'. As such the loan contract creates an equitable charge through the rule in *Walsh v Lonsdale*[20] (assuming the availability of specific performance), with the legal charge coming to fruition on registration. The loan contract may also shape the nature of the legal charge as a property right by expressly varying and/or supplementing the inherent rights and powers of the mortgagee conferred by the legal charge as a property interest.[21]

Clarke has observed that the relationship between the contract and the mortgage is not static.[22] The value of the mortgage 'fluctuates depending on the likelihood of the

[19] ibid.

[20] *Walsh v Lonsdale* (1882) 21 Ch D 9.

[21] For instance, the right of a legal chargee to take immediate possession see: Law of Property Act 1925, s 87 (1) and *Four Maids Ltd v Dudley Marshall (Properties) Ltd* [1957] Ch 317; *Birmingham Citizen Permanent Building Society v Caunt* [1962] Ch 883 and a chargee's powers implied into all mortgages created by deed: see Law of Property Act 1925, s 101.

[22] A Clarke, 'Security Interest in Property' in JW Harris (ed), *Property Problems: From Genes to Pension Funds* (London, Kluwer, 1997).

mortgagor repaying the debt in full and on time':[23] the greater the likelihood of default, the more valuable the mortgage. The status of the loan contract is thus fundamental to the strength of the mortgage as an immediate proprietary interest. Indeed, Clarke argues that the 'mortgage' is no more than a contingent right of management and alienation that constitutes less of a 'bundle' of rights than is often assumed. In her view, if it falls on the 'right side of the property line', then it does not do so by far.[24] Generally, it is at the point of default that the property relationship comes to the fore. Prior to default, the mortgage outlines controls to preserve the value of the security, for example by imposing upon the mortgagor obligations to insure and repair and to limit competing disposals.

(ii) The 'Bizarre' Property Relationship

Given the call for certain and logical property rules governing commercial transactions between strangers,[25] one might expect to find a clearly articulated property relationship between mortgagor and mortgagee. This is far from the case. The property rules governing the mortgagor and mortgagee's internal relations are obscured by the historical fictions that have dogged the mortgage relationship. The combined effect of the Law of Property Act 1925 and Land Registration Act 2002 dictates the use of the legal charge by way of mortgage as the sole form of legal security interest over registered land.[26] It is both the pre-eminent property relationship between mortgagee and mortgagor in the residential context and also frequently forms an integral element of a security package in commercial borrowing. For instance, an SME may be required to create a mortgage over any land it owns or, where an SME has insufficient assets to support its borrowing, a lender may call for collateral security over land (often their home) owned by the SME's directors and/or shareholders.

Under the legal charge, the mortgagee obtains a charge (ie, a new property interest), but enjoys the same protection, powers and remedies as if it held a mortgage by demise for 3,000 years.[27] This hybrid form of security creates a bizarre relationship which 'still operates in the world of make-believe.'[28] The mortgagee, as a notional tenant, is entitled to immediate possession and thus, strictly speaking, its interest is not contingent upon default as Clarke suggests. Meanwhile the rights of the mortgagor, as the holder of the legal estate and notional landlord, remain ill defined.[29] In the absence of express provision, statutory default rules supplement this property relationship, for instance with implied powers of sale and to appoint a receiver,[30] and provide the mechanics for the smooth transfer of title to a purchaser.[31] Some semblance of reality may be achieved by the consensual relationship shaping the nature of the legal charge as a property right by expressly varying and/or supplementing the legal chargee's inherent rights. For instance, the mortgagee may agree to suspend its right to possession until default.

[23] ibid 119.
[24] ibid 121.
[25] See the meta-principle of rationality in dealings with strangers in Gray and Gray (n 14 above) 246.
[26] Law of Property Act 1925, ss 85 and 86 and Land Registration Act 2002, ss 23(1) and 51.
[27] Law of Property Act 1925, s 87. A mortgagee is treated as though it held a lease of 3,000 years.
[28] Watt (n 1 above) 87.
[29] See S Nield, 'Charges, Possession and Human Rights, A Reappraisal of s.87(1) Law of Property Act 1925' in E Cooke (ed), *Modern Studies in Property Law*, vol 3 (Oxford, Hart Publishing, 2005) 155.
[30] Law of Property Act 1925, ss 101–103.
[31] ibid, ss 88 and 89.

(iii) Equity's Marginal Contribution

Equity's contribution to facilitative relations was historically vital but is now much diminished. The equitable right to redeem (or discharge) remains significant but the continuing utility of the concept of an equity of redemption is largely redundant under a legal charge,[32] and with it the maligned and largely moribund 'clogs and fetters' doctrine.[33] Two features of equity's contribution remain worthy of comment. Intertwined fiduciary duties to act in good faith for the purpose of recovery of their debt,[34] and to account, not only for what is received, but also for what ought to be received[35] discourage mortgagees from taking possession and require reasonable steps to be taken to obtain a realisation value that withstands judicial scrutiny.[36] Although the contribution of the regulatory sphere has largely superseded equity's contribution to the danger of exploitation, its control of unconscionable and oppressive terms[37] and penalties[38] provides an ultimate backstop.

(iv) Meeting Contractual and Property Norms?

Looking to the relational contractual norms and social obligation norm already referred to, it is useful to consider how the facilitative sphere measures up. Within a loan relationship the distinction between the parties' performance expectations can be stark. The lender is selling just another financial product, but for the borrower it is the purpose of the loan that is of primary significance, whether that be to buy a home or fund a business. The import of these respective expectations can lead to a motivational imbalance in favour of the lender acting as a gatekeeper both to home ownership and entrepreneurship. Preservation of the relationship largely lies with continuing performance by the borrower of their repayment obligations. The borrower bears the risk that conditions may change to affect their capacity to repay, eg, because of disruptions to their income flow through job loss, ill health or relationship breakdown.[39] Nevertheless, preservation of the relationship is important to the lender. Repayment of the loan may be achieved by enforcement of the mortgage but, as the 2007/08 financial crisis has demonstrated, doing so may compromise lenders' funding models, liquidity and ultimately their balance sheets.

Power imbalance between lenders and borrowers is further underlined by experiential differences between the parties. Lenders are experienced and repeat players within the credit market, whilst, for borrowers, large loan contracts are likely to be infrequent, long-term transactions. This inexperience compromises a borrower's ability to evaluate loan products and thus make a rational choice between competing terms. Inevitably they often

[32] See nn 1 and 29.

[33] See, for example, the Law Commission's proposal to abolish the doctrine: Law Commission, *Transfers of Land – Land Mortgages* (Law Comm No 204, 1991) Part VIII.

[34] *Quennell v Maltby* [1979] 1 WLR 318.

[35] *White v City of London Brewery* (1889) 42 Ch D 237; *Medforth v Blake* [1991] 2 All ER 97.

[36] *Cuckmere Brick Co Ltd v Mutual Finance* [1971] Ch 949; *Tse Kwok Lam v Wong Chit Sen* [1983] 1 WLR 1349; *Silven Properties Ltd v Royal Bank of Scotland* [2003] EWCA Civ 1409, [2004] 1 WLR 997.

[37] *G&K Kreglinger v New Patagonia Meat and Cold Storage Co Ltd* [1914] AC 25; *Multi Service Bookbinding Ltd v Marden* [1979] Ch 84.

[38] *Makdessi v Cavendish Square Holdings BV; ParkingEye Ltd v Beavis* [2015] UKSC 67, [2016] AC 1172.

[39] A Wallace, '"Feels like I am doing it on my own": Examining the Synchronicity Between Policy Response and the Circumstances and Experience of Mortgage Borrowers in Arrears' (2012) 11 *Social Policy and Society* 117.

place greater reliance on the knowledge and experience of the lender,[40] which may lead to a heightened risk of exploitation and substantial unfairness both in standards of behaviour and economic exchange. All of these factors point to the need for external regulation of the parties' credit relationship to support the norms necessary to sustain enduring contractual relations.

The vast majority of loan contracts are satisfactorily performed but where the borrower defaults the focus will turn to the mortgage as a property right. Default highlights the allocation of risk and the associated remedies attendant upon breach. Neo-liberal theories confine their attention to transactional equality in negotiating such matters within the confines of the contract. Non-performance inevitably raises the prospect of mortgage enforcement. By contrast, both relational contract theory and progressive property display a concern for the outcome of relations within which risk and responsibility are viewed from a wider perspective. They are prepared to take an instrumentalist approach to risk and its consequences. This approach may incorporate backward-looking measures which redefine contractual obligations and, in recognition of a social obligation norm, restrain the exercise of property rights to ameliorate risk and the impact of default upon communities, including financial markets.[41]

C. The Regulatory Sphere

At its core, regulation encompasses three functions – to set standards of desired behaviour, to monitor compliance with such standards and then to modify unwanted behaviour.[42] Financial services regulation has been influenced by a number of regulatory techniques which adopt a decentred approach to regulation. Within the decentred model, the regulator, the regulated and other bodies all have a role in seeking to ensure that the regulated comply with regulatory objectives. The regulatory field encompasses all those within the market rather than concentrating attention solely on the regulator, and the interactions between regulatory actors are as important as individual regulatory contributions. For instance, adjudicators and borrowers are both regulatory actors and can precipitate change when they enforce regulatory norms by holding financial service providers to account.

Closely associated with standard setting within a decentred regulatory model is principles-based regulation, which defines desired behaviour in broad aspirational, but inevitably uncertain, terms.[43] It is for the regulated to organise their operations to effectively meet

[40] See J Wightman, 'Beyond Custom: Contract, Contexts, and the Recognition of Implicit Understandings' in D Campbell, H Collins and J Wightman (eds), *Implicit Dimensions of Contract: Discrete, Relational and Network Contracts* (Oxford, Hart Publishing, 2003) 145.

[41] Wightman (ibid) 176 calls these 'potentially relational contracts'. Evidence of such norms is longstanding and finds regulatory expression for example in the Administration of Justice Act 1970, s 36 and MCOB.

[42] J Black, 'Enrolling Actors in Regulatory Systems: Examples from UK Financial Services Regulation' [2003] *Public Law* 63, 67 and see generally B Morgan and K Yeung (eds), *An Introduction to Law and Regulation: Text and Materials* (Cambridge, Cambridge University Press, 2007).

[43] See J Black et al, 'Making a Success of Principles Based Regulation' (2007) 1 *Law and Financial Markets Review* 191; J Black, 'Tensions in the Regulatory State' [2007] *Public Law* 58; J Black, 'Forms and Paradoxes of Principles-Based Regulation' (2008) 3 *Capital Markets Law Journal* 425; J Black, 'The Rise (and Fall?) of Principles Based Regulation' in K Alexander and N Moloney (eds), *Law Reform and Financial Markets* (Cheltenham, Edward Elgar, 2011); J Black, 'Paradoxes and Failures: New Governance Techniques and the Financial Crisis' (2012) 75 *MLR* 1037.

those standards. There are overarching regulatory principles defined by the Financial Services and Markets Act 2000 (FSMA)[44] but these principles do not stand alone. There are detailed rules governing market participants' conduct, found in the Financial Conduct Authority (FCA) Handbook.[45] Nevertheless, '[t]he Principles "occupy the field"':[46] they are 'the ever present substrata upon which specific rules are added'.[47] Accordingly, rule compliance is insufficient if the principles are not observed.

Also aligned with the decentred model is responsive regulation, which prioritises consensus tools to modify behaviour. The aim is to achieve compliance through negotiated conversations between the regulated and the regulator, which persuade, rather than coerce, changes in behaviour.[48] Within responsive regulation, it is thus necessary to understand and navigate the regulated's culture and structure to identify the most effective mix of regulatory tools ('smart regulation')[49] and to effectively harness the potency of the firm's strengths ('meta-regulation').[50] These regulatory techniques are inevitably open textured, leaving room for individual firms to develop their own practices and policies to interpret and meet the required regulatory norms. Their success depends both on how closely regulatory objectives dovetail with the business goals of the regulated and the willingness of the regulator, as well as other prominent regulatory actors, to evaluate and challenge firms' interpretation and attainment of regulatory norms.[51]

(i) Legislative Intervention

Legislation has little effect upon the relationship between commercial lenders and borrowers but the residential mortgage relationship is impacted at two levels.

First, in the pursuit of substantial fairness, the Consumer Rights Act 2015 imposes controls over unfair loan terms in an attempt to rebalance the contractual relationship.[52] The target is the mortgagee's standard-form documentation (individually negotiated terms are excluded) and the imbalance of bargaining power that together mean that the mortgagor must simply 'take it or leave it'. An unfair terms challenge may come from dual sources – the regulator(s)[53] or the borrower who may challenge a term as unfair and so unenforceable. As such it provides a blending of the facilitative and regulatory spheres.[54]

[44] See *FCA Handbook*, High Level Standards, PRIN Principles for Business, available at: https://www.handbook.fca.org.uk.

[45] ibid.

[46] *R (British Bankers Association) v Financial Services Authority* [2011] EWHC 999, [2011] Bus LR 1531, [166] Ousseley J.

[47] ibid [162].

[48] See the pioneering work of I Ayres and J Braithwaite, *Responsive Regulation* (Oxford, Oxford University Press, 1991).

[49] See for instance N Gunningham and P Grabosky, *Smart Regulation* (Oxford, Oxford University Press, 1998).

[50] See for instance L Salamon, *The Tools of Government* (Oxford, Oxford University Press, 1992).

[51] J Black, 'Paradoxes and Failures: New Governance Techniques and the Financial Crisis' (n 43 above).

[52] See in relation to mortgages *Newham London Borough Council v Khatun* [2004] EWCA Civ 55, [2005] QB 37.

[53] For example, the Competition and Markets Authority or FCA: see Unfair Contract Terms and Consumer Notices Regulatory Guide for the FCA's regulatory guidance, available at: https://www.handbook.fca.org.uk/handbook/UNFCOG/1.

[54] For example, an unfair terms challenge may impact upon the mortgagee's right to claim possession: see *Aziz v Caixa d'Estalvis de Catalunya, Tarragona i Manresa (Catalunyacaixa)* [2013] 3 CMLR 5.

Secondly, section 36 of the Administration of Justice Act 1970 confers a well-known discretionary jurisdiction on the courts to control the exercise of the mortgagee's right to possession of dwelling houses. This jurisdiction enables the court to adjourn possession proceedings or delay the execution of the possession order where the mortgagor can prove that he or she is able to pay the sums due under the mortgage within a reasonable period.[55] The legislation has been the subject of extensive academic commentary.[56] Although it provided an early and valuable route for a mortgagor to seek forbearance, it suffers from procedural weaknesses, both in terms of its reach[57] and its position at the end of the repossession journey, where its import is over-shadowed by the earlier forbearance steps required by the MCOB.[58]

(ii) Regulation: The Financial Services and Markets Act 2000

Since the realignment of regulatory responsibilities prompted by the Mortgage Credit Directive, lending secured on dwelling houses is largely regulated by the FCA pursuant to the FSMA.[59] In addition, the FCA is responsible for conduct of business regulation of other financial services providers, including banks and insurers.

The foundational principles of financial services regulation have been inspired by neo-liberalist principles, according to which lenders and borrowers who enter into a loan contract are perceived as rational and autonomous decision-makers, able to assess the risk attendant upon performance of their contractual obligations.[60] Regulation has thus focused on transactional equality through three broad objectives. The first is to create an open and competitive market of ex ante licensed providers offering a range of products in the expectation that rational selection will favour 'better' products and leave 'poorer' products to fail.[61] Secondly, a borrower's rational decision-making is promoted by mandating disclosure of standardised information of competing terms and 'educating' less experienced borrowers to become financially astute. Lastly, to promote integrity in the market, experiential asymmetries between the parties are balanced through the regulation of financial service providers' market conduct.

Since the financial crisis there has been some row back in reliance on the neo-liberal ideal by a recognition, inspired by behavioural economics, that financial decision-making is not

[55] See *Cheltenham & Gloucester Building Society v Norgan* [1996] 1 WLR 343.

[56] For example M Haley, 'Mortgage default: Possession, Relief and Judicial Discretion' (1997) 17 *Legal Studies* 483 and L McMurtry, 'Mortgage Default and Repossession: Procedure and Policy in the Post Norgan Era' (2007) 58 *Northern Ireland Legal Quarterly* 194.

[57] See A Clarke, 'Further Implications of Section 36 of the Administration of Justice Act 1970' [1982] *Conv* 293 and *Ropaigealach v Barclays Bank Plc* [2000] QB 263.

[58] For an insight into the reality of the section 36 jurisdiction see S Bright and L Whitehouse, *Information, Advice and Representation in Housing Repossession Cases* (University of Oxford and University of Hull, 2014).

[59] Directive 2014/17/EU of the European Parliament and of the Council of 4 February 2014 on credit agreements for consumers relating to residential immovable property and amending Directives 2008/48/EC and 2013/36/EU and Regulation (EU) No 1093/2010 and Mortgage Credit Directive Order 2015.

[60] See I Ramsay, 'Consumer Law, Regulatory Capitalism and the "New Learning" in Regulation' (2006) 28 *Sydney Law Review* 9.

[61] ibid.

always rational.[62] This has prompted some realignment of decision-making responsibilities.[63] For example, in seeking to minimise the risk and impact of default, regulated mortgage providers are required to take greater responsibility through regulatory norms to assess loan affordability and suitability, and to explore ways of avoiding the trauma of home repossession where repayment remains sustainable through managed forbearance.[64]

In adopting principles-based regulation, a cluster of the overarching principles to which financial service providers are expected to adhere articulates 'fairness' as a governing standard.[65] This standard finds more detailed expression in the FCA's Treating Customer Fairly (TCF) initiative, which is influential not just in standard setting, with its own set of consumer outcomes,[66] but also in targeting the FCA's compliance activities.[67] The conduct of business rules and guidance are found in the generic Conduct of Business Rules (Conduct of Business Sourcebook (COBS)) and sector-specific handbooks, including the MCOB.[68]

Persuasion underlies the FCA's compliance approach, with much of their work devoted to producing guidance to encourage banks to meet conduct standards and the monitoring of lenders' behaviour against those expectations.[69] The FCA's investigatory and disciplinary armoury is impressive. It encompasses not just fines but undertakings by financial services providers as to their future conduct and a consumer redress scheme to provide compensation to those adversely affected.[70] Coercion is generally viewed as a last resort.[71]

(iii) The Borrower and Adjudicators as Regulatory Actors – Section 138D FSMA and the Financial Ombudsman Service (FOS)

Of additional import are the steps by which a purchaser of financial services may take direct action to obtain redress and, in so doing, become a regulatory actor.[72] Section 138D (previously section 150) of the FSMA confers a right for an individual to obtain damages, by way of breach of statutory duty, for the loss they may have suffered where a conduct of business rule is breached. It thus provides a significant link between the facilitative and regulatory spheres.

The limited feasibility of consumers seeking court redress is recognised by the creation of the FOS as the foremost redress forum. The FOS is able to resolve complaints according

[62] FCA, 'Journey to the FCA' (15 October 2012) 45 and FCA, 'Applying behavioural economics at the Financial Conduct Authority', Occasional Paper No 1 (April 2013).

[63] By the Mortgage Market Review: see Financial Services Authority (FSA), 'Mortgage Market Review: Arrears and approved persons' (FSA PS10/9, 2010) and FSA, 'Mortgage Market Review' (FSA PS12/16, 2012).

[64] MCOB Rules 11 and 13 respectively. See S Nield, 'Mortgage Market Review: "Hard-wired Common Sense?"' (2015) 38 *Journal of Consumer Policy* 139.

[65] Financial Services and Markets Act 2000 s 64 and see *FCA Handbook* (n 45 above).

[66] See FSA, 'Treating Customers Fairly – Towards Fair Outcomes for Consumers' (July 2006).

[67] T Williams, 'Open the Box, an Exploration of the Financial Services Authority's Model of Fairness in Consumer Financial Transactions' in M Kenny, J Devenney and L Fox O'Mohony (eds), *Unconscionability in Private European Transactions: Protecting the Vulnerable* (Cambridge, Cambridge University Press, 2010) 82.

[68] Available at: https://www.handbook.fca.org.uk/handbook/COBS/ and www.handbook.fca.org.uk/handbook/MCOB/. Made pursuant to the FCA's rule- and guidance-making powers under Financial Services and Markets Act 2000, Part X.

[69] See for instance FCA, 'Transforming Culture in Financial Services' (FCA DP18/2, 2018).

[70] See generally Financial Services and Markets Act 2000, Part XIV.

[71] The FCA are reviewing their approach: see FCA, 'Our Approach to Enforcement' (March 2018).

[72] See for example R Samuel, 'Tools for Changing Banking Culture: FCA Are You Listening' (2016) 11 *Capital Markets Law Journal* 129.

to a fair and reasonable standard and at no cost to the borrower through a process that is relatively informal, quick and accessible.[73] It can thus provide additional detail to, and even look beyond, the legal frame by setting out the norms of fairness that an experienced yet independent observer might expect. It publicises its views through guidance and case summaries and, by reporting common problems to other regulators. Its impact can thus extend beyond individual dispute resolution, although its jurisdiction is limited by a £150,000 award ceiling.[74]

(iv) Soft Law – Industry, Procedural and Self-Generated Norms

Principles-based regulation, and its close partner smart regulation (in all its forms), leave considerable discretion to financial services providers to meet the stated outcomes, for instance in treating their customers fairly. The conduct of business rules constrain that discretion but nevertheless leave room for different compliance approaches. For example MCOB 13.3 provides one of many instances where the rules call upon mortgage providers to generate their own norms.

> (1) A *firm* must deal fairly with any *customer* who:
>
> (a) has a *payment shortfall* on a *regulated mortgage contract* …;
>
> (2) A *firm* must put in place, and operate in accordance with, a written policy (agreed by its respective *governing body*) and procedures for complying with (1) …

A mortgage provider must thus develop its own internal policy on how payment shortfalls are to be treated, against the benchmark of 'fairness'. In formulating such policy they may look to the practice of the sector, as that may be shaped by the guidance of industry bodies.[75]

The range and influence of these industry- and self-generated norms should not be underestimated. They clothe the bare bones of the regulatory framework. Whitehouse has noted that the apparent stability of the legal rules governing mortgages is deceptive. Mortgagees have preferred to leave 'the substance of the mortgage relationship to be "regulated" through more malleable processes such as contractual "negotiation", "discretion" and "soft law"',[76] to avoid more fundamental legal reform.

The difficulty is the lack of transparency of *unilateral* self-generated norms. A mortgagor is not a member of the industry 'club' or privy to the policy of an individual mortgage provider. Mortgagors must negotiate this shifting world blindfold at a stressful time both financially and personally,[77] when evidence suggests that they often fail to take advantage

[73] See generally Part XVI Financial Services and Markets Act 2000.

[74] Although their experience and independence has come under adverse scrutiny which triggered an independent review see R Lloyd, *Report of the Independent Review of the Financial Ombudsman Service* (July 2018).

[75] See, for instance, CML guidance as to when a receiver might be appointed, available at: https://www.cml.org.uk/policy/guidance/all/the-role-of-law-of-property-act-lpa-receivers/ and issued following the disquiet triggered by *Horsham Properties Group Ltd v Clark* [2008] EWHC 2327, [2009] 1 WLR 1255.

[76] L Whitehouse, 'A Longitudinal Analysis of the Mortgage Repossession Process 1995–2012: Stability, Regulation and Reform' in S Bright (ed), *Modern Studies in Property Law*, vol 6 (Oxford, Hart Publishing, 2011) 152.

[77] Wallace (n 39 above).

of available safety nets.[78] The Pre-action Protocol for Possession Claims based upon Mortgage … Arrears of Residential Property provides a degree of openness.[79] This protocol replicates much of what might be expected of forbearance required by MCOB 13 but with a degree of court oversight. Yet it remains soft law, with no sanctions beyond the possibility of an adjournment, until its substance has been met, or limiting the mortgagee's entitlement to costs.[80]

This chapter now turns to consider two case studies which illustrate the interface between these different sources in two respects. First, is the fit between the parallel norms of the facilitative and regulatory spheres. The second is the interaction between the two spheres where regulation contributes directly to the parties' private law relationship.

III. The Mortgagee's Right to Possession and Mortgage Conduct of Business (MCOB) Rules

In the case of *Thakker v Northern Rock plc*[81] the High Court was asked to consider the interface between the mortgagee's right to possession and MCOB's regulatory standards. The Thakkers bought their home with the aid of a mortgage and subsequently obtained further advances totalling £259,000. However, by 2010 they were £53,000 in arrears. Northern Rock, also in financial difficulty, sought possession. The Thakkers argued that Northern Rock had not observed MCOB's regulatory standards by failing to advise them on the suitability of the further advances and without conducting any affordability checks or a further valuation of their home.[82] Furthermore, there was a failure to show any forbearance pursuant to MCOB 13 – Northern Rock had refused to meet the Thakkers. These allegations, if proved, would have entitled the Thakkers to damages for breach of statutory duty under section 138D FSMA, which, they argued, should be set-off against the arrears.

However, the Thakkers encountered the *Mobil Oil* principle,[83] which does not allow a counterclaim or set-off to affect the mortgagee's right to possession. The principle demonstrates the continued strength of the right to possession despite the various measures requiring forbearance where home ownership remains sustainable. The court was not persuaded that the MCOB made any inroads into the principle. They characterised a mortgagee's claim for possession in two stages. The first stage considers whether or not the mortgagee has a right to possession which might be defended, for instance because the mortgage was invalid or unenforceable. The second stage looks to whether the court has jurisdiction to stay the execution of the possession order, eg under section 36. It is at this

[78] Bright and Whitehouse (n 58 above).

[79] Civil Procedure Rules Pre-Action Protocol for Possession Claims based on Mortgage or Home Purchase Plan Arrears in Respect of Residential Property.

[80] L Whitehouse, 'The Mortgage Arrears Pre-action Protocol: An Opportunity Lost' (2009) 72 *MLR* 793 and J Lean, 'A Practical Guide to Enforcing the Mortgagee's Security' (Landmark Chambers, 2009) available at: http://www.landmarkchambers.co.uk/userfiles/documents/resources/Possession_Claims_Procedure_-_JAL.pdf.

[81] *Thakker v Northern Rock plc* [2014] EWHC 2107.

[82] The brief case report does not specify the particular rule but it is likely to have been MCOB 11.

[83] *Mobil Oil Co Ltd v Rawlinson* (1982) 43 P&CR 22. See also *National Westminster v Skelton* [1993] 1 WLR 72; *Citibank Trusts Ltd v Ayivor* [1987] 1 WLR 1157; *Ashley Guarantee v Zacaria* [1993] 1 WLR 62.

second stage that an alleged breach of MCOB could be considered. Thus, it is the contractual, rather than the property, relationship that is affected by regulatory norms granting a right to damages.

The decision demonstrates the disconnect between the facilitative and regulatory norms. The clear regulatory message is that regulated mortgage providers should explore forbearance *before* initiating legal proceedings for possession. Yet, given the bizarre mortgage relationship, that intention has been trumped by the court's finding in *Thakker* that the regulatory norms are not relevant in deciding whether the mortgagee can establish a right to possession. In contrast, is the employment of unenforceability as a compliance tool in the Consumer Credit Act 1974.[84] This tool, which *does* bite when the mortgagee is seeking to establish a right to possession, harks back to when coercion was more in tune with regulatory thinking and contrasts with the consensus tools that underlie the FCA's compliance strategies.[85]

A qualification of the *Mobil Oil* principle is possible where the mortgage expressly or impliedly qualifies the mortgagee's right to possession, for instance by requiring prior default. *Thakker* does not explore this avenue by considering either the express terms of the mortgage or whether at least some of the MCOB rules should be implied into the parties' relationship.[86] Implication of other conduct of business rules has been contemplated in insurance cases. Perhaps the strongest hint comes in *Parker v National Farmers Union*[87] when Teare J, accepted that 'whether or not they are implied terms of the policy, the NFU cannot claim to be entitled to exercise a right to reject a claim … otherwise than in accordance with those [ie ICOB] standards.'

The status of regulatory norms upon mortgage repossession has also been considered by the Irish courts. The issue found its way to the Irish Supreme Court in *Irish Life and Permanent Plc v Dunne*.[88] The pertinent regulatory norms were those contained in the Code on Mortgage Arrears, issued pursuant to section 117 of the Central Bank Act 1989 (the Code).[89] These norms set out a range of measures including a moratorium on commencing possession proceedings (varyingly six and 12 months)[90] and a requirement for mortgagees to show reasonable forbearance. A mortgagee who failed to observe the Code could face regulatory disciplinary action but, in contrast to the FSMA, the Code did not outline any private law consequences.

The lower courts had been minded to accept that the Code did impact on the mortgage relationship so as to prevent a non-compliant mortgagee from obtaining possession.[91]

[84] Unenforceability faced an Article 1 Protocol 1 challenge in *Wilson v First County Trust Ltd (No 2)* [2003] UKHL 40, [2004] 1 AC 816, which led to amendment of the impugned Consumer Credit Act 1974, s 127.

[85] The courts are wary of resort to unenforceability see: *Carey v HSBC Bank Plc* [2009] EWHC 3417, [2010] Bus LR 1142; *Phoenix Recoveries (UK) Ltd v Kotecha* [2011] EWCA Civ 105, [2011] ECC 13.

[86] At least these grounds are not evident from the report; possibly because they were not pleaded.

[87] *Parker v National Farmers Union Mutual Insurance Society Ltd* [2012] EWHC 2156, [197]. The interface between regulatory, statutory and industry standards is also explored in *Plevin v Paragon Personal Finance Ltd* [2014] UKSC 61, [2014] 1 WLR 4222.

[88] *Irish Life and Permanent Plc v Dunne* [2015] IESC 46.

[89] Like the MCOB, there have been various iterations of this code.

[90] Depending on the version of the Code in force.

[91] *Stepstone Mortgage Funding Ltd v Frizell* [2011] IEHC 142; *Zurich Bank v McConnon* [2011] IEHC 75; and *Irish Life and Permanent Plc v Duff* [2013] IEHC 43.

Before the Irish Supreme Court two approaches were argued. The first was that the Code should be implied into the mortgage relationship; the second was that non-compliance with the Code gave rise to a breach of the mortgagee's duty of care, and accordingly a subsequent possession order would be tainted with illegality.

The implied term argument was given short shrift on the basis that the Code, in contrast to other terms implied by consumer-based legislation, was subject to change. This is hardly a convincing ground when it must be open to the parties to agree to observe a set of obligations from time to time in force should they be minded to do so.

The illegality argument turned not on the fact that the mortgage itself was illegal but that its enforcement, in which the court was asked to play its part, was infected by illegality. Here a distinction was drawn between: black and white provisions of the Code whereby compliance could clearly be determined, eg, whether or not the moratorium had been observed; and the majority of the Code where value judgements were required, for instance as to the reasonableness of behaviour. Where the moratorium had not been observed, the Court refused to facilitate 'illegal' enforcement. However, where other provisions of the Code were in issue, the Court fell back on constitutional deference in the absence of a legislative conferral of judicial responsibility.

The Court's different approach to the moratorium and other provisions of the Code is unsatisfactory. Compliance with the moratorium is easier to establish, but courts are well versed in assessing reasonable behaviour in many diverse contexts. The constitutional grounds are more convincing, but only in the Irish context. In England and Wales the Financial Services and Markets Act, sections 36 and 138D both empower the court to take account of regulatory standards. There seems little point in setting behavioural standards if they have limited impact on the dynamics of the mortgage relationship, particularly when the mortgagor has entered into that relationship in the comfort that the mortgagee's business is regulated by the FCA.

IV. Interest Rate Hedging Product Mis-selling to SMEs

The second case study relates to the redress available to SMEs for the mis-selling of IRHPs. The IRHPs in question were sold to hedge against interest rate rises under the floating rate terms prevalent in commercial lending. In the low interest environment which followed the 2007/08 financial crisis these IRHPs triggered payments to lending banks or exorbitant exit fees.

IRHPs take a number of forms. Interest rate caps place a limit on the maximum rate of interest that can be charged and are sold for a premium. Interest rate collars provide a cap and a floor by also setting a minimum rate of interest which triggers a payment from the borrower to the lender. Swaps, as their name suggest, swaps one type of interest for another: for instance a floating rate for a fixed rate. Typically, if interest rates rise the borrower receives a payment that can be used to off-set the increase in loan repayments but if rates fall the borrower is obliged to make a payment to the lender although benefits from lower repayments.

It became evident that the nature and associated risks of these complex financial instruments were not fully appreciated by many SMEs to which they were sold as part of a financing package.[92] In particular, banks pushed the more complex 'structured collars', which, in contrast to caps, did not attract the payment of a premium but carried the risk of payments to the lender in the events that transpired of ultra-low interest rates. In the early part of the new millennium when many IRHPs were sold, this risk was peddled as 'remote', given the relative stability of interest rates in preceding years. A number of poor sales practices were prevalent, the most significant of which were: banks' failure to adequately disclose the break or exit costs or to ensure SMEs' understanding of the risks associated with IRHPs; the failure to distinguish between information-only and advised sales; inappropriate sales incentives; and the over-hedging of risk exposures.[93]

All of these practices ran counter to the COBS conduct of business standards.[94] These standards call (inter alia) for banks: to act honestly, fairly and professionally in the best interests of their client;[95] and to provide a general description of the nature and risks of products being sold,[96] as well as appropriate and comprehensible information – that is fair, clear, accurate and not misleading[97] – to enable their client to understand the nature and risks of the product being sold.[98] The standards also require banks to assess the appropriateness of products offered to their clients and determine that they have the necessary experience and knowledge to understand the risks involved.[99]

It might be thought that the most obvious route to redress was the section 138D right of a 'private person' to sue for breach of statutory duty for non-compliance with COBS. But this proved a dead end for corporate SMEs. The courts' interpretation of 'private person' under the Financial Services and Markets Act 2000 (Rights of Action) Regulations 2001 excluded recovery for losses suffered by persons who were not individuals 'in the course of carrying on business of any kind.'[100] Even though the buying of an IRHP was a one-off transaction for many SMEs, a wide interpretation has been given to this business exclusion to encompass IRHP purchases.[101] A complaint to the FOS is also unavailable to many SMEs. Only micro-enterprises with an annual turnover of £2 million and fewer than 10 employees can make a complaint to the FOS.[102]

This lack of redress exposed a regulatory deficit which triggered such political disquiet that the regulator was pressurised into action. In 2012 they 'persuaded' some leading banks to carry out a Pilot Review of a sample of IRHPs sold to 'non-sophisticated' SMEs.[103]

[92] Some banks required SMEs to take out an IRHP as a pre-condition to the grant of loan facilities.

[93] FSA, *Interest Rate Hedging Products Pilot Findings* (March 2013) 10.

[94] Tailored business loans, in which an IRHP is embedded as part of a business loan, are not regulated by the FSMA: see T Riley-Smith, 'FCA Regulation of Interest Rate Hedging Products: One Rule for Some?' (2015) 7 *Butterworths Journal of International Banking and Finance Law* 425.

[95] COBS 2.1.1 (see n 68 above).

[96] ibid 14.3.2.

[97] ibid 4.2.1.

[98] ibid 2.2.1 and 4.5.2.

[99] ibid 10.2.1.

[100] Financial Services and Markets Act 2000 (Rights of Action) Regulations 2001, reg 3 (1)(b).

[101] *Titan Steel Wheels Ltd v Royal Bank of Scotland Plc* [2010] EWHC 211, [2010] 2 Lloyd's Rep 92; *Sivagnanam v Barclays Bank Plc* [2015] EWHC 3985; *Grant Estates Ltd v Royal Bank of Scotland Plc* [2012] CSOH 133. For discussion see R Zepeda, 'Derivatives Mis-selling by British Banks and the Failed Legacy of the FSA' (2013) 28(6) *Journal of International Banking Law and Regulation* 209.

[102] A complaint based upon the withdrawal of a settlement offer was also beyond the FOS jurisdiction see *R (Mazarona Properties Ltd) v Financial Ombudsman Service* [2017] EWHC 1135 (Admin), [2017] ACD 94.

[103] FSA (n 93 above).

Over 90 per cent of sales failed to comply with regulatory standards. There followed an agreement with banks to review IRHPs sales made to 'unsophisticated customers' since December 2001.[104] The review encompassed all sales of structured collars, the sale of other IRHPs (except caps) on a case-by-case basis and the sale of caps where a complaint was made. Redress was provided on 'a fair and reasonable' basis. Each bank's reviews were overseen by 'an independent' reviewer approved by the regulator under section 166 FSMA – usually a well-known audit firm.

The key categorisation of a non-sophisticated customer was intended to capture small businesses that were unlikely to have the specific expertise to understand the risks associated with IRHPs.[105] The test of such entities was based upon their turnover, balance sheet and number of employees – being more than £6.5 million, more than £3.2 million and more than 50, respectively, with some adaption for SMEs that formed part of a group or employed part-time employees. Even so, banks could escape a review if they could establish that an SME was a sophisticated entity and able to comprehend the complexity of the IRHP sold.

The reviews took over two years to complete, with a staggering £2 billion paid out by way of compensation and an estimated 90 per cent of claims accepted.[106] Nevertheless, this redress scheme drew criticism, most notably from Members of Parliament representing the interests of SMEs within their constituencies.[107] Both the Backbench Business Committee[108] and the House of Commons Treasury Committee[109] criticised the review for inconsistency, lack of transparency and lack of fair and reasonable redress.[110] The FCA has made conciliatory noises but taken little action. Attempts to hold banks to a duty of care in the conduct of the reviews[111] and an independent reviewer to account by way of judicial review have both failed.[112]

The remaining hope of compensation for SMEs rests with common law causes of action of the facilitative sphere. Such actions have not proved fruitful, but rather highlighted the mismatch between regulatory and facilitative norms.

The key feature that has emerged from these cases is whether the bank is giving advice rather than mere information. Where the bank is giving advice the courts recognise a duty of care and they have looked to regulatory standards as a useful reference point. In *Green & Rowley v Royal Bank of Scotland*[113] the court noted that the content of an advisory duty

[104] The banks voluntarily accepted the reviews, as a consumer redress scheme pursuant to Financial Services and Markets Act 2000, s 404 was unavailable – SMEs are not classified as consumers.

[105] FSA (n 93 above).

[106] See SK Afghan 'Should Private Opt-Out Collective Redress Actions Be Introduced for the Resolution of Widespread Consumer Financial Services Claims Part 1' (2016) 31(4) *Journal of International Banking Law and Regulation* 194.

[107] Commentators have also complained see R Samuel, 'Tools for Culture Change: FCA, Now You are Listening! Time to Build and Independent, Low Cost Forum for Conduct Dispute Resolution' (2016) 12 *Capital Markets Law Journal* 277.

[108] HC Deb 4 December 2014, vol 589, col 477.

[109] Treasury Committee, *Conduct and competition in SME Lending* (HC 2014–15, 204).

[110] See SK Afghan 'Commercial Financial Dispute Resolution Platform: a Palliation or Panacea for Consumer Financial Services?' (2017) 32(5) *Journal of International Banking Law and Regulation* 200.

[111] *CGL Group Ltd v Royal Bank of Scotland* [2017] EWCA Civ 1073, [2018] 1 WLR 2137, but see *Suremime Ltd v Barclays Bank Plc* [2015] EWHC 2277; *Elite Property Holdings Ltd v Barclays Bank Plc* [2016] EWHC 3294.

[112] *R (Holmcroft Properties Ltd) v KPMG LLP* [2016] EWHC 323, [2017] Bus LR 932.

[113] *Green & Rowley v Royal Bank of Scotland* [2013] EWCA Civ 1197, [2014] Bus LR 168. See also *Thornbridge Ltd v Barclays Bank Plc* [2015] EWHC 3430.

would be informed by COBS, given that the 'care and skill to be expected of a reasonably competent financial adviser ordinarily includes compliance with the relevant regulatory rules'.[114] However, the Court of Appeal rejected the argument that COBS standards triggered a co-extensive duty of care to provide accurate and full information.

In non-advised sales, redress for negligent misstatement may arise where there has been an assumption of responsibility by the bank which satisfies the test in *Hedley Byrne & Co Ltd v Heller & Partners Ltd*.[115] However, the courts have rarely found such a duty on the evidence.[116] The selling of an IRHP will almost inevitably involve the provision of information or an explanation of the product. In *Crestsign Ltd v National Westminster Bank Plc*,[117] whilst the court rejected a duty to explain, it suggested that, if the bank had assumed responsibility, their explanation should be accurate and not misleading. They describe this duty as an intermediate or 'mezzanine' duty. Subsequent cases[118] have explored this duty but the Court of Appeal in *Property Alliance Group Ltd v Royal Bank of Scotland*[119] stated that 'the expression "mezzanine" duty or intermediate duty … is best avoided' and with it 'the notion that there is a continuous spectrum of duty, stretching from not misleading, at one end, to full advice at the other end'.[120] In non-advised sales there seems to be merely a duty not to misstate information that is given voluntarily or in response to questions from a potential purchaser. The likelihood of redress is thus remote.

It is evident that the interaction between the COBS regulatory standards and any common law liabilities is complex and lacks clarity. Whilst the courts acknowledge the inter-relationship between the standards expected of those providing advice, on several occasions they have referred to Parliament's intention to confine section 138D regulatory redress so as to limit any development of facilitative recourse in non-advised sales.[121] The process interface is also troubling. The regulatory review of IRHP mis-selling has impacted upon common law claims. Many claims have become statute-barred[122] and possible causes of action compromised by settlement.[123]

V. Conclusion: Regulatory Challenges

The case studies demonstrate the operation of the complex network sources that constitute the parties' enduring relationship. This network is not simply one-dimensional but is

[114] *Green & Rowley v Royal Bank of Scotland* (ibid) [18].

[115] *Hedley Byrne & Co Ltd v Heller & Partners Ltd* [1964] AC 465.

[116] For an example, see *Crestsign Ltd v National Westminster Bank Plc* [2014] EWHC 2144, but was excluded by the terms of business.

[117] ibid.

[118] See *Thornbridge Ltd v Barclays Bank Plc* (n 113 above); *Marz Ltd v Royal Bank of Scotland Plc* [2017] EWHC 3618; *London Executive Aviation Ltd v Royal Bank of Scotland Plc* [2018] EWHC 74.

[119] *Property Alliance Group Ltd v Royal Bank of Scotland* [2018] EWCA Civ 355, [2018] 1 WLR 3529.

[120] ibid [67].

[121] Most notably in *Green & Rowley v Royal Bank of Scotland Plc* (n 113 above) [30]; *CGL Group Ltd v Royal Bank of Scotland Plc* (n 111 above) [83]–[87]; *London Executive Aviation Ltd v Royal Bank of Scotland Plc* (n 118 above) [166]–[172] and [235]–[237].

[122] *Qadir v Barclays Bank Plc* [2016] EWHC 1092; *Orchard Developments (Holdings) Plc v National Westminster Bank Plc* [2017] EWHC 2144; *Kay Hotels Ltd v Barclays Bank Plc* [2014] EWHC 1927.

[123] *Marsden v Barclays Bank Plc* [2016] EWHC 1601, [2016] 2 Lloyd's Rep 420; *WW Property Investments Ltd v National Westminster Bank Plc* [2016] EWCA Civ 1142, [2017] 2 All ER (Comm) 624; *Cameron Developments (UK) Ltd v National Westminster Bank Plc* [2017] EWHC 1884.

constituted by the different levels of the facilitative and regulatory spheres, the intersection of which is far from seamless. In so doing they raise a number of regulatory challenges.

The Thakkers' story illustrates the mismatch between the facilitative and regulatory norms. Despite the clear import of the MCOB standards, the parties' relationship continues to be dominated by their property relationship and the strength of the mortgagee's right to possession. The courts have struggled to find an appropriate rationale to reconcile regulatory norms with this property relationship. Regulatory redress looks only at the parties' *in personam* financial obligations, yet in a security relationship the mortgagee's property rights and the mortgagor's personal obligations should be interdependent. In the case of other security interests, usually they are. The fundamental problem is that in the legal charge they are not – the mortgagee's right to possession is not dependent on default. Although practical mechanisms are employed to try and turn this right into a default remedy, its effects lurk in the shadows through such doctrines as the *Mobil Oil* principle. It is time for the legal charge to become a security interest in substance (not just name) whether through legislative reform or judicial activism.

The IRHPs story illustrates the remedial deficit of both the facilitative and regulatory sphere. Despite a backdrop of regulatory norms, where there is no feasible route for a borrower to obtain redress,[124] political pressure has precipitated limited regulatory action. The question is whether this change is a one-off or should lead to a more fundamental rethink of the credit relationship (both facilitative and regulatory) between SMEs and their bankers?

The FCA's overall strategic objective is to ensure that financial markets function well,[125] in which ensuring the integrity of the financial system, promoting effective competition and providing an appropriate degree of consumer protection are the key drivers.[126] Political concern over the vulnerability of SMEs to financial oppression continues and the FCA acknowledges that some SMEs are deserving of 'consumer' protection.[127] They have issued proposals to allow more SMEs access to FOS dispute resolution.[128] Other commentators call for additional measures, including the amendment of section 138D to allow claims by SMEs,[129] and more radically, the establishment of a specialist financial services tribunal (a proposition that is gaining traction).[130] Who is 'a consumer' in the purchase of ever-more

[124] See N Beale, 'Access to Financial Justice: Three Financial Services Conduct Scandals, and a Proposal for Reform' (2018) 33(5) *Journal of International Banking Law and Regulation* 153 on the consequences of this lack of access to justice.

[125] Financial Services and Markets Act, s 1B (2).

[126] ibid, ss 1B(3)–1E.

[127] FCA, 'Our Approach to SMEs as Users of Financial Services' (FCA DP15/7, 2015). A problem is working out which SMEs should qualify see SK Afghan, 'What is the Purpose of Section 138D of the FSMA 2000 (As Amended)?' (2018) 33(5) *Journal of International Banking Law and Regulation* 163.

[128] The proposal is to expand the FOS's remit to SMEs with not more than 50 employees, an annual turnover of under £6.5m and an annual balance sheet total of under £5m: see FCA and Bank of England Prudential Rating Authority, 'Financial Services Compensation Scheme – Management Expenses Levy Limit 2018/19' (FCA CP3/18, PRA CP3/18, 2018). The FCA Policy Statement is expected in Summer 2018.

[129] SK Afghan (n 127 above) and D McIlroy, 'Unexpected, Illogical and Unfair: the Distinction Between Who Can and Who Cannot Sue for Breaches of Financial Services Rules' (2017) 32(9) *Butterworths Journal of International Banking and Finance Law* 548.

[130] R Samuel (nn 72 and 107 above). His work has sparked parliamentary interest see the All Party Parliamentary Group on Fair Business Banking: http://www.appgbanking.org.uk/our-work/dispute-resolution/.

complex financial products is a slippery concept, but there seems little doubt that some SMEs are unable to exercise informed choice and thus play their part within the neo-liberal ideal. Their vulnerability is evident not just in having to accept credit on take-it-or-leave-it terms but in having few other avenues by which to obtain finance.

Workable redress also would enable SMEs to play their part as regulatory actors, both to enhance the integrity of the financial system and to participate effectively as decision-makers in a competitive market through access to more probing product information. Banks may have won a number of battles, but peace and prosperity will only be achieved by restoring and maintaining confidence in financial services' conduct standards after the severe battering meted out by the financial crisis and subsequent scandals, including the mis-selling of IRHPs. Regulation does not just benefit 'consumers': financial service providers can gain too.[131]

[131] For example, see the arguments in R Samuel, 'The FCA Has Listened: Banks, It is in Your Interests to Listen Too' (2018) 13 *Captial Markets Law Review* 3.

PART IV

Land Registration: Problems and Solutions

15

Updating Land Registration Law and Practice: Some Lessons from China

LU XU

I. Introduction

For those interested in Chinese property law, the past few years have been exciting for two reasons. Firstly, China established the world's largest system of land registration, comprising over 3,300 registry offices, in less than three years.[1] Given the short timeframe, the overhaul pushed ahead without settling several important principles of registration. Around the same period, the Supreme Court of China started to upload millions of judgments to its online platform open for free general access.[2] These include decisions by all levels and all types of court in China. A simple keyword search on land registration would reveal thousands of cases all over China in the past few years, providing some wonderful insights into the implementation of the unified registration system and the challenges it currently faces.

English property law and the system of land registration, established and refined over a much longer period, are fundamentally different from their Chinese counterparts. The Land Registration Act 1925 was in operation for 77 years before being replaced by the Land Registration Act 2002. Nevertheless, there has been a steady stream of cases in recent years on a number of key issues, such as rectification of mistakes, and this continues to expose what remains unsettled or unclear despite decades of registration. The Law Commission has recently published its report on updating the 2002 Act.[3]

Notwithstanding the significant differences between the English and Chinese law and practice of registration, this chapter aims to examine some of the common problems and difficulties in both systems. Understanding the approach and theory of the more experienced English framework can be of great benefit for the new Chinese system. At the same time, the sheer number of cases and materials from China on issues such as registration mistakes or conveyancing fraud provide ample food for thought for English law on several interesting questions, such as whether the current system of registration and indemnity could withstand the potential rise of fraud in an increasingly globalised and digitised world.

[1] For consistency, the term 'land registration' is preferred to 'real estate registration' in all discussion, except in the translation of the title of Chinese legislation or registration departments.

[2] China Judgements Online, available at: http://wenshu.court.gov.cn.

[3] Law Commission, *Updating the Land Registration Act 2002* (Law Com No 380, 2018).

II. Land Registration in China

A. Unified Registration

Some forms of registration of proprietary rights in land have been operating in parts of China since the 1980s. But they were governed by a complex web of primary legislation and secondary regulations, which often overlapped or contradicted each other, while allocating the administration of registration to an array of different governmental departments at different levels.[4] The Property Law of the People's Republic of China (PRC), enacted in 2007, stated the aim of unified registration for the first time.[5] In November 2014, the State Council issued the Interim Regulations on Real Estate Registration, putting the Ministry of Land and Resources in charge of establishing unified registration across the country. Full implementation commenced in 2015, with the ambitious targets of establishing the registration system within three years and constructing a national registration information management platform in four.[6] This entails a new registration department or registry office in each of mainland China's 31 provincial-level, 335 prefecture-level and 2855 county-level governments. It also means that much of the registration information accumulated in different parts of the country over the past decades would need to be handed over to these new registration authorities, with any paper-based documents digitised and all information safely stored and uploaded onto the national information platform.

And that is exactly what China managed to achieve, ahead of schedule. The city of Xuzhou in Jiangsu, with a population of 8.7 million, issued the first unified registration certificate on 1 March 2015 as the first prefecture to implement unified registration. On 19 June 2017, Ge'gyai, Ngari in Xizang (or Tibet), population 10,000, became the last county to implement unified registration.[7] This signified the establishment of over 3000 registration departments or registry offices in every corner of the country. The Ministry of Land and Resources also reported that the registration authorities in all counties and prefectures were connected to the national information platform by the end of August 2017, with more than 200,000 registry entries being uploaded every day.[8] Towards the end of 2017, over 90 per cent of registration materials, both digital and paper-based, had been handed over to the new system of unified registration. The largest land registration system in the world, built in less than three years, is now fully operational.

[4] For a more detailed account of the status of property rights registration in China prior to the recent reform, see L Xu, 'The New Real Property Registration Structure in China: Progress with Unanswered Questions' (2016) 5(1) *Global Journal of Comparative Law* 91.

[5] Property Law of the People's Republic of China 2007, Art 10.

[6] S Wee, 'China Says Pushing for Unified Property Registration by Year-end', *Reuters* (London, 10 January 2016) available at: https://www.reuters.com/article/us-china-property/china-says-pushing-for-unified-property-registration-by-year-end-idUSKCN0UO04W20160110.

[7] 李倩, '不动产统一登记：初心不改 拾级而上' (25 August 2017): http://www.mlr.gov.cn/xwdt/xwpl/201708/t20170825_1578085.htm.

[8] 李倩 赵蕾, '全国所有市县接入国家级不动产登记信息平台' (22 September 2017): http://www.mlr.gov.cn/xwdt/jrxw/201709/t20170922_1595829.htm.

B. The Online Judgments Database

Around the same time, largely unrelated to the implementation of unified registration, the Supreme People's Court of China started to construct an online database of judgments from all levels of courts in China. This development has the potential to fundamentally change the study of Chinese law, far beyond the current context of property registration.

Chinese law does not have any system or rules of case law or precedent. Even decisions of the Supreme Court are not binding on the lower courts. Moreover, there are 3,525 courts in China.[9] Records of judgments used to be maintained by these courts separately. Though they are public documents, in practice few people would have the time and resources to locate and access them. There have been series of case reports over the years organised by various bodies, but these often take a couple of years to be published as books and cover only a very limited number of cases. Since 2012, the Supreme Court has been periodically publishing a number of 'guiding cases', which are edited reports of cases with legal significance decided by various appellate courts.[10] Still, by the end of 2017, there were only 92 guiding cases in total, spanning different areas of criminal, civil and administrative law. While leading legal scholars have been calling for some system of case law,[11] the shortage of usable cases would have been a major obstacle for those keen to look into previous decisions.

The creation of 'China Judgements Online' by the Supreme People's Court completely changed the landscape of case study in China. Cases from over 3000 courts are made available on this free online platform. A small number of these are older cases dating as far back as 1996. The vast majority of the cases now in the database are from 2014 onwards. The decisions are made available in searchable full text with minimum editing, mostly to protect privacy by redacting details such as residential addresses. Subject to such minor changes, the decisions are uploaded promptly, quite often on the same day that they are handed down.

The number of cases available is staggering. This database now contains over 42 million judgment documents, making it the largest of its kind in the world, according to the Supreme Court.[12] Some of the cases would have more than one judgment document associated with them and there are redundant entries of the same document by mistake. Nevertheless, the reality is that there are over 10 million cases reported in each of 2016 and 2017, and over 5 million cases in the first half of 2018. Moreover, 50,000 new cases are being uploaded on a typical day. Based on the number of cases available, these would still only represent about half of all cases decided in China. For example, the court system of China decided 19.77 million cases in 2016,[13] but there are only 11.48 million judgment documents dated 2016 included on the database. There is no information as to whether

[9] 周强, '最高人民法院工作报告' (9 March 2018): http://www.court.gov.cn/zixun-xiangqing-87832.html.

[10] Supreme People's Court, 'Notice of the Supreme People's Court on Issuing the Provisions on Case Guidance' (26 November 2010).

[11] eg 王利明, 民法疑难案例研究 *Research on Ambiguous Difficult Civil Cases* (Beijing, China Legal Publishing House, 2002) xvii.

[12] Supreme People's Court, '最高法院召开司法公开工作座谈会 中国裁判文书网公布裁判文书4260余万篇访问总量逾132亿次' (28 February 2018): http://www.court.gov.cn/zixun-xiangqing-82532.html.

[13] 周强, '最高人民法院工作报告' (12 March 2017): http://www.court.gov.cn/zixun-xiangqing-37852.html.

there is any selection mechanism before cases are uploaded, or whether the system is simply uploading everything that is digitally available.

Although there are very helpful functions for filtering and sorting these decisions, the amount of material available, even on clearly defined topics such as land registration, is simply overwhelming. After many years of being starved of useful case reports, practitioners and scholars are now experiencing the opposite extreme of having far too many cases to know where to start. Even a slight tweak of the keyword search, such as replacing one word with a close synonym, often produces a very different list of cases, full of surprises and new discoveries. Any discussion in the remainder of this chapter is heavily qualified by this humbling understanding that it may be impossible to give a comprehensive account of the case law on very specific issues and it is entirely foreseeable, even probable, that any examination could have missed some important development somewhere in the vast court system of China.

C. The Missing Components of Chinese Land Registration

In the tight timeframe for establishing unified registration, there was not much time to address some of the important legal principles underlying this massive structure. The system came into full operation without settling a number of issues which are arguably fundamental to its integrity and value.

One notable example of the gap in legal principles is the nature and extent of any liability on the part of the registration authority when there are errors in registration entries. This would include cases where these errors were caused or induced by fraud or misrepresentation of third parties, such as the 'transfer' of registered land to a purchaser by a fraudster impersonating the registered proprietor. For the past two decades, both before and after the enactment of the Property Law of the PRC in 2007, Chinese legal scholars argued for three different models in allocating liability:

i) where the registration authority is liable only if it acted against law or regulations in its practice, for example in processing an application without requesting all the prescribed documents;
ii) where the registration authority is liable only if it is at fault or substantially at fault for the registration errors, for example in failing to expose an obvious forgery;
iii) where the registration authority is liable regardless of fault.[14]

The Property Law of the PRC states that the registration authority should compensate for any loss caused by errors in registration, while recovering from the person responsible for causing the error afterwards.[15] This would seem to imply that compensation is available without having to establish any fault on the part of the registration authority, though it does leave the interesting and unanswered question of where the money comes from in

[14] 申惠文, 物权登记错误救济论 *Theory on Remedies for Errors in Property Registration* (Beijing, Law Press China, 2015) 187.
[15] Property Law of the PRC, Article 21.

the absence of any provision or mechanism for establishing an indemnity fund. On the other hand, the Supreme People's Court issued its judicial interpretation in 2010, finding liability only if the registration authority did not discharge its duty carefully in examining registration applications, with compensation payable only in proportion to the extent of fault of the registration authority as to the overall loss.[16] The Interim Regulations on Real Estate Registration, which started the unified registration move in 2014, simply referred to the Property Law of the PRC,[17] without clarifying any of the uncertainty caused by the ostensible inconsistency between the primary legislation and the Supreme Court's judicial interpretation. A few months later, the Ministry of Land and Resources, in charge of unified registration, issued a consultation draft of implementation rules, which re-enacted the 2010 Supreme Court's interpretation that construed compensation only on the basis of and in proportion to any fault on the part of the registration authority.[18] Yet when the final version of the Implementation Rules came out in 2016, this provision was completely dropped from its text,[19] leaving a conspicuous vacuum on this fundamental question of whether fault is required for any compensation claim against the registration authority.

Unsurprisingly, this rather interesting pendulum swing on a basic registration principle that ended with silence from the central state powers leaves the court with little reliable guidance when faced with litigation. Where registration errors were induced by third parties under comparable circumstances, the decisions to award compensation vary greatly from full compensation to no compensation as well as numerous articulations of partial compensation at a seemingly artificial percentage such as 10 per cent,[20] 30 per cent[21] and 50 per cent,[22] or an arbitrarily appointed sum awarded 'under the circumstances' without any explanation as to its calculation.[23] Some decisions refused to consider any claim for compensation as a matter of civil law and gave direction for administrative lawsuits seeking state compensation instead.[24] Yet this would largely preclude the possibility of the registration authority having to pay out compensation before recovering from third parties as envisaged by the Property Law of the PRC, due to the understanding that state compensation is only available after exhausting civil claims against third parties.[25]

[16] '最高人民法院关于审理房屋登记案件若干问题的规定' 'Rules of the Supreme People's Court on Several Problems in the Trial of Building Registration Cases' (Law Interpretation No 15 of the Supreme People's Court, 5 November 2010), Article 12.

[17] Interim Regulations on Real Estate Registration, Article 21.

[18] Ministry of Land and Resources, 不动产登记暂行条例实施细则（草案征求意见稿）'Draft Implementation Rules of Interim Regulations on Real Estate Registration', available at: http://zqyj.chinalaw.gov.cn/readmore?listType=2&id=685, Article 129.

[19] Implementation Rules of Interim Regulations on Real Estate Registration, Order 63 of the Ministry of Land and Resources, 1 January 2016.

[20] 岳西县土库生态林业发展有限公司 v 岳西县人民政府，安庆市中级人民法院，(2017)皖08行赔初6号，8 December 2017.

[21] 遵义市国土资源局 v 江秀英, 遵义市中级人民法院, (2015)遵市法行终字第263号, 6 November 2015.

[22] 周林美 v 丹阳市国土资源局, 丹阳市人民法院, (2017)苏1181行初43号, 26 June 2017.

[23] 重庆市云阳县国土资源和房屋管理局 v 冉龙全，重庆市第二中级人民法院，(2017)渝02行赔终8号，21 June 2017, which awarded a round figure of RMB 130,000 for loss calculated at RMB 590,269 (roughly 22.02%).

[24] 邹火珠 v 贺州市国土资源局，贺州市八步区人民法院，(2016)桂1102民初2214号，20 March 2017; 金石小额贷款股份有限公司 v 石柱土家族自治县国土资源和房屋管理局，重庆市第四中级人民法院，(2017)渝04民终418号，24 April 2017; 成都华新国际实业有限公司 v 乐山市沙湾区人民政府，乐山市中级人民法院, (2017)川11民终1643号, 2 November 2017.

[25] 遵义市国土资源局 v 江秀英，遵义市中级人民法院，(2015)遵市法行终字第263号，6 November 2015; 王海燕 v 济南市国土资源局, 济南市中级人民法院, (2016)鲁01行赔终10号, 30 March 2017; 刘香 v 济南市国土资源局, 济南市中级人民法院, (2017)鲁01行赔终11号, 29 November 2017.

D. Bona Fide Acquisition

In addition to the need for clearer principles on compensation, the current registration law and practice of China also heavily rely on the concept of bona fide acquisition to settle the proprietary rights of parties. The Property Law of the PRC is the source of bona fide acquisition, which allows acquisition of ownership of immovables if a transferee is in good faith, has paid a reasonable price, and has completed the registration of the transfer, even if the transferor has no right to dispose of the property.[26] This mode is broadly extended to proprietary rights other than ownership '*mutatis mutandis*'.[27]

In the current Chinese system, the completion of registration gives little in terms of additional rights or protection. If the transaction or transfer leading to the registration was subsequently rescinded for whatever reason, the registration would be seen as baseless and duly rescinded. Even if there is only a defect in an earlier transfer, all subsequent transactions and registration would be viewed as flawed and challengeable. Bona fide acquisition thus stands as the only substantive protection for the registered proprietor. On satisfaction of the test, the proprietary right acquired is no longer seen as invalid or defective. The completion of registration is an important step in establishing bona fide acquisition. At the same time, bona fide acquisition facilitates some level of confidence in the system of registration, so that not every error can come back and haunt registered rights.

Despite this pivotal role for the concept of bona fide acquisition, there is nevertheless no definition or clarification on key components such as good faith or a reasonable price. For many years academics argued about the exact meaning and requirement of such concepts.[28] This flexible and vaguely defined test unsurprisingly gave rise to much litigation and inconsistent interpretation by the courts. In 2016, the Supreme People's Court handed down its Judicial Interpretation of the Property Law of the PRC, making the effort to elaborate on the issue for the first time in almost a decade since the commencement of the statute.[29] The threshold and onus of proof are heavily in favour of a transferee claiming bona fide acquisition. If the transferee did not know that the transferor had no right of disposition and the transferee is not at substantial fault, then it shall be deemed that the transferee is in good faith. The original owner who argues that the transferee is not in good faith will have to prove it.[30] The requirement of a reasonable price is to be assessed by taking into consideration a variety of factors including the nature and quantity/volume of the subject-matter, methods of payment, market value at the time and place of the transaction, and the customs of trade.[31]

It may be observed that this long-awaited Judicial Interpretation in essence replaced one set of uncertainties with another. Although the absence of either substantial fault or proof

[26] Property Law of the PRC, Article 106.

[27] Translation by the National People's Congress: http://www.npc.gov.cn/englishnpc/Law/2009-02/20/content_1471118.htm.

[28] eg 程啸, '论不动产善意取得之构成要件 — 《中华人民共和国物权法》第106条释义' (2010/5) *ZUEL Law Journal* 74.

[29] Supreme People's Court, Judicial Interpretation 2016 No 5.

[30] ibid Article 15.

[31] ibid Article 19.

of bad faith would support a presumption of good faith, there is very little guidance on the notion of 'substantial fault'. This term was used only once in 247 articles of Property Law of the PRC, on a completely unrelated topic.[32] In the context of the transfer of immovables, the only guidance on the concept of 'substantial fault' is that if the owner can prove that the transferee ought to have known that the transferor had no right of disposition, then it shall be deemed that the transferee is at substantial fault.[33] But this is arguably a redundant rule, as the proof of such knowledge would invalidate any claim of good faith in the formulation by the Supreme People's Court already, without the need for establishing substantial fault. In any event, the law supposedly expects any challenger against bona fide acquisition to prove either knowledge of the inconsistent right or the existence of substantial fault, which seems a rather significant hurdle to clear.

Yet in practice many cases display a very different approach by the lower courts in assessing this issue from that of the binding Judicial Interpretation from the Supreme People's Court. The courts take into consideration what is expected in a typical land transaction and dislike significant departure from the norm by anyone claiming good faith. For example, it is commonly expected for the purchaser to visit the property and assess its physical and occupation status prior to the transaction. *Not* visiting the property that one is buying is typically seen as an indication of some knowledge that all is not well, and consequently fatal in claims of good faith.[34]

While the reliance on customary behaviour is uncontroversial, there are many instances of more creative ventures into what could compromise good faith. In a typical case of fraud through notarised agency,[35] a third-party fraudster arranged for someone to impersonate the registered proprietor at a notary public office, and obtained a notarised agency authorising another accomplice to dispose of the property concerned. The transferee duly completed registration of the disposition from the 'agent' and argued for bona fide acquisition when the plot was exposed. The court, however, decided that the transferee did not discharge his 'duty of careful attention', a term mentioned by neither the statute nor the Judicial Interpretation, and was not in good faith. The main reason given for such finding was that the photograph of the impersonator taken at the notary public looked rather different from the photograph on the identity document of the proprietor. The decision made no reference to the Judicial Interpretation that had come into force some nine months before,[36] nor did it explain whether not noticing the differences between a person and his identity photo constituted 'substantial fault'. Perhaps the most impressive but unsuccessful argument came from the transferee, who pointed to the fact that the impersonation fooled both the notary public and the registration authority and questioned how an ordinary citizen could have spotted the discrepancy.

The tendency to raise the threshold of what is expected from a transferee claiming bona fide acquisition is seen in many other cases. In another case of fraud through notarised agency, the court refused the claim of good faith by the transferee because the notary was

[32] Property Law of the PRC, Article 111, on the liability of the authority in safekeeping lost property under its custody.

[33] Supreme People's Court, Judicial Interpretation 2016 No 5, Article 16.

[34] 钱信儒 v 黄春涛, 南通市中级人民法院, (2015)通中民终字第02934号, 1 June 2016.

[35] 张志森 v 宋颀, 北京市朝阳区人民法院, (2016)京0105民初62504号, 21 December 2016.

[36] On 1 March 2016, in accordance with Article 22 of the Judicial Interpretation.

too far away from the property.[37] With the property in dispute located in Shanghai, the court held that the transferee should have questioned, as a matter of common sense, the authenticity of a notary's certificate of agency obtained from Henan Province. Another ground which the court picked out was that the transferee had worked as an estate agent for a number of years. She was consequently expected to demonstrate a higher level of awareness of the risks in property transactions than an ordinary member of the public. However, it was unclear how such factors could have contributed to any 'substantial fault', which the decision again ignored. If the owner of a Shanghai property is physically in Henan, it is entirely logical for a notarised agency to be given in Henan for the transaction to be carried out in Shanghai by the agent. And if a higher standard is expected from estate agents, then what about employees of land registration departments, police officers, judges, or property law professors?

In a system with no principle of case law or precedent, such a liberal and flexible approach by the court would often lead to surprising decisions, even for experienced lawyers. In another case, the transferor sold the matrimonial home behind the back of his wife whom he was in the process of divorcing.[38] The trial and appellate court both held that the transferee did not act in good faith, as he was a former colleague of the transferor and should have been aware of his marital status. This prompted the Beijing People's Procuratorate to formally appeal against the decision, triggering a retrial, which is highly unusual in a civil dispute between two private individuals. The retrial was nevertheless assigned by the Beijing High People's Court back to the Beijing Second People's Intermediate Court, which upheld its own decision.[39]

Aside from inconsistent application and controversial interpretation on the issue of bona fide acquisition, the tendency by the lower courts to rely on common sense or customary transactions also seems to set the threshold heavily in favour of some parties. Most notably, banks hold very advantageous positions when they claim bona fide acquisition as mortgagees. Unlike other purchasers mentioned above, banks are not expected to visit the property to ascertain its current use or occupancy status. The standard procedure for banks in processing post-acquisition mortgage loans normally requires the would-be mortgagor to submit a real estate valuation report compiled by a qualified appraiser. Such valuation is routinely carried out on the basis of market data of comparable property in the vicinity, without the need for a site visit. In any case, the valuation report is produced by the appraiser as an agent for the mortgagor, not the mortgagee bank. This largely prevents any defect in the valuation report or in the practice of the appraiser from implicating the good faith of the bank. In essence, the absence of any duty to make enquiry or physical inspection of the actual mortgaged property leaves the bank free to deal with a loan application on the sole basis of documents submitted by the mortgagor. If the mortgagor is a fraudster or otherwise conceals from the bank the existence of rights of third parties, the bank could simply claim bona fide acquisition. A large number of cases were thus decided in favour of banks on the grounds that there was no evidence of bad faith on the part of the bank.[40]

[37] 吴家妹 v 朱星云, 上海市第二中级人民法院, (2016)沪02民再5号, 1 July 2016.
[38] 李柔美 v 汪军, 北京市第二中级人民法院, (2009)二中民终字第02105号, 10 December 2009.
[39] 李柔美 v 汪军, 北京市第二中级人民法院, (2015)二中民再终字第06849号, 7 September 2015.
[40] eg 王荣英 v 丹阳市国土资源局, 镇江市中级人民法院, (2017)苏11行终130号, 20 November 2017; 葛月姣 v 南京市国土资源局, 南京市中级人民法院, (2017)苏01行终929号, 4 January 2018; 平安银行 v 李林, 大连市中山区人民法院, (2017)辽0202民初6256号, 8 February 2018.

Given the serious detriment to many proprietors, it seems imperative for Chinese law to at least consider how the proprietors could protect themselves from such perils. In one of the extreme cases,[41] an elderly couple in Beijing lived in their only apartment. A third party forged a notarised agency and transferred the apartment to the couple's seemingly gullible daughter and took out a loan from the bank in the name of the daughter secured against the apartment. The bank was held to have acted in good faith both at trial and on appeal, despite having never made any effort to discover that the couple were the true owners and occupied the apartment throughout these events.

E. Overview of the Chinese Position

The establishment of a massive system of unified real estate registration within three years is a remarkable achievement as well as an impressive demonstration of the power of implementation in modern Chinese law and governance. A unified platform of registration law and practice facilitated by the latest information technology is a huge step forward in the development of Chinese property law. At the same time, however, it should be recognised that under the mandate to have everything ready and operational by a tight deadline, several important legal principles were afforded neither enough attention nor sufficient time for consideration. As discussed above, when the Implementation Rules could not decide between the difficult choice of following the Property Law of the PRC or the Judicial Interpretation of the Supreme People's Court, the Ministry of Land and Resources simply omitted the relevant provision from the Rules. And when the Supreme Court had the chance to interpret the Property Law of the PRC, it merely replaced the uncertainty of good faith with the unclarified element of 'substantial fault'. It may be fair to say that no difficulty in legal principles can be satisfactorily addressed by turning away from any discussion of it.

Such hesitation or reluctance to take a clear stance on key property law principles expectedly led to serious confusion and inconsistency of the law, seen in the large number of cases from all over the country. Judges have to rely a lot on common sense and their own creativity in interpreting and applying uncertain property law principles. There are plenty of indications that the courts are very aware of the broader policy and doctrinal implications of their decisions. There are, for instance, notable references to the choice between static and dynamic security for land registration in recent decisions,[42] which has never been discussed in any legislative or governmental documents. But in the absence of a case law system and against the background that primary sources of law opt to say as little as possible about potentially controversial principles, even the most learned judicial discussion could hardly provide the clarity and certainty that the law desperately needs. Another example would be the issue of compensation for errors in registration. To borrow from the Australian Torrens terminology, the question is whether Chinese registration law prefers the 'last resort' model or the 'first resort' model.[43] At the moment, the answer by the legislator

[41] 焦平安 v 中国建设银行, 北京市第二中级人民法院, (2017)京02民终10854号, 30 November 2017.

[42] eg 陈新义 v 郭如意, 徐州市中级人民法院, (2016)苏03民终5966号, 22 September 2017; 林磊 v 王琰, 上海市奉贤区人民法院, (2017)沪0120民初19490号, 21 November 2017.

[43] P Carruthers, 'A Tangled Web Indeed: The English Land Registration Act and Comparisons with the Australian Torrens System' (2015) 38(4) *University of New South Wales Law Journal* 1261, 1267.

and central powers of Chinese law seems to be an astounding 'don't know' or 'undecided'. It would be harsh to criticise the court for giving contradictory decisions on these issues with such uncertainty looming over the system.

In some senses this uncertainty becomes more unwelcome now with the unified registration system in place across the whole country, than when there were eight or nine different registration schemes that varied greatly from province to province. Furthermore, the immense database of China Judgements Online could easily expose these problems in the current law and their very real impact on individuals expecting a reliable and efficient system of land registration. It is to be hoped that the implementation of unified registration and the making available of millions of court decisions will instil a sense of urgency on the legislative and judicial authorities of China, to tackle the difficulty and uncertainty in the current law head-on.

III. Lessons from, and for, English Land Registration

In comparison with the relatively new system of Chinese registration, English law is much more experienced and better established to deal with almost all the problems and difficulties identified above. Although there is still scope for discussion on a number of specific issues, the overall structure of the legal framework is clearly stipulated in primary legislation. On the issue of compensation, for instance, the Land Registry provides indemnity for loss suffered first, with the possibility to recover the amount paid from the responsible person.[44] The Land Registry maintains an Indemnity Fund to meet existing and potential claims.[45] In contrast and despite having the world's largest property registration system, taking in hundreds of thousands of registrations every day, China has yet to decide on whether to maintain a fund, to rely on insurance or to draw upon a general government budget for such inevitable liability.[46]

On the issue of deciding between competing claims where there is a mistake on the register, English law clearly favours the registered proprietor who is in possession. Unless the registered proprietor has by fraud or lack of proper care caused or substantially contributed to the mistake, or it would be for some other reason unjust not to change the register, the law will protect the registered proprietor and compensate the other innocent party monetarily.[47] There is no need to prove or disprove the difficult concept of good faith, which, as explained above, has caused great difficulty and inconsistency in Chinese law.

At the same time, English law strikes a balance in the protection of vulnerable parties, for example those who occupy their homes without any knowledge or understanding of what was going on in the world of registration. Property rights of a person in actual occupation will generally override registration,[48] which in turn makes it necessary for purchasers or mortgagees to ascertain if anyone actually occupies the property they are buying or lending on. The elderly couple in Beijing mentioned above would not have lost out to the

[44] Land Registration Act 2002, Sch 8, para 10.
[45] HM Land Registry, *Annual Report and Accounts 2016/17* (London, HM Land Registry, 2017) 115.
[46] See eg 陈思静 & 陈耀东, '不动产登记机构赔偿责任研究' (2015/2) *Guangxi Social Sciences* 94, 98.
[47] Land Registration Act 2002, Sch 4, paras 3(2) and 6(2).
[48] ibid Sch 3, para 2.

bank, which is expected to make the effort to discover occupiers rather than just relying on documents submitted at the behest of a fraudster.

It is important to appreciate from the outset that there are significant and wide-ranging differences between the English and Chinese systems, from the role of the state in administering a citizen identity card scheme, to the involvement of professionals such as solicitors in property transactions. Often the very different environments in which the two systems operate make the divide between them unbridgeable and this leaves any comparison lacking a comprehensive theoretical structure. Nevertheless, both systems increasingly face comparable challenges that transcend the underlying legal framework, such as the increase in sophisticated fraud which targets land registration. Despite its rather unsatisfactory foundation in legal principles, the Chinese system has accumulated considerable experience in dealing with such practical challenges in a short period of time, thanks to its scale of operation and the number and variety of incidents, which can serve as valuable lessons for its English counterpart.

A. Strengthening Identity Verification

For anyone who has examined hundreds of cases of registration fraud in China that took place in only a couple of years, it is perhaps understandable to form an impression that fraud is overwhelming the helpless system. This kind of perception could mask some of the strengths in the system, such as the role performed by an electronically verified identification system in combating fraud.

China implements a system of citizen identification cards for its population. The current generation of ID cards is embedded with a chip that stores encrypted information such as name, date of birth, a digital photo and fingerprints of the person. It is practically an everyday necessity to carry the ID card, as one needs it for bank transactions, mobile phone contracts, trains, hotels and so on. At the same time, the government authorises many ID card readers to be commercially available for use by various entities and organisations, such as government departments and banks. Although we should never underestimate the capability of hackers and fraudsters, there is almost no reported incident of someone successfully creating a fake chip to fool the system.[49] All those hundreds of fraudsters in reported cases that attempted or succeeded in defrauding land registration over the past couple of years had to rely on two different methods that did not involve the creation of a forged ID card. The first requires a fraudster to get hold of the genuine ID card of the person he is impersonating. But given the importance and everyday usage of ID cards, most people would only temporarily leave it in the hands of family and close associates when necessary.[50] Another method is for the fraudster to impersonate the victim and claim that the ID card has been lost. But this requires not only access to other safeguarded documents such as the household registration book, but also for the fraudster to be personally questioned and

[49] 蔡新正 v 临朐县国土资源局，临朐县人民法院，(2017)鲁0724行初6号，27 March 2017, was a rare case where the particular real estate registration office had no card reader equipped at the time to expose a forged ID card.

[50] eg 蒋柳柳 v 周庆中，南京市秦淮区人民法院，(2013)秦民初字第1918号，29 September 2014, where a husband asked the sister of his wife to impersonate the wife with the genuine ID card.

photographed at a police station pretending to be someone else, which is in itself a crime.[51] Consequently, the vast majority of registration fraud perpetrated in those cases was by close family and friends of the victim, or with the help of such persons who had access to ID cards or household registration books. Although that provides little emotional comfort to the victim, it makes the job of law enforcement much easier in pursuing those responsible. Hopefully the high likelihood of being caught sooner rather than later would deter would-be fraudsters, other than the most desperate or reckless.

In contrast, the current framework and practice of English law does not provide any comparable mechanism that could be safely relied upon. The wider debate of whether the UK should introduce ID cards, heard recently in the Parliament,[52] is beyond the scope of this chapter. Nevertheless, the immediate concern is that the current English system does not readily allow verification of identity and exposure of fraud by the persons primarily entrusted with such responsibility. In the commonplace fraud by an impersonator attempting to sell or mortgage the registered property, it is the solicitor acting for the 'vendor' or 'mortgagor' who has to verify the identity of the client, currently as part of the solicitor's obligations under anti-money laundering law. In its latest report, the Law Commission proposes a new statutory duty of care on professionals involved in a conveyance to take reasonable steps to identify the parties they are acting for.[53] Yet in *Purrunsing v A'Court & Co*, when the fraudster presented to the solicitor 'what appeared to be a British passport', it was accepted by all that the solicitor could not have detected that the passport was a forgery.[54] In China, any bank employee or attorney could have popped a forged ID card onto a card reader and been alerted within seconds.[55] Yet an English solicitor, who is also the only person with the opportunity to meet the fraudster and handle the forged passport, has no comparable mechanism for help. Instead the court expected the solicitor to possibly uncover the fraud by asking more questions about the fraudster's alleged employment in Dubai.[56] Between a forged British passport in hand and a foreign employer who has little incentive to respond to any enquiry from an English conveyancer, it is intriguing that the current system expects more to be uncovered from the latter than the former.

The fraud occurred in 2012 and it was unclear whether the passport was a new-style 'e-passport' or not. But even if it is a biometric passport presented today, it is unclear how the solicitor could have verified it by any method other than reading what is printed on the passport, rather than what is encrypted in the biometric chip. The Law Commission proposes enhanced powers for the Land Registry to prescribe mandatory requirements for professionals to follow in identify verification, including electronic verification, as part of discharging a proposed statutory duty of care in conveyancing transactions.[57] It is imperative

[51] eg 郑睿 v 郎涛, 上海市第一中级人民法院, (2016)沪01民终2232号, 25 April 2016; 北京市丰台区人民检察院 v 邓杰, 北京市丰台区人民法院, (2017)京0106刑初82号, 28 April 2017.

[52] HL Deb 20 July 2017, vol 783, cols 1732–34.

[53] Law Commission (n 3 above) [14.73].

[54] *Purrunsing v A'Court & Co (a firm)* [2016] EWHC 789 (Ch), [2016] 4 WLR 81, [5].

[55] 毛春 v 唐嫣华, 上海市第一中级人民法院, (2017)沪01民终字3492号, 14 June 2017. The fraudster paid for someone to forge an ID card. She was exposed the first time when she tried to use it at a bank and was duly remanded in custody after bank staff alerted the police.

[56] *Purrunsing v A'Court & Co* (n 54 above) [18].

[57] Law Commission (n 3 above) [14.89].

that law and practice should keep up with technological advances, and the latest technology should be an integral part of fraud prevention.

B. Reforming the Inadequacy of Registration Based on Name and Address

The inability to reliably identify a forged document may be more of a concern for individuals charged with the responsibility. It is even more worrying that there are instances where it would almost be impossible under current practice to tell whether anybody is the true owner in the absence of forgery. In the case of any natural person rather than a corporation, the current system of land registration identifies the registered proprietor by only two means: the full name and the address. Neither element nor their combination serves as a particularly reliable mechanism for identification, especially when targeted by fraudsters.

Different individuals can have identical names, whether due to family relations, by coincidence, or through deliberate changes. In *Rashid v Rashid*,[58] the person guilty of forgery had identical names to the true owner of the property and forged a transfer when the owner was abroad for a prolonged period. There were many complications in the case such as prior dealings between the namesakes and the owner being threatened never to return to the UK. And there was no question that the transfer was forged or as to who the true owner of the property should be. Nevertheless, while the owner was scared away and the fraudster was applying to register the transfer, could the system in place detect anything untoward? The property was owned by a Mohammed Rashid. Anyone observing could only conclude that the property is now being transferred by someone who has all the genuine documentation to prove that he is indeed Mohammed Rashid. How does the Land Registry know which Mohammed Rashid is applying for registration?

P&P Property Ltd v Owen White & Catlin LLP[59] is another illustration of the inadequacy of relying on only the name and address of a person for identification as an owner. The disputed house was registered to Clifford Harper. The solicitor for the 'vendor' met an impersonator who produced a passport in the name of Clifford Harper and up-to-date utility bills in relation to the property, addressed to Clifford Harper. At trial, it was alleged that the person in the passport photograph looked younger than his date of birth would suggest. A further point was raised that if that was the proprietor Clifford Harper, then he would have acquired an expensive West London estate at the age of 23, which should have alerted the solicitor.[60] The practical question is, provided the solicitor was meeting someone called Clifford Harper, would the solicitor be able to find out how old the proprietor Harper should be? Could even the Land Registry readily tell between the two Harpers? Similarly to the decision of *Purrunsing*, the judge also felt that the solicitor should have asked more questions about the alleged residence and work of the fraudster

[58] *Rashid v Rashid* [2017] UKUT 332 (TCC).

[59] *P&P Property Ltd v Owen White & Catlin LLP* [2016] EWHC 2276 (Ch), [2016] Bus LR 1337, which was overturned in part on appeal *P&P Property Ltd v Owen White & Catlin LLP* [2018] EWCA Civ 1082, [2018] Lloyd's Rep FC 445. The case is mentioned by Dame Elizabeth Gloster in her keynote address: see Chapter 1 of this volume.

[60] ibid (HC) [263].

(coincidentally also in Dubai), as these questions could possibly have revealed the true position or discouraged the fraudster.[61] This point will be revisited below in relation to the risk for fraudsters.

Perhaps the highlight of these doppelganger scenarios came in *Bakrania v Souris*.[62] The North London house in dispute was registered to Vallabh, Hansa and Jayanti Bakrania, three siblings from Kenya. The house was unoccupied and in a state of disrepair for several years with all the owners living in Kenya. Then a married couple, Vallabh and Hansa Bakrania arrived at the property and started to market the house. They also had a Kenyan death certificate for Jayanti Bakrania. The sale went through and the purchasers duly registered as the proprietors. The siblings learned of what happened later and applied for the register to be rectified to restore their proprietorship. This was rejected by the First-Tier Tribunal as the purchasers were already in possession and had not caused or substantially contributed to the mistake by fraud or lack of proper care, and it would not be unjust not to rectify for any other reason. Although there was little difficulty in the application of legal principles, the practical question is whether anyone within the registration and conveyancing system could have discovered such fraud before it succeeded. The fraudsters Vallabh and Hansa Bakrania apparently used their real names, so would have passed any identity check. They were husband and wife rather than brother and sister, but the Land Registry held no relevant information anyway. They were much younger than the siblings, but again the system did not reveal that. Finally, it would seem feasible to find a genuine death certificate of someone called 'Jayanti Bakrania' from all over Kenya with a population of 48 million. Even with hindsight, such fraud appears almost undetectable and unavoidable in the current system.

All these cases expose some or other systemic vulnerability in the current land registration structure for England and Wales due to its dependency on names and addresses of the proprietor. The thinking underlying some of the rules and practice is plainly outdated. Utility bills, for example, are still heavily relied upon as proof of address and would form an essential part of the checks against fraud. Yet many service providers, such as energy suppliers, have long switched to electronic bills delivered as PDF documents, which are easy to tamper with. Even when a postal bill is requested by the customer, many suppliers simply print out the PDF and post it. How would conveyancers be able to tell whether the utility bill they are presented with as proof of address came from the printer of the client/fraudster, or the printer of one of more than 60 energy suppliers, half of which did not even exist three years ago?[63]

Yet there could be some simple and efficient method to close most of the loopholes. The Registry could retain key information about applicants and registered proprietors without necessarily publishing such information on the register. The registration system in China only shows the name of the proprietor on any registration certificate it issues. This would have created huge problems, as namesakes are extremely common in China thanks to its population size as well as naming conventions. It is estimated that more than one million people could share some of the common full names. But Chinese registration keeps

[61] ibid [278].

[62] *Bakrania v Souris* [2017] UKFTT 0364.

[63] OFGEM, 'Number of Active Domestic Suppliers by Fuel Type' (2018): https://www.ofgem.gov.uk/data-portal/number-active-domestic-suppliers-fuel-type-gb.

much more up its sleeves than what it shows on public records. Chinese registration rules require the registration authority to record not only the outcome of registration, but also the 'original materials' for registration applications, including identification of applicants and proprietors.[64] When someone applies to deal with the registered property next time, their identity is routinely compared with the archived original identification. It is highly unlikely anyone would succeed in impersonating a proprietor on the sole basis of having the same name.

And that would be a realistic leaf that the English system could take out of the book of Chinese registration practice. A background record of the date of birth of the registered proprietor, for example, would effectively eliminate 99 per cent of the possible name-based fraud, without compromising the privacy of registered proprietors. Addresses change often and are frequently shared with multiple parties, such as tenants or fraudsters who take out short leases to gain access in preparation of fraud. Names can be changed, sometimes with sinister motives. But how feasible is it for anyone to apply to change his or her date of birth? Considering the potential benefit the recording of such crucial information could offer in combating fraud and preventing mistakes on the register, arguably it is irresponsible for the current system to not keep a record of it. The latest Law Commission report makes no recommendation of such a nature, but it is never too late to consider any effective and practical improvement to the current system.

C. Transferring Risks from the System to the Fraudster

The English system is carefully designed on the basis of sound legal principles. Most notably in this context, the insurance principle first identified by Ruoff is still of fundamental importance for the current structure of land registration. The indemnity offered by the Land Registry, funded by the fees paid on applications for registration, is a matter of first recourse for parties who suffer loss in cases of fraudulent registration.[65] Under the Law Commission's proposal, even if the conveyancers involved acted in breach of their statutory duty of care, this would not affect the indemnity claim by the parties against the Land Registry, but the Land Registry would be able to claim against the conveyancers.[66]

The creativity of fraudsters should not be underestimated. In *Nationwide Building Society v Davisons Solicitors*,[67] the fraudsters managed to fabricate a new branch of an established solicitors' firm on the website maintained by the Law Society and the Solicitors Regulation Authority. Sloan and Hudson, in their contribution to this volume, highlight the vulnerability of registered titles after the death of the proprietors, especially where many executors or personal representatives often choose not to take the title themselves, leaving fraudsters many months to impersonate the deceased and dispose of the properties.[68] There is no reason to think that fraudsters would need to wait for death as an opportunity to strike. If one can 'bring back' a dead person to life through forgery, why not forge the death certificate

[64] Implementation Rules of Interim Regulations on Real Estate Registration, Art 94.

[65] *Patel v Freddy's Ltd* [2017] EWHC 73 (Ch), [76].

[66] Law Commission (n 3 above) [14.89].

[67] *Nationwide Building Society v Davisons Solicitors (a firm)* [2012] EWCA Civ 1626, [2013] 3 Costs LO 464.

[68] B Sloan and S Hudson, 'Death, Lies and Land Registration', Chapter 16 in this volume.

of a person alive where there is advantage to be had? There were, for instance, three separate cases within two months in Beijing involving the forgery of multiple documents corroborating the death of registered proprietors, as well as a waiver from potential successors to obtain registration in favour of the fraudsters.[69] Some of the forgeries were so impressively thorough that in addition to the usual death certificates and notarisation documents, there were even certificates of cremation of the registered proprietors! If practitioners in England and Wales are typically unable to expose forged British passports, it would seem legitimate to question how they would be able to guard against such sophisticated fraud involving multiple systems of personal identity and records.

In this regard the Land Registry certainly deserves credit for being increasingly vigilant against the risk of fraud. In *Dreamvar (UK) Ltd v Mischon De Reya*,[70] for example, the fraudster-vendor fooled his solicitors and the purchasers but the Land Registry asked for additional checks before registration, which quickly exposed the fraud through successfully reaching the true registered proprietor. In other cases, the Registry could simply get lucky and avoid any liability through events beyond its control, such as in *P&P Property*, mentioned above, where the true owner happened to visit the vacant property subject to the fraud and noticed builders instructed by the purchasers working on it. There is certainly 'an element of serendipity' identified by the Law Commission in whether fraud is exposed before or after registration.[71]

Even if fraud is discovered before registration, negating any liability on the Land Registry, it is hardly a victory for the system, as a fraudster purporting to be a vendor of the registered title would still have disappeared with the money on completion of the transaction. The question then is who should bear the loss in the absence of an indemnity from the Land Registry. At the moment, English law seems to favour liability on the defrauded purchaser's solicitor on the basis of breach of trust, often independent of any wrongdoing.[72] The rationale for such finding is that the solicitor held the purchase money on trust for the purchaser to pay out only on a genuine completion. Any completion with a fraudster who impersonates the vendor is only 'pretended completion',[73] and paying out under such pretended completion constitutes a breach of trust.[74] Although the solicitor may apply for relief from any liability under section 61 of Trustee Act 1925, this is at the discretion of the court. In *Dreamvar*, for example, the judge took the view that the solicitors were adequately insured and would be better placed financially to absorb the loss caused by the fraud than the purchaser, and refused relief, even if the solicitors acted both honestly and reasonably.[75]

[69] 赵惠兰 v 北京市规划和国土资源管理委员会, 北京市西城区人民法院, (2017)京0102行初460号, 26 June 2017; 彭政明 v 北京市规划和国土资源管理委员会, 北京市昌平区人民法院, (2017)京0114行初54号, 30 June 2017; 胡庆 v 北京市规划和国土资源管理委员会, 北京市丰台区人民法院, (2017)京0106行初218号, 25 July 2017.

[70] *Dreamvar (UK) Ltd v Mischon De Reya (a firm)* [2016] EWHC 3316 (Ch), [39]. The case was overturned in part by *Dreamvar (UK) Ltd v Mischon De Reya* [2018] EWCA Civ 1082, [2018] Lloyd's Rep FC 445.

[71] Law Commission, *Updating the Land Registration Act 2002: A Consultation Paper* (Law Com CP No 227, 2016) [14.9].

[72] *Nationwide Building Society v Davisons Solicitors* [2012] EWCA Civ 1626, [2013] 3 Costs LO 464; *Dreamvar (UK) Ltd v Mischon De Reya* (n 70 above (HC)).

[73] As termed by Briggs LJ in *Santander UK Plc v RA Legal Solicitors* [2014] EWCA Civ 183, [2014] Lloyd's Rep FC 282.

[74] See n 70 above (HC) [95].

[75] ibid [182]–[188].

On appeal, Lady Justice Gloster disagreed with such contemplation that the court should exercise its discretion on the basis of which commercial parties have insurance, but this was overruled by the majority.[76] In any case, the fraudster won and disappeared with the money, so someone will have to lose, be it the Land Registry or the conveyancer. Being honest and diligent does not protect either of them from such fraud.

This stands in sharp contrast to the risk faced by the fraudster. In most of these registration fraud cases, the fraudster hardly ever appears in person and mostly moves everything forward with emails and phone calls. Even if the fraud is exposed at this stage, it will be incredibly difficult to track down an individual hiding behind telecommunication and a forged identity. The riskiest activity for a fraudster would be visiting the solicitor's office for identity verification. This is the only occasion that the fraudster appears in person, perhaps with highly incriminating evidence such as forged passports and documents. Nevertheless, as discussed above, the solicitors or paralegals handling the process crucially have no technical capability to detect the fraud at that preciously short meeting. Once that window has passed, the fraudster will again disappear into the void of the online world, pulling the strings with email instructions. There is often very little evidence to assist in finding the suspect after the crime is committed. In *P&P Property*, for example, the police even suggested it would be better not to freeze the remainder of the money already wired to an account in Dubai so that they could investigate the case.[77] The judge in *Bakrania* summed up the common situation, where the fraudsters seemingly travelled to Dubai, India, Australia and Singapore as: '[i]n short, the fraudsters have gone, as has the money'.[78] And the system pays for the consequences, whether through the Land Registry or some innocent conveyancers.

In this regard, the practice of the Chinese system could potentially tip the balance of risk between the system and fraudsters. The process for identity verification, whether at the real estate registration office or a notary public's office, is routinely recorded on camera.[79] An impersonator will have a high definition front photo taken that will go straight to the police when the fraud is discovered. Leaving aside the potential use of a digital photo in combating crime with the help of facial recognition surveillance technology, it seems likely that the knowledge that graphic evidence will be recorded while a crime is being committed would be a strong deterrent to would-be fraudsters. The availability of such evidence will also help the victims in raising a claim, as it would be immediately apparent that fraud has taken place without the need to go through processes such as handwriting analysis.[80] Moreover, if the person photographed is noticeably different from the photo of the identity document presented, this could be a ground to find that the person carrying out the verification process was not doing the job properly and so is potentially liable in upcoming claims.[81]

[76] See n 70 above (CA) [125].

[77] See n 59 (HC) [64].

[78] See n 62 above [50].

[79] 全林正 v 延吉市房产局, 延吉市人民法院, (2016)吉2401行初67号, 12 July 2016; 徐富英 v 北京市规划和国土资源管理委员会, 北京市第三中级人民法院, (2017)京03行终755号, 28 December 2017.

[80] 李梅英 v 江门市不动产登记局, 江门市中级人民法院, (2017)粤07行终138号, 28 December 2017. On the other hand, a dishonest person cannot simply challenge a disposition on the grounds of questionable signature if there was a video recording of himself submitting the documents, eg 司宇智 v 大连市国土资源和房屋局, 大连市中级人民法院, (2017)辽02行终351号, 23 July 2017.

[81] *cf P&P Property* (n 59 above) [263] where there is only a photocopy of the passport available to the court.

With these obvious advantages that a simple photograph would offer, taking a photograph and storing it digitally for a prescribed period should be one of the mandatory steps required by the Land Registry in identity verification, when it receives the enhanced powers recommended by the Law Commission.[82] Such a change will have minimal impact on practice, since most solicitors can afford digital cameras, but it will start to redress the current imbalance between the risk borne by the system and the risk faced by the fraudster. There are far more technically advanced possibilities on the horizon, such as the use of blockchain encryption in land registration alluded to by Dame Elizabeth Gloster in her contribution to this volume.[83] But English law and practice could certainly demonstrate its willingness to use technology by starting from something as simple as taking photos.

As things stand, English land registration sets out a principled and well-designed system so that parties can deal with registered land efficiently and confidently. Nevertheless, when faced with the increasingly serious problem of fraud, this legal framework is often let down by out-of-date practice and becomes nothing more than a target for exploitation. The system expects solicitors to uncover forged identity, but it does not give them the technical capability to perform the important task that safeguards the whole conveyancing structure behind it. The system relies on information that can be manipulated such as names and addresses and inexplicably ignores reliable constants such as the date of birth. Its perception of what proves the address of an individual shows no appreciation as to how people or banks actually manage bank statements nowadays. The innocent purchasers and their conveyancers, as well as the Land Registry, have much to lose under current practice. A fraudster walks into a solicitor's office with a complete set of lies and is allowed to disappear forever without any genuine record of this person being taken. Overall, the system and these practices have yet to arrive in the twenty-first century, whereas fraudsters certainly have gone digital and global in their operations.

IV. Conclusion

It is perhaps fair to say that the Chinese system of unified real estate registration was hurried along by the administration. There was little time to address the uncertainty and difficult policy decisions in the system before the set deadline of implementation. Unsurprisingly a large number of cases streamed into the courts, which had to work on the basis of equivocal or even contradictory guidance from legislators and the Supreme Court. The system calls for clearer principles on issues such as the expectation of purchasers' diligence or the availability of indemnity provided by the registration authority, where there is much to be learnt from English law. Notwithstanding these difficulties with basic legal principles, the practice of Chinese registration is often impressive in some regards, such as its efficiency and use of technology.

[82] See above text at n 57.

[83] Dame Elizabeth Gloster, 'Property Law and Technology: Putting You on Notice' Chapter 1 in this volume.

The English system of land registration is much more experienced and more established with the accumulated wisdom and knowhow of over a century. Nevertheless, the practice of registration is sometimes hindered by weakness or defects in the system, whether due to its original design, or the fact that it has not adapted quickly enough to social and technological changes. There are very practical measures that English land registration can consider by looking at the newer, bigger, busier and technologically adventurous Chinese system. The Land Registry should record more information, away from the public register if appropriate, including things such as proprietors' date of birth. Professionals who carry out identity verification should have, and be required to use, the appropriate technology, such as electronic verification and the opportunity to take photographs of the person being identified. With these practical improvements, English land registration can take full advantage of the upcoming updating of the law recently proposed by the Law Commission and will continue to thrive in a modern world full of both challenges and opportunities.

16

Death, Lies, and Land Registration

SIÔN HUDSON AND BRIAN SLOAN

I. Introduction

Real property is the most valuable and potentially contentious property owned by many people at the point of death.[1] The recent debate surrounding the so-called 'dementia tax' highlights the significance of the family home from an inheritance perspective,[2] as does as the emphasis on the importance of passing it on under the new residence nil rate band legislation for inheritance tax purposes.[3] More immediately, land formerly (co-)owned by a deceased person may already be a home for surviving family members.[4] This may create some tensions between testamentary freedom on the one hand, and the notion of 'dynamic' security for the protection of purchasers prioritised by the land registration system on the other.

This chapter analyses the law on dealings with registered land after a registered proprietor has died, alongside relevant Land Registry practice, identifying several potential conceptual and practical problems in the area. Section II discusses the tension between the basic conclusiveness of the register under the Land Registration Act 2002 and the logical impossibility of the dead owning property, the possibility that registered title will not devolve onto personal representatives and the associated risks of fraud. Section III highlights the particular difficulties related to (previous) co-ownership and the position of surviving trustees in light of the personal representative's duty to retain control of estate property until it is distributed to genuinely intended (or mandated) beneficiaries.

The chapter considers whether law and practice are fit for purpose from the perspective of the interests of the now-deceased person, surviving co-owners, estate beneficiaries, personal representatives, practitioners and their professional indemnity insurers, as well as considering the objectives of land registration, including by comparing the treatment of registered land with that of other forms of significant property owned by now-deceased

[1] See, eg, B Sloan, *Borkowski's Law of Succession*, 3rd edn (Oxford, Oxford University Press, 2017) 9.

[2] See, eg, B Sloan, '"Disregards", Deferred Payment Agreements and the "Dementia Tax"' (*UK Care Guide Blog*, 12 September 2017) available at: https://ukcareguide.co.uk/disregards-deferred-payment-agreements-dementia-tax/; B Sloan, 'Charges for Charges: Home Sales under the Care Act 2014' in H Conway and R Hickey (eds), *Modern Studies in Property Law*, vol 9 (Oxford, Hart Publishing, 2017).

[3] Inheritance Tax Act 1984, s 8D. See, eg, J Brook, 'Testamentary Freedom – Myth or Reality?' [2018] *Conv* 19.

[4] See, eg, G Morrell, M Barnard and R Legard, *The Law of Intestate Succession: Exploring Attitudes among Non-traditional Families: Final Report* (London, National Centre for Social Research, 2009) 26.

persons. Section IV makes several tentative suggestions for reform in light of the conceptual difficulties relating to the accuracy of the land register, risks of fraud and threats to testamentary freedom identified.

II. Dealings with Registered Title Following the Death of a Registered Proprietor

A. The Dead Owning Property and the Conclusiveness of the Register

This subsection highlights the conceptual inconsistency between the impossibility of the dead owning property and the basic conclusiveness of the land register.

Blackstone wrote that 'the instant a man ceases to be, he ceases to have any dominion'.[5] It is a matter of logic that a dead person cannot own property, as distinct from her (qualified)[6] ability to direct what happens to her property on death by making a will while still alive.[7] Nevertheless, a recently deceased person may still be the registered proprietor of land, and the appearance of her name in the register is treated as conclusive proof that she is the landowner.[8] Conceptually, neither the basic conclusiveness of the land register, nor the principle of 'title by registration',[9] nor the existence of statutory owner's powers[10] can alter the logical fact that the dead cannot own property. This is true notwithstanding the fact that a major purpose of the Land Registration Act 2002 is to ensure that the land register 'provides a decisive attribution of proprietorship' such that '[e]state owners are conclusively identified on the face of an authoritative public record'.[11] The idea is that 'titles … derive from the register itself, rather than from the external rules of general property law',[12] such that the Land Registrar possesses a 'metaphorical "Midas Touch"'.[13] This conceptual inconsistency contributes to what Goymour has called the 'myth' of 'title by registration'.[14]

When a person dies, her property will devolve onto her personal representative(s) under the Administration of Estates Act 1925,[15] executors in the case of testate succession and

[5] W Blackstone, *Commentaries on the Laws of England* (1765–69), Book II, ch 1, 10. *cf*, eg, R Paisley, 'The Effect of Death in the Context of the Law of Succession' (Queen's University Belfast School of Law Seminar, Belfast, 1 March 2013) available at: https://www.youtube.com/watch?v=7EVDRsqxHcE.

[6] See, in particular, the Inheritance (Provision for Family and Dependants) Act 1975.

[7] See also R Probert, 'Disquieting Thoughts: Who Will Benefit When We Are Gone?' in B Häcker and C Mitchell (eds), *Current Issues in Succession Law* (Oxford, Hart Publishing, 2016) 31.

[8] Land Registration Act 2002, s 58.

[9] HM Land Registry and Law Commission, *Land Registration for the Twenty-First Century: A Conveyancing Revolution* (Law Com No 254, 1998) [10.43].

[10] Land Registration Act 2002, s 23; *cf* s 24(b); see, generally, S Watterson and A Goymour, 'A Tale of Three Promises: (3) The Empowerment Promise' in A Goymour, S Watterson and M Dixon (eds), *New Perspectives on Land Registration: Contemporary Problems and Solutions* (Oxford, Hart Publishing, 2018).

[11] K Gray and SF Gray, *Elements of Land Law*, 5th edn (Oxford, Oxford University Press, 2009) [2.2.5].

[12] A Goymour, 'Mistaken Registrations of Land: Exploding the Myth of "Title by Registration"' (2013) 72 *CLJ* 617, 618.

[13] Watterson and Goymour (n 10 above) 282.

[14] Goymour (n 12 above) See also, eg, Scottish Law Commission, *Discussion Paper on Land Registration: Void and Voidable Titles* (Discussion Paper No 125, 2004) [2.14].

[15] Administration of Estates Act 1925, ss 1–2.

administrator(s) in the case of (broadly) intestate succession.[16] Such property in principle includes real property, although the relevant property should be considered the *estate* in land since a concept of *dominium* over land has historically been 'alien' to English Law.[17]

There is, however, a difficulty in the case of registered land with the notions that a dead person cannot own property and that legal title to her assets vests in her personal representatives. The difficulty essentially relates to the authority of the register. The basic conclusiveness of the register at any given time does not of course mean that it is static. A major purpose of the system is precisely to aid the *transfer* of land, even if full electronic conveyancing (allowing simultaneous completion and registration) looks unlikely to materialise in the near future.[18] The legislation has been described as 'very clearly "transaction driven"',[19] and it has been said that 'registration of title is the cornerstone of land marketability'.[20] Therefore, the 2002 Act allows for alteration of the register for the purposes of 'correcting a mistake', 'bringing the register up to date', 'giving effect to any estate, right or interest excepted from the effect of registration', or 'removing a superfluous entry',[21] with rectification being a more tightly controlled form of alteration that 'involves the correction of a mistake' and 'prejudicially affects the title of a registered proprietor'.[22] The notion of 'bringing the register up to date' in the context of the death of a registered proprietor would clearly derive its authority from the general law contained in the Administration of Estates Act 1925.

In the absence of full electronic conveyancing, there will inevitably be a point in time with any transfer of land where the transferee has a right to be registered under the general law but has not yet been entered as the proprietor (and the transferor remains as such). In inter vivos situations, this 'registration gap' produces the difficulty that, as a matter of land registration law, the transferee remains vulnerable to rights created by the transferor before that transferor is removed,[23] although in a transactional context this vulnerability is tempered by the protection of an Official Search with Priority in favour of the transferee.[24] Admittedly, the creation of interests during the registration gap is not an option for a deceased person herself, which in some respects makes the succession context less problematic than the inter vivos one.

Despite the conceptual difficulties referred to above, the deceased person will remain on the register as the registered proprietor unless and until removed via alteration,[25]

[16] The vesting in the case of the executor occurs at the moment of death (rather than the grant of probate), while for an administrator this does not occur until the grant of letters of administration. In the interim, the estate of an intestate will vest in the Public Trustee, who has a limited role in respect of the property: JR Martin and N Caddick (eds), *Williams, Mortimer & Sunnucks – Executors, Administrators and Probate*, 20th edn (London, Sweet & Maxwell, 2013) [41-01]–[41-08].

[17] Gray and Gray (n 11 above) [2.2.7].

[18] See, eg, Law Commission, *Updating the Land Registration Act 2002: A Consultation Paper* (Consultation Paper No 227, 2016) ch 20.

[19] M Dixon, 'The Reform of Property Law and the Land Registration Act 2002: A Risk Assessment' [2003] *Conv* 136, 136.

[20] S Cooper, 'Resolving Title Conflicts in Registered Land' (2015) 131 *LQR* 108, 108.

[21] Land Registration Act 2002, s 65, sch 4, paras 2 and 5.

[22] Land Registration Act 2002, sch 4, para 1.

[23] *Stodday Land Ltd v Pye* [2016] EWHC 2454 (Ch), [2016] 4 WLR 168.

[24] Land Registration Act 2002, s 70.

[25] See, eg, *Barclays Bank PLC v Guy* [2008] EWCA Civ 452, [2008] 2 EGLR 74 [9] (Lloyd LJ).

and a personal representative cannot be registered as the proprietor without a grant of probate or letters of administration or a court order appointing the applicant as a personal representative.[26] It is significant that it can take some time before a grant of representation is obtained after death (albeit that the process is generally quick once an application has been made),[27] and in 2015 it was said in particular that '[i]ntestate estates can be very slow to be dealt with and there may be some … estates [relating to deaths after 1995] still unadministered'.[28] This creates particular conceptual difficulties since, unlike in inter vivos conveyancing, it is not merely that the (deceased) former owner *ought* no longer to be recognised as the legal owner and registered proprietor, but that she *cannot* be the legal owner under the general law and therefore cannot logically be the registered proprietor either.

To add to the conceptual difficulties and tensions, as the Land Registry explains in its Practice Guide on death:

> The personal representative(s) of a deceased sole proprietor of the registered estate, or of a charge or mortgage may, without first being registered themselves in that capacity, deal with that registered estate or charge. They may do this by way of a transfer, or a transfer by way of an assent or appropriation using the appropriate form in either case.[29]

Where this occurs, the personal representative must still produce the same evidence of his entitlement to dispose of the property as if he had been registered,[30] such that he cannot deal with registered land until the grant of probate or letters of administration. In any event, registered title to the land might not therefore ever be transferred into the names of the personal representatives (such a course of action potentially being considered to involve unnecessary complication and cost), even though the Land Registry's own Practice Guide states that 'the legal estate vests in the personal representatives on the death of the sole proprietor',[31] although admittedly the Act extends owner's powers to those who are 'entitled to be registered as the proprietor' as well as those who are actually so registered.[32] A 'transfer on the death … of an individual proprietor' is specifically excluded from the list of dispositions that are *required* to be registered (somewhat misleadingly described as registr*able* dispositions),[33] such that the 'disposition will operate at law immediately'.[34] Where title is voluntarily transferred to a personal representative, however, the registrar must add 'executor or executrix (or administrator or administratrix) of [name] deceased' to the register entry.[35]

[26] Land Registration Rules 2003, SI 2003/1417, r 163(1)–(2).

[27] See, eg, G Owen, 'How Long Does it Take to Issue a Grant of Representation?', *Today's Wills & Probate* (31 March 2017), available at: www.todayswillsandprobate.co.uk/news/grant-representation-time-taken/.

[28] C Sawyer and M Spero, *Succession, Wills and Probate*, 3rd edn (Abingdon, Routledge, 2015) 167.

[29] HM Land Registry, 'Practice Guide 6: Devolution on the Death of a Registered Proprietor', available at: https://www.gov.uk/government/publications/devolution-on-the-death-of-a-registered-proprietor/practice-guide-6-devolution-on-the-death-of-a-registered-proprietor [2.2].

[30] Land Registration Rules 2003, SI 2003/1417, r 162(1).

[31] Land Registry (n 29 above) [6]. See also *Williams, Mortimer & Sunnucks* (n 16 above) [46-03]; *Ijacic (executor of the estate of Tripkovic) v Game Developments Ltd* [2009] EWLandRA 2008_1081, [2009] EWLandRA 2008_1083 [2] (Deputy Adjudicator Simon Brilliant).

[32] Land Registration Act 2002, s 24(b).

[33] Land Registration Act 2002, s 27(5)(a).

[34] *Helman v John Lyon Free Grammar School Keepers and Governors* [2014] EWCA Civ 17, [2014] 1 WLR 2451 [21] (Rimer LJ).

[35] Land Registration Rules 2003, SI 2003/1417, r 163(4).

Significantly, the Land Registration Rules specifically provide that:

> The registrar shall not be under a duty to investigate the reasons a transfer of registered land by a personal representative of a deceased sole proprietor or last surviving joint proprietor is made nor to consider the contents of the will and, provided the terms of any restriction on the register are complied with, he must assume, whether he knows of the terms of the will or not, that the personal representative is acting correctly and within his powers.[36]

This picture, including the possible delays in obtaining a grant, creates conceptual difficulties which detract from the internal coherence of the law. It also produces a risk of fraud in light of information easily obtainable about a deceased person.[37]

B. The Risk of Fraud

The situation described in the last subsection creates a possibility that a fraudster could impersonate the deceased person, and transfer the property to a purchaser or mortgage the property to a lender who is unaware of the death.[38] The Land Registry has said that '[i]n most instances of fraud it is the purported disponor, rather than the applicant [for registration], who acts fraudulently'.[39] If such impersonation is possible in the context of a person who is still alive,[40] with one commentator describing it as 'astonishingly simple',[41] it may be all the easier on death. Even if the purchaser (or a chargee) takes the trouble to inspect the property (as may now be expected in order to secure a full indemnity)[42] there may be no-one with a proprietary interest in discoverable actual occupation for the purposes of schedule 3, paragraph 2 of the Land Registration Act 2002. It follows that the purchaser may take free of any legitimate interests of those whom the deceased left behind because the interests do not override.[43] This constitutes a significant interference with the deceased's testamentary freedom.

The theft of a deceased person's identity (or 'ghosting') is 'made possible by a lag between the decedent's death and the date that financial institutions, agencies … and credit-reporting bureaus update their databases'.[44] Identity theft is said to be 'more likely' in situations such as 'where a relationship breaks down', 'where a property is empty or is bought

[36] ibid, r 162(2).

[37] S Kirchheimer, 'Protecting the Dead From Identity Theft', *AARP Bulletin* (2013), available at: www.aarp.org/money/scams-fraud/info-03-2013/protecting-the-dead-from-identity-theft.html.

[38] See, eg, *Ijacic v Game Developments* (n 31 above), considered in detail below.

[39] HM Land Registry, 'Practice Guide 67: Evidence of Identity; Conveyancers', available at: https://www.gov.uk/government/publications/evidence-of-identity-conveyancers/practice-guide-67-evidence-of-identity-conveyancers [2]. See further L Xu, 'Updating Land Registration Law and Practice: Some Lessons From China' Chapter 15 in this volume.

[40] See, eg, *Swift 1st Ltd v Chief Land Registrar* [2015] EWCA Civ 330, [2015] Ch 602.

[41] S Evans, 'Was Privacy in Land Ownership Such a Bad Thing?' [2017] *Conv* 357, 358.

[42] J Pownall and R Hill, 'The Land Registry's Perspective: The Practical Challenges of Land Registration' in Goymour (n 10 above) 13.

[43] Land Registration Act 2002, s 29.

[44] H Davidson, 'Aftermath of the Fight Over Fiduciary Access to Digital Assets: The Revised UFADAA and its Implications for Legislators and Professional Advisors' (2017) 7 *Tax Development Journal* 58, 61.

to let', 'where the owner is abroad or absent', and 'where the owner is infirm or in a home'.[45] A situation where a sole registered proprietor has died has something in common with each of these.

If the 'vendor' in these circumstances is represented by a conveyancer, the purchaser is unlikely to take independent steps to verify the vendor's identity,[46] and the vendor's conveyancer's standard identity checks[47] may be ineffective if the conveyancer has been duped because the fraudster has the same name (potentially having changed it by deed poll)[48] as the deceased and claims that (for example) the property being sold was previously rented out, or simply produces to the conveyancer forged identification documents in the name of the deceased.[49] There are of course occasions where the conveyancer him/herself is a party to the fraud, or may inaccurately *appear* to be such a party because it is an increasingly common tactic for legitimate law firms to be impersonated by the fraudster, making clever use of headed notepaper and subtle differences in an email address.[50]

A fraudster could also simply transfer the land to himself or an associate for no consideration. The Land Registry will make some attempt to verify identity if a party to the transaction is unrepresented via its ID1 form, involving verification by a solicitor or similar.[51] That said, however well-versed a busy high-street solicitor may be in taking copies of a person's identification documents, solicitors are not trained to be forgery experts. The unconnected solicitor completing the ID1 form on behalf of an entirely unknown person who walks in apparently possessing all the correct documents can do no more than make the declaration on the ID1 that the person is a true likeness to their photograph, and that they have produced the required documents.[52] It is also, of course, easy for the fraudster simply to impersonate a legitimate solicitor or conveyancer on the ID1. The risk of fraud therefore remains, and the Law Society claims that '[r]ecorded incidents of fraud are rising' in relation to real property.[53] Even though the Land Registry apparently 'prevented frauds on properties valued in excess of £92 million' between September 2009 and mid-January 2017, it accepts that 'no system can be 100 per cent fraud-proof'[54] and this will

[45] HM Land Registry, 'Public Guide 17: How to Safeguard against Property Fraud' (2008) 1; see now HM Land Registry and Law Society, 'Property and Title Fraud' (2017) 2.

[46] See, eg, S Cooper, 'Seller Fraud and Conveyancers' Liabilities' [2017] *Conv* 325, 325; S Cooper, 'Lack of Proper Care' in Goymour et al (n 10 above) 193.

[47] Legal Sector Affinity Group, 'Anti-Money Laundering Guidance for the Legal Sector' (2018).

[48] HM Land Registry and Law Society (n 45 above) 3; Law Commission (n 18 above) [14.94].

[49] In light of the Money Laundering, Terrorist Financing and Transfer of Funds (Information on the Payer) Regulations 2017, SI 692/2017, r 33(5), it is becoming increasingly common in practice to undertake an additional online identity check with a specialist agency in order to corroborate the identification documents produced, a trend which is certainly welcome.

[50] HM Land Registry and Law Society (n 45 above) [2.1].

[51] HM Land Registry, 'Form: Verify Identity: Citizen (ID1)', available at: www.gov.uk/government/publications/verify-identity-citizen-id1. See further SR Coveney et al, *Ruoff and Roper: Registered Conveyancing* (London, Sweet & Maxwell, 2017) [24.001.02].

[52] Indeed, it is surely true that solicitors or conveyancers are no more qualified to verify somebody's identity documents than any other person: yet the social status of the solicitor gives a false perception of credibility to the documents and the person whose identity is being verified.

[53] Law Society and HM Land Registry, 'Joint Property and Title Fraud Advice Note' (2017) available at: www.lawsociety.org.uk/policy-campaigns/articles/property-and-title-fraud-advice-note/. See, generally, *P&P Property Ltd v Owen White & Catlin LLP* [2018] EWCA Civ 1082, [2018] Lloyd's Rep FC 445.

[54] J Prasad, 'High-Profile Case Shows how Property Fraud Can Happen' (*HM Land Registry Blog*, 16 January 2017) available at: https://hmlandregistry.blog.gov.uk/2017/01/16/high-profile-case-shows-how-property-fraud-can-happen/.

remain true even if the Law Commission's recommendations in relation to identity checks are implemented.[55] A Land Registrar and Assistant Land Registrar confirm that '[i]n the past 10 years, registration fraud has increased considerably', and that this is particularly the case with identity fraud.[56]

An example of the sort of fraud that is possible on the *death* of a registered proprietor is provided by the Land Registry Adjudicator's decision in *Ijacic v Game Developments*.[57] The case is apparently rare in being *reported* and concerning fraud involving a deceased registered proprietor, but this should not be taken as an indication that more such instances do not occur or that the risks are not significant, even if the reported cases suggest that other forms of fraud are more common. At the time of his death in October 2006, Cetko Tripkovic was the sole registered proprietor of the property in which he lived. Probate was granted to his executor, Mr Ijacic, in 2007, but the executor chose not to become registered as the proprietor. In fact, Mr Tripkovic remained as the registered proprietor at the time of the adjudicator's decision in 2009. The executor instructed a solicitors' firm, MED, to sell the property and account to the beneficiaries under the will, who lived abroad. But in December 2007, a fraudster purporting to be Mr Tripkovic successfully applied to Link Lending (which was in administration at the time of the adjudicator's decision)[58] for a three-month bridging loan secured on the property. The fraudster declared that the property was unoccupied, giving addresses in Central London and Spain. He purported to supply copies of a page of Mr Tripkovic's passport, his driving licence and his counterpart driving licence. All had been apparently certified by a solicitor (who, it appears, had been struck off by the time of the adjudicator's decision).[59] Copies of utility bills stamped by a bank and a bank statement were also supplied, addressed to Mr Tripkovic's property, although the account number was different from the one that the fraudster had given on the mortgage application form. The fraudster managed to execute a mortgage deed in the name of Mr Tripkovic, Link Lending was registered as the proprietor of a charge, and the loan money was advanced to the fraudster's solicitors.

After the approximately £400,000 loan was not repaid in March 2008, Link Lending exercised its power of sale in favour of Game Developments. Although in January 2008 MED had begun to send a trainee to the property around once a week to check that nothing untoward was happening, the fraud was not discovered until the day after Link Lending and Game Developments had completed the transfer, when estate agents instructed by MED failed to gain access to the property for a viewing because it had been secured by Link Lending's agents. Game Developments did not apply to be registered as the proprietor until April 2008, and following Mr Ijacic's objection was never so registered.

The adjudicator rectified the register by removing the charge in favour of Link Lending, with that decision deemed to take effect before Game Developments' registration application, there being no 'exceptional circumstances' justifying the refusal of rectification in

[55] Law Commission, *Updating the Land Registration Act 2002* (Law Com No 380, 2018) [14.34]–[14.91].

[56] Pownall and Hill, 'The Land Registry's Perspective: The Practical Challenges of Land Registration' in Goymour (n 10 above) 12.

[57] *Ijacic v Game Developments* (n 31 above).

[58] Companies House, https://beta.companieshouse.gov.uk/company/01568365/insolvency.

[59] *In the Matter of Harilal Susantha Fernando and Purantharan Rajoo, solicitors*, findings of the Solicitors Disciplinary Tribunal, No 10078-2008, 28 May 2009.

circumstances where the chargee was not in possession.[60] Consequently he refused to register Game Developments as the new proprietor and Mr Tripkovic remained. The adjudicator was also confident that Game Developments would receive an indemnity as 'a refusal to register the transfer because the charge no longer existed at the date of Game's original application would be a direct consequence of rectification of the register'.[61] While all may have been well that ended well, a preventative approach would surely be preferable: things would have been more difficult if the estate beneficiaries had been interested in the property per se or Link Lending had been a purchaser able to go into possession rather than a mere chargee.

Some protection against fraud would be provided if the registered proprietor had entered a Form LL restriction (specifically designed to combat identity theft) while alive, which would prevent a disposition of an estate by the purported registered proprietor 'without a certificate signed by a conveyancer that that conveyancer is satisfied that the person who executed the document submitted for registration as disponor is the same person as the proprietor'.[62] But if no such restriction has been entered then the estate beneficiaries are vulnerable, and even then the conveyancer could be in cahoots with, or duped by, a fraudster. This restriction (free of charge if the property is not occupied)[63] could apparently be entered post-death if the personal representative was registered as proprietor, but it has been seen that this may not happen at all and requires a grant of probate or letters of administration before it can happen. For similar reasons, a restriction in Form C, relating to dispositions by personal representatives other than by way of assent being declared to be in accordance with the will or intestacy rules,[64] would not solve the difficulty identified here.

The routine use of a restriction Form Q by personal representatives may be a partial solution. This provides:

> No disposition [*or specify type of disposition*] of the
>
> [*choose whichever bulleted clause is appropriate*]
>
> - registered estate by the proprietor of the registered estate
> - registered charge dated [*date*] referred to above by the proprietor of that registered charge
>
> is to be registered after the death of [*name of the current proprietor(s) whose personal representatives' consent will be required*] without the written consent of the personal representatives of the deceased.[65]

It is also possible to apply for a restriction that is not in standard form, and the application will be approved if it appears to the registrar that 'the terms of the proposed restriction are reasonable' and that 'applying the proposed restriction' would 'be straightforward', and 'not place an unreasonable burden on him'.[66] A standard form restriction would, however, be

[60] Land Registration Act 2002, sch 4, para 3(3).
[61] *Ijacic v Game Developments* (n 31 above) [73] (Deputy Adjudicator Simon Brilliant); Land Registration Act 2002, sch 8.
[62] Land Registration Rules 2003, SI 2003/1417, sch 4.
[63] HM Land Registry, 'Form: Restriction by Owner not Living at Property Request: Registration (RQ)', available at: www.gov.uk/government/publications/restriction-by-owner-not-living-at-property-request-registration-rq.
[64] Land Registration Rules 2003, SI 2003/1417, sch 4.
[65] ibid.
[66] Land Registration Act 2002, s 43(3).

preferable in the sense of being something that could be routinely used in the context of estate administration and would attract a lower fee.[67]

The basic difficulty remains even with a standard form restriction, however. Personal representatives are not expressly listed as '[p]ersons regarded as having a sufficient interest to apply for a restriction'.[68] A person who is 'entitled to be registered' as the relevant proprietor is so listed, but a problem might be that a personal representative can prove that he is so entitled only once he has obtained a grant of probate or letters of administration, and we have seen that a vulnerability is present during an intervening period.

The fundamental issue is that the Land Registry may be completely unaware that a registered proprietor has died, at least until a grant of probate or letters of administration is obtained. *Ijacic* demonstrates that this ignorance can extend beyond the grant if the personal representative takes no relevant action in relation to the property. It is not immediately clear how the Registry would react to receiving a death certificate relating to a registered proprietor without (ie before) a grant of probate or letters of administration. It is to be hoped that such a certificate would not simply be ignored even if the personal representative does not yet have authority to deal with the land, such that a fraudster purporting to be the deceased person could subsequently do so. It must nevertheless be conceded that there is a chance that the risk of fraud might be *increased* if the Land Registry makes it too obvious that a proprietor has died, which might justify a distinction between information that the Registry holds and that which it publishes.[69] In section IV of the chapter, the advantages of a new standard form restriction are considered.

Of course, as illustrated by *Ijacic*, the Land Registration Act 2002 does contain mechanisms for rectification[70] (demonstrating that indefeasibility of title is not taken to 'extremes')[71] and indemnity[72] (albeit that the Law Commission's suggested 'long stop' will to some extent reduce the scope for rectification as against an innocent purchaser).[73] These mechanisms are logically set up to prejudice those who 'by fraud or lack of proper care caused or substantially contributed to the mistake' (in the case of rectification)[74] or where loss is suffered wholly or partly as a result of fraud or lack of proper care.[75] Moreover, Ferris has said that '[a] system of prima facie effective title, subject to possible rectification, is in principle a better system' than one involving '[p]rovisions that deny legal effect to the registration of forged documentation'.[76] But as suggested above, it would be preferable to take more measures to prevent the fraud in the first place rather than to attempt to cure it afterwards, particularly given the onerous consequences of dealing with fraud for estate beneficiaries at an upsetting time (even if they will ultimately be able to reverse its effect), the effect on public finances of the generous nature of the indemnity provisions under the

[67] Compare Land Registration Fee Order 2013, SI 2013/3174, sch 3, para 1(1) and para 1(2).
[68] Land Registration Rules 2003, SI 2003/1417, sch 4, r 93; Land Registration Act 2002, s 43(1)(c).
[69] See further Xu (n 39 above).
[70] Land Registration Act 2002, sch 4.
[71] Cooper (n 20 above) 108.
[72] Land Registration Act 2002, sch 8.
[73] Law Commission (n 55 above) ch 13.
[74] Land Registration Act 2002, sch 4, para 6(2)(a).
[75] ibid, sch 8, para 5.
[76] G Ferris, 'How Should a System of Registered Title to Property Respond to Fraud and Sharp Practice?' in Conway and Hickey (n 2 above) 224.

2002 Act,[77] and indeed the cost to solicitors' firms due to professional indemnity insurance claims (often the first port of call when a beneficiary has lost out). Such professional indemnity issues would become particularly acute if, as the Law Commission has recommended, a specific statutory duty of care in relation to identity verification were introduced.[78]

A bank will freeze the account of a deceased person on receipt of a death certificate, usually very early on in the administration of the estate.[79] It is well established that one of the reasons that there exists a specific body of Land Law is the particular value and importance of land,[80] and it is strongly arguable that more effort should be made by the land registration system to secure registered land for the benefit of true beneficiaries. In *Ijacic*, for example, it is noteworthy that the fraud had occurred *after* the grant of probate and Mr Ijacic and/or his advisors had probably decided not to involve the Registry in the administration of Mr Tripkovic's estate until they had completed the intended (legitimate) sale. Moreover, it must also be conceded that elements other than the land register and fraudsters themselves contribute to fraud. If the fraudster's solicitor or the lender had acted differently on the facts of that case, the fraud might not have been initially successful.

In addition to the use of standard form restrictions suggested above, one option would be to require the personal representatives to be registered as legal owners in circumstances (at least) where a sole registered proprietor has died, or within a certain period of the death if the land is not otherwise dealt with. This would be consistent with the general rule in the Administration of Estates Act 1925, and its implications will be considered further once co-owned land has been discussed in the next section.

III. Co-Owned Land

A. Co-Owned Property on Death

Particular risks that property will be misappropriated arise where registered land was co-owned (and therefore increasingly likely to be held on trust in the modern era) before death and there remain(s) one or more registered proprietor(s) after a registered proprietor has died. This is especially true in circumstances where the deceased previously held the beneficial title to the property as a tenant in common with a person or people who survive her. It is axiomatic that, where there was such a tenancy in common, the deceased's entitlement passes under the will or intestacy rules rather than accruing to the remaining co-owner(s) by survivorship (as it would in the case of a joint tenancy).[81] It will be seen, however, that the land registration system might in some circumstances assist the surviving

[77] See, eg, M Dixon, *Modern Land Law*, 11th edn (Abingdon, Routledge, 2018) 37; Law Commission (n 55 above) [14.16]–[14.21].

[78] Law Commission, ibid [14.62]–[14.73].

[79] Law Society, Society of Trust and Estates Practitioner and British Bankers' Association, 'Banking Practices Protocol: Estate Administration' (2016) [15].

[80] B McFarlane, *The Structure of Property Law* (Oxford, Hart Publishing, 2008) [3.1].

[81] See, eg, B McFarlane, N Hopkins and S Nield, *Land Law: Text, Cases and Materials*, 4th edn (Oxford, Oxford University Press, 2018) 505.

legal co-owner(s) in illegitimately asserting beneficial entitlement to the property where they are *not* entitled under the will or intestacy rules and someone else is instead, with profound consequences for both testamentary freedom and the rule of law.

That said, it must be conceded that the position with respect to land here reflects that of other property subject to trusts, in that the personal representatives of a now-deceased trustee will not acquire the legal title to the property unless the deceased was herself the sole surviving trustee,[82] such that there is no need to transfer the legal title where there are surviving co-owners.[83] As regards jointly held bank accounts, for example, 'it is well established that, upon a joint account holder's death, the legal title to the chose in action representing the joint account vests entirely in the remaining account holder(s) by virtue of a right of survivorship'.[84] As it was recently put by Lord Briggs in the Privy Council decision in *Whitlock v Moree*, '[s]urvivorship, that is the devolution of … legal rights upon the survivor or survivors of joint owners is an inevitable, indeed inherent, aspect of joint legal title'[85] (albeit that 'joint tenancy … is only one of numerous ways in which property may be co-owned beneficially').[86] This creates a tension with the general principle that the legal title to the deceased's assets vests in the personal representatives on death, and the duties that the personal representatives owe to the estate beneficiaries in circumstances where the deceased was also a trust beneficiary, but not one unique to land. Lord Briggs and the others in the majority in *Whitlock* were anxious that essentially the same principles be applied to co-ownership regardless of the type of property involved,[87] although in dissent Lord Canwath expressed concern about this approach.[88]

B. Tenancy in Common and Restrictions

While restrictions are in principle designed to protect those beneficially entitled to land who are not on the legal title, this sub-section will demonstrate that they are not always able to perform this function where a registered proprietor dies. Where two or more persons are the registered proprietors of an estate in land, the registrar will be obliged to enter a Form A restriction unless the registrar is informed that the proprietors are trustees for themselves as beneficial joint tenants, or that they are being registered in their capacity as personal representatives.[89] The entry of this restriction will therefore occur inter alia in circumstances where a tenancy in common is intended and the Land Registry has not been told otherwise, and the restriction's purpose is to ensure that beneficial interests are

[82] Trustee Act 1925, s 18.
[83] Land Registration Act 2002, s 27(5)(a).
[84] EP Ellinger, E Lomnicka, and C Hare, *Ellinger's Modern Banking Law*, 5th edn (Oxford, Oxford University Press, 2011) 324, implicitly approved in *Whitlock v Moree* [2017] UKPC 44 [60] (Lord Carnwarth, dissenting).
[85] *Whitlock v Moree* (ibid) [21].
[86] ibid [22].
[87] ibid [26].
[88] ibid [55].
[89] Land Registration Act 2002, s 44; Land Registration Rules 2003, SI 2003/1417, r 95; HM Land Registry, 'Practice Guide 24: Private Trusts of Land', available at: www.gov.uk/government/publications/private-trusts-of-land/practice-guide-24-private-trusts-of-land [1.3]; *Ruoff and Roper* (n 51 above) [37.007]; *Megarry & Wade: The Law of Real Property*, 8th edn (London, Sweet & Maxwell, 2012) [13-053].

overreached on a purchase or charge,[90] meaning that the purchaser or chargee will take free of any beneficial interests even if their holders would otherwise have had an overriding interest under schedule 3, paragraph 2 of the Land Registration Act.[91] The restriction provides: 'No disposition by a sole proprietor of the registered estate (except a trust corporation) under which capital money arises is to be registered except under an order of the Court.'[92]

Significantly for present purposes, a Form A restriction 'will be cancelled automatically … when a transfer which overreaches any interests under a trust is registered'.[93] Such cancellation would therefore occur straightforwardly following a death where there is a disposition by two or more surviving trustees (even if not all conveyancers will seek to rely on such overreaching), potentially prejudicing beneficiaries under the deceased's will or the intestacy rules who find their interests overreached. It could be said that this is a straightforward operation of the Act in a manner that reflects the 'curtain principle'[94] and protects 'dynamic' security (ie when the property moves to the ownership of an innocent purchaser)[95] as intended.[96] Such purchaser protection has been described as 'the very foundation of land registration' according to the orthodox point of view.[97] Significantly, the Law Commission concluded in its recently completed project on land registration that 'given the curtain principle …, the existing mechanisms for the protection of beneficial interests under trusts are sufficient and … no further protection is appropriate'.[98] That said, the distinction between dynamic and static security (ie protecting those people with existing interests in the property from being deprived of those interests against their will)[99] is arguably less clear-cut with succession than in the inter vivos context because, while the surviving joint tenant or estate beneficiary is not a *purchaser* per se, the legal and beneficial ownership of the land must inevitably move (or change) on death, and it could be seen as an important function of the land registration system to ensure that testamentary freedom, or alternatively the intestacy rules, are properly respected.

The current position does not necessarily deny a remedy to a wronged heir where overreaching validly occurs, but leaves the deceased's heirs to pursue proprietary remedies in respect of the sale proceeds and personal remedies for breach of trust where appropriate.[100] This risk of such a transaction taking place without the involvement of the deceased's executor, however, is perhaps difficult to square with the executor's duties to get in, manage and distribute the property according to the terms of the will,[101] particularly where the purpose of the will was to give the beneficiary an interest in the home per se. In this respect,

[90] Law of Property Act 1925, ss 2, 27(2).
[91] *City of London Building Society v Flegg* [1988] AC 54 (HL).
[92] Land Registration Rules 2003, SI 2003/1417, sch 4.
[93] HM Land Registry (n 29 above) [6].
[94] See, eg, TBF Ruoff, 'An Englishman Looks at the Torrens system: Part II – Simplicity and the Curtain Principle' (1952) 26 *Australian Law Journal* 162.
[95] E Cooke, *The New Law of Land Registration* (Oxford, Hart Publishing, 2003) 100.
[96] See, eg, Law Commission (n 18 above) [10.43].
[97] Cooper (n 20 above) 108. *cf*, eg, *HSBC Bank Plc v Dyche* [2009] EWHC 2954 (Ch), [2010] BPIR 138.
[98] Law Commission (n 18 above) [10.47].
[99] Cooke (n 95 above) 100.
[100] See, eg, G Virgo, *Principles of Equity and Trusts*, 3rd edn (Oxford, Oxford University Press, 2018) Part VIII.
[101] Administration of Estates Act 1925, s 25; see, eg, B Sloan, *Borkowski's Law of Succession* (n 1 above) ch 11.

it is worth noting Owen and Cahill's claim in relation to overreaching that 'in 1925 the legislature was not trying to capture any features concerning the use of property primarily *as a home*'.[102]

The current approach to trust property once a death occurs reflects a distinctly formalistic and administrative position. Whatever protection is usually provided by conveyancers, the Land Registry is effectively permitted to ignore the fact that a Form A restriction essentially signals a tenancy in common rather than a joint tenancy, and the substantive law implications of that, as long as overreaching occurs, (ie the correct number of trustees are selling the property). Of course, the remaining co-owners *may* be beneficiaries under the will or the intestacy rules, but in other circumstances the very purpose of the creation of a tenancy in common will have been to give the deceased's share by her will to people who are not existing co-owners. Yet the land registration system is uninterested in that fact, even though the presence of the Form A restriction renders it particularly important for it to be clear that the registered proprietors are behaving properly. Of course, the current limitations on the registrar's interest are consistent with the express statutory statement that '[t]he registrar shall not be affected with notice of a trust'.[103] It might also be said that, where the surviving co-owners are content to sell the property over the heads of the estate beneficiaries, that indicates a level of animosity such that an application under the Trusts of Land and Appointment of Trustees Act 1996 will be inevitable,[104] and that such an application is likely to produce a sale in any event by virtue of the courts' usual preference.[105] But a court application would at least allow the beneficiary properly to put the case for retention of the property, and a court-ordered sale might reduce the risk that the sale proceeds will be dissipated and therefore rendered unavailable to the beneficiary. This is another situation where prevention is better than cure.

In the perhaps more usual situation where there is only one remaining trustee (such as a surviving spouse) once a co-owner has died, the Form A restriction will not be cancelled automatically and will catch any attempted disposition unless another trustee is appointed.[106] This at least gives the personal representative an opportunity to become involved in a transaction if he becomes a legal owner (or to block it if no other legal owner can be found). The Land Registry's Practice Guide nevertheless expressly states that even where a Form A restriction has not been automatically cancelled, 'consideration should be given to applying to cancel any existing Form A restriction', even if only where 'following the death of a joint proprietor a sole surviving proprietor has become the sole beneficial owner'.[107] The Guide actively advises that 'applying to cancel the restriction at the earliest opportunity may avoid problems arising on a future disposition when the necessary evidence is no longer readily available'.[108] The application would be made on Form RX3, 'accompanied by evidence of the

[102] G Owen and D Cahill, 'Overreaching – Getting the Right Balance' [2017] *Conv* 26, 33.
[103] Land Registration Act 2002, s 78.
[104] Trusts of Land and Appointment of Trustees Act 1996, ss 14–15.
[105] M Dixon, 'To Sell or not to Sell: That is the Question – The Irony of the Trusts of Land and Appointment of Trustees Act 1996' (2011) 70 *CLJ* 579.
[106] HM Land Registry (n 29 above) [6].
[107] ibid.
[108] ibid.

equitable title to show that the sole survivor has become the sole beneficial owner'.[109] The evidence 'usually' accepted is:

> a statutory declaration or statement of truth ... by the sole surviving proprietor which shows how they have become the sole beneficial owner by:
>
> - explaining what has happened to the beneficial interest protected by the restriction
> - if it has devolved to the surviving proprietor, explaining how this happened
> - confirming, if it is true, that no one other than the registered proprietor now has a beneficial interest in the property
> - confirming, if it is true, that no beneficial interest in the property has been separately mortgaged or charged, and that no beneficial owner is or was subject to a charging order or bankruptcy proceedings (a registered mortgage does not count).[110]

The Land Registry confirms that

> [i]nstead of a statutory declaration or statement of truth, we will accept a certificate to [the] effect [of the evidence above] from the conveyancer acting for the surviving proprietor if they are able to speak from personal knowledge of the facts,

or 'a court order requiring the registrar to cancel the restriction may be lodged'.[111]

It is noteworthy that there is no necessary consideration of the will or intestacy rules themselves in this procedure, which would demonstrate the fact (if true) that the surviving co-owner is actually beneficially entitled to the whole property despite the fact that it was previously subject to a tenancy in common. This is consistent with the express negation of the Land Registry having a duty to enquire into the will, highlighted in the case of sole ownership above. It nevertheless seems odd to rely on the surviving co-owner's word rather than the documentary evidence actually *establishing* entitlement, or indeed to rely on the word of someone other than the personal representatives, whose duty it is to investigate the full facts and ensure that the will and/or the intestacy rules are properly implemented. Although it would be a dangerous strategy for a surviving co-owner to misrepresent the terms of a will (itself not immune from forgery)[112] in light of its status as a public document, this is a possibility and the Law Society and Land Registry have noted the existence of 'intra-family frauds that are perpetrated by family members, friends or partners'.[113] In particular, the fact that the Land Registry does not even require a grant of representation as evidence in these cases means that there are circumstances (when no other assets in the estate require a grant) where a co-owner may entirely conceal the existence of a will disposing of the property to other (true) beneficiaries, whereas the registration of the death itself is obligatory.[114]

There is also the issue that the verification process applies only where the surviving co-owner is seeking to cancel the restriction. If the sole surviving owner were to appoint another trustee with whom he was in cahoots (perhaps a new partner), he could formally

[109] ibid [7].
[110] ibid.
[111] ibid.
[112] See, eg, *In re the Estate of Patel* [2017] EWHC 133 (Ch).
[113] HM Land Registry and Law Society (n 45 above) 6.
[114] Births and Deaths Registration Act 1953, Part II.

comply with the restriction and more easily circumvent the terms of the will or the intestacy rules. In such circumstances a survivor could (legitimately under the current law) avoid even obtaining a grant of probate where all the other significant assets[115] in the estate are co-owned.

The next section considers some potential solutions to the problems identified in this chapter.

IV. Possible Solutions

If there are thought to be problems with the law's approach to registered land (whether previously co-owned or not) following a death, what might be the solutions?

One possibility would be to *require* personal representatives to be registered as legal owners. This would be consistent with the general rule that the legal title to the deceased's assets vests in personal representatives on death and places the personal representative in a better position to perform their duties towards the beneficiaries, even if it is not consistent with the general law's approach to trusts per se where there remains a surviving trustee. It could be argued that land is very important, that trusts and co-ownership are particularly common in relation to land, that trustees of residential land are also likely to be beneficiaries, and that these factors justify a distinctive approach to co-owned land. Such an approach is arguably already reflected in the distinctive requirements for overreaching imposed in relation to land.[116] The requirement of registration of the personal representatives would also be less radical than (for example) requiring the consent of the beneficiary to the disposition of the property in all instances, and would thus protect dynamic security to some extent. That said, while the fiduciary and other duties owed by a personal representative are potentially more likely to be performed where the personal representative is a professional third party such as a solicitor, the beneficiary's position is unlikely to be improved significantly where the personal representative is also a surviving co-owner (such as a spouse) intent on selling the property against the interests or wishes of an estate beneficiary.

A compromise falling short of the requirement of registration of the personal representatives would be the ability, once the death has been registered but well before the issue of the grant of representation, for the personal representative to send the death certificate to the Land Registry and apply for a standard form restriction to be entered on the register. This restriction would purport to prevent anybody other than the personal representatives named on the eventual grant from disposing of the property (whether by sale or assent). A possible wording might be:

> No disposition of the registered estate shall be registered unless accompanied by a Grant of Representation appointing personal representatives to administer the estate of [*insert name of deceased*], and the disposition is made by those personal representatives named in the Grant.

[115] See also, eg, Administration of Estates (Small Payments) Act 1965.

[116] See generally, D Fox, 'Overreaching' in P Birks and A Pretto (eds), *Breach of Trust* (Oxford, Hart Publishing, 2002).

A variation would be to use a Form Q restriction, requiring *consent* of the personal representative(s), but allow it to be sought upon production of a death certificate and before a grant of representation.

This standard form restriction proposal would reflect the system adopted by banks, investment companies and most other financial institutions,[117] and so logically it should be available for land. If such a step became an industry standard within estate administration, solicitors' firms who fail to protect the estate's interests in the land in this way could be liable in negligence and the loss covered by their indemnity insurance, therefore perhaps increasing the options for beneficiaries in seeking a remedy. The proposal would be a compromise between preventing fraud and reflecting the fact that the personal representative does not yet have authority to deal with the land. Obligations to enter restrictions are not unknown to the land registration system, as shown by the joint proprietorship obligation discussed in the previous section of this chapter.[118] If an obligation is thought inappropriate, this may be a situation where the registrar should exercise his power to enter a restriction that is 'necessary or desirable' for the purpose of 'preventing invalidity or unlawfulness in relation to dispositions of a registered estate or charge'.[119]

A personal representative is not himself immune from impersonation, and the Law Society and Land Registry specifically recognised 'a personal representative responsible for a property where the owner has died and the property is to be sold' as a vulnerable client for these purposes.[120] That said, if a restriction were entered from the moment a death certificate is received, requiring production of the grant of probate or letters of administration before the land can be dealt with, the true personal representative will have little trouble in transferring the land to either true beneficiaries or legitimate purchasers. The land will in all likelihood be used by those truly entitled and the risk of fraud is reduced.

One further step could be to include the Land Registry within the Government's 'Tell Us Once' system.[121] When registering a death, the informant can (with the help of the registrar of births and deaths) complete a short application such that 'parts of the DWP and other organisations such as HMRC, Local Authorities' Family Information Services and Library Services' are essentially automatically informed of the death.[122] It would not be unrealistic for the Land Registry also to be informed under this scheme, and a notice or restriction then automatically entered on each title for which the deceased is a registered proprietor. This would serve the desirable objective of an up-to-date register.

As regards previously co-owned land held on trust, one possibility might be to pull back the 'curtain' and allow the substantive registration of trust interests (or their protection by notice), which creates the potential for the true nature of interests under trusts[123] to be reflected on the register.[124] In addition to the potential for greater protection for the interests concerned, this would also be consistent with the drive towards transparency in

[117] See, eg, Law Society et al (n 79 above).
[118] Land Registration Act 2002, s 44(1).
[119] Land Registration Act 2002, s 42(1)(a).
[120] HM Land Registry and Law Society (n 45 above) 9.
[121] Welfare Reform Act 2012, s 135, inserting Registration Service Act 1953, s 19A; Gov.uk, 'What to do after Someone Dies: Tell Us Once', www.gov.uk/after-a-death/organisations-you-need-to-contact-and-tell-us-once.
[122] Explanatory Notes to the Welfare Reform Act 2012 [692].
[123] Implied, resulting and constructive trusts aside.
[124] See, eg, Owen and Cahill (n 102 above) 37–40.

trust interests.[125] The effect of a registration requirement would be limited, however, by the fact that an estate beneficiary does not acquire a fully-fledged proprietary interest in the estate assets until the process of estate administration is complete (unless he was previously an inter vivos trust beneficiary),[126] although the equity to compel due administration of the estate may currently be protectable by notice.[127] Registration of a beneficiary's interest would in any case require accurate information to be made available in the first place to would-be trust beneficiaries following a death.

Finally, it could be possible to require the Land Registry to examine the grant of probate or of letters of administration, together with any will and trust document and having appropriately verified relevant identities. Such evidence could be scrutinised in any circumstance where surviving co-owner(s) are claiming that no one other than themselves is beneficially entitled following a death, at least in circumstances where there is reason to believe that the property was held subject to a tenancy in common rather than a joint tenancy by the time of the death. This suggestion would involve more substantive examination of trust terms than is currently the case, but is arguably simply a stronger form of evidence than is currently required for the Registry's existing verification processes.

V. Conclusion

We have demonstrated that in both sole- and co-owner situations the current law and practice place greater emphasis on the importance of the conclusiveness of the land register than on the need to protect the rights of true testamentary or intestacy beneficiaries in the context of registered land, in some cases placing the land registration system at odds with the general law, logic and normative principle. This sidelining of testamentary freedom becomes more acute in the current climate where sophisticated property fraud is on the rise, and the lack of simple protective mechanisms could easily result in the true beneficiary losing out.

On the orthodox account, the current land registration system's focus is to protect the innocent third-party purchaser, but Cooper has said that 'a fixed purchaser protection rule … might perversely take the land from a party who cherishes its uniqueness in order to reallocate it to a party who regards it only as a characterless repository of wealth'.[128] Such an approach would be in clear tension with succession law's principles of testamentary freedom and passing on property as a home to loved ones. While testamentary freedom is not and should not be an absolute principle, it should be qualified through transparent and lawful mechanisms rather than the possibility of fraud and breach of trust. Although innocent purchasers must of course be offered security, and although the judiciary have found ways

[125] See the debates (discussed ibid) surrounding Directive 2015/849 on the prevention of the use of the financial system for the purpose of money laundering or terrorist funding, amending Regulation 648/2012 and repealing Directive 2005/60 and Commission Directive 2006/70 [2015] OJ L141/73. *cf* F Noseda, 'For or Against the Registration of Trusts – Why it Matters: Balancing Regulatory Concerns and the Right to Privacy' [2014] *Private Client Business* 137 and Evans (n 41 above).

[126] *Commissioner of Stamp Duties (Queensland) v Livingston* [1965] AC 694 (PC).

[127] Land Registration Act 2002, s 115; *cf* s 33.

[128] Cooper (n 20 above) 131.

to reduce innocent purchaser protection where arguably appropriate,[129] perhaps Owen and Cahill have a point when they say that 'the scales need resetting' when balancing overreaching with beneficial interests that can be applied to the succession context.[130]

The ease with which beneficial ownership can prima facie be extinguished on the land register adds to this tension. The most recent Land Registration Act is now 17 years old, and the blasé attitude shown by the Act towards beneficial interests is perhaps starting to look outdated in the current climate of transparency propounded by recent anti-money laundering legislation, and advocated directly in the land registration context by Owen and Cahill. Furthermore, as Ferris puts it: 'Land registration cannot be reduced to the single objective of lowering transaction costs at the cost of static security and principles of justice. The system has a fundamental interest in the protection of static security'.[131]

Whilst the Money Laundering Regulations have tightened up the identification requirements for conveyancers, the Law Commission has proposed reforms to identity verification and the Land Registration Act 2002 provides mechanisms for rectification and indemnity in the case where a true owner or chargee has lost out due to fraud, there is surely a case for introducing a simple preventative mechanism such as the entry of a restriction on the register on production of a death certificate to reduce the ease with which fraud can be perpetrated. This must be preferable to the protracted and upsetting process of untangling the mess once it has happened. Given the huge monetary and societal value placed on land, most of our suggestions do not seek fundamentally to change the nature of land registration, but rather to assist the land registration system to provide a just, rather than merely a procedurally correct, outcome. Our proposals would also have the by-product of increasing the accuracy of the register, and thus help to reduce the tension between testamentary freedom and dynamic security identified in this chapter.

[129] See, eg, Goymour (n 12 above).
[130] Owen and Cahill (n 102 above).
[131] Ferris (n 76 above) 234.

PART V

Trusts: Nature and Operation

17

The Paradox of the Equitable Proprietary Claim

SINÉAD AGNEW AND BEN McFARLANE

I. Introduction

Equitable property rights can be seen as paradoxical: how can a system based on conscience have developed rights that operate *in rem*? In *Akers v Samba Financial Group*,[1] for example, Lord Sumption states that that 'an equitable interest possesses the essential hallmark of any right in rem',[2] yet goes on to say that when an asset subject to an equitable interest is transferred to a third party, 'the question becomes whether the conscience of the transferee is affected'.[3]

Our aim here is to resolve this paradox, at least in relation to rights under a trust.[4] Where T holds on trust for B, we argue that conscience is crucial when considering how and when B may make an equitable proprietary claim against C, a successor in title to the original trustee. Such a claim can only be made in relation to property which is held by C at a point in time when C's conscience is affected by knowledge of the initial trust relationship between T and B, in such a way as to subject C to a duty to B.[5] In other words, the proprietary effect of the trust is based squarely on an initial relationship between B and T, and a later, similar relationship between B and C, rather than any abstract, depersonalised interest of B.[6]

The resolution of the paradox depends on accepting that, when B's beneficial interest is described as proprietary, 'proprietary' must be understood in a special, limited sense.[7]

[1] *Akers v Samba Financial Group* [2017] UKSC 6, [2017] AC 424.

[2] ibid [82].

[3] ibid [89]. For similar remarks, see *Investec Trust (Guernsey) Ltd v Glenalla Properties Ltd* [2018] UKPC 7, [2018] 2 WLR 1465, [228] (Lord Mance).

[4] It is possible that a slightly different analysis may be required in relation to other equitable interests: see, eg, B McFarlane, 'The *Numerus Clausus* Principle and Covenants Relating to Land' in S Bright (ed), *Modern Studies in Property Law*, vol 6 (Oxford, Hart Publishing, 2010) 311.

[5] For an account of the role of conscience in private law, see: S Agnew, 'The Meaning and Significance of Conscience in Private Law' (2018) 77(3) *CLJ* 479. Other recent discussions of conscience in equity include, eg, D Klinck, 'The Unexamined "Conscience" of Contemporary Canadian Equity' (2001) 46 *McGill Law Journal* 571; M Macnair, 'Equity and Conscience' (2007) 27 *OJLS* 659; I Samet, 'What Conscience Can Do For Equity' (2012) 3 *Jurisprudence* 13, 20; G Virgo 'Whose Conscience? Unconscionability in the Common Law of Obligations' in A Robertson and M Tilbury (eds), *Divergences in Private Law* (Oxford, Hart Publishing, 2016).

[6] This accords with the idea that all 'equitable proprietary rights' require two people: L Smith, 'Trust and Patrimony' (2008) 38(2) *Revue Générale de Droit* 379, [16].

[7] See Smith (n 6 above) [15]–[16], who suggests equitable title is a 'metaphor' in the sense that it is 'not literally true'; and B McFarlane and R Stevens, 'The Nature of Equitable Property' (2010) 4(1) *Journal of Equity* 1, who argue that an equitable interest arises where A holds a right and owes a duty to B in relation to that right.

The key to Lord Sumption's observation in *Akers* is the particular, and idiosyncratic, sense in which his Lordship used the term 'in rem', defining the essential hallmark of such a right as being that it is 'good against third parties into whose hands the property or its traceable proceeds may have come, subject to the rules of equity for the protection of bona fide purchasers for value without notice'.[8] We agree that the ability to affect C is what justifies regarding a beneficial interest under a trust as more than a mere personal right. It is possible to recognise that a beneficial interest has such an effect whilst also distinguishing it from rights, such as a legal property right, which are 'in rem' in the more orthodox sense of imposing an immediate, strict duty on the rest of the world.[9]

II. Beneficial Interests and Third Parties: The Current Position

A. The Innocent Volunteer

> Example 1: T holds a painting on trust for B. Acting in breach of her duties to B, and without any authority from B or under the terms of the trust, T makes a gift of the painting to C. C is unaware of the relationship between T and B and honestly believes that T simply owned the painting outright.

(i) The Scope of B's 'Proprietary Claim'

What is meant if it is said that B has, in addition to a personal claim against T, a proprietary claim? The point is that, following C's receipt of the trust property (or its traceable proceeds), it may be possible for B to show that C holds the property subject to a duty to B. So, in Example 1, if, at the time of B's claim, C still holds the painting received from T or its traceable proceeds, B's claim is simply that C must give it up, either by transferring it to a new trustee or, in the case of a bare trust, transferring it directly to B. It is this claim that is most commonly referred to as the equitable proprietary claim.[10] In such a case, it has been said that, whether the initial trust was express or not, C holds the property on constructive trust for B.[11]

If, however, C no longer holds the property or its traceable proceeds, so the trust cannot be given effect to *in specie*, B may be able to claim that C is liable to account to B as a

[8] *Akers* (n 1 above) [82].

[9] Although the existence of a trust imposes a duty on the rest of the world not to dishonestly assist the trustee in a breach of trust (*Royal Brunei Airlines v Tan* [1995] 2 AC 378 (PC)), the duty is not strict and thus it offers less protection than a legal property right. Furthermore, its existence does not distinguish the trust from other *in personam* rights, as similar duties exist, eg, not to assist in a breach of fiduciary duty and not to procure a breach of contract (*OBG Ltd v Allan* [2007] UKHL 21, [2008] 1 AC 1). See, further, B McFarlane, 'Equity, Obligations, and Third Parties' [2008] *Singapore Journal of Legal Studies* 308.

[10] *Foskett v McKeown* [2001] 1 AC 102 (HL), 129–30; *Independent Trustee Services Ltd v GP Noble Trustees Ltd* [2012] EWCA Civ 195, [2013] Ch 91, [75]–[76].

[11] *ITS v Noble* (n 10 above) [80].

constructive trustee.[12] If such a 'knowing receipt' claim succeeds then, as Mitchell and Watterson have shown,[13] C is subject to exactly the same remedies as an express trustee, and, whilst no longer able to hand over the trust property or its traceable proceeds, must do the next best thing and so, for example, must account to B for value which C should have acquired from the property. In our view, the knowing receipt claim depends on showing that C previously held such property subject to a duty to B, and was *in that sense* a trustee.[14] We therefore argue that each of the knowing receipt claim, and the claim that C must give up particular property, is founded on exactly the same duty of C to B, and, indeed, is simply a different means to give effect to that duty. We therefore argue that cases discussing the knowing receipt claim can provide valuable insights into the nature of, and limits to, the equitable proprietary claim.[15]

As to the content of C's duty, B's ability to make a claim against C does not mean that C is under all the same duties as T may have owed to B.[16] To that extent, B's interest, as against C, differs from B's pre-existing rights against T. Nevertheless, B can show that C is under the same core duty as T: a duty, owed to B, not to use the property other than for the benefit of B.[17] In that sense, a core aspect of the initial trust relationship can be said to persist, notwithstanding the transfer to C. Moreover, C, like T, is unable to meet B's claim by simply offering to pay B the value of the trust property:[18] C's duty can be enforced in relation to the specific trust property, or its traceable proceeds, through an order that C transfer that very property to a new trustee, or to B, as appropriate.

As to the timing and basis of C's duty, it is clear that C's duty need not arise immediately on C's receipt of the relevant right from T. This was confirmed, for example, in *Independent Trustee Services Ltd v GP Noble Trustees Ltd*,[19] where Lloyd LJ stated that B's proprietary claim against C: 'only extends to money (or its traceable proceeds) which was in her hands at the time she was given notice of [B's] claim.'[20] Adopting the analysis of Millett J in *Agip (Africa) Ltd v Jackson*,[21] Lloyd LJ stated that: 'to the extent that, before she

[12] *Re Montagu's Settlement Trusts* [1987] Ch 264 (Ch), 276 (Megarry VC).

[13] C Mitchell and S Watterson, 'Remedies for Knowing Receipt' in C Mitchell (ed), *Constructive and Resulting Trusts* (Oxford, Hart Publishing, 2010) 115, 138, discussing *In re Rothko* 43 NY 2d 305, 372 NE 2d 291 (1977) (Court of Appeals of New York).

[14] In *Williams v Central Bank of Nigeria* [2014] UKSC 10, [2014] AC 1189, [31], Lord Sumption stated that a party liable in knowing receipt is not a 'trustee', either generally or in the sense used by the Limitation Act 1980, s 21(1)(a), as such a party has not been entrusted by a settlor to hold assets on trust. That is one means of defining the term 'trustee', and is not inconsistent with a finding that such a recipient does hold specific assets subject to a duty to B.

[15] There is continuing academic debate as to the proper characterisation of a knowing receipt claim: eg, W Swadling, 'The Nature of "Knowing Receipt"' in P Davies and J Penner (eds), *Equity, Trusts and Commerce* (Oxford, Hart Publishing, 2017). Our analysis is closest to that of R Chambers, 'The End of Knowing Receipt' (2016) 2 *Canadian Journal of Contemporary and Comparative Law* 1, which explains C's liability as depending on the fact that C held property at some point on trust for B. However, we differ from Chambers in that we agree with Mitchell and Watterson (n 13 above) that C's liability does not depend on proof of a breach of trust; we regard conscience as an important idea in understanding why C holds on trust for B; and we draw an explicit link between knowing receipt and the equitable proprietary claim.

[16] R Nolan, 'Equitable Property' (2006) 122 *LQR* 232.

[17] See eg *ITS v Noble* (n 10 above) [81] (Lloyd LJ).

[18] An important point, noted by Lionel Smith in a paper for the Philosophical Foundations of Equity Law conference, King's College, London, June 2017.

[19] *ITS v Noble* (n 10 above).

[20] ibid [76].

[21] *Agip (Africa) Ltd v Jackson* [1990] Ch 265 (Ch), 290–91.

had notice of the claim to the funds, she had disposed of any of the money without receiving traceable proceeds, she would not be liable [to B].'[22] It is therefore clear that, in a case such as Example 1, even though C has received property transferred by T in breach of trust, C is under 'no relevant duty as regards the [property] until she [has] notice of the interest of [B].'[23] This means that C 'cannot be made accountable for relevant assets disposed of at a time when he had no notice of the adverse interest'.[24]

The key point is that even in a case such as Example 1, where B has a pre-existing beneficial interest in an asset received by C, C's receipt of the property, by itself, does not subject C to an immediate duty to B. Rather, B must point to further facts to show why there is a good reason for C to come under such a duty: specifically, B needs to show that C's conscience is affected by knowledge (from whatever source) of the pre-existing trust relationship between T and B. This does not mean that, in the period after C's receipt, and before C acquires such knowledge, B no longer has any interest in the trust property or its traceable proceeds. Rather, the possibility of C's coming under a duty to B in relation to that property justifies regarding B as having a persisting interest in the property which is protected, for example, if C goes into insolvency.[25]

There may seem to be a tension between this point and the House of Lords' analysis in *Foskett v McKeown*,[26] where it is said that B's claim to traceable proceeds of the initial property in the hands of T or of C depends on 'hard-nosed property rights'.[27] That analysis suggests that B's protection depends simply on the assertion of B's initial beneficial interest, and that B need *not* point to any additional facts. On our view, two points can be made in response to that analysis. First, our question – when does a third party, C, come under a duty to B – is different from the question, addressed in *Foskett*, of to what property a claim against T or C relates. Secondly, and more broadly, the essence of the *Foskett* analysis lies in the idea of *obviousness*: if T holds particular property on trust for B, then it is obvious (and can be explained without reference to ideas such as unjust enrichment) that T also holds property acquired in exchange for that trust property on trust for B. The irony is that 'hard-nosed property rights' provide a poor way to explain such obviousness: an essential feature of a property right is that it must relate to a specific asset, and so it is not clear why holding a property right in one asset should necessarily entitle B to a property right in a different asset.[28]

[22] *ITS v Noble* (n 10 above) [76].

[23] ibid [81].

[24] ibid [84].

[25] There is a question as to whether, in the period before C acquires knowledge of the trust, B is best described as having a 'power' to impose a duty on C: certainly, B can impose such a duty by communicating the existence of the trust to C, but such a duty will also arise if C discovers that trust by other means, and so by informing C, B is simply ensuring that a particular fact with legal consequences occurs. In Raz's terms, B's act can be seen as having legal effect causatively not normatively (J Raz, *Practical Reason and Norms*, 2nd edn (Oxford, Oxford University Press, 1999) 103). For the distinction between such actions and the exercise of a power, see too A Halpin, 'The Concept of a Legal Power' (1996) 16 *OJLS* 129, C Essert, 'Legal Powers in Private Law' (2015) *Legal Theory* 136, 139–45.

[26] *Foskett* (n 10 above).

[27] ibid 109.

[28] See eg R Chambers, 'Tracing and Unjust Enrichment' in JW Neyers, M McInnes and SGA Pitel (eds), *Understanding Unjust Enrichment* (Oxford, Hart Publishing, 2004) 263.

A different, and better, explanation is to see the *Foskett* analysis as recognising that whatever reason justifies T or C being under a duty to B in relation to the initial trust property also justifies that party's being under a duty to B in relation to its traceable proceeds. This is clearest in a case where T holds on an express trust for B and makes an authorised substitution of that initial trust property: T has consented to hold not only the initial property, but also its substitutes, on trust for B. Even if T makes an unauthorised substitution, the reason for T's initial duty can continue and justify T's coming under a duty to B in relation to the substitute, as a 'next best' means to enforce T's initial duty.[29] On this view, it is a focus on the duty of the defendant, rather than on any abstract property interest of the claimant, that best explains not only the ability of B to make a claim against C in Example 1, but also the ability of B to make a claim in relation to traceable proceeds of trust property.

(ii) The Distinction between Legal and Equitable Interests

Care must be taken when it is said that B's beneficial interest is binding on C: first, not all of the duties of T will also be owed by C; second, the binding effect of B's interest in equity is different from, and more limited than, the binding effect of a legal property right on a third party. For example, Honoré used the term 'immunity from divesting' to describe one important feature of a legal property right. So if O has a freehold estate and grants a lease to L, for example, then L is not divested of her property right if O transfers the freehold estate to O2.[30] The position in equity is starkly different. In the case of the innocent volunteer receiving trust property, B clearly cannot claim that C, like T, was under an immediate duty not to use the trust property for C's own benefit. For this reason, B does not enjoy the same immunity from divesting as L does at common law, and the transfer to C, even if it is not authorised by the terms of the trust, *does* affect B's position.

There is nothing strange in the fact that T's unauthorised action can thus change B's position. If T holds a right on trust for B, then T, by virtue of holding that right, has a general power to deal with it, for example by transferring it to C. That power arises independently of, and irrespective of, the terms of the trust, as it depends simply on T's holding the right: it is the same power as held by O, an unencumbered owner of property. The terms of the trust may give T *authority*, as *against* B,[31] to deal with the trust property in particular ways, and those powers are relevant when considering the operation of overreaching.[32] Nonetheless, the point is that the existence of the trust does not strip T of any of T's general rights or powers in relation to the trust property; it rather imposes duties on T, owed to B,

[29] This argument adopts the 'continuity thesis' as explained by J Gardner, 'What is Tort Law For? Part 1. The Place of Corrective Justice' (2011) 30 *Law and Philosophy* 1. See too B McFarlane and R Stevens, 'What's Special About Equity? Rights About Rights' (Philosophical Foundations of Equity Law conference, King's College, London, June 2017).

[30] A Honoré, 'Rights of Exclusion and Immunities Against Divesting' (1960) 34 *Tulane Law Review* 453.

[31] A point also noted by Jessica Hudson in a work in progress presentation at the Modern Studies in Property Law Conference 2018.

[32] C Harpum, 'Overreaching, Trustees' Powers and the Reform of the 1925 Legislation' [1990] *CLJ* 277. Where overreaching occurs, C can take free from a proprietary claim of B even if C has knowledge that T holds on trust for B, as B's right can be regarded as always vulnerable to the exercise by T of a specific power under the trust: the overreaching defence is thus distinct from the general bona fide purchaser for value defence.

in relation to that property.[33] So if, for example, the terms of the trust state that T can dispose of the trust property only with the consent of X, then a sale by T to C with X's consent will mean that B cannot make an equitable proprietary claim against C, as T has exercised the specific authority under the trust, and B's right is thus extinguished. If, however, T sells to C without the consent of X, then the sale is still effective to pass title to C, but, if B can show that C's conscience is affected, B will be able to make the equitable proprietary claim against C.[34]

The key Hohfeldian point that all legal relations exist only in relation to specific other parties is highly relevant here.[35] In the example just discussed, it might be said that, owing to the terms of the particular trust, T has no power to dispose of the trust property without the consent of X; but that simply means that T has no power *in relation to B* to extinguish B's right by making such a disposition. T does not need to rely on the terms of the trust to have a power *in relation to C* to transfer the trust property to C; rather, T (and C) can simply rely on the fact that T holds that trust property. Similarly, consider a case, such as *Keech v Sandford*,[36] in which it is said that T has no power to acquire, for T's own benefit, a renewal of a lease held by T on trust for B. Of course, T does have a power, as an adult with capacity, to take on a lease; it is just that T will then hold such a lease subject to a duty to B. As far as any other party is concerned, however, it is indeed T's lease: it is T, rather than B, who is liable on any leasehold covenants; and it is T, rather than B, who can bring a claim against a third party who interferes with the lease. The point is that the nature of T's initial duty to B means that T is disabled, *as against B*, from renewing the lease for T's own benefit.

Our analysis of the case of the innocent volunteer is consistent with the view of the Supreme Court, expressed in *Akers v Samba Financial Group*,[37] of the effect of a transfer by T to C. In such a case, T simply transfers T's right to C: there is no disposition of any right or interest of B. The question is simply whether C then comes under a duty to B in relation to the right now held by C. It is not that C needs to show any defence against a prima facie binding interest of B; it is rather that B needs to show a good reason why C should be under a duty to B. It is this dependence of equitable interests on the existence of an initial duty owed by one party to another that explains their inherent vulnerability.

(iii) Determining When C's Conscience is Affected

In our view, the case-law on knowing receipt provides the best evidence of the test used to determine whether C's conscience is affected by knowledge of the initial trust relationship in such a way as to subject her to a duty to B. This is because C's liability depends precisely on C's coming under the core trust duty not to use property held by C for C's own benefit,

[33] See, eg, P Matthews, 'The Compatibility of the Trust with the Civil Law Notion of Property' in L Smith (ed), *The Worlds of the Trust* (Cambridge, Cambridge University Press, 2013).

[34] See eg *ITS v Noble* (n 10 above) [101] (Lloyd LJ); see also *Rolled Steel Products (Holdings) Ltd v British Steel Corporation* [1986] Ch 246 (CA), 304 for similar comments made by Browne-Wilkinson LJ in relation to the position of a third party who receives company property transferred in excess or abuse of the company's powers.

[35] W Hohfeld, 'Some Fundamental Legal Conceptions as Applied in Judicial Reasoning' (1913–14) 23 *Yale Law Journal* 16; J Finnis, 'Some Professorial Fallacies About Rights' (1972) 4 *Adelaide Law Review* 377.

[36] *Keech v Sandford* (1726) Sel Cas Ch 61, 25 ER 223.

[37] *Akers* (n 1 above).

and there are significant judicial suggestions that the test to be applied to a knowing receipt claim also applies to a proprietary claim.[38]

In deciding whether C is liable in knowing receipt, the key question is whether C's conscience is 'sufficiently affected for it to be right to treat him as bound by obligations in equity giving rise to an *in personam* claim against him as recipient to account for the money which came into his hands.'[39] As to *what* C must know, it is said that she must know that the property is traceable to, or was transferred in, breach of trust.[40] This test is fairly expansive. It does not require C to know who B is, or even what a trust is, and may be satisfied in any one of the following cases: where C knows that (i) the property was diverted from someone else without legitimate reason;[41] or (ii) the property represents the proceeds of fraud;[42] or (iii) the property was 'entrusted by [B] to [T] and not lent to him';[43] or (iv) 'there was a possibility that [T] did not have title to, or authority to sell' the property.[44] It appears that the crucial fact which C must know is that someone else (such as B) has a pre-existing right in respect of the property, which may be breached by T's exercise of her general power to transfer the property to C, and that T is in fact dealing without that person's authority when she transfers the property to C.

As to the level of knowledge required for C to be liable in knowing receipt, the test is whether that knowledge is 'such as to make it unconscionable for [C] to retain the benefit of the receipt' of the trust property.[45] This formulation appears to be question-begging, but it is not without significance. Five points are worth noting for present purposes. First, the relevant date for assessing whether it would be unconscionable for C to retain the property is not the date of receipt, but the earliest date at which she holds the property *and* has knowledge of the circumstances of its transfer. This is consistent with our analysis that an innocent volunteer is not subject to an immediate duty to B.[46] Second, the reference to unconscionability supports our view that conscience plays an important role in signalling that a specific reason must exist before C can come under a duty to B: mere receipt of property transferred in breach of trust does not suffice. Third, the broad phrasing of the test is a deliberate attempt to avoid the intricacies of the distinctions between the five gradations of knowledge set out in the *Baden, Delvaux* case.[47]

[38] *Re Loftus* [2005] EWHC 406 (Ch), [2005] 1 WLR 1890 [177] (Lawrence Collins J); *Papadimitriou v Crédit Agricole and Investment Bank* [2015] UKPC 13, [2015] 1 WLR 4265, [33] (Lord Sumption, obiter).

[39] *Relfo v Varsani* [2012] EWHC 2168 (Ch), [78] (Sales J).

[40] *El Ajou v Dollar Land Holdings Ltd* [1994] 1 BCLC 464 (CA), 478 (Hoffmann LJ).

[41] *Relfo v Varsani* [2012] EWHC 2168 (Ch), [81], [82] (Sales J).

[42] *El Ajou* (n 40 above) 472 (Nourse LJ).

[43] *Ali v Al-Basri* [2004] EWHC 2608 (QB) [194] (Tugendhat J).

[44] *Armstrong DLW GmbH v Winnington Networks Ltd* [2012] EWHC 10 (Ch), [2013] Ch 156, [278] (Stephen Norris QC).

[45] *Bank of Credit & Commerce International (Overseas) Ltd v Akindele* [2001] Ch 437 (CA), 455 (Nourse LJ).

[46] A similar point can be made in relation to proprietary estoppel: the question is not whether the defendant was under an immediate duty to honour a promise to the claimant; it is rather whether, given the defendant's reliance, it would now be unconscionable for the defendant to breach the promise and not provide any redress to the claimant: B McFarlane, 'Equitable Estoppel as a Cause of Action: Neither One Thing Nor One Other' in S Degeling, J Edelman and J Goudkamp (eds), *Contract in Commercial Law* (Sydney, LawBook Co, 2017).

[47] *Baden, Delvaux and Lecuit v Société Générale pour Favoriser le Developpement du Commerce et de l'Industrie en France* [1993] 1 WLR 509, 575–87.

Fourth, the use of conscience does not dictate that C can only come under a duty where C has actual knowledge.[48] Of itself the idea of conscience does not mandate a specific level of knowledge which must be established before a duty will arise.[49] If what C knows would prompt a reasonable person to make enquiries, which in turn would reveal the material facts which would ground the duty, it can still be said that her conscience is affected, albeit more weakly than if she had actual knowledge.[50] C knows enough to enable her, through the process of moral reasoning, to work out that she ought to make further enquiries, which in turn would give her the information she needs in order to decide how to behave in the particular situation she finds herself in. Therefore, it is not particularly helpful to say that the idea of conscience *per se* requires a particular level of knowledge. Rather, the question of what and how much C must know depends on the nature of her moral and legal relations with B, and is itself a question of moral (and legal) principle.

Finally, recent high-level authority[51] appears to require something more than mere knowledge of facts that would put someone on enquiry, which suggests that the degree of knowledge required for C to come under a duty to B in relation to the property is higher than the degree of knowledge or notice that would be required simply to deprive C of the defence we will now examine: the bona fide purchaser defence.

B. The Purchaser for Value

> Example 2: T holds a painting on trust for B. Acting in breach of her duties to B, and without any authority from B or under the terms of the trust, T sells the painting to C. C is unaware of the relationship between T and B and honestly believes that T simply owned the painting outright. C pays a fair market price for the painting.

The result in such a case is clear: B has no claim against C. There are, however, some benefits to be gained by precisely analysing the operation of the bona fide purchaser defence.

The language of conscience has been used to describe the operation of the bona fide purchase defence.[52] If C could show that at the time of giving value, her conscience was unaffected by notice of B's prior right, her title was said to be unimpeachable[53] and B's right

[48] We therefore disagree with suggestions to the contrary in, eg, *Consul Development Pty Ltd v DPC Estates Pty Ltd* (1975) 132 CLR 373 (HCA) 410–11 (Stephen J); R Havelock, 'The Transformation of Knowing Receipt' (2014) 22 *Restitution Law Review* 1, 15.

[49] Agnew (n 5 above) 11.

[50] See eg *The Law Society of England and Wales v Habitable Concepts Ltd* [2010] EWHC 1449 (Ch); *Armstrong* (n 44 above) [286] (Stephen Morris QC, obiter).

[51] See eg *Akindele* (n 45 above); *Arthur v Attorney General for Turks and Caicos* [2012] UKPC 30, [40] (Sir Terence Etherton).

[52] See eg *Bailey v Barnes* [1894] 1 Ch 25 (CA), 34 (Lindley LJ); *Taylor v London and County Banking Company* [1901] 2 Ch 231 (CA), 256 (Stirling LJ); *Midland Bank Trust Company Ltd v Green* [1981] AC 513 (HL), 528 (Lord Wilberforce); D Fox, 'Purchase for Value Without Notice' in P Davies, S Douglas and J Goudkamp (eds), *Defences in Equity* (Oxford, Hart Publishing, 2018) 66 notes that the defence was 'recast' in the 'familiar Chancery rationale of conscience' in the last quarter of the 18th century (see eg *Hoare v Parker* (1785) 1 Bro CC 578, 581, 28 ER 1308, 1310), as previous formulations had emphasised a different rationale.

[53] R Eastwood, *Strahan's Digest of Equity*, 6th edn (London, Butterworth & Co. Ltd, 1939); *Pilcher v Rawlins* (1872) LR 7 Ch 259 (CA), 269 (James LJ).

was extinguished.[54] C was 'entitled to hold that which, without breach of duty [on her part]' she had had conveyed to her,[55] and it was said that 'equity declines all interference with the purchaser, having, as is said, no ground on which it can affect [her] conscience.'[56] This language clearly suggests that a bona fide purchaser for value without notice is under no duty at all to B.

Even if there were no such thing as the bona fide purchaser defence, C's lack of knowledge of the initial trust relationship means that C would not in any case come under an immediate duty to B. The point of the defence is that even if C subsequently acquires knowledge of the initial trust relationship, C never comes under any duty to B. C's bona fide purchase thus gives C a form of immunity: C acquires the property from T free from any prospect of coming under a duty to B in relation to that property. This helps to explain why, if C then sells the property to C2, who *does* have knowledge of the initial trust relationship, B has no claim against C2 either.[57] At the time of the transfer to C2, C's right to the property is unburdened by any duty to B, and so C2 receives it free of any such duty. C2's position differs from that of an initial purchaser from T as, unlike such a purchaser, C2 does not deal with someone who holds a right subject to a duty to another.

It has been suggested that the bona fide purchaser defence 'clears the title' received by C and thus operates as an exception to the *nemo dat* principle.[58] Such a characterisation may be apt in those rare cases (such as when money passes into currency)[59] where such a defence is available against a pre-existing legal property right; but not in the context of the equitable proprietary claim. First, the requirements of the defence in equity differ from those applying where legal title is 'cleared'.[60] This is not surprising. In equity, the mere fact that C cannot rely on the defence does not necessarily mean that C will owe a duty to B: any such duty will only arise if C subsequently acquires knowledge of the initial trust relationship whilst still holding the trust property or its traceable proceeds.[61] By contrast, at common law, if title is not cleared, a third party will be prima facie liable in tort. Second, the effect of the defence in equity is not necessarily to 'clear' title: if the trust property is re-conveyed to T, then T will again hold on trust for B.[62] Third, when T transfers trust property to C, it is not the case that T purports to transfer distinct legal and equitable titles to C, and only succeeds in transferring equitable title where the defence applies. Rather, as discussed above, T simply exercises her general power, as holder of the trust property, to transfer that property to C. Even where C is a bona fide purchaser, the operation of the defence does not constitute

[54] W Cornish, *An Essay on Uses* (London, J Butterworth & Son, 1826) 17–18; W Hayes, *An Introduction to Conveyancing*, vol 1, 5th edn (London, S Sweet, 1840) 42–43.

[55] *Pilcher v Rawlins* (n 53 above).

[56] ibid 266 (Lord Hatherley LC).

[57] By analogy to *Wilkes v Spooner* [1911] 2 KB 473 (CA), a case involving a restrictive covenant.

[58] P Birks, 'Notice and Onus in *O'Brien*' (1998) 12 *Tolley's Trust Law International* 2, 5.

[59] See eg *Miller v Race* (1758) 1 Burr 452, 97 ER 398.

[60] In equity, notice is tested at the time when value is provided, rather than always at the time when the right is acquired, and the giving of a promise does not in itself count as value: see eg *ITS v Noble* (n 10 above), where the setting aside of the arrangement under which C acquired title prevented C from using the defence.

[61] This point is made by Lloyd LJ in *ITS v Noble* (n 10 above) [112].

[62] *Re Stapleford Colliery Co* (1880) 14 Ch D 432, 44; *ITS v Noble* (n 10 above) [47], [89].

a disposition of B's interest to C.[63] This is because C never acquires *B's* right, as B's right depended on the existence of a duty between B and T, and C does not benefit from any such duty.

If C wishes to avail herself of the immunity offered by the defence, she must demonstrate that, when she paid the purchase price and took the transfer of the legal estate,[64] she lacked actual and constructive notice that a third party (such as B) had a pre-existing 'proprietary right' in respect of the property.[65] In our view, the relevant facts of which C may or may not have notice are precisely the same facts as are relevant when determining liability in knowing receipt. The degree of knowledge or notice required to prevent C invoking the defence is, however, different, and lower than that required for C to come under a duty to B. The effect of notice (in preventing C from taking advantage of a purchase for value so as to acquire an immunity) is different from the effect of knowledge (in leading C to come under a duty to B in relation to property held by C).[66] Given those different effects, there is no necessary reason why the same test must be applied. After all, where C is a purchaser for value, the effect of actual or constructive notice is simply to place C in the same position as an innocent volunteer, ie, it removes her immunity from claims by B, so that she is liable to restore what is left of the property in her hands *if* C later acquires the required knowledge of the initial trust relationship. The court will therefore ask what C actually knew and what further enquiries an honest and reasonable person, with her knowledge and experience, would have made in the circumstances.[67] Further, whereas the evidential burden is on B to show that C had sufficient knowledge to come under a duty to B for the purposes of a knowing receipt claim,[68] the position is reversed where C seeks to show that she can avail herself of the bona fide purchaser defence.[69]

III. The Significance of the Idea of Conscience

In section II we set out the circumstances in which an equitable proprietary claim is available to B, a beneficiary of a trust, against a third party, C, to whom T transfers the trust property. The mere fact of receipt by C is insufficient. B's interest will bind C only if the circumstances in which C received and then holds the property are such as to bring her under a duty not to deal with the property other than for B's benefit. Although the language of conscience does not reveal the moral reasons why C comes under a duty to B in respect of

[63] *Akers* (n 1 above) [65] (Lord Neuberger). That result is also consistent with the analysis of the term 'disposition', as used in the different context of s 53(1)(c) of the Law of Property Act 1925 by the House of Lords in *Vandervell v Inland Revenue Commissioners* [1967] 2 AC 291 (HL): if T simply transfers the trust property to C, with B's permission, there is no disposition of B's beneficial interest to C.

[64] *Story v Lord Windsor* (1743) 2 Atk 630, 631, 26 ER 776, 777–78.

[65] *Sinclair Investments (UK) Ltd v Versailles Trade Finance Ltd (in administrative receivership)* [2011] EWCA Civ 347, [2012] Ch 453, [97] (Neuberger LJ); *Papadimitriou* (n 38 above) [18], [20] (Lord Clarke JSC).

[66] See, eg, *Re Montagu* (n 12 above); Fox (n 52 above) 79–80.

[67] *Sinclair Investments* (n 65 above) [100], [109] (Neuberger LJ); see also *Papadimitriou* (n 38 above) [15] (Lord Clarke of Stone-cum-Ebony JSC).

[68] eg, *Re Montagu* (n 12 above) 272–73.

[69] See eg *Barclays Bank v Boulter* [1999] 1 WLR 1919 (CA), 1925 (Lord Hoffmann, obiter).

the property, it does tell us something about the importance of knowledge in the generation of that duty, and examining conscience may therefore assist us in understanding the current approach of the courts.

A. The Meaning and Explanatory Role of Conscience

Broadly speaking, the idea of conscience captures both the process by which we reach moral judgements and the standards by which we make them. Aquinas regarded conscience as an act of applied knowledge, capturing the idea that an individual's innate moral understanding combines with knowledge of material facts to enable her to reach a conclusion as to the moral quality of her actions.[70] The Thomist idea of conscience was influential in the development of both our contemporary understanding of conscience and the idea of conscience in equity, and it is particularly helpful in explaining the incidence of moral and equitable duties.[71] If an individual's conscience is affected by knowledge, ie, if she has knowledge of the material facts, she can reason morally as to what she *ought* to do, and thus it is not unjust to treat her as bound by a moral duty to do it. Therefore, moral duties may be experienced as 'demands of conscience'.[72]

The language of conscience in equity may be interpreted in the same way. To say that an individual's conscience is affected by knowledge tells us that if she has knowledge of the relevant facts, her capacity for moral reasoning is activated. It is only through the process of moral reasoning – ie, through the operation of her conscience – that she can ascertain what she ought, morally, to do in the circumstances. At this point, it becomes reasonable to treat her as being subject to a moral or conscientious duty, which equity then underwrites and enforces.[73] To say that an individual has behaved unconscionably is therefore to indicate that she has breached a moral duty, which equity recognises and to which it gives effect.

This interpretation of conscience fits well with the way in which the courts deal with knowing receipt and the equitable proprietary claim: they are reluctant to treat C's conscience as sufficiently affected to justify the imposition of the core trust duty unless C either has knowledge of particular facts or has deliberately avoided acquiring that knowledge. It informs our analysis of the limited and special proprietary nature of B's beneficial interest under a trust, as discussed below.

B. Conscience and the Moral Position of Innocent Volunteers

If, at the date of receipt, C neither knows nor has any reason to know about B's rights in respect of the property, she does not owe a duty to B. Therefore, B cannot complain about

[70] Agnew (n 5 above) 481.

[71] Agnew (n 5 above) 481–92. For consideration of a different aspect of Aquinas's writings on the development of the use as a right capable of affecting third parties, see L Smith, 'Philosophical Foundations of Proprietary Remedies' in R Chambers, C Mitchell and J Penner (eds), *Philosophical Foundations of the Law of Unjust Enrichment* (Oxford, Oxford University Press, 2009).

[72] J Finnis, *Natural Law and Natural Law Rights*, 2nd edn (Oxford, Oxford University Press, 2011) 297.

[73] Agnew (n 5) 487.

C's actions if C deals with the property for C's own benefit.[74] Whilst C has the property but no knowledge of B's interest, her conscience is unaffected: she does not have the necessary information to work out what she ought to do with the property vis-à-vis B, and it is unreasonable to treat her as owing any moral duty towards B in respect of it. At most, she bears the risk that she ought to restore the property if she learns that B has a prior right to it. This explains why, as an innocent volunteer, C may mix the trust assets with her own and dispose of them freely, despite B's potential claim.

However, once C acquires knowledge of B's right, her conscience is affected. Then, she has all the information she needs to discern how she ought to deal with the property – eg, not to deal with it other than by restoring it – and it becomes reasonable to regard her as owing a moral duty to B to do just that. Equity underwrites this moral duty with an equitable duty 'not to part with the remaining funds (and the traceable proceeds in her hands of any which had already gone) otherwise than by restoring them to or for the benefit of the beneficiaries'.[75] C may fulfil this duty by restoring the property *in specie*; if she is unable to do so, she will be required to give substitutive performance by personally making good its value.[76] Note that C has no choice in the matter: if she has the property when B seeks to recover it, she must perform her obligation to restore the property,[77] and thus she is treated as a trustee.

C. Conscience and the Moral Position of Purchasers for Value

The language of conscience has also been used to describe the impact of notice on C, where C acquires the trust property for value. If C's conscience is affected by notice, she may not avail herself of the bona fide purchase defence. If our analysis is correct, the only effect of notice is to place C in the same position as an innocent volunteer: both are under a liability, which will not concretise into a duty unless and until they acquire knowledge of the initial trust relationship. If C, a purchaser for value, can demonstrate the absence of notice, she enjoys an immunity from this liability and thus from the prospect of *ever* coming under a duty to B in respect of the property.

Our analysis makes it possible to untangle any confusion that may arise from the invocation of the language of conscience in the context of both knowing receipt and the bona fide purchase defence. The key point, made above, is that whilst 'notice' by itself may suffice to prevent C from establishing the bona fide purchaser defence it need not suffice to impose on C a duty to B. First, if, as we contend, an innocent volunteer is subject only to a liability from the date she receives the property, then the same is true of C as a purchaser for value with notice. Even if notice is sufficient to subject C to a moral duty from the date she receives the property, any such duty is not strong enough to be directly enforceable as an equitable obligation. Instead, C is merely precluded from availing herself of the immunity which the

[74] *ITS v Noble* (n 10 above) [84].

[75] *ITS v Noble* (n 10 above) [78], [81] (Lloyd LJ).

[76] Mitchell and Watterson (n 13 above) 122–26.

[77] Noted by Lionel Smith, in a paper for the Philosophical Foundations of Equity Law conference, King's College, London, June 2017.

bona fide purchase defence offers. If this is right, then the impact of notice on C's conscience should be understood as excluding her from enjoying an immunity rather than subjecting her to an equitable duty: such a duty will arise only if C acquires further knowledge of B's position.

The second point is that it may be for historical reasons that the language of conscience and duty has been used to describe both: (i) the impact of notice on a purchaser for value; and (ii) the impact of knowledge on *all* recipients of trust property. At one point in time, the test for establishing constructive notice for the purposes of the bona fide purchase defence turned on whether C had wilfully abstained from enquiry to avoid finding out about B's interest.[78] The general principle was that the courts would not permit C to take a legal estate if when she took it she was aware of a fact which would make it 'unconscionable' for her to take it: this required evidence of a 'desire or fixed purpose to avoid knowing more'.[79] Although the language of gross or wilful negligence was sometimes used,[80] the key question was whether C was trying to avoid knowledge of the true state of the title.[81] In our view, this would be enough to subject C to a duty to B, and thus for both the equitable proprietary claim and knowing receipt. By the early twentieth century, however, the test for constructive notice had been relaxed. For C to be deprived of the bona fide purchase defence, gross negligence in her investigation of title would suffice.[82] The question was no longer whether C could show the absence of wrongdoing on her part, but rather whether she had done enough to protect her own legal title from pre-existing equitable interests.[83]

During the nineteenth century, the threshold for liability in knowing receipt appears to have been constructive notice rather than knowledge, although if C acquired the property in the ordinary course of business, proof of fraud or collusion was required.[84] Thus, it seems likely that for some time the threshold tests for knowing receipt and the absence of notice for the bona fide purchase defence were very similar, if not the same. If C had constructive notice of the initial trust, not only was she disabled from claiming immunity from B's equitable proprietary claim, she also came under an immediate custodial duty in respect of the property. Since then, the tests have diverged, with the result that now it is possible for C to be barred from claiming immunity as a bona fide purchaser without also coming under a duty not to deal with the property other than for B's benefit.

[78] *Espin v Pemberton* (1859) 3 De J & J 547, 554, 44 ER 1380, 1383 (Lord Chelmsford LC); *Jones v Smith* (1841) 1 Hare 43, 55–56, 66 ER 943 (Wigram VC).

[79] *Kettlewell v Watson* (1884) 26 Ch D 501 (CA), 707 (Fry J).

[80] Eg, *Hewitt v Loosemore* (1851) 9 Hare 449, 458, 68 ER 586 (Turner VC).

[81] *Hunt v Elmes* (1860) 2 DeF & J 578, 586–87, 45 ER 75 (Turner LJ); *The Agra Bank Ltd v Barry* (1874) LR 7 HL 135, 157 (Lord Selborne).

[82] *Oliver v Hinton* [1899] 2 Ch 264 (CA), 273–74 (Lindley MR); *Hudson v Viney* [1921] 1 Ch 98 (Ch), 104 (Eve J).

[83] See, eg, the remarks of Lord Selborne in *The Agra Bank Ltd v Barry* (n 81 above) 157; R Chambers and J Penner, 'Ignorance' in S Degeling and J Edelman (eds), *Unjust Enrichment in Commercial Law* (Pyrmont, LawBook Co, 2008) 256–66.

[84] *Bodenham v Hoskyns* (1852) 2 De GM & G 903, 42 ER 1125; *Mayor, etc of Berwick-upon-Tweed v Murray* (1856–57) 7 De GM & G 496, 44 ER 194; *Ernest v Croysdill* (1860) 2 De GF & J 175, 45 ER 589; *Gray v Lewis* (1869) LR 8 Eq 526; *Russell v Wakefield Waterworks Company* (1875) LR 20 Eq 474; *Blundell v Blundell* (1888) 40 Ch D 370 (Ch); *Thomson v Clydesdale Bank Ltd* [1893] AC 282 (HL), 290 (Lord Watson); *Bank of New South Wales v Goulburn Valley Butter Company Proprietary Ltd* [1902] AC 543 (HL); C Harpum, 'The Stranger as Constructive Trustee' (1986) 102 *LQR* 112, 273, 276, 278, 281–82, 290; P Birks, 'Misdirected Funds: Restitution from the Recipient' [1989] *Lloyd's Maritime and Commercial Law Quarterly* 296, 318, 320.

D. Conscience and the Replication of the Initial Trust Relationship

There is a very close relationship between the idea of conscience and the adage that equity acts *in personam*; this also sheds light on the way in which B's right under a trust is given protection against C. A core aspect of the initial trust relationship – T's duty not to deal with the property other than for the benefit of B – is replicated in the relationship between B and C.

The central idea common to uses and trusts was that the recipient of the property came under a duty to apply it in accordance with the purpose stipulated by the feoffor and, later, the settlor.[85] Initially, that duty was enforceable only as a matter of honour and conscience,[86] ie, it was a personal moral duty, which arose out of the trust and confidence placed by the feoffor in the feoffee to administer the property for the *cestui que use*. According to Strahan,

> an equitable interest is merely an interest affecting the conscience of the legal owner. If the legal owner obtains his title in such a way that his conscience is not affected by the equitable interest, he is in no way bound by it.[87]

As Simpson explains, '[T]here could be no use which attached simply to the land and not to some person.'[88]

Over time, the ecclesiastical courts[89] and subsequently the courts of Chancery underwrote the feoffee's moral obligation with institutional force and allowed the *cestui que use* to enforce the use against the feoffee personally 'in the name of good conscience'.[90] The Chancellor's role in relation to uses

> was to see that persons acted honestly according to the precepts of good morality, and, in accordance with the principle that equity acts *in personam*, he did not hesitate to proceed against feoffees who disregarded the moral rights of the *cestui que use*.[91]

Initially the right of a *cestui que use* was a personal right[92] enforceable against the feoffee alone.[93]

Gradually, the use began to take on proprietary characteristics as equity extended the personal liability of the feoffee to other recipients of the property.[94] The key to the

[85] W Holdsworth, *A History of English Law*, vol IV, 7th edn (London, Methuen, Sweet and Maxwell, 1966) 410; O Holmes Jr, 'Early English Equity' (1885) 1 *LQR* 162, 163; A Simpson, *A History of the Land Law*, 2nd edn (Oxford, Clarendon Press, 1986) 173.

[86] Simpson (n 85 above) 176.

[87] Eastwood (n 53 above) 29.

[88] Simpson (n 85 above) 181.

[89] R Helmholz, 'The Early Enforcement of Uses' (1979) 79 *Columbia Law Review* 1503; R Helmholz, *The Oxford History of the Laws of England*, vol I (Oxford, Oxford University Press, 2004) 422–23.

[90] Simpson (n 85 above) 176.

[91] E Burn and J Cartwright, *Cheshire and Burn's Modern Law of Real Property*, 18th edn (Oxford, Oxford University Press, 2011) 67.

[92] Sir Francis Bacon, *Reading on the Statute of Uses*, reprint edn (New York, Garland Publishing Inc, 1979) 401.

[93] HJ Stephen, *Stephen's Commentaries on the Laws of England*, vol 1, 21st edn (London, Butterworth & Co, 1950) 119.

[94] *Gilbert on Uses and Trusts*, 3rd edn (London, W Reed, 1811) 51; J Penner, 'The "Bundle of Rights" Picture of Property' (1995) 43 *University of California, Los Angeles Law Review* 711, 813, fn 242.

extension of liability beyond the trustee was whether the third party had been affected by the personal confidence originally reposed by the feoffor in the feoffee to hold the property for the benefit of the *cestui que use*;[95] if not, the use would not be enforced against her.[96] In the case of purchasers with notice, Story tells us that the courts were prepared to 'force the trust upon the conscience of the guilty party, and compel him to perform it, and to hold the property subject to it, in the same manner as the trustee himself held it.'[97] Those who inherited the property from the feoffee[98] and those who received it from her by way of gift[99] were also bound to carry out the use, even though they may have had no actual or constructive notice of it at the time of receipt. Equity appears to have treated the feoffee's gratuitous transfer of the property to a volunteer as insufficient to interrupt the obligations of trust and confidence that went with it.[100] The transaction was regarded as 'a change of the person of the legal owner, without any alteration of the legal title. That confidence which had been expressly reposed in [the feoffee], was tacitly communicated to [the third party].'[101] Not having paid, the volunteer could not have been in a better position than the feoffee.[102] Then, as now, however, the *cestui que use* could only recover whatever property remained in the volunteer's hands at the date she became aware of the former's claim to the property.[103]

The history shows that equity required a key aspect of the initial trust relationship – the core trust duty – to be present in B's relationship with C before it would allow B to recover the property from C. Thus, although B's right could be described as having proprietary effect, equity generated this effect by ascertaining whether C's conscience had been affected by knowledge and, if so, fastening an enforceable moral duty upon C. This distinctive approach to justifying liability had practical consequences. For example, the decision in *Burgess v Wheate*[104] emphasised that 'the trust is an institution based on the conscience of the trustee being affected':[105] if the beneficiary died intestate without heirs, so that there was no-one with a claim on T's conscience, the property would not pass to the Crown, but could rather be enjoyed by T. The limit on T's ownership comes from an obligation owed to B, and where there is no-one to whom such a duty can be owed, the trust ceases to exist. The result

[95] Hayes (n 54 above) 42.
[96] Burn and Cartwright (n 91 above) 81.
[97] W Grimsby, *Story's Commentaries on Equity Jurisprudence*, 2nd English edn (London, Stevens and Haynes, 1892) 867, [1257].
[98] YB 14 Hen VIII, pl 5.
[99] Stephen (n 93 above) 119–20; W Blackstone, *Commentaries on the Laws of England*, vol 2, 4th edn (London, J Murray, 1876) 282; Burn and Cartwright (n 91 above) 81, citing *Chudleigh's Case* 1 Co Rep 113b, 122b, 76 ER 261.
[100] Hayes (n 54 above) 43; Fox (n 52 above) 55–57 suggests that this conclusion was based on the (actual or presumed) intentions of the original feoffor to use and those who took from him.
[101] ibid.
[102] P Matthews, 'From Obligation to Property and Back Again? The Future of the Non-Charitable Purpose Trust' in D Hayton (ed), *Extending the Boundaries of Trusts and Other Similar Ring-Fenced Funds* (London, Kluwer Law International, 2002) 203, 208. Fox (n 52 above) 57–59 notes that, in sixteenth century cases, the absence of consideration allowed the court to assume that the feoffee, in transferring title to C, intended C to be bound by the initial use.
[103] Burn and Cartwright (n 91 above) 76.
[104] *Burgess v Wheate* (1759) 1 Wm Bl 123, 96 ER 67, 1 Eden 177, 28 ER 652.
[105] P Matthews, '*Burgess v Wheate* (1759)' in C Mitchell and P Mitchell (eds), *Landmark Cases in Equity* (Oxford, Hart Publishing, 2012) 115, 144.

in *Burgess* would not obtain today,[106] but the distinctive means by which equity achieves a 'proprietary' effect remains important.

In *R Griggs Group Ltd v Evans*,[107] Peter Prescott QC commented on the idea that equity had always acted *in personam* by fastening on C's conscience and requiring her to act accordingly. In his view:

> If equity had tried to make [C] liable, irrespective of any notice, it would not have been acting in personam. It would have been creating a title in [B] good as against the whole world. Thus it would have been acting in rem. It would have been ousting the common law, not supplementing it.[108]

Or, as Lord Mance recently put it, 'The rights of beneficiaries operate on the conscience of those party to or having notice of them.'[109] Were the 'bindingness' of B's interest not limited by reference to whether C's conscience is affected by knowledge, equity would not be following the law. Instead, it would be usurping it by setting up a parallel, competing system of rights *in rem*. The fact that the proprietary effect of B's rights under a trust depend on the existence of a particular relationship between B and C confirms that B's interest under a trust is 'a kind of personal claim that has proprietary effects because it can be enforced against any trustee, including transferees of the trust property who become trustees by operation of law.'[110]

IV. Conclusion

The purpose of this chapter has been to explain *how* B's rights under a trust bind third parties, and in particular to consider the role of C's conscience in the rules currently applied by the courts. We have not sought to offer a definitive justification as to *why* the rules operate in this way, or to consider what the rules tell us about the operation of equity more generally: this would be the next stage of our inquiry. One possibility is that equity often acts as an extra-legal moral standard or brake, preventing one party from taking opportunistic advantage of another:[111] on this view, the role of conscience, and the focus on C's knowledge, is to determine when C is seeking an opportunistic advantage from a transfer made by T in breach of T's duty to B. Another possibility is that equity often aims to protect those who are in the process of acquiring, or at risk of losing, particular rights:[112] on this view, the focus on C's knowledge may be a means of balancing protection of B's expectation of acquiring the benefit of legal property rights[113] with protection of C's more immediate expectation of acquiring the same benefit.

[106] Law of Property Act 1922, s 148, Administration of Estates Act 1925, ss 45(1)(d), 46(1)(iv).

[107] *R Griggs Group Ltd v Evans (No 2)* [2004] EWHC 1088 (Ch), [2005] Ch 153.

[108] ibid [43]. For similar comments on knowing receipt, see *Selangor United Rubber Estates Ltd v Cradock and Others (No 3)* [1968] 1 WLR 1555 (Ch), 1583, 1615 (Ungoed-Thomas J).

[109] *Investec* (n 3 above) [228].

[110] Smith (n 6 above) 10.

[111] HE Smith, 'Property, Equity, and the Rule of Law' in L Austin and D Klimchuk (eds), *Private Law and the Rule of Law* (Oxford, Oxford University Press 2014) 232–33.

[112] For this suggestion, we are grateful to Larissa Katz, in a paper for the Philosophical Foundations of Equity Law conference, King's College, London, June 2017.

[113] As a trust is generally a form of delayed gift, through which the trust property, or part of it, is ultimately channelled to B: see eg J Penner, 'The (True) Nature of a Beneficiary's Proprietary Interest Under a Trust' (2014) 27 *Canadian Journal of Law and Jurisprudence* 473, 485.

It can also be noted that equity, as a secondary and supplementary jurisdiction, often intervenes to control the acquisition or enforcement of primary rights; it need not respond to a wrong committed by the defendant, but can instead aim to prevent the defendant acting in a way that can be seen as involving an unconscionable assertion of a right.[114] Similarly, the scope of B's proprietary claim is informed by whether C has come under an equitable duty to B in respect of the property, even though that duty need not exist immediately upon C's receipt of the property. Understanding this is key to resolving the paradox raised at the start of this chapter. B's rights under a trust have 'in rem' effect in a limited sense only. That sense depends on their distinctive ability to bind a particular set of third parties: anyone who holds the trust property or its traceable proceeds at a point when her conscience is affected by knowledge of the initial trust relationship, so that she (like the initial trustee) may be said to owe B a moral and equitable duty in respect of the property.

[114] See eg *Hughes v Metropolitan Railway* (1877) 2 App Cas 439, 448 (Lord Cairns LC); *Crabb v Arun District Council* [1976] Ch 179 (CA), 187–88 (Lord Denning MR); McFarlane and Stevens (n 29 above).

18

'So How Should I Presume?': Loan, Resulting Trust, or Discharge of a Prior Obligation

JOHN MEE

I. The Issue

This chapter considers the legal starting point in cases where one person has paid money to another and there is a dispute as to the reason for the payment, and therefore as to its legal consequences.[1] There are, obviously, a number of possible explanations for a payment. The payor might have been making a gift of the money to the payee. Alternatively, the payment might have been made in discharge of a debt or obligation owed by the payor to the payee. In both of these cases, the payment would not lead to any legal liability on the part of the payee (unless the payor was mistaken in thinking that a debt was owed, in which case the payee could become liable in the law of restitution).[2] Another possibility is that the payment was a loan, in which case the payee would be under a contractual liability to repay the debt. Yet another explanation is that the money was transferred on trust, so that the payee would have to hold it as a trustee.

Which of the above explanations does the law presume when it is proven simply that one person has made a payment of money to another? Surprisingly, there are three candidate answers to this question. First, a number of nineteenth-century authorities hold that 'when money is paid by one man to another the legal presumption is that it was paid in discharge of some prior debt or obligation'.[3] This would mean that, in the absence of any further evidence, the recipient would be under no liability in relation to the payment. Secondly, both Professor James Penner and Professor William Swadling have recently argued that proof that one person made a payment or other transfer to another is sufficient to trigger the presumption of resulting trust.[4] On this view, in the absence of any further evidence, equity

[1] The quotation in the title is from TS Eliot, 'The Love Song of J. Alfred Prufock': www.poetryfoundation.org/poetrymagazine/poems/44212/the-love-song-of-j-alfred-prufrock.

[2] See eg *Barclays Bank Ltd v WJ Simms, Son and Cooke (Southern) Ltd* [1980] 1 QB 677.

[3] *Ex parte Cooper; Re Foster* [1882] WN 96, 96 (Jessel MR).

[4] J Penner, 'Resulting Trusts and Unjust Enrichment: Three Controversies' in C Mitchell (ed), *Constructive and Resulting Trusts* (Oxford, Hart Publishing, 2010) 238–41; W Swadling, 'Legislating in Vain' in A Burrows, D Johnston and R Zimmermann (eds), *Judge and Jurist: Essays in Memory of Lord Rodger of Earlsferry* (Oxford, Oxford University Press, 2013) 655, 659.

would presume that the payee would hold the payment on a resulting trust for the payor.[5] Thirdly, in 1968 in *Seldon v Davidson*,[6] the Court of Appeal considered the question of 'what is to be inferred as to the nature of the transaction when the simple payment of money is proved or admitted'.[7] Its conclusion was that 'on that bald state of affairs, proof of payment imports a prima facie obligation to repay the advancement'.[8] In other words, in the absence of any other evidence, the payment would be categorised as a loan and the recipient would be liable to repay the debt. The approach in *Seldon v Davidson* has been accepted in a series of subsequent English cases.[9]

Obviously, it would not be coherent for the law to presume three different things – discharge of a prior obligation, a resulting trust, a loan – on the same basic facts. This chapter will attempt to reconcile the apparently competing approaches by showing that they do not, in fact, apply in the same scenario. It will be argued that the presumption of discharge of a prior obligation is the one that applies where all that has been proven is that a payment has been made by one person to another. The presumption of resulting trust, notwithstanding the views of Penner and Swadling, is not triggered unless, in addition to the fact that a payment has been made, the claimant shows that the transfer was 'voluntary', ie made without consideration. Similarly, the rule in *Seldon v Davidson* is not properly to be regarded as being triggered simply by the making of a payment but must be understood as applying only where the evidence and the pleadings have reduced the possibilities to a choice between 'gift' and 'loan' (in which case the rule dictates that a loan is presumed). Having made these distinctions, the chapter will move from the analytical to the normative and, by way of conclusion, consider briefly the merits of the three different rules in order to assess whether they represent an appropriate legal response in the circumstances in which they apply.

Before moving on to address the questions of substance, the chapter will consider, in section II, an important preliminary question – how much does any of this matter?

II. What is at Stake?

It has been suggested that presumptions and/or the location of the burden of proof only matter in rare cases where there is no available evidence or in the unlikely event that the evidence on each side is equally balanced. For example, in *Ex parte Cooper; Re Foster*,[10] Lindley LJ stated that '[w]hen the parties to such a transaction [a disputed payment] are

[5] Although there has been academic controversy on the matter, the better view is that the fact which is presumed when the presumption of resulting trust applies is that the recipient was intended to be a trustee. See generally J Mee, 'Presumed Resulting Trusts, Intention and Declaration' (2014) 73 *CLJ* 86; J Mee, 'The Past, Present, and Future of Resulting Trusts' (2017) 70 *Current Legal Problems* 189.

[6] *Seldon v Davidson* [1968] 1 WLR 1083.

[7] ibid 1090 (Edmund Davies LJ).

[8] ibid. As will be discussed in the text to and following n 111 below, a gift would instead be presumed if the circumstances were such that the presumption of advancement would arise.

[9] See text to nn 76–79 below. The rule has been rejected in Australia (see text to nn 129–130) and in Hong Kong (see text to nn 22–26 below). The rule has, however, been accepted in New Zealand: see eg *Re Matthews* [1993] 2 NZLR 91.

[10] n 3 above.

alive, and give evidence, there is no occasion to resort to any presumption; the question is one of fact.'[11] Similarly, Professor Robert Chambers has argued that the presumptions of resulting trust and of advancement 'do not matter much as evidentiary devices, since they rarely determine the outcome of cases'.[12] Until recently such arguments had to concede that, in the context of illegality, the presumptions could play a crucial role under the test established by the House of Lords in *Tinsley v Milligan*.[13] However, in *Patel v Mirza*[14] the Supreme Court departed from *Tinsley*, eliminating the special significance that the presumptions of resulting trust and of advancement once had in the illegality context.[15]

The difficulty with the argument that presumptions rarely matter is that, in practice, 'lawyers and judges treat [presumptions] as having great importance'.[16] Yablon suggests that

> the perceived importance of burden-shifting doctrinal rules may be due to their role in framing questions for the judge or other legal decisionmaker and the implicit recognition of judges and lawyers, now made explicit by behavioral theory, that the way such questions are presented has a significant impact on the answers that are provided.[17]

He argues that, in the case of a presumption whereby fact Y is rebuttably presumed upon proof of X, it may be that

> the effect of the presumption will be to cause the judge or other fact finder to focus more on X in the determination of Y than he or she might otherwise be inclined to do. Accordingly, when Y is present, the likelihood of a finding of X increases significantly, and decreases when Y cannot be shown.[18]

This effect, whereby people who are deciding under conditions of uncertainty are heavily influenced by a starting point (even when they know it to have been arbitrarily selected), has been described by leading behavioural psychologists Daniel Kahneman and Amos Tversky as 'anchoring'.[19]

A somewhat different argument for the importance of the allocation of the burden of proof is that the situation where the evidence is in equipoise may not be as rare as one might assume. Logically, it depends on the 'granularity' of the process whereby a judge weighs evidence. If it were the case, for example, that evidence could be weighed on a scale from 1 to 1,000, then it would be very unlikely that the evidence on each side would be equally balanced. There would, however, be a very much higher chance of this occurring if the scale only ran from 1 to 10. It has been argued that, in making the relevant

[11] ibid 96–97.

[12] R Chambers, 'Is There a Presumption of Resulting Trust?' in Mitchell (n 4 above) 268. See also *Marr v Collie* [2017] UKPC 17, [2017] 3 WLR 1507 [54] (Lord Kerr).

[13] *Tinsley v Milligan* [1994] 1 AC 340.

[14] *Patel v Mirza* [2016] UKSC 42, [2017] AC 467.

[15] See generally PS Davies, 'Ramifications of *Patel v Mirza* in the Law of Trusts' in S Green and A Bogg (eds), *Illegality after Patel v Mirza* (Oxford, Hart Publishing, 2018).

[16] C Yablon 'A Theory of Presumptions' (2003) 2 *Law, Probability and Risk* 227, 228.

[17] ibid.

[18] ibid 234.

[19] Note, in particular, the 'wheel of fortune' experiment described in D Kahneman, P Slovic and A Tversky (eds), *Judgments Under Uncertainty: Heuristics and Biases* (Cambridge, Cambridge University Press, 1982) 14–17, referred to by Yablon (n 16 above) 232 (at the first stage of the experiment, subjects were presented with a number they believed to have been randomly generated; the size of this number significantly affected the subjects' subsequent answer to a factual question that they knew had absolutely no connection with the number).

sort of judgement, people do not in fact have an highly-graduated scale of certainty but, rather, have a much more limited number of 'settings'.[20] Clermont refers to seven options: '(1) slightest possibility, (2) reasonable possibility, (3) substantial possibility, (4) equipoise, (5) probability, (6) high probability, and (7) almost certainty.'[21]

A recent case in Hong Kong's highest court, *Big Island Construction (HK) Ltd v Wu Yi Development Co Ltd*,[22] provides an illustration of the potential importance of the allocation of the burden of proof, even in circumstances where both sides have given evidence in the course of a long trial.[23] *Big Island* also contains a detailed consideration of the status of the rule in *Seldon v Davidson*, and a discussion of the case now will prepare the ground for references to the case in the analysis in later parts of this chapter. The claimant in the case, BIC, had paid over HK$100 million[24] to the defendants. BIC claimed repayment on the basis that the money had been lent. The defendants, on the other hand, insisted that the money had been paid on the basis of various Fund Exchange Agreements, in return for equivalent payments by the defendants in RMB, the Chinese currency. At first instance, after a 43-day trial, Poon J held that BIC had failed to discharge the burden of proving that there had been a loan agreement. He went on to state that, although this did not affect the result, he also rejected the defendants' account of events as improbable. The judge's view was that there was '[s]omething more than meets the eye' to the situation and that the true explanation for the relevant transactions had been concealed from the court.[25] The plaintiffs appealed, inter alia on the basis that, following the rule in *Seldon v Davidson*, the burden of proof should have been on the defendants to prove that the payments had not been loans. The appeal was rejected by the Court of Appeal and the plaintiffs appealed again to the Court of Final Appeal. In rejecting the appeal, the Court held unanimously that the first instance judge ought to have found that the payments had been made on the basis of the Fund Exchange Agreements, since this account of events was well supported by documentary evidence. However, the Court of Final Appeal also considered the status of the rule in *Seldon v Davidson*. The majority view, expressed by Anthony Mason NPJ, was that the rule did not form part of Hong Kong law, although Tang PJ took a different view.[26]

For the reasons discussed in this section, the practical importance of presumptions and of the location of the burden of proof in civil cases may be greater than is sometimes assumed. There seems to be no objection to a presumption playing a significant role in determining decisions if there is a strong logical connection between the fact which triggers the presumption and the fact which is presumed. However, if a particular presumption is outdated or for other reasons is not reflective of reality, then the presumption's influence cannot be defended. Along these lines, it will be suggested in the conclusion to this chapter

[20] KM Clermont, 'Procedure's Magical Number Three: Psychological Bases For Standards of Decision' (1986–87) 72 *Cornell Law Review* 1115.

[21] ibid 1156.

[22] *Big Island Construction (HK) Ltd v Wu Yi Development Co Ltd* [2015] HKCFA 47, available at: https://www.hongkongcaselaw.com/big-island-construction-hk-ltd-v-wu-yi-development-co-ltd-and-another-4/; noted by M Kok and K Kwok, 'The Rule in *Seldon v Davidson* and the "Absence of Basis" Approach Revisited in Hong Kong' [2015] *Restitution Law Review* 128.

[23] For an illustration of the practical importance of the presumptions of resulting trust and of advancement, see *Antoni v Antoni* [2007] UKPC 10, [2007] WTLR 1335.

[24] Roughly £10 million.

[25] See n 22 above, [11]–[16] (Tang PJ).

[26] Aspects of the case are discussed in the text to nn 64–65, 104–107, 124–127, and 131–133 below.

that neither the presumption of resulting trust upon a voluntary transfer, nor the rule in *Seldon v Davidson*, has a sufficient foundation in probability to be acceptable as a matter of principle.

III. The Presumption of Discharge of a Prior Debt or Obligation

As has been mentioned, a number of older decisions suggest that the making of a payment will, in the absence of further evidence, be presumed to have been in discharge of a prior debt or obligation. In the first of these decisions, *Cary v Gerrish*,[27] it had been proven that the testator had drawn a draft on his bank in favour of the defendant and that the bank had paid the money to the defendant on the basis of the draft. In his briefly reported judgment, Lord Kenyon reasoned that 'a naked transaction' like this, was 'no evidence to establish a debt':

> No evidence is offered of the circumstances under which the draft was given, it might be in payment of a debt due by the testator; or the defendant might have been given cash for it at the time.[28]

In *Aubert v Walsh*,[29] the defendant in an action for money had and received gave notice of set-off and proved 'numerous checks drawn by the Defendants on their bankers, and delivered to the Plaintiff, to whom the bankers had paid them'.[30] The plaintiff objected

> that it was necessary to shew on what consideration, or for what purpose these checks were delivered, in order to apply them to this set-off; and that they did not prove any payment, without evidence of the circumstances under which they were given.[31]

Mansfield CJ is reported as having said simply: 'I am sure I remember a case before Lord Mansfield CJ in which a check given was produced as evidence of a debt, and his Lordship held that that alone was not sufficient.'[32] Chambre J is reported as having added 'All our accounts would be in inextricable confusion if such evidence were allowed.'[33]

The next case in the series is *Welch v Seaborn*,[34] where £100 had been lent by a man named Simpson to Rice Evans, who had in turn paid it to Evan Evans, who was now bankrupt. It was argued by Rice Evans that he was a creditor of Evan Evans to the amount of £100. In the brief report of the case, it is simply stated that:

> Lord Ellenborough was of opinion that there was not sufficient evidence to leave it to the jury, whether this money had been advanced to Evan Evans, by way of loan, since the presumption of law was, that money when paid is paid in liquidation of an antecedent debt.[35]

[27] *Cary v Gerrish* (1801) 4 Esp 9, 170 ER 624.
[28] ibid 10.
[29] *Aubert v Walsh* (1812) 4 Taunt 293, 128 ER 342.
[30] ibid 293.
[31] ibid 293–94.
[32] ibid 294. Here Sir James Mansfield, Chief Justice of the Common Pleas, was referring to a decision of the more famous William Murray, Earl of Mansfield, Lord Chief Justice of the King's Bench from 1756–88.
[33] ibid.
[34] *Welch v Seaborn* (1816) 1 Stark 474, 171 ER 534.
[35] ibid 474.

A final case from later in the nineteenth century, *Ex parte Cooper; Re Foster*,[36] does not seem to have been noticed in the present context before. Once again the report of the case is very brief, with the following being the full report of Jessel MR's judgment:

> When money is paid by one man to another the legal presumption is that it was paid in discharge of some prior debt or obligation, and not that it was meant as a gift, and if money is paid by a father to a son, and nothing beyond the fact of payment is proved, there is no legal obligation on the son to repay it, and the equitable doctrine, that there is a presumption that moneys advanced by a father to a son are intended as a gift, has no application. The onus of proof then is on the person who claims the repayment of the money, to shew that there was some contract rendering the payee liable to repay it. If there is such a contract, the payee is liable to repay at law as well as in equity.[37]

Two of these four cases, *Cary v Gerrish* and *Welch v Seaborn*, were commented upon in *Seldon v Davidson*. Edmund Davies LJ stated that '[t]hey are old cases; they are none the worse for that, but they are extremely briefly reported, and the extent to which they throw light on the circumstances of the present case is, with all respect, doubtful.'[38] Distinguishing the facts of *Seldon* from *Cary v Gerrish*, Edmund Davies LJ emphasised that it was

> clear from the assertion contained in the defence [in *Seldon*] that the advancements were made by way of gift, that no question here arises of the plaintiff repaying by the advancements a debt which she owed to her employee, nor is there any question of the defendant having given cash in return for the cheques drawn by the plaintiff.[39]

Referring to *Welch v Seaborn*, Edmund Davies LJ reiterated that 'the state of the pleadings in the present case rules out any … presumption' that the money had been paid in liquidation of an antecedent debt.[40] Willmer LJ commented only on *Cary v Gerrish* and he also concluded that it was distinguishable because the defendant had clearly admitted the payment of the money and there was 'no suggestion that it was paid in settlement of an existing debt, or that it was given in return for cash, or anything of that sort.'[41]

To sum up, beyond Edmund Davies LJ's observation that they were briefly reported, the authority of the older cases was not doubted in *Seldon*, and both Edmund Davies LJ and Willmer LJ went to the trouble of distinguishing the older cases on the facts. In light of this, and bearing in mind that there are two further cases to the same effect that were not discussed in *Seldon*, it seems reasonable to reach the provisional conclusion that the presumption established by the older cases remains part of the law, at least if it can be satisfactorily reconciled with the rule in *Seldon* and with the doctrine of resulting trusts.

IV. The Presumption of Resulting Trust

The conventional view has been that the primary fact triggering the presumption of resulting trust is that the claimant made a voluntary transfer (ie, a transfer without consideration)

[36] n 3 above.
[37] ibid 96. The report also includes a sentence from Lindley LJ (which was quoted above as text to n 11).
[38] n 6 above, 1089.
[39] ibid 1090.
[40] ibid.
[41] ibid 1088.

of personal property[42] or advanced the purchase money for a purchase in the name of another. The upshot, in the voluntary transfer situation, is that the presumption would not arise where all that has been proven is that X has made a payment to Y. This orthodox view allows the operation of the presumption discussed in section III to be reconciled with the operation of the presumption of resulting trust: where the only evidence is the making of a payment, the presumption is that the payment was made in discharge of a prior obligation but, once the claimant goes further and proves that the payment was voluntary (ruling out inter alia the conclusion suggested by the previously mentioned presumption), then the presumption of a resulting trust in favour of the transferor comes into play.

That the presumption of resulting trust would arise only upon a transfer that was voluntary does not appear to have been doubted until a relatively recent contribution by Professor James Penner,[43] which supported a view which Penner attributed to Professor William Swadling. This view was that, in order to trigger the presumption of resulting trust, 'all a claimant needs to show is that he transferred property to the defendant or contributed to the purchase price (up to paying the entire price) of property transferred by the seller to the defendant'.[44] Swadling has since explicitly adopted this view, stating that '[i]t is not necessary to obtain the benefit of the presumption … that the transferor prove by evidence that the transferee gave nothing in return'.[45] Swadling acknowledged his debt to Penner's contribution on the point, which Swadling stated that he had failed to make clear in a previous article.[46]

Penner does not offer an argument of principle but suggests that he favours Swadling's position (or what has now become Swadling's position) 'for the simple reason that he has the cases on his side'.[47] The first two cases upon which Penner relies, to establish that 'there is no need to show that there was an absence of any quid pro quo',[48] involve the presumption of resulting trust that is triggered by contributions to the purchase price of property which is transferred into the name of another.[49] The relevant cases have nothing specific to say about the point under discussion. Penner does not engage with the argument that the indirect transfer to the defendant is 'voluntary' in the sense that the claimant has provided the purchase price for property that was transferred to someone else. Rather, he emphasises the fact that the cases do not go on expressly to rule out the possibility that the defendant might have provided some other *quid pro quo* for the transfer.

The final authority relied upon by Penner is *Tinsley v Milligan*,[50] from which he quotes a passage which he sees as the 'nail in the coffin'[51] for the view that the presumption of

[42] Although there is ongoing controversy over the proper interpretation of this provision, s 60(3) of the Law of Property Act 1925 appears to ensure that there is no presumption of resulting trust in relation to voluntary conveyances of land. See J Mee, 'Resulting Trusts and Voluntary Conveyances of Land' [2012] *Conv* 307; J Mee, 'Voluntary Conveyances of Land: The Presumption of Resulting Trust Redux?' [2018] *Conv* 184.

[43] J Penner, 'Resulting Trusts and Unjust Enrichment: Three Controversies' in Mitchell (n 12 above) 238–41.

[44] ibid 238.

[45] Swadling (n 4 above) 659.

[46] ibid. Swadling's previous article was W Swadling, 'Explaining Resulting Trusts' (2008) 124 *LQR* 72.

[47] Penner (n 43 above) 239.

[48] ibid 240.

[49] *The Venture* [1908] P 218; *Mehta Estate v Mehta Estate* (1993) 104 DLR (4th) 24.

[50] n 13 above.

[51] Penner (n 43 above) 240.

resulting trust will arise only if the recipient has provided no consideration.[52] In the relevant passage, Lord Browne-Wilkinson states that what triggers the presumption is the fact 'that the plaintiff provided part of the purchase money, or voluntarily transferred the property to the defendant'.[53] The phrase 'voluntarily transferred' here clearly means that the recipient was a volunteer, who gave no consideration. Nonetheless, Penner comments, in respect of the relevant passage, that '[t]here is nothing here about any further requirement of having to show that the recipient of the title to the property provided no consideration for it'.[54] This comment is puzzling; it would only make sense if the word 'voluntarily' could be read to mean 'not as a result of compulsion', a position which is obviously unsustainable in light of the way in which the word 'voluntary', and variations thereon, is used in the case law concerning this category of resulting trust.[55]

Penner's argument explicitly applies to both the 'voluntary transfer' resulting trust and the purchase money resulting trust. Following on from the remarks in the previous paragraph, it will now be argued that in relation to the first of these two categories – the one with which this chapter is concerned – the argument is simply untenable.[56] The first difficulty is that it does not mention, and is inconsistent with, the four nineteenth-century authorities discussed earlier in this chapter, which indicate that bare proof of a payment from A to B does not trigger a presumption of resulting trust but rather a presumption that the payment was made in discharge of a prior liability. Secondly, the requirement mentioned in *Tinsley* that, in order to trigger the presumption of resulting trust, the transfer to the defendant must have been voluntary, in the sense of 'without consideration', is repeated in other leading cases. For example, in his explanation in *Westdeutsche Landesbank Girozentrale v Islington London Borough Council*[57] of the situations in which resulting trusts can arise, Lord Browne-Wilkinson stated that 'Where A makes a *voluntary* payment to B … there is a presumption that A did not intend to make a gift to B.' (emphasis added)[58] Similarly, in discussing the relevant aspects of the law of resulting trusts in *Lavelle v Lavelle*,[59] Lord Phillips MR outlined the rules applicable '[w]here one person, A, transfers the legal title of a property that he owns or purchases to another, B, *without receipt of any consideration*' (emphasis added).[60] This echoes the description of the facts triggering the presumption that was advanced by Lord Upjohn in *Vandervell v Inland Revenue Commissioners*,[61] where he discussed the 'well-settled principles' that apply '[w]here A transfers … the legal estate in property to B *otherwise than for valuable consideration*' (emphasis added).[62]

[52] The rejection, in *Patel v Mirza* (n 14 above), of the *Tinsley v Milligan* approach to the doctrine of illegality (see text to nn 13–15 above) does not affect Penner's argument, since he was relying on the general description in Tinsley of the circumstances in which a resulting trust arises, rather than on any point concerning illegality.

[53] n 13 above, 371.

[54] Penner (n 43 above) 240.

[55] On the two meanings of 'voluntary', see *Overseers of the Savoy v Art Union of London* [1896] AC 296, 305 (Lord Halsbury LC).

[56] The position in relation to the purchase money resulting trust is more complex. Due to constraints of space, it is not possible to pursue the point in the current chapter.

[57] *Westdeutsche Landesbank Girozentrale v Islington London Borough Council* [1996] AC 669.

[58] ibid 708. Lord Goff's explanation was in similar terms: ibid 689D.

[59] *Lavelle v Lavelle* [2004] EWCA Civ 223, [2004] 2 FCR 418.

[60] ibid [13].

[61] *Vandervell v Inland Revenue Commissioners* [1967] 2 AC 291.

[62] ibid 312. Note also *Re Vandervell's Trusts (No 2)* [1974] Ch 269, 294 (Megarry J).

This understanding of the law continues to be reflected in judicial statements of the relevant principles in the English case law.[63] It is also noteworthy that Tang PJ expressly stated in *Big Island Construction (HK) Ltd*[64] that 'it is only when a payment is voluntary that a resulting trust may arise'.[65]

It is also possible to point to examples where the requirement of voluntariness is not merely stated as a point of principle but is also applied to the facts of the case at hand. In *Crown Prosecution Service v Malik*,[66] Richards J stated that '[t]here could be no presumption of a resulting trust since … this was not a voluntary conveyance but a conveyance for a consideration of £35,000'.[67] In *Collier v Collier*,[68] Chadwick LJ stated that:

> [T]he creation of the leases in 1986 is not to be regarded as a voluntary transfer of property such as to give rise to any presumption of resulting trust. The leases, on their face, are granted for consideration. No presumption of resulting trust arises.[69]

Turning to considerations of principle, it may be pointed out that both the history and internal logic of the 'voluntary transfer' resulting trust doctrine show that the idea of voluntariness is crucial to its operation. At the time that the courts developed the rules on resulting uses,[70] replicated in the modern rules on resulting trusts, most voluntary conveyances of land were not intended as gifts but rather were made with the intention that the recipient would take as a trustee, to hold on the basis of instructions to be given later by the settlor. This led to the rule that, upon a voluntary transfer of property, the fate of the beneficial interest depends on the motivation of the transferor in entering into the transaction (on the 'consideration' for the transaction, in a different sense to the one now prominent in the law of contract), ie, on whether or not the settlor intended to pass the beneficial interest to the transferee. This idea is at the heart of the modern law in relation to presumed resulting trusts. Thus, the presumption applies in the case of what Chambers has called 'apparent gifts'[71] and what Swadling has referred to as 'ambiguous transactions';[72] it cannot sensibly apply to *all* transfers. The voluntary transfer resulting trust focuses on the unilateral intention of the claimant,[73] as is illustrated by the fact that a resulting trust has

[63] Note eg *KK v MA* [2012] EWHC 788, [2012] BPIR 1137, [112] (Charles J); *High Commissioner for Pakistan in the United Kingdom v Jah* [2016] EWHC 1465, [2016] WTLR 1763, [139] (Henderson J). Note also the reference to a 'voluntary conveyance' in s 60(3) of the Law of Property Act 1925.

[64] n 22 above.

[65] n 22 above, [44]. See also ibid, fn 43 to [61].

[66] *Crown Prosecution Service v Malik* [2003] EWHC 660, [2003] All ER (D) 33.

[67] ibid [30].

[68] *Collier v Collier* [2002] EWCA Civ 1095, [2002] BPIR 1057.

[69] ibid [80]. See also ibid [64] (Chadwick LJ). Note *Prest v Petrodel Resources Ltd* [2013] UKSC 34, [2013] 2 AC 415, [49], where, although a consideration of £1 had been paid, Lord Sumption described the relevant transfers as 'gratuitous' (another word for 'voluntary') and applied the presumption.

[70] See generally, Mee, 'Presumed Resulting Trusts, Intention and Declaration' (n 5 above) 94–97.

[71] R Chambers, *Resulting Trusts* (Oxford, Oxford University Press, 1997) 11.

[72] Swadling (n 46 above) 86.

[73] Note that matters have been complicated in the context of the purchase money resulting trust by the emergence of the common intention constructive trust which, on one view, has swallowed up the older doctrine entirely: see Mee, 'The Past, Present, and Future of Resulting Trusts' (n 5 above) 213–21. Note also, in the voluntary transfer context, the remarks of Chief Master Marsh in *National Crime Agency v Dong* [2017] EWHC 3116, [2018] Lloyd's Rep FC 28, [35]–[38].

been held to arise in cases where the recipient was unaware of the transfer to him or her.[74] However, if a transfer has been made in return for consideration, there is no logical reason to afford decisive significance to the (possibly undisclosed) intention of the transferor. Once the transfer has been paid for by the transferee, it is entirely reasonable for the beneficial interest to pass to the transferee in the absence of any express declaration of trust or some understanding between both parties that might trigger some other equitable doctrine.[75]

The foregoing discussion leads to the conclusion that, as it applies to the voluntary transfer resulting trust, the argument of Penner and Swadling is not sustainable either as a matter of authority or as a matter of principle.

V. The Rule in *Seldon v Davidson*

The rule in *Seldon v Davidson* appears to be established in English law, having been applied, or (more frequently) mentioned favourably, in a number of modern cases. These have often arisen in the context of disputes between cohabitants[76] but have also involved, eg, a dispute between a football club and its chairman,[77] a course of dealing between two wealthy business associates,[78] and a payment by a wealthy claimant and his wife to a friend whose business had run into difficulties.[79] This section examines the nature and basis of the rule in *Seldon v Davidson*.

A. The Reasoning in *Seldon v Davidson*

The defendant in *Seldon* had been employed by the claimant as a chauffeur and handyman. The defendant and his wife wanted to buy a house and, to help them to do so, the claimant gave two cheques amounting to £1,550 to solicitors acting on behalf of the defendant and

[74] See eg *Duke of Norfolk v Browne* (1697) Pr Ch 80, 24 ER 38; *Re Vinogradoff* [1935] WN 68. Note also, in the purchase money resulting trust context, *Shephard v Cartwright* [1955] AC 431; *Sidmouth v Sidmouth* (1840) 2 Beav 447, 48 ER 1254.

[75] Swadling (n 4 above) 659 comments that: 'Many judges and textbooks talk of the presumption arising in cases of proved by evidence gratuitous transfers, but that collapses issues of the facts necessary to be proved by evidence to raise the presumption and the sorts of evidence which will rebut it. The fact that consideration was given, ie that the transfer was not gratuitous, is something which rebuts the presumption.' However, proof of the existence of contractual consideration would not tell the court anything direct about the subject-matter of the presumption, ie about the nature of the claimant's intention (or, if one accepted Swadling's understanding of the nature of the presumption – advanced in Swadling (n 46 above) and criticised in Mee, 'Presumed Resulting Trusts' (n 5 above) – about whether the claimant made an express declaration of trust). It does not seem logical to argue that the presumption arises upon the making of any transfer, including one that is not voluntary, but that bare proof that the transfer is not voluntary serves automatically to rebut the presumption.

[76] *Freeman v Tems* (CA, 27 January 1993); *Clark v Mandoj* [1998] Lexis Citation 2366; [1998] EWCA Civ 505; *Markham v Karsten* [2007] EWHC 1509, [2007] BPIR 1109; *Woodward v Taylor* [2011] EWCA Civ 1729; *Favor Easy Management Ltd v Wu* [2011] EWHC 2017 (the rule was not mentioned on appeal: *Favor Easy Management Ltd v Wu* [2012] EWCA Civ 1464); *Chapman v Jaume* [2012] EWCA Civ 476, [2012] 2 FLR 830.

[77] *Re Nuneaton Borough Association Football Club Ltd (No 2)* [1991] BCC 44.

[78] *International Commercial Finance (UK) Ltd v K & K Knitwear Ltd* (HC, 18 June 2001).

[79] *Edwards v Dallyn* [1998] Lexis Citation 3489 (CA, 17 December 1998).

his wife. Subsequently, the claimant fell out with the defendant and he was dismissed from his employment. The claimant then sought repayment of the money. The defendant argued that the payment had been a gift or that, if it had been a loan, it was not repayable yet. The county court judge held, in response to a submission on behalf of the claimant, that the legal burden was on the defendant to prove one of the two defences on which he was relying. The judge then acceded to an application on behalf of the defendant for the trial to be adjourned so that the judge's ruling on the burden of proof could be appealed to the Court of Appeal. The two judges in the Court of Appeal had 'considerable doubts' as to whether an appeal lay on the point in question[80] given the potential for such adjournments to lead to 'a chaotic state of affairs'.[81] However, they did not rule conclusively on that point and, not wanting the parties to 'go away empty-handed',[82] proceeded to consider and dismiss the appeal on the merits.

The judgments in *Seldon* were given ex tempore and were relatively brief. Both judges noted the scarcity of relevant authorities. As mentioned previously, both judges discussed *Cary v Gerrish*,[83] and Edmund Davies LJ also referred to *Welch v Seaborn*.[84] Willmer LJ observed that:

> [Counsel for the defendant] was constrained to admit that the house which had been bought with the aid of the money paid by the plaintiff was no doubt prima facie subject to a resulting trust in favour of the plaintiff. That being so, it would be strange indeed if the same considerations did not apply to the money paid by the plaintiff to the defendant to assist him in the purchase of the house.[85]

Similarly, Edmund Davies LJ emphasised the fact that counsel for the defendant had been 'forced to concede that … the house must, prima facie, be regarded as being held by the defendant by way of a resulting trust for the benefit of the plaintiff'.[86]

The analogy with the resulting trust doctrine was the only argument expressly advanced by the judges to justify their decision that the burden of proof lay on the defendant to establish that the payment was a gift rather than a loan. However, a second argument may have had some influence on the minds of the judges. In the later Australian case of *Joaquin v Hall*,[87] Jenkinson J commented that the Court of Appeal in *Seldon* 'appears to treat the defence pleaded as a confession and avoidance'.[88] In argument in *Seldon*, counsel suggested that 'the mere handing over of money' should not 'always mean that there was an automatic obligation to repay'.[89] Willmer LJ asked in response: 'Why is the position not the same as in the case of a claim for breach of contract where it is pleaded that an exception clause applies?'[90] and Edmund Davies LJ followed this up with the observation that 'Confession

[80] n 6 above, 1088 (Edmund Davies LJ); ibid 1087H (Willmer LJ).
[81] ibid 1089 (Edmund Davies LJ).
[82] ibid.
[83] n 27 above.
[84] n 34 above.
[85] n 6 above, 1088.
[86] ibid 1089.
[87] *Joaquin v Hall* [1976] VR 788.
[88] ibid 789.
[89] n 6 above, 1085.
[90] ibid.

and avoidance occurs every day of the week.'[91] An example of confession and avoidance would be a case where a defendant conceded that the money had been lent but claimed to have repaid the loan; in such a case, the burden of proof would lie on the defendant to establish the repayment of the loan.[92] However, Jenkinson J appears to have been correct to point out in *Joaquin* that the defence in *Seldon v Davidson* was of a different nature to confession and avoidance and involved the 'denial of an essential ingredient in the cause of action.'[93] The admission by the defendant that he or she has received a payment from the claimant does not in itself – unlike the admission that a contract of loan existed between the parties – 'confess' a liability to repay that must be 'avoided' by the defendant's producing evidence that explains away that liability.[94]

B. Contract of Loan or Unjust Enrichment

It seems clear that the effect of the rule in *Seldon v Davidson* is that, when it applies, it places an onus of proof on the defendant which, if not discharged, will lead to a finding that the payment was a loan. The result would be that the defendant is contractually obliged to repay the loan. In his interesting discussion of *Big Island Construction (HK) Ltd*,[95] Professor Peter Watts appears to view the rule in a different light.[96] He suggests that it could be seen as providing support for the 'absence of basis' view of the law of unjust enrichment. Under this approach, favoured in civil law jurisdictions and in Canada, and advocated in the English context by Professor Peter Birks, 'once the transferor asserts "no basis" the onus moves to the recipient to prove a valid ground for the transfer of value.'[97] This is contrary to the current position in English law, whereby a person seeking restitution for unjust enrichment must be able to point to a specific 'unjust factor', such as mistake or failure of basis. According to Watts, while Birks looked for support for his position in the law of resulting trusts,[98] Birks 'appears to have overlooked that much more direct support for this view can be found in *Seldon v Davidson*'.[99] However, it does not seem to be accurate to suggest, as Watts does, that *Seldon* imposes the burden on the defendant 'of showing that the claimant intended to make a gift of the money or that otherwise there is a valid reason why restitution should be denied'.[100] If the defendant is unable to discharge the burden of proof laid on him by *Seldon*, the result will not be that 'restitution' will follow. Rather, there will be a finding of fact that the money was advanced as a loan and the defendant will be contractually liable to repay the debt.

[91] ibid.
[92] See *Young v Queensland Trustees Ltd* (1956) 99 CLR 560 (HCA).
[93] n 87 above, 789.
[94] As pointed out by Mason NPJ in *Big Island Construction (HK) Ltd* (n 22 above) [91].
[95] n 22 above.
[96] P Watts, 'The Onus of Proof in Restitutionary Claims' (2016) 132 *LQR* 11.
[97] ibid 12, citing P Birks, *Unjust Enrichment*, 2nd edn (Oxford, Oxford University Press, 2005) 136–37.
[98] See ibid 150–52, 304–07, developing an argument first presented in detail in P Birks, 'Restitution and Resulting Trusts' in S Goldstein (ed), *Equity and Contemporary Legal Developments* (Jerusalem, Hebrew University of Jerusalem, 1992). Note also Chambers (n 71 above).
[99] Watts (n 96 above) 12.
[100] ibid.

This emerges clearly from *Seldon v Davidson*, where Edmund Davies LJ stated that 'proof of payment imports a prima facie obligation to repay the advancement' and went on to explain that

> [Willmer LJ] has expressed the view that *the loan* would be repayable on demand. I would say, if not repayable on demand, at least repayable within a reasonable time of a request for repayment, and, of course, if it be the case that mere loans were made and, later on, the borrower repudiates the loans and asserts that the advancements were by way of out-and-out gifts, that repudiation of *the true nature of the transaction* would upon any view render the loans immediately repayable (emphasis added).[101]

This passage shows that, where the defendant is unable to prove that a gift was intended, the court will presume that the transaction involved a loan. As Swinton Thomas LJ put it in the later case of *Clarke v Mandoj*, what is at issue is a 'presumption in favour of a loan'.[102] It seems clear that the existence, in some factual circumstances, of a presumption that there was an actual contract of loan between the parties offers no support to Birks' general argument as to the circumstances in which restitution for unjust enrichment should be available.[103]

C. The Analogy with the Resulting Trust

As has been mentioned, the judges in *Seldon* laid emphasis on the proposition that a presumption of resulting trust would have been triggered by the fact that the defendant used the money to fund the purchase of a house. In *Big Island*,[104] Sir Anthony Mason NPJ commented that:

> The Court of Appeal's reasoning, based on the *prima facie* proposition that D held the house property on a resulting trust for the benefit of S, leading to the conclusion that the moneys paid by S to D should be repaid, is difficult to explain. The imposition of a resulting trust was designed evidently to justify an order for the repayment of the money paid on the footing that it was a loan. The relationship of resulting trust and loan in the circumstances of the case was inconsistent … What is more S did not claim that there was a resulting trust.[105]

The inconsistency referred to by Sir Anthony Mason NPJ arises from the well-established principle that an intention to lend on the part of the claimant is inconsistent with the creation of a resulting trust.[106] Sir Anthony Mason NPJ referred in the above passage to the

[101] n 6 above, 1090.

[102] *Clark v Mandoj* (n 76 above) (no pagination in original, penultimate paragraph). See also *Arif v Anwar* [2015] EWHC 124, [2016] 1 FLR 359, [87] (Norris J): 'the presumption of loan under *Seldon v Davidson*'.

[103] It is not entirely obvious how the rule in *Seldon v Davidson* might be seen as supporting an absence of basis theory of unjust enrichment but perhaps the argument is that the rule involves a presumption that the transfer was not a valid gift, so that the alternative possibilities are not just that the transfer was a loan but also that it was a gift made on the basis of a mistake or other invalidating factor, or that it was intended to satisfy some obligation that did not exist. However, there is no trace of a suggestion to this effect in the case law on *Seldon v Davidson*. Furthermore, the view that emerges in the case law is that the rule is only triggered when the evidence and the pleadings show that the transfer was either a gift or a loan (see text to nn 115–127 below) and that it operates to allocate the burden of proof as between these two possibilities.

[104] n 22 above.

[105] ibid [91]. Similar points were made by Tang PJ, ibid [42]–[47].

[106] *Re Sharpe* [1980] 1 WLR 219, 223B (Browne-Wilkinson J). See also *Big Island* (n 22 above) [44] (Tang PJ); [92]–[97] (Sir Anthony Mason NPJ).

'imposition' of a resulting trust in *Seldon v Davidson*.[107] However, as Watts points out, 'although Willmer LJ and Edmund Davies LJ's respective statements about resulting trusts were certainly elliptical',[108] they probably did not intend to suggest that a resulting trust actually arose over the house.[109] Watts goes on to suggest that:

> What the judges had in mind, it is suggested, is that, had the plaintiff alleged a resulting trust of the land bought with the money, instead of a loan, equity would have placed an onus on the defendant to deny the trust. It then seemed odd to them that the position would be different where only a loan of the money was being asserted.[110]

Watts's interpretation is convincing. Nonetheless, the rule emerging from Seldon draws significantly on the doctrine of resulting trusts in that it co-opts the concept of the presumption of advancement.[111] Professor Robert Chambers has suggested that *Seldon* 'demonstrates the independent nature of the presumption of advancement',[112] which 'being an inference that a gift was intended, can be applied in cases having nothing to do with the resulting trust'.[113] On the other hand, the point could be looked at differently, and it could be argued that *Seldon* is anomalous in its willingness to uproot the presumption of advancement from its home in the doctrine of resulting trusts and to give it an independent life. The range of relationships that attract the presumption of advancement has often been criticised. This is largely because of its sexist nature (since it applies from husband to wife and not the other way around and, historically at least, it only applied from father to child and not from mother to child).[114] It has also sometimes been argued that the presumption should also apply in the context of quasi-matrimonial cohabitations. It seems to be an undesirable feature of the rule in *Seldon v Davidson* that it imports the baggage associated with the presumption of advancement. If the rule were discarded, the burden of proof would (as usual) be allocated to the claimant, and the focus would be on assessing the actual evidence in the case, thus avoiding the disadvantages associated with drawing a 'bright line' between those relationships that attract the presumption of advancement and those that do not.

[107] And did so again, ibid [98].

[108] Watts (n 99 above) 13.

[109] Note that the facts of *Seldon* had the special feature that the claimant used the money to purchase a house. This diverted attention to the purchase money resulting trust and away from the voluntary transfer resulting trust (and the possible clash between the presumption of a resulting trust over the money and the *Seldon* presumption of a loan).

[110] Watts (n 99 above) 13.

[111] In another respect, however, the rule in *Seldon v Davidson* and the resulting trust appear to be different in nature. Although the point is surprisingly unclear, it seems that the presumption of resulting trust is an evidential presumption, which does not reverse the burden of proof but merely creates a burden of production on the other side (on such presumptions, see *Murphy on Evidence*, 15th edn (Oxford, Oxford University Press, 2017) 153). See eg *Fowkes v Pascoe* (1875) 10 Ch App 343, 352 (Mellish LJ); *O'Kelly v Davies* [2014] EWCA Civ 1606, [2015] 1 WLR 2725, [19] (Pitchford LJ); *Swadling* (n 46 above) 80, fn 49. In contrast, the rule in *Seldon v Davidson* seems to reverse the burden of proof: see eg, *Seldon* (n 6 above) 1088G (Willmer LJ); *Edwards v Dallyn* (n 79 above) (no pagination in original; penultimate paragraph (Roch LJ)); *Nel (suing as executrix of Nel) v Kean* [2003] EWHC 190, [2003] All ER (D) 206, [97] (Simon J); contrast *Markham v Karsten* (n 76 above) [58] (Briggs J): an 'evidential presumption'.

[112] Chambers (n 71 above) 32.

[113] ibid 33.

[114] See J Glister 'The Presumption of Advancement' in Mitchell (n 4 above); J Glister 'Section 199 of the Equality Act 2010: How Not to Abolish the Presumption of Advancement' (2010) 73 *MLR* 807.

D. When, Precisely, is the Rule Triggered?

Given the way in which the older authorities were distinguished in *Seldon*, the question arises as to when the rule comes into operation. Having reviewed *Cary v Gerrish*,[115] and *Welch v Seaborn*,[116] Edmund Davies LJ commented that, in light of their lack of relevance to the facts of the case before him,

> one is really driven back to consider this matter without the assistance of authority and, being so unassisted, I ask myself what is to be inferred as to the nature of the transaction when the simple payment of money is proved or admitted between strangers.[117]

His conclusion was that 'on that bald state of affairs, proof of payment imports a prima facie obligation to repay the advancement in the absence of circumstances from which the presumption of advancement can or may arise'.[118] Edmund Davies LJ's references to 'the simple payment of money' and 'that bald state of affairs' might suggest a broad scope for the rule in *Seldon*, whereby the inference of a loan would follow in any case where the payment of money is proven between strangers, with the obligation being on the defendant to prove the existence of additional factors in the case which would raise the possibility of the payment being in discharge of a pre-existing debt (and which would, on this view, cause the burden of proof to shift back to the claimant).

Willmer LJ, having discussed the approach of Lord Kenyon in *Cary v Gerrish*, pointed out that

> [n]o such considerations arise in the present case; indeed they are clearly ruled out, because we have from the defendant in this case a clear admission of the payment of the money, and no suggestion that it was paid in settlement of an existing debt, or that it was given in return for cash, or anything of that sort.[119]

Willmer LJ's conclusion was that:

> In the absence of any such circumstances, money paid by the plaintiff in circumstances such as these is prima facie repayable on demand. If the defendant seeks to evade repayment of the money which was paid to him, it seems to me that the judge was right in placing the onus on him to prove the facts which he alleges show that the money was not repayable.[120]

These remarks seem to suggest a narrower scope for the rule, whereby it will only apply in circumstances where the state of the evidence and the pleadings in the case rules out the possibilities considered in *Cary v Gerrish*; in other words, the rule would only apply where it fell to the court to decide between gift and loan.

Given that *Seldon* is open to two interpretations in terms of the scope of the rule it establishes, it is necessary to look to the subsequent English case law for clarification. Sometimes the rule is stated in these cases by reference to quotations from the judgments of Willmer

[115] n 27 above.
[116] n 34 above.
[117] n 6 above, 1090.
[118] ibid.
[119] ibid 1088.
[120] ibid.

and Edmund Davies LJJ, thus offering little or no assistance concerning the interpretation of the relevant statements.[121] In most of the cases, however, the rule is described by reference to the choice between gift and loan, as for example in *Markham v Karsten*,[122] where Briggs J stated that

> where there is a dispute between the payer and recipient of a sum of money as to whether it was a loan or gift, and no presumption of advancement arises between them, the onus is on the recipient to prove that it was a gift.[123]

Along the same lines, in his minority judgment in the Hong Kong case of *Big Island*, Tang PJ took a narrow view of the scope of the rule, insisting that it means only that the burden of proof is on the defendant 'to prove that the payment was a gift'.[124] He was 'firmly of the view that the burden is not on the defence to prove, for example, that the payments were in repayment of an earlier debt or in return for cash.'[125] In his majority judgment, Sir Anthony Mason NPJ stated that, in light of the language used by the judges in *Seldon*, it 'would be possible to so confine the implied obligation to repay so that it has no application at all to commercial transaction[s]'.[126] Presumably, the point being made by Sir Anthony Mason NPJ was that, in the commercial context, it will not generally be plausible to argue that the payment in question was intended as a gift and so, on the assumption that its function is to allocate the burden of proof where there is a dispute as to whether a payment was a gift or a loan, the rule in *Seldon* would have no application. In fact, Sir Anthony Mason NPJ went on to hold that, even in this form, there was no room for the rule in *Seldon v Davidson* in Hong Kong law.[127]

In the current author's view, the English case law suggests that, in line with the position of Tang PJ in *Big Island*, the rule in *Seldon v Davidson* is not triggered simply by the making of a payment, but rather applies to cases where the court is faced with a choice between gift and loan.

VI. Conclusion

The view that has just been taken of the scope of the rule in *Seldon v Davidson* suggests that it is compatible with the presumption of resulting trust, which applies where (since

[121] *Freeman v Tems* (n 76 above); *Clark v Mandoj* (n 76 above) (see the judgment of Hobhouse LJ; Buxton LJ concurring).

[122] n 76 above.

[123] ibid [42]. See also *Briggs v Rowan* [1991] Lexis Citation 2759 (no pagination in the original): 'there is an onus of proof on the recipient to prove that it was a gift if he seeks to defend the claim for repayment on the footing that it was a gift' (Jules Sher QC, sitting as a Deputy High Court Judge); *Edwards v Dallyn* (n 79 above) (no pagination in the original): 'the burden of proof on [D] to establish that these payments were gifts and not loans' (Roch LJ); *Nel (suing as executrix of Nel) v Kean* (n 111 above) [97] (Simon J); *Aspect Capital Ltd v Revenue & Customs* [2012] UKFTT 430, [2012] SFTD 1208, [194] (Judge Mosedale); *Shop Direct Group v Commissioners for HM Revenue and Customs* [2013] EWHC 942, [2013] STC 1709, [120] (Asplin J). Note also the reference by Swinton Thomas LJ in *Clark v Mandoj* (n 76 above) (no pagination in the original) to the issue of whether the transaction 'was a gift or a loan'.

[124] n 22 above, [53].

[125] ibid [53].

[126] ibid [99].

[127] See text following n 130 below.

the payment has been proven to be voluntary) the choice is between gift and trust. This view also allows the rule in *Seldon* to be reconciled with the existence of the presumption of discharge of a prior debt discussed earlier in this chapter; that presumption arises upon proof of a payment and the rule in *Seldon* arises only if, beyond that, the evidence and pleadings establish that the possibilities are gift or loan. This is consistent with the fact that there was no suggestion in *Seldon* that the older cases were wrongly decided. This analysis provides a method of rationalising the three presumptions that feature in the case law and, it is submitted, represents the best way to make sense of the current law and to avoid the problem of competing presumptions.

The final task of this chapter is to comment briefly on the normative desirability of this position. The current author has argued elsewhere that presumed resulting trusts, including the voluntary transfer resulting trust, are explicable on historical grounds and that their continued existence is difficult to justify in modern times.[128] When a person makes a gratuitous transfer of property, his or her likely intention is that the recipient should take the benefit of the property for himself or herself, so that the presumption of resulting trust does not reflect the probability of the matter. Therefore, although this is a comparatively radical position which cannot be defended in detail here, it would probably be best to discard the voluntary transfer resulting trust, including the presumption of resulting trust that currently arises upon a voluntary transfer.

If the voluntary transfer resulting trust were to be dispensed with, this would have implications for the logic underlying the rule in *Seldon v Davidson*, since the only justification offered by the court in *Seldon v Davidson* was the analogy with the presumption of resulting trust. It is significant that in Australia, where the voluntary transfer resulting trust has been held by the High Court of Australia not to apply in relation to chattels passing by delivery,[129] the rule in *Seldon v Davidson* has never been accepted.[130] Even if (as seems likely) the relevant form of resulting trust continues to be tolerated by English law, there would seem to be a strong case for following the approach of the Hong Kong Court of Final Appeal in *Big Island* and dropping the less well-entrenched rule in *Seldon v Davidson*.

The reasoning in *Seldon v Davidson* itself is unimpressive and there does not appear to be any strong justification for the rule it established. Writing extra-judicially, Tang NPJ has commented that, while he favoured retaining the rule (in its narrower form),[131]

> most probably, it makes little practical difference whether the English or Australian view is adopted. Just as it does not matter whether one drives on the right or left, so long as one knows on which side one is supposed to drive.[132]

[128] J Mee, 'The Past, Present, and Future of Resulting Trusts' (n 5 above) esp 220–21.

[129] *Heydon v Perpetual Executors, Trustees and Agency Co (WA) Ltd* (1930) 45 CLR 111, relying on *George v Howard* (1819) 7 Price 646, 146 ER 1089. On the status of the voluntary transfer resulting trust in Australia, see eg, *Ford and Lee: The Law of Trusts Online* (Sydney, Thomson Reuters Australia, 2016) [21.100].

[130] See *Joaquin v Hall* (n 87 above). See also eg *Sherwin v Commens* [2008] NTSC 45, [7] (Southwood J); *Alexiadis v Zirpiadis* [2013] SASCFC 64, [62]–[69] (judgment of the Full Court of the Supreme Court of South Australia); *Voce v Deloraine* [2012] NSWSC 1187, [12] (Lindsay J); *Steiner v Strang* [2016] NSWSC 395, [113]–[116] (Slattery J).

[131] One possible objection to the rule, mentioned by the Hon Mr Justice Tang in 'Developing Common Law in Hong Kong' (Common Law Lecture Series 2015, University of Hong Kong, 27 October 2015), tinyurl.com/ycgjjj95, [50], is that it is unfair to place the onus of proof on the payee because a lender is more likely to retain an 'IOU' than a payee is to retain a receipt.

[132] ibid [51] (footnote omitted).

The difficulty with this argument is that, as was suggested earlier in this chapter, presumptions have significant practical influence. The standard rule is that the burden of proof lies on the person seeking to establish a claim and, in the absence of any compelling justification, it is undesirable to create an exception to this general rule. There seems to be wisdom in the comments made by Sir Anthony Mason NPJ in his majority judgment in *Big Island*, which eliminated the rule from Hong Kong law, to the effect that:

> The making of a bare payment to another may in the nature of things be explicable by reference to a wide variety of possibilities. To my mind, the probability that there is an obligation to repay the amount is not so strong that it should become the subject of a presumption … Presumptions lend themselves to tactical ploys in litigation; it is better that parties be encouraged to present the totality of their case, particular[ly] in cases arising out of commercial transactions.[133]

While, for these reasons, the current author favours discarding the rule in *Seldon v Davidson*, there seems to be no objection to retaining the presumption that a payment, in the absence of any evidence beyond the fact that it is has been made, represents the discharge of a prior obligation. Although described as a presumption, the effect of this long-standing rule is simply to place the normal burden of proof on a claimant who seeks to make the case that another person is contractually obliged to repay money to him or her.

[133] n 22 above, [106].

19

Trusts and Legal Transplants: Lessons from Japan

JAMES C FISHER

I. Introduction: Trusts and Transplantation

Global interest in the trust is rising, evidenced by the adoption of the trust in individual civil law jurisdictions,[1] and by attempts to create an internationally applicable trust model.[2] Responding to the anticipated difficulties in introducing the trust to jurisdictions which do not accommodate the division between legal and equitable title, in terms of which the common law trust is classically described, some suggest that the trust's effects can be replicated using mechanisms already known to the civil law, while others challenge traditional understandings of the trust to show that they can in fact readily be absorbed by civilian jurisdictions.[3] Prior analysis of trusts in Asian civil law jurisdictions confirms that novel rights and obligations required to reproduce the trust can successfully be legislated into existence.[4] But this leaves unsatisfied the demands of *doctrine* – the organising 'grammar' of the law,[5] which stands 'outside of and above the law as it exists at any given time',[6] and justifies positive law in the sense of 'explain[ing] it rationally' as more than an arbitrary aggregation of disparate rules.[7] Commitment to doctrinal integrity seems to require that the tensions allegedly presented by the civil law trust be overcome if the entrance of trusts into new systems is to be legitimate.

[1] For example, trusts were introduced in a moderated form into Romania in 2011 (see eg L Tuleaşcă, 'The Concept of the Trust in Romanian Law' (2011) 6 *Romanian Economic and Business Review* 150) and the Czech Republic in 2014 (Czech Civil Code, ss 1448–1474); K Ronovská, '"Svěřenský fond" (Trust Fund): A Daring New Legal Transplant in Czech Law' in S Farran, J Gallen, J Hendry and C Rautenbach (eds), *The Diffusion of Law: The Movement of Laws and Norms Around the World* (Farnham, Ashgate Publishing, 2015).

[2] Examples include the Hague Convention on the Law Applicable to Trusts and on their Recognition, Book X of the Draft Common Frame of Reference, and movements towards a European 'protected fund' (see SCJJ Kortmann, K Reid, DJ Hayton, NED Faber and JWA Biemans (eds), *Towards an EU Directive on Protected Funds* (The Hague, Kluwer, 2009)).

[3] See eg T Honoré, 'Trusts: The Inessentials' in J Getzler (ed), *Rationalizing Property, Equity and Trusts: Essays in Honour of Edward Burn* (Oxford, Oxford University Press, 2003).

[4] L Ho and R Lee, 'Reception of the Trust in Asia: An Historical Perspective' in L Ho and R Lee (eds), *Trust law in Asian Civil Law Jurisdictions: A Comparative Analysis* (Cambridge, Cambridge University Press, 2013) 22.

[5] FH Lawson, 'Legal Orthodoxy' (1968) 6 *Houston Law Review* 1, reprinted in FH Lawson, *Many Laws: Selected Essays, Volume I* (Amsterdam, North-Holland, 1977) 79.

[6] ibid 63.

[7] J Gardner, 'What is Tort Law For? Part 1. The Place of Corrective Justice' (2011) 30 *Law and Philosophy* 1, 3.

The trust's proliferation is an archetypal case of legal transplantation. Drawing on studies of the diffusion of classical Roman law and the *ius commune*, Alan Watson famously argued that legal rules can be reliably transplanted into new legal systems notwithstanding the societal differences inherent in geography and the passage of centuries.[8] Watson's influential theory emphasises the autonomy of law as a self-contained normative system. In insisting that law develops or endures principally under its own internal logical forces, this theory presents *doctrine* not just as the justificatory principle behind positive law, but also as its principal agent of change. Both legal transplant theory and accounts of the trust's reception into civil law jurisdictions are concerned with the reception of foreign law and the central importance of doctrine in legal development. Much may therefore be gained by considering them together.

This chapter links the Japanese experience of trust reception to wider debates about legal transplantation. It considers the reception of the trust device into Japanese law in the early twentieth century, some of the distinctive doctrinal features of the Japanese trust, and its capacity to disrupt foundational axioms of the wider law of property and succession, in order to reflect on the success of the Japanese trust as a legal transplant. It concludes that it is wrong to consider the trust a particularly problematic legal form for emulation, by locating the inevitable disruption caused by introduction of the trust into Japanese law within a general account of legal change.

II. Japanese Trust Legislation

Japan was the first purely civil law jurisdiction to adopt the trust, and has been a crucial nodal point in the trust's spread across the civil law world, with its trust legislation being emulated by East Asian jurisdictions such as South Korea,[9] Taiwan[10] and China.[11] Space permits only a cursory outline of the process by which Japan adopted a codified civil law system that nonetheless includes trusts.[12] In the mid-nineteenth century, military pressure from Western states forced Japan out of its two centuries of isolationism and into a series of unequal treaties which, in addition to exploitative trade provisions, ensured extraterritoriality for the laws of the Western powers in disputes concerning foreign nationals in Japan. The situation galvanised internal dissatisfaction with Japan's fragmented feudal government, and the resultant civil war led to a centralised Imperial state. The new government sought rapidly to emulate Western statehood in order to resist foreign designs on Japanese

[8] A Watson, *Roman Law and Comparative Law* (Athens GA, University of Georgia Press, 1991) 97; A Watson, 'Legal Transplants and Law Reform' (1976) 92 *LQR* 79, 80.

[9] Trust Act of the Republic of Korea 1961, Act No 900 of 1961. Korea amended the law with the Korean Trust Act 2011 to reflect almost all the reforms Japan had made in the 2006 reforms.

[10] Trust Act of the Republic of China (Taiwan) (promulgated 26 January 1996, amended 30 December 2009).

[11] Trust Law of the People's Republic of China (Order No 50 of 2001).

[12] For accounts of modern Japanese legal history and the overall process of reception of foreign law, see eg W Röhl (ed), *History of Law in Japan since 1868* (Leiden, Brill, 2005). On the legislative history of Japanese trusts in English, see M Tamaruya, 'Transformation of Trust Ideas in Japan: Drafting the Trust Act 1922' (2013) 88 *Rikkyō Law Review* 97; S Tofaris, 'Trust Law Goes East: The Transplantation of Trust Law in India and Beyond' (2015) 36 *The Journal of Legal History* 299; and M Tamaruya, 'Japanese Law and the Global Diffusion of Trust and Fiduciary Law' (2018) 103 *Iowa Law Review* 2229.

sovereignty. A major objective was revision of the unequal treaties, but the Western powers insisted that revision required comprehensive reform of Japanese law on a Western model,[13] particularly its commercial law, to guarantee the safety of foreign investments in Japan.[14] Political demands for fast, comprehensive reform made the uncodified common law an unrealistic model,[15] and a series of codes (of largely German and some French influence) emerged as the basis of modern Japanese law.

In the early twentieth century, at the instigation of the Japanese banking sector,[16] and with a view to succeeding in the international competition for investment capital to support Japan's continued industrialisation,[17] the Japanese government enacted the Secured Bond Trusts Act 1905 to permit large banks to act as trustees for the exclusive purpose of facilitating large-scale investment. 'Trust-bank' status proved popular, and around 500 institutions were trading under this regime by the early 1920s. Most conducted no trust business, a regulatory failing that prompted more thorough legislation in 1922. The new Trust Act set out and explained in detail the substantive law of trusts in Japan, while the associated Trust Business Act provided for the thorough regulation of trustees. Tight regulation of trusts meant that they occupied only a minor role in Japanese law for decades, but with deregulation in the 1980s, the trust became the new legal architecture for high-value capital investments. These regulatory changes are now reflected directly in the revised Trust Business Act 2004 and Trust Act 2006.

III. The Trust's Effect on the Wider Japanese Law of Property

Japan's trusts legislation has always focused on the interests of commerce, and almost all legislative change in Japanese trusts law is economically motivated, equipping trusts for use in an ever-increasing array of sophisticated investment products.[18] But despite conspicuously little *official* interest in expanding the use of trusts in civil legal life, judicial exegesis has probed the implications of the Japanese trust, revealing its power markedly to affect the wider private law.

Although Japanese law recognises wills, the Civil Code nonetheless guarantees extensive forced heirship rights,[19] and does not recognise successive interests. However, since

[13] FC Jones, *Extraterritoriality in Japan and the Diplomatic Relations Resulting in its Abolition, 1853–1899* (New Haven CT, Yale University Press 1931) 100.

[14] D Howland, *International Law and Japanese Sovereignty: The Emerging Global Order in the 19th Century* (London, Palgrave Macmillan, 2016) 29.

[15] K Takayanagi, 'Contact of the Common Law with the Civil Law in Japan' (1955) 4 *The American Journal of Comparative Law* 60, 61.

[16] Close symbiosis between the civil bureaucracy and large corporate interests characterised the formation of the modern Japanese state: see BS Silberman, 'The Bureaucratic State in Japan: The Problem of Authority and Legitimacy' in T Najita and JV Koschmann (eds), *Conflict in Modern Japanese History: The Neglected Tradition* (Princeton NJ, Princeton University Press, 1982) 226, 242–43.

[17] Tamaruya, 'Transformation of Trust Ideas in Japan: Drafting the Trust Act 1922' (n 12 above) 98.

[18] Tamaruya, 'Japanese Law and the Global Diffusion of Trust and Fiduciary Law' (n 12 above). Please note that, unless otherwise indicated, all statutory provisions referred to in this chapter come from Japanese legislation.

[19] Civil Code, Articles 887 and 1028.

the early 1980s the Japanese courts have recognised trusts' power to oust these otherwise non-excludable rights, particularly by sanctioning successive interests under trusts. Japan's Civil Code invalidates any legal act incompatible with public policy,[20] which includes the mandatory provisions of law recorded in the Code itself, subject to derogation in statute. The courts' willingness to uphold successive beneficial interests even though the Trust Act 1922 did not expressly sanction them suggests that they understood the ability to create successive beneficial interests as intrinsic to the trust form. Following these judicial developments, the financial sector foresaw demand for 'estate-planning' trusts, calculated specifically to circumvent the forced heirship rules, and the 2006 legislative reforms explicitly sanctioned the use of trusts as will-substitutes,[21] and the creation of successive beneficial interests.[22] The Japanese courts have even applied trusts analysis indirectly to effectuate purported outright testamentary gifts to successive donees – presenting an attempt to give to successive donees as, by its very nature, an exercise in settlement.

More generally, the courts have held that a trust may be constituted by the mere transfer of assets with a view to their application to a particular purpose, even without proof of an express intention on the part of the settlor to create a trust. In the leading case, a transferor was able to recover a sum paid to an insolvent transferee.[23] The Supreme Court found that the transfer constituted a trust of the funds because the transferor had not intended to expose that money to the risk of the transferee's insolvency. Such an intention was transparently constructive: in the absence of any indication that the transferor had considered the results of insolvency, the Court simply *deemed* a transfer in such circumstances to have been made with the intention that the money should not be vulnerable to the transferee's insolvency and (implicitly) with the intention that it should be held on trust.

This decision developed and ratified earlier jurisprudence, much of it from an insurance context. Where an insurance policy is concluded through an agent, Japanese regulations require that sums paid to the agent in advance and intended to be used as premiums must be clearly segregated from the agent's general assets.[24] In two decisions concerning the insolvency of insurance agents,[25] the Tokyo District Court held that such sums were not subject to insolvency distribution along with the agent's other assets, provided: (i) the holding account was so named as to show that its contents were outside the agent's general assets, (ii) the funds were not, and were not understood to be, divertible to any other purposes, and (iii) the contents of the account clearly represented the unpaid premiums. These criteria can only be rationalised as evidence for the nature of the payment – that the principal paid the money to the agent for the specific purpose of paying the insurer.

When reaching these decisions, courts have not expressly invoked the language of trusts, but nothing else in Japanese private law can explain why simply placing funds in

[20] ibid, Article 90.

[21] Trust Act 2006, Article 90.

[22] ibid, Article 91.

[23] Supreme Court, Case No 1671 of 2000.

[24] A rule now incorporated into the Insurance Business Act 1996.

[25] Tokyo District Court, decisions of 29 March 1988 (reported in *Hanrei Jiho* 1306) 121, and 27 September 1988 (reported in *Kinyu Homo* 1220) 34.

a discrete bank account makes them unavailable to creditors on insolvency.[26] In recognising trusts simply on transfer or segregation of assets with a view to their application to a particular purpose, Japanese law independently emulated the common law in ways that the perfunctory 1922 legislation did not contemplate. It allowed something similar to the English *Quistclose* trust[27] to emerge organically, despite the fact that Japan's 1922 legislative framework did not countenance trusts' creation without the specific consent of the settlor.[28]

IV. Legal Transplantation Assessed

While analyses of various legal systems have utilised and endorsed Watson's theory of legal transplantation,[29] for ardent detractors such as Legrand, legal transplantation on Watson's model is conceptually impossible,[30] because a rule's meaning is specific to the culture that produces it,[31] and the rule's 'meaning cannot survive the journey' to a new jurisdiction.[32] As others have observed,[33] many debates in comparative law are really disagreements of legal philosophy. To deny that legal rules have a content articulable in isolation from other planes of social existence – to insist that legal rules have no 'determinate content apart from a given culture'[34] – clearly expresses an anti-positivist orientation. Comparative law cannot answer these primordial jurisprudential questions, because they logically precede, and indeed define, the parameters of the comparative enquiry. But it is possible to engage with a less absolute rendition of this critique – with 'contextualist' voices that emphasise the influence the social environment exerts on the content of legal rules, while not denying that the law thus produced is comprehensible in its own terms. Watson's theory proved controversial because it 'flies in the face of some of the most treasured preconceptions of modern legal thought',[35] namely 'that the law changes in response to forces *external*

[26] Unjustified enrichment analysis hardly applies, since the outcome in both cases was not the repayment of the sums to the principal, but that they should be paid to the insurer as originally countenanced.

[27] *Barclays Bank Ltd v Quistclose Investments Ltd* [1970] AC 567.

[28] See further JC Fisher, 'The Trust as Trojan Horse: A Comparative Perspective on Trusts' Role in Japanese Succession Law' (2018) 103 *Iowa Law Review* 1945.

[29] Chen-Wishart draws on contract law in Asia to insist 'the legal system is shaped by the elite priesthood of legal professionals who … look principally to the legal tradition itself': M Chen-Wishart, 'Comparative Asian Contract Law on the Remedies for Breach of Contract: Transplant, Convergence, and Divergence' in M Chen-Wishart, A Loke and B Ong (eds), *Studies in the Contract Laws of Asia I: Remedies for Breach of Contract* (Oxford, Oxford University Press, 2016) 425.

[30] P Legrand, 'The Impossibility of Legal Transplants' (1997) 4(2) *Maastricht Journal of European and Comparative Law* 111.

[31] P Legrand, 'What "Legal Transplants"?' in D Nelken and J Feest (eds), *Adapting Legal Cultures* (Oxford, Hart Publishing, 2001) 55–57.

[32] Others have gone so far as to posit a 'law of non-transferability of law': A Seidman and RB Seidman, *State and Law in the Development Process: Problem Solving and Institutional Change in the Third World* (London, Palgrave Macmillan UK, 1994) 44–46.

[33] W Ewald, 'The Jurisprudential Approach to Comparative Law: A Field Guide to "Rats"' (1998) 46 *The American Journal of Comparative Law* 701.

[34] M Graziadei, 'Comparative Law as the Study of Transplants and Receptions' in M Reimann and R Zimmermann (eds), *The Oxford Handbook of Comparative Law* (Oxford, Oxford University Press, 2006) 467.

[35] W Ewald, 'Comparative Jurisprudence (II): The Logic of Legal Transplants' (1995) 43 *The American Journal of Comparative Law* 489, 490.

to law'[36] – variously the politics, economics or culture of the jurisdictions in question. This contextual focus is particularly strong among economists of law. Lawrence Friedman, for instance, posits that the substance of law is basically economically determined, explaining why developed legal systems resemble each other far more than their own pre-modern ancestors.[37] But in fact, the gulf between the formalist and contextualist accounts of legal development and transplantation is narrower than is often assumed.

Many critics read Watson as denying that externalities *ever* influence positive law,[38] a claim so 'ludicrous' that contradicting it is 'like shooting fish in a barrel'.[39] But on its strongest construction Watson's thesis accepts that 'to some extent a people's law is peculiar to it … [and] reflects the interests of the ruling élite',[40] asserting only that these things do not inevitably predict all concrete legal rules and institutions – a claim with which almost all 'contextualists' concur.[41] Even the most classical determinist accounts of law understand it as 'no mechanical superstructure arising atop the economic base', but a peculiar normative system, with 'law and legal reasoning … having, to some degree, a life of their own.'[42] As David Nelken notes, the discourse on transplantation needs to 'find a better route to capture how law both does and does not "fit" its context.'[43] Watson's work contributes to this by identifying examples of how law endures and develops independently of a changing social environment. But his reasoning does not, and cannot, deny a relationship of any kind between law and society. His conclusions about law's insulation from its environment rely on the specific characteristics and practices of the juridical community responsible for the development of legal content in Roman – and later – society.[44] His conclusion therefore rests on the fact that legal discourse is a rarefied rather than popular process. That hardly disproves a relationship between social fact and the rules that eventually emanate from this rarefied discourse, because the concentration of 'legal culture' in a technocratic elite *is itself* a political fact. That a layer of internally self-validating legal formalism mediates between the raw facts of social relations and specific judicial outcomes does not rebut claims of a relationship between law and society – it is precisely what (sophisticated) explications of that relationship allege.

[36] ibid.

[37] L Friedman, 'Borders: On the Emerging Sociology of Transnational Law' (1996) 32 *Stanford Journal of International Law* 65.

[38] Ewald (n 35 above) 505–06. See eg L Friedman, 'Some Comments on Cotterrell and Legal Transplants' in Nelken and Feest (n 31 above).

[39] Friedman ibid.

[40] A Watson, *Society and Legal Change* (Edinburgh, Scottish Academic Press, 1977) 4.

[41] Watson has been accused of attacking a view that no sociologist of law actually holds: R Abel, 'Law as Lag: Inertia as a Social Theory of Law' (1982) 80 *Michigan Law Review* 785, 790. Legal sociologists accept that 'law may be out of phase with social change, whether it is behind … or ahead of other developments.': D Nelken, 'Towards a Sociology of Legal Adaptation' in Nelken and Feest (n 31 above), 14.

[42] P O'Connell, 'Engels, Law and Dialectics' (*Legal Form: A Forum for Marxist Analysis of Law*, 12 December 2017): https://legalform.blog/2017/12/12/engels-law-and-dialectics-paul-oconnell/. As even Engels observed, although legal content is hyper-conditioned by social relations – meaning that the law will necessarily 'correspond to the general economic situation and be its expression' – nonetheless the very 'concept of law' means that 'it must of itself constitute a coherent expression', with the development of a *legal system* properly so called being 'the attempt to eliminate the contradictions arising from the *direct* translation of economic conditions into legal principles' (emphasis added): Letter to Conrad Schmidt (27 October 1890), in *Marx–Engels Collected Works*, vol 49 (London, Lawrence and Wishart, 2010) 57. Sound general treatments of the Marxist approach to law include P Phillips, *Marx and Engels on Law and Laws* (Oxford, Martin Robertson, 1980).

[43] D Nelken, 'Legal Transplants and Beyond: Of Disiplines and Metaphors' in A Harding and E Örücü (eds), *Comparative Law in the 21st Century* (London, Kluwer Law International, 2002) 29.

[44] A Watson, *The Evolution of Law* (Baltimore MD, John Hopkins University Press, 1985) 119.

V. Doctrine and Context as Engines of Transplantation and Change

The presence of the trust in Japan's codified civil law is hard to reconcile with a Watsonian 'internalist' account of legal development. The Japanese trust results from political-economic concerns external to the law. The trust represented a means to attract foreign investment into Japan that was particularly attractive to powerful commercial interests intimately connected with the state bureaucracy. The state's interest in the trust extended only to its ability to support stable, secure and controlled commercial investment,[45] to which doctrinal niceties were immaterial. That said, the subsequent expansion of the trust beyond its original peripheral role is principally a product of 'internal' legal logic, which has occurred in a complex relationship with the changing social and economic environment.[46]

As explained above, the Japanese courts have accepted the trust's ability to achieve free testation in defiance of the Civil Code's provisions on forced heirship. The common law derives much of its traditional support for free testation from the proposition that freely chosen distributions of property on death will on the whole be 'more accurately adjusted to the requirements of each particular case, than could be obtained through a distribution prescribed by the stereotyped and inflexible rules of a general law.'[47] Like other developed economies, Japan is experiencing major social and demographic change. Its notoriously ageing population and declining birth-rate mean an ever-increasing demand for pensions and medical care, but also a decreasing number of economically productive individuals who can provide the tax revenue on which social welfare depends. It is therefore increasingly problematic that the Civil Code reserves large amounts of wealth for heirs who may not need it, obstructing testators' ability to mitigate poverties or social issues that would otherwise burden the community at large.

It is unclear how far judicial decisions confirming the unstated potential of the 1922 trust regime result from conscious judicial sensitivity to the economic case for flexible succession law. The judgments themselves do not reference these issues, but the *ratio* of Japanese courts is famously opaque, and Japanese judges are not immune from the temptation to deploy apparently formalist reasoning to reverse-engineer a preferred outcome. Other recent judicial developments in connected areas of Japanese law do incontrovertibly result from judicial sensitivity to social change, for instance concerning challenges to the Civil Code provisions giving illegitimate children only half the inheritance rights of their legitimate siblings.[48] In 1995 the Supreme Court held this to be consistent with the constitutional guarantee of equality,[49] but in 2013 it declared the provisions unconstitutional.[50] The majority saw in the Code's succession provisions a general norm that children should

[45] H Dōgauchi, 'The Theoretical Outlook and Other Issues in the New Trust Act' (2007) 1261 *Kinyū Shōji Hanrei* 66 (in Japanese).

[46] See more fully Fisher (n 28 above) 1946–57.

[47] *Banks v Goodfellow* (1870) LR 5 QB 549, 564–65. See J Brook, 'The Neighbour, The Carer and the Old Friend – The Complex World of Testamentary Capacity' in H Conway and R Hickey (eds), *Modern Studies in Property Law*, vol 9 (Oxford, Hart Publishing, 2017) 120–24.

[48] Civil Code, Article 900.

[49] Supreme Court (Grand Bench), Decision of 5 July 1995, reported in *Minshū* 49-7-1789.

[50] Supreme Court (Grand Bench), Decision of 4 September 2013, reported in 67 *Minshū* 1320.

inherit equally (the result of the American Occupation's abolition of primogeniture), and regarded the rule halving inheritance for illegitimate children as a specific derogation, reflecting social attitudes about marriage in the mid-twentieth century. The Court concluded that attitudes and practices concerning family life had changed since the War, such that this derogation was no longer constitutionally compliant.

Such open-textured reasoning is to be expected in a challenge to the constitutionality of primary legislation, and there is no direct evidence that recognising the trust's unstated potential is the work of an 'activist' judiciary consciously developing the law to advance a given agenda. Indeed, empirical research on the Japanese judiciary consistently reports an ideologically homogeneous institution that is politically and juridically conservative,[51] wedded not to instrumentality but to doctrine. Judicial recognition of the trust's unarticulated potential to recalibrate the wider Japanese law of property and succession is certainly adaptive to changes in the social environment. However, the engine of the trust's development was its own juridical logic. Socio-economic changes simply provided the opportunity for the trust's disruptive potential to unfold in this way, by incentivising jurists to probe the trust form in search of new, better answers to disputes about the use of wealth. 'Although the 1922 legislation did not expressly provide for many of the things that courts have accepted trusts can do', the courts simply took the 'embryonic Japanese trust device to [the] logical conclusions' implicit in the 1922 legislation, 'applying not what the individual lawmakers of 1922 subjectively believed they were enacting, but what the Act that legislature in fact enacted entails as a matter of legal logic.'[52]

Ultimately though, how far subjective judicial attention to non-legal factors explains the Japanese courts' development of the law of trusts is incidental. The purpose here is not to explain particular legal developments by reference to judicial psychology, but to show Japanese law's *systemic* adaption to its extra-legal environment through the disruptive effect of the trust, regardless of who – if anyone – is consciously linking these together. With the debate between doctrinal and contextual accounts of legal transplants in mind, it is interesting that the changes bringing Japanese property and succession law into closer resonance with the common law derive from 'internal' judicial exegesis probing the logical implications of the trust. Conversely, as discussed below, subsequent developments which divide the Japanese trust from those familiar to English equity lawyers have been *legislative* in origin – the work of Japanese government ministries with a famously symbiotic relationship with the business sector, aimed at making trusts increasingly 'shapeless' in light of the interests of financial operators.[53]

[51] Although they offer competing explanations: *cf* eg, JM Ramseyer and E Rasmusen, *Measuring Judicial Independence: The Political Economy of Judging in Japan* (Chicago IL, Chicago University Press, 2003); JO Haley, 'The Japanese Judiciary: Maintaining Integrity, Autonomy and the Public Trust' in DH Foote (ed), *Law in Japan: A Turning Point* (Seattle WA, University of Washington Press, 2008); DS Law, 'The Anatomy of a Conservative Court: Judicial Review in Japan' (2009) 87 *Texas Law Review* 1545.

[52] Fisher (n 28 above) 1964.

[53] The stated purpose of the 2006 reforms was to equip trusts to be used to meet Japan's increasingly broad economic and social requirements: Economic Legal Research Institute of Japan, *The Practice of the Reformed Trust Act* (Tokyo, ELRI, 2007) 5.

VI. The Success of the Japanese Trust?

Watson claimed that 'legal rules may be very successfully borrowed where the relevant social, economic, geographical and political circumstances of the recipient are very different from those of the donor system.'[54] But his work barely considers what it means for a legal transplant to succeed, rather than fail – he regards transplants as 'socially easy' and barely accommodates the potential for failure.[55] Emphasising that a transplanted rule 'will grow in its new body, and become part of that body, just as … [it] would have continued to develop in its parent system',[56] Watson accepted that 'a rule once transplanted is different in its new home',[57] and that the local context will affect the direction of this development.[58] But this adaption is treated as separate from the transplantation itself, which Watson insists occurs unencumbered by environmental forces. This clean division between (invariably successful) transplantation and subsequent evolution results from Watson's formalist understanding of transplantation – the transplant itself is complete as soon as a rule enters the positive law of the recipient system.[59] Watson is surely right that law in the books is easy to transplant, but that is so obviously true as to be theoretically uninformative, and Watson's textual understanding of the act of transplantation has attracted criticism – its formal focus 'stands in stark contrast to traditional comparative scholarship'.[60]

Comparatists typically understand a 'complete' transplant as involving both a rule's establishment as formal law and its reception and 'adaptation'.[61] They require of a *successful* transplant some evidence that the rule's incorporation has affected legal life in its new environment – things should, in some observable sense, *work differently* following a successful transplant. Kanda and Milhaupt describe success as the 'use of the imported legal rule in the same way that it is used in the home country, subject to adaptations to local conditions',[62] but do not indicate *how much* change to the rule or its application is tolerated as 'adaptations to local conditions' before this is regarded as a signal that the rule is not being used 'in the same way' as in the donor jurisdiction. The same authors identify failure when 'the application and enforcement of the [transplanted] rule lead to unintended consequences.'[63] Again, crucial questions remain. What about consequences that are unintended but beneficial? The shortcomings of these and similar formulae are clear in that

[54] Watson, 'Legal Transplants and Law Reform' (n 8 above) 80.

[55] A Watson, *Legal Transplants: An Approach to Comparative Law* (Athens GA, University of Georgia Press, 1974) 95.

[56] ibid, 27.

[57] A Watson, 'Legal Transplants in European Private Law' (2000) 4 *Electronic Journal of Comparative Law* 1, 2.

[58] A Watson, 'Legal Change, Sources of Law and Legal Culture' (1983) 131 *University of Pennsylvania Law Review* 1121; A Watson, *Law Out of Context* (Athens GA, University of Georgia Press, 2000).

[59] A Watson, *Legal Origins and Legal Change* (London, Hambledon Press, 1991) 86–87. Watson regards leading critiques as being at cross purposes: Watson (n 57 above) 9; see also Watson, 'Legal Change, Sources of Law and Legal Culture' (ibid).

[60] J Zekoll, 'Kant and Comparative Law – Some Reflections on a Reform Effort' (1996) 70 *Tulane Law Review* 2719, 2747; L Friedman, 'Society and Legal Change' (1979) 6 *British Journal of Law and Society* 127, 128.

[61] W Twining, 'Diffusion of Law: A Global Perspective' (2004) 49 *Journal of Legal Pluralism and Unofficial Law* 1, 24.

[62] H Kanda and CJ Milhaupt, 'Reexamining Legal Transplants: The Director's Fiduciary Duty in Japanese Corporate Law' in Foote (ed) (n 51 above) 440.

[63] ibid.

it is possible for the same legal transplant to be both a success *and* a failure according to these criteria – for example, if the transplanted rule is used superficially in the same way as in the donor system, but its use has produced unintended consequences in the recipient system at large.[64] It is important also not to abandon attention to doctrine. Those who do so struggle to distinguish success from the *practical utility* of a transplant, or even from the general competitiveness of the jurisdiction into which a rule has been introduced, which may have no direct link with the rule itself. For instance, commentary on Japan's adoption of codified civil law celebrates this as a successful legal transplant with 'very little analysis of what this means, beyond the fact that … [Japan subsequently] developed into a highly prosperous and politically stable nation.'[65] Recalling the doctrinal element may permit a more scientific understanding of the 'success' of legal transplantation than an impressionistic consequentialist enquiry into whether things are better after a rule's reception.

Although the trust has brought Japanese property and succession law incrementally closer to a characteristically common law position, the Japanese trust itself is distinct from the trust as it exists in England and Wales or any other common law jurisdiction – whatever one's preferred account of the 'nature' of the common law trust. Trusts can be understood as either settlor-focused or beneficiary-focused structures. On the former understanding, trusts operate to empower settlors, expanding what can be done with their wealth beyond the dichotomy of (i) retaining it or (ii) disposing of it. Central therefore to the trust in operation is not the beneficiary but the trustee, as it is through the trustee's duties that the settlor's intentions are effectuated. On the latter understanding, a trust comprises, ultimately, a gift to the beneficiary, 'projected on the plane of time and so subject to a management regime.'[66] These conceptions are at least partially competing, and their respective influence on the positive law of trusts varies with time and place. The settlor-focus has been particularly influential in the United States,[67] but has also affected English law in developments such as the loosening of certainty rules for discretionary trusts,[68] advancing the view that trusts should be valid provided the intentions of the settlor can be reasonably protected through enforcement of trustees' duties.[69] The beneficiary-focus has been particularly dominant in England and Wales, manifesting itself variously in the idea that trusts confer equitable property rights on beneficiaries,[70] the rule that trusts not for purposes recognised as charitable are valid only if 'for the benefit of individuals',[71] and the rule in *Saunders v Vautier*, allowing a beneficiary of majority and capacity to demand the trust capital notwithstanding contrary terms established by the settlor.

[64] Similar questions are raised by Nelken (n 43 above) 38–39.

[65] ibid.

[66] B Rudden, 'Book Review of J.P. Dawson, Gifts and Promises: Continental and American Law Compared (New Haven CT, Yale University Press, 1989)' (1981) 44 *MLR* 610.

[67] J Getzler, 'Transplantation and Mutation in Anglo-American Trust Law' (2009) 10 *Theoretical Inquiries in Law* 355, 375. cf TP Gallanis, 'The New Direction of American Trust Law' (2011) 97 *Iowa Law Review* 215.

[68] *Re Baden's Deed Trusts (No 1), McPhail v Doulton* [1971] AC 424.

[69] The same notion underlies the sporadic decisions upholding trusts for non-charitable purposes (eg *Re Thompson* [1934] Ch 342 (directly) and *Re Denley's Trust Deed* [1969] 1 Ch 373 (obliquely)) provided the obligations are of a nature that can be overseen and enforced.

[70] Agnew and McFarlane discuss the limited and idiosyncratic proprietary effect of a beneficiary's entitlement under a trust: S Agnew and B McFarlane, 'The Paradox of the Equitable Proprietary Claim' in this volume.

[71] *Bowman v Secular Society* [1917] AC 406; *Re Endacott* [1960] Ch 232.

Japanese trusts likewise represent a fusion of beneficiary-focused and settlor-focused ideas, but they have coalesced into a balance peculiar to Japan. In many ways the Japanese trust centres on the settlor and echoes contractual logic, with the trust defined as 'an arrangement in which a specific person … administers or disposes of property in accordance with a certain purpose'.[72] The law therefore expressly permits trusts for purposes with no identified beneficiary.[73] Likewise a trustee's consent was traditionally necessary not just for their own assumption of trustee's duties, but for the creation of the trust itself. However, the 2006 reforms for the first time allowed declarations of trust,[74] by the 'manifestation of an intention' to be a trustee.[75] Although unremarkable in common law jurisdictions, the entrance of self-declared trusts into Japanese law frustrates the rationalisation of trusts as a subspecies of bilateral contract. Other, older features of the Japanese trust further isolate it from the wider law of obligations by presenting a beneficiary as in some sense analogous to an owner of the trust assets, not merely a third party benefited under a contract between two others. Japanese trusts provide the familiar 'ring-fencing' effect that protects trust assets from the trustee's personal creditors and removes it from her estate in the event of death,[76] and Japanese beneficiaries also have the power to rescind dispositions in breach of trust.[77]

Yet in other ways the 2006 Act further subsumes trusts within contract law principles – for instance, it declares that trusts are fully constituted at the moment of agreement between settlor and trustee, even before transfer of the trust assets.[78] This development results from trusts' role in providing the legal architecture for high-value investment products. The goal was to accelerate the moment at which trustee institutions fall subject to the (quasi-)fiduciary duties that accompany trusteeship, since they may acquire commercially valuable knowledge about the trust property even before its transfer, from which they should not be able unscrupulously to profit.[79] Other features, such as the presumptive inalienability of beneficial interests,[80] further distinguish the Japanese trust from the notion of equitable property that still represents the most reliable account of the English trust.

The multiple attempts to maximise the trust's commercial utility in multiple directions preclude a logically satisfactory account of its relationship with wider Japanese private law – the trust has become a 'law unto itself' as economically-motivated innovations in the operation of trusts change their nature. This is not to say the Japanese trust is drawing closer to the English. For example, post-2006 Japanese trust law tolerates a sole settlor declaring herself sole trustee for herself as sole beneficiary,[81] which is anathema in English law. This outlandish feature was designed to facilitate efficiency in investments – trust banks wanted the ability to declare themselves trustees and initial beneficiaries of assets, and then sell their own beneficial interests to investors.

[72] Trust Act 2006, Article 2 (1).
[73] ibid, Article 258(1). Such trusts must be subject to third-party oversight.
[74] ibid, Article 3(3). This is subject to formality requirements.
[75] ibid.
[76] ibid, Article 5.
[77] ibid, Article 27.
[78] ibid, Article 3(1). The 1922 Act echoed English law in regarding the trust as formed only on transfer.
[79] T Ryan, 'The Trust in Ageing Japan: Has commercialisation precluded the trust from reaching its welfare potential?' (2012) 7(1) *Asian Journal of Comparative Law* 1, 28.
[80] In practice, however, Japanese trusts generally do permit this, since beneficial interests are intended to be traded.
[81] Such trusts automatically terminate after one year if it is still for the same sole beneficiary.

Many have tried to reconcile the Japanese trust with the logic of the Civil Code. Adopting the analysis of the French comparatist Pierre Lepaulle,[82] Kazuo Shinomiya suggested that, although legal title to trust assets lies with the trustee, neither the trustee nor the beneficiary *owns* them in a meaningful sense.[83] Rather the trust itself is a legal person, against which the beneficiary holds ordinary personal rights. This analysis accounts for some features of Japanese trusts, such as the independence of trust property from the trustee's personal assets, and the fact that third parties whom the trustee engages in service of the trust have rights against the trust assets similar to those of beneficiaries,[84] while the trustee's personal creditors do not.[85] The analysis also sits naturally with the trust's legislative reshaping in accordance with commercial norms – many of the 2006 reforms were modelled explicitly on Japanese company law – since it understands trusts as almost perfectly analogous to companies, but cannot explain why trusts are exempt from the rules limiting the creation of non-human legal persons.

An alternative view regards a trust as a 'special patrimony' curated by the trustee.[86] A trust patrimony 'operates very like a person, as an autonomous, quasi-personal, fund.'[87] The beneficiary's rights are 'personal rights against the trustee, enforceable against the special patrimony.'[88] On this account, beneficiaries are not *privileged* over the trustee's ordinary creditors – their claims are simply discrete, lying against a different patrimony. To the extent that a theoretical account of the Japanese trust is necessary, this is the most promising, but as Lionel Smith has shown, it is inapplicable to common law trusts in which a 'trust creditor' has no claim against the trustee in any special capacity.[89] The trustee can pay him out of her own pocket and reimburse herself from the trust assets, or out of the trust assets directly, but if the trustee neglects to pay such creditors, they have no interest in the trust assets should the trustee become insolvent,[90] since 'the trust creditor's access to the trust assets can never be stronger than the trustee's own claim to them.'[91]

For want of a single model accommodating the English and Japanese trust, it is clear that the trust itself has changed significantly during its transplantation, whilst also causing changes to other parts of Japanese private law, echoing the common law. What is to be

[82] P Lepaulle, *Traite theorique et pratique des trusts en droit interne, en droit fiscal et en droit international* (Paris, Rousseau et Cie, 1932) 31; P Lepaulle, 'Review of Roberto Molina Pasquel's *La Propriété dans le Trust: Essai de droit comparé*' (1952) 4 *Revue Internationale de Droit Comparé* 377.

[83] K Shinomiya, *Trust Law*, 2nd edn (Tokyo, Yuhikaku, 1989), 61–81 (in Japanese).

[84] Trust Act 2006, Article 16.

[85] A prominent example of a civil-law trust formulated on such lines is to be found in Quebec, where no person has real interests in the assets subject to *fiducie*: Civil Code, Article 1261. Such assets are formally ownerless; the trustee merely has powers to administer the property under the articles of the Civil Code that permit administrators to deal with the property of others (Civil Code, Articles 1299 to 1370).

[86] GL Gretton, 'Trusts Without Equity' (2000) 49 *International & Comparative Law Quarterly* 599, 610.

[87] ibid, 614.

[88] ibid, 612.

[89] L Smith, 'Trust and Patrimony' (2009) 28 *Estates, Trusts & Pensions Journal* 332.

[90] *Jennings v Mather* [1902] 1 KB 1. The trustee and trust creditor may agree that the creditor will have no claim against the trustee's assets except those held on trust. On default the creditor will sue the trustee to oblige her to reimburse herself from the trust assets in order to satisfy the debt. This agreement might even comprise the grant to the creditor of a charge over the trustee's right of reimbursement: *Re Pumfrey* (1882) 22 Ch D 255, but this is distinct from a claim to the trust assets themselves. Even this will fail if the terms of the trust exclude the trustee's right of reimbursement. Moreover, unless a charge has been granted in favour of the specific creditor, the trustee's right of reimbursement forms part of the bankruptcy estate: while it offers up an amount necessary to pay a specific trust creditor, the funds are available to all trustee's creditors (both personal and 'trust creditors').

[91] Smith (n 89 above) 341.

made of this from the perspective of legal transplantation? Jan Smits regards transplants as successful only 'if they create some degree of uniformity between the laws of the importing and the exporting country', and unsuccessful 'if they do not lead to any uniformity at all or, even worse, pose a threat to the consistency of the importing system.'[92] This suggests that a successful transplant of the trust must achieve both (i) a doctrinal match between the trust law of the original jurisdiction and that of the recipient jurisdiction, and (ii) compatibility between the trust and the wider law of the recipient jurisdiction. But these two aspirations are inconsistent: the trust can only come to operate in the same way in the new system as it did in the old by producing a major change in the overall law of the recipient system that previously lacked the trust. That change can scarcely occur *without* affecting 'the consistency of the importing system'. This fact forms a central element of Gunther Teubner's important intervention in the transplantation debate. Urging comparatists to reject 'the false dichotomy of repulsion or interaction which is a result of thinking with this metaphor' of transplantation,[93] Teubner talks not of transplants but of 'legal irritants'. He explains that the introduction of an extra-systemic element necessarily loosens the 'binding arrangements' of the law in the recipient jurisdiction. The system subsequently reconstructs itself *in relationship with* the additional legal element – a process in which both the legal environment and the incorporated foreign element will necessarily change, producing 'new divergences'.[94] While 'pure' doctrinalism is suspicious of alterations produced by transplantation, Teubner identifies the disruptive effect of 'irritation' as a valuable 'evolutionary dynamic'.[95] Entirely faithful transplantation is therefore impossible, but Teubner demonstrates that success or failure is a fruitless enquiry: the real issue is sensitivity to the production of new and potentially unforeseen legal content. Irritants are valuable precisely because of the change they induce in both the receiving jurisdiction and the imported rule – in other words, specifically because they do *not* correspond with the recipient jurisdiction's original conditions.

The Japanese experience raises doubts whether it is possible to import into a new jurisdiction a reliably self-contained trust device, or whether the novel legal notions that must be introduced for the trust to be a distinctive and useful legal form necessarily import into the receiving system a vulnerability to wider disruption of the law of property. Teubner's insights are valuable in explaining why this does not mean that the introduction of the trust into Japanese law has been a failure.

VII. The Ineluctable Disruption of Legal Change

The literature on legal transplantation contains more explanations for why transplants are attempted than why they succeed or fail.[96] This in turn comprises two linked sub-questions: (i) why does legal change so often occur by transplantation rather than domestic

[92] J Smits, 'On Successful Legal Transplants in a Future *Ius Commune Europaeum*' in Harding and Örücü (n 43 above) 140.

[93] G Teubner, 'Legal Irritants: Good Faith in British Law or How Unifying Law Ends up in New Divergences' (1998) 61 *MLR* 11, 17.

[94] ibid 12.

[95] ibid.

[96] Smits (n 92 above) 146.

innovation,[97] and (ii) why do particular rules get transplanted but not others? Answers to the first sub-question look to prestige ('the desire to have what others have, especially if it is deemed superior'[98]) and especially economic efficiency:[99] transplantation is attractive because 'it usually costs less (in money and time) to buy ready-made goods than to make them yourself'.[100] Concerning the second sub-question, there is a tendency to conflate the motive for transplantation with the supposed reasons for a transplant's success, especially among economists of law, who argue that the global diffusion of particular legal forms 'must be linked to their competitive advantage over alternative institutions associated with higher transaction costs.'[101] For such voices, doctrinal scholars' 'emphasis on "borrowing" or "transplants" tends to obscure what has really been happening, which is modernisation'.[102]

Certainly legal rules and institutions arise, spread and endure other than for reasons of 'quality',[103] since they are not free to compete Darwinianly but rather exist in relationship with material factors and the existence of socially privileged interests.[104] Economic advantage is clearly relevant in answering why *particular* rules are desirable transplants, but cannot be the whole story. Synthesising doctrinal and contextual approaches, Kanda and Milhaupt present the crucial determinant of success as the degree of 'fit' between the new rule and the recipient legal system: specifically the degree of 'micro-fit' ('how well the imported rule complements the preexisting legal infrastructure') and 'macro-fit' ('how well the imported rule complements the preexisting institutions of the political economy').[105] These authors differentiate between imports due variously to practical utility, politics (specifically following 'colonization or military occupation') and symbolism,[106] suggesting that 'the more prominent practical utility is in the mix of motives for the transplant, the more likely it is that the transplant will be successful'.[107] To some extent the motivation for transplanting a particular rule is likely to correlate with its subsequent treatment in the receiving jurisdiction. For example, following 'symbolic' (elsewhere called 'legitimacy-generating'[108]) transplants, adopted to signal improvement or modernisation of

[97] Forcibly imposed transplants must be treated somewhat differently: E Örücü, 'Mixed and Mixing Systems: A Conceptual Search' in E Örücü, E Attwooll and S Coyle, (eds), *Studies in Legal Systems: Mixed and Mixing* (London, Kluwer Law International, 1996), 349.

[98] Graziadei (n 34 above) 457; A Watson, 'Comparative Law and Legal Change' (1978) 37(2) *CLJ* 313. This links also to the 'need for authority': A Watson, 'Aspects of Reception of Law' (1996) 44 *The American Journal of Comparative Law* 335, 345.

[99] U Mattei, 'Efficiency in Legal Transplants: An Essay in Comparative Law and Economics' (1994) 14 *International Review of Law and Economics* 3.

[100] Friedman (n 38 above) 94.

[101] Graziadei (n 34 above) 459.

[102] Friedman (n 38 above) 94.

[103] Koschaker has problematised traditional assumptions that Roman law swept continental Europe because of its intrinsic superiority: P Koschaker, *Europa und das Römisches Recht*, 2nd edn (Munich, CH Beck, 1953) especially 79–81, 137–38. English lawyers are used to explaining the comparative resilience of English law to Romanistic influence by reference not to the juridical quality of the common law but to the political and professional power of the Inns of Court: see eg JH Baker, *The Oxford History of the Laws of England (1483–1558)*, vol VI (Oxford, Oxford University Press, 2003) 3ff.

[104] Legal ideas spread not just because they are 'better', but due to factors such as politics and symbolism: E Örücü, 'Law as Transposition' (2002) 51(2) *International & Comparative Law Quarterly* 205, 214.

[105] Kanda and Milhaupt (n 62 above) 440–41.

[106] ibid 439. See also M Dean, 'Legal Transplants and Jury Trial in Japan' (2011) 31 *Legal Studies* 570, 590.

[107] Kanda and Milhaupt (n 62 above) 441.

[108] J Miller, 'A Typology of Legal Transplants: Using Legal History and Argentine Examples to Explain the Transplant Process' (2003) 51 *The American Journal of Comparative Law* 839.

the political economy, localising adaptations are minimised because too much divergence from the original model defeats the object of the transplantation.[109] But more generally, factors such as the motivation for a transplant collapse into the holistic question of 'fit'. For instance, the observation that fewer 'available substitutes for the transplanted rule' in the recipient legal system make it 'more likely that … [it] will be adapted to local conditions and thus used by relevant actors'[110] is hardly distinguishable from the wider enquiry into how far the import 'complements the preexisting legal infrastructure' – whether an imported rule treads virgin soil or instead competes with prior rules is simply part of the question of 'fit'.

Many similar commentaries in transplant theory are really competing attempts to dissect the same central observation: that the results of legal transplantation turn on the conditions – both legal and extra-legal – in the recipient jurisdiction. That is hardly a surprising claim, and moreover it is not uniquely characteristic of legal *transplants*. It is certainly not unique to inter-jurisdictional transplantation – domestic private lawyers have shown how distinct economic circumstances affect the fate of 'interdoctrinal' domestic transplants[111] – but more crucially still, it is equally true of purely domestic legal innovation.

Whenever new legal doctrines are introduced – either by invention *in situ* or transplantation – they do not materialise inside appropriately shaped legal voids. They emerge into legal systems that already provided an answer to the legal questions on which the new doctrine will come to bear, even if that answer was that no legal remedy existed. The answer the law gave in the absence of the imported rule will necessarily diverge from the one that the new rule requires – after all, the purpose of introducing (by whatever means) a new legal rule is to displace the results of its continued absence. Such displacement is intrinsic to all legal change, and it is 'naïve to think that a legal innovation is bound to take firmer roots where it was first produced, rather than elsewhere'.[112] Watson's insistence that transplants are 'socially easy' is redeemable if understood as meaning only that contextual factors in the recipient legal system are *no more* determinative of the fate of a given legal innovation merely because that innovation is in the form of a transplant rather than *in situ* legal change.

Indeed the story of the trust is, in a meaningful sense, the same in England as in recipient jurisdictions like Japan. While the precise development of the English *use* is contested,[113] its emergence incontrovertibly results from desires to achieve ends that could not be realised under the orthodox law of property.[114] Landowners sought to devise land to religious institutions but the Statutes of Mortmain made this subject to expensive royal permission. They desired freedom of testation but the common law imposed compulsory primogeniture

[109] ibid 860.

[110] Kanda and Milhaupt (n 62 above) 441.

[111] E Rock and M Wachter, 'Dangerous Liaisons: Corporate Law, Trust Law, and Interdoctrinal Legal Transplant' (2002) 96 *Northwestern University Law Review* 651.

[112] Graziadei (n 34 above) 467.

[113] *cf* eg OW Holmes, 'Early English Equity' (1885) 1 *LQR* 162; FW Maitland, 'The Origin of Uses' (1894) 8 *Harvard Law Review* 18; 'The Origin of Uses' in JB Ames, *Lectures on Legal History* (Cambridge MA, Harvard University Press, 1913); JL Barton, 'The Medieval Use' (1965) 81 *LQR* 562; J Biancalana, 'Thirteenth-Century Custodia' (2001) 22 *Journal of Legal History* 14.

[114] The Islamic *waqf* has likewise been linked to a desire to circumvent restrictions on testamentary freedom: D Powers, 'The Islamic Family Endowment (Waqf)' (1999) 32 *Vanderbilt Journal of Transnational Law* 1167.

on all but chattel wealth. And they wanted their heirs to receive their inheritance undiminished but the common law attached costly feudal incidents to breaks in seisin. In short, individuals contemplated futures for their wealth preferable to the future imposed by the existing law. The emergence of a novel legal instrument capable of circumventing orthodox law – the *feoffment to use* – precipitated a conflict between the social forces and interests in favour of innovation and inertia, as legal orthodoxy resisted its evasion, a conflict which ultimately conditions the outcome of every legal innovation.[115] Eventually, after 'subtle inventions' had caused 'the utter subversion of the ancient common laws of this realm',[116] political contingency gave the person most disadvantaged by these developments – namely 'the King's highness [who] hath lost the profits and advantages' of feudal incidents – the opportunity forcibly to reinstate old legal orthodoxy, in the form of the Statute of Uses of 1535. Subsequent changes to the political and social environment likewise underlie the survival of the 'active use' and the 'use upon a use', and their evolution into the modern trust.[117]

VIII. Conclusion: Trusts are Not Special

Legal irritation, then, and the relevance of varied social forces in shaping the outcome of such irritation and determining how far innovation triumphs over inertia, are not unique to the transplantation of legal rules from abroad. They are, furthermore, not unique to the trust specifically. No non-trust jurisdiction contains a trust-shaped void – no matter how 'civil-law-friendly' we think the common law trust will be once stripped of its quaint equitable clothing.

The issues confronting Japan in adopting the trust echo those in other codified civil law jurisdictions. A *numerus clausus* principle provides that no real rights can exist except those listed in the Civil Code or other statutes.[118] But, if desired, this objection can be overcome by legislatively adding trusts to the canonical list of property rights. More difficult to overcome are assumptions about the *nature* of property.[119] Coralie Raffenne attributes the tribulations of the modern French *fiducie* to features of 'the French epistemic tradition',[120] namely 'a certain civilian way of understanding, articulating and regulating ownership',[121] which produces a 'deep-seated epistemic resistance to the trust'.[122] Supplying an important nuance to Watson's account of lawyerly culture as an agent of legal transplantation,

[115] As Kahn-Freund observed, the transmissibility of rules and institutions is affected by the distribution of power in the relevant jurisdictions, whose interests are promoted or harmed by particular legal innovations: O Kahn-Freund, 'Uses and Misuses of Comparative Law' (1974) 37 *MLR* 1, 12–13.

[116] Statute of Uses 1535.

[117] This is distinct from a doctrinal account of the legal mechanisms by which the trust emerged from the ashes of the use, on which see eg, SFC Milsom, Historical Foundations of the Common Law, 2nd edn (London, Butterworths, 1981) 236–39.

[118] Civil Code, Article 175.

[119] R Zhang, 'A Better Understanding of Dual Ownership of Trust Property and its Introduction in China' (2015) 21 *Trusts & Trustees* 501.

[120] C Raffenne, 'Why (Still) No Trust in French Law?' in Harding and Örücü (n 43 above) 83.

[121] ibid 77.

[122] ibid.

Raffenne's work presents modern civilian juridical ideology as the crucial *obstacle* to the reception of trusts into French law – specifically, French jurists' attachment to a 'myth to which legal logic is subsumed', namely 'that of the unity and transparency of a gapless Law, echoing the characteristics of the power of its mystical Originator – once God, the King, and in the modern era, the Legislator, or Man.'[123]

In accommodating the inevitable 'irritation' of the *use* or trust, English law benefited from the law–equity divide, which provided a means to conceptualise and (at least superficially) defuse the conflict between legal orthodoxy and innovation – an example of the jurisdictional divide functioning not as the obstructive bogeyman of fusionist nightmares, but as a midwife to legal evolution. The different structure of the codified civilian environment forces its lawyers to grapple with the 'irritation' of trust transplantation directly.

While common lawyers often see a doctrinaire obsession with taxonomical purity as a characteristic of the civilian heritage, in fact the pre-codified civil law included notions of property far more nebulous than those in the modern Codes. It is for this reason that civil law jurisdictions less affected by the codificatory impulse – such as Scotland, South Africa and Quebec – readily assimilated the trust on contact with English law.[124] Vera Bolgar demonstrated that the civil law's resistance to the trust owes far more to the nineteenth-century European mind than the Roman. The *Code Napoléon* substituted a nebulous law of property entitlements and encumbrances broadly familiar to a common lawyer 'with the simple seductive concept of … an absolute power of enjoyment and disposition vested in the owner',[125] calculated specifically to 'consolidate the objectives of the Revolution' through 'abolition of the feudal burdens of the *ancien régime*.'[126] While French law has been obstructed by the need to integrate the *fiducie* into the *jurisprudence* of the *Code Civil*,[127] Japan provides a striking counter-example of the trust being received as a functionalist anomaly in creative tension with the Civil Code.

The Japanese trust problematises common assumptions that 'cultural' resistance to foreign transplants must be particularly high in the context of trusts. While few share Legrand's extreme view that all law comprises an inseparable 'social totality' with all of social life,[128] most follow Kahn-Freund in considering some areas of law highly 'organic' and intimately linked with society, and therefore difficult faithfully to reproduce in other environments.[129] Comparatists traditionally assume that property and succession are among the areas of law most 'deeply rooted in locally developed legal traditions',[130] and therefore resistant to transplantation.[131] But the Japanese experience suggests we cannot always 'rely on [these] simple categorisations of law'.[132] The intimacy between formal law

[123] ibid 83.

[124] V Bolgar, 'Why No Trusts in the Civil Law?' (1953) 2 *The American Journal of Comparative Law* 204, 208.

[125] ibid 218.

[126] ibid 210; see also Raffenne (n 120 above) 84.

[127] Raffenne (n 120 above) 77.

[128] Legrand (n 30 above) 122.

[129] Kahn-Freund (n 115 above) 5–6; Teubner (n 93 above) 19.

[130] A Gambaro, 'Perspectives on the Codification of the Law of Property: an Overview' (1997) 5 *European Review of Private Law* 497.

[131] E Levy, 'The Reception of Highly Developed Legal Systems by Peoples of Different Cultures' (1950) 25 *Washington Law Review* 233, 244. See also Smits (n 92 above) 147.

[132] R Cotterrell, 'Is There a Logic of Legal Transplants?' in Nelken and Feest (n 31 above) 80.

and wider culture is liable to be different in (i) societies that cultivated their own law (albeit, as Watson and his successors emphasise, in constant dialogue with historical legal heritage and other legal traditions); and (ii) societies that imported their modern law in a deliberate and performative departure from indigenous norms and social relations. Thus, it may be significant that the Japanese trust represents just one more transplant into an entirely transplanted legal system. Ultimately, the key problem facing the import of trusts into codified civil law jurisdictions is not the trust, but the habit of regarding the axioms of the codes as immutable dictates of natural reason rather than the products of historical contingency and social forces. That 'myth … of the unity and transparency of a gapless Law' may have less strength in a jurisdiction where the civilian legal idiom is itself a functionalist modern import rather than a distillation of the jurisdiction's own legal heritage,[133] which may inform Japan's receptivity to the trust as a legal transplant – inevitable disruptiveness and all.

[133] Japanese sociologists of law identify in contemporary Japanese social consciousness a 'sense of the hollow core of the modern' that is 'characteristically found in any country in which the modern apparatus like the law is imported.': T Tanase, 'The Empty Space of the Modern in Japanese Law Discourse' in Nelken (n 31 above) 193.

INDEX

Note: Alphabetical arrangement is word-by-word, where a group of letters followed by a space is filed before the same group of letters followed by a letter, eg 'access to justice will appear before 'accessible housing'. In determining alphabetical arrangement, initial articles and prepositions are ignored.

www.ingramcontent.com/pod-product-compliance
Ingram Content Group UK Ltd.
Pitfield, Milton Keynes, MK11 3LW, UK
UKHW051449290926
15471UKWH00008B/1097

9 781509 974238